Lecture Notes in Computer Science   11319

Commenced Publication in 1973
Founding and Former Series Editors:
Gerhard Goos, Juris Hartmanis, and Jan van Leeuwen

More information about this series at http://www.springer.com/series/7409

Günter Fahrnberger · Sapna Gopinathan
Laxmi Parida (Eds.)

Distributed Computing and Internet Technology

15th International Conference, ICDCIT 2019
Bhubaneswar, India, January 10–13, 2019
Proceedings

 Springer

Editors
Günter Fahrnberger ⓘ
University of Hagen
Hagen, Germany

Laxmi Parida
IBM Thomas J. Watson Research Center
Yorktown Heights, NY, USA

Sapna Gopinathan
Coimbatore Institute of Technology
Coimbatore, India

ISSN 0302-9743 ISSN 1611-3349 (electronic)
Lecture Notes in Computer Science
ISBN 978-3-030-05365-9 ISBN 978-3-030-05366-6 (eBook)
https://doi.org/10.1007/978-3-030-05366-6

Library of Congress Control Number: 2018963980

LNCS Sublibrary: SL3 – Information Systems and Applications, incl. Internet/Web, and HCI

This Springer imprint is published by the registered company Springer Nature Switzerland AG
The registered company address is: Gewerbestrasse 11, 6330 Cham, Switzerland

Preface

The 15th edition of the International Conference on Distributed Computing and Internet Technology (ICDCIT) was held in Bhubaneswar, Odisha, India, during January 10–13, 2019. The conference was hosted and sponsored by the Kalinga Institute of Information Technology (KIIT).

Continuing in the tradition of previous ICDCIT events, the conference focused on three areas: distributed computing, Internet technologies, and societal applications. The conference attracted both national and international delegates from academia and industry providing participants with a platform to present and publish research findings as well as to discuss and deliberate on topics and advances in the area of computer science and its application in society.

ICDCIT 2019 received a total of 115 submissions. A strong, well-qualified and committed Program Committee (PC) comprising 52 members from nine countries (of whom 42 were from academia and 10 from industry) was constituted for reviewing papers. Each submission was peer-reviewed by an average of four PC members. Papers were accepted on the basis of technical merit, presentation, and relevance to the conference. A total of 32 papers (27%) were accepted, 18 as full papers and 14 as short papers; 30 final versions were received and registered for presentation in the conference. This volume also contains five invited papers authored by well-respected scholars. ICDCIT was enriched by the lectures and insights given by the following five distinguished invited speakers: Meenakshi D'Souza (Indian Institute of Information Technology Bangalore, India), Christian Erfurth (University of Applied Sciences Jena, Germany), Hacène Fouchal (University of Reims Champagne-Ardenne, France), Ulrike Lechner (Bundeswehr University Munich, Germany), and Hrushikesha Mohanty (Kalinga Institute of Industrial Technology Bhubaneswar, India). We thank the invited speakers for sharing the enthusiasm for research and accepting our invitation to share their expertise as well as contributing papers for inclusion in the proceedings.

ICDCIT was able to maintain standards in terms of the quality of papers thanks to the contribution made by many stakeholders. First, thanks are due to all the authors for their contributions as well as to the 52 PC members and additional reviewers for the effort taken in reviewing the papers. We are grateful to the PC chairs of the 2018 edition of ICDCIT, Raj Bhatnagar and Atul Negi for their guidance and valuable inputs. We sincerely thank Hrushikesha Mohanty and Raja Natarajan for the continuous guidance, support, and insights at every step.

We are grateful to Dr. Achyuta Samanta (Founder of KIIT and KISS) for his continued patronage and constant support for the ICDCIT conference series. We are thankful to the vice-chancellor, management, and staff of KIIT for providing the infrastructure and resources to organize the conference. Particularly, we thank D. N. Dwivedy for his contribution to ICDCIT since its inception. Thanks are due to the Advisory Committee members for their guidance related to the conference. We would also like to thank all the PC chairs of previous editions of the conference for setting a benchmark for the conference. Satellite events to ICDCIT include the Student Research Symposium, the Industry Symposium, and the Project Innovation Contest. These events qualitatively add to attracting participants of different categories to ICDCIT. We acknowledge the program chairs and PC members of these events. We owe our thanks to the Organizing Committee: Chittaranjan Pradhan (conference management chair), Manjusha Pandey (organizing chair), Harish Pattniak (finance chair), Hrudaya Ku. Tripathy (publicity chair), Krishna Chakravarty (registration chair), Manas Ranjan Lenka (session chair), Bhaswati Sahoo (publication chair), Arup Abhinna Acharya (student symposium co-chair), Satarupa Mohanty (student symposium co-chair), Santosh Ku. Pani (industry symposium chair), Siddharth S. Rautaray (project innovation contest co-chair), Jagannath Singh (project innovation contest co-chair), and all members of the sub-committees who made an invaluable contribution to the conference.

We sincerely thank Alfred Hofmann and Anna Kramer from Springer for their cooperation and constant support throughout the publication process of this LNCS volume. From the very inception of the ICDCIT series, the conference proceedings have been published by Springer as *Lecture Notes in Computer Science*: vol. 3347 (2004), 3816 (2005), 4317 (2006), 4882 (2007), 5375 (2008), 5966 (2010), 6536 (2011), 7154 (2012), 7753 (2013), 8337 (2014), 8956 (2015), 9581 (2016), 10109 (2017), and 10722 (2018). We wish to specifically acknowledge the financial support received from Springer. We acknowledge the contribution of EasyChair in enabling an efficient and effective way of managing the paper submissions, reviews, and preparation of proceedings. Finally, we thank all the authors and participants for their enthusiastic support.

We sincerely hope that you find the book to be of value in the pursuit of academic and professional excellence.

January 2019

Günter Fahrnberger
Sapna Gopinathan
Laxmi Parida

Organization

Program Committee

Rafah Almuttairi	University of Babylon, Iraq
Kavitha Ammayappan	Robert Bosch Engineering and Business Solutions, India
Rajiv Bagai	Wichita State University, USA
Bettina Baumgartner	University of Vienna, Austria
Raj Bhatnagar	University of Cincinnati, USA
Nikolaj Bjorner	Microsoft, USA
Venkatesh Choppella	International Institute of Information Technology Hyderabad, India
Hung Dang Van	Vietnam National University Hanoi, Vietnam
Manik Lal Das	Dhirubhai Ambani Institute of Information and Communication Technology Gandhinagar, India
Chiara Di Francescomarino	Fondazione Bruno Kessler, Italy
Gerald Eichler	Deutsche Telekom, Germany
Christian Erfurth	University of Applied Sciences Jena, Germany
Günter Fahrnberger	University of Hagen, North Rhine-Westphalia, Germany
Katarina Fahrnberger	University of Vienna, Austria
Hacène Fouchal	University of Reims Champagne-Ardenne, France
Marc Frincu	West University of Timisoara, Romania
G. R. Gangadharan	Institute for Development and Research in Banking Technology Hyderabad, India
Sapna Gopinathan	Coimbatore Institute of Technology, India
Karthick Jayaraman	Microsoft, USA
Vineet Joshi	University of Cincinnati, USA
Pisipati Radha Krishna	Infosys Technologies Hyderabad, India
Pasupuleti Syam Kumar	Institute for Development and Research in Banking Technology Hyderabad, India
Pradeep Kumar	Indian Institute of Management Lucknow, India
Ulrike Lechner	Bundeswehr University Munich, Germany
Kamesh Madduri	Pennsylvania State University, USA
Venkata Swamy Martha	@WalmartLabs, USA
S. Mini	National Institute of Technology Goa, India
Hrushikesha Mohanty	Kalinga Institute of Industrial Technology, India
Nageswara Rao Moparthi	Velagapudi Ramakrishna Siddhartha Engineering College, India
Srabani Mukhopadhyaya	Birla Institute of Technology Mesra, India

Yogesh Murarka	SAIT, India
Dmitry Namiot	Lomonosov Moscow State University, Russia
Raja Natarajan	Tata Institute of Fundamental Research, India
Atul Negi	University of Hyderabad, India
N. Parimala	Jawaharlal Nehru University New Delhi, India
Jagadeesh Patchala	Kohl's Departmental Stores, USA
Manas Ranjan Patra	Berhampur University, India
Dana Petcu	West University of Timisoara, Romania
Anupama Potluri	University of Hyderabad, India
Sanjiva Prasad	Indian Institute of Technology Delhi, India
Rajendra Raj	Rochester Institute of Technology, USA
Ramaswamy Ramanujam	Institute of Mathematical Sciences Chennai, India
Srinivan Ramaswamy	Asea Brown Boveri, USA
Hemant Rathore	Birla Institute of Technology and Science Pilani, India
Divya Sardana	University of Cincinnati, USA
Neha Sharma	Vidya Pratishthan Institute of Information Technology Baramati, India
Nagesh Bhattu Sristy	National Institute of Technology Andhra Pradesh, India
Sithu Sudarsan	Asea Brown Boveri, India
Ibrahim Tabash	University of Palestine, Palestine
Rajeev Wankar	University of Hyderabad, India
Da Yu	Brown University, USA
Liguo Yu	Indiana University South Bend, USA

Additional Reviewers

Almuttairi, Rafah M.	Ramapantulu, Lavanya
Banda, Sandhya	Rao, Subba
Barjis, Joseph	Raza, Khalid
Choudhary, Sachin	Rengasamy, Vasudevan
Dang, Duc-Hanh	Sadakane, Kunihiko
Das, Ashok	Sau, Buddhadeb
Mahajan, Manish	Srinivasan, Seshadhri
Mukherjee, Kuntal	Sudarsan, Sithu
Mukhopadhyaya, Krishnendu	Suresh, Varsha
Nguyen, Thuy	Vidya Sagar, Ponnam
Patra, Moumita	Vikranth, B.
Phani, Chitti	Yoshigoe, Kenji
Phanikanth, K. V.	Yu, Liguo

Contents

Emerging Areas

Networks

XII   Contents

Invited Papers

Avionics Self-adaptive Software: Towards Formal Verification and Validation

Meenakshi D'Souza[1(✉)] and Rajanikanth N. Kashi[1,2]

[1] International Institute of Information Technology, Bangalore, Bangalore, India
meenakshi@iiitb.ac.in
[2] Dayananda Sagar University, Bangalore, India
rajanikanth.kashi-cse@dsu.edu.in

Abstract. One of the future trends in the aerospace industry for ground and air operations is to make aircrafts self-adaptive, enabling them to take decisions without relying on any control authority. We propose a Belief, Desire, Intention (BDI) based multi-agent system for modelling avionics Self-Adaptive Software (SAS). Our BDI models are formally specified using Z notation and include a library of learning algorithms to cater to adaptability. Apart from satisfying various self-* properties that define adaptability features, avionics SAS, being safety critical systems, also have to satisfy safety and provide deterministic response meeting real-time constraints. We propose a validation framework to check for self-* properties. We also present a formal verification framework based on abstractions and model checking for verifying safety properties. The framework is illustrated through an avionics case study involving an adaptive flight planning system.

1 Introduction

It is well known that there is a steady growth in air traffic this causes an increase of workload for all related systems including pilots, air traffic control etc. There is also an increase in the development and use of unmanned air vehicles for surveillance and emergency response. A recent road-map [6] recommends use of intelligent adaptive systems to address this growth. While development of intelligent and adaptive systems will partly address the demand, there is also a related problem of making these systems safe and reliable. It is acknowledged to be one of the biggest challenges in the development and use of adaptive systems in avionics [1,2].

Self-adaptive systems need to cater to self-* properties [5] which specify the various categories under which a system can adapt itself like self-healing, self-configuring etc. Apart from these, in the context of avionics applications, safety and determinism are of primary importance [1]. Avionics software needs to be certified as per DO-178C [8] (earlier DO-178B [7]) guidelines which require rigorous testing and analysis of the software, including use of formal methods and model based development wherever necessary.

© Springer Nature Switzerland AG 2019
G. Fahrnberger et al. (Eds.): ICDCIT 2019, LNCS 11319, pp. 3–23, 2019.
https://doi.org/10.1007/978-3-030-05366-6_1

We propose a framework for design and verification of self-adaptive systems for avionics. Our models are based on BDI (Belief, Desire and Intention) models of multi-agent systems [14,16] which have been used for design and development of intelligent systems in several other areas [3,4]. Agents in a multi-agent system possess several features that aid in being adaptive—they are autonomous, can implement different reasoning and analysis mechanisms including learning algorithms and can work in a dynamically changing environment. Our BDI models have different kinds of agents: *strategic agents* accomplish adaptivity by using learning algorithms, *tactical agents* ensure safety by catering to faults and sudden changes, an important requirement for avionics systems, *normal agents* provide routing functionality for an avionics application and *moderator agents* ensure deterministic and real-time response. A scheduler takes care of executing the agents within the framework. Our framework is amenable for prototyping using tools like NetLogo [13]. The BDI models and the various functions that each agents use (without learning algorithms) have been formally specified using the formal language Z [17].

Functional requirements, safety properties, requirements to ensure deterministic and real-time response and self-* properties in our framework are written in CTL [11]. We work with Boolean abstractions of BDI models of avionics self adaptive software to specify requirements and also to model check them. Model checking is done using the NuSMV model checker [23] and since our abstraction is sound, a property reported as satisfied in the abstract model will be satisfied in the BDI model too. Counter examples reported could be spurious, we manually re-do abstractions and repeat the model checking to eliminate spurious counter examples. For measuring adaptivity to cater to a few self-* properties, we propose various measures that evaluate the extent of adaptability by an individual agent and by a collection of agents. NetLogo, the prototype tool environment that we use can be configured to compute these measures.

We have worked on two large case studies to evaluate our proposed approach end-to-end—an adaptive flight planning system and an unmanned air vehicle system. We present the adaptive flight planning system in this paper with details of its prototype implementation in NetLogo including learning algorithms used by strategic agents of this application. Measures of co-operativeness for being adaptable are evaluated within NetLogo tool. Boolean abstractions and NuSMV modelling are presented with model checker results for verification of some of the properties.

This paper summarizes work from [20–22] and finally [12]. The rest of the paper is organized as follows. Section 2 introduces self adaptive software, self-* properties and also discusses avionics self adaptive software. BDI models, their design, our proposed BDI models for avionics self adaptive software are discussed in Sect. 4. We also present the TD-learning algorithm used by strategic agents in our BDI models. Section 5 discusses formal verification and validation of our BDI models. Adaptive flight planning system case study is presented in Sect. 6. A brief comparison with related work is done in Sect. 7 and Sect. 8 presents the conclusion and future work.

2   Self Adaptive Software

As per the survey article [5], a DARPA broad agency announcement defines *self-adaptive software* as one that evaluates its own behavior and changes behavior when the evaluation indicates that it is not accomplishing what the software is intended to do, or when better functionality or performance is possible. Such software has an operating environment that includes the platform on which it runs and its interactions with sensors and actuators. Self-adaptive software modifies its own behaviour in response to dynamic changes in its operating environment. They are also sometimes referred to as self-managing systems or autonomous systems.

Self-* Properties. Requirements about self adaptive software are specified using the so-called self-* properties [5]. Self-* properties describe the various elements of adaptability that self adaptive software cater to. The following is a list of some of the well-known self-* properties:

- *Self-healing:* This property represents the capability to discover and react to disruptions in the operating environment. Fault diagnosis and self repair to recover from faults and failures are included.
- *Self-configuring:* This property represents the capability of re-configuring automatically and dynamically in response to changes by installing, updating, and integrating various software entities.
- *Self-optimizing:* This property represents the capability of managing some of the non-functional attributes like performance, latency, throughput etc.
- *Self-protecting:* This property is related to security requirements and includes defensive mechanisms for protection against malicious attacks.

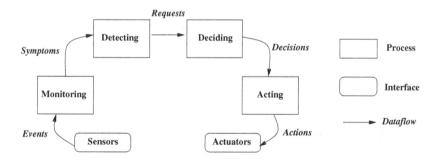

Fig. 1. Adaptation process in self-adaptive-software

Typically, self adaptive software follow a four step adaption process to cater to various requirements including self-* properties [5]. As given in Fig. 1, it begins with monitoring sensor and other inputs, detecting parameters related to functionality and retaining self-* properties, taking decisions to cater to them and finally, communicating the decisions to various end outputs. The various design and architecture decisions follow the high level four step adaptation process towards satisfying self-* properties.

3   Avionics Self Adaptive Software

In this paper we consider self adaptive software in the avionics domain. Avionics domain broadly constitutes the various air and ground operations associated with aircrafts and their flights that are controlled by software. Across the globe, steady increase in air traffic has fuelled the need for complex avionics systems. Intelligent and autonomous systems, operations and decision making, human integrated systems, and networking and communications has been identified as one of the five research and technology areas that requires high priority work to be done for conquering many of challenges in this area [6]. There is imminent scope for adaptivity in each of these areas within avionics.

Avionics domain being safety critical imposes many additional constraints on the underlying self adaptive system. Apart from catering to the specified self-* properties, such systems also need to be deterministic, guarantee safety requirements that include real-time response to requests. Certification of avionics software, a mandatory procedure to be followed is another area of focus. RTCA standards DO-178B [7] and its updated version DO-178C [8] dictate the process of certification of software. This involves subjecting the software to stringent testing achieving various coverage criteria and producing documentation as evidence for the same. Self adaptive avionics software needs to be amenable for certification.

Formal methods, especially model checking [11] is one of the techniques that is popularly used to prove safety and is also highly recommended by the above certification standards. Annex DO-333 [9] to DO-178C recommends various formal methods techniques for certifying high integrity systems. Applying these techniques to formally verify avionics software has been well studied [10].

Our model for avionics self-adaptive software based on BDI-based multi-agent systems is amenable to formal verification through model checking and abstraction. In addition, we also validate the self-* properties by proposing measures for them and prototype implementation to evaluate the proposed measures.

4   BDI Model for Avionics Self-adaptive Software

We present our BDI-based multi-agent system models for avionics self-adaptive software in this section. The models are amenable to formal specification [12] and two case studies have been implemented using the tool NetLogo [13]. We begin with a brief introduction to BDI models.

4.1   BDI Model: A Brief Introduction

BDI model as a multi-agent system model was introduced in [14] and has been well studied and formalized since its conception [15]. Fundamental entities in BDI models are *agents*. An agent is an autonomous software entity that interacts with other agents and the environment. Agents adjust their actions dynamically based on inputs they receive from the environment and other agents. Agents are modelled using the concepts of beliefs, intentions and desires and execute plans based on these. Figure 2 depicts how each agent works within a BDI model.

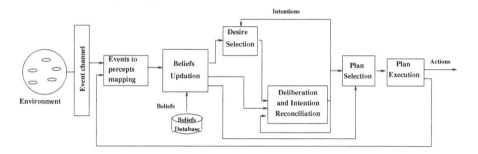

Fig. 2. Generic BDI model of an agent

- *Beliefs* are facts about the agent's environment and may also represent some internal assumptions. Beliefs are generated by a belief generation function that operates on *percepts* received from the environment, other agents and their internal status.
- A set of options or *desires* is generated by a desire generation function that either works from the beliefs or directly from events received by the agent. These represent the *goals* that each agent wishes to achieve.
- The *desires* are then deliberated based on some apriori mechanism or a rule set that chooses one of the desires which is committed by an agent as *intention*. Intentions are processed in some order.
- Simultaneously a set of *events* is also collected in an event queue. A *plan* corresponding to the intention and the event at the top of the event queue is chosen for performing actions by the agent. Plans need to be re-planned if environment inputs change. This process is repeated forever.

Several semantics of BDI-based multi-agent systems are available [15,16]. In particular, the paper [15] provides a semantics for BDI-based multi-agent systems using the formal language Z [17], which in turn, is based on set theory and predicate calculus. Such a semantics makes a BDI-based system amenable to reasoning using a variety of formal verification methods.

4.2   BDI Model Based Framework for Avionics Self-adaptive Software

We propose and explain our BDI model for avionics self-adaptive software in this section. Our avionics BDI model has components that coincide with the generic BDI model but there are also differences in the architecture to cater to the needs highlighted in Sect. 3.

Figure 3 describes the proposed BDI model for avionics self-adaptive software. The set of agents is partitioned into five kinds: *strategic agents*, *normal agents*, *tactical agents* and *moderator agents*. Each agent has its own set of beliefs, desires, intentions and plans as in the generic BDI model. In addition, to ensure safety, there is a *monitor agent*. To ensure determinism, a *scheduler* is also added to the avionics BDI model.

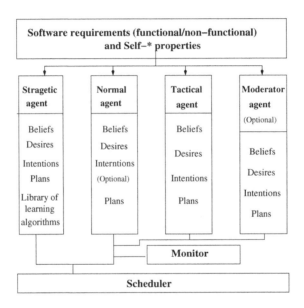

Fig. 3. BDI model for avionics self-adaptive software

We now describe each of the agents and their main role in the design of an avionics BDI model.

- Strategic agents, as their name indicates, work towards providing long term strategic response. Such responses are needed to cater to some of the self-* properties and to meet many functional and non-functional requirements. Strategic agents use a library of learning algorithms that can dynamically change the strategic plan in response to changes in the other agents, towards meeting the functionality. Two such learning algorithms (from well-known ones) and their use to generate goals and plans below are given below.

- Tactical agents cater to meeting safety requirements. In case of an emergency, upon an appropriate event being detected as their beliefs, tactical agents provide quick response. The beliefs of tactical agents map to safety and other real-time requirements. Goals of these agents prioritize the tactical plans upon detecting critical events. For each application, based on the prescribing safety standards, tactical agents can deploy plans that will implement their intention to maintain safety.
- Normal agents cater to normal functional behaviour of a system, in response to the functionality related properties. Functional requirements are mapped to beliefs and the beliefs, in turn, directly map to functions that implement these as goals. There might not be a need for intentions in normal agents. The set of functions used by normal agents are application specific and will be designed by avionics domain experts for each application.
- Moderator agents might not be needed by all applications. The main function of moderator agents is to supplement the strategic agents when a moderation function is needed by them. These constitute the primary goals of the moderator agent. Standard moderation protocols can be deployed as plans of moderator agents.
- Monitors are not first-class agents but, are included in the BDI model to cater to fault tolerance. Many standards for avionics systems demand that faults be identified and mitigated by the various components and in the case of a component failing to mitigate a fault, it needs to be passed on to another component for further fault handling. Monitors collect failures from various agents and report them to tactical agents for fault handling. Standard algorithms for detecting and reporting faults can be deployed in these agents [18]. Tactical agents will handle faults in the process of catering to safety.
- Scheduler is the core part of the framework, it statically schedules the various agents. This implies that agents don't posses complete autonomy. The presence of a scheduler is necessary to ensure determinism in implementation of the avionics software.

The above BDI model has been formally specified using the Z language [12]. Such a specification includes specifying the events, the various agents, functions for beliefs, desires, intentions and plans for each agent. In addition, exception handling, monitor and scheduler have also been formally specified. Once a formal specification is available, the model can be refined to add details about how intentions or goals are chosen, plans are implemented, re-planning is done etc. Such a refined model constitutes a low-level design that can serve as a skeleton implementation for any application that uses the model. We use the Z model to arrive at finite state abstractions that are subject to model checking against functional requirements and safety properties.

4.3   Learning Algorithms in Strategic Agents

We now elaborate on how strategic agents use learning algorithms to cater to adaptivity in BDI models for avionics self-adaptive software. To start with, beliefs of strategic agents constitute facts that the agent knows about its environment as it is working on its plan. A *belief update function* takes sensory inputs and computes such beliefs. Desires, for ease of representation, are bucketed into a finite set of partitions. For example, if the desire is to continue a flight path, it is simply partitioned as being high, moderate or low. An initial desire option is chosen and learning algorithms are used to deliberate and arrive at an intention of which desire option to continue.

We have chosen two kinds of learning algorithms that have been implemented with strategic agents in the two case studies: Temporal Difference (TD) learning and Q-learning.

A TD learning algorithm [19] is characterized by the following equations:

$$sample = R(s, \pi, s') + \gamma V\pi(s'), V\pi(s') = V\pi(s) + \alpha(sample - V\pi(s))$$

where R is a reward function, S is a set of states $s, s' \in S$, s' is the next state of s, $a \in A$, a set of actions, $\pi : S \to A$ is a policy, γ is a discount factor and α is the learning rate. The second equation is called the update equation and updates the value of states each time a new experience is obtained (s, a, s', r). V is a value function that associates a value to each state. TD learning algorithm is considered beneficial in situations where there is no model involved, converges quickly and in our application, the policy π can be aptly mapped to the plan of strategic agent. A suitable notion of an "optimal" policy is desired by an agent as its goal.

We illustrate the use of TD learning algorithm in strategic agents in flight planning case study in Sect. 6.

Q-learning is another kind of TD-learning where an agent tries to learn the optimal policy π from the history of interactions with its environment. History of an agent is a sequence of state, action, rewards depicting that an agent in a particular state s did an action a and received a particular reward r. This results in an experience (s, a, r, s'). An agent tries to learn from its experiences and maximizes its value.

Our strategic agents follow a one step Q-learning algorithm given by

$$Q(s, a) = Q(s, a) + \alpha(r + \gamma maxQ(s', a) - Q(s, a))$$

where Q is the utility function, α, γ, s, s', a, and r are as before, $maxQ$ denotes the maximum Q value over all actions possible from the next state. Even though Q-learning algorithm is not used in the case study presented in this paper, we use it in the case study involving unmanned air vehicle [22].

4.4 Prototype Implementation in NetLogo

Netlogo [13] is a popular open source tool to model the design of multi-agent systems. A proto-type implementation of the considered multi-agent system can be modeled including agents and their environment. Simulations of the multi-agent system can be tracked, displayed and visualized using various plots, 2D and 3D models etc.

We have implemented two case studies of avionics self-adaptive software as BDI models as per the above architecture in Netlogo. Details of the adaptive flight planning case study are presented in Sect. 6.

5   Formal Verification and Validation of Avionics Self-adaptive Software

As mentioned earlier, one of the goals of the proposed BDI models for avionics self-adaptive software is to make them amenable to verification and validation. These are essential steps towards any concept being put to use in a safety critical domain like avionics.

For checking the most important requirement of safety and other functional aspects, we propose model checking. Figure 4 describes the process of model checking BDI models of avionics self adaptive software. Functional and safety requirements and some self-* properties are specified using the temporal logic CTL (Computation Tree Logic) [11]. CTL is expressive enough to specify several different requirements. The atomic propositions in CTL used here deal with Boolean entities that we use during abstraction.

Z models are not finite state models and cannot be subject to model checking as it is. We define predicate abstractions (mainly Boolean) that will retain the essential functional features and define a finite state system corresponding to the BDI model. This system can be formally verified against safety properties and other functional requirements. Our abstractions are sound in the sense that if a model checker reports that the property is true against the abstract finite state system, it will indeed be true in the original BDI model. If the model checker reports that the property is false along with a counter example, we simulate the counter example scenario within the BDI model. It could be the case that the counter example is spurious, i.e., it exists only in the abstraction and not in the original BDI model. In such a case, we need to attempt a refinement of the

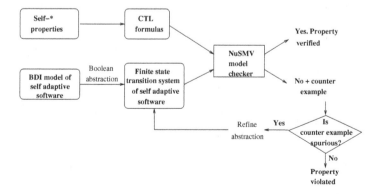

Fig. 4. Abstraction and model checking of BDI models of avionics self adaptive software

abstraction and repeat the exercise. Details are presented for the adaptive flight planning case study in Sect. 6.

Self-* properties constitute the core of avionics self-adaptive software. They need to be validated to ensure that the desired set of self-* properties are met. Strategic agents are the main set of agents responsible to meet self-* properties related to adaptivity. They contain a library of learning algorithms to plan and re-plan based on inputs from the environment and other agents. Tactical agents are designed to cater to some self-* properties like self-protecting. We detail some measures that can be used to validate some of the self-* properties in Sect. 6. These measures can be obtained by implementing the agents and learning algorithms in NetLogo and running appropriate simulations.

A simple measure involves measuring if using a learning algorithm for adapting an agent's decisions was effective or not. This does not map to any specific self-* property but gives an indication of how effective learning for adaptivity was. We call such a measure *cooperative gain*. Assuming that time and distance are two basic parameters that can be measured for an avionics self-adaptive system, the following two measures are proposed.

Measure of Co-operative Gain 1

$$= \frac{\text{Time to complete an episode without Learning}}{\text{Time to complete an episode with Learning}},$$

Measure of Co-operative Gain 2

$$= \frac{\text{Distance travelled to complete an episode without Learning}}{\text{Distance travelled to complete an episode with Learning}}$$

These measures can be directly used to judge the performance and efficiency of a learning algorithm used to adapt by strategic agent. Measuring co-operative gain for an implementation in Netlogo is presented for the adaptive flight planning system case study in the next section.

6   Case Study: Adaptive Flight Planning System

We have evaluated the proposed BDI model for avionics self-adaptive software on two case studies: adaptive flight planning and unmanned aircraft vehicle system [12,20–22]. We present the adaptive flight planning case study in this paper. Unmanned aircraft vehicle system case study details can be found in [22] and [12]. We begin with a brief description of the adaptive flight planning system, list the various safety properties, functional requirements and self-* properties. The BDI model structure for both the case studies is the same as in Fig. 3. The main focus is on modelling of strategic agents that incorporate learning algorithms to cater to adaptability. We present some measures for self-* properties, discuss measuring co-operative gain and also detail formal verification using the model checker NuSMV as described in Fig. 4.

Avionics Self-adaptive Software   13

6.1 Adaptive Flight Planning

Aircrafts flying in the terminal airspace need to get clearance from the corresponding Air Traffic Controller (ATC) to complete the flight paths that they wish to perform. Consider an aircraft using instrument aids and arriving to land at a runway. It follows what is called a Standard Arrival Chart (STARS) on which various segments of the flight path and the altitude levels that the aircraft has to adhere to are indicated [20]. Figure 5 depicts a sample STARS chart of Chennai (India) Terminal airspace at the top right corner of the STARS chart (north east direction) around the HYDOK Waypoint. The goal is to reach any of the endpoints MM515 or MM513 or MM 512 or MM510 given in the figure.

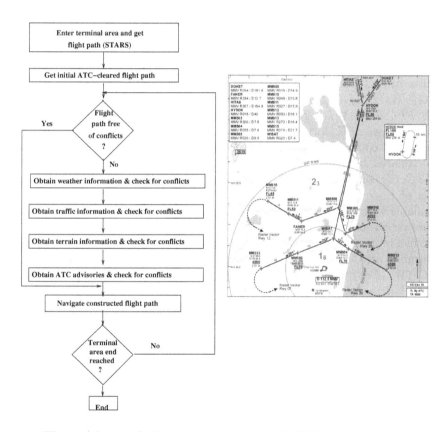

Fig. 5. Adaptive flight planning process and STARS clearance chart

The figure also describes the process of obtaining flight clearance. The pilot needs to evaluate clearances from the ATC and then accept or reject such clearances. The pilot also evaluates conditions that will prevent the pilot from accepting the clearance: Weather, approaching traffic, and obstacles (terrain) and follow the route to the runways indicated on the STARS chart. Therefore the path that the aircraft needs to take will need to be adapted suitably based on constraints of weather, traffic and terrain. We make two assumptions for our hypothetical system: (1) The pilot is free to choose an endpoint on the STARS chart as the final destination once he enters the terminal area. The end point so chosen can change based on weather, traffic and terrain constraints. (2) We allow the aircraft to choose a different route when conditions on a route chosen become unfavorable due to any of the constraints of weather/traffic/terrain. The associated pilot workload under such circumstances motivates the need for the system to be self-adaptive.

Requirements and Self-* Properties. Two requirements for the adaptive flight planning system are given below, along with their CTL specifications. Many other such requirements can be specified using CTL and subject to model checking [12].

- The system shall find a path to the next way-point in the terminal area that is free of conflicts from weather, traffic and terrain constraints.
  $\mathbf{AG}(\neg Wx\_Conf \wedge \neg Tr\_Conf \wedge \neg Te\_Conf \wedge ATC\_Clr \wedge \neg FPL\_RouteAVL) \implies \mathbf{EF}(FPL\_RouteAVL \wedge TMB)$
  In the above CTL formula XX_Conf is a Boolean variable indicating that there is no conflict as far as XX parameter is concerned. XX could be parameter related to traffic (Tr), terrain (Te), weather (Wx) or ATC clearance (ATC_Clr) or flight plan route being available ($FPL\_RouteAVL$). If the negation of these hold, then, the formula says that a flight plan route will be available within a specified time bound (TMB).
- The system shall issue a warning (to divert to an alternate airport) when with the fuel remaining on-board the aircraft, it appears impossible to find a route (terminal area way-point) that is weather, traffic, and terrain constraint free.
  $\mathbf{AG}((Wx\_Conf \vee Tr\_Conf \vee Te\_Conf \vee \neg ATC\_Clr) \wedge (\neg FPL\_Route\_AVL) \wedge (Fuel\_Remaining > Qty\_Reqd\_Reach\_LWPT)) \implies \mathbf{EX}(Abandon\_Warn)$
  Here again, the conflict Boolean variables are the same as in the earlier formula. In addition, if $Fuel\_Remaining$ (the quantity of fuel remaining in the aircraft) is greater than the $Qty\_Reqd\_Reach\_LWPT$ (the quantity required to reach waypoint), then, a warning to abandon the current route and reach the nearest waypoint is given. This is a safety property that forces the self adaptive software to become deterministic in its response to ensure safety.

BDI Model of Adaptive Flight Planning System. In the BDI model for the flight planning system, there are strategic agents for weather, traffic and terrain monitoring and management, a normal agent for ATC and a moderating negotiation agent that represents the aircraft controller. Each of these agents are implemented in NetLogo as per the architecture given in Fig. 3. Each agent, in turn, follows the BDI process described in Fig. 2.

- Strategic agents: Weather, traffic and terrain are all strategic agents, we describe them generically by detailing their beliefs, desires and intentions.

We begin with a finite state machine description of a strategic agents given in Fig. 6. Each cycle of the agents starts with a check of flight plan and fuel sufficiency in the state $s0$. In the state $s1$, the availability of sensor updates for weather, traffic and terrain are checked. The states $s2$, $s7$ and $s12$ begin computations of weather, traffic and terrain agents respectively.

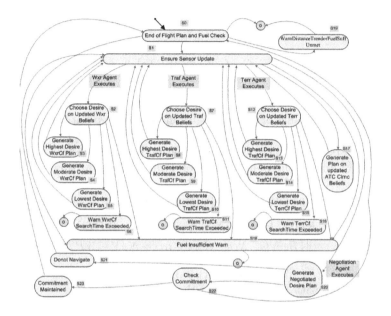

Fig. 6. Finite state transition system of adaptive flight planning system

Beliefs: Each strategic agent maintains two kinds of beliefs about intermediate and terminal way-points associated with states $s2$, $s7$ and $s12$. The first is on whether a way-point is constraint (weather/traffic/terrain) free and is available for navigation to it currently. The second is about whether a way-point is constraint free and is available for navigation for the next (say) 5 min window. The latter is a set of predicted beliefs. Sensors provide the 'percepts' of the current and predicted weather situation. The strategic agents directly maps these percepts onto beliefs.

Desires: The base beliefs are used to generate feasible waypoint lists which are segregated according to the desires. We bucket them into three categories: highest, moderate, and lowest desire lists, corresponding to (Distance + Heading) prioritization, (Distance) prioritization, and (Heading) prioritization. The desire generation and selection operates in two stages: In the first stage, partial plans (options generation function, Opf-1) are generated by each agent (computations in states $\{s3, s4, s5\}$, $\{s8, s9, s10\}$ and $\{s13, s14, s15\}$ for weather, traffic and terrain agents respectively). In the second stage, the 'Best Desire List' is chosen among the three using TD-learning algorithm (Opf-2). A utility value

is appended to each of the generated lists within the individual agents looking at 'Negotiated Final Desire List' that is provided by the Moderator Agent
(Controller/Negotiation agent).

We describe the function `Opf-2`, which computes the values associated with
states $s3, s4, s5$ for weather agent. The other values are computed similarly.

$$V(si) = K_1/(\|\{Beliefs - Xx - Conf - free - WPTs\}_t\|),$$

for $i = 3, 4, 5$ where

$$\|\{Beliefs - Xx - Conf - free - WPTs\}_t\| = \sum_{n=1}^{m} d * n,$$

K_1 is a constant (set to 100 in our experiments), m is the number of way-
points and d is the distance of each of the conflict free way-point from the runway.
The values in the sequence $\{Beliefs - Xx - Conf - free - WPTs\}_t$ are bucketed
into three sets based on way-point prioritization order (distance+heading, distance, heading) and results in a sequence of desire values over time t. These map
to the policies π_1, π_2 and π_3.

Rewards for each agents are calculated as follows:

$$R_{t+1} = K_1/(\|\{Beliefs - Xx - Conf - free - WPTs\}_t\|)$$
$$\sim (\|\{Beliefs - Neg - Conf - free - NAV - WPTs\}_t\|)$$

where $\{Beliefs - Neg - Conf - free - NAV - WPTs\}_t$ represents set of waypoints
found conflict free with respect to all of the constraints.

Now,

$$V(si') = K_2/(\|\{Beliefs - Xx - Conf - free - WPTs\}_t\|),$$

for $i = 3, 4, 5$ where $\{Beliefs - Xx - Conf - free - WPTs\}_{t+1}$, we use the same
formula as above but the distances are decreased by an amount that the aircraft
would have travelled in the intermediate time unit. K_2 is another constant, again
set to 100 in our experiments.

Intentions: Looking at the 'Negotiated Final Desire List', each strategic agent
learns what would be the most preferred list to send to the negotiation agent,
so that its list is maintained as the intention. The 'Best Desire Lists' (way-point
lists from multiple agents) are reconciled within the negotiation agent which uses
a simple one-shot negotiation for real-time considerations.

– Moderator agent: This the agent that does negotiation. It is formulated with
  two filter functions `filter-neg` (for negotiation) and `filter-int` (for intention). `filter-neg` implements the one shot negotiation between strategic
  agents corresponding to weather, traffic, and terrain, wherein the way-point
  lists from each agent is compared with the other to find agreeable common
  way-points. This common way-point list forms the 'Negotiated Way-point
  List'. During each execution cycle, the current way-point to which the aircraft is heading is set to the head of the 'Negotiated List'. The Intention

function (commitment) checks if there are changes brought about during an execution cycle to the negotiated list that introduces a new way-point in the list that is currently not in it. Only when this happens the intention changes. Also, during execution of an agent cycle, time constraints are checked and a warning is generated if it is exceeded. The fuel remaining within the system is also tracked within a global cycle that evaluates it continuously and a warning is issued if there is an exceedance. A distance trending check is also evaluated to monitor whether the final solution is converging. A simple execute function navigates the current way-point (housed within negotiation agent or with a separate and distinct entity).

The complete flight planning system has been implemented in NetLogo. This includes all the agents, their initialization, the TD-learning algorithm for strategic agents, the filter functions for negotiations, check for fuel limit warning and abandoning the flight plan if necessary. Figure 7 shows the code snippets of our model containing code corresponding to some of the functions of the negotiation agent.

Fig. 7. Negotiation agent code in NetLogo

Each agent is invoked in a simulation cycle within the NetLogo model. The image of Chennai STARS chart can be imposed on the implementation of the model and 'Availability' of the way-points for each of weather, traffic and terrain constraints can be set. This is dynamically changed by random means based on a slider setting that conceptually maps to the severity of the constraint, for weather, traffic and terrain. The GUI implementation also provides an option to set our own aircraft speeds in the terminal area. Yet another option provides the ability to switch on/off a random selection of the terminal chosen for path navigation (intention selection) within the final negotiated list.

We have experimented with three implementation variations of algorithms for strategic and moderator agents: one without the use of any form of learning, another using TD-learning as explained above. In yet another implementation of the system, we have added another algorithm that provides additional reinforcement learning that uses the experience gained from episodes. An episode is one complete run of the system from start to a terminal end point. The method involves remembering (via writing into a file) the shortest navigable path to the terminal way-points after arriving at a node. This 'desire.txt' file is updated after every episode to update any of the lists (navigable strings) that need to be changed due to discovery of new shorter paths. We have simulated multiple runs with our NetLogo implementation of the flight planning system with these three implementations. Figure 8 is a snapshot of the desire changes in a single episode with TD learning implementation of strategic weather agent.

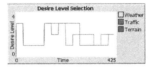

Fig. 8. Behaviour of strategic weather agent

Abstraction and Model Checking. We now highlight how the above properties are formally verified as per the process given in Fig. 4. As described earlier in this section, we characterized the desires for the strategic agents into three buckets and the states of the strategic agents were also partitioned into these three sets directly. For all other parameters, we used Boolean abstraction and defined a Boolean variable that can be used to indicate whether the corresponding parameter or a predicate involving the parameter is true or false at a particular state of the agent. The finite state transition system that results as a sound abstraction of the Netlogo model is presented in Fig. 6.

The variables corresponding to each state are directly used to specify the self-* properties of the system, two such properties were specified earlier in this section.

We used the model checker NuSMV [23] to model the finite state transition system in Fig. 6. NuSMV can model check a finite state transition system against CTL specifications using techniques of symbolic model checking. Figure 9 shows a small snapshot of our model within NuSMV. To test the model checking process, we removed the fuel check criterion from the model and verified it against the second formula regarding the system shall issue a warning (to divert to an alternate airport) when with the fuel remaining on-board the aircraft becomes critically low. As expected, the model checker produced a property violation and produced a counter example depicting a run wherein the aircraft was continuously in a loop of adapting against changing traffic, terrain and weather conditions without finding a flight path [20]. This was not a spurious counter example and could be simulated in the NetLogo model too.

```
ASSIGN

    init(Hd_Wx) := {TRUE,FALSE};  -- Initializing Hd_Wx randomly, either true or false
    next(Hd_Wx) :=
        case
            state = s2 : {TRUE,FALSE};  -- Updating Hd_Wx, only at state s2
            TRUE : Hd_Wx;
        esac;
    init(Hd_Tr) := {TRUE,FALSE};  -- Initializing Hd_Tr randomly, either true or false
    next(Hd_Tr) :=
        case
            state = s7 : {TRUE,FALSE};  -- Updating Hd_Tr, only at state s7
            TRUE : Hd_Tr;
        esac;
    init(Hd_Te) := {TRUE,FALSE};  -- Initializing Hd_Te randomly, either true or false
    next(Hd_Te) :=
        case
            state = s12 : {TRUE,FALSE};  -- Updating Hd_Te, only at state s12
            TRUE : Hd_Te;
        esac;
```

Fig. 9. Code snippet of NuSMV model

The fuel warning check and subsequent actions by negotiation agents were added as remedial measures to overcome the counter example behaviour. The model checking process for the same requirement was repeated and this time, the property was reported to be satisfied.

Validation of Self- Properties.* One of the measures proposed in Sect. 5 is that of co-operative gain that indicates if the learning algorithms helped in gaining adaptivity. We analyzed experimental data obtained from NetLogo simulation that recorded data on aircraft conditions (height, distance travelled during simulation time), data about changing weather, traffic and terrain and ATC clearance. It is straightforward to obtain data for the two measures of co-operative gain with and without the two learning algorithms.

In addition, to analyze to what extent the flight planning system is being adaptive to changes, we propose the following measures:

Coefficient of co-operation for an agent (for an episode)

$$= \frac{(\text{highest desire level} * \text{T}) - (\text{instantaneous desire level} * \text{T})}{(\text{highest desire level} * \text{T})},$$

where T denotes time ticks. The coefficient of co-operation provides a measure of the extent to which an agent can adjust to accommodate its desire level.

Relative coefficient of co-operation between two different agents x and y is the ratio of coefficient of co-operation for agent x and the coefficient of co-operation for agent y. This provides a quantitative measure of the amount of mutual co-operation that exists between agents x and y relative to the disturbances in the environment for an episode and also helps compare the learning algorithms.

To measure the above, we provided numerical values of 1, 2, and 3 for lowest, moderate and highest desire levels. We then vary α, γ and the availability to measure the coefficient of co-operation and the relative coefficient of co-operation. By recording the values of desire levels over simulation time, we can obtain the coefficient of co-operation for each agent.

To measure the relative coefficient of co-operation between agents, we set up an experiment for 67 episodes and captured experimental data for which K_1 and K_2 were set to 100, α and γ were each set to 0.9. The availability of way-points in the STARS chart for each constraint (weather, traffic, and terrain) was varied from 100% (always available) to 55% (half available). As mentioned earlier, we have built-in functions to record the number of time ticks, and compute the distance travelled and to measure the individual coefficients of co-operation for each episode. The results were populated into a spreadsheet and the relative coefficients of cooperation for each pair of agents was computed and tabulated. Table below shows the summary of our experimental results.

Measures for adaptability		
Measure	Mean value	Standard deviation
Coeff. of co-op (TD-learning)	0.294 (Wx Ag)	0.141 (Wx Ag)
	0.287 (Tr Ag)	0.139 (Tr Ag)
	0.278 (Te Ag)	0.135 (Te Ag)
Coeff. of co-op (TD-learning and RL learning)	0.282 (Wx Ag)	0.118 (Wx Ag)
	0.281 (Tr Ag)	0.124 (Tr Ag)
	0.265 (Te Ag)	0.124 (Te Ag)
Relative coeff. of co-op (TD and RL learning)	1.097,1.059 (Wx/Tr)	0.51,0.33 (Wx/Tr)
	1.121,1.36 (Wx/Te)	0.50,1.73 (Wx/Te)
	1.13,1.393 (Tr/Te)	0.59, 2.06 (Tr/Te)
Co-op gain 1 and 2 (TD-learning)	2.99 (G1)	7.16 G2)
	2.99 (G1)	7.16 (G2)
Co-op gain 1 and 2 (TD and RL learning)	4.42 (G1)	13.579 (G2)
	4.42 (G1)	13.579 (G2)

We can plot the data in this table and arrive at the percentage of co-operation. We arrive at the conclusion that we can obtain about 30% co-operation from every agent on the average. Maximum co-operation of about 60% is when the availability of terminals is high (85–100%) i.e, when the terminals are not heavily constrained. Minimum co-operation of about 10% is obtained when the availability of terminals is low (55%) i.e, when the terminals are heavily constrained. We can also experiment with other suitable learning algorithms and see which of the will yield the desired measures.

7   Related Work

Our work spans the entire life-cycle of avionics self-adaptive software touching requirements specified in CTL, design and architecture through the BDI formalism and learning algorithms for adaptivity planning, prototype implementation in NetLogo, formal verification through abstraction and model checking and validation through evaluating measures for adaptivity. An exhaustive literature survey is available in the report [12].

We briefly discuss research that has looked at BDI models in avionics, and approaches to verification and validation. The work that is closest to ours is that of [24] where the authors consider autonomous systems in unmanned aircrafts that use the notion of rational agents (not necessarily modelled as BDI models). They document an exhaustive list of properties some of which can be specified using Linear Temporal Logic (LTL) [11] and propose a methodology for providing certification evidence for testing these properties using model checking. However, they don't provide any formal semantics and also their agents don't use learning algorithms to scale up the autonomy. Very early work on using BDI models for avionics for specific problems can be found in [25] and [26].

Moving on to agents and model checking, [27] presents Gwendolen, a prototype language used in developing an agent infrastructure language which enables model checking. Another case study using model checking for autonomous aircraft that is similar to ours can be found in [28]. The author deals with safety but doesn't discuss ensuring deterministic design and other real-time requirements. Work in [29] relates to an avionics display system, discusses state space reduction techniques and model checking. Our work uses similar principles.

8   Conclusion and Future Work

We have provided a summary of design of self-adaptive avionics software with aspects touching upon every aspect of its development life-cycle. Functional and safety requirements along with self-* properties have been identified and suitably specified using CTL. BDI models based architecture with learning algorithms to implement adaptivity are proposed. Formal verification using abstraction and model checking and measures to convince the extent of adaptability are also proposed.

Moving forward, we would like to strengthen our work by integrating other fault mitigation frameworks into it. Our framework has been formally specified using Z, making it amenable to refinement and direct formal verification. We are also considering other case studies that further illustrate the viability of our proposed framework.

References

1. Helle, P., Strobel, C., Schamai, W.: Testing of autonomous systems - challenges and current state-of-the-art. In: Proceedings of 26th Annual INCOSE International Symposium (IS 2016), Winter Simulation Conference, pp. 150–158 (2016)
2. Goodloe, A.: Challenges in the verification of flight-critical systems. In: CPS V&V I& F Workshop 2014-Talks. National Science Foundation (2014)
3. Adam, C., Gaudou, B.: BDI agents in social simulations: a survey. Knowl. Eng. Rev. **31**(3), 207–238 (2016)
4. Müller, J.P., Fischer, K.: Application impact of multi-agent systems and technologies: a survey. In: Shehory, O., Sturm, A. (eds.) Agent-Oriented Software Engineering, pp. 27–53. Springer, Heidelberg (2014). https://doi.org/10.1007/978-3-642-54432-3_3
5. Salehie, M., Tahvildari, L.: Self-adaptive software: landscape and research challenges. ACM Trans. Auton. Adapt. Syst. **4**(2), 14:1–14:42 (2009)
6. Roadmap for intelligent systems in aerospace. American Institute of Aeronautics and Astronautics (AIAA), pp. 1–111 (2016)
7. RTCA DO-178B: Software Considerations in Airborne Systems and Equipment Certification (1992)
8. RTCA DO-178C: Software Considerations in Airborne Systems and Equipment Certification (2011)
9. RTCA DO-333: Formal Methods Supplement to DO-178C and DO-278A (2011)
10. Cofer, D., Miller, S.: DO-333 certification case studies. In: Badger, J.M., Rozier, K.Y. (eds.) NFM 2014. LNCS, vol. 8430, pp. 1–15. Springer, Cham (2014). https://doi.org/10.1007/978-3-319-06200-6_1
11. Baier, C., Katoen, J.-P.: Principles of Model Checking. The MIT Press, Cambridge (2008)
12. Kashi, R.N., D'Souza, M.: VERMILLION: Verifiable MultIagent Framework for DependabLe and AdaptabLe AvIONics (2018, submitted)
13. NetLogo: A multi-agent programmable modelling environment. http://ccl.northwestern.edu/netlogo/
14. Rao, A.S., George, A.P.: BDI agents: from theory to practice. Technical Note 56, Australian Artificial Intelligence Institute (1995)
15. D'Inverno, M., Luck, M., George, M., Kinny, D., Wooldridge, M.: The dMARS architecture: a specification of the distributed multiagent reasoning system. Auton. Agents Multi-Agent Syst. **9**(1–2), 5–53 (2004)
16. Wooldridge, M.: An Introduction to MultiAgent Systems, 2nd edn. Wiley, Hoboken (2009)
17. Davies, J., Woodcock, J.: Using Z: Specification, Refinement and Proof. International Series in Computer Science. Prentice Hall, Upper Saddle River (1996)
18. Siewiorek, D.P., Narasimhan, P.: Fault-tolerant architectures for space and avionics. http://citeseerx.ist.psu.edu/viewdoc/summary?doi=10.1.1.108.5369
19. Sutton, R.S., Barto, A.G.: Temporal difference learning. In: Reinforcement Learning: An Introduction, chap. 6. MIT Press (2005)
20. Kashi, R.N., D'Souza, M., Baghel, S.K., Kulkarni, N.: Formal verification of avionics self-adaptive software: a case study. In: Proceedings of ACM ISEC, pp. 163–169 (2016)
21. Kashi, R.N., D'Souza, M., Baghel, S.K., Kulkarni, N.: Incorporating adaptivity using learning in avionics self adaptive software: a case study. In: Proceedings of IEEE ICACCI 2016, pp. 220–229 (2016)

22. Kashi, R.N., D'Souza, M., Kishore, K.R.: Incorporating formal methods and measures obtained through analysis, simulation testing for dependable self-adaptive software in avionics systems. In: Proceedings of 10th ACM Compute (2017)
23. NuSMV: A symbolic model checker. http://nusmv.fbk.eu/
24. Webster, M., Cameron, N., Fisher, M., Jump, M.: Generating certification evidence for autonomous unmanned aircraft using model checking and simulation. J. Aerosp. Inf. Syst. **11**(5), 258–279 (2014)
25. Georgeff, M., Ingrand, F.: Monitoring and control of spacecraft systems using procedural reasoning (1989)
26. Ljungberg, M., Lucas, A.: The OASIS air traffic management system (1992)
27. Dennis, L.A., Farwer, B.: Gwendolen: a BDI language for verifiable agents. In: Löwe, B. (ed.) Logic and the Simulation of Interaction and Reasoning, AISB 2008 Workshop (2008)
28. Raimondi, F.: Case study description: avionic scenario. Dagstuhl Reports, vol. 3, pp. 180–184 (2013)
29. Whalen, M., et al.: ADGS-2100 adaptive display & guidance system window manager analysis. Technical report, NASA. http://shemesh.larc.nasa.gov/fm/fmcollinspubs.html

The Digital Turn: On the Quest for Holistic Approaches

Christian Erfurth[(✉)] [iD]

Ernst Abbe University of Applied Sciences Jena, 07745 Jena, Germany
christian.erfurth@eah-jena.de

Abstract. Companies, especially SMEs, are struggling with the digital turn. Technologies are ready for use. Industrial Internet of Things (IIoT) is not new anymore. Apparently, the change is not straightforward. For a better digital future, a bigger perspective and greater responsibility for decisions around digital technologies seems to be necessary. Digitization has now become a social issue. A look at the basics and principles of digitalization will lead us to some theses. With the help of some insights into companies, we embark on a search for successful practices and challenges in digital change.

Keywords: Digital transformation · Industry 4.0 · New work

1 Digital Transformation and State of Innovation

1.1 Difference Between Digitization, Digitalization and Digital Transformation

Nowadays often catchphrases are used without a definition of their meaning but with a common understanding felt. There seems to be a persistent confusion regarding the difference between the terms digitization, digitalization and digital transformation. While digitization is process of making analog information available and accessible in a digital format, digitalization uses digitalized data in applications that facilitate standard work practices. The path to digital transformation is made possible by the increasing networking and linking of digital data in applications and processes. But where does the transition from digitalization to digital transformation begin?

1.2 Digital Transformation - Analogy to Optics

The existence of cut quartz crystals in Egypt can be traced back to the 8th century BC. It is controversial whether the use of quartz crystals was more likely as a burning glass or as an optical lens. Modern optics with the explanation of the optical properties of lenses did not begin until the 9th century AD, when seeing was understood as the incidence of light into the eye. Everyday use for the correction of sight defects began in the late 13th century. The multiple use (cascading) of lenses led to the invention of the microscope and the telescope in the 16th and 17th centuries respectively. The original lens became an instrument of research and opened up new qualitative spaces that had previously been imperceptible, study able, usable or marketable. The optical

G. Fahrnberger et al. (Eds.): ICDCIT 2019, LNCS 11319, pp. 24–30, 2019.
https://doi.org/10.1007/978-3-030-05366-6_2

magnification had been observed, theoretically described, gradually refined and finally strengthened by several powers of ten through multiple applications. The development took place over centuries, so that changes over generations led to a change in working and living habits as well as further innovations. If the digital transformation is understood in analogy to this example from optics as a qualitative change, then a quantitative leap - a scale effect - must be a prerequisite for it. (This analogy is taken from a German publication [1].)

1.3   Innovations in Industry

With the increasing use of technology in industry, there is a growing need to reduce media discontinuities through digital imaging of objects integrated in processes [2]. For instance, the use of AR technologies can support such places where people are active in the processes. Exemplary reasons for the introduction of AR technologies are technological developments [3], the diversity of service employees in terms of training, language, experience [4] as well as demographic change and the increasing individualization of products [2] due to increasing customer orientation [5]. For digital transformation decisive reasons also include declining batch sizes [2 , 6] up to batch size 1 [7], an increasing number of parts [8] as well as increasing pressure to perform [3], among others due to a growing number of special information and high demands on the skills of factory workers.

The most important factor in a company is still the human being. Humans are creative, the most flexible element in production, have experience and are able to make decisions [2]. A digital assistance system serves to support people in their role as employees. There can be up-to-date information relevant for action and decision-making [2] and step-by-step instructions [4] in order to close the gap between the employee's abilities and the required competencies at the workplace [9]. The success factor here is employee acceptance, which need to be taken into account during the development and introduction of innovations. The affected employees should be involve from the very beginning [5]. User-friendliness also plays a major role [10]. The assistance system should be adaptable to the environment, the cognitive abilities of the employee, the user experience and knowledge (incl. multilingualism) [3 , 4 , 7].

At the same time, networked machines and systems for the planning and control of production processes collect a large amount of data. The manufactured parts themselves produce data on their condition during the production process and have to be clearly identifiable for the purposes of quality assurance. In an empirical study on the handling of shop floor data (analysis and development) from approx. 100 companies (Germany, Switzerland), it is evident that only a few companies carry out cross-company data analyses and only 6% use this data for decisions [11]. However, it is found that only five percent of small and medium-sized manufacturing companies comprehensively network their machines, plants and systems [12]. Due to the significantly lower degree of digitalization among small and medium-sized enterprises (SMEs), they have an increased need to catch up in Industry 4.0 implementation.

Important fields of application for data analysis are predictive maintenance (35%), process optimization (26%), quality control (13%), production planning and scheduling (12%), and track and tracing (6%). In the course of digitization, data analysis will play an important role. The actual potential of the AR systems has not yet been exploited in most areas and might be used as an assistance system in the shop floor. According to Groggert et al. [11] the main topics are:

1. Train and educate current employees (84%),
2. Integrate existing IT infrastructure better (64%), and
3. Strong collaborations with external partners (55%).

2 Some Studies on Digital Transformation

As part of our research project "Healthy work in pioneer industries", we have investigated the situation in various companies (Germany). Approximately 20 case studies were investigated after intensive surveys and inspections. The companies have embarked on the path of digitization, but are struggling with various problems [13]. These challenges do not only relate to the technology used by a company, but also affect all areas equally. The following findings were obtained from the material collected on the qualitative case studies:

1. The phenomenon of "digital transformation" is a global phenomenon: society, the economy and businesses as a whole are penetrated by it and lastingly changed. For example, companies must establish new innovative methods, change a new culture and an established organization and structure.
2. It is a process characterized by revolution and evolution: Established processes and technologies are confronted with new technologies - new processes are developed evolutionarily. Old and new are newly combined and create the revolution through disruption.
3. A key driver of the pressure to change is the emergence of new opportunities, which are attacking the established business models of companies in particular.
4. The consequences of these changes are not sufficiently reflected in the practice of companies. The cause is seen as a deficit in the lack of awareness, particularly in the area of technology and impact assessment (social and corporate).
5. Successful factors for the digitization of companies are characterized by: (1) a change of mentality in the management. (2) in the creation of innovative areas and (3) in the increasing collection, networking and integration of data by IT.
6. Companies that have recognized innovation as important always have to cope with similar challenges: How can innovative techniques and processes be successfully established in an institution with fixed structures? There is a lack of areas of innovation where new ideas can be tried out independently of established structures that ensure operative business.
7. Another major problem is seen especially in data silos in companies. It begins with paper-based work or spreadsheet files available in individual areas - data that are located in individual areas or in persons, but are not visible in the entire company. Here, companies must take fundamental steps towards digitization in order to be able to work with the data.

8. Particular difficulties are also to be seen in the current legal frameworks, which do not adequately provide for digital services as a substitute for papers. Similarly, committees are challenging: In particular, data protection (e.g.: assessment of employee performance) is often a particular focus of works councils, which can have an inhibiting effect on the introduction of new technologies. Transparency and methods that prevent misuse must be used to counteract this.
9. Another obstacle is the complexity of change and technology. In order to be able to act, promising technologies and processes must be applied and adapted experimentally.
10. An essential factor is also the binding of knowledge in companies: Experience and solutions to problems are often highly dependent on individuals. With the professional world becoming more and more specialized, a loss of know-how is increasingly a critical problem for companies. This can be counteracted by operating an active feedback and knowledge management system in companies.

Beside technological challenges we found organisational, legal and in some cases ethical obstacles. According to the study, main barriers are a lack of strategy, a shortage of resources, a lack of standards and a lack of data security. In addition, SMEs often lack an overview of all available technologies [14]. A current research map for CPS research was compiled for this purpose [15]. Due to the fast pace of change, digitalization approaches must be continuously developed further [16]. The speed of digitalization is perceived as too slow, even by large companies [17].

Often, due to greater heterogeneity in the machinery of medium-sized companies, the cost of digitalization is greater [18]. Vertical integration through the digital exchange of production data between typical areas such as sales, planning, service and controlling is already difficult. An even greater challenge is the exchange of data with external partners such as suppliers and customers, especially for SMEs, which generally have fewer resources and know-how than large companies [19]. Smart services are still not very widespread among SMEs.

The literature addresses the alignment of IT to business needs and thus the appropriate IT support. However, individual technology solutions such as ERP or MES are often considered [20]. For the digital transformation, the interaction of various technologies/functional areas [21] is necessary. They offer solutions from the following areas [22]: (1) Solutions for innovative manufacturing, (2) Additive manufacturing, (3) Assistance systems with augmented reality, among others, (4) Simulation, (5) Networking and integration (horizontal/vertical), (6) Industrial Internet, (7) Cloud, (8) Cyber security, (9) Data acquisition and processing (Big Data and data analysis). This requires new knowledge in the field of IT [16] and increased interdisciplinary cooperation between IT and the production environment in order to successfully implement data-based decisions in companies [6] and learn from them [23].

In the literature, a maturity level assessment in relation to Industry 4.0 can be found as an introduction to digital transformation [24]. Recommendations for action within the framework of a digitalization strategy are derived from assessments. In particular, solutions that are easy to implement with corresponding business advantages are prioritized and a transformation concept with concrete step-by-step measures is created [22, 25]. Soft factors that address the role of people in tomorrow's production and digital work environment, such as the creation of new work processes and forms of work organization, are becoming increasingly important in digitalization. [2, 21].

3 Discussion and Summary

Scaling appears to be a critical factor for digital transformation. Platforms like Uber and AirBnB would not be successful without the high number peoples using the services provided by these platforms. Can such scaling effects also be found in the industrial sector? Are there other enabling factors for a digital transformation?

In industry, scaling through sensor technology, increasing networking and the avoidance of media disruptions is more likely to be found in the area of data generation. However, these data from the "Data Lake" only acquire a certain value through an analysis. Integrated into production processes, the information gained in this way enables greater transparency and, as a result, new possibilities for controlling complex processes. The opportunity arises to design completely new processes - to have a creative destructive effect.

Digital transformation also requires cultural change. Whereas previously the focus was on stability with regard to production processes. Nowadays flexibility with high quality demands and competitive prices is becoming important due to a stronger focus on the customer. Automation will thus become new dimensions. This affects the organization of companies: Strategy and adaptability are possibly vital factors for survival. A valuable asset in this context are the company's employees, who rank second after the customer in terms of priority - even ahead of the company's economic interests. Sustainable digital transformation therefore means taking the human factor more into account in addition to the technical basis.

There is no blueprint for digital transformation, no best practice developed as a standard. New forms of work such as agility, coordinated IT, governance, some courage and farsightedness as well as a holistic view, openness and diversity help on the way to digital transformation. As always: Start with the changes in areas that bring recognizable benefits.

Acknowledgement. The author is very thankful for the support in the research especially Arlett Semm and Marcus Wolf. This work was supported in part by the German Federal Ministry of Education and Research (BMBF) under the grant number 02L14A073.

References

1. von der Heyde, M., Hartmann, A., Auth, G., et al.: Zur disruptiven Digitalisierung von Hochschulforschung: Faktoren der Skalierung und ein Zukunftsszenario. Informatik Spektrum **41**(5), 1–10 (2018). https://doi.org/10.1007/s00287-018-01126-1
2. Stocker, A., Brandl, P., Michalczuk, R., et al.: Mensch-zentrierte IKT-Lösungen in einer Smart Factory. Elektrotech. Inftech. **131**(7), 207–211 (2014). https://doi.org/10.1007/s00502-014-0215-z

3. Hinrichsen, S., Riediger, D., Unrau, A.: Development of a projection-based assistance system for maintaining injection molding tools. In: 2017 IEEE International Conference on Industrial Engineering and Engineering Management (IEEM), pp. 1571–1575. IEEE (2017)
4. Schlagowski, R., Merkel, L., Meitinger, C.: Design of an assistant system for industrial maintenance tasks and implementation of a prototype using augmented reality. In: 2017 IEEE International Conference on Industrial Engineering and Engineering Management (IEEM), pp. 294–298 (2017)
5. Spath, D. (ed.): Produktionsarbeit der Zukunft - Industrie 4.0: Studie. Fraunhofer-Verl., Stuttgart (2013)
6. Bauer, D., Maurer, T., Henkel, C., et al.: Big-Data-Analytik: Datenbasierte Optimierung Produzierender Unternehmen. Zenodo (2017)
7. Funk, M.: Augmented reality at the workplace. Dissertation, Universitätsbibliothek der Universität Stuttgart (2016)
8. Liu, Y., Li, S., Wang, J., et al.: A computer vision-based assistant system for the assembly of narrow cabin products. Int. J. Adv. Manuf. Technol. 76(1–4), 281–293 (2015). https://doi.org/10.1007/s00170-014-6274-9
9. Hold, P., Erol, S., Reisinger, G., et al.: Planning and evaluation of digital assistance systems. Procedia Manuf. 9, 143–150 (2017). https://doi.org/10.1016/j.promfg.2017.04.024
10. Huck-Fries, V., Wiegand, F., Klinker, K., et al.: Datenbrillen in der Wartung. Gesellschaft für Informatik, Bonn (2017)
11. Groggert, S., Wenking, M., Schmitt, R.H., et al.: Status quo and future potential of manufacturing data analytics—an empirical study. In: 2017 IEEE International Conference on Industrial Engineering and Engineering Management (IEEM), pp. 779–783 (2017)
12. Schröder, C.: Herausforderungen von Industrie 4.0 für den Mittelstand. Gute Gesellschaft - soziale Demokratie #2017plus. Friedrich-Ebert-Stiftung, Abteilung Wirtschafts-. und Sozialpolitik, Bonn (2016)
13. Wolf, M., Semm, A., Erfurth, C.: Digital transformation in companies – challenges and success factors. In: Hodoň, M., Eichler, G., Erfurth, C., et al. (eds.) Innovations for Community Services, vol. 863, pp. 178–193. Springer International Publishing, Cham (2018). https://doi.org/10.1007/978-3-319-93408-2_13
14. Jordan, F., Bernardy, A., Stroh, M., et al.: Requirements-based matching approach to configurate cyber-physical systems for SMEs. In: 2017 Portland International Conference on Management of Engineering and Technology (PICMET), pp. 1–7 (2017)
15. Klotzer, C., WeiBenborn, J., Pflaum, A.: The evolution of cyber-physical systems as a driving force behind digital transformation. In: 2017 IEEE 19th Conference on Business Informatics (CBI), pp. 5–14 (2017)
16. Ten Hompel, M., Cirullies, J., Engelmeier, G., et al.: Kompetenzentwicklungsstudie Industrie 4.0: Erste Ergebnisse und Schlussfolgerungen (2016)
17. etventure.de: etventure-Studie Digitale Transformation 2017: Die deutschen Unternehmen sind zu langsam und zu unflexibel (2017). www.etventure.de/blog/etventure-studie-digitale-transformation-2017-die-deutschen-unternehmen-sind-zu-langsam-und-zu-unflexibel/
18. Forstner, L., Dümmler, M.: Integrierte Wertschöpfungsnetzwerke – Chancen und Potenziale durch Industrie 4.0. Elektrotech. Inftech. 131(7), 199–201 (2014). https://doi.org/10.1007/s00502-014-0224-y
19. Wischmann, S., Wangler, L., Botthoff, A. (eds.): Industrie 4.0: Volks- und betriebswirtschaftliche Faktoren für den Standort Deutschland : eine Studie im Rahmen der Begleitforschung zum Technologieprogramm Autonomik für Industrie 4.0. Bundesministerium für Wirtschaft und Energie (BMWi), Berlin (2015)

20. Jung, K., Kulvatunyou, B., Choi, S., Brundage, Michael P.: An overview of a smart manufacturing system readiness assessment. In: Nääs, I., Vendrametto, O., Reis, J.M., Gonçalves, R.F., Silva, M.T., von Cieminski, G., Kiritsis, D. (eds.) APMS 2016. IAICT, vol. 488, pp. 705–712. Springer, Cham (2016). https://doi.org/10.1007/978-3-319-51133-7_83
21. Bischoff, J.: Studie "Erschließen der Potenziale der Anwendung von 'Industrie 4.0' im Mittelstand" (2015). https://www.bmwi.de/Redaktion/DE/Publikationen/Studien/erschliess en-der-potenziale-der-anwendung-von-industrie-4-0-im-mittelstand.html
22. de Carolis, A., Macchi, M., Negri, E., et al.: Guiding manufacturing companies towards digitalization a methodology for supporting manufacturing companies in defining their digitalization roadmap. In: 2017 International Conference on Engineering, Technology and Innovation (ICE/ITMC), pp. 487–495 (2017)
23. Schuh, G., Fuß, C. (eds.): ProSense: Ergebnisbericht des BMBF-Verbundprojektes; hochauflösende Produktionssteuerung auf Basis kybernetischer Unterstützungssysteme und intelligenter Sensorik, 1st edn. Apprimus Verl, Aachen (2015)
24. Hübner, M., Malessa, N., Nyhuis, P., et al.: Vorgehensmodell zur Einführung von Industrie 4.0: Vorstellung eines Vorgehensmodells zur bedarfsgerechten Einführung von Industrie 4.0-Methoden. wt. Werkstattstechnik online(4), 266–272 (2017)
25. Rosell, A., Salomonsson, L.: Towards a framework for identifying digital improvement opportunities: utilizing information flow and its stakeholder value. Master thesis, Linköping University (2018)

Secured Communications on Vehicular Networks over Cellular Networks

Hacène Fouchal$^{(\boxtimes)}$, Emilien Bourdy, Geoffrey Wilhelm, and Marwane Ayaida

CReSTIC, Université de Reims Champagne-Ardenne, Reims, France
{Hacene.Fouchal,Emilien.Bourdy,Geoffrey.Wilhelm,
Marwane.Ayaida}@univ-reims.fr

Abstract. On VANETs (Vehicular AdHoc Networks) mobile stations communicate with other stations (fixed or mobile ones). IEEE 802.11p (denoted also ETSI ITS-G5) is a WiFi designed for mobile networks, it is used for these communications. ITS-G5 is used by real vehicles over the world within deployment projects. These communications could be between vehicles denoted V2V communications or between vehicles and RSUs denoted V2I. The coverage of RSUs will never sufficient to cover all ares and roads. In the meantime cellular networks are evolving very quickly using various technologies (3G, 4G, LTE) waiting for next revolution through 5G. We believe that the future of VANETs will be achieved by cellular networks.

The aim of this study is present a framework which permits to stations to communicate which others using cellular networks when G5 networks are not available. Data protection is a very important feature nowadays on any shared system. This issue should be considered on deployed VANETs in order to avoid tracking drivers who send their locations in awareness messages. The anonymity is ensured by changing the identity of users frequently using a strict process. Indeed, the new identities shall be authenticated and trusted. An adapted PKI (Public Key Infrastructure) solves this issue. We have considered also authenticity and anonymity in this paper inherited from [5]. Evaluation of the work has been by means simulations and has proven that the end-to-end latency is similar to G5 network ones.

Keywords: C-ITS · VANETs · Cellular networks · Security · Privacy

1 Introduction

Connecting vehicles is a hot topic either for researchers and for car industry. These actors work on various issues (autonomy, safety, security, connectivity, etc,...). The connectivity issue is considered at different levels: architecture, protocols, coverage, etc,.. The well known ITS-G5 (IEEE 802.11p) is a dedicated WIFI for connected vehicles working in a short range radio. In order to enhance the connectivity of these networks, it is worthy to take profit of cellular networks which are widely deployed and will be surely guarantee a very wide coverage.

© Springer Nature Switzerland AG 2019
G. Fahrnberger et al. (Eds.): ICDCIT 2019, LNCS 11319, pp. 31–41, 2019.
https://doi.org/10.1007/978-3-030-05366-6_3

In this paper, we intend to use the cellular network (3G, 4G, LTE) in order to ensure the collection and the delivery of warning messages to and from vehicles. Each vehicle sends continuously Awareness Messages (CAM) to a central manage which records the new location of the vehicles When a vehicle needs to notify an event, it will send an appropriate event to the manager which will forward the event to all relevant vehicles. In addition to communications over cellular networks, we deal with authenticity of senders to avoid untrusted actors to notify non proper events and privacy in order to avoid driver tracking. These two issues are solved by using a PKI in charge of distributing pseudonyms certificates (PC) to all involved vehicles. All messages are sent along with their signature computed using their actual PCs.

This paper contains the following sections: Sect. 2 describes some works dedicated to vehicular networks and cellular networks In Sect. 3 we present our architecture able to ensure communications between vehicles through cellular networks. Section 4 is dedicated to measure key performance indicators (KPI) about the proposal. Section 5 give some conclusions and ideas about future enhancements of the study.

2   Related Works

[16] presents a detailed study on performance evaluation of IEEE 80211.p networks versus LTE vehicular networks. The authors analyse some performance indicators like end-to-end delay for both networks in different scenarios (high density, urban environments, etc.). Many important issues have been measured as network availability and reliability. The authors have proved through simulations that LTE solution meets most of the application requirements in terms of reliability, scalability, and mobility. However, IEEE 802.11p provides acceptable performance for sparse network topologies with limited mobility support.

[21] presents another alternative to WAVE/DSRC using this time Wi-Fi Direct, ZigBee and Cellular Network. Wi-Fi Direct is used as a direct link between nodes. ZigBee is used to connect roadside sensors and Cellular Network for long distance communication. In this study, the ITS-G5 is also ignored. In [8], the authors provide their network architecture which has been deployed in Spain on vehicles communicate switching between 802.11p and 3G, depending on RSU's availability.

[17] is dedicated to routing over VANETs in an urban environments. [15] is a study about movement prediction of vehicles. Indeed, an adapted routing algorithms are proposed in [11] and in [11]. [10] gives an overview of strategies to use for routing on VANETs. [19] reviews much more actual strategies on vehicular networks.

Authors of [20] presents an alternative to WAVE/DSRC using an hybrid system, which uses Wi-Fi Direct and Cellular Network. They show that such a system could work for C-ITS. However, this paper does not take into account the hybridation between ITS-G5 and Cellular Network suggest a prediction method for unicast routing over VANETS.

[13] studies throughput over VANETs system along an unidirectional traffic for different conditions and transmission ranges of wireless equipments. All studied vehicles are randomly connected. The paper gives few results of simulation studies achieved on NS-2 toolbox. They have measured performances indicators in case of congestion. A comparison of the obtained results with the expected connectivity has been done and have shown that the throughput over simulation is lower due to packet losses caused by collisions.

In [14], an evaluation of vehicular communications networks through car sharing scenarios is detailed. It has investigated three parameters. They adopted a specific mobility model which has been imported to a simulator. They have worked on a grid Manhattan network and they observed some performance parameters such as delay, packet loss, etc. The most important objective of the study is to show that vehicular communication is feasible and realistic under some conditions.

[7] gives an overview of how research on vehicular communication evolved in Europe and, especially, in Germany. They describe the German field operational test sim TD. The project sim TD is the first field operational test to evaluate the effectiveness and benefits of applications based on vehicular communication in a setup that is representative for a realistic deployment environment. It is, therefore, the next necessary step to prepare for an informed deployment decision of cooperative systems.

These studies show that we need an architecture for VANETs over cellular networks in order to cover wider areas. In addition to that trust, privacy and efficiency has never been studied in the same time. We try to give some answers in this paper.

3   System Architecture

3.1   Preliminaries

In the area of C-ITS (Cooperative Intelligent Transportation System), a protocol stack has been defined and standardised by the ETSI standardisation institute in Europe [1]. Over the *Transport-Networking* layer (defined as geo-networking layer), the *Facilities* layer has been designed in order to be an efficient interface between the application layer (close to the driver and the vehicle sensors) and the *Transport-Networking* layer. Many types of messages are provided by this layer and we will focus in this study only on 2 main messages: CAM (Cooperative Awareness Message) [6] and DENM (Decentralised Environmental Notification Message) [9]. The aim behind sending CAM messages is to give dynamic information about the vehicle (i.e. position, speed, heading, etc.). A vehicle sends CAMs to its neighbourhood using Vehicle-to-Vehicle (V2V) or V2I communications. Depending on the vehicle speed, the frequency of CAM messages varies from 1 Hz to 10 Hz. A vehicle sends DENM messages is to notify about any type of event (i.e. accident, traffic jam, etc.). The event could be triggered automatically thanks to the connexion to the vehicle CAN Bus (which runs smart rules and generates appropriate messages) or manually for sensitive cases as animal on the road.

3.2   Privacy and Authenticity

C-ITS security considers two main aspects:

- Authenticity: this aspect allows to consume only messages coming from trusted sources.
- Privacy: this aspect permits to protect drivers data and avoid driver tracking.

The well know solution is to use a Public Key Infrastructure (PKI). Each involved vehicle in the eco-system has to be registered which allows to it get a recognition on the PKI server. A long term certificate (LTC) is provided to this vehicle (signed by a root PKI).

A vehicle could sign all its messages using this LTC by means of a hardware security module (HSM) which manages cryptographic processes and keys with care. Authenticity is ensured but privacy is not considered at all. Indeed, from LTC we could extract private informations which give opportunity to external observers to track drivers. The usual solution to solve privacy is the use of pseudonym certificates (PC) for small period. A node should own a pool of PCs which should be up to date in order to be able to switch to another PC accordingly. Having a pool of PCs could be a problematic when the vehicle is stolen by misbehaving user which will send fake messages. The usual PKI revocation mechanism in this case is solved by the distribution of Certificate Revocation Lists (CRLs) to vehicles. This solution is not applied because the CRLs may be too large and very dynamic. Then it needs to be updated frequently.

In this paper, we propose to upload a set of pseudonyms certificates for a long period (some years into the vehicle). This period should the maximum required delay for a car manufacturer to maintain a vehicle. That means that after this period, another set of certificates should be uploaded again in a trusted reparring garage of the car manufacturer. The set of certificates is a list of sorted pools. A pool is expected to be valid for a week. These certificates should not be used alone. Each certificate needs an additional data in order to be valid. The missing information is denoted as a validation code. This issue will not be detailed in this paper, we use the validation code process almost similar to the process defined in [5]. Each pool needs to get the same validation code which is uploaded for each week. It has to be uploaded at maximum one week before using a cellular network through a specific procedure using appropriate protocol. When a station has to be revoked, the validation code could not be downloaded, then it will not be trusted by all other stations.

3.3   ITS G5 Communications

The general architecture is presented on Fig. 1. Each station is supposed to have a set of pseudonym certificates.

A vehicle is able to send a message through a G5 network in order to reach its neighbours. The message could reach other vehicles thanks to multi-hop forwarding (Fig. 2).

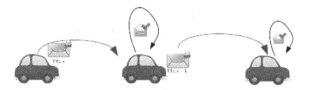

Fig. 1. A general scheme for vehicle to vehicle communication

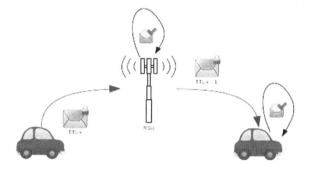

Fig. 2. A general scheme for vehicle to infrastructure communication

An RSU plays the same role than a vehicle for the forwarding aspect. In addition to that, the RSU handles all received messages from vehicles in order to run road operator's computations as traffic management, event recording. In some cases the RSU disseminates events towards other RSUs within operator's network. The ETSI has defined an ITS stack where the forwarding mechanism is achieved with the geo-networking protocol [3]. This layer plays the role of the networking layer. The message signing is done in the geo-networking PDU is shown on Fig. 3.

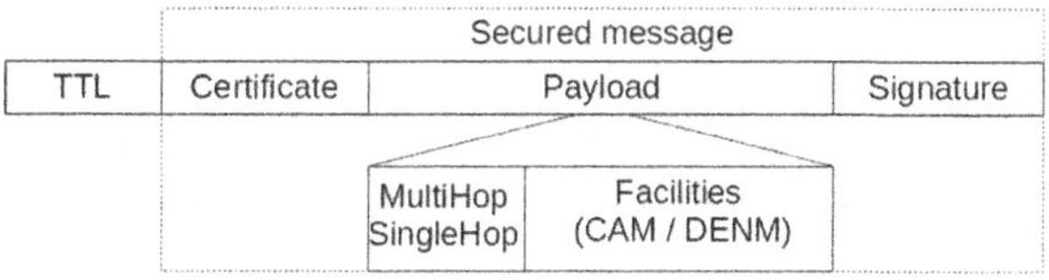

Fig. 3. A secured geonet packet

Geonetworking messages collect in the payload part a facilities message (in our case CAM or DENM). It is transmitted through ITS-G5 messages in order to be sent in the local area. When such a message is resent by a station, its TTL is decreased by one unit without modifying the message signature. It is worth to notice that the secure message is composed of the payload and the signature as in usual authentication schemes. But in our case the certificate is also sent. It is needed to check immediately the signature. However, additional verification steps are needed in order to ensure the source trust (the validity of the certificate of the pseudonym issuing authority, the PKI root CA, ...).

3.4   Extension to Cellular Communication

One of the main contributions of the study is the use of a TCP connection in order to emulate an ITS-G5 channel.

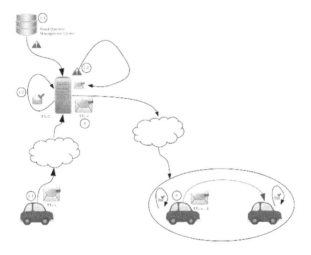

Fig. 4. Cellular communication

In order to build a broadcast mechanism over TCP, we split the message sending in two parts:

– The usual message is first encapsulated (action 1.1 on Fig. 4) into an TCP segment to be sent to a server (Cellular ITS server) which is able to receive messages from ITS stations. The central station decapsulate the ITS-G5 message (action 1.2 on Fig. 4) from TCP segment. It should be decoded using the same rules than those used on a regular ITS station. The payload of the TCP packet is simply a Geonetworking message. After de-capsulation, the message is exactly as the one received through G5 access. In this case, the Cellular ITS server checks the messages and verifies their validity. It considers CAM messages for updating the vehicle's position and DENM messages through some tasks that will be detailed below. In fact, the vehicle works in the same network environment than for the ITS-G5 one, it has just an additional interface over cellular networks on which it sends ITS-G5 messages when required.
– The central station will run two main tasks: updates vehicle positions periodically and forwards event messages (action 3 on Fig. 4) to all vehicles for which these messages are relevant (those stations which are in the area of

the event and which have already sent a CAM message to the Cellular ITS server). The broadcast mechanism is then ensured.

Our original proposal is to forward from the central station the whole Geonetworking message as it has been sent from the notifier station for many reasons:

– The next receiver could forward with ease the message to its neighbours which could not access to cellular networks through ITS-G5. This issue is very sensitive for road operators or authorities which care very much about the safety of road users (action 5 on Fig. 1).
– The message signing is still valid since the message authentication is achieved into the Geonetworking layer.
– The originating sender (the signer of the message) has not been changed. Then, liability issues are maintained and the computation load has been reduced (Fig. 5).

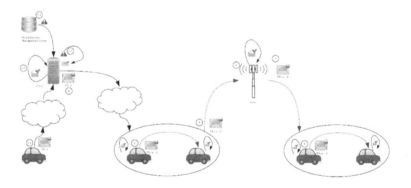

Fig. 5. The general hybrid architecture: ITS G5 + cellular networks

When an event has to be sent from the road operator to road users, it triggers this event from the the road operator server (action 2.1 on Fig. 4), then central station will build a geo-networking message containing the appropriate event. This central station will sign the message as a regular station. This station does not need to change its pseudonym certificates since it is not related to a driver which could be tracked by any external observer. In this case, the road operator signs the message (validates somehow the event) since it is the issuer.

4   Evaluation and Performance Analysis

We have experimented our solution into vehicles within the InterCor project (see the acknowledgment part for details).

We have used a set of certificates for 20 vehicles. We have observed the performances of these vehicles during a week driving through covered zones by RSUs together in order to emulate the ITS-G5 coverage and also driving in other uncovered zones.

We have measured an end-to-end communications mainly the duration between the event is triggering in a mobile OBU (On-Board Unit) and the reception of this event by all the other connected OBUs.

First, we studied the delay of the TCP connection as shown on the Fig. 6.

Fig. 6. End-to-end delay

The average delay presented by Fig. 6 is 250 ms using 3G/4G networks. These values are considered as high compared to ITS-G5 networks but are still acceptable for most of C-ITS use cases. Just notice that the signature/verifications processes are achieved by a software component. Further studies are needed in order to give more precise results.

Fig. 7. HTTP average delay

We have also experimented the connections with the central station through web-sockets using HTTP protocol. The reason is to be close to real deployment

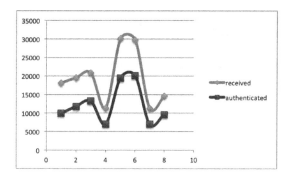

Fig. 8. Authenticated messages vs. received messages

of C-ITS in an industrial environment. Using HTTP will help network managers to setup load balancing mechanisms when several servers are used. However, the observed average HTTP delay on Fig. 7 is around 400 ms.

We have observed a delay of 400 ms. We are still in acceptable delays for C-TS applications (most of applications accept one second delay as a maximum delay).

As a consequence of this evaluation, the delay of the cellular communication for such road application (i.e. road works and hazardous warning) is satisfactory. Even with HTTP connections, the delay seems reasonable.

We have observed on a single RSU the authentication process and have analysed the authentication rate. Fig. 8 shows that almost 40% of messages are not authenticated by the RSU. This is due mainly to fact that receiving rate (10 messages per second from a single station) is very high compared to the message verification rate (nearly 20 messages per second). Since the experimentation has run with 20 vehicles which are supposed to send 200 messages per second. As we observe the authentication of all messages could not be achieved.

5 Conclusion

In this paper we have proposed a hybrid architecture for C-ITS which considers security (mainly authentication of messages and privacy of drivers). We have also shown how a simple revocation mechanism could be used without handling a complex CRL updates. The revocation is implemented thanks to simple validation codes uploaded periodically by vehicles. Our proposal is quite simple to implement for vehicles. They only need to open a connection with a server and sends to it the regular Geonetworking packets used in ITS-G5 networks. However, a dedicated server from a road operator shall be setup. We have shown the main features of such a server. We have explained the results obtained from our experimentations with 20 vehicles. The obtained delays are acceptable in the domain of C-ITS.

As a future works, we intend to test better the scalability of our system by launching simulations. In the meantime we intend to analyse the security performances of signing and verifying processes. They are very sensitive for the performance of the whole system.

Acknowledgement. This work was made possible by EC Grant No. INEA/CEF/ TRAN/A2014/1042281 from the INEA Agency for the SCOOP project. The statements made herein are solely the responsibility of the authors.

References

1. European Telecommunications Standards Institute (ETSI). http://www.etsi.org
2. IEEE Draft Standard for Amendment to Standard [for] Information Technology-Telecommunications and information exchange between systems-Local and Metropolitan networks-Specific requirements-Part II: Wireless LAN Medium Access Control (MAC) and Physical Layer (PHY) specifications-Amendment 6: Wireless Access in Vehicular Environments, in IEEE Std P802.11p/D11.0 April 2010, pp. 1–35, 15 June 2010
3. Intelligent Transport Systems (ITS); Vehicular Communications; GeoNetworking; Part 4: Geographical addressing and forwarding for point-to-point and point-to-multipoint communications; Sub-part 1: Media-Independent Functionality. ETSI EN 302 636-4-1 V1.2.1, July 2014
4. Intelligent Transport Systems (ITS); Vehicular Communications; GeoNetworking; Part 5: Transport Protocols; Sub-part 1: Basic Transport Protocol. ETSI EN 302 636-5-1 V1.2.1, August 2014
5. Eric, R.: Verheul, Issue First Activate Later Certificates for V2X. Presentation InterCor project, June 2017
6. Intelligent Transport Systems (ITS); Vehicular Communications; Basic Set of Applications; Part 2: Specification of Cooperative Awareness Basic Service. ETSI EN 302 637–2 v.1.3.2, November 2014
7. Weiß, C.: V2X communication in Europe: from research projects towards standardisation and field testing of vehicle communication technology. Comput. Netw. **55**(14), 3103–3119 (2011)
8. Santa, J., Fernandez, P.J., Perenaguez-Garcia, F.: Deployment of vehicular networks in highways using 802.11p and IPv6 technologies. I JAHUC **24**(1/2), 33–48 (2017)
9. Intelligent Transport Systems (ITS); Vehicular Communications; Basic Set of Applications; Part 3: Specifications of Decentralized Environmental Notification Basic Service. ETSI EN 302 637-3 V1.2.2, November 2014
10. Lochert, C., Hartenstein, H., Tian, J., Fussler, H., Hermann, D., Mauve, M.: A routing strategy for vehicular ad hoc networks in city environments. In: Proceedings (Cat. No. 03TH8683) IEEE IV2003 Intelligent Vehicles Symposium, pp. 156–161, June 2003
11. Ayaida, M., Barhoumi, M., Fouchal, H., Ghamri-Doudane, Y., Afilal, L.: PHRHLS: a movement-prediction-based joint routing and hierarchical location service for Vanets. In: IEEE International Conference on Communications (ICC), Budapest, Hungary, May 2013, pp. 1424–1428 (2013)
12. Ayaida, M., Barhoumi, M., Fouchal, H., Ghamri-Doudane, Y., Afilal, L.: HHLS: a hybrid routing technique for VANETs. In: Global Communications Conference (GLOBECOM), Anaheim, December 2012, pp. 44–48. IEEE (2012)

13. Lu, W., Bao, Y., Sun, X., Wang, Z.: Performance evaluation of inter-vehicle communication in a unidirectional dynamic traffic flow with shockwave. In: Proceedings of the International Conference on Ultra Modern Telecommunications, ICUMT 2009, 12–14 October 2009, St. Petersburg, Russia, pp. 1–6 (2009)
14. Lu, W., Han, L.D., Cherry, C.R.: Evaluation of vehicular communication networks in a car sharing system. Int. J. Intell. Transp. Syst. Res. **11**(3), 113–119 (2013)
15. Menouar, H., Lenardi, M., Filali, F., A movement prediction-based routing protocol for vehicle-to-vehicle communications. In: V2VCOM: 1st International Vehicle-to-Vehicle Communications Workshop, Co-located with MobiQuitous 2005, 21 July 2005, San Diego, USA, San Diego, USA, 07 2005
16. Mir, Z.H., Filali, F.: LTE and IEEE 802.11p for vehicular networking: a performance evaluation. EURASIP J. Wirel. Commun. Netw. **2014**, 89 (2014)
17. Seet, B.-C., Liu, G., Lee, B.-S., Foh, C.-H., Wong, K.-J., Lee, K.-K.: A-STAR: a mobile Ad Hoc routing strategy for metropolis vehicular communications. In: Mitrou, N., Kontovasilis, K., Rouskas, G.N., Iliadis, I., Merakos, L. (eds.) NETWORKING 2004. LNCS, vol. 3042, pp. 989–999. Springer, Heidelberg (2004). https://doi.org/10.1007/978-3-540-24693-0_81
18. Taleb, T., Ochi, M., Jamalipour, A., Kato, N., Nemoto, Y.: An efficient vehicle-heading based routing protocol for VANET networks. In: Wireless Communications and Networking Conference, 2006. WCNC 2006, vol. 4, pp. 2199–2204. IEEE, April 2006
19. Zeadally, S., Hunt, R., Chen, Y.-S., Irwin, A., Hassan, A.: Vehicular ad hoc networks (VANETS): status, results, and challenges. Telecommun. Syst. **50**(4), 217–241 (2012)
20. Jeong, S., Baek, Y., Son, S.H.: A hybrid V2X system for safety-critical applications in VANET. In: 2016 IEEE 4th International Conference on Cyber-Physical Systems, Networks, and Applications (CPSNA), Nagoya, pp. 13–18 (2016)
21. Bhover, S.U., Tugashetti, A., Rashinkar, P.: V2X communication protocol in VANET for co-operative intelligent transportation system. In: International Conference on Innovative Mechanisms for Industry Applications (ICIMIA), Bangalore, pp. 602–607 (2017)

IT-Security in Critical Infrastructures
Experiences, Results and Research Directions

Ulrike Lechner[(✉)]

Fakultät für Informatik,
Universität der Bundeswehr München, Neubiberg, Germany
Ulrike.Lechner@unibw.de

Abstract. IT security in critical infrastructures is one of the main challenges in informatics today. This contribution shares results and experiences from the research project VeSiKi. The discussion begins with the human factor in cybersecurity, with economic and strategic approaches to cybersecurity and presents selected results form a case study series on Cybersecurity and an eclectic summary of results from a Cybersecurity research program.

Keywords: Critical infrastructures · IT security · Case studies
Serious games · State-of-the-Art · Risk · Risk perception

1 Introduction and Motivation

Security of critical infrastructures, in particular IT security in critical infrastructures is one of today's major challenge in informatics. "Critical infrastructures (CI) are organizational and physical structures and facilities of such vital importance to a nation's society and economy that their failure or degradation would result in sustained supply shortages, significant disruption of public safety and security, or other dramatic consequences." [1] Critical infrastructure provide the products and services for the modern civilian society as energy, transportation, food, health services, water as well as telecommunication, media and public administration. Availability of products and services is paramount and integrity and confidentiality of information are other concerns in the domain of IT security in critical infrastructures. The increasing use of information and communication technology creates new areas of vulnerability and dependencies and current geopolitical developments add to the levels of risk. Critical infrastructure providers need to increase the level of security and they also need to meet – in our case – requirements from German and European legislation as, e.g., the German IT Security Act [2].

"Today's reality and yesterday's understanding" is according to Loch et al. [3] a seemingly inherent concern in cybersecurity as the white hats, i.e. the "good cybersecurity guys", tends to be a step behind the black hats, the "bad guys". We analyze in this paper in how far strategy and joint societal efforts to increase the level of security change the game to ensure that critical infrastructures are secure and the civil society is safe. We share in this contribution experiences and results from project VeSiKi that coordinated thirteen research projects with over 80 partners in a collaborative research process in IT security in critical infrastructures (cybersecurity). Cybersecurity is a topic

G. Fahrnberger et al. (Eds.): ICDCIT 2019, LNCS 11319, pp. 42–59, 2019.
https://doi.org/10.1007/978-3-030-05366-6_4

that has both regional and global aspects and that is determined by existing structures, the sociomateriality of critical infrastructures and the need to raise the level of security effectively and efficiently. We discuss what it takes to change the black and white hat game in cybersecurity.

The paper is organized as follows. First, we motivate this research and present the context – the research program "IT Sicherheit in Kritischen Infrastrukturen" (IT Security in Critical Infrastructures, itskritis) funded by the German Federal Ministry of Education and Research in Sect. 2. We argue that human perception of risk and economic decision making do not suffice in the domain of IT-Security and also that cybersecurity should not alone be guided by economic methods and tools (Sects. 3 and 4). In Sect. 5, we analyze strategies and cybersecurity as a joint societal challenge. Experiences about successful solutions in practice from the case study series case|kritis and next generation solutions – the state of the art– conclude our analysis (Sects. 6 and 7).

2   The Context – Project VeSiKi and Research Program itskritis

The context of this review of cybersecurity approaches is the research program "IT-Sicherheit in Kritischen Infrastrukturen" (IT Security in Critical Infrastructures, itskritis) and the research project "Vernetzte IT-Sicherheit Kritischer Infrastrukturen" (Networked IT Security for Critical Infrastructures, VeSiKi) funded by the German Ministry of Education and Research (BMBF) from 2014 to 2018.

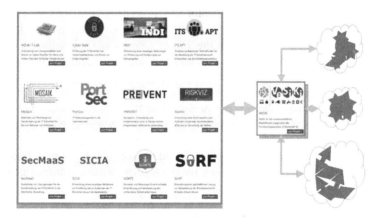

Fig. 1. Thirteen research projects Aqua-IT-Lab, CyberSafe, INDI, ITS.APT, Mosaik, PortSec, Prevent, RiskViz, SecMaaS, SICIA, Sidate, Surf and VeSiKI with a total of about 80 research partners collaborate in itskritis (www.itskritis.de)

In thirteen projects (Fig. 1), about 80 critical infrastructure operators, technology providers and research institutions collaborate from 2014 to 2018 in research on innovative concepts and technologies for IT security in critical infrastructures. The collaborative research process of the thirteen projects is coordinated by project VeSiKi.

Fig. 2. Monitor, Monitor 2.0, CASE|KRITIS, ITS|KRITIS platform, State of the Art and IT Security Navigator (www.itskritis.de, www.security-standards.de)

Results of VeSiKi and the collaborative research process include the two studies "Monitor" [4] and "Monitor 2.0" [5] with insights on threat level, threat landscape, IT security strategies and perceptions of risk and security. The interpretations of, e.g., the German IT security act [6] or the NIS directive are essential themes in the collaborative research process and the security navigator (www.security-standards.de) provides a collection of German, European, and international norms, standards, and legal acts. The IT security matchplay series with the games Operation Digital Snake, Owl and Chameleon [7] developed as serious games makes awareness training a fun experience. The itskritis "State of the Art" summarizes selected research results of the thirteen research projects. Platform www.itskrits.de supports knowledge transfer among the projects and, furthermore, between the projects and the general public. The paper at hand relies on the research results of VeSiKi and the collaborative research process of itskritis. Particular to the topic of IT security in critical infrastructures is that human factor, organization and technology need to be addressed and the human factor is the aspect with which we start the discussion on IT security of critical infrastructures.

3   The Human Factor in Cybersecurity

Do humans make the right, the future oriented decisions? – is a very relevant question when it comes to cybersecurity, to innovations in cybersecurity and to strategy. The socalled Human Factor -traditionally- is a major concern in the IT security [8]. We asked IT security experts in the two studies Monitor [4] and Monitor 2.0 [5] of IT security in critical infrastructures for an assessment of the threat level of their own organization, of their industrial sector and for the economic region Germany (Fig. 3).

The data analysis distinguishes all participants, KRITIS, i.e., German Critical Infrastructure according to the German IT Security Act and small and medium sized enterprises (SMEs).

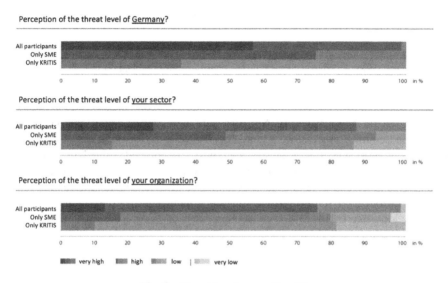

Fig. 3. Threat level perception [5]

There is a distinctive pattern in the data. On average, study participants rate the threat level to their own organization lower than the risk to their sector and this threat level again lower than threat level for Germany (Fig. 3). For the ability to defend against cyberattacks the converse applies: the capabilities of their own organization are rated higher than the capabilities of the sector and these capabilities are again higher than the capabilities of the economic region Germany [4].

This is a known pattern in risk perception: people in general estimate their own risk rather optimistic and are oblivious about this – a phenomenon known as optimism bias [9]. People also tend to overestimate the value of their own work – a phenomenon known as IKEA effect [10] and IT security experts put a lot of effort into the security of their organization. That such perception of individual risks and value of effort is a deeply rooted human trait illustrates the Nobel Memorial Prize in Economic Sciences 2017 that was awarded to Richard Thaler for his work in behavioral economics on risk perception and irrational risk response to abstract risks in the future [9].

A next topic in our studies are the factors that influence the IT security measures in an organization (Fig. 4), i.e. the risk assessment and response on organizational level.

We find that attacks against the organization and regulations have the strongest impact on IT security in an organization. The impact of risk analysis on IT security in an organization seems to be weaker. This is interesting as, e.g. the German IT Security Act as well as international standards and norms require organizations to do risk analysis as part of information security management. We argue, that not only individual

In how far have the following factors influenced IT security in your organization?

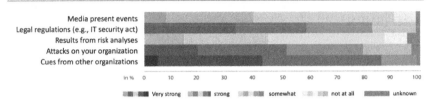

Fig. 4. Impact factors on IT security in an organization [5]

risk perception but also the systematic risk management in organizations seem not to be the driving factor in cybersecurity. Note also that other studies report, that IT security information scouting processes e.g., on novel threats, novel malware or campaigns against the own organization or the sector are typically not well defined, not automated and not systematic. In a study on cybersecurity processes, we find that for many organizations it seems rather unclear on whether IT security related information to the outside contributes to the security within an organization and what the processes eventually look like [11].

Reaction to specific threats? (All particpants)

	Wannacry	Mirai	Industroyer	(Not)Petya
The threat was known in advance and measures could be taken	51%	26%	20%	38%
No measures were taken	13%	30%	30%	20%
New measures were taken	18%	7%	7%	12%
Existing measures were checked	62%	39%	37%	50%
I do not know	7%	23%	25%	15%

Fig. 5. Reactions of an organization to specific threats [5]

Figure 5 depicts the results on our questions for reaction to news on a Cyberthreat. For a significant percentage of organizations, the threat – in all four cases – was known in advance and measures were already taken in advance, most organizations however reviewed their existing measures, while only a minority took either no action or implemented new IT security measures. One of the IT experts in critical infrastructures commented on that figure that – "yes, for every new malware we look what that means for our processes". Note that critical infrastructure providers, i.e. that are categorized as KRITIS according to the German IT Security Act are in general more active – they review processes more often and they take more often new measures than providers of (non-critical) infrastructures [5]. This illustrates that critical infrastructure providers take their responsibility seriously and become active whenever there is information on a novel malware. It seems that the confidence in security in their own organization does not prevent the IT security experts to check measures and processes in place. This result seems to contradict – to some extent – the optimistic risk perception and capability perception presented in Fig. 1.

Psychology and marketing literature point out that it is a deeply human trait to be optimistic, to underestimate risks, to respond not rationally to abstract risks in the future. This optimism bias is found in both men and women as well as throughout cultures. Our results from the Monitor studies seem to suggest that the optimism bias applies in cybersecurity and also that the institutionalized systematic risk management as part of the information security management in organizations hardly provide the energy to change the black hat - white hat game in IT security while the critical infrastructure provides need to put effort into their systems with every novel malware and threat.

The Nobel laureate Richard Thaler suggests that such risk response is somewhat inherent for abstract risks in the future: it takes smart decision architectures and a nudge strategy [9] to ensure that humans make the right, the safe and future oriented decisions. "Nudge is a concept in behavioral science, political theory and economics which proposes positive reinforcement and indirect suggestions as ways to influence the behavior and decision making of groups or individuals. Nudging contrasts with other ways to achieve compliance, such as education, legislation or enforcement. A nudge makes it more likely that an individual will make a particular choice, or behave in a particular way, by altering the environment so that automatic cognitive processes are triggered to favour the desired outcome." [9] In subsequent sections, we review whether economic theories and instruments provide guidance in risk response, the global and national approaches to Cybersecurity and technology to enable smart decision architectures and nudges.

4   The Economy of Cybersecurity – a Brief Review

In security of critical infrastructures costs and other burdens of both technological and organizational measures are crucial. Various studies argue that the damage from cybersecurity incidents is on the rise and that this is a global phenomenon (cf. e.g. [12]). Studies suggest that there is a well established yet hidden market for, e.g., zero-day exploits, malware tools, malware-as-a-service as well as for stolen data ranging from credit card data, financial data, employee credentials, compromising pictures or films to Netflix accounts or bonus cards [13].

Determining the necessary investments in IT security measures is far from obvious. The "Calculus of Negligence" suggests $PL > B$ where B is the cost of taking precautions, P is the probability of loss and L is the gravity of the loss. The product

$P * L$ must be a greater amount than B to create a duty of due care. This rule was coined by Judge Learned Hand [14].

The "Return on Security Investments" (ROSI) uses ((ALE*Mitigation ratio – Cost of solution)/Cost of Solution) to determine the return on investments. ALE is the annual loss expectancy [15]. ROSI assumes that investments mitigate risks and potential losses and can be utilized to compare the efficiency for security investments.

The renowned model by Gordon and Loeb allows to reason about the efficiency of security investments: "Our analysis shows that for two broad classes of security breach probability functions, the optimal amount to spend on information security never exceeds 37% of the expected loss resulting from a security breach (and is typically much less that 37%). Hence, the optimal amount to spend on information security would typically be far less than even the expected loss from a security breach." [16, 17].

These three methods for assessing the necessary investments all deal with rather low or unknown likelihoods and potentially huge damage and damages that can hardly be quantified. The question remains whether results of such economic models eventually trigger investments and the right decisions. Yet, there are critical infrastructures to which investments are more of a burden then in others. E.g. the health care sector - at least according to the German health care system - cannot just transfer the costs for IT security to medical bills. The energy sector is less restrained to transfer the costs to protect the infrastructure to its customers. Anyway, customers or end users are reluctant to pay for security and decision makers are equally reluctant to invest in topics that are not honored by the market.

However, discussions on cybersecurity as, e.g., on blackouts or fake news illustrate that cybersecurity has implications to split society. Prof. Dirk Heckmann coined the term "Concordization" for tragedies that – in analogy to the tragic accident of the Concorde that caused to stop not only all flights of the Concorde but defacto all developments of supersonic commercial airplanes – change the trust in technology and developments of technology [18]. Again, this is an argument that investments in cybersecurity should not be measured by economic means alone. Prof. Peter Burgess argued at the first conference of its|kritis in 2015 as keynote speaker for the notion of "social value" of critical infrastructure, i.e., critical infrastructures have the value that society ascribes to them. This underlines the strategic importance of politics and legislation in the domain of critical infrastructures. The subsequent section in this analysis is about society and how legislation addresses the topic of cybersecurity.

5   Strategies in Cybersecurity – Selected Examples

Cybersecurity is a topic of strategic relevance and both a regional and a global phenomenon: The first instances of malware (in the 80s of the past century) spread then globally – according to what was considered global at that time. In the 90s, number and variety of malware increased significantly and infections of mainly personal and desktop computers as Windows PCs, Macintosh, Atari and Amiga desktops spread. Today, the threat landscape of current malware is found to be differentiated with malware that may spread globally or that aims at a particular technology, say of one or more manufacturers, of a particular system integrator or technology provider, or to target a particular region or nation state, a particular kind of organization or even a single organizations. E.g., Stuxnet as the first prominent malware designed to infect Industrial Control Systems (ICS) was designed to operate and spread in a particular region and address technology from one manufacturer [19]. Social engineering or ransomware that relies on (spear) phishing as primary attack vector relies on knowledge about language and processes as well as of the look-and-feel of forms or emails or a particular exploitation chain to monetarize or make other use of information collected by malware or control gained through malware. This means in practice that technology providers, manufacturers, sectors, region states need to develop capabilities to detect cyberthreats as novel malware or campaigns, to prevent attacks and respond to attacks – as the risk for any of these players could be different and because any of these actors need to provide information to detect and prevent attacks. In our case the strategies of nation states or economic regions are of particular interest as this shapes how authorities and private organizations work together in cybersecurity.

Nation states take different approaches to ensure security of critical infrastructures. This brief review summarizes work x from D. Kipker and Kipker & Müller in project VeSiKi [6, 20, 21]:

Germany implements a rather collaborative public-private partnership approach: the Federal Office for Information Security (cf. bsi.bund.de) is "the national cyber security authority" which "shapes information security in digitization through prevention, detection and reaction for government, business and society" as the central public institution for cybersecurity. "The UP KRITIS National initiative" implements the collaboration of critical infrastructures and public administration. The German IT Security Act [2] articulates the requirements for critical infrastructures: the need to report "critical" cyber incidents to the BSI, certify their measures and establish points of contact for authorities. The CRITIS directive defines thresholds which infrastructure providers are considered to be critical and critical infrastructure providers register themselves as critical infrastructures. These critical infrastructure operators are entitled to information and consultation on security issues. Sectors of critical infrastructures may define sector specific security standards to be approved by the BSI.

Other states employ different approaches. E.g., France uses a more centralized approach: the critical infrastructures are been determined in a process led by public administration. The strategic goal of the French national Digital Security Strategy articulates as the first one is "Fundamental interests, defence and security of State information systems and critical infrastructures, major cybersecurity crisis". (cf. article 22 of the French CIIP law ("Loi de programmation militaire 2014-2019")).[1] Europe's strategy for "An Open, Safe and Secure Cyberspace" represents EU's vision on how best to prevent and respond to cyber disruptions and attacks and articulates priorities[2]. The NIS directive requires the member states to have certain national cybersecurity capability, e.g. a national Computer Security Incident Response Team (CSIRT) and it

---

[1] https://www.enisa.europa.eu/topics/national-cyber-security-strategies/ncss-map/strategies/information-systems-defence-and-security-frances-strategy.

[2] http://europa.eu/rapid/press-release_IP-13-94_en.htm.

requires cross-border collaboration between EU countries, e.g. the operational EU CSIRT network and national supervision of critical sectors.

The US strategy is articulated in the National Security Action Plan (CNAP) and the Executive Order 13636 "Improving Critical Infrastructure Cybersecurity" from 2013 articulates the measures for the protection of critical infrastructures, as e.g. information sharing between public authorities and critical infrastructure operators and facilitates self-regulation. Accordingly, the National Institute of Standards and Technology (NIST) published a "Cybersecurity Framework", with voluntary standards, measures and best practices in cybersecurity. The Cybersecurity Enhancement Act (2014) fosters a voluntary private-public collaboration. Sector specific regulations on federal level are, e.g., the Health Insurance Portability and Accountability Act (HIPAA, 1996) for health related data, the Financial Services Modernization Act (Gramm-Leach-Bliley Act, 1999) for personal financial data or the Federal Information Management Act (FISMA, 2002) for information processing in federal administration and the Cybersecurity Information Sharing Act (CISA, 2015) for sharing IT security relation information between private organization and administration. The Federal Trade Commission (FTC) is the central public authority in the Cyber Security Strategy.

Russia articulated with its second Cyber-Security-Doctrine in 2016 its response to the increasing cyber threat levels. The main focus of this doctrine is not so much on economic aspects but on political and military interests and it is connected with the national security strategy of the Russian Federation and its defense strategy. [6] The "Federal Law on Security of Critical Russian Federation Information Infrastructure" sets not only the frame for security of critical infrastructures, but also lays the foundation for a national IT security system, ranging from detection, prevention to the elimination of the aftereffects of cyber incidents. It defines rights and obligations to service providers as critical service providers take place in an information exchange with authorities and it defines an expansion of official control and instruction rights to review the new legal requirements. Among other, critical infrastructure providers inform public administration on cyber incidents and support public authorities in detection of the state of security, prevention and reaction to Cyber incidents.

In China, the Cybersecurity Law from 2016 and an additional catalogue for operational IT security measure articulate an approach to privacy and information security. Key network technology and services need to be certified in a national security review by the Cybersecurity Review Committee and the Cybersecurity Review Expert Committee in a public-private partnership.

The various cybersecurity strategies differ in scope and focus as well as in the role of public administration and private organizations. Minimum security standards throughout sectors and the preparation for more digitalization with more networked structures for information sharing and common operational pictures is common to all the national cybersecurity initiatives. The German approach relies on collaboration between public authorities and private organizations and therefore it is interesting to see what critical infrastructures do in cybersecurity and what they consider to be successful approaches. It is an open question to be answered in the future which approach will facilitate more innovation and creativity – to get ahead in the game of black hats vs. the white hats.

6 Security in Practice - the Case Study Series CASE|KRITIS Revisited

IT security in critical infrastructures is a complex topic that involves decision making about investments and the right balance in a strategy for human, organizational and technical security measures. This section revisits the CASE|KRITIS case study series [18, 22] to analyze the world of processes in IT security.

Case studies are considered to be a method to study complex, real world phenomena and therefore a suitable method to study IT security measures in critical infrastructures with technology, human factor and organizational processes. Focus of our case studies are business processes and the technology necessary to implement and support them. Our approach is inspired by the eXperience method for case studies [23]. The case studies were conducted from 2015 to 2017 and the cross-case study in 2017 and 2018.

6.1 The Cases of CRITIS

The nine cases with organization, title, case study authors and the case type (successful project, technology or organizational culture) together with a cross case analysis are summarized in Table 1. Note that one case study (Dairy) is anonymized. The cases are presented briefly below.

Table 1. The CASE|KRITIS case studies

	Title (original title)	Authors
Bundeswehr	Working Group IT-SecAsBw – How a working ground fosters IT Security Awareness inland and abroad (*AG IT-SecAwBw – Wie eine Arbeitsgruppe IT-Security Awareness im In- und Ausland fördert*)	A. Rieb, G. Opper
genua gmbh	Remote Maintenance in Critical Infrastructures (*Fernwartung Kritischer Infrastrukturen*)	A. Rieb
itWatch GmbH	A Secure Standard Process for Digital Crime Scene Photography with DeviceWatch (*Ein sicherer Standardprozess für die Digitale Tatortfotografie mit DeviceWatch*)	S. Lücking, S. Dännart
kbo	Balanced Risk Management for Sustainable Security (*Ausgewogenes Risikomanagement für nachhaltige Sicherheit*)	T. Kehr, S. Dännart
Dairy	IT Security in a Dairy: Family Tradition and High Availability (*IT-Sicherheit in der Molkerei: Familientradition und Hochverfügbarkeit*)	S. Dännart
PREVENT	IT Security for Business Processes in the Financial Sector: The Management Solution PREVENT *IT-Sicherheit für Geschäftsprozesse im Finanzsektor: die Managementlösung PREVENT)*	S. Rudel, T. Bollen

(*continued*)

Table 1. (*continued*)

	Title (original title)	Authors
SAP SE	Information Security at SAP SE: The Longest Human Firewall in the World (*Informationssicherheit bei SAP SE: Die längste Human Firewall der Welt*)	U. Lechner, T. Gurschler, A. Rieb
Stadt Gera	Coordination Center East Thuringia: IT-Security in a Coordination Center (*Zentrale Leitstelle Ostthüringen: IT-Sicherheit in einer Leitstelle*)	T. Gurschler, A. Rieb, M. Hofmeier
ugarbe software	Information Security with ClassifyIt: Information Security through Digital Classification of Documents and Emails (*Informationssicherheit durch ClassifyIt: Informationssicherheit durch gestützte Klassifizierung von Dokumenten und E-Mails*)	A. Rieb

The case **"Working Group IT-SecAsBw – How a working ground fosters IT Security Awareness inland and abroad"** is about an IT security awareness campaign: Key visual of the campaign is a power plug with the symbol of a face – a symbol that IT security is both about technology measures and the human factor alike. The PIA campaign exemplifies a collaborative, longitudinal IT security activity with a tradition to engage IT security staff and with a minimum of dedicated resources.

Case **"Remote Maintenance in Critical Infrastructures"** tackles with remote access for maintenance one of the 10 most relevant IT security topics in Critical Infrastructures according to BSI [24]. The remote, secure login for maintenance purposes is the core process considered in the case study. Remote access via a single interface, the functionality to control and monitor "sessions" for remote maintenance increases the security level of critical infrastructures. The single interface for all maintenance service providers and all service operation decreases complexity in securing remote access while the solution is easy to integrate in existing IT landscape in a critical infrastructure.

The case **"A Secure Standard Process for Digital Crime Scene Photography"** presents an innovative secure-by-design solution for crime scene photography and the handling of digital crime scene photos in police work. Police officers may use any digital camera, the photos are watermarked with a signature when transferred in the police information system such that authenticity of pictures is maintained throughout police work. Amortization took only three years and the new process is considered to be modern as well as user friendly as it saves time and resources.

Case **"Balanced Risk Management for Sustainable IT Security"** analyses the reaction to ransomware threats against hospitals. While the first reaction to an imminent ransomware was a complete separation of the hospital from the Internet, the hospital established to a more refined strategy later with a considerable speed up of IT security processes and an increased priority for IT security investments. The novel process of security incident response includes all stakeholders in the hospital as well as external service providers. Joint responsibility for IT security measures as well as a proved and tested communication policy rounds up the process. A few months after the process was first implemented in the reaction to the ransomware threat: the hospital group was successful in the defense against a considerable threat.

Case **"IT Security in the Food Industry: Tradition and High Availability"** reports on a safety and security culture of a family owned dairy in a rural area. The processing of sensitive primary products as raw milk requires high availability of production lines. The case is about the strategy of the CIO – he integrates traditional organizational and modern IT security measures in a successful digitalization strategy. Cornerstone of his strategy are close relations to IT staff, the integration of IT staff and technicians into one team with uniform IT inspired processes, training of staff and the loyalty of staff over generations to the company as the main employer in town. Employees practice essential IT security routines as e.g., restoring data from backups in their daily work, new IT technology is only implemented when staff feels confident to handle disruptions and IT staff is encouraged to identify and experiment with potentially useful IT innovations. The case explores also IT security measures to ensure high availability as real time backups of the core SAP system or VLan encapsulation of production lines.

The case **"IT Security for Business Processes in the Financial Sector – The Management Solution PREVENT"** demonstrates real-life complexity of a comprehensive enterprise level risk management. In this case study, the business process is the unit of analysis in risk management. The underlying business case is a (fictitious) computing center of a bank that provides business processes as a service to several (fictitious) client banks. The risk management approach comprises a unified way to source all risk relevant data and a collection of tools (simulations, analytic methods) for risk analysis. The case exemplifies the novel risk management approach which an analysis of interdependencies between infrastructure, information system and business process level. The case argues about the advantages such a comprehensive risk management and the business models for which such a comprehensive risk management is a prerequisite.

"Information Security at SAP SE: The Longest Human Firewall in the World" is a case study on the information security campaign at SAP SE. Key visual of the campaign is a chain of SAP employees with a group handshake with crossed arms – a symbol for the joint effort to protect the company. Employees take part in an individual (mandatory) information security training and can then become part of the human firewall with a picture and an individual statement on information security. The case study highlights the pivotal role of employees in information security and that information security eventually benefits from "fun" but also from perseverance.

Case study **"Coordination Center East Thuringia: IT-Security in a Coordination Center"** discusses availability of emergency services: The alarm process from an emergency call to alerting the emergency services need to be available despite outage of IT components. The case study presents fallbacks and redundancies as well as IT security concepts to ensure highest availability of the emergency number 112 with emergency services. It addresses questions in the further development of information and communication technologies in a coordination center of emergency services. Success factors are the volition of staff not only to use but to understand the infrastructure with its technologies and to get to the bottom of any problem to solve it.

Case **"Information Security by Digital Classification of Documents and E-Mails"** is about a tool to ensure confidentiality of information. ClassifyIt is a PlugIn for Microsoft Office that support users in the classification of documents and emails. Together with a firewall it ensures that only documents and emails with adequate classification can leave the organization and that encryption that is adequate for the document is used for sending it via email. The software is distributed via standard software distribution tools, and it can be customized individually, interfaces for users and administrators are perceived to be user friendly and it needs no Internet connection.

The nine cases illustrate strategic decisions made by critical infrastructure providers and operators. They illustrate that the field of IT security provides a plethora of challenges for novel technical or organizational measures and that technologies, processes, leadership and strategy matter in the domain of Cybersecurity. What distinguishes these projects that can be considered good or best practices? This question is to be answered in a cross-case analysis in the subsequent section.

6.2 Success Factors for IT Security in Critical Infrastructures

This section presents selected topics from the cross-case analysis to identify success factors beyond the apparent contribution to IT security. For the paper at hand we selected codes and arguments from the full cross case analysis presented in [18] and focus on the topics of risk response and the human factor (cf. Sect. 3).

The first analysis perspective is the one on risk perception (cf. Sect. 3). We have looked for information in how far IT security is being measured and what we can learn from the cases on risk management. This perspective is captured in the code "**Measurement of IT Security**". To be able to measure or assess the level of IT security is an important capability – critical infrastructure operators as well as public institutions look actively for methods and tools to "measure security".

The cross-case analysis identifies various perspectives: The case on the "Management Solution PREVENT" exemplifies the complexity of a comprehensive risk assessment. The SAP case illustrates that measurements of the level of IT security can be relatively simple (SAP uses only a couple of questions) – what matters is perseverance over several years to see how the level of security changes over time. However, measuring security to increase the level of security seems not to be the main driver in the cases: It is a qualitative assessment of vulnerabilities and the need to address them that is the dominant pattern throughout the cases.

The economic perspective is captured in code "**Cost efficiency of IT security measures**". Cost efficiency of IT security measures is an important factor in particular for the small and medium sized critical infrastructure operators. The cases offer different perspectives on cost efficiency and investments: The case on the Secure Standard Process for Digital Crime Scene Photography by itWatch is on a secure-by-design solution and this case study is the only one that reports on return of investment: the new process is more efficient than the "old, analogous" way of handling photographs. The case study on the Toolbox for an awareness campaign argues first, that such a toolbox is more cost efficient than individual campaigns developed from scratch and costs for running the working group and providing awareness campaign material are reasonable. The cases on IT security products (Remote Maintenance, ClassifyIt by ugarbe.de software) argue with limited costs for trainings and –qualitatively– that well designed solutions, solutions with little integration and training efforts and with standard processes have economic advantages in the long run.

A second code that captures the economic perspective is "**Simplicity of IT security measures**". No one wants "over-complex" security projects – this is common sense – and ideally, successful IT security projects should be simple, in particular as small and medium-sized critical infrastructure operators are reluctant to adopt seemingly "complex" measures. The code "simplicity of measure" in the cross case analysis captures the resources necessary to implement and operate IT security measures. The coding and the inductive analysis process identify three criteria as the ones that are used in practice to capture "simplicity": (1) user friendliness (2) implementation effort and (3) training effort for end users, IT staff as system administrators. These three criteria are the ones of which our interview partners are proud of as technology providers or as security experts and which they consider to be success factors in cybersecurity.

Other codes analyze interdependencies between security solutions and other information systems and their processes and the analysis identifies little interdependency as a success factor as well as the prerequisites, i.e., the "homework that needs to be done" to make a solution effective. The trade-off between availability and IT security of the IT landscape is a core topic in case "Stadt Gera" and availability is also the driver in the design of the whole security organization in case "Dairy". The cases Dairy and SAP and the case of the research project PREVENT illustrate the size and complexity of IT security solutions: the leadership necessary to take a family owned business into the digital age with the necessary level of security, the fun and effort to raise awareness in a global organization and the complexity of collecting and analyzing data for risk management at business process level in the research of project event. This leads us to the next section of future security, i.e. on research projects in the domain of cybersecurity.

7   The State of the Art in Cybersecurity – Selected Results and Experiences from Research in itskritis

The cases focus on successful projects and the case analysis identifies simplicity and costs as important factor – the projects of the research program have been selected for research on systemic approaches to IT security. The State-of-the-Art [25] summarizes selected results from the research program itskritis with its thirteen projects (cf. Sect. 2). In this brief and eclectic review we emphasize again the topics risk perception and response.

The IT security topics particular to the domain of Cybersecurity with its industrial control systems and its particular focus on availability of products and services is addresses by several projects: PortSec develops methods to analyze and increase dependability of the software hubs in ports that process incoming and outgoing messages. These pieces of software are to some extent legacy, heterogenous and with software architectures from times, in which dependability and security were less of importance. Furthermore, they operate in an open setting with connections to other hubs and technology. Methods to analyze and retrofit such complex software projects are crucial not only in the port use case. Project INDI develops methods and tools to monitor networks with protocols from the pre-Internet era to analyze whether communication is compliant with the protocols. Project SURF uses trusted elements to harden devices and develop an holistic approach to increase the level of security as well as an holistic information security approach.

The risk perception, risk assessment and the risk response are the core research results of several research projects. Project SecMaaS goes beyond technology and develops concepts and tools for security services in the domain of public administration. Tools that allow risk assessment to provide services are a essential contribution by SecMaaS. Mosaic does the risk analysis at architecture level and provides respective methods and tools. The solutions of project Aqua-IT-Lab include a method and tool for self-assessment of the level of security that provides recommendations for methods necessary to reach the sector specific state of the art in IT security. This research by project Aqua-IT-Lab is done in particular for the sector water with the many small and medium sized water suppliers in Germany in mind. Project SICIA assess the level of risk from components, relates these risks via connectedness graphs and allows a comparative and time series analysis. This research was done with the complexity of energy plants and energy sector in mind. The approach of project ITS.APT addresses the risks of end users and employees in the open setting of hospitals and provides an innovative concept and solution for testing awareness of users: software that emulates attacks as phishing is being deployed and users experience attacks and typical malware behavior and the test allow to analyze the cybersecurity awareness of users, i.e., will they identify malware, abnormal behavior of their computer and report to the service desk for security incident response. The method of project RiskViz relies on a search engine to identify devices on the Internet or Intranet and relate this information to vulnerabilities databases and other information sources, as well as methods from the risk assessment in insurance industry that allows to determine the level of risk for critical infrastructures. Project Sidate provides a networking platform for small and medium sized critical infrastructure providers and tools to assess the level of security and provide recommendations. The systemic projects of itskritis facilitate a risk assessment and relate the abstract risks to concrete IT security measurements or measures.

A brief presentation of one of VeSiKi's research results, the IT security game series "IT-Matchplays" with the games Operation Digital Chameleon, Operation Digital Owl and Operation Digital Snake concludes the review of research results. Red and blue teams develop attack chains and IT security measures. Figure 6 depicts the game board with typical IT components of a critical infrastructure.

The red team's task is to develop an attack against the critical infrastructure protected by the blue team. Team red chooses a threat actor as a role and they declare a goal related to their role. In addition to that, red teams are instructed to justify their attack before designing their attack chain and before deciding on a goal. I.e. red teams have to think about motivation and technique of neutralization of the threat actor that they enact. The blue team knows which kind of actor is going to attack. The development of attack chains and defense strategies is followed by a presentation and the decision about which team(s) win(s). Red teams present goal, technique of neutralization and attack chain. Results of teams red and blue are assessed in a group

Fig. 6. The board of "Operation Digital Chameleon"

discussion led by the game master regarding plausibility of the concepts with the chosen threat actor and feasibility. The gaming phase is followed by a debriefing which aims to solicit emotions, proposals on improvements of the gaming experience, and a self-assessment of IT security awareness levels. A discussion of the threat actor including their attacks and team blue's defense strategies is part of the debriefing. For more details regarding the model of the game, see [26]. This game allows to analyze the level of awareness and to raise awareness about concerns of IT security specialists about current tools and procedures. Furthermore, it allows to make intangible, weak signals about forthcoming topics tangible and a look ahead – by thinking out of the box in a creative format. We argue that the technology implements smart decision architectures and give impulses to assess risk and react in a future oriented way.

8 Summary

IT security for critical infrastructures is an enticing field – the level of security needs to be increased and we argue that this is a societal challenge. Risk perception and risk response are considered to be inherently difficult – they can be considered human factors for the domain of critical infrastructures. The article briefly reviews selected economic models which seem to fall short in supporting adequate decision making and risk response. The various strategies of regions and state take different society approaches to cybersecurity and it remains open, which strategy eventually fosters innovation and creativity beyond networking and information sharing. The results from the case study series illustrate experiences from practice in Cybersecurity projects while the results of the project illustrates the future dimension of systemic approaches to cybersecurity. Risk reaction and risk response are the focus in this brief and very subjective review. The security of critical infrastructures currently is a relevant topic, yet novel approaches and more research is needed for creativity to change the white hat vs. black hat games and to develop a better understanding for today's challenges.

Acknowledgements. This research is funded by the German Federal Ministry of Education and Research under Grant Number FKZ: 16KIS0213K.

I would like to thank all case study partners and interviewees for the insights as well as our project partners from VeSiKi and our fellow projects from ITS|KRITIS for their engagement in the collaborative research process of itskritis. I am indebted to the VeSiKi Team and in particular Steffi Rudel as well as Sebastian Dännart, Andreas Rieb, Thomas Diefenbach, Tamara Gurschler, Manfred Hofmeier, and Tim Reimers as well as Kathrin Möslein, Albrecht Fritzsche, Max Jalowski, Matthias Raß, Benedikt Buchner and Andreas Harner for their work on the research results of VeSiKi and itskritis. Dennis Kipker and Sven Müller contributed with their work on norms, standards and Cybersecurity law in VeSiKi to this article.

References

1. BSI - Critical Infrastructure Protection in Germany. https://www.bsi.bund.de/EN/Topics/Criticalinfrastructures/criticalinfrastructures_node.html
2. Bundesgesetzblatt: Gesetz zur Erhöhung der Sicherheit informationstechnischer Systeme (IT-Sicherheitsgesetz, Bundesgesetzblatt Jahrgang 2015 Teil I Nr. 31) (2015)
3. Loch, K.D., Carr, H.H., Warketin, M.E.: Threats to information systems: today's reality, yesterday's understanding evolution of computer security. MISQ. **16**, 173–187 (1992)
4. VeSiKi: Monitor IT-Sicherheit Kritischer Infrastrukturen. Universität der Bundeswehr München, Neubiberg (2017)
5. Lechner, U.: Monitor 2.0 IT-Sicherheit Kritischer Infrastrukturen (2018)
6. Kipker, D.-K., Müller, S.: Internationale Cybersecurity-Regulierung (2018)
7. Rieb, A., Gurschler, T., Lechner, U.: A gamified approach to explore techniques of neutralization of threat actors in cybercrime. In: Schweighofer, E., Leitold, A., Mitrakas, A., Rannenberg, K. (eds.) APF 2017, vol. 10518, pp. 87–103. Springer, Heidelberg (2017). https://doi.org/10.1007/978-3-319-67280-9_5
8. Badke-Schaub, P., Hofinger, G., Lauche, K.: Human Factors - Psychologie sicheren Handels in Risikobranchen. Springer, Heidelberg (2012)
9. Thaler, R.H., Sunstein, C.R.: Nudge: Improving Decisions About Health, Wealth, and Happiness. Yale University Press, New Haeven (2008)
10. Norton, M., Mochon, D., Ariely, D.: The "IKEA Effect": When Labor Leads to Love (2011)
11. Bhanu, Y., et al.: A cyberthreat search process and service. In: Proceedings of the 2nd International Conference on Information Systems Security and Privacy, ICISSP 2016 (2016)
12. Ponemon Institute and Accenture: 2017 Cost of Cyber Crime Study, p. 56 (2017)
13. McFarland, C., Paget, F., Samani, R.: The hidden data economy - the marketplace for stolen digital information (2015)
14. Brown, J.P.: Toward an economic theory of liability. J. Legal Stud. **2**, 323–349 (1973)
15. Enisa: Introduction to Return on Security Investment, p. 18 (2012)
16. Gordon, L.A., Loeb, M.P.: The economics of information security investment. ACM Trans. Inf. Syst. Secur. **5**, 438–457 (2002)
17. Gordon, L.A., Loeb, M.P., Zhou, L.: Investing in cybersecurity: insights from the Gordon-Loeb model. J. Inf. Secur. **07**, 49–59 (2016)
18. Lechner, U., Dännart, S., Rieb, A., Rudel, S.: IT-Sicherheit in Kritischen Infrastrukturen: Fallstudien zur IT-Sicherheit in Kritischen Infrastrukturen. Logos Verlag, Berlin (2018)
19. Zetter, K.: Countdown to Zero Day: Stuxnet and the Launch of the World's First Digital Weapon. Broadway Books, Portland (2015)
20. Kipker, D.-K.: VPN-Tunnelabschaltung und „Chinese Cybersecurity Law" – wohl mehr Mythos als Realität. DuD - Datenschutz und Datensicherheit **42**(9), 574–575 (2018)

21. Kipker, D.-K.: Pläne für ein Datenschutzgesetz in Indien: Untersuchung des White Paper des Expertenkomitees (2018, to appear)

22. Dännart, S., Diefenbach, T., Hofmeier, M., Rieb, A., Lechner, U.: IT-Sicherheit in Kritischen Infrastrukturen – eine Fallstudien-basierte Analyse von Praxisbeispielen. In: Drews, P., Burkhardt, F., Niemeyer, P., Xie, L. (eds.) Konferenzband Multikonferenz Wirtschaftsinformatik 2018: Data driven X - Turning Data into Value. Leuphana Universität Lüneburg, Lüneburg (2018)

23. Schubert, P., Wölfle, R.: The experience methodology for writing IS case studies. In: Americas Conference on Information Systems, pp. 19–30 (2006)

24. BSI: Industrial Control System Security: Top 10 Bedrohungen und Gegenmaßnahmen 2016 (2016)

25. Lechner, U., Rudel, S.: IT-Sicherheit für Kritische Infrastrukturen. Ergebnisse des Förderschwerpunkts IT-Sicherheit für Kritische Infrastrukturen ITS|KRITIS des BMBF. VeSiKi - Vernetzte IT-Sicherheit Kritischer Infrastrukturen (2018)

26. Rieb, A., Lechner, U.: Operation digital chameleon – towards an open cybersecurity method. In: Proceedings of the 12th International Symposium on Open Collaboration (OpenSym 2016), Berlin, pp. 1–10 (2016)

Digital Society: A Computing Science Prospective

Hrushikesha Mohanty[1,2(✉)]

[1] KIIT Deemed University, Bhubaneswar, India
h.mohanty@kiit.ac.in
[2] University of Hyderabad, Hyderabad, India
hmcs@uohyd.ac.in

Abstract. Unprecedented connectivity over Internet has given rise to digital society where individuals turn to netizens in cyberspace. The support that computing science can offer enabling netizens to active citizens is of interest for computing professionals. From computing science perspective, this paper addresses some of the issues like modelling a netizen, communication, pressure group creation, electronic voting, law making and education for digital society; scopes the research challenges the issues offer.

Keywords: Digital society · Netizen modelling
Social communication · Pressure group management
Electronic voting and law making

1 Introduction

Internet has brought changes to every walk of life in contemporary world. It has provided different digital platforms and so connectivities bringing people of far distance digitally close defying geographical separations. A citizen on Internet has turned to a netizen. However, though a netizen's presence is spread across cyberspace defying limits of sovereign boundary lines still a netizen is also a citizen. This paper puts interest on facilitating netizens to perform as a smart citizen. The emerging digital society is predominantly technology driven for faster growth. It also brings in different aspects of digital society that needs to redefine existing social theory and inventing new. Now computing science being an enabler has greater challenge to face and provide specific solutions to the challenges digital society facing.

Digital world provides instantaneous access to information and so people unlike before are more and fast aware of happenings around. Soon after new information available, people evolve strategy to make use of information for their betterments. Thus a digital society is endowed with dynamic changes. In order to make a digital society smart, not only people and society but also governance is to be relooked. In order to be timely responsive, technology has to provide a framework that enables netizens to turn themselves into smart citizens.

G. Fahrnberger et al. (Eds.): ICDCIT 2019, LNCS 11319, pp. 60–70, 2019.
https://doi.org/10.1007/978-3-030-05366-6_5

A netizen's behaviour is viewed as changes in its three dimensional status space. In this space a netizen is viewed by its objectives. An objective of a netizen is viewed as achievable possibility based on its knowledge, location and resources. As we see social groups among citizens so also a digital society has groups of netizens based on their status similarities. As in a functional democracy, these netizen groups now make pressure groups in digital society. Such pressure groups, we see in forms of tweet troll, facebook post trail and video viral. So our study here focusses on modelling of a netizen and their groups. Further in this chapter we touch upon netizen communication and their participation in governance like voting and law making. Considering importance of education we discuss on upcoming changes and challenges in this sector and its importance to digital society.

Behavioural aspects of digital society are of interest for understanding the society and strategising programmes accordingly to meet the challenges setting in. The relations being built on social platforms and their social impacts are of research interest. These relations can be used for marketing purposes and even can be used for developing emotional quotients in a digital society. Studying human relations though of interests of social scientists but for digital society the role of computing scientists are not less as they provide enabling technology and social analytics for better strategy formulations to meet the social changes effectively. Finding relations, relative online presence predictions, profiling netizens behaviour, predicting risk with relations are some of the many exciting issues that attract expertise of computing scientists.

The next section presents an abstraction that provides a basis to model netizens and their activities. Following the section netizen governance comprising electronic voting, pressure group management and law making for digital society is taken up. Further three sections in sequence present communication, education eSocial life in digital societies. Then the paper ends with a conclusive remark.

2   Modelling Netizens

With fast access of information a person in a digital society sets its objectives derivable by its knowledge K, resource R and location L. That means a person being at a location, having certain resource and knowledge may define its objectives that are achievable. This is an abstraction of a netizen in digital society proposed in [9]. Below, we present some functions to express behavioural aspects of the model. An objective of a person is achievable if and only if there exists a composition of these functions that derives the objective. Thus functions help in modelling dynamic behaviour of a netizen in this abstract space $<K, L, R>$.

2.1   Dynamic Behaviour

On modelling dynamic behaviour of a netizen the following twelve functions with respect to a person P having knowledge $k \in K$, resource $r \in R$ at location $l \in L$ and objective q, are defined as follows:

1. $<P, q, k>:: needK(P, q) \longrightarrow k$
2. $<P, q, r>:: needR(P, q) \longrightarrow r$
3. $<P, q, l>:: needL(P, q) \longrightarrow l$
4. $<P, k, q>:: addQ(P, k) \longrightarrow q$
5. $<P, k, r>:: genR(P, k) \longrightarrow r$
6. $<P, k, l>:: moveL(P, k) \longrightarrow l$
7. $<P, r, k>:: acqK(P, r) \longrightarrow k$
8. $<P, r, q>:: addQ(P, r) \longrightarrow q$
9. $<P, r, l>:: moveL(P, r) \longrightarrow l$
10. $<P, l, k>:: acqK(P, l) \longrightarrow k$
11. $<P, l, q>:: addQ(P, l) \longrightarrow q$
12. $<P, l, r>:: genR(P, l) \longrightarrow r$

The first three functions returns knowledge, resource and location respectively for a person P wishing to achieve an objective q. The next three functions are designed to assess what a person with a given knowledge can achieve. The fourth function proposes an objective that a person with a given knowledge can achieve. Similarly the fifth and sixth functions respectively return resource and location. That means one person with given knowledge can earn certain resources and move to certain locations suitable. The seventh, eighth and ninth functions model behaviour of a person with certain resource. These functions return an objective(s) what a person with given resource can achieve, the knowledge it can acquire and to location it can move. The last three functions model what a person can do being at a given location. These functions essentially model locational advantages in achieving an objective, acquiring knowledge and earning resources.

Usability of such a model is in manifolds when person specific digital data are now available and in future will be available more. For example for planning and development any developmental agency can compose a person specific plan as a composition of the above defined functions. How efficient could be a composition is both computational as well as socio-economic problems for research. Having told this, the computational challenge is enormous not only for enormous size of population but to derive a resonance of individual developmental plans so that the desirable socio-development metrics are achieved. The challenges include both in abstraction as well as realisation of netizen models. The abstraction presented may need a revision adding emotional quotients to it. Further clan and ism associations can also be modelled into the abstraction. The question how does aggregation of such netizens reflect a society is not only of interest of sociologists but for computing science it is also of an importance because that aggregation makes an eco-system that induces netizens of a digital society. So modelling such influences and getting a unified model for a digital society can be considered from computing science perspective.

2.2 Facilitators

A person needs an eco-system that helps it to realise its objectives following a composition of functions defined in the previous subsection. Facilitators add to an eco-system and help people to carry out their aspirations as visualised by them. The way a person works in personal space to meet its objective is given in steps as follows:

1. For a given goal finding required functions and their composition.
2. Top down refinement of the composition to create a goal achieving process.
3. For process execution seeking collaborations from service providers and risk predictions
4. Evaluation and monitoring of goal achieving process
5. Learning from experience

All these throw research challenges for computing scientists. The model here is a simple abstraction of a netizen of a digital society. The researchers challenge is to find a further unified abstraction encompassing all the aspects of a person in a digital society. The model should be endowed with mechanism of self-generation and refinement so that different instantiations of a person for its different objectives can be realised and these are complimenting to each other. The research issues include modelling of agents for a person in digital society, defining refinement procedures for verifiable process creations for each agent to accomplish a defined objective, synchronisation of processes in digital spaces of agents, and endowing intelligence to agents for auto learning and using the learnt knowledge in future for realising objectives of a person in future. Some of these research issues are addressed in the realm of distributed multi-agent systems. But, not much have been done in the domain of digital society. First concrete specification of digital society and then that of agents those who work in a digital domain of a society are of prime concern. This research will lead to design of digital humanoid systems [10] that not only automates actions for a person but also sensitive enough to interface with real human society. Coding of human characters to computing systems is a research challenge for computing scientists.

Digital society promotes service economy at the peak. Here, all these software agents turn to be service providers instead of humans. Then the present service based society will gradually turn to humanoid service society and the governance of this emerging society projects a new world that requires a new governance system possibly totally different. In the next section we will touch upon this issue.

3   Governance

Governance of inorganic bodies like software agents can also be thought of policy driven when required policies are encoded within. A society of DHS, not only performs works for people but also behaves humanly. It means, an authorised software agent being a DHS adapts to the behaviour of its owner. Before going to that extent of DHS, let's first see what offing in the near future in early times of digital society. Among those we have picked up voting, pressure group management and law making considering their immediate applications and importance to governance. In order to make our discussion focussed readers' attention is drawn on exploring aspects of computing science needing research and development.

3.1 Electronic Voting

Electronic voting has been in use in current times, though it brings in brick-bats particularly from losers. Leaving aside this kind of political upheavals as we see now, the use of electronic voting machines has been more or less accepted. Now the next step is, can a voter vote at any time from any where. Now citizens may feel encouraged to participate in democratic process on Internet. Technology being an enabler has also its limitation to address. The issues like secrecy, impersonation, confidentiality and verifiability are some aspects need to be studied. There have been research on electronic voting. We will refer some of these papers to provide possibly an extended view on research carried out in this area.

A voter now wants to be a remote voter for casting its vote on its choice in such a way that while its privacy is guarded, it should be assured that its vote has been indeed counted. While this aspect of voting is desirable at the same time secrecy and privacy, two vital aspects of voting must not be compromised. Among those scantegrity is a technique [2] that allows for end-to-end verification of voting. It also assures a voter that its ballot is not modified. A voter gets a pre-filled ballot with a unique serial number. The ballot paper contains a crypto code for each candidate. The voter on casting its vote gets a part of the ballot paper with its serial number and the crypto code of the candidate to whom it voted. On publication of the election result the voter can check the published codes against the candidate it voted. If its code is not among the published codes then the voter can put its complain raising ireregularity in the voting process. This kind of electronic ballot based voting mainly depends on the three aspects. The first one is of the voters to understand the voting process and to verify its creation, the second one is crypto witness generation and voting result publication with corresponding witnesses and the third aspect is voting verification. Thus the voting scheme puts emphasis on voter's participation. Recently [13] proposes a trusted third party intervention that takes away drudgery of voters. However, in changing world with Internet spread and supporting mobility voters wish to vote anytime from anywhere. This needs to be encouraged to improve people participation in voting. Internet based voting though fairly easy to participate but remains security challenge being online and allowing voting remotely. The first concern is about impersonation which to some extent can be taken up by using citizen database as Aadhar database in India. But, the fear of coercion of voters is to be mitigated. Secured transmission of a vote and its verification are essential to assure resiliency in voting process. In case of remote online voting, the process must ensure the free will participation of voters i.e. without coercion. Challenge for computing scientists is to ensure resiliency and sanctity in voting process.

3.2   dPresure Groups

Pressure groups are often seen as tools used in a functional democracy. Ofcourse, sometimes pressure groups can blackmail a system but ideally are meant for effective functioning of the system. It all depends how these pressure groups are constituted and functioning. In an evolving digital society digital technology is to leverage functioning of democracy. Later for full blown digital society with digital humans how these pressure groups are to evolve is now though a hypothetical question still in near future it demands an answer.

Currently, pressure groups are seen using information technology particularly social media to reach out people so to increase their strength in terms of group membership as well as making impact on governance system. Unlike before social uprising does not take months and years of time but turns instantaneous as seen in China and Egypt. For example, Arab Spring in Egypt and Jasmine walk in China are two digital revolutions carried out in social media. India has its share too. Such dPressure (digital Pressure) groups' activities though discussed in sociology and governance perspectives but not studied in computing science perspectives.

The computing science issues in studying dPressure groups include the following

1. Group structure forecasting
2. Structure nucleus finding
3. Strategy for Information flow
4. Structure dynamics and stability study
5. dPressure analytics

The above points highlight on development of algorithms that find a suitable structure among people in a digital society so that information on the structure flow seamlessly. The properties of such structures like dynamic equilibrium, stability and nuclei findings are of interest in the new paradigm of digital social structures. There have been studies on forecasting of online appearance of netizens on social platforms. Many social aspects like inclusiveness, consensus, emergent view, pressure impact study, destabilizing pressure prediction, genesis and spread of pressures, maintenance of pressure groups are some interesting phenomena to be studied for digital society. These studies may look for new variants of data structures suitable for online study of group behaviour. Some classical subjects like graph theory, Randomized algorithms, Synchronisation, Byzantine agreement, Election algorithms are to be relooked in the context of digital society.

A scenario that may emerge in near future as DHSs working for humans on being endowed with their agencies may tend to form pressure groups, is a problem of different kind than what we just discussed before. There pressure groups are among people who are connected on Internet but here instead of people these are software entities working on behest of people. The way these DHSs i.e. cyber human systems would behave and the science as well as engineering of realisation of such systems are issues for research. Such a system needs to be auto-programmed in real-time on reading the minds of a person. This though sounds a bit of science fiction but sooner or later will come true judging the speed of development we are witnessing in contemporary world. These humanoid cyber human systems on reflecting their masters' minds how would they get engaged themselves in formation of pressure groups and achieving their objectives through these groups, require a rethinking on the abstract model proposed earlier in this paper. We also require modelling of a human mind and projection of it to DHS model. From engineering point of view brain-computer interface engineering model needs to be realised for making of a cyber humanoid. Cyber humanoid is to be governed by a reconfigurable asynchronous automata that not only mimic functioning of a human but also learn from experience and apply it in its decision making. DHSs i.e. a cyber human systems reflecting minds of its owners form pressure groups to achieve a common goal. This offers a paradigm of computing that seamlessly integrates human and cyber humanoids. For the same purpose other than automata, applicability of deep neural networks, rule based systems, randomized algorithms and probably totally different computing paradigms may be investigated.

3.3   dLawMaking

Governance needs laws and lawmakers have responsibility to formulate or revise laws those are applicable and fruitful for a contemporary society. For a digital society characterised by its fast changes, mobility of lawmakers and people the process of law making is to be relooked.

A lawmaker's life becomes easier if a tool comes to an aid for its functioning. There has been a consensus on electronic voting for people to exercise their franchise. Law makers have started using electronic gadgets mostly for communication. Streaming of parliament proceedings in realtime on Internet has been there. Uses of Internet in law making has caught researchers' imagination in '90s. A seminal work [7] presents a protocol formalizing the rules of Paxons part-time lawmakers. [4] presents an idea of mobile parliament that not only emphasizes the role of regional participations but also adds mobility factor in the process of law making. Currently, at the advent of Internet the idea has now much relevance. Digital society can outsmart the traditional law making process by providing some features viz. part-time parliament,mobile parliament and provision for public referendum.

These requirements of digital society bring in exciting research problems inviting interventions of computing scientists. Some of these are:

– Protocol for part-time parliament
– Hybrid protocol for both part-time and mobile parliament
– Protocol for referendum

A part-time parliament requires a protocol for consistency in law making process while ensuring liveness of the parliament. It also requires a digital platform to provide this smart digital service excelling that of regular parliament secretariat. Mobile parliament can be thought of houses that are being conducted at different places giving priority to localities to which the issue in question matters. So that while local and other interested law makers can participate in parliament proceedings not being present in parliament house but being at the place(s) where the event in discussion is of interest. In this paradigm law makers and people could be part-time participants too. This requires a protocol for parliament business ensuring on time and on the spot participation opportunity, liveness and correctness of participations. Digital society will gradually look for online referendum for speedy solution of pressing issues. Computing scientists are certainly looking forward to take up such challenges.

Governance is well achieved by free flow of information from governing entities to people governed. Further people communicate among themselves on business of common interests. The next section takes up issues on communication among netizens.

4 Communication

Communication being a basic activity for a human being carries a lot of importance particularly in digital society when most of the communication is being done electronically over Internet. Instant exchanges of messages over social media like WhatsApp, Tweeter and Facebook have brought extra dimension to digital communication. While contouring communication in digital society we see three forms in changes offing ahead. The first one is social media and communication there on, the second one is modelling communication phenomena and the third one is the communication among cyber humanoids.

The research on social networking comes in the first category of changes. This research work concentrates on people network spun on social media. Because of people interactions, hundreds of thousands of random dynamic graphs are being generated over social media providing scopes for business promotions, but for computing scientists the phenomena provide rich scope of research. Problems that are actively pursued are event detection and summarisation [12,15], link (friend) prediction [3], sentiment analysis [1,5] and etc. The interest in general lies in studying the dynamic nature of evolving social media to know when a person may appear on social media and at that time who else could be there. Further, it also predicts on what issues these people will discuss on at a given time and at a given date. Terror as well as illegal engagements on social media are to deciphered. That needs monitoring as well as deciphering of communications on social media. In order to analyse online and to deal with huge data, computing scientists need to invent powerful algorithms and new data structures for fast data access and semantic interpretations. Will there be a universal language for netizens communications, that future will say.

5 Education

Education particularly in India has gone a long way. So also is for all the ancient civilisations. It has been always teacher centric starting from yesteryears gurus to today professors. In advent of technology ranging from printing press to Internet, instruction delivery has been taking different forms like tool aided class room teaching, instruction by correspondence, virtual class room and etc. But, the point is the challenge teachers face from Internet search engines by making teaching material and videos available at clicks of buttons. This has made teachers role in education redundant. Teachers can still lead education process with valuable contribution by personal and precise instruction delivery to students based on their requirements, capability and interest. This projects a huge challenge to teachers. While finding its solution is an academic engagement, its implementation can be facilitated by introduction of technology. Some of the issues needing technology intervention are:

- Academic profile management
- Identifying needed academic services
- Academic service delivery and evaluation

A teacher can have software bots that can get engaged with individual students on behalf of the teacher. Similarly, the vice versa could be a possibility too. A student software bot can swim across Internet and negotiate with teacher software bots and choose the one who can match to the student characteristics and requirements. This solution could be a blend of webservices and agent technologies. But, this requirement goes beyond the domain of software bots for those requiring human characteristics to represent teachers and students. In addition to traditional intelligence and learning, these software bots should have emotional quotients for humane interactions.

5.1 eSocial Life

Humans are social at the virtue of beings; they will remain so even for a digital society. But, the mode of being social has taken digital forms as we see in use of variety of emoticons and linguistic expressions that are at times puzzling to old timers. This difference brings in digital divisions in society that needs to be met socially as well as technically. Technological solutions include ready composition of contextual smart messages, just in time delivery and easy understanding of languages. Digital society has taken to the imaginations of youth as well as senior citizens to create their individual social networks and almost live in it. Though this sounds odd to conventionalists still is a reality as well as practical. Being in such digital societies, the issues of interest include

- Social network creation and maintenance
- Emotion management
- Humane service management

There has been research works on social network management like link predictions and estimating spread of networks. Analytics of social networks are being used for commercial purposes. But now for digital society, relation management has to be way ahead towards emotion management. Extracting emotion quotient from one's social media postings and interactions there of is a matter of research. Some research work on this are also reported as in [6,8]. Development of Online algorithms for emotion discovery and responding to emotions is a useful research. This requires interdisciplinary research encompassing computing science and social science. Services required in distress can be sourced in digital society by soliciting trusts of netizens. For the purpose assuring trust factor in digital society is essential. Developing algorithms to estimate trust based on netizens' behaviour on digital society is an area of study. In a work we report a method on assessment of trust in webservices [11].

Excellence in a digital society depends on quality eSocial life. It's achievable on studying emergent behaviour and its impact, establishing ethics and creating ecosystem providing transparency and nurturing leadership in eSocial life.

Interestingly netizens exhibit typical cultural behaviour like exchanging conventional daily greetings, digital celebrations of anniversaries and get-together on cyberspace by going live, sending digital emoticons, exchanging pleasantries through webservices and etc. A trilogy on Internet apocalypse has already appeared [14]. Soon, there will be many more such fictions and non-fiction works on netizens' lives in cyberspace.

6   Conclusion

In this paper we have discussed on some aspects on lives in digital societies. We have not focussed on services that can be provided to citizens using Internet. Rather our interest is in understanding netizens that's how people behave in cyberspace. On presenting a paradigm for modelling netizen behaviours we have taken up governance issues in digital society. Particularly, the way netizens can participate in voting, forming groups to sensitise governance and get engaged with their law makers so lawmakers can resort to online negotiation with people from any where and at any time while participating in parliament sessions. The idea of mobile parliament has also been discussed. Strategies for education in digital society are also listed. Though the discussion here on aspects of digital society is not exhaustive but indicative to show the research challenges computing science has to face and offer solutions for better of digital society. This study brings a new area of research known as computational social science [10] that needs to move with developments in computing science to address research challenges of digital societies. Critique may warn of Cyber Frankestein but it has to arrive one day or other. Taming Frankenstein is also the challenge for computing scientists.

References

1. Bifet, A., Frank, E.: Sentiment knowledge discovery in twitter streaming data. In: Pfahringer, B., Holmes, G., Hoffmann, A. (eds.) DS 2010. LNCS (LNAI), vol. 6332, pp. 1–15. Springer, Heidelberg (2010). https://doi.org/10.1007/978-3-642-16184-1_1
2. Chaum, D., Essex, A., Carback, R.: Scantagrity: End-to-End voter-verifiable optical-scan voting. IEEE Secur. Priv. (2008)
3. He, C., Li, H., Fei, X., Yang, A., Tang, Y., Zhu, J.: A topic community based method for friend recommendation in large scale online social networks. Concurr. Comput.: Pract. Exp. **29**, 1–20 (2017)
4. Borch, C., Lind, U.: The mobile parliament: taking regional matters of concern seriously; Scandinavian. J. Soc. Theory **10**(1), 69–86 (2009)
5. Platglaou, G.: Sentiment-based even detection in Twitter. J. Assoc. Inf. Sci. Technol. **67**(7), 1576–1587 (2016)
6. Persson, G.: Love, affiliation, and emotional recognition in *kmpamalm*: the social role of emotional language in twitter discourse. Soc. Media+ Soc. January-March 2017, 1–11 (2017)
7. Lamport, L.: The part-time parliament. ACM Trans. Comput. Syst. **16**(2), 133–169 (1998)
8. Bing, L., Chan, K.C.C., Ou, C.: Public sentiment analysis in tweeter data for prediction of a company's stock price movements. In: IEEE 11th International Conference e-Business Engineering, pp. 232–239 (2014)
9. Mohanty, H.: Person habitat and migration modeling. In: IEEE INDICON (2011)
10. Mohanty, H.: Computational social science: a bird's eye view. In: Hota, C., Srimani, P.K. (eds.) ICDCIT 2013. LNCS, vol. 7753, pp. 319–333. Springer, Heidelberg (2013). https://doi.org/10.1007/978-3-642-36071-8_25
11. Mohanty, H., Prasad, K., Shyamasundar, R.K.: Trust assessment in web services: an extension to jUDDI. In: ICEBE, pp. 759–762 (2007)
12. Imran, M., Castillo, C., Diaz, F., Vieweg, S.: Processing social media messages in mass emergency: a survey. ACM Comput. Surv. **47**(4), 1–38 (2015)
13. Simpson, R., Storer, T.: Third-party verifiable voting system: addressing motivation and incentives in e-voting. J. Inf. Secur. Appl. **38**, 132–138 (2018)
14. Wayne Gladstone' The Internet apocalypse Trilogy, Novel
15. Fang, Y., Zhang, H., Ye, Y., Li, X.: Detecting hot topics from Twitter: a multiview approach. J. Inf. Sci. **40**(5), 578–593 (2014)

Distributed Computing

A Hybrid Meta-heuristic Approach for Load Balanced Workflow Scheduling in IaaS Cloud

Indrajeet Gupta[✉], Shivangi Gupta, Anubhav Choudhary,
and Prasanta K. Jana

Department of Computer Science and Engineering,
Indian Institute of Technology (ISM), Dhanbad, Dhanbad, India
indrajeet7830@gmail.com, shivangi24gupta@gmail.com,
anubhav.choudhary@live.com, prasantajana@yahoo.com

Abstract. Workflow scheduling is one of the most-focused research problems in the field of cloud computing. This is a well known NP-complete problem and therefore finding an optimal solution in respect of various parameters such as makespan, resource utilization, energy, QoS or their combination is computationally very expensive. Nevertheless, load balancing among the virtual machines (VMs) is one of the most important aspects while scheduling tasks of the workflow. In this paper, we propose a hybrid meta-heuristic approach for workflow scheduling for IaaS cloud which is shown to be load balanced. The proposed algorithm is based on hybridization of genetic algorithm (GA) and particle swarm optimization (PSO). The algorithm takes advantages of both the algorithms by avoiding slower convergence rate of GA and local optimum problem in PSO. The objective of the proposed algorithm is to map the tasks of the workflow to the VMs, such that the overall workflow execution time (makespan) is minimized and the assigned load on each VM is also balanced. With the rigorous experiments on scientific workflows, we show that the proposed approach performs better than PSO, GA and MPQGA (multiple priority queues genetic algorithm) based workflow scheduling algorithms. We also validate the better performance through a statistical test, i.e., paired t test with 95% confidence interval.

Keywords: Workflow scheduling · Cloud computing · Meta-heuristic
Load-balancing · Makespan

1 Introduction

Scheduling of workflow in cloud computing is a challenging problem which is widely studied due to its NP-complete nature. Workflow applications demand infrastructure with huge storage space and a high degree of parallelism for faster execution. Cloud computing is the most suitable platform for scheduling large workflows as it can provide this infrastructure through virtualized resources by

© Springer Nature Switzerland AG 2019
G. Fahrnberger et al. (Eds.): ICDCIT 2019, LNCS 11319, pp. 73–89, 2019.
https://doi.org/10.1007/978-3-030-05366-6_6

using pay-per-use model [1–3]. However, in order to provide smooth services, we need an effective scheme for scheduling workflows while fulfilling various objectives such as minimization of makespan, minimization of cost, load balancing, energy conservation and so on. Numerous algorithms for workflow scheduling have been developed in the recent years. Note that, for a given workflow of n tasks and a set of m VMs, the total number of possible solutions is m^n for scheduling them, which is very large. Thus, generating an optimal schedule for a large workflow involves huge computational time and storage. Therefore, meta-heuristic approaches such as genetic algorithm (GA) [4] and particle swarm optimization (PSO) [5] may be very effective as they can find near optimal solution in reasonable time and space. However, latest studies [6] show that hybridizing more than one algorithm shows better performance as compared to a stand-alone algorithm.

This article presents a hybrid workflow scheduling algorithm for IaaS cloud which considers two basic objectives, (1) minimization of makespan and (2) load balancing. The proposed algorithm is based on the combination of two well-known meta-heuristics, i.e., GA and PSO. Some of the existing algorithms [7,8] also hybridize the PSO and the GA for task scheduling. However, these algorithms are developed for task scheduling of independent tasks only and therefore they cannot be applied for workflow scheduling for cloud infrastructure which consists of dependent as well independent tasks. The proposed algorithm takes two core operation, crossover and mutation from GA, which are embedded into each iteration of PSO. Note that the PSO has a faster rate of convergence as compared to GA. But the limitation of PSO includes a local optimum problem in high-dimensional search space. Also, GA suffers from the problem of slow convergence rate. The proposed algorithm exploits the advantage of GA and PSO in such a way that it can avoid the limitations of both the algorithms. To evaluate the performance of the proposed algorithm, we perform extensive simulation on scientific workflows [9] and compare the results with the standard PSO, GA and MPQGA based workflow scheduling algorithms. Simulation results show that the proposed algorithm performs better in terms of makespan and load balancing. We summarize the major contributions as follows.

- Development of a hybrid meta-heuristic algorithm for workflow scheduling along with an efficient encoding scheme for task-VM mapping.
- Derivation of bi-objective fitness function with respect to makespan and load balance.
- Generation of optimal schedule which minimizes makespan and balances the load among the VMs using hybridization of PSO and GA.
- Comparison of fitness value, makespan and balanced load of the proposed algorithm with state of art the existing approaches.
- Validation of the experimental results using paired *t-test*.

The rest of the paper is organized as follows. Section 2 describes the related and existing works. Section 3 presents models of resource and workflow application. Section 4 describes terminology, constraints and problem formulation. The proposed algorithm is presented in Sect. 5 with illustration. Experimental results, performance evaluation and statistical validation are discussed in Sect. 6 followed by conclusion in Sect. 7.

2   Related Work

In the recent past, various algorithms have been proposed to solve the workflow scheduling problem. Many heuristic and meta-heuristic schemes have also been proposed. Simulated annealing and Tabu search are applied to solve the scheduling problems in Grid [10, 11]. In [12], makespan and energy are considered as the scheduling objective which uses two-phase genetic algorithm that involves multi-parent crossover parameter. In [13], the authors have proposed an algorithm based on improved GA (IGA) which picks VMs on the basis of surplus policy and shows to perform better than basic GA based algorithm. In [14], the authors have presented a hybrid heuristic for scheduling the workflow. Here, the proposed scheduling techniques first prioritized the tasks then GA is used for improvement in the task-VM mapping. Recently, a bi-objective hybrid workflow scheduling proposed by Choudhary et al. in [15]. They have hybridized meta-heuristic gravitational search algorithm (GSA) with a popular heuristic namely, heterogeneous earliest finish time (HEFT). In their work, a cost to time equivalent factor has been introduced to make the scheduling objective as the cost-effectiveness. Min-Min and Max-Min both are the conservative scheduling algorithm for the grid system. However, these algorithms are applied frequently in the cloud computing environment. Min-Min [16] is a heuristic algorithm which starts with a set of all unmapped tasks and finds the task and the resource on which it gets minimum expected time for complete execution. The drawback of this algorithm is that the bigger tasks have to wait for the completion of smaller ones which results in the starvation problem.

In max-min heuristic algorithm [17], the task having maximum completion time is selected from the set of unmapped task and assigned to the resources with minimum execution time. The drawback of this scheduling algorithm is that, tasks with maximum completion time is executed first. So, it may increase the makespan and also tends to increase the response time of tasks with smaller completion time. In [18], Zhan et al. have presented a load balance aware genetic algorithm for task scheduling in cloud computing. They consider two scheduling parameters first is makespan and the second is load balancing. Objective of this algorithm is to balance the load over all the resources and to minimize makespan. In [19], the authors have presented a task scheduling algorithm which is based on GA. The algorithm is the critical path genetic algorithm (CPGA). It is based on rescheduling the critical path nodes encoded in chromosome through different generations using two fitness functions applied one after another. The HGA [1] proposed by Ahmad at el. is primarily a single objective workflow scheduling algorithm. It minimizes only the makespan. Wang et al. [20] proposed reliability-driven (RD) reputation to effectively measure the reliability of a VM. They use RD reputation and proposed an algorithm called look-ahead genetic algorithm (LAGA) to optimize both the reliability of VM and makespan. However, the communication overhead is not considered in this work, which is a crucial factor for scheduling workflows. An algorithm presented in [8] introduces a mutation operator into PSO. This concept helps the PSO algorithm overcome the local optimization problem. It has been observed that the hybridization of two or more algorithms shows better performance than a stand-alone algorithm. We propose a hybridization of GA and PSO which is shown to perform better than the existing algorithm in terms of makespan and load balancing.

3   Workflow and Cloud Model

A workflow W (in Fig. 1(a)) is represented by a directed acyclic graph (DAG) $W = (T, E)$ where T is the set of tasks, i.e., $T = \{T_1, T_2, T_3, \ldots, T_n\}$ and E denotes a set of edges, where, $E_{i,j} = (T_i \rightarrow T_j)$ shows the precedence constraint between T_i and T_j. This means that a task T_j cannot start until the task T_i is completed.

We consider a cloud model in which m number of VMs are deployed based on the size of the workflow. We assume that the cloud server always has the available resources for provisioning the required number of VMs. Note that execution of the workflow incurs execution time as well as communication time between two dependent tasks. We assume that the communication time between two dependent tasks is zero if they are assigned to the same VM. The execution time of each task may vary from one VM to another VM. It is represented by a matrix called expected time to compute (ETC) [21, 22] given as follows.

$$ETC = \begin{array}{c} \\ T_1 \\ T_2 \\ \vdots \\ T_n \end{array} \overset{\begin{array}{cccc} VM_1 & VM_2 & \cdots & VM_m \end{array}}{\begin{bmatrix} ETC_{1,1} & ETC_{1,2} & \cdots & ETC_{1,m} \\ ETC_{2,1} & ETC_{2,2} & \cdots & ETC_{2,m} \\ \vdots & \vdots & \vdots & \vdots \\ ETC_{n,1} & ETC_{n,2} & \cdots & ETC_{n,m} \end{bmatrix}} \tag{1}$$

where, $1 \leq i \leq n$, $1 \leq j \leq m$ and $ETC_{i,j}$ represents the estimated execution time of task T_i on VM_j.

The communication time among the VMs is represented by CO (communication overhead) matrix. As the communication time between two dependent tasks assigned on same VM is assumed to be zero, all the diagonal elements of the CO matrix are zero. This matrix is given as follows.

$$CO = \begin{array}{c} \\ VM_1 \\ VM_2 \\ \vdots \\ VM_m \end{array} \overset{\begin{array}{cccc} VM_1 & VM_2 & \cdots & VM_m \end{array}}{\begin{bmatrix} 0 & CO_{1,2} & \cdots & CO_{1,m} \\ CO_{2,1} & 0 & \cdots & CO_{2,m} \\ \vdots & \vdots & \vdots & \vdots \\ CO_{m,1} & CO_{m,2} & \cdots & 0 \end{bmatrix}} \tag{2}$$

where, $CO_{k,l}$ represents the communication overhead time, when a task is being executed on VM_k needs to communicate with another task, which is to be executed on VM_l.

4 Terminologies and Problem Formulation

4.1 Constraints and Assumptions

Here, we consider some constraints and assumptions which are followed in [21] and similar to Amazon EC2 (Elastic Compute Cloud) to make the proposed work more realistic. These constraints and assumptions are described as follows.

(a) The communication time for up-link and down-link denoted by '$\leftrightarrow$' may be different for a pair of VMs such that $VM_k \leftrightarrow VM_l$ as they are not equal in the practical scenario.
(b) An initial boot time cannot be ignored when any VM is provisioned. Likewise, we can not forget the VM shut down time while releasing any VM.

In the proposed scheduling algorithm, we consider makespan and load balancing as the performance parameters for optimization which are described as follows.

Definition 1 (Makespan (MS)): Makespan can be described as the total time elapsed for the execution of an entire workflow. It makes the assumption that a VM cannot execute a task while data is being transferred. Thus, makespan can be formulated as follows.

$$MS = VM\_Boot\_Time + max\,(VM\_On\_time(VM_j)\, + VM\_Shutdown\_Time) \tag{3}$$

where, $j \in \{1, 2, \ldots, m\}$ and $VM\_On\_time(VM_j)$ denotes the total time that VM_j requires to complete all the tasks assigned to it.

Definition 2 (Load balancing (LB)): Load balancing can be defined as the assignment of tasks over the VMs such that all the active VMs have almost equal load. Generally, load is termed as the actual working time (AWT) of that VM to accomplish a set of assigned tasks of a given workflow. If load is almost equally distributed over all the VMs, variation of the load among all VMs will be less. To measure the variation among the load on each VM, we calculate the standard deviation (SD) of AWT of VMs. So, Load Balancing Factor(LBF) can be maximized by minimizing the SD of AWT of VMs. AWT is defined as follows.

$$AWT\,(VM_j) = \sum_{i=1}^{n} ETC\,(i, j) \times B\,(i, j). \tag{4}$$

$$where\;B(i,j) = \begin{cases} 1, \text{ if } T_i \rightarrow VM_j \\ 0, \quad \text{Otherwise} \end{cases} \tag{5}$$

For calculation of SD, we require average value of AWT of all the VMs, which is calculated as follows.

$$avg\,(AWT) = \frac{\sum_{j=1}^{m} AWT\,(VM_j)}{m} \tag{6}$$

$$Thus, \quad SD = \sqrt{\frac{\sum_{j=1}^{m} \left(AWT_j - avg\left(AWT\right)\right)^2}{m}} \quad (7)$$

If SD is minimized then load balancing will be maximized, so LBF can be written as follows.

$$LBF = \frac{\mid avg(AWT) - SD \mid}{avg(AWT)} \times 100\% \quad (8)$$

Remark: If standard deviation (SD) of load on all VMs is zero, then LBF will be 100% and this implies that load distribution over all the VMs is uniform.

4.2   Problem Formulation

Given set of m active virtual machines $VM = \{VM_1, VM_2, \ldots, VM_m\}$ and a set of n tasks $T = \{T_1, T_2, \ldots, T_n\}$ in a workflow, it is to assign all the tasks to the available VMs so that the MS (Eq. 3) is minimized and the LBF (Eq. 8) is maximized. Note that maximization of LBF implies minimization of SD (Eq. 7). Therefore, the problem can be formulated as the minimization of the liner combination of makespan and SD as follows.

$$minimize \ z = \alpha \times MS + (1 - \alpha) \times SD \quad (9)$$

subject to:

$$(1) \quad \sum_{j=1}^{m} B(i,j) = 1, \quad \forall \ i \in \{1, 2, \ldots, n\}$$

$$(2) \quad 0 \leq \alpha \leq 1$$

where $B(i,j)$ is defined in Eq. 5. The constraint (1) ensures that each task must be assigned to a single VM only and the constraint (2) provides weight to SD and makespan in the objective function.

5   Proposed Algorithm

The basic idea of the proposed algorithm is as follows. We first generate an initial population of particles randomly. Then we apply the PSO algorithm to the generated population. We now adopt crossover and mutation operation from GA as iterative steps of PSO. In each iteration, we first apply all the steps of PSO and identify the best particle (*Gbest*) in the current population. The steps of the proposed algorithm are described in details as follows:

1 **Particle Representation:** We represent a particle in such a way that each particle provides a solution for scheduling the tasks on VMs. A particle is represented as follows.

$$P_i = \begin{bmatrix} X_{i,1} \ X_{i,2} \ \ldots \ X_{i,n-1} \ X_{i,n} \end{bmatrix} \quad (10)$$

where, $X_{i,t}$ denotes the position of P_i in the tth dimension. Dimension of all the particles are kept same as the number of task in the given workflow. We initialize each component, i.e., $X_{i,t}$, $0 < i \leq Pop\_size$, $0 < t \leq n$, with a randomly generated number which lies in the interval $(0, 1]$. Using the value of $X_{i,t}$, $MAP_{i,t}$ determines the VM mapped to t^{th} task as encoded in P_i. The $MAP_{i,t}$ is defined as follows.

$$MAP_{i,t} = \lceil X_{i,t} \times m \rceil \tag{11}$$

where m is the number of VMs. If $MAP_{i,t} = k$, then t^{th} task is assigned to k^{th} VM, i.e., $T_t \rightarrow VM_k$.

2 **Update Velocity and Position of the Particle:** The velocity and position of every particle updated in each iteration using Eqs. 12 and 13 [5] respectively. The updated value of velocity and position for some dimension t may go out of the interval $(0, 1]$ due to algebraic step of addition and subtraction operations in Eqs. 12 and 13. In our scenario, the position of the particle in each dimension must satisfy the boundary condition. Otherwise, some tasks will be mapped to unavailable VMs. To overcome this problem we update velocity and position by using Eq. 14.

$$\begin{aligned} V_{i,t}(k) = w \times V_{i,t}(k-1) + c_1 \times r_1 \times (X_{Pbest,t}(k-1) - X_{i,t}(k-1)) \\ + c_2 \times r_2 \times (X_{Gbest,t}(k-1) - X_{i,t}(k-1)) \end{aligned} \tag{12}$$

$$X_{i,t}(k) = X_{i,t}(k-1) + V_{i,t}(k) \tag{13}$$

where, r_1 and r_2 are two constants, whose values lies between 0 and 1. The constants c_1 and c_2 are the acceleration coefficients and w is the inertia weight.

$$X_{i,t} = \begin{cases} 0.001, & \text{if } X_{i,t} \leq 0 \\ 1, & \text{if } X_{i,t} > 1 \\ X_{i,t}, & \text{Otherwise} \end{cases} \tag{14}$$

After the updation of the position of the particle, we generate the mapping to evaluate fitness function of each particle. If its current fitness value is better than its $Pbest_i$ fitness then its personal best ($Pbest_i$) is replaced by itself. Thus,

$$Pbest_i = \begin{cases} P_i, & \text{if } fitness(P_i) < fitness(Pbest_i) \\ Pbest_i, & \text{Otherwise} \end{cases} \tag{15}$$

3 **Selection and Crossover:** In this operation, we select two particles, first is *Gbest* and second one is any random particle from the current population. Then we generate two child particles by performing single point crossover whereby crossover point is chosen at random.

4 **Mutation:** The purpose of mutation in GA is to preserve and introduce diversity. The mutation prevents the child particles from becoming too similar to parent particles to avoid local minima. To mutate $child_i$, we select any two indices j and k of the $child_i$ such that j^{th} task and k^{th} task does not map to same VM. Then we swap the values of the selected index to get a mutated child.

5.1   Fitness Function

The objective function defined in Eq. 9 can be used to evaluate the quality of the solution. A solution having a smaller value of the objective function is preferable. Thus, we use the objective function as our fitness function to evaluate each particle. Therefore, the fitness function to evaluate i^{th} particle is given as follows.

$$F(P_i) = \alpha \times MS_i + (1 - \alpha) \times SD_i \tag{16}$$

Note that for evaluation, we have the same fitness function for the particle of the PSO and chromosome of the GA and MPQGA.

Table 1. Notations and their description.

Notation	Description
Pop_size	Size of population
P_i	i^{th} particle or chromosome
POP	It is a set of all the particles
$F(P_i)$	Fitness value of particle P_i based on its makespan and load balancing factor
$crossover(P_i, P_j)$	Crossover operation over two chromosomes (particle) P_i and P_j
ch_i	i^{th} child particle or chromosome
$mutation(ch_i)$	Mutation operation on child ch_i
$Pbest_i$	It represents the local best position of ith particle known so far.
$Gbest$	It represents the global best particle known so far
$worst\_fit$	Variable that is used to store fitness value of worst particle.
fit_ch_i	store the fitness value of child ch_i
$max\_ietration$	Total number of iteration
n	Total number of tasks in a workflow W
m	Number of available VMs
$random()$	It returns a random number which lies in interval $(0, 1]$
$Predr(T_i)$	Predecessor task node of task T_i
$Succr(T_i)$	Successor task node of the task T_i
T_i	i^{th} task
VM_j	j^{th} VM

The proposed scheme is presented through Algorithms 1 and 2. The notation used in these algorithms are shown in Table 1. The Algorithm 1 is the main procedure of the proposed scheme, which takes the DAG, ETC, CO matrix as input and gives a schedule for workflow as output. Algorithm 2 which is called by the Algorithm 1, performs the GA operation by calling crossover and mutation function respectively and produces two child particles. Then, it finds the worst particle in the current population in order to replace it with best-generated children particles. Replacement is done only when the best child particle is better.

The rationality behind the hybridization of the above steps of the PSO and GA is as follows. PSO suffers from the local minimum problem which is resolved by crossover and mutation operation of the GA as these two operations bring randomness in the particle. This is worth noting that the crossover operation takes place between the *Gbest* and a randomly selected particle which produces the better result (chromosome/particle) due to the involvement of the *Gbest*. Again the population is filtered out by replacing the worst particle with the best child chromosome after the aforementioned crossover and the mutation. Note that after obtaining the task-VM mapping by the Algorithms 1 and 2, the final schedule is generated by Algorithm 3 with minimum makespan (MS) and maximum LBF. The detailed steps involved in the scheduling process are explained in the Algorithm 3 by considering overall task nodes dependencies and communication overhead among the VMs.

Algorithm 1. Main Procedure

Input: Workflow (W), ETC matrix, Communication overhead (CO) matrix
Output: Task-VM Mapping ($MAP_{i,t}$)

---

initialize population (POP) randomly of size Pop_size
$Pbest_i = P_i$, $\forall i$, $1 \le i \le Pop\_size$
$Gbest = P_k$, where $F(P_k) = \min\limits_{j=1}^{Pop\_size} \{F(Pbest_j)\}$
for $Iter = 1$ *to* $max\_iteration$ **do**
  for $k \leftarrow 1$ *to* Pop_size **do**
    Update velocity and position of P_k using Eq. 12 and Eq. 13
    Calculate $F(P_k)$
    Update $Pbest_k$ using Eq.15
  end
  $Gbest = P_k$, where $F(P_k) = \min\limits_{j=1}^{Pop\_size} \{F(Pbest_j)\}$
  $Update\_byGA(POP, Gbest)$
end
Obtain the Mapping as encoded by the *Gbest* particle
return $MAP_{i,t}$

Algorithm 2. $Update\_byGA(POP, Gbest)$

$r = \lceil random() \times Pop\_size \rceil$
$crossover(P_r, Gbest)$ to produce two children ch_1 and ch_2
$ch_3 = mutation(ch_1)$; $ch_4 = mutation(ch_2)$
$best\_child = ch_k$, where $F(ch_k) = \min\limits_{j=1}^{4} \{F(ch_j)\}$
$worst\_fit = 0$
for $i \leftarrow 1$ *to* Pop_size **do**
  if $worst\_fit < F(P_i)$ **then**
    $worst\_fit = F(P_i)$
    $worst\_particle = i$
  end
end
if $F(best\_child) < worst\_fit$ **then**
  $P_{worst\_particle} = best\_child$
end

Algorithm 3. Calculation of Makespan

Input: Workflow (W), Mapping ($MAP_{i,t}$), ETC matrix, CO matrix.
Output: Makespan (MS)

---

for *each* $VM_j \in VM$ **do**
  | $VM\_On\_time[VM_j]=0$
end
for *each task* $T_i \in W$ *in the topological order* **do**
  if $T_i.Predr\_Count! = 0$ **then**
    | $Predr\_finish\_time = \max\limits_{T_p \in Predr(T_i)} \left(Task\_actual\_finsh\_time[T_{p_i}] \right)$
  end
  if $T_i.Succr\_Count! = 0$ **then**
    $Data\_Transfer\_Time = 0$
    for *each task* T_j, $\forall\ T_j \in Succr(T_i)$ *and* $MAP[i] \neq MAP[j]$ **do**
      if *the output data is not transferred to* $VM_{MAP}[j]$ *from the task* T_i **then**
        | $Data\_Transfer\_Time = Data\_Transfer\_Time + CO_{i,j}$
      end
    end
  end
  Execution Time of task T_i on $VM_j = ETC_{i,j}$
  $actual\_start\_time(T_i) = max(Predr\_finish\_time, VM\_On\_time[MAP[i]])$
  $actual\_finish\_time(T_i) = actual\_start\_time(T_i) + ETC_{i,j} + Data\_Transfer\_Time$
  $VM\_On\_time[MAP[i]] = actual\_finish\_time(T_i)$
end
Makespan(MS)= $VM\_boot\_time + VM\_On\_time[VM_j] + VM\_shudown\_time$
return Makespan (MS)

5.2 Illustration

Consider the sample workflow as shown in Fig. 1, which has 10 task nodes and a set of three active VMs $VM = \{VM_1, VM_2, VM_3\}$. The scheduling objective is to schedule all the tasks on these 3 VMs as per the proposed approach. The expected time to compute (ETC) matrix and VM to VM communication overhead (CO) matrix are also given.

Let the population size be 5. We initialize each particle of the population with random values in the range of $(0, 1]$. Randomly generated initial population matrix (POP) is shown as Fig. 2(a). Mapping of the task to VM corresponding to each particle (referred as MAP matrix) is calculated using Eq. 11 and shown in Fig. 2(b) along with the fitness value of each particle (using Eq. 16). Note that $MAP_{2,5} = 3$ means that task T_5 is scheduled on VM_3 according to solution provided by particle P_2. As P_1 has lowest fitness value, we treat it as the *Gbest* of the current population as shown in Fig. 2(c).

We next illustrate the rest of the steps in the current iteration as follows:

1. Update the particle's position with respect to *Gbest* and *Pbest* using Eqs. 12 and 13. It is shown in Fig. 2(d).
2. The fitness values ($F(P_i)$) are calculated corresponding to updated particles using Eqs. 11 and 16 respectively and the corresponding MAP matrix shown in Fig. 2(e).
3. Update $Pbest_i$ using Eq. 15 and find the *Gbest* particle and worst particle of the population. P_1 is the global best particle and P_5 is the worst particle of the current population as shown in Fig. 2(f).

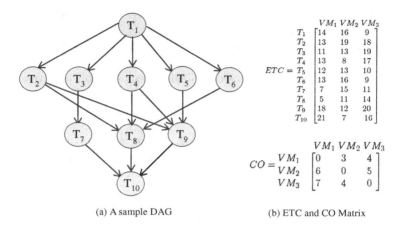

(a) A sample DAG

(b) ETC and CO Matrix

Fig. 1. A sample workflow with ETC and CO matrix.

(a)

	T_1	T_2	T_3	T_4	T_5	T_6	T_7	T_8	T_9	T_{10}
P_1	0.84	0.39	0.78	0.80	0.91	0.20	0.34	0.77	0.28	0.55
P_2	0.48	0.63	0.36	0.51	0.95	0.92	0.64	0.72	0.14	0.61
P_3	0.02	0.24	0.14	0.80	0.16	0.40	0.13	0.11	0.99	0.22
P_4	0.51	0.84	0.61	0.29	0.64	0.52	0.49	0.97	0.29	0.77
P_5	0.53	0.77	0.40	0.89	0.28	0.35	0.81	0.92	0.07	0.95

(b)

MAP	T_1	T_2	T_3	T_4	T_5	T_6	T_7	T_8	T_9	T_{10}	$F(P_i)$
P_1	3	2	3	3	3	1	2	3	1	2	64.45
P_2	2	2	2	2	3	3	2	3	1	2	71.68
P_3	1	1	1	3	1	2	1	1	3	1	75.56
P_4	2	3	2	1	2	2	2	3	1	3	74.67
P_5	2	3	2	3	1	2	3	3	1	3	92.45

(c)

$Pbest_i$	P_1	P_2	P_3	P_4	P_5
$F(Pbest_i)$	64.45	71.68	75.56	74.67	92.45

$Gbest \quad P_1$

(d)

	T_1	T_2	T_3	T_4	T_5	T_6	T_7	T_8	T_9	T_{10}
P_1	0.84	0.39	0.78	0.80	0.91	0.20	0.34	0.77	0.27	0.55
P_2	0.72	0.31	0.49	0.99	0.88	0.42	0.62	0.79	0.16	0.55
P_3	0.51	0.30	0.41	0.81	0.66	0.19	0.26	0.61	0.50	0.68
P_4	0.96	0.54	0.70	0.31	0.99	0.03	0.21	0.68	0.28	0.58
P_5	0.61	0.27	0.90	0.82	0.61	0.27	0.31	0.90	0.20	0.72

(e)

MAP	T_1	T_2	T_3	T_4	T_5	T_6	T_7	T_8	T_9	T_{10}	$F(P_i)$
P_1	3	2	3	3	3	1	2	3	1	2	64.45
P_2	3	1	2	3	3	2	2	3	1	2	72.01
P_3	2	1	2	3	2	1	1	2	2	3	106.43
P_4	3	2	3	1	3	1	1	3	1	2	73.63
P_5	2	1	3	3	2	1	1	3	1	3	101.36

(f)

$Pbest_i$	P_1	P_2	P_3	P_4	P_5
$F(Pbest_i)$	64.45	71.68	75.56	73.63	92.45

$Gbest \quad P_1$
$Worst \quad P_5$

(g)

MAP	T_1	T_2	T_3	T_4	T_5	T_6	T_7	T_8	T_9	T_{10}	$F(child_i)$
$Child_1$	2	1	2	3	2	1	1	2	1	2	87.07
$Child_2$	3	2	3	3	3	1	2	3	2	3	95.02

(h)

T_1	T_2	T_3	T_4	T_5	T_6	T_7	T_8	T_9	T_{10}
VM_1	VM_2	VM_3	VM_3	VM_1	VM_2	VM_1	VM_3	VM_2	VM_1

Fig. 2. Illustrative steps involved in the proposed algorithm, (a) Initial population of particle, (b) Mapping of particles, (c) Fitness value of *Pbest* at initial stage, (d) Update position of the particles (e) Mapping of the updated particle, (f) Fitness values of *Pbest* in the 1st iteration, (g) Mapping of the child particles and (h) Optimum task-VM mapping.

4. Select any random particle and perform crossover with *Gbest* particle and generate two child particles as $child_1$ and $child_2$.
5. Then the fitness value of the generated children particles are calculated, which is demonstrated in Fig. 2(g).
6. Mutate both children particles as described in Sect. 5. After mutation fitness value of both children particles are 96.72 and 87.89 respectively.
7. Fitness value of $Child_2$ is improved after mutation. So, we keep mutated $child_2$ and undo mutation for $child_1$.
8. Out of both the children particles, $child_1$ is best and also better than the *worst* particle (P_5) of the current population, So replace particle P_5 by $child_1$. We repeat the above steps upto a maximum number of iterations. Final schedule is shown in Fig. 2(h).

After finding the optimal task-VM mapping the scheduling takes place according to the Algorithm 3 and load balancing factor (LBF) is calculated by Eq. 8.

6   Performance Evaluation and Results Analysis

This section shows the simulation environment, specifications of the workflow used as input and the comparison of results with PSO and GA based scheduling algorithms. We use makespan (refer Eq. 3), balanced load in (%) (refer Eq. 8) and fitness value (refer Eq. 16) as performance metrics.

6.1   Simulation Setup and Experimental Parameters

We evaluate the proposed algorithm using C++ programming language, which is executed on Intel(R) Core(TM) i3-2310M CPU @ 2.10 GHz having 4 GB RAM and Ubuntu 16.04 as an operating system. For the purpose of effective validation of the proposed work, we use core structure of five different benchmark workflow applications namely, Cybershake, Epigenomic, Inspiral, Montage and Sipht as characterized by Juve et al. [9] and shown in Fig. 3.

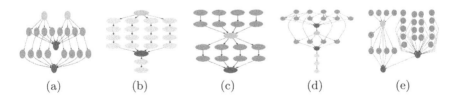

(a)   (b)   (c)   (d)   (e)

Fig. 3. Structure of scientific workflows used in simulation (a) Cybershake, (b) Epigenomic, (c) Inspiral, (d) Montage and (e) Sipht.

All the parameters which are used in the simulations are listed in Table 2. In the Table 2, w indicates inertial weight and lies in interval [0, 1]. Also,

c_1 and c_2 represents cognitive acceleration constant and social acceleration constant respectively, which are used to determine particle's acceleration in search space and r_1, r_2 are randomly generated number using the function $random()$ in the range of $(0, 1]$. The important parameters as VM_boot_time and $VM\_shutdown\_time$ are considered $0.5\,s$ for each VMs.

Table 2. Experimental parameters.

	Parameters and their value						
	Pop_{size}	c_1	c_2	w	$max\ Iteration$	r_1 and r_2	p_c probability of crossover
Proposed	20	2.05	2.05	0.5314	300	[0–1]	
PSO	20	2.05	2.05	0.5314	300	[0–1]	
GA and MPQGA	20				300		0.6

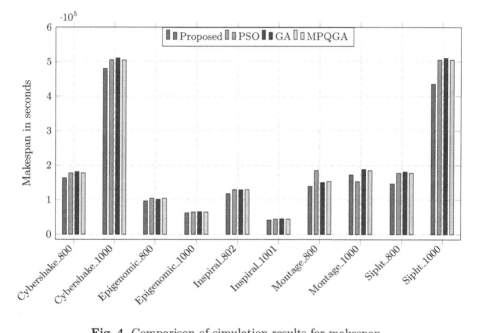

Fig. 4. Comparison of simulation results for makespan.

6.2 Result Comparison and Analysis

We compared the performance of the proposed algorithm with PSO [7], GA [18] and MPQGA [23] based workflow scheduling. We executed all the algorithms by considering the same simulation environment and the same parameter values. The comparison of results with respect to makespan, load balancing factor and

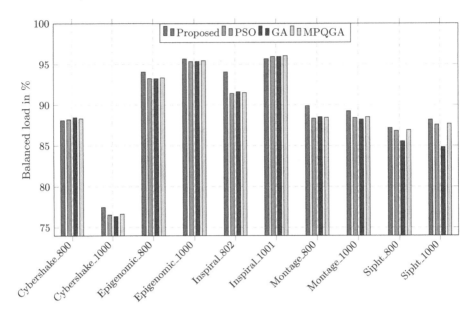

Fig. 5. Comparison of simulation results for load balanced factor.

fitness value are shown in Figs. 4, 5 and 6. Each figure shows comparison of 800 and 1000 tasks against 40 and 50 VMs respectively for all five scientific workflows. Although we have shown the comparison results only for the large sized of workflows i.e., 800 and 1000 tasks. Moreover, the simulation runs give far better results for all the task ranges i.e., 30, 50, 100, 200, and 400 tasks against the 5, 10, 20, 25 and 30 VMs respectively.

It can be observed from Fig. 4, the makespan of the proposed algorithm is better than other algorithms for almost all the sizes of all the workflows. It is noteworthy that the improvement in terms of makespan is significant for all the sizes as compared to other scientific workflows. Also, large workflows of sipht shows the same improvement. We also observe that, the load balancing factor (LBF) for *cybershake_800* and *Inspiral_1001* are not better than the other algorithms (referred Fig. 5). However, for the other workflows, the LBF is remarkable for the proposed algorithm. For all other scientific workflows of different sizes, we also get improved load balancing factor. The Fig. 6 presents the fitness value for each scientific workflow which shows the overall quality of the solution produced by considering both makespan and LBF. We witness the fact that the fitness value produced by the proposed algorithm outperforms the other algorithms, even for the case of cybershake where the makespan is higher.

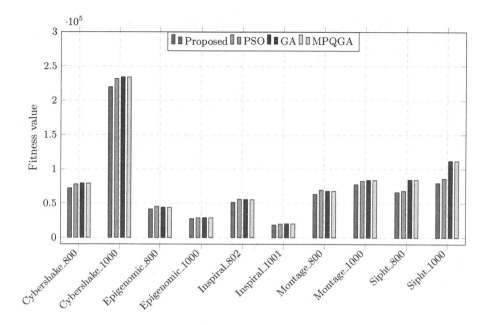

Fig. 6. Comparison of simulation results for fitness value.

6.3 Statistical Test

We performed the paired t-test for all five benchmark workflows of different sizes upto 35 simulation runs. The sample considered in the test consists of the value of makespan, load balancing factor, and the fitness function. Here we also calculate the 95% confidence interval (CI) of the population means by assuming the alpha value (error) as .05 or 5%. If the means of two, unlike populations, are equal, it falls under the null hypothesis. For the sake of mathematical expression null hypothesis can be represented as: $H_0 : \mu_1 - \mu_2 = 0$ to the contrary of $H_1 : \mu_1 - \mu_2 \neq 0$ as alternate hypothesis. Table 3 depicts the output of the fitness value which is made by paired t-test. The table shows the pairwise difference in the means of the simulated results from the runs of PSO and proposed, GA and Proposed, MPQGA and proposed. Significant difference between the paired algorithms (hypothesis) is measured by rejecting the null hypothesis. If the t $static > t$ $critical$ one tail and t $static > t$ $critical$ two tail then null hypothesis (H_0) is rejected which implies that the means(μ) of both the algorithms are different. The significant difference is also dignified by p one-tailed value and p two-tailed value in the Table 3. A lesser p value (≤ 0.05) directs that the null hypothesis is overruled, i.e., there is no noteworthy difference amongst two results. Therefore, the null hypothesis is rejected, whereas the larger p value will be accepted by null hypothesis. From the above conditions, we can conclude that p one-tailed value and p two-tailed value always smaller than p value (≤ 0.05) of the paired. Therefore, the pairing of the proposed algorithm with the existing algorithms one by one is significantly different. In the Table 3, higher value of t for a specific degree of freedom (df) implies that how strongly these pair differ and they are positively correlated.

Table 3. Comparison of mean, variance, t statistic, df, p values, t values and CI for PSO, GA, MPQGA and proposed algorithm for all workflows.

Algorithm	Population	Mean	Variance	t statistic	df	p one-tail	t critical one-tail	p two-tail	t critical two-tail	CI (0.95)
PSO	35	30287.93857	1854227902	4.132900159	34	0.00011044	1.690924255	0.00022088	2.032244509	±1.409
Proposed	35	28247.80914	1640198840							±1.406
GA	35	32586.02857	2002901085	3.748664615	34	0.000330641	1.690924255	0.000661282	2.032244509	±1.427
Proposed	35	28247.80914	1640198840							±1.406
MPQGA	35	32354.02857	2002901085	3.548192923	34	0.000578301	1.690924255	0.001156601	2.032244509	±1.409
Proposed	35	28247.80914	1640198840							±1.406

7   Conclusion and Future Work

In this paper, we have presented a load balanced workflow scheduling in cloud computing. The primary concern of our proposed work is to balance the load among the VMs and minimization of makespan. The proposed algorithm has the combined flavor of PSO and GA. The experimental results have been compared with GA, PSO and MPQGA based workflow scheduling. Through simulation results, we have shown that the proposed algorithm performs better than these existing algorithms in terms of makespan and load balancing factor (LBF). We have also validated the simulation results statistically by means of paired t-test. However, the algorithm lacks the dynamic provisioning of the VMs to develop more efficient algorithms. The future work will focus on development of dynamic workflow scheduling schemes with considering cost and budget minimization.

References

1. Ahmad, S.G., Liew, C.S., Munir, E.U., Ang, T.F., Khan, S.U.: A hybrid genetic algorithm for optimization of scheduling workflow applications in heterogeneous computing systems. J. Parallel Distrib. Comput. **87**, 80–90 (2016)
2. Buyya, R., Yeo, C.S., Venugopal, S., Broberg, J., Brandic, I.: Cloud computing and emerging IT platforms: vision, hype, and reality for delivering computing as the 5th utility. Futur. Gener. Comput. Syst. **25**(6), 599–616 (2009)
3. Alkhanak, E.N., Lee, S.P., Rezaei, R., Parizi, R.M.: Cost optimization approaches for scientific workflow scheduling in cloud and grid computing: a review, classifications, and open issues. J. Syst. Softw. **113**, 1–26 (2016)
4. Man, K.-F., Tang, K.-S., Kwong, S.: Genetic algorithms: concepts and applications in engineering design. IEEE Trans. Ind. Electron. **43**(5), 519–534 (1996)
5. Eberhart, R., Kennedy, J.: A new optimizer using particle swarm theory. In: 1995 Proceedings of the Sixth International Symposium on Micro Machine and Human Science, MHS 1995, pp. 39–43. IEEE (1995)
6. Keshanchi, B., Souri, A., Navimipour, N.J.: An improved genetic algorithm for task scheduling in the cloud environments using the priority queues: formal verification, simulation, and statistical testing. J. Syst. Softw. **124**, 1–21 (2017)

7. Awad, A.I., El-Hefnawy, N.A., Abdel_kader, H.M.: Enhanced particle swarm optimization for task scheduling in cloud computing environments. Procedia Comput. Sci. **65**, 920–929 (2015)
8. Li, R., Huang, W., Yuan, Q.: Grid task scheduling using mutation particle swarm algorithm. In: IEEE Conference Anthology, pp. 1–3. IEEE (2013)
9. Juve, G., Chervenak, A., Deelman, E., Bharathi, S., Mehta, G., Vahi, K.: Characterizing and profiling scientific workflows. Futur. Gener. Comput. Syst. **29**(3), 682–692 (2013)
10. Zhu, Z., Zhang, G., Li, M., Liu, X.: Evolutionary multi-objective workflow scheduling in cloud. IEEE Trans. Parallel Distrib. Syst. **27**(5), 1344–1357 (2016)
11. Cho, K.-M., Tsai, P.-W., Tsai, C.-W., Yang, C.-S.: A hybrid meta-heuristic algorithm for vm scheduling with load balancing in cloud computing. Neural Comput. Appl. **26**(6), 1297–1309 (2015)
12. Tao, F., Feng, Y., Zhang, L., Liao, T.W.: CLPS-GA: a case library and Pareto solution-based hybrid genetic algorithm for energy-aware cloud service scheduling. Appl. Soft Comput. **19**, 264–279 (2014)
13. Zhong, H., Tao, K., Zhang, X.: An approach to optimized resource scheduling algorithm for open-source cloud systems. In: 2010 Fifth Annual ChinaGrid Conference (ChinaGrid), pp. 124–129. IEEE (2010)
14. Delavar, A.G., Aryan, Y.: HSGA: a hybrid heuristic algorithm for workflow scheduling in cloud systems. Clust. Comput. **17**(1), 129–137 (2014)
15. Choudhary, A., Gupta, I., Singh, V., Jana, P.K.: A GSA based hybrid algorithm for bi-objective workflow scheduling in cloud computing. Futur. Gener. Comput. Syst. **83**, 14–26 (2018)
16. He, X.S., Sun, X.H., Von Laszewski, G.: QoS guided min-min heuristic for grid task scheduling. J. Comput. Sci. Technol. **18**(4), 442–451 (2003)
17. Mao, Y., Chen, X., Li, X.: Max–min task scheduling algorithm for load balance in cloud computing. In: Patnaik, S., Li, X. (eds.) CSAIT 2013. AISC, vol. 255, pp. 457–465. Springer, New Delhi (2014). https://doi.org/10.1007/978-81-322-1759-6_53
18. Zhan, Z.-H., Zhang, G.-Y., Gong, Y.-J., Zhang, J., et al.: Load balance aware genetic algorithm for task scheduling in cloud computing. In: Dick, G., et al. (eds.) SEAL 2014. LNCS, vol. 8886, pp. 644–655. Springer, Cham (2014). https://doi.org/10.1007/978-3-319-13563-2_54
19. Omara, F.A., Arafa, M.M.: Genetic algorithms for task scheduling problem. J. Parallel Distrib. Comput. **70**(1), 13–22 (2010)
20. Wang, X., Yeo, C.S., Buyya, R., Su, J.: Optimizing the makespan and reliability for workflow applications with reputation and a look-ahead genetic algorithm. Futur. Gener. Comput. Syst. **27**(8), 1124–1134 (2011)
21. Rodriguez, M.A., Buyya, R.: Deadline based resource provisioning and scheduling algorithm for scientific workflows on clouds. IEEE Trans. Cloud Comput. **2**(2), 222–235 (2014)
22. Kumar, M.S., Gupta, I., Panda, S.K., Jana, P.K.: Granularity-based workflow scheduling algorithm for cloud computing. J. Supercomput. **73**(12), 5440–5464 (2017)
23. Xu, Y., Li, K., Hu, J., Li, K.: A genetic algorithm for task scheduling on heterogeneous computing systems using multiple priority queues. Inf. Sci. **270**, 255–287 (2014)

Duplication Based Budget Effective Workflow Scheduling for Cloud Computing

Madhu Sudan Kumar$^{(\boxtimes)}$, Indrajeet Gupta, and Prasanta K. Jana

Department of Computer Science and Engineering, Indian Institute of Technology
(Indian School of Mines) Dhanbad, Dhanbad, Jharkhand, India
mdhsdnkumar88@gmail.com, indrajeet7830@gmail.com, prasantajana@yahoo.com

Abstract. Running a large scientific or web application in cost oriented manner is the present day's demand in cloud computing. Workflow scheduling with minimum runtime and within the user budget is an important reserach area in cloud environment. In this paper, we propose a budget constrained task duplication based scheduling algorithm for infrastructure as a service (IaaS) cloud that utilizes user's remaining budget to a greater extent for reducing the schedule length. We simulate the proposed algorithm on various scientific and random workflows of different size and category. The simulation results show that the proposed algorithm outperforms the existing scheduling algorithms.

Keywords: Budget · Workflow scheduling · Task duplication
Schedule length · Cloud computing

1 Introduction

Handling a large and complex application that needs a lot of computing resources always remain a challenging task in cloud computing. It is also considered to be a NP-complete problem [1]. In cloud computing, specially infrastructure as a service (IaaS), resources in the form of virtual machines (VMs) are leveraged on-demand to the end users through Internet to support the execution of such applications. The service providers charge for these resources on a pay-per-use [2] basis. The users with a limited budget can run their application(s) on the leased resources if it is feasible with the cost incurred by the service provider.

Complex applications are well represented in the form of workflows that has a set of tasks connected with several edges representing the data flow dependencies among the tasks [3,4]. Scheduling algorithms are designed for mapping these workflows to the VMs offered by the cloud service providers. The purpose of a budget constrained algorithm is to minimize the execution time while preserving the user's budget. Many algorithms have been developed for this purpose but they work on one-to-one basis [2,5,6]. Such algorithms utilizes the user budget to an extent while giving certain schedule length. If the application runtime is

© Springer Nature Switzerland AG 2019
G. Fahrnberger et al. (Eds.): ICDCIT 2019, LNCS 11319, pp. 90–98, 2019.
https://doi.org/10.1007/978-3-030-05366-6_7

not satisfactory to the user within that budget, it counts for the QoS. A possible solution is to run multiple instances of critical tasks on different VMs wherever required. It does not require additional VMs to be provisioned.

In this paper, we propose a duplication based workflow scheduling scheme which is also budget efficient for scheduling workflows. The overall algorithm can be divided into two phases. The first phase of the algorithm uses the schedule generated with a budget conscious workflow scheduling algorithm (MSLBL) [6]. Then the second phase of the algorithm duplicates some of the critical tasks to reduce the overall running time of the workflow the remaining budget obtained from the first phase is sufficient and there is a scope for duplication, otherwise algorithm returns the schedule generated in the first phase. The performance of the proposed algorithm is shown by comparing it with MSLBL [6], a variation of the proposed algorithm on the basis of average schedule length, execution cost, algorithm runtime and resource utilization.

Major contributions in this paper are summarized as follows:

◇ We propose a budget-constrained duplication algorithm for workflow scheduling scheme for IaaS cloud environment.
◇ It extends the budget distribution strategy given in [6].
◇ We also implement two variations of the budget distribution with level-wise task selection based on effectiveness ratio cost to remaining budget.
◇ We compare the simulation results of the above algorithms based on several parameters to show improvement of the proposed algorithm.

The rest of this paper consists of the following sections. Section 2 contains the reviews of some related works. The system model and formulation of the problem are given in Sect. 3. The proposed schemes and the simulation results are detailed in Sect. 4 and 5 respectively. Section 6 concludes the paper.

2   Related Work

For last few years, many researchers have been motivated towards cloud computing and its related issues. One of the major issue among others is the workflow scheduling problem. Many heuristic techniques have been developed for solving this problem with respect to various constraints. Some of the works that are closely related to this work are being discussed here. Arabnejad and Barbosa [2] proposed HBCS algorithm for scheduling wokrflows in a heterogeneous computing environment. It follows b-level [7] for deciding the execution sequence while for processor selection it uses a worthiness factor based on the initial assignment of the tasks with the minimum execution cost. It focuses on minimizing the schedule length while satisfying the user budget. Although it has been further optimized by Chen et al. in [6]. They proposed MSLBL method that distributes the user budget to every task proportionately to each task. It also minimizes the schedule length while saving some amount of the user budget. In [8], a duplication based approach has been proposed for minimizing the makespan of the workflow schedule. Although they did not considered the budget constraint while duplication the tasks. A hybrid approach that combines task clustering with duplication has been proposed in [9]. We propose budget constrained duplication based workflow scheduling algorithms that works on the schedule generated by MSLBL for further minimizing the schedule length by utilizing the remaining budget. We have also proposed another method that uses only the budget distribution technique used in MSLBL but differs in task selection criteria.

3   System Model and Problem Statement

This section elaborates the system model considered in the proposed scheme along with the problem statement and its formulation.

3.1   System Model

The system model is composed of two parts: (a) the cloud resource model and (b) the application model. The cloud resource model considered for our proposed scheme consists of several cloud servers (CSs) that hosts m number of available virtual machines (VMs) with different capacity with respect to processing speed, memory, bandwidth and so on. The processing capacity of each VM are given in terms of million instructions per second (MIPS). Any VM can execute only one task at any moment of time and the execution will be non-preemptive in nature. The bandwidth for communicating data files among these VMs is assumed to be equal and constant so that the communication time between any two VMs becomes dependent on the size of the data file only. Furthermore, we also assume that every VM can receive data from multiple sources simultaneously. As the VM costing is based on pay-per-use policy, the user is charged only for the time duration they are using the VM depending on the VM's capacity. A user application considered in our work, is represented in the form of a directed acyclic graph (DAG) $G = (T, E)$, where T is the set of n tasks and E is the set of edges $e_{i,j}$ such that $1 \leq i < n, 1 < j \leq n$ and $i < j$. Every edge $e_{i,j}$ denotes the data flow dependency $(t_i \rightarrow t_j)$ such that the execution of task t_j can start only after the availability of required data from task t_i.

We use the following terminologies in our work:

◇ *Task Runtime*, $(TR_{i,j})$: It can be described as the estimated runtime of a task t_i, having task length in MI for virtual machine VM_j, having certain processing speed in MIPS. So, $TR_{i,j} = TaskLength_i/VMSpeed_j$ and it can be organized as a task-VM runtime matrix, $[TR_{i,j}]_{n \times m}$, where $1 \leq i \leq n, 1 \leq j \leq m$ for n number of tasks in the given workflow and m number of available VMs along the cloud servers.
◇ *Average Task Runtime*, $(AvgTR_i)$: It is the average of the estimated execution time of a task t_i and is given as $\sum_{j=1}^{m} \frac{TR_{i,j}}{m}$.
◇ *Earliest Time to Start and Finish*, $(EST_{i,j}$ and $EFT_{i,j})$: These can be described as the earliest time when a task t_i can start or finish its execution

on VM_j depending upon the availability of the required data files from their predecessor tasks to the VM_j. It can be expressed as follows:

$$EST_{i,j} = \begin{cases} avl_j & \text{if } |pre(t_i)| = 0; \\ max\{avl_j, \max\limits_{t_y \in pre(t_i)} \{FT_y + dt_{y,i}\} & \text{otherwise,} \end{cases} \tag{1}$$

$$EFT_{i,j} = EST_{i,j} + TR_{i,j} \tag{2}$$

where, avl_j is the availability time of VM_j when it can start the execution of a new task, $pre(t_i)$ is the set of predecessor task(s) for task t_i and FT_y is the finish time of task t_y on its allocated resource. $dt_{y,i}$ is the time consumed for transferring the required data files from task t_y to t_i.

◇ *Workflow Cost, (W_{cost})* : It is the sum of cost incurred by all VMs with BT_j and C_j as the total busy time and the cost rate using VM_j for executing their allocated task. It is calculated as follows:

$$W_{cost} = \sum BT_j \times C_j \quad \forall \, j \in m \tag{3}$$

Moreover, W_{exe} and Bud are taken as overall time to finish the execution of user application and the user budget provided respectively while $Cost_i$ and $Task\_bud_i$ are considered as the cost of execution and the budget assigned for task t_i.

3.2 Problem Statement

Based on the above terminologies the problem statement can be formulated as follows. *Given n number of tasks in the user application and m number of VMs, with their corresponding cost rate of usage, the cloud scheduler needs to find an optimal mapping of tasks to the available VMs and the order of execution of the allocated tasks by the corresponding VM such that the overall workflow runtime, W_{exe} can be minimized while maintaining the cost of workflow execution lesser than the user budget.* Formally, it can shown as:

$$minimize(W_{exe}) = minimize(\max\limits_{t_i \in G}(FT_i)) \tag{4}$$

while satisfying the constraint: $W_{cost} < Bud$.

4 Proposed Algorithm

The proposed algorithm i.e., the duplication based workflow scheduling under budget constraint, basically works on a one-to-one task-VM mapping and the execution sequence which is calculated initially with the help of a budget based algorithm. The second phase follows the task sequence obtained in the first phase for finding critical tasks suitable for duplication on one or more VMs other than the preallocated VM. So the output of the second phase is a one-to-many task-VM mapping. While finding the critical task and the VM for duplicating the task, the algorithm takes care of the remaining budget left from the first phase. Before discussing the proposed algorithm, we will give a brief overview of the existing work i.e., MSLBL, proposed in [6]. It first finds the budget level by normalizing the budget given by the user based on the minimum and maximum possible cost of the workflow.

$$budgetlevel = (Bud - CostMin(G))/(CostMax(G) - CostMin(G)) \qquad (5)$$

where the $CostMin(G)$ and $CostMax(G)$ are calculated by selecting the resources with least cost and maximum cost for the tasks respectively. This budget level is used for distributing the user budget to each task in a fair manner.

$$Task\_bud_i = CostMin_i + (CostMax_i - CostMin_i) \times budgetlevel \qquad (6)$$

Here, $CostMin_i$ and $CostMax_i$ are the minimum and maximum possible cost for task t_i. It then selects the tasks on the basis of b-level values of the tasks [7] and map them to the VM that results in least EFT (Eq. 2) within the task budget ($Cost_i <= Task\_bud_i$). It also adds the spare budget left from the previous task's allocation to the budget of the next task in the sequence.

We propose here two duplication based variations of MSLBL algorithm.

◇ *Proposed Algorithm 1*: The first variation is based on the modification of task selection process. Instead of using b-level, it uses a task selection factor $TaskSelFactor_i$ for all tasks in workflow as shown in Eq. 7.

$$TaskSelFactor_i = (Task\_bud_i - AvgCost_i)/AvgTR_i \quad \forall\, t_i \in T \qquad (7)$$

where $AvgCost_i$ is computed as $\sum_{j=1}^{m}(TR_{i,j} \times C_j)/m \quad \forall\, t_i \in T$. It is then followed by the budget constrained duplication in second phase.

◇ *Proposed Algorithm 2*: The other variation directly uses the MSLBL in the first phase followed by budget constrained duplication in the second phase.

Both variations can be well justified with help of Algorithms 1 and 2. Both the algorithms together shows the steps to be followed by the MSLBL_Var1. Algorithm 1 will work as existing MSLBL approach by replacing the task selection criteria and using b-level [7] and by removing the step that calls ScheduleDup function at the end. Moreover, if the priority scheme is replaced to the b-level and ScheduleDup function is used then both algorithms will work as MSLBL_Var2.

5   Numerical Results

5.1   Simulation Settings

The simulations were carried out by using Matlab R2013a on Intel Core2Duo processor, 2.20 GHz CPU and 2 GB RAM with Microsoft Windows 7 platform. For simulation, we have used several synthetic workflows that are based on well known scientific applications [3] such as Montage, Cybershake, Inspiral and

---

Algorithm 1. MSLBL_Var1

Require: A DAG $G(T, E)$ for user application with n tasks, and m VMs.
Ensure: Schedule Plan having $TaskVMmap$ and $TaskSeq$.
  Calculate $CostMin(G)$ using cheapest resources to all tasks in G.
  if $CostMin > Bud$ **then**
    Return Budget Infeasible
  else
    Calculate $AvgFT_i$ and $TaskSelFactor_i$ $\forall$ $t_1 \in G$
    Initialize $TaskSeq$, $Task\_bud_i$, $TaskVMmap_i$ and $ExecStatus_i$ to $NULL$
    Initialize $avl_j \leftarrow 0$ $\forall$ $VM_j \in M$
    for level $l = 1 \rightarrow totalLevel$ **do**
      while $\exists\{t_i : level\ of\ t_i\ is\ l, ExecStatus_i = 0\}$ **do**
        Select $tid \leftarrow t_i$ with maximum $TaskSelFactor_i$ value
        Add $TaskSeq \leftarrow tid$
        Calculate $Task\_bud_{tid}$ /*refer equations 5 and 6*/
        Calculate $EST_{tid,j}$ and $EFT_{tid,j}$ $\forall$ $j \in M$ /*refer equations 1 and 2*/
        Calculate $Cost_j \leftarrow TR_{tid,j} \times C_j \forall VM_j \in M$
        Select $VMalloc \leftarrow (VM_j : EFT_j$ is minimum and $Cost_j < Cost\_bud_{tid})$
        $TaskCost_{tid} \leftarrow Cost_{tid,VMalloc}; \{ST_{tid}, FT_{tid}\} \leftarrow \{EST, EFT\}_{VMalloc}$
        $TaskVMmap_{tid} \leftarrow VMalloc$; $avl_{VMalloc} \leftarrow FT_{tid}$; $ExecStat_{tid} \leftarrow 1$
      end while
    end for
    Calculate W_{cost} /* refer equation 3*/
    Calculate Schedule length $W_{exe} \leftarrow max(FT)$
  end if
  Calculate $BudgetLeft \leftarrow Bud - W_{cost}$
  Call **ScheduleDup(TaskVMmap, TaskSeq, FT, SL, BudgetLeft)**

Epigenomic, and some random workflows. These workflows vary in tasks' size, number of tasks and edges, and the data transfer times that represent task dependency. For random workflows, we have considered 50 (small), 100, 400 (medium) and 1000 (large) number of tasks. Moreover, each algorithm have been simulated for different communication to computation ratio (CCR) [4] value of workflows that ranges from 0.1 to 2. In addition to this, the performance of the algorithms is also tested against the variation in budget level (from 1.1 to 2.0 with step size 0.1) of the user budget. Every performance parameters have been averaged over all CCRs to get the performance against a single budget level.

5.2 Performance Evaluation

For comparison, we have used normalized values of each parameters with respect to the maximum value found among all the algorithms. The results in Figs. 1a and 1b show the performance of given algorithms with respect to overall schedule length and budget consumed respectively. As shown in Fig. 1a, the normalized average schedule length for MSLBL and MSLBL_Var2 are nearly equal for budget level 1.1 and 1.2. But for budget level 1.3 onwards MSLBL_Var2 shows

Algorithm 2. ScheduleDup(TaskVMmap, TaskSeq, FT, W_{exe}, BudgetLeft)

$tempSL \leftarrow W_{exe}; tempVMmap \leftarrow TaskVMmap$

for $i : 1 \rightarrow n$ **do**

　$tid = TaskSeq_i$

　if $|pre_{tid}| > 0$ **then**

　　Select $ptid \leftarrow t_p$ with max data arrival from t_p to tid, $\forall\ t_p \in pre_{tid}$

　end if

　if $Cost_{ptid,TaskVMmap_{tid}} <= BudgetLeft$ **then**

　　Add $tempVMmap_{ptid} \leftarrow TaskVMmap_{tid}$

　　Calculate new schedule length tSL for $tempVMmap$ and $TaskSeq$

　　if $tSL < tempSL$ **then**

　　　$tempSL \leftarrow tSL$

　　else

　　　Remove $tempVMmap_{ptid} \rightarrow TaskVMmap_{tid}$

　　end if

　end if

end for

$TaskVMmap \leftarrow tempVMmap; BudgetLeft = Bud - W_{cost}$

Calculate W_{cost} for $TaskVMmap$

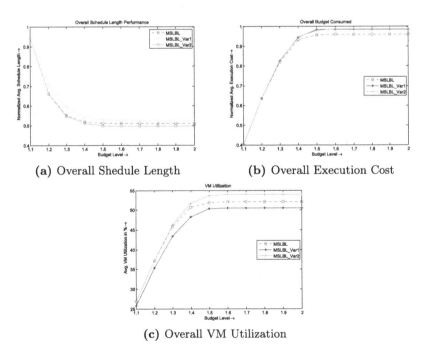

(a) Overall Shedule Length　　　　**(b)** Overall Execution Cost

(c) Overall VM Utilization

Fig. 1. Performance of scheduling algorithms

significant improvement in comparison to MSLBL. Due the increase in the user budget several tasks will come in feasibility range of the remaining budget for that particular budget level. While on the other side, MSLBL performs well in very few number of workflow cases. Hence its performance in Fig. 1a is not good in comparison of other algorithms. In the same way, as seen in Fig. 1b, both variations utilize almost similar budget which is greater than existing algorithm. Although, by analyzing both parameters together, we can consider that MSLBL_Var2 performs better than the other algorithms. When we consider the resource utilization aspect of the algorithms as shown in Fig. 1c, MSLBL_Var2 algorithm utilizes the VMs to a greater extent.

6   Conclusion

In this paper, we have proposed a budget constrained workflow scheduling algorithm which is shown to be an improvement over the existing algorithm MSLBL. All the algorithms have been simulated rigorously. The comparisons have been done mainly on the basis of four parameters that are worklow schedule length (application runtime), consumed budget, scheduler runtime and the resource utilization (average VM utilization). The second proposed algorithm MSLBL_Var2 performs better with respect to the application runtime and average VM utilization. While a comparable but not a significant performance is seen for MSLBL_Var1. The simulation results also show the improvement done by the applying the duplication strategy in the proposed algorithms but at cost of degraded scheduler performance. Further improvements are possible by allocation of some extra budget to the tasks that are comparatively more critical tasks in an application.

References

1. Buyya, R., Yeo, C.S., Venugopal, S., Broberg, J., Brandic, I.: Cloud computing and emerging it platforms: Vision, hype, and reality for delivering computing as the 5th utility. Future Gener. Comput. Syst. **25**(6), 599–616 (2009)
2. Arabnejad, H., Barbosa, J.G.: A budget constrained scheduling algorithm for workflow applications. Future Gener. Comput. Syst. **12**, 665–679 (2014)
3. Juve, G., Chervenak, A., Deelman, E., Bharathi, S., Mehta, G., Vahi, K.: Characterizing and profiling scientific workflows. Future Gener. Comput. Syst. **29**(3), 682–692 (2013)
4. Kanagaraj, K., Swamynathan, S.: Structure aware resource estimation for effective scheduling and execution of data intensive workflows in cloud. Future Gener. Comput. Syst. **79**, 878–891 (2018)
5. Fuhui, W., Qingbo, W., Tan, Y.: Workflow scheduling in cloud: a survey. J. Supercomput. **71**(9), 3373–3418 (2015)
6. Chen, W., Xie, G., Li, R., Bai, Y., Fan, C., Li, K.: Efficient task scheduling for budget constrained parallel applications on heterogeneous cloud computing systems. Future Gener. Comput. Syst. **74**, 1–11 (2017)

7. Kwok, Y.-K., Ahmad, I.: Static scheduling algorithms for allocating directed task graphs to multiprocessors. ACM Comput. Surv. (CSUR) **31**(4), 406–471 (1999)
8. Gupta, I., Kumar, M.S., Jana, P.K.: Task duplication-based workflow scheduling for heterogeneous cloud environment. In 2016 Ninth International Conference on Contemporary Computing (IC3), pp. 1–7, August 2016
9. Dubey, S., Jain, V., Shrivastava, S.: An innovative approach for scheduling of tasks in cloud environment. In: 2013 Fourth International Conference on Computing, Communications and Networking Technologies (ICCCNT), pp. 1–8, July 2013

Dr. Hadoop: In Search of a Needle in a Haystack

Sabuzima Nayak[(⊠)] and Ripon Patgiri[(⊠)]

National Institute of Technology Silchar, Assam 788010, India
sabuzimanayak@gmail.com, ripon@cse.nits.ac.in

Abstract. Dr. Hadoop is a framework to achieve the infinite scalability of metadata, hot-standby, high availability, automatic fault-tolerance, least hiccup time upon failure. The design is based on the Doubly Circular Linked List. However, the Dr. Hadoop considers the conventional hashing scheme of metadata. In this paper, Bloom Filter is integrated with Dr. Hadoop to boost up the metadata service performance. The conventional hashing is replaced by Bloom Filter in Dr. Hadoop to reduce extra space consumption. We propose to implement an existing Bloom Filter on the platform of the Dr. Hadoop. The rFilter is a variant of Bloom Filter, that is considered for the Dr Hadoop framework. We deploy rFilter in Dr. Hadoop platform and rFilter exhibits very good performance as compared to other variants of Bloom Filter. We conduct a series of rigorous experiments using Microsoft Traces to investigate the behavior of the rFilter on the Dr. Hadoop framework.

Keywords: Dr. Hadoop · In-memory replication · Bloom Filter
Cuckoo filter · rFilter · Big data · Metadata server · Microsoft Traces
Distributed system

1 Introduction

The Big data is the most researched topics in today's research world. The requirement of Big Data came from the voluminous data produced by various sectors. Storage of such voluminous data requires a cluster of machines. However, the efficient searching and retrieval of data from these clusters is a galling and time consuming task. So, now the focus is shifted to metadata. Compared to data the size of metadata is very small, hence, it is kept in RAM for faster retrieval of data. The metadata is stored in Metadata server (MDS) [6]. The MDS is the server to serve information about data [6]. Every node in the cluster does search operation to find the requested metadata. However, the client request comes at a rate of millions in a minute. So, performing the search operation for every client request consumes resources. Hence, eliminating this searching overhead can further improve the efficiency of the MDS cluster. Thus, our research problem begins with some research questions on this search operation-[**Q1**] Should all MDS nodes waste their resources in the search operation every time a client

© Springer Nature Switzerland AG 2019
G. Fahrnberger et al. (Eds.): ICDCIT 2019, LNCS 11319, pp. 99–107, 2019.
https://doi.org/10.1007/978-3-030-05366-6_8

makes a request? [**Q2**] Does the BF has the answer that we are looking for? The Q1 inspire us to use a methodology that can return the membership of the metadata in the MDS within a constant time. And, Q2 inspires us to judge the worthiness of BF in the MDS field. This paper proposes embedding of BF to Dr. Hadoop to provide a solution to avoid initial searching overhead of finding the node having the metadata in MDS. BF is integrated with Dr. Hadoop to boost up the metadata service performance. Moreover, The conventional hashing is replaced by BF in Dr. Hadoop to reduce extra space consumption.

Contribution: This paper corroborates the worthiness of Dr. Hadoop by embedding BF to implement MDS. The BF enhances the memory space consumption with an order of magnitude. The contribution of BF embedded Dr. Hadoop are- (a) BF gives a fast query response that also helps the Dr. Hadoop in performing quick searching, and (b) BF inherits the infinite scalability property of the Dr. Hadoop.

2   Background and Related Work

A Cuckoo Bloom Filter [2] is a variant of the BF [3]. It uses a variation of Cuckoo hash table [5], called partial-key cuckoo hashing. Cuckoo BF stores fingerprint of the element. In the Cuckoo hash table, the hash function discovers two locations for insertion of an element. The element is inserted in any one of the empty location. If both are occupied, then the older element of any one location is kicked and the new element is inserted. For storing the old element the same kicking process is followed. The kicking process continues till an empty slot or a threshold value is reached. The advantages of Cuckoo BF are less collisions, efficient table utilization, and dynamic insertion and deletion of elements. In delete operation, content of any one location which matches with the fingerprint is removed.

A rFilter is a $2D$ position based membership tester variant of BF. It is highly space efficient. It uses a reduced number of hash which helps in avoiding complex hashing algorithms. The rFilter does the bitwise operation in its BF. It has the advantage of very less time complexity in insert, query and delete operation. Initially, all slots are assigned 0. In insert operation, every character is extracted and stored in an array slot. The OR operation is performed to find the position of the bit and assign 1. Similarly, the same process is repeated for all characters in the word. In query operation, after finding location for each character if a single slot is 0, true negative response is returned. In delete operation, 0 is assigned to each character location. All operations in the rFilter have a time complexity of $O(1)$. Its advantages are- (a) highly adaptable, (b) flexible in changing BF size, and (c) reduces the FPR using reversing and shattering the placing of the character. However, in some cases such as words are palindrome or have consecutive repeated characters, the rfilter returns false positive response.

The Dr. Hadoop [1] is an MDS that provides infinite scalability. The design of Dr. Hadoop is based on Hadoop framework. It uses Dynamic Circular Metadata Splitting (DCMS) protocol. The DCMS is based on circular doubly linked list.

Hence, each node contains its two neighbors replicas. Dr. Hadoop is a decentralized MDS. Dr. Hadoop has availability of 99.99%. When a node fails, its neighbors automatically connect to each other. It is a self-healing, self-managing, and self-Locality-preserving MDS. The Dr. Hadoop overcomes many issues such as scalability, load balancing, hotspot, and small file problem. Dr. Hadoop can tolerate single, two consecutive, and multiple non-consecutive node failure at a given time. However, Dr. Hadoop cannot tolerate three consecutive node failure.

3 Proposed Model

In our proposed model, a BF is embedded to Dr. Hadoop to boost up the performance of MDS. In the updated Dr. Hadoop cluster, every node has its own BF. The BF maintains the unique metadata elements. Every node keeps both the metadata and the BF in RAM. It helps in faster membership checking by BF. When a new metadata is inserted into the MDS node, then it is stored both in RAM and BF. The BF is always kept up-to-date. In Dr. Hadoop along with the replicas, the neighbor nodes also store the BF. During a node failure, replica BF helps in membership checking. Conventionally, BF consumes very less amount of memory space. Hence, the BF removes an important overhead while compromising a small amount of memory. New features in the updated Dr. Hadoop are (a) Client-funded- When a client makes a request to Dr. Hadoop, the list of IP addresses of the nodes in the cluster is funded to the client. It helps the client to contact the nodes directly. (b) No complex hashing technique- Previously, Dr. Hadoop uses complex hashing techniques for uniform key distribution. However, in our updated Dr. Hadoop, the Client-funded feature eliminate this requirement (c) Completely decoupling MDS from the storage system, and (d) Highly adaptable- The use of BF, and the complete decoupling of storage system makes the new Dr. Hadoop highly adaptable.

4 Experiment and Results

Experimental Environment: The experimental environment is set up using low-cost commodity machines. These machines are interconnected through Layer 3 switch with $1GB/S$ Ethernet. The experimental setup is as follows- (a) Intel(R) Core(TM) i7-4770 CPU 3.40 GHz, (b) 4 GB RAM, (c) 500 GB HDD, (d) Ubuntu 16.10 64-bit, and (e) five nodes.

Latency: Figure 1 illustrates the rotational latency measurement of each node. The x axis represents the name of the node. The $NODE\_AE$ means the latency is measured from node A to node E. The y axis represents the time taken (milliseconds). The Figure illustrates the latency between A and B is the lowest. However, the latency from B to C is the highest compared to other nodes. But, the reverse is not true.

Data and Methods: The experiment is conducted on Microsoft Metadata Trace [4]. The trace data are pre-processed to obtain the metadata operation

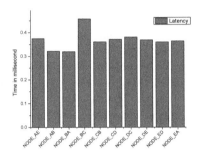

Fig. 1. Rotational latency measurement from each node.

and its respective disk memory address. The metadata operations are Diskread, Diskwrite and HardFault. The Diskwrite and Diskread operation initiate the insert and query operation in BF respectively. The HardFault is considered as an error. Figure 2a describes the Microsoft metadata traces used in our experiment. The Figure comprises of file of- (a) actual metadata, (b) pre-processed metadata, (c) read operation, and (d) write operation. The x axis represents the trace file name. The y axis represents the file size (MB). From the figure, it is concluded that the metadata size is very less compared to the original file. The original file is in the range of 52–60 MB whereas the metadata file size is in the range of 7.5–10.6 MB. The figure also illustrates the number of write operations is more compared to the read operations.

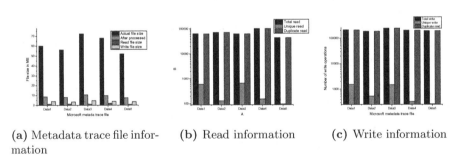

(a) Metadata trace file information   **(b)** Read information   **(c)** Write information

Fig. 2. Metadata trace file information.

Figures 2b and c illustrates the read and write operations of the metadata traces. The x axis represents the trace file name. The y axis represents the number of read operations in Fig. 2b and write operations in Fig. 2c. The Fig. 2b comprises of total number of read, unique read, and duplicate read operations. The difference between the unique and the duplicate data is huge. From this, we can conclude that the frequency of the client reads requests on some data is huge. Figure 2c comprises of the total number of write, unique write and duplicate write operations. The difference between the number of unique and duplicate write is very less. It illustrates that client file update request to some files is huge. Hence, the overhead of searching MDS nodes for frequent read or write operation to some particular nodes can be reduced by using BF.

Cuckoo vs rFilter: One of the most important task in the BF embedded Dr. Hadoop is to find a good BF with less or none false positive rate (FPR). We compare the rFilter [7] with one of the famous BF i.e. cuckoo BF [2]. Figure 3a illustrates the comparison between the two BFs. The x axis represents the trace file name. The y axis represents the size and the number of operations performed by the two BFs. The metadata trace files are the merger of five metadata trace files. The file size is in the range of 19.9–49.9 MB. The write operations on merged metadata files are input to the BF and the number of unique write operation is obtained as the output. When the file size is lowest, in case of Data_merge1, the difference between the cuckoo BF and the rFilter is same. However, when the size increases the difference becomes significantly visible. This difference confirms the presence of false positive in cuckoo. The cuckoo BF is showing false positive values for 2194 elements. Compared to the total number of elements, this value is less. However, the presence of false positive decreases the efficiency of a BF. But, in case of rFilter the number of false positive is 1 or none using similar configuration. We again compared the Cuckoo BF and rFilter based on the time taken in the processing of the operation. The x axis represents the trace file size. The y axis represents the time to process the operation (seconds). With the gradual increase in metadata file size the huge time difference of both filters is observed.

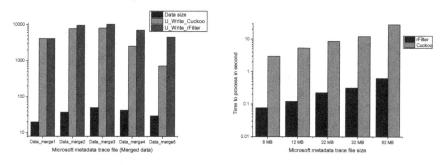

(a) Based on number of operations processed

(b) Based on processing time of operations

Fig. 3. Cuckoo vs rFilter

rFilter Embedded Dr. Hadoop: The comparison helped us to consider rFilter as the BF for Dr. Hadoop. We set up Dr. Hadoop in five commodity low cost hardware. The steps followed for the experiment are- (a) Setup Dr. Hadoop in five nodes, (b) Write BF data structure to file, (c) Transfer the file to neighbor nodes, and (d) Reconstruct the BF data structure in neighbor nodes. The data structure file also need to be resent periodically. We have considered 10 s as resend period. Normally the resent time should be for a little long duration (nearly 5 min) considering the network traffic.

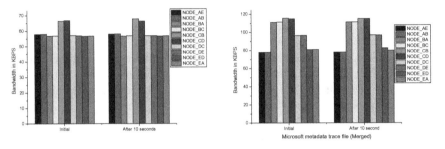

(a) Bandwidth taken by metadata trace files   (b) Bandwidth taken by merged metadata trace files

Fig. 4. Bandwidth

Figures 4a and b illustrates the bandwidth used by various nodes for file transfer to their neighbor nodes. The x axis represents the two types of file transfer- the first time and resend after 10 s delay. The color of the bar indicates the nodes among whom the transfer has done. The y axis represents the bandwidth (KBPS). Figure 4a illustrates the bandwidth taken for transfer of files to their neighbor nodes. We have given the write operation data of metadata trace files (3.5–4 KB) as input to the file transfer. Usually, the bandwidth used remain same during all transfers, within a range of 58–70 KBPS. However, the bandwidth does not depend on the metadata trace file size, rather it depend on the BF(rFilter) size. Referring to Fig. 4b, 5-data i.e five merged files are given as input to rFilter. The figure illustrates the bandwidth is in the range of 77.8–115.6 KBPS. Again, the bandwidth is independent of the metadata trace files. It depends on the BF size. However, the rFilter size is same as in the case of a single trace file. The file size becomes nearly double due to less non-zero values. But, after increasing the metadata trace file size by five times, the transfer file size becomes double. It helps to conclude that less bandwidth is used for transfer of much big sized file. Figures 5a and b depicts the time taken for transfer of metadata trace files. The x axis represents file transfer during first time and update transfer. The y axis represents the file transfer time (seconds). In Fig. 5a, during the first time connection with neighbor node, the file transfer takes more time compared to the file resent for the update. From this, it is concluded that the updating takes less time. Hence, network traffic generation is less. Figure 5b illustrates the transfer time of 5-data. The comparison between the Figs. 5a and b shows the less time difference between the file transfer. From this, it is concluded that the increase in file size increases the file transfer time in less magnitude. Hence, the BF transfer time produces less network traffic with increase in file size. We also conducted experiments on larger files. Table 1 illustrates the information recorded about the files. The 10-data file is obtained after merging 10 metadata trace files with size 56.7 MB. However, the insertion to rFilter took only less than a second. On the contrary, Cuckoo BF takes more than a minute. We sent the rFilter data structure to the neighbor nodes. The bandwidth taken is less compared to transfer of five merged files. Moreover, the transfer time of these files is very close to the time taken for transfer of five merged files. In addition, we conducted experiments on 20 merged metadata trace file with size 148.7 MB, and the time taken for construction of rFilter is only 2 s. In this case, it uses more bandwidth for file transfer. It also takes little longer time for file transfer. From our experiment, it is concluded the rFilter uses less bandwidth and takes less time for file transfer. It is also showing good performance upon increment of the metadata trace file size. Hence, embedding the BF with MDS is more efficient.

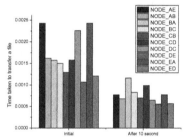 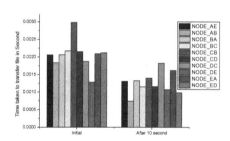

(a) Transfer time taken by metadata trace files   (b) Transfer time taken by five merged metadata trace files

Fig. 5. Time taken for transfer of file

Table 1. Information on large merged files

File name	File size (MB)	Construct time (ses)	Filter size (KB)	Bandwidth (KBPS)	Transfer time (secs)
10-data	56.7	0.8	161.8	91.8	0.0025 0.001258
20-data	148.7	2.14065	161.8	365	0.02 0.00402

5   Discussion and Future Work

False positive is the biggest problem in using BF. Using rFilter, we have reduced the FPR to very low or none. However, rFilter have some limitations, such as, sparse matrix, unable to remember the capability of the uniqueness of a bit string. Moreover, Dr. Hadoop also has some limitation. It has re-adjustment overhead during insertion and deletion of nodes in the cluster. Another issue is synchronization cost. In BF embedded MDS, both inherit the properties from each other. Hence, rfilter embedded Dr Hadoop also have the limitations of both rFilter and Dr. Hadoop. These limitations can be handled in the future. Moreover, many parameters remains to observe in rFilter embedded Dr. Hadoop. The BF is implemented in many research areas, but never in MDS to solve initial searching overhead. It proves to be better in reducing a big overhead in exchange for a small extra memory.

6 Conclusion

This paper presented an updated Dr. Hadoop. The rFilter is deployed on the Dr. Hadoop platform to enhance the performance. Moreover, Dr. Hadoop is capable of handling hot-standby, and high scalability. The BF reduces the memory overhead. The Bloom Filter embedded Dr. Hadoop inherits the properties of each other. Dr. Hadoop offers high scalability, efficient balancing of metadata storage, and no bottleneck with negligible additional overhead. Whereas, the rfilter is highly adaptable, flexible about changing the data structure size, space efficiency, and reduces the false positive. In Dr. Hadoop, the neighbors are hot standby. Hence, along with the replica of metadata, the replica of the rfilter is sent. A huge volume of metadata is sent as the rfilter is able to store the data without giving a false positive response. The bandwidth taken to send a single trace file of size 3–4.5 KB is 58–70 KB/sec. The bandwidth becomes double when the metadata traces file size increases by five times. In this updated Dr. Hadoop, the bandwidth is independent of the metadata trace files. Even ten merged trace files takes less bandwidth compared to five trace files. Moreover, the time taken by five merged trace file is same compared to transfer of a single trace file. In addition, the time taken to transfer the rFilter containing 20 merged trace file is less than a second i.e. 0.00402.

References

1. Dev, D., Patgiri, R.: Dr. Hadoop: an infinite scalable metadata management for Hadoop-how the baby elephant becomes immortal. Front. Inf. Technol. Electron. Eng. **17**(1), 15–31 (2016)
2. Fan, B., Andersen, D.G., Kaminsky, M., Mitzenmacher, M.D.: Cuckoo filter: practically better than bloom. In: Proceedings of the 10th ACM International on Conference on emerging Networking Experiments and Technologies, pp. 75–88. ACM (2014)
3. Grandi, F.: On the analysis of bloom filters. Inf. Process. Lett. **129**, 35–39 (2018)
4. SNIA: IOTTA: Storage networking industry's association. Accessed 20 Apr 2018. http://iotta.snia.org/tracetypes/6
5. Pagh, R., Rodler, F.F.: Cuckoo hashing. J. Algorithms **51**(2), 122–144 (2004)

6. Patgiri, R.: MDS: in-depth insight. In: 2016 International Conference on Information Technology (ICIT), pp. 193–199, December 2016
7. Patgiri, R., Borgohain, S.K., Bhattacharjee, A.: rFilter: a scalable and space-efficient membership filter. In: 2018 5th International Conference on Signal Processing and Integrated Networks (SPIN), pp. 478–485 (2018)

Parallel High Average-Utility Itemset Mining Using Better Search Space Division Approach

Krishan Kumar Sethi[1], Dharavath Ramesh[1(✉)], and M. Sreenu[2]

[1] Indian Institute of Technology (ISM) Dhanbad, Dhanbad 826004, Jharkhand, India
{kksethi,ramesh.d.in}@ieee.org
[2] Ashoka Institute of Engineering and Technology,
Hyderabad 500082, Telangana, India

Abstract. Since the last decade, High Utility Itemset (HUI) mining has emerged as a popular pattern mining approach. HUI mining discovers a set of itemset with their profit more than a user defined profit threshold. High Average-Utility Itemset (HAUI) mining is an improvement over HUI mining that involves the length of items to refine the patterns and keep a fair mining process. In the era of big data, traditional HAUI mining algorithms are not suitable to process large transaction dataset on standalone system due to limitation of processing resources. Therefore, several distributed frameworks have been developed to process big data on cluster of commodity hardwares. This paper presents a parallel version of the traditional HAUI-Miner algorithm and names it as Parallel High-Average Utility Itemset Miner (PHAUIM). PHAUIM is a Spark-based distributed algorithm which splits the dataset into multiple chunks and distributes on cluster nodes to process each data chunk in parallel. In addition, an improved approach for search space division is developed. Proposed search space division technique fairly assigns the workload to each node and upgrades the performance. Comprehensive experiments have been performed to measure the performance of PHAUIM in terms of speedup and data scalability. PHAUIM is also compared with traditional HAUIM.

Keywords: High average-utility itemset mining · Big data
Apache-Spark · Search space

1 Introduction

Discovery of useful patterns from a dataset is the task of pattern mining techniques [7,10]. Association rule and frequent itemset are two major constructs in the traditional pattern mining approaches that are still used for several real-life applications. Frequent Itemset Mining (FIM) [1,2,8,11] searches all frequent

Supported by Indian Institute of Technology (ISM) Dhanbad.

© Springer Nature Switzerland AG 2019
G. Fahrnberger et al. (Eds.): ICDCIT 2019, LNCS 11319, pp. 108–124, 2019.
https://doi.org/10.1007/978-3-030-05366-6_9

itemsets from a transaction dataset which have frequency(also called as support) more than a user defined support threshold. Apriori algorithm is a fundamental algorithm which performs a level-wise searching to discover a set of frequent itemsets [2]. It applies a Downward Closure (DC) property to prune the unpromising candidate itemsets from the search space. The DC property states that if any item in the search space is not frequent then none of its superset can be frequent. However, support is not an important measure to define useful patterns for various organizations. Therefore, FIM is extended by incorporating two new parameters called utility and quantity of itemset. Utility of an itemset means the profit obtained by that itemset. This new field of pattern mining is named as high utility itemset mining [3,28]. An itemset is termed as high utility itemset if its utility is no less than a user defined minimum utility threshold. Utility measure does not follow the DC property unlike the apriori algorithm. Therefore, a novel measure called Transaction Weighted Utility (TWU) [22] is introduced to retain the DC property in HUI mining. Several two-phase algorithms [17,23,26] have adopted TWU model to apply pruning. All two-phase algorithms search a set of strong candidate itemsets at the end of first phase and calculate the actual utility value to find the HUIs in the second phase. HUI-Miner [21] is the earliest algorithm which discovers HUIs from a dataset in one-phase. It has introduced a list structure called utility list to store utility of itemset and required information to apply pruning method. Thereafter, several improved one-phase algorithms [9,13,14,31] have been developed.

HUI miner suffers from a major limitation that length of the itemset affects the quality of the patterns. It is most likely that an itemset with larger length will has more chances to be a HUI regardless its usefulness. Therefore, an alternative of utility measure called average-utility is introduced to remove the impact of length constraint from the HUI miner. Average-utility of an itemset is measured by dividing the utility by its length. Pattern mining using average-utility is named as high average-utility itemset mining [12,15,16]. TWU is not applicable in HAUI mining algorithms. Therefore, a novel measure called Average Utility Upper-Bound (AUUB) [12] is introduced to acquire the downward closure property. Several HAUI mining algorithms [15,18] have adopted AUUB model to serve the pruning method. However, these algorithms are two-phase in nature and require more time and computing resources to search HAUIs. HAUI-Miner [18] is the first one-phase algorithm which produces candidate itemsets and HAUIs together. It has presented a list structure called Average-Utility (AU) list. Average-utility list is similar concept like utility list of HUI-Miner [21]. It requires a dataset scan to construct the AU-list of 1-itemset. Then, joining of AU-list of $(k-1)$-itemset is performed to build the AU-list of k-itemset. Various advanced HAUI mining algorithms [19,29] have been developed with tighter upper-bounds and efficient pruning methods.

A big explosion in technology and data industries have generated huge volume of data, lying on the servers. This data is termed as big data [4]. To apply pattern mining techniques on big transaction data is a challenging task because of two factors. First, big transaction data generates massive number of candidate itemset which might not fit in the system memory. Second, most of the pattern mining algorithms are developed for the standalone system which might not suitable to store and process big data. Many distributed frameworks such as hadoop [27], Spark [30] have been developed to effectively process big data with cluster computing approach. Many studies [5,20,24,25] have been performed to apply pattern mining techniques such as FIM, HUI mining on big data. Mining in distributed systems requires to divide and distribute the processing load on multiple machines so that processing can be achieved independently in a parallel manner. Therefore, search space division is a challenging task for data processing in distributed manner.

In this paper, parallel version of HAUI-Miner algorithm [18] named parallel HAUI-Miner is proposed. PHAUIM is a Spark based distributed algorithm. Apache Spark is considered as one of the best distributed framework for iterative data processing. Its in-memory processing and flexible programming environment uplift it over the hadoop framework. It introduces a new data structure called Resilient Distributed Dataset (RDD) that is collection of immutable distributed objects. Data in RDD is automatically distributed across the cluster nodes by spark framework to parallelize data processing. Moreover, a better search space division method is introduced to fairly divide the workload on each node. This method considers both AUUB values of items and length of subspace to define a weight factor for each node. It assures that no node with higher weight gets more workload than lower weight node. This paper has the following contributions.

1. A parallel algorithm PHAUIM is presented which models the traditional HAUI-Miner to work in distributed framework, i.e., Spark. Apache-Spark provides fast processing for iterative algorithms.
2. A better search space division method is introduced to assign the workload fairly on each computing node.
3. Substantial experiments have been conducted to evaluate the performance of proposed algorithm PHAUIM. It has also been compared with the base algorithm HAUI-Miner. It is observed that PHAUIM outperforms HAUI-Miner in speedup.

Remaining paper is arranged in the following manner. Section 2 explains the terms and definitions to describe HUI-mining and HAUI-mining. The proposed algorithm PHAUIM is discussed in Sect. 3. Section 4 contains experiments and performance evaluation of the PHAUIM. Section 5 concludes the paper.

2 Prerequisites

2.1 High Average-Utility Itemset Mining

Let $D = \{t_1, t_2, ..., t_n\}$ be a transaction dataset with n transactions and m distinct items $I = \{i_1, i_2, ..., i_m\}$. Each transaction $t_p \in D (p \in [1, n])$ is denoted as a unique identifier called as Transaction identifier (Tid) and contains a set of items from I. Let $X = \{i_1, i_2, ..., i_k\}$ be a set of k distinct items from I that is called k-itemset. Each item $x \in I$ in a transaction t_p is associated with a positive integer called as purchasing quantity or internal utility of x. Internal utility of the item x in transaction t_p is denoted as $IU(x, t_p)$. Each item also acquires a positive integer for the whole dataset that is called per unit profit or external utility. External utility of item x is denoted as $EU(x)$. External utility values for all the itemsets are stored in the profit table such as $PT = \{EU(i_1), EU(i_2), ..., EU(i_m)\}$. A sample transaction data and profit table are shown in respective Tables 1 and 2. These tables are used as running example throughout the paper.

Table 1. A sample dataset

Tid	item:quantity
t_1	a:2, c:3, d:1, e:5
t_2	a:3, b:4, c:1, e:2
t_3	b:4, c:1, d:4, e:2, f:1
t_4	a:2, b:3, c:3, d:1, e:4
t_5	a:1, b:3, c:2, d:2
t_6	a:2, b:5, c:2, f:2

Table 2. Profit table

Items	Per unit profit
a	2
b	3
c	3
d	2
e	4
f	1

Definition 1 (Item utility). Let x be an item in a transaction t_p, utility of x in t_p is denoted as $U(x, t_p)$ and defined as follows.

$$U(x, t_p) = IU(x, t_p) \times EU(x) \tag{1}$$

Definition 2 (Itemset utility). Let X be an itemset in transaction t_p, utility of X in t_p is denoted as $U(X, t_p)$ and defined as follows.

$$U(X, t_p) = \sum_{x \in X \& X \subseteq t_p} U(x, t_p) \tag{2}$$

Utility of itemset X in dataset D is denoted as $U(X)$ and defined as:

$$U(X) = \sum_{X \subseteq t_p \& t_p \in D} U(X, t_p) \tag{3}$$

Definition 3 (Average-utility). Average-utility of a k-itemset X in transaction t_p is denoted as $AU(X, t_p)$ and defined as follows.

$$AU(X, t_p) = \frac{U(X, t_p)}{|X|} = \frac{\sum_{x \in X \& X \subseteq t_p} U(x, t_p)}{k} \tag{4}$$

Where, $|X|$ is the cardinality of itemset X, i.e. $|X| = k$. Average-utility of X in dataset D is denoted as $AU(X)$ and computed as follows.

$$AU(X) = \sum_{X \subseteq t_p \& t_p \in D} AU(X, t_p) \tag{5}$$

For example, in the running dataset, $AU(\text{ac}) = AU(\text{ac}, t_1) + AU(\text{ac}, t_2) + AU(\text{ac}, t_4) + AU(\text{ac}, t_5) + AU(\text{ac}, t_6) = 6.5 + 4.5 + 6.5 + 4 + 5 = 26.5$.

Definition 4 (Total dataset utility). Total dataset utility of the dataset D is denoted as $TDU(D)$ and defined as follows.

$$TDU(D) = \sum_{t_p \in D} TU(t_p) \tag{6}$$

Where, $TU(t_p)$ is transaction utility of t_p that is computed as:
$TU(t_p) = \sum_{x \in t_p} U(x, t_p)$.

Definition 5 (Minimum average-utility threshold). Minimum average-utility threshold is a user defined percentage value of TDU. Let δ be the user defined percentage value, then minimum average-utility threshold (denoted as $minUtil$) is defined as follows.

$$minUtil = TDU \times \delta \tag{7}$$

For example, in the running dataset, $TDU(D) = 182$. Let δ be 18% then $minUtil = 182 \times 0.18 = 32.76$.

Definition 6 (High average-utility itemset). The itemset X is called as High Average-Utility Itemset (HAUI) if $AU(X) \geq minUtil$.

$$HAUIs \leftarrow \{X | AU(X) \geq minUtil\} \tag{8}$$

For example, in the running dataset, $AU(\text{ac}) = 26.5 < minUtil$. Therefore, itemset (ac) is not a HAUI.

Definition 7 (Transaction maximum utility). Transaction maximum utility (TMU) for a transaction t_p is denoted as $TMU(t_p)$ and defined as the maximum utility value in t_p.

$$TMU(t_p) = max(U(x, t_p) | x \in t_p) \tag{9}$$

Definition 8 (Average-utility upper bound). The average-utility upper bound for itemset X is denoted as $AUUB(X)$ and defined as follows.

$$AUUB(X) = \sum_{X \subseteq t_p \& t_p \in D} TMU(t_p) \tag{10}$$

For example, in the running dataset, AUUB values of the items are as follows. $AUUB(a) = 72$, $AUUB(b) = 64$, $AUUB(c) = 84$, $AUUB(d) = 57$, $AUUB(e) = 60$, $AUUB(f) = 27$.

Property 1 (Downward closure property using AUUB). If an itemset X has AUUB value lesser than $minUtil$ then neither X nor any superset of X is HAUI.

Property 1 is used to apply the pruning step in HAUI-mining algorithms. AUUB provides the upper-bound of average-utility for itemsets to remove the weak candidate itemsets. For example, in the running dataset, $AUUB(f) = 27 < minUtil$. Therefore, item f is a weak candidate and can be removed from the search space.

Definition 9 (Processing order and revised dataset). In the first scan of dataset, AUUB of all the items is computed. Then, the dataset is revised and used in place of original dataset. There are following two constrains for the dataset revision.

1. All the items with AUUB value lesser than $minUtil$ are removed. As per the Property 1, such items are no longer needed.
2. Items in a revised transaction are arranged as per the ascending order of the AUUB values.

Definition 10 (Average-utility list). Average-utility list for an itemset X is a list of tuples $<Tid, U, TMU>$, where Tid is the transaction ID which stores X, U is the utility of X in Tid and, TMU is the maximum utility of transaction Tid. AU-list of 1-itemset is constructed by a scan of revised dataset. Thereafter, AU-list of k-itemset $(k \geq 2)$ can be constructed by joining the AU-list of $(k-1)$-itemset. Hence, no extra dataset scans are required to built the AU-list of larger itemsets. Let $X.AUL$ (m length) and $Y.AUL$ (n length) be the AU-list of two itemsets X and Y. To construct the AU-list of itemset XY, i.e. $XY.AUL$ requires following rules to be employed.

1. All the common Tids in both the AU-lists are put in $XY.AUL$. Tid in both the AU-lists are sorted, therefore searching of common Tids requires $(m+n)$ comparison.
2. For each common Tid, U field is measured as $X.U + Y.U$.
3. $Y.TMU$ value is assigned to $XY.TMU$.

Property 2 (Pruning using AU-list). Let X be an itemset and $SUM(X.TMU)$ be the sum of all TMU values in the AU-list of X. If $SUM(X.TMU)$ is lesser than $minUtil$, then neither X nor any superset of X can be HAUI. Therefore, X and all its extensions can be pruned from the search space.

3 Proposed Algorithm: Parallel High Average-Utility Itemset Miner

Parallel High Average-Utility Itemset Miner (PHAUIM) is a Spark based algorithm which is suited to run on big transaction dataset in a distributed manner. PHAUIM works on divide and conquer concept where large problem is divided into smaller problems and solved individually by each node to make mining process faster. Execution flow of the PHAUIM is depicted in Fig. 1. Transaction data are partitioned into smaller and equal size of chunks and distributed across the cluster nodes. The distribution is part of Hadoop framework where we used HDFS as file system. The Data are loaded in a RDD $<Transaction>$ and each node processes the assigned data in parallel. Then, each item is associated with TMU value to form a paired RDD $<item, TMU>$. Thereafter, TMU values of each item across all the nodes is summed to produce another RDD $<item, AUUB>$ and collected at the master node. The transaction data is revised as per the List($[item, AUUB]$) where, each transaction omits all the items with AUUB value lesser than $minUtil$ and remaining items are sorted in ascending order of their AUUB values. All the items from the List($[item, AUUB]$) are extracted and mapped to the number of nodes in the cluster. Thus, a List($[item, Node]$) is obtained which is used for search space division such that only assigned items and their extensions are explored by each node. Moreover, the required transactions from the revised dataset are extracted for each node to reduce the processing complexity. Each node constructs average-utility list, i.e., $items.AUL$ for each assigned item. Then a recursive HAUI mining procedure is applied on $items.AUL$ to produce a set of HAUIs. The HAUIs produced by all the nodes are combined to produce the final output.

The pseudo code of PHAUIM is shown in Algorithm 1. It takes three inputs: transaction dataset D, number of nodes N, minimum average-utility threshold $minUtil$ and produces a list of HAUIs as output. In the first dataset scan, it applies flatmap() method to the D and each item x in transaction t_p is mapped to a key-value form (x, TMU) (line 4). TMU values of each item across the cluster nodes is summed to built another RDD $<x, AUUB>$ using reduceByKey() method (line 5). All the items with AUUB lesser then $minUtil$ are pruned out (line 6) and remaining items along with their AUUB are assigned to RDD $itemAUUB$. Thereafter, a list of items $items$ from the RDD $itemAUUB$ is extracted where items are sorted in ascending order of their AUUB values (line 11). Then, mapping() method is invoked to assign a set of items to each node, i.e., $itemNode$ so that the node can search the HAUIs from all the extensions of assigned items (line 12). Both the $itemAUUB$ and $itenNode$ are broadcasted to each node using broadcast variable (line 13). In the second dataset scan, the dataset is revised and the AUUB value of each item is recalculated from the revised dataset (lines 14–16). Thereafter, revised dataset is again scanned to assign required data to each cluster node using DataGenerator() method (lines 17–18). Each cluster node constructs the AU-list for every assigned item x (lines 19–22). Then, the HAUIMiner() method is recursively called to generate a set of

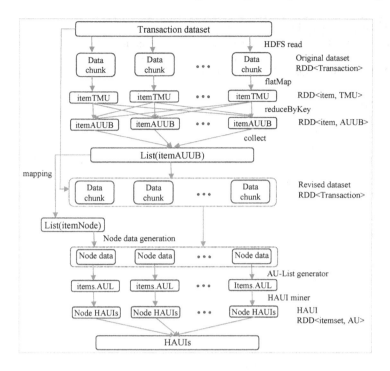

Fig. 1. Execution flow of PHAUIM

HAUIs. All the three methods mapping(), DataGenerator() and HAUIMiner() are discussed in detail in the following subsections.

3.1 Search Space Division

Entire Search space is divided into several subspaces and processed by individual cluster node to speedup the mining. For example, in the running dataset, after the first scan, five items (along with their AUUB values) {d: 57, e: 60, b: 64, a: 72, c: 84} are discovered and sorted in ascending order of their AUUB values. The search space is represented in form of enumeration tree [21] as shown in Fig. 2. Each Node with an item is responsible to mine a set of HAUIs such that any node with item d discovers all the itemsets with item d, node with item e mines all the itemsets having e but not d, node with item b mines itemsets having b but not item d and e, and so on. A fair division of search space is a difficult task. PHAUI-Miner [5] is the first algorithm to implement the HUI-Miner [21] in Spark framework. It assigns the items to cluster nodes in the following sequence. Let $\{1, 2, ..., N\}$ be the number of nodes in the cluster and $\{i_1, i_2, ..., i_k\}$ be the items to be assigned to the nodes. Items are assigned to nodes 1, 2,..., N and, then N, N − 1, ..., 1 and so on. For example, let there are 2 nodes in the cluster then, items assignment will be like this: {Node 1: d, a, c; Node 2: e, b}.

Algorithm 1. PHAUIM

INPUT: D: Transaction dataset, N: number of nodes
              $minUtil$: Minimum average-utility threshold
OUTPUT: $HAUI$: List of high average-utility itemsets
    //First dataset scan
 1: **flatMap** (D)
 2: **for each** transaction t_p in D **do**
 3:     **for each** item x in t_p **do**
 4:         map $(x \rightarrow (x, TMU))$
 5:         redeuceByKey $(\_ + \_)$
 6:         filter $(x \rightarrow x.\_2 \geq minUtil)$
 7:         $itemAUUB \leftarrow (x, AUUB)$
 8:     **end for**
 9: **end for**
10: **end flatMap**
11: $items = itemAUUB.\text{toList.sortBy}(x \rightarrow (x.\_2, x.\_1)).\text{map}(x \rightarrow x.\_1)$
12: $itemNode=$ mapping$(itemAUUB, N)$
13: Boradcast the hashmap $itemAUUB$ and $itemNode$
    //Second dataset scan
14: Revise the dataset: remove the items whose $AUUB < minUtil$
15: Each transaction is sorted in ascending order of AUUB values.
16: Recalculate the AUUB values.
    //Third dataset(revised) scan
17: $NodeTrasnactions=$ DataGenerator$(revisedData, itemNode)$
18: $NodeData=NodeTrasnactions.\text{groupByKey}()$
19: **flatMap** $(NodeData)$
20: **for each** Node N in $NodeData$ **do**
21:     **for each** item x at the Node N **do**
22:         P= $x.AUL$
23:     **end for**
24:     $HAUI \leftarrow$ HAUIMiner$(Null, P, minUtil, itemNode, NodeID, 1)$
25: **end for**
26: **end flatMap**
27: Output $(HAUI)$

It is observed that the existing search space division method may not perform efficiently because of two factors. First, There is a big difference in number of itemsets in each subspace, e.g., items d, e, b, a, c has 16, 8, 4, 2, 1 itemsets in their respectively subspaces. Second, there may be a large gap in AUUB values of the subspace itemsets. A large AUUB value means more entries in AU-list. Therefore, processing of a larger AU-list requires some extra time. To accommodate these constraints, in this paper, a novel search space division method is proposed that considers both subspace size and items AUUB value for a fair division. Each node is assigned a weight that is computed by using both size of subspace and AUUB value of items. An item is assigned to a node which has the lowest weight after that item assignment. Search space division method mapping() is depicted in Algorithm 2. It takes two inputs: $itemAUUB$ and number of nodes N and,

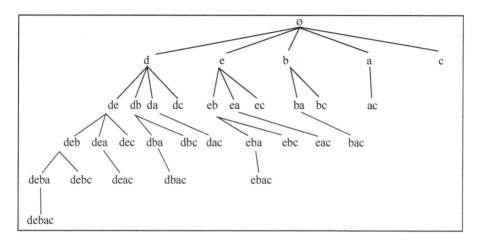

Fig. 2. Search space for the running dataset

produces a hashmap *itemNode* which maps each item to a node. For each item x in *itemAUUB*, the weight of x is computed by adding the subspace size to AUUB value of item (lines 3–4). If a node is not assigned any item then x is assigned to that node and nodeWeight is also updated (lines 8–11, 19–20). Otherwise, for each node, *afterWeight* is measured which is weight of the node after assignment of x (line 12). Item x is assigned to a node which has lowest value of *afterWeight* (lines 13–16, 19–20). In the end, *itemNode* is returned as an output. In the running dataset, search space division after applying the proposed method is as follows: {Node 1: d, a; Node 2: e, b, c}.

3.2 Data Generation on Node

Each node is responsible to discover HAUIs from the assigned subspace. Therefore, only required transactions or subset of transactions are stores at each node. If a node is assigned an item x then only those transactions are stored which have x. Moreover, if x is not the first item in revised dataset then subset of transaction, i.e., from x to end of the transaction will be stored.

The method DataGenerator() for node data generation is depicted in Algorithm 3. It takes two inputs: *revisedData* and *itemNode* and, produces a paired RDD *NodeTransaction* <*NodeID, transaction*> as an output. For each transaction t_p in *revisedData*, algorithm searches each item x of t_p in *itemNode* and grabs the NodeID (lines 1–5). If *NodeID* has not been delivered as output then subset of t_p from the item x to the end of the t_p is associated with *NodeID* to make a key-value pair and given in the output (lines 6–10).

Algorithm 2. Search space division: mapping()

INPUT: $itemAUUB$: List of items along with AUUB values
                   N : Number of nodes
OUTPUT: $itemNode$: A hashmap that maps each item to a NodeID
 1: $itemNode$ = empty hashmap
 2: len=Length of $itemAUUB$
 3: **for each** item x in $itemAUUB$ **do**
 4:     $weight = 2^{len-1} + x.AUUB$
 5:     NodeID=-1
 6:     $minimum = Int.MaxValue$
 7:     **for** each node n in N **do**
 8:         **if** $nodeWeight(n)$ is equal to 0 **then**
 9:             $NodeID = n$
10:             break
11:         **else**
12:             $afterWeight = nodeWeight(n) + weight$
13:             **if** $nodeWeight(n)$ is lesser than $minimum$ **then**
14:                 $minimum = afterWeight$
15:                 $NodeID = n$
16:             **end if**
17:         **end if**
18:     **end for**
19:     $itemNode \leftarrow (item, NodeID)$
20:     $nodeWeight(NodeID)+ = weight$
21:     $len = len$ -1
22: **end for**
23: return $itemNode$

3.3 HAUI Mining

The HAUIMiner() procedure is similar as described in HAUI-Miner [18]. However, Each cluster node runs its own HAUIMiner() for the assigned search space. The Pseudo code for the HAUI mining method is depicted in Algorithm 4. Initially, P is set to null and $extensionOfP$ is assigned the AU-list of all 1-itemset. For assigned items to a node, the search space is explored in top-down manner. If the itemset X from the $extensioOfP$ have average-utility more than $minUtil$ then it is assigned to output set $HAUI$ (lines 3–4). Then, pruning strategy is applied such that, if $X.AUUB = SUM(X.TMU) \geq minUtil$ then extensions of X are explored in the search tree (line 6). Each itemset Y after X in $extensionOfP$ is concatenated with X and a construct() method is called to build the AU-list of itemset XY (lines 7–9). Construct() method is not separately defined in this paper, as it is already given in HAUI-Miner [18]. Thereafter, HAUIMiner() method is called recursively to explore the extensions of itemset XY (line 11). At the end of the algorithm, a set of HAUIs is discovered.

Algorithm 3. Node data generation: DataGenerator()

INPUT: *revisedData*: Revised dataset
                itemNode: mapping of item to NodeID
OUTPUT: *NodeTransaction*: 0 or more $<NodeID, transaction>$
1: **flatMap** (*revisedData*)
2: **for each** transaction t_p in *revisedData* **do**
3:     *added* ← *emptyhasmap*
4:     **for each** item x in each t_p **do**
5:         search item x in *itemNode* and grab its *NodeID*
6:         **if** $NodeID$ is not in *added* **then**
7:             *added* ← *NodeID*
8:             T ← subset of transaction t_p from item x to the end
9:             output $(NodeID, T)$
10:        **end if**
11:    **end for**
12: **end for**
13: **end flatMap**

---

4   Experiments and Results Analysis

In order to evaluate the performance of PHAUIM, a comparison with HAUI-Miner [18] is performed. All the experiments were conducted on a Spark cluster of six nodes. Four nodes were having CPU Xeon(R) CPU E3-1225 v5 clocked @ 3.30 GHz and two nodes were configured with core i7-7700HQ clocked @ 3.8 GHz. Each node was equipped with 8 GB of DDR4 RAM and 2 TB of hard drive. Each node was having following software modules: Ubuntu 16.04 OS, Spark version 2.2.1, Java v-8.01 and Scala v-1.12.4. PHAUIM is evaluated in terms of run time performance and scalability.

4.1   Datasets

Both the algorithms were run for four distinct real-life datasets: accidents, chess, retail and mushroom. Attributes of each dataset are shown in Table 3. All the datasets were taken from the SPMF library [6].

Table 3. Datasets

Dataset	# of transactions	# of items	*avg.len.*	Type
Accidents	340,183	468	33.8	Dense
Chess	3,196	75	37	Dense
Retail	88,162	16,407	10.3	Sparse
Mushroom	8,124	119	23	Dense

Algorithm 4. HAUI Mining on node: HAUIMiner()

INPUT: P: AU-list of itemset P, $extensionOfP$: AU-list of all 1-extensions of P,
                $itemNode$: mapping of item to NodeID, $minUtil$: Minimum
                average-utility threshold, $NodeID$: Node ID of current node,
                $length$: length of current itemset

OUTPUT: $HAUI$: A set of high average-utility itemsets with P prefix

 1: **for each** AU-list X in $extensionOfP$ **do**
 2:      **if** P is not empty OR $itemNode(X.itemset)$ is equal to $NodeID$ **then**
 3:           **if** $\frac{SUM(X.U)}{length} \geq minUtil$ **then**
 4:                $HAUI \leftarrow HAUI \cup X$
 5:           **end if**
 6:           **if** $SUM(X.TMU) \geq minUtil$ **then**
 7:                $exAUL \leftarrow Null$
 8:                **for each** AU-list Y in $extensionOfP$ **do**
 9:                     $exAUL \leftarrow exAUL \cup construct(P.AUL, X, Y)$
10:                **end for**
11:                HAUIMiner($X, exAUL, minUtil, itemNode, NodeID, length + 1$)
12:           **end if**
13:      **end if**
14: **end for**

4.2   Runtime Performance

Run time performance of PHAUIM is evaluated by comparing it with traditional HAUI-Miner. Moreover, to measure the performance of search space division strategy, three distinct variations of PHAUIM were implemented: PHAUIM-Rnd, PHAUIM-Ex and PHAUIM. PHAUIM-Rnd divides the search space items in random manner. On the other hand, PHAUIM-Ex includes the existing method discussed in PHUI-Miner [5], while PHAUIM includes the proposed search space division technique. All three provide same functionality with different search space division technique. Run time of both the algorithms was measured with respect to different value of $minUtil$, as depicted in Fig. 3. It can be observed from the results that each version of PHAUIM outperforms the HAUI-Miner. The reason is that, HAUI-Miner performs all the computation on a single machine while PHAUIM assigns the workload to multiple nodes to search the HAUIs faster. PHAUIM-Rnd takes more time to terminate than the other two PHAUIM-Ex and PHAUIM. Random division of search space may assign some nodes more workload than others. Therefore, such nodes produces the results lately than other nodes and increase job completion time. PHAUIM-Ex takes slightly more time than the PHAUIM. PHAUIM handles the items with large gap in AUUB value and make a fair assignment. On the other hand, there is a fix pattern of item assignment in PHAUIM-Ex. It is also observed that PHAUIM shows the best performance for chess and accidents datasets.

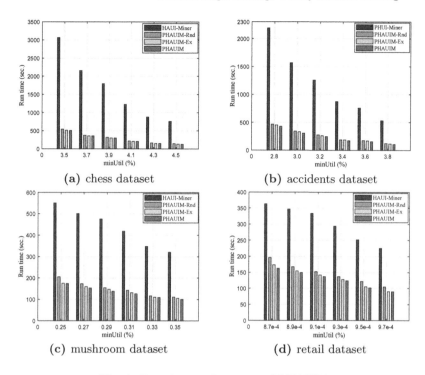

Fig. 3. Run time performance of PHAUIM

4.3 Scalability Test

Scalability test is performed to analyze nature of both the algorithms while data size is linearly increased. To evaluate the scalability of PHAUIM, both the algorithms were run by varying the data size in a certain proportion. The run time of each algorithm was measured to check the performance. Each dataset is replicated by a factor f such that experiment data = original data $\times f$, where $f = 1, 2, .., 5$. Both the HAUI-Miner and PHAUIM were run with replicated benchmark datasets. The results were taken with a fixed value of $minUtil$ for each dataset. Value of $minUtil$ for chess, accidents, mushroom and retail dataset was set to respectively 3.9%, 3.2%, 0.29 % and 9.1e−4 % of the total dataset utility. The results are depicted in Fig. 4. From the results, it can be noticed that, with increase in data size, run time also grows linearly. The reason is that, with the increase in number of transactions, there are more entries in the AU-list of itemset and requires additional run time. Run time of the HAUI-Miner for all datasets increases sharply with rise in data size. In contrast, PHAUIM run time increases slowly and remains close to x-axis.

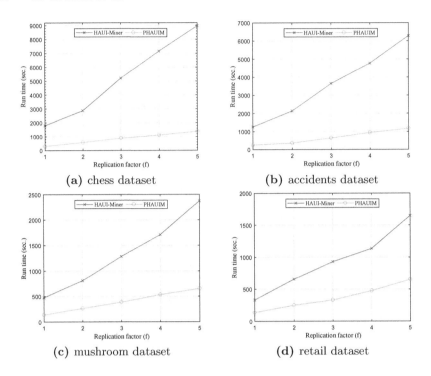

(a) chess dataset   (b) accidents dataset

(c) mushroom dataset   (d) retail dataset

Fig. 4. Scalability test of PHAUIM

5   Conclusion

This paper presents a detailed study about the pattern mining approaches such as HUI (High utility itemset) mining and HAUI (High-average utility itemset) mining. With the introduction to big data, pattern mining has acquired many challenges such as searching of high average-utility itemsets from a big transaction dataset. Huge number of candidate itemsets are generated while HAUI searching which requires massive computing resources and memory. Standalone system is not suitable to process big data in efficient manner. In this paper, a parallel version of traditional HAUI-Miner called PHAUIM is proposed to discover HAUIs from big transaction datasets. PHAUIM is a Spark-based distributed algorithm that model the HAUI-Miner to work in parallel on a multi node cluster. Search space is divided into subspaces and distributed to cluster nodes. Each node individually processes its subspace and produces a set of HAUIs. A novel search space division method is also presented that considers the AUUB of items along with the subspace size to divide the search space fairly. Various experiments have been conducted to evaluate the performance of PHAUIM with respect to four benchmark datasets. Moreover, it is also compared with HAUI-Miner. Experimental results show that PHAUIM outperforms the HAUI-Miner with a huge margin.

Acknowledgment. This research work is supported by Indian Institute of Technology (ISM), Dhanbad. The authors wish to express their gratitude and heartiest thanks to the Department of Computer Science & Engineering, Indian Institute of Technology (ISM), Dhanbad, India for providing their research support.

References

1. Agrawal, R., Imieliński, T., Swami, A.: Mining association rules between sets of items in large databases. ACM SIGMOD Rec. **22**, 207–216 (1993)
2. Agrawal, R., Srikant, R.: Fast algorithms for mining association rules. In: Proceedings of the 20th International Conference on Very Large Data Bases, VLDB, vol. 1215, pp. 487–499 (1994)
3. Chan, R., Yang, Q., Shen, Y.-D.: Mining high utility itemsets. In: 2003 Third IEEE international conference on Data mining, ICDM 2003, pp. 19–26. IEEE (2003)
4. Chen, C.L.P., Zhang, C.-Y.: Data-intensive applications, challenges, techniques and technologies: a survey on big data. Inf. Sci. **275**, 314–347 (2014)
5. Chen, Y., An, A.: Approximate parallel high utility itemset mining. Big Data Res. **6**, 26–42 (2016)
6. Fournier-Viger, P., Gomariz, A., Gueniche, T., Soltani, A., Cheng-Wei, W., Tseng, V.S.: SPMF: a Java open-source pattern mining library. J. Mach. Learn. Res. **15**(1), 3389–3393 (2014)
7. Fournier-Viger, P., Lin, J.C.-W., Kiran, R.U., Koh, Y.S., Thomas, R.: A survey of sequential pattern mining. Data Sci. Pattern Recognit. **1**(1), 54–77 (2017)
8. Fournier-Viger, P., Lin, J.C.-W., Vo, B., Chi, T.T., Zhang, J., Le, H.B.: A survey of itemset mining. Wiley Interdisc. Rev.: Data Mining Knowl. Discov. **7**(4), e1207 (2017)
9. Fournier-Viger, P., Wu, C.-W., Zida, S., Tseng, V.S.: FHM: faster high-utility itemset mining using estimated utility co-occurrence pruning. In: Andreasen, T., Christiansen, H., Cubero, J.-C., Raś, Z.W. (eds.) ISMIS 2014. LNCS (LNAI), vol. 8502, pp. 83–92. Springer, Cham (2014). https://doi.org/10.1007/978-3-319-08326-1_9
10. Han, J., Pei, J., Kamber, M.: Data Mining: Concepts and Techniques. Elsevier, Amsterdam (2011)
11. Han, J., Pei, J., Yin, Y.: Mining frequent patterns without candidate generation. ACM SIGMOD Rec. **29**, 1–12 (2000)
12. Hong, T.-P., Lee, C.-H., Wang, S.-L.: Effective utility mining with the measure of average utility. Expert Syst. Appl. **38**(7), 8259–8265 (2011)
13. Krishnamoorthy, S.: Pruning strategies for mining high utility itemsets. Expert Syst. Appl. **42**(5), 2371–2381 (2015)
14. Krishnamoorthy, S.: HMiner: efficiently mining high utility itemsets. Expert Syst. Appl. **90**, 168–183 (2017)
15. Lan, G.-C., Hong, T.-P., Tseng, V.S.: Efficiently mining high average-utility itemsets with an improved upper-bound strategy. Int. J. Inf. Technol. Decis. Making **11**(05), 1009–1030 (2012)
16. Lan, G.-C., Hong, T.-P., Tseng, V.S., et al.: A projection-based approach for discovering high average-utility itemsets. J. Inf. Sci. Eng. **28**(1), 193–209 (2012)
17. Li, Y.-C., Yeh, J.-S., Chang, C.-C.: Isolated items discarding strategy for discovering high utility itemsets. Data Knowl. Eng. **64**(1), 198–217 (2008)
18. Lin, J.C.-W., Li, T., Fournier-Viger, P., Hong, T.-P., Zhan, J., Voznak, M.: An efficient algorithm to mine high average-utility itemsets. Adv. Eng. Inform. **30**(2), 233–243 (2016)

19. Lin, J.C.-W., Ren, S., Fournier-Viger, P.: MEMU: more efficient algorithm to mine high average-utility patterns with multiple minimum average-utility thresholds. IEEE Access **6**, 7593–7609 (2018)
20. Lin, Y.C., Wu, C.-W., Tseng, V.S.: Mining high utility itemsets in big data. In: Cao, T., Lim, E.-P., Zhou, Z.-H., Ho, T.-B., Cheung, D., Motoda, H. (eds.) PAKDD 2015. LNCS (LNAI), vol. 9078, pp. 649–661. Springer, Cham (2015). https://doi.org/10.1007/978-3-319-18032-8_51
21. Liu, M., Qu, J.: Mining high utility itemsets without candidate generation. In: Proceedings of the 21st ACM International Conference on Information and Knowledge Management, pp. 55–64. ACM (2012)
22. Liu, Y., Liao, W., Choudhary, A.: A fast high utility itemsets mining algorithm. In: Proceedings of the 1st International Workshop on Utility-Based Data Mining, pp. 90–99. ACM (2005)
23. Liu, Y., Liao, W., Choudhary, A.: A two-phase algorithm for fast discovery of high utility itemsets. In: Ho, T.B., Cheung, D., Liu, H. (eds.) PAKDD 2005. LNCS (LNAI), vol. 3518, pp. 689–695. Springer, Heidelberg (2005). https://doi.org/10.1007/11430919_79
24. Sethi, K.K., Ramesh, D.: HFIM: a Spark-based hybrid frequent itemset mining algorithm for big data processing. J. Supercomput. **73**(8), 3652–3668 (2017)
25. Sethi, K.K., Ramesh, D., Edla, D.R.: P-FHM+: parallel high utility itemset mining algorithm for big data processing. Procedia Comput. Sci. **132**, 918–927 (2018). International Conference on Computational Intelligence and Data Science
26. Tseng, V.S., Wu, C.-W., Shie, B.-E., Yu, P.S.: Up-growth: an efficient algorithm for high utility itemset mining. In: Proceedings of the 16th ACM SIGKDD International Conference on Knowledge Discovery and Data Mining, pp. 253–262. ACM (2010)
27. White, T.: Hadoop: The Definitive Guide. O'Reilly Media, Inc., Newton (2012)
28. Yao, H., Hamilton, H.J., Butz, C.J.: A foundational approach to mining itemset utilities from databases. In: Proceedings of the 2004 SIAM International Conference on Data Mining, pp. 482–486. SIAM (2004)
29. Yun, U., Kim, D.: Mining of high average-utility itemsets using novel list structure and pruning strategy. Future Gener. Comput. Syst. **68**, 346–360 (2017)
30. Zaharia, M., et al.: Resilient distributed datasets: a fault-tolerant abstraction for in-memory cluster computing. In: Proceedings of the 9th USENIX Conference on Networked Systems Design and Implementation, pp. 2. USENIX Association (2012)
31. Zida, S., Fournier-Viger, P., Lin, J.C.-W., Wu, C.-W., Tseng, V.S.: EFIM: a highly efficient algorithm for high-utility itemset mining. In: Sidorov, G., Galicia-Haro, S.N. (eds.) MICAI 2015. LNCS (LNAI), vol. 9413, pp. 530–546. Springer, Cham (2015). https://doi.org/10.1007/978-3-319-27060-9_44

Supporting Transaction Predictability in Replicated DRTDBS

Pratik Shrivastava$^{(\boxtimes)}$ and Udai Shanker

M.M.M.U.T, Gorakhpur, India
pratik.shrivastav10@gmail.com, udaigkp@gmail.com

Abstract. The design and implementation of replicated distributed real time database system (RDRTDBS) must meet two rigorous requirements; deadline of real time transactions (RTTs) and preserving of the mutual consistency of replicated data. Previous researches in RDRTDBS have been concentrated mainly on designing of replica update techniques (RUTs) for soft and firm RTTs with sole correctness criteria of serializability and epsilon serializability. No work has been reported for predictable processing of real time transaction (RTT) with guaranteeing the mutual consistency of replicated data. Therefore, this paper first addresses the factors of predictability and mutual consistency in RDRTDBS and then briefly discusses the features and requirements of RDRTDBS and presents a processing plan that supports predictable execution of hard, soft and firm RTT along with maintaining the mutual consistency. The simulation results demonstrate that the proposed processing scheme enhances the performance of RDRTDBS beyond that offered by the existing RUTs.

Keywords: Replication · Real time transaction · Predictability
Mutual consistency

1 Introduction

In RDRTDBS, RTTs have explicit requirements of timing constraint and mutual consistency. The correctness of RTT depends on logical consistency along with timeliness [1]. Therefore, scheduling must be done in such a way that RTTs are completed within the specified deadline. In some cases, missing the deadline of RTTs may cause serious harm or heavy economical loss. This type of tight time constrained RTT is called hard one. There exist some other real-time applications that have deadline requirement but are noncritical in nature. RTT working for such application is termed as soft type. Finally, firm RTT gives no value [2] if the output is generated after crossing its deadline.

Previously reported works such as MIRROR, RT-RCT, ORDER, and others [3–16, 27–29] have focused on designing replica update technique (RUT) for soft and firm RTT. In these works, the processing of RTTs follows different correctness criteria such as strict serializability and epsilon serializability. However, no result has been reported for predictable processing of RTT along with maintaining mutual consistency in RDRTDBS. In current scenario, there exist many real time applications where RDRTDBS must be equipped with a technique to minimize the latency occurred in

© Springer Nature Switzerland AG 2019
G. Fahrnberger et al. (Eds.): ICDCIT 2019, LNCS 11319, pp. 125–140, 2019.
https://doi.org/10.1007/978-3-030-05366-6_10

RTT processing making its execution predictable. For example, some of the control systems require highly perishable data and hard deadline RTT for their application [17–20]. On the other hand, information management systems [21, 22] support only soft and firm deadline RTT. The predictability depends on a range of factors such as interaction with indeterministic sub-system, the data requirements of RTT, resources and data conflicts between different processing RTT, traditional recovery mechanism and mutual consistency between replicated data.

The issues of interaction with indeterministic subsystem and data requirement of RTT have been solved via solutions presented in [23, 24]. Therefore, our focus is mainly on the other three issues i.e. recovery technique for predictable recovery of failed site, dual version data object for solving the problem of blocking or abort and maintaining the mutual consistency of replicated data. To achieve our goal, a new recovery technique has been proposed that shares the load of recovery among existing healthy sites. Through sharing the load of recovery among healthy sites and updating from urgently needed data objects in recovering site, the predictable execution of RTT on healthy sites and recovering site can be easily predicted. During processing of RTT, single version data objects are present. Due to this, blocking or abortion of low priority RTT in favor of high priority RTT during conflict condition has to be done. The ultimate result of blocking and abortion of low priority RTT causes wastage of resources. Therefore, concept of dual version data object [4] is being used for both real time and non-real time data objects. This dual version data object eliminates unpredictable issue and allows different RTTs to concurrently work on a same data object. These RTTs can be of any type (i.e. write, update or read one). Also, our proposed predictable processing scheme of RTT must provide both predictability and mutual consistency such that each submitted RTT in the RDRTDBS is assured to complete within deadline. To maintain the mutual consistency between replicated sites, we propose a system model consisting of multiple master sites that predictably maintains the mutual consistency between replicated data. Overall, our proposed predictable processing of RTT provides both predictability and mutual consistency such that it will work for existing and forthcoming real time applications.

The rest of the paper is organized as follows. Section 2 describes requirements of RDRTDBS and Sect. 3 different issues that makes RTT processing more difficult. Section 4 presents designing of proposed system involving data and transaction model that is considered in this study. Section 5 outlines the predictable processing of RUT for different types of RTTs. Again, Sect. 6 deals with literature review and Sect. 7 discusses the results of the experimental study. Finally, Sect. 8 concludes the study.

2 Requirements for RDRTDBS

2.1 Predictability

In RDRTDBS, predictability for the RTT execution is considered as one of the most important requirements. Predictability confirms whether hard RTT will be completed within its deadline or not. Confirming transaction completion requires its comprehensive knowledge; however, not possible to gather this comprehensive knowledge feasibly because of various factors involved stated above contributing to the unpredictability of RTT execution. Such a prediction cannot be made available for all RTTs.

2.2 Mutual Consistency

Mutual consistency means that all the replicated data placed at different sites will converge to the same value. Moreover, this data value will remain consistent until the update transaction does not change its value. Replica update transactions must be periodically executed on replicated sites to ensure mutual consistency. This situation becomes worse when the number of update RTT increases as compare to read RTT.

2.3 Correctness Criteria

Correctness criteria are followed by the scheduler. Serializability is considered as one of the most accepted correctness criteria for RUT in distributed database system. It ensures that the output generated from a concurrent schedule of RTT is equivalent to serial schedule [25]. There exist other different correctness criteria such as eventual consistency, strict consistency and so on to provide flexibility in correctness criteria. In this paper, strict correctness criterion i.e. serializability has been considered to provide consistent value for the executing RTT.

3 Sources of Unpredictability in RDRTDBS

Table 1. represent different factors for predictable execution of RTT in RDRTDBS.

Table 1. Issues in predicting RTT completion time

S. No	List of issues	Subcategories of issues	Solutions
1.	Interaction with indeterministic subsystem	1. Page fault	Existing solution of [23]
		2. Unpredictable I/O scheduling	
		3. Buffer management	
		4. Disk scheduling	
2.	Data requirements by RTT	1. Unable to predict time elapsed for I/O	Existing solution of [24]
3.	Data and resource conflict between RTT	1. Lock allocation policy	Existing concept of dual version data object [4]
		2. Transaction abort	
		3. Transaction block	
4.	Recovery techniques	1. Unconditional delay for RTT execution	Proposed recovery solution
5.	Mutual consistency between replicated data objects	1. Unpredictable communication delay	Proposed system model
		2. Replication type (i.e. full, partial or no replication)	

3.1   Interaction with Indeterministic Subsystem

This is one of the most important issues that creates difficulty in predicting RTT completion time. It includes the factors such as dynamic page fault, disk I/O, I/O scheduling and unpredictable buffer residence. These limiting factors can be overcome through designing real time sublayer. This sublayer can be appended to the operating system to address the need for predictable RTT execution. In our proposed system model, replicated site is integrated with real time sublayer proposed in [23]. By integrating such sublayer on the replicated site, unpredictability with respect to indeterministic subsystem can be overcome and predicting RTT execution time becomes easier.

3.2   Data Requirement by RTT

This is another issue that also creates difficulty in predicting RTT completion time. For instance, I/O scheduling algorithm schedules the I/O request of RTT to process completely. Although I/O scheduler knows in advance about the data items to be accessed but it is unable to predict I/O elapsed time. Similarly, unpredictable buffer residence and process switching during processing of I/O causes predicting I/O elapsed time more difficult. Therefore, to solve the issue of data requirement by RTT, we propose to use the approach presented in [24] so that predictable execution of RTT can be done more easily.

3.3   Data and Resource Conflict Between RTT

To effectively identify data and resource conflict between RTT, RDRTDBS needs local and global control over the movement of replicated data across the system. If conflict detection and resolution mechanism is not followed during concurrently executing RTT on same data object, it may lead to inconsistency in replicated data. Therefore, correctness criteria are used to overcome the occurrence of inconsistency in replicated data object. Serializability is considered as one of the strict correctness criteria. It does not allow reading inconsistent data by any transaction. Transaction abort or block operations are used to implement this strictness. Following serializability correctness criteria in RDRTDBS is not an easy task because of stringent requirement between deadline and consistency. On the other hand, eventual consistency allows RTT to read inconsistent data. Therefore, we propose to use dual version data object to follow strict consistency criteria which works for write, update and read RTTs as shown in Figs. 1 and 2. Through utilizing dual version data object, it is possible that write, update and read RTTs can work together, so that wastage of resource can be stopped.

3.4   Recovery Techniques

Predictable performance of RTT in case of failure is of paramount importance in RDRTDBS. The failure of a replicated site may cause the running RTT to miss its deadline. Therefore, logging with checkpointing (i.e. one of the ancient techniques) is used to overcome such unpredictability. Some applications use logging with fuzzy

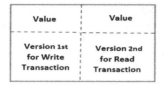

Value	Value
Version 1st for Write Transaction	Version 2nd for Read Transaction

Fig. 1. Dual version data object working in between write and read RTT.

Value	Value
Version 1st for Update Transaction	Version 2nd for Read Transaction

Fig. 2. Dual version data object working in between update and read RTT.

checkpointing that allows synchronously execution of both the transaction and recovery. Shadows based recovery is also an alternative that includes two directories i.e. current directory and scratch directory to recover from crash easily. However, Predicting RTT completion time with failure recovery mechanism is a challenging task. Failure recovery mechanism is one to one process that degrades the performance of both the sites. In the current paper, we will distribute the workload of recovery among currently available sites such that all available sites parallelly prepare their partial log and propagate it to the failure site concurrently. At recovering site, the process of recovery starts from that partial log such that timeliness of the waiting high priority transaction can be fulfilled.

3.5   Mutual Consistency Between Replicated Data Objects

This is one of the mandatory issues that occurs only in RDRTDBS. Prediction for RTT completion time in replicated environment requires keeping the system working even though system network failed or partitioned. Apart from network partitioning, replica design, replica size, replication type, replication propagation strategy and network communication delay also play a role for predicting RTT completion time. Therefore, this paper proposes a system model that can efficiently maintain the mutual consistency, so that unnecessary abort of RTT can be prevented and performance in terms of transaction miss ratio can be improved. The detailed description of our proposed system and transaction model is presented in Sect. 4.

4   System Model for RDRTDBS

Most RUTs [3–16] have been developed and tested in their respected simulation environment with their defined settings. In majority of simulation settings, RTT are assumed to arrive in a Poisson stream at a specified rate. The data requirements of RTT consist of random number of request to access the pages. Such simulation environment is reasonable for soft and firm RTT. However, they lack predictability in existing system model and do not support hard RTT. In the current paper, our objective is to design the system model that can tackle all types of RTT i.e. hard, soft and firm type.

4.1   Data Model for RDRTDBS

In our proposed system model, RDRTDBS consists of two types of data objects: real time and non-real time data objects. Real time data object is related to external world continuously changing with time. Whenever external world changes its value, it is represented as real time data object and replicas must also get updated with this new value. In addition to this, real time data object is linked with an absolute validity interval, relative validity interval and timestamp that suggest that after certain interval of time, its value will automatically become inconsistent. Therefore, it is necessary to update its value before expiring of its validity interval. On the other hand, non-real time data object does not have such strict requirement. The data value of non-real time data object will remain valid until it is being modified by any write transaction.

In our proposed system model, RDRTDBS consists of a set of real time data objects $X = \{X_1, X_2, X_3, ..., X_n\}$, and non-real time data objects $Y = \{Y_1, Y_2, Y_3, ..., Y_n\}$. In the rest of the paper, this notation will be used.

4.2   Transaction Model for RDRTDBS

In our proposed system model, RTT has the following attributes: arrival time (A_T), circulation (i.e. periodic (P), sporadic (S) or random (R)), deadline (D_L), priority (P_T), worst case execution time (E_T), data requirement (D_R), criticalness (C_T), slack value (S_V), response time (R_T) and value function (V_F). Depending on the values of such attributes and information available, an RTT can be characterized into hard, soft or firm type.

Hard RTT

Hard RTTs are periodic in nature and have hard deadline. Data requirements of hard RTTs are always predefined and they are always used to update the real time data objects. Due to strict requirement of time constraint property, scheduler always assigns the high priority to hard RTT. During processing stage of hard RTT, conflict can have occurred between hard RTT and soft or firm read RTT. Therefore, conflict resolution gives hard RTT high priority to execute and soft or firm RTT is blocked or restarted later. Overall, it is necessary to predict hard RTT completion time, so that guarantee in terms of completion time can be provided.

Soft RTT

Soft RTT are periodic or sporadic in nature and their data requirements are unknown. However, this type of RTTs do not have strict requirement of deadline fulfillment. Its output does not get zero value even after its deadline misses. Due to availability of limited resource in RDRTDBS, it is not possible to guarantee deadline fulfillment of soft RTT because different RTTs compete for CPU and the allocation of other resources.

Firm RTT

The firm RTTs are also aperiodic or sporadic in nature. The RDRTDBS does not get any value due to missing the deadline of the firm RTT. Therefore, firm RTT is immediately aborted on missing its deadline. As compare to hard RTT, it offers more leeway because of flexibility for deadline fulfillment. Apart from this, firm RTT involves various complexities such as scheduling, conflict detection and resolution that make the deadline fulfillment more complex.

4.3   Dual Version Data Object

The reason for introducing dual version data object is to support the processing of write, update and read RTTs concurrently. When RTT executes a write operation to a real time and non-real time data object, data object is associated with two values; after-value and before-value. After value is used by write and update RTTs to update value. Whereas before value is used by read RTT to get completed within deadline. Through using dual version, read RTTs have never to wait or get blocked for data object. Overall, wastage of resources through using dual version data object will never happens because at a time either update/write RTT or read RTT gets the opportunity to commit. Due to following strict correctness criteria, only one RTT between update/write or read RTT gets the opportunity to commit. Figures 1 and 2 show the snapshot of dual version data object.

Suppose that firm RTT T_W (i.e. write RTT), hard RTT T_U (i.e. update RTT) and soft RTT T_R (i.e. read RTT) are submitted on a master site. Here, T_U will update the real time data object X, T_W will write the non-real time data object Y and T_R is submitted to read the X and Y value. Based on RTT type, T_U will get the high priority to execute and T_W will get comparatively low priority for processing. As it is well known that T_W and T_U work on different data objects, the possibility for the occurrence of conflict between T_W and T_U is nil. Therefore, T_W and T_U can execute without checking of the conflict. Moreover, during processing of T_R, occurrence of conflict between T_R, T_W and T_R is more because T_R needs those real-time and non-real time data object that are being updated by T_U and T_W respectively. To overcome the consistency issue between T_R & T_U and T_R & T_W, we propose to use the concept of dual version data object. Dual version data object allows two values to be operated at a time. During conflict occurrence, T_R can work on before version value and T_U/T_W can modify the after-version value. The ultimate reason for proposing dual version data object is that, if in future T_W or T_U need to commit, then T_R will get restarted so that strict consistency criteria cannot be compromised. But, if T_W or T_U need to abort, then T_R gets a chance to commit. Overall, utilization of resources is never wasted.

In case of replicated master sites, coordinator master site will immediately broadcast T_U and T_W to remaining master sites to initiate the processing of RTT. Due to broadcasting of T_U and T_W sites in its initial stage, remaining master sites will reach to the common stage prior to starting of commit phase.

4.4   Proposed Recovery Mechanism

As defined in the Sect. 3, recovery technique raises unpredictability during RTT processing. In the real-world scenario, RDRTDBS can suffer from different types of failures such as transaction failure, system failure and media failure. During system recovery time, it creates large overhead in terms of runtime. Therefore, this overhead need to overcome/minimize, so that, replicated site can be recovered in a predictable manner. In this paper, our focus is on media failure. Media failure occurs when the content of the volatile memory is corrupted or lost [26]. To resolve recovery issue in the proposed system model, we propose recovery mechanism that improves predictability with respect to RTT processing.

In RDRTDBS, recovery techniques are mainly influenced by four factors; Recovery Algorithm, Replication Management, Concurrent Control Protocol and Sustainability Protection. Therefore, keeping these four factors in mind, in our proposed system model, a restarted replicated site (i.e. recovery target) will request to the entire healthy site (i.e. recovery sources) to pull the partial updates. Through pulling partial updates from all healthy sites, recovery load gets shared. After pulling all updates, recovery target will start updating from urgently required partial update so that waiting RTT can be completed within its deadline. Overall, predictable behavior for the currently submitted RTT can be feasibly identified. Instantaneous view of our proposed system model is given below in Fig. 3.

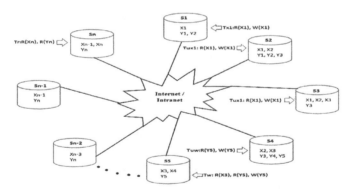

Fig. 3. Proposed system model

As specified in this section, our system model consists of above defined data and transaction model. This data and transaction model will be employed on partially RDRTDBS and is shown in Fig. 3. In Fig. 2, S1, S2, ..., Sn are representing master sites which are responsible for executing hard, soft and firm RTTs. These replicated master sites hold real time and non-real time data objects, so that, possibly user demands can be fulfilled locally. In Fig. 2, S1 is the owner of real time data object X1 and non-real time data object Y1 & Y2. For maintaining the strict consistency of real-time data object X1, Tx1 is periodically executed to maintain its consistency. To maintain the mutual consistency between different replicas holding X1, Tux1 is executed on different replicas, so that, inconsistency can be prevented for other RTT. The propagation of replica, update RTT is started at the preliminary stage of RTT commit phase, so that all the replicated sites reach to a common state synchronously. Similarly, S5 holds X3, X4 and Y5 data objects and firm RTT Tw is submitted to update non-real time data object Y5. Likewise, soft RTT Tr is submitted on Sn to read real time and non-real time data object. Altogether, our system model can concurrently process different types of RTTs. Conclusively, we can argue that our proposed system can predictably process hard, firm and soft RTTs.

5   To Support Predictable Processing of RUT for Different Types of RTTs

The primary goal of RDRTDBS is to guarantee predictable execution of different types of RTTs i.e. Hard, soft and firm. This predictable execution can be used as decision parameter to identify the number of RTTs that are completed within its deadline. At the same time, all the temporal and mutual consistency for real and non-real time data objects should also converge to consistent state. Therefore, to guarantee predictable completion of RTTs, we propose RUT that can leverage slack value of transaction processing. This slack value is used in assigning the deadline to the RTT. The reason behind using this slack value in our RUT is to use the unutilized time slot of completed RTT, so that, another waiting RTT can get the chance to complete within its deadline. Overall, we present a RUT that supports predictable processing of RTT along with maintaining temporal & mutual consistency of data objects and satisfies the performance requirement for different types of RTT.

5.1   Predictable Execution of Different Types of RTTs

In RDRTDBS, existing priority assignment policy of hard RTT transforms its temporal consistency requirement into deadline constraint because the real demand is to satisfy the deadline property of hard RTT. Hence, we assign high priority to hard RTT, low priority to firm RTT, and comparatively very low priority to soft RTT. Our system model provides statically guarantee to hard and firm RTT and uses a slack value stealing algorithm for dynamically scheduling soft RTT so that its miss ratio can be improved. Let us suppose that RDRTDBS consists of a set of RTTs = {T_{HARD} U T_{FIRM} U T_{SOFT}}, where T_N is a set of N RTTs. N belongs to hard, firm and soft RTT. We denote the set of all guaranteed RTTs T_{HARD} as $T_{GUARANTEED}$. In our system model, each type of RTTs in T will be scheduled in such a way that the underlying system model provides deterministic services to RTTs and hence data objects (i.e. real time and non-real time) can be accessed with deterministic service time.

Guarantee on Hard RTTs
RTTs belonging to the category of T_{HARD} have their computation and data requirements already known and priority assignment policy always assigns high priority to hard RTT as compare to soft and firm RTT. In our system model, master site will employ a deadline-monotonic strategy for predictable execution of hard RTT.

Maintaining mutual consistency in RDRTDBS requires predictable time from both network and master site. Therefore, to solve network unpredictability issue, we employ high speed network with total order broadcast. Here, message will be received by the recipient in a predictable amount of time and total order broadcast will ensure that the entire replicated site will receive the message in the same order. Suppose that hard RTT T_1 is submitted on master site S, its predictable execution requires predictable value from both master site and network (i.e. total computation time from all the replicated sites and network communication time). Coordinator master site computes this value and compares it with absolute validity interval (AVI) of real time data object (i.e. X). If this computed value is less than AVI then T_1 will be allowed to proceed for completion. However, if this computed value is more than AVI, the set of master sites will be identified that can be synchronously updated so that consistent value can be provided to the upcoming RTT on their site. Remaining non-updated master site will apply the best effort policy to guarantee predictable execution. Total computation cost for predictable processing in RDRTDBS is calculated through the formula given below.

$$C_{TOTAL} = (T_{INIT} + (TSD_{FETCH} * TSDC_{COST}) * N + T_{CLOSE}) * R + NWC_{COST} \quad (1)$$

Where C_{TOTAL} is total computation that involves $T_{INILIALIZATION}$ (i.e. RTT initialization), TSD_{FETCH} is the single data fetching cost, $TSDC_{COST}$ is operation cost (i.e. read cost, write cost or both), N is the number of data operation belonging to single RTT, T_{CLOSE} is the transaction closing time, R is number of replica where this RTT must be executed to maintain the mutual consistency and finally NWC_{COST} is the predictable amount of communication cost.

> if (C_{TOTAL} <= AVI(X)) then
>   proceed the RTT to process;
> else
>   identify the list of replicas that can be updated;
>   non-updated replica sites will restart the RTT after getting updated;

Priority assignment to hard RTT is high as compare to other RTT (i.e. firm and soft). RTT belonging to the same type (i.e. hard RTT), priority assignment is based on the urgency of deadline.

Guarantee on Firm RTTs
The correctness of firm RTT depends on logical consistency and timely completion. During RTT processing, if the data requirement for firm RTT is already known, then the worst-case execution for firm RTT can be easily predicted. Unfortunately, this is not possible for all firm RTTs: predictability becomes more complex when the data requirement for firm RTT and computation is unknown. Missing the deadline of firm

RTT does not create the serious damage in the system. But it also doesn't leave any value for the system. Therefore, to guarantee the predictable execution of firm RTT, we assign the low priority to firm RTT as compare to hard RTT and use the equation given below.

$$C_{TOTAL} = (T_{INIT} + (TSD_{FETCH} * TSDC_{COST}) * N * S_T + T_{CLOSE}) * R + NWC_{COST} \qquad (2)$$

Equation 2 contains the parameters defined in Eq. 1. We involve one important parameter S_T for predictable processing of firm RTT. Here, S_T denotes random variable that is selectively distributed. Due to availability of cumulative distribution for S_T, it is possible to predictably identify the worst-case execution of firm RTT. Overall predictable processing for firm RTT depends on S_T and its probability for timely is as follows.

$$P(C_{TOTAL} < WC_{ET}) = P(S_T < s) = P_S \qquad (3)$$

Where WC_{ET} represents worst case execution time.

Guarantee on Soft RTTs
In RDRTDBS, a number of research papers have been published for executing soft RTT along with maintaining mutual consistency. In the current paper, our approach is to process soft RTT during unused slack period of completed hard RTT. Processing soft RTT during unused slack period shows better performance in terms of miss ratio.

The processing of soft RTT is as follows: Identify the availability of unused slack period during time interval t1–t2. At completion of hard RTT or firm RTT, identify the most urgent soft RTT that needs to complete. Schedule the selected soft RTT in the unused slack period; so that soft RTT can be completed within its deadline and rest of waiting RTTs get the chance to complete.

6   Related Work

Over the past few years, RDRTDBS have gained more interest in research. Experimental results of [17–22] are very comprehensive and cover most important issues of RTT processing. However, they do not consider predictable execution of different types of RTT in replicated real time environment. Therefore, realizing predictability of RTT in RDRTDBS can definitely increase its performance.

RDRTDBS in which time constraint property are associated with data consistency are discussed in [3]. This system also introduces the need to maintain data temporal consistency in addition to mutual consistency between replicated data item placed at different replica sites. The performance of RUT for maintaining mutual consistency is studied in [3]. Token based scheme for replication control is proposed in [4] and integrated version of replication protocol together with scheduling is presented in [5, 6]. These all proposed protocols follow epsilon correctness criteria i.e. a weaker one than one copy serializability (1SR). A parallel and distributed DBMS named as ClustRa [7] has been designed to provide real-time capabilities for telecom applications. This database does not guarantee quality of services (QoS) during overloaded situation. Apart from QoS, 1SR based replication protocol named as Managing Isolation in Replicated Real-time Object Repositories (MIRROR) is proposed in [8]. This protocol is augmented version of Classical Optimistic Two-Phase Locking (O2PL) and novel state-based real time conflict resolution mechanism. MIRROR suffers from the issue of deadlock, unbounded delay and overload. Just-In-Time Real-Time Replication (JITRTR) protocol designed for distributed real time object-oriented database presented in [9] performs well in static environment. However, it is unable to handle dynamic request. Solution of continues conflict detection and resolution based on conflict sets is proposed in [10]. But, eventually this solution also does not support strict consistency. Continuous convergence protocol for distributed real time database [11] has three main terms; local consistency, local predictability and eventual global consistency. This protocol has been designed to tolerate inconsistency for read transaction. Replication protocol PRiDe [12] based on optimistic approach with deterministic detection and forward resolution of conflicts is designed. This protocol was developed to maintain the mutual consistency of the real-time data object but the Real Time Replication Control Protocol (RT-RCT) [13] works to manage the stability for non-real time objects. Simulator for examining the performance of different replication protocols/RCTs for small and medium scale RDRTDBS is proposed in [14]. Virtual full replication based on adaptive segmentation [15] resolves the serious drawbacks of full replication but such approach also suffers from overloading issue. Recently MBRCT following 1SR is proposed in [16] for improving the performance and scalability. This protocol was designed for multi masters and slave sites approach where master will execute write & update transactions and slave are only responsible to execute read transactions.

7 Simulation and Experimental Results

In this section, we conduct number of experiments to identify the impact of our proposed predictable processing scheme for RTTs compared to traditional approach. The most important performance metric is Transaction Miss Ratio (TMR), i.e., the percentage of RTT that are not completed within deadline. This is a conventional parameter metric used to check the performance in RDRTDBS. Let T_{MISS} denotes the number of RTT that miss their deadline, and $T_{SUCCEED}$ denotes the number of RTT that get successfully completed in their deadline. The TMR represents the transaction miss ratio and is given by.

$$TMR = (T_{MISS})/(T_{MISS} + T_{SUCCEED}) * 100 \qquad (4)$$

7.1 Cost for Predictable Processing of RTTs

Figures 4 and 5 shows the result between different scheduling technique (i.e. EDF) in replicated and non-replicated environment for soft, firm and hard RTT. For getting clear cut understanding, we also include the result of traditional scheduling technique (i.e. Blind/EDF and Guaranteed/Spare Capacity Finding (SCF)).

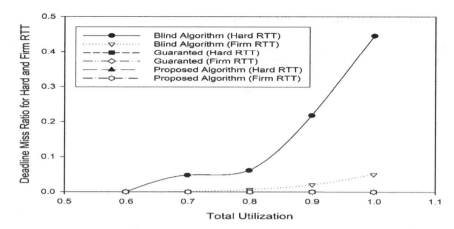

Fig. 4. Deadline miss ratio for hard and firm RTT

As shown in the Fig. 4, some of submitted hard and firm RTT miss their deadline during following Blind policy in non-replicated environment whereas all the submitted hard and firm RTT get completed within its deadline using our proposed system model.

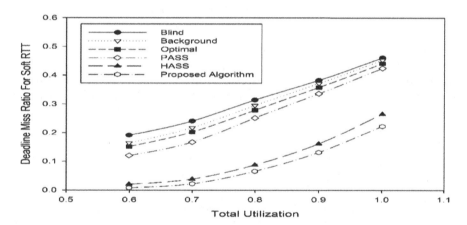

Fig. 5. Deadline miss ratio for soft RTT

Figure 5 shows the transaction miss ratio for soft RTT under Background Processing (Background), Optimal Slack Stealing (Optimal) and Approximate Slack Stealing (ASS). The deadline miss ratio of our system model is low as compared to other scheduling policies because of use of unused slack time of hard and firm RTT completed before deadline by soft RTT to get completed earlier.

7.2 Cost for Maintaining Mutual Consistency

Enforcing the mutual consistency between replicated data objects of RDRTDBS may eventually results in a greater number of RTT to miss their deadline. Therefore, we perform an experiment by using unused slack period of completed hard RTT. Processing soft RTT during unused slack period shows better performance.

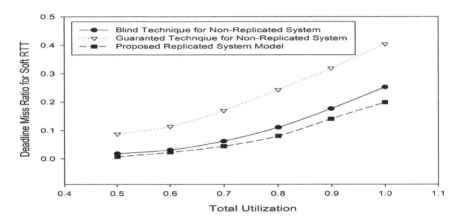

Fig. 6. Deadline miss ratio for soft RTT

Figure 6, shows that mutual consistency between replicated data objects in RDRTDBS is highly maintained through our proposed predictable processing scheme of RTT. However, if we follow existing technique to maintain consistency to the given set of hard and firm RTT, significant number of soft RTTs will violate internal consistency.

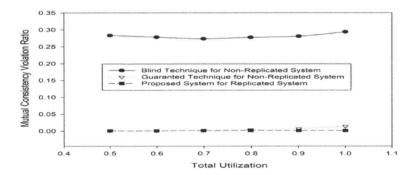

Fig. 7. Deadline miss ratio for soft RTT.

In Fig. 7, the performance difference between proposed system model and existing technique represents the cost of maintaining mutual consistency.

8 Conclusion

In this paper, we have proposed a predictable processing plan of RTT that is applicable to work for several real time applications. This proposed processing works for different types of RTTs (i.e. hard, firm and soft) that can concurrently maintain the mutual consistency between different replicated sites and satisfies the deadline requirement of RTTs. To improve the predictability of RTT, we have proposed two solutions in which first solution improves the recovery process, and another is system model that maintain the mutual consistency. Experimental results show that following such predictable processing in RDRTDBS improves the predictability for write, update and read RTT.

This research work can be extended in different direction to accommodate different real time application from different environments such as real time banking, real time control in nuclear power plant and so on. Although our proposed predictable processing model might be conservative, we are working on different conditions to guarantee logical consistency and mutual consistency.

References

1. Yu, P.S., Wu, K.L., Lin, K.J., Son, S.H.: On real-time databases: concurrency control and scheduling. Proc. IEEE **82**(1), 140–157 (1994)
2. Wang, F., Yao, L.W., Yang, Y.L.: Efficient verification of distributed real-time systems with broadcasting behaviors. Real-Time Syst. **47**(4), 285 (2011)
3. Son, S.H.: Using replication for high performance database support in distributed real-time systems. In: RTSS, pp. 79–86 (1987)
4. Son, S.H., Kouloumbis, S.: A token-based synchronization scheme for distributed real-time databases. Inf. Syst. **18**(6), 375–389 (1993)
5. Son, S.H., Zhang, F.: Real-time replication control for distributed database systems: algorithms and their performance. In: DASFAA 1995, 11 April, pp. 214–221 (1995)
6. Son, S.H., Zhang, F., Hwang, B.: Concurrency control for replicated data in distributed real-time systems. J. Database Manag. (JDM) **7**(2), 12–23 (1996)
7. Kim, Y.-K.: Towards real-time performance in a scalable, continuously available telecom DBMS (1996)
8. Xiong, M., et al.: MIRROR: a state-conscious concurrency control protocol for replicated real-time databases. Inf. Syst. **27**(4), 277–297 (2002)
9. Peddi, P., DiPippo, L.C.: A replication strategy for distributed real-time object-oriented databases. In: Proceedings. Fifth IEEE International Symposium on Object-Oriented Real-Time Distributed Computing, ISORC 2002, pp. 129–136. IEEE (2002)
10. Gustavsson, S., Andler, S.F.: Real-time conflict management in replicated databases. In: Proceedings of the Fourth Conference for the Promotion of Research in IT at New Universities and University Colleges in Sweden, PROMOTE IT 2004, Karlstad, Sweden, vol. 2 (2004)
11. Gustavsson, S., Andler, S.R.: Continuous consistency management in distributed real-time databases with multiple writers of replicated data. In: Proceedings of the 19th IEEE International Parallel and Distributed Processing Symposium. IEEE (2005)
12. Syberfeldt, S.: Optimistic replication with forward conflict resolution in distributed real-time databases. Diss. Institutionen för datavetenskap (2007)

13. Haj Said, A., Sadeg, B., Amanton, L., Ayeb, B.: A protocol to control replication in distributed real-time database systems. In: Proceedings of the Tenth International Conference on Enterprise Information Systems, ICEIS, vol. 1, pp. 501–504 (2008). ISBN 978-989-8111-36-4
14. El-Bakry, H.M., Sultan, T.: Design of replicated real-time database simulator. In: Proceedings of the 6th WSEAS International Conference on Computer Engineering and Applications, and Proceedings of the 2012 American conference on Applied Mathematics. World Scientific and Engineering Academy and Society (WSEAS) (2012)
15. Mathiason, G., Andler, S.F., Son, S.H.: Virtual full replication by adaptive segmentation. In: 13th IEEE International Conference on Embedded and Real-Time Computing Systems and Applications, RTCSA 2007. IEEE (2007)
16. Shrivastava, P., Shanker, U.: Replica control following 1SR in DRTDBS through best case of transaction execution. In: Kolhe, M.L., Trivedi, M.C., Tiwari, S., Singh, V.K. (eds.) Advances in Data and Information Sciences. LNNS, vol. 38, pp. 139–150. Springer, Singapore (2018). https://doi.org/10.1007/978-981-10-8360-0_13
17. Audsley, N.C., Burns, A., Richardson, M.F., Wellings, A.J.: Absolute and relative temporal constraints in hard real-time databases. In: Proceedings of 1992 IEEE Euro Micro Workshop on Real Time Systems, February 1992
18. Lin, K.-J., Jahanian, F., Jhingran, A., Locke, C.D.: A model of hard real-time transaction systems. Technical report RC No. 17515, IBM T. J. Watson Research Center, January 1992
19. Sha, L., Rajkumar, R., Son, S.H., Chang, C.: A real-time locking protocol. IEEE Trans. Comput. **40**(7), 793–800 (1991)
20. Song, X., Liu, J.: Performance of multiversion concurrency control algorithms in maintaining temporal consistency. In: Proceedings of the IEEE 14th Annual International Computer Software and Applications Conference (COMPSAC), October 1990
21. Abbott, R., Garcia-Molina, H.: Scheduling real time transactions: a performance evaluation. ACM Trans. Database Syst. **17**(3), 513–560 (1992)
22. Haritsa, J.R.: Transaction scheduling in firm real time database systems. Ph.D. thesis, University of Wisconsin, Madison, August 1991
23. Kim, Y.-K., Son, S.H.: An approach towards predictable real-time transaction processing. In: RTS (1993)
24. O'Neil, P.E., Ramamritham, K., Pu, C.: A Two-Phase Approach to Predictably Scheduling Real-Time Transactions, pp. 494–522 (1996)
25. Ruiz-Fuertes, M.I., Munoz-Escoı, F.D.: Refinement of the one-copy serializable correctness criterion. Technical report ITI-SIDI-2011/004, Instituto Tecnológico de Informática, Valencia, Spain (2011)
26. Bernstein, P.A., Hadzilacos, V., Goodman, N.: Concurrency Control and Recovery in Database Systems. Addison-Wesley, Boston (1987)
27. Shrivastava, P., Shanker, U.: Replica update technique in RDRTDBS: issues & challenges. In: Proceedings of the 24th International Conference on Advanced Computing and Communications (ADCOM-2018), Ph.D. Forum, Bangalore, India, 21–23 September 2018 (Accepted and Presented)
28. Shrivastava, P., Shanker, U.: Real time transaction management in replicated DRTDBS. In: Proceedings of the Australasian Database Conference (ADC-2019), Sydney, Australia, 29th January–1st February 2019 (Accepted)
29. Shrivastava, P., Shanker, U.: Replication protocol based on dynamic versioning of data object for replicated DRTDBS. In: Proceedings of the International Conference on Computational Intelligence & Internet of Things (ICCIIoT) Agartala, India, 14–15 December 2018 (Accepted)

Data Scheduling and Resource Optimization for Fog Computing Architecture in Industrial IoT

Wei Wang[1,2,3(✉)], Guanyu Wu[1], Zhe Guo[2,3], Liang Qian[1], Lianghui Ding[1], and Feng Yang[1]

[1] Department of Electronic Engineering, Shanghai JiaoTong University, Shanghai, China
{116034910083,wuguanyu,lqian,lhding, yangfeng}@sjtu.edu.cn
[2] Shanghai Microwave Research Institute, Shanghai, China
guozhe@foxmail.com
[3] CETC Key Laboratory of Data Link Technology, Shanghai, China

Abstract. In the actual industrial environment, how the system processes and analyzes big data stably in real time is the main challenge of industrial Internet of Things (IIoT) currently. Although fog computing, as a significant extension of cloud computing, provides a distributed solution to real-time data processing in the industrial environment, it is an unavoidable problem that non-negligible network latency and fluctuations in the industrial network and limited computing power of fog nodes make it difficult to process big data timely and stably. We integrate the decentralized resources of fog nodes to form a cluster which can deliver sufficient processing power to deal with a complicated computational task. And then we propose an optimal data scheduling policy with multiple communication channels to minimize real-time processing delay and increase stability of the system. A series of experiments are designed to evaluate the behaviors with three different scheduling policies. Simulation results show that over 15% performance gain, in the system adopted optimal data scheduling policy, can be achieved according to different working scenarios, in which network communication conditions and processing power make the decisive contributions. Meanwhile, the fluctuating range of system delay curve is lower with the fluctuating of the network than the other two, which means the system has a better stability.

Keywords: Fog computing · IIoT · Real-time · Stability · Optimal scheduling

1 Introduction

Industrial Internet of Things (IIoT) collects various sound, light, heat, electricity and other information generated by real-time monitoring, connection and interaction in the industrial field through various information sensing devices such as sensors, RFID, global positioning systems (GPS), high-definition cameras, infrared sensors, and gas sensors [1], analyzes and processes industrial field data information in real time, realizes intelligent production, monitoring and management, and finally achieves on-demand

© Springer Nature Switzerland AG 2019
G. Fahrnberger et al. (Eds.): ICDCIT 2019, LNCS 11319, pp. 141–149, 2019.
https://doi.org/10.1007/978-3-030-05366-6_11

production of personalized products. IIoT has the characteristics of large number and wide distribution of sensing devices, large amounts of sensing data and high real-time performance, which requires a reliable, stable, and fault-tolerant communication networks and adequate real-time processing power [2].

At present, the most outstanding computing paradigm for large-scale data processing is cloud computing. However, due to global centralization, high bandwidth constraints and uncertain response time from the cloud, current cloud model hardly meets the need of IIoT. A new computing paradigm, namely fog computing [7], is designed to extend cloud computing power to the edge of the network. Compared to the Cloud, the Fog is much closer to end devices at the network edge and has lower latency, which makes it effective for real-time tasks [9]. Some other non-trivia benefits of fog computing bringing to IIoT include large-scale distributed fog nodes geographically and decentralized data processing mode, which means the Fog is suitable for large and widely distributed sensor networks [3].

However, there are still some crucial problems existing in the actual industrial environment using fog computing in IIoT. One is that isolated fog nodes have relatively finite resources and logging computing power, making it difficult to process big data timely [5]. The other is network in a harsh industrial environment is unstable, and even some networks will be interrupted, which is a fatal problem for industrial safety.

This work proposes a fog-based architecture for IIoT to minimize latency and enhance stability of the real-time processing system. Alibaba JStorm is applied to integrate fog nodes at the edge of network to form a JStorm cluster, which can take full advantage of the computing resources available [4] in the fog nodes to provide processing power of big data. Some of the features inherent in JStorm, such as high fault-tolerance, reliable message processing mechanisms, distributed and extensible features, make it ideal for fog computing scenes. An optimal data scheduling policy is proposed to solve the problem of the non-negligible network latency and fluctuations in the industrial environment.

The remainder of this paper is structured as follows. In Sect. 2, we introduce the related work on fog computing applied to IIoT. In Sect. 3, we describe the fog-based scheme proposed and explain its four layers deeply, and then we develop system mathematical models. In Sect. 4, we compare the delay and the stability of the systems by applying different policies. Finally, we report the conclusions of this paper.

2   Related Works

Cloud computing provides an excellent solution for the processing of big data. In many smart city scenarios such as [10], the cloud is used for the management, storage, and processing of big data. Authors in [13] distinguish cloud platform to three parts, storage, cloud computing and sharing, which can efficiently upgrade the speed of production management. However, using cloud computing merely in IIoT, in the most of the preview studies, can't meet the real-time requirements in industrial environments.

Currently, more and more studies combine fog computing with IIoT. [3] suggests a low-cost and highly scalable solution by using machine learning to predict coming data with MQTT, which could minimize additional delay and operational expenses of the system and make system very efficient. [6] proposed a framework based fog computing which uploads gathered data from edge device with the predefined threshold of fog nodes. These studies take advantage of fog computing to reduce traffic overhead. Nonetheless, they do not consider the network fluctuations in the industrial environment.

Fog computing is applied to many other scenarios such as logistics centers [12], the Internet of Vehicles [11], monitoring system [9] and so on. Although the aforementioned studies apply fog computing to industrial environment, the edge network is still hard to meet the requirements of big data real-time processing. Thus, we present a novel architecture to provide a processing-efficient solution for IIoT.

3   Real-Time Processing-Efficient Fog-Based IIoT Scheme

3.1   Architecture

In this paper, we propose a four-layer scheme, consisting of Cloud layer, JStorm Clusters layer, Data Scheduler layer, and Devices layer in a top-down fashion, which is shown as Fig. 1. In the scheme, JStorm Clusters layer and Data Scheduler layer belonging to fog computing architecture are responsible for distributed computing of real-time big data. The four main parts of the scheme are explained in more depth as follows.

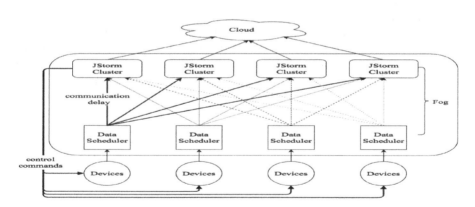

Fig. 1. The four-layer scheme

1. Devices layer

Devices layer is comprised by multifarious end devices of IIoT. They collect abundant valuable data by heterogeneous sensors and perform related operations according to control commands. Industrial big data generated by multisource sensors [8] will be uploaded for processing timely, and big data should contain information of the source devices so that these devices can receive correct control commands.

2. **Data Scheduler Layer**

On account of the non-negligible communication delay in the industrial environment, we propose an optimal data scheduling policy based on multi-channel transmission, taking into account the condition of communication channels and the processing power of the corresponding JStorm clusters provided by JStorm Clusters layer. The policy proposed in Data Scheduler layer splits big data collected by Devices layer into multiple blocks in an optimal method and transmits them to different JStorm clusters.

3. **JStorm Clusters Layer**

JStorm Clusters layer, using JStorm to integrate geographically large-scale distributed fog nodes into multiple clusters so that these clusters can process big data while isolated fog nodes cannot, is in charge of processing data uploaded by Devices layer timely. Output data of this layer will be used for real-time control or uploaded to Cloud layer.

4. **Cloud Layer**

Cloud Layer is the highest level of the architecture, with large-scale storage and computing power, providing a centralized computing model. The data transmitted to this layer are stored to support data retrieval and mining in the future.

3.2   System Model

In this section, we describe system model. For a device node, we assume there are N communication channels to upload data. A channel and the subsequent JStorm cluster are called a data route. On the i-th data route, communication delay of the channel is denoted by $C_i(x)$, and cluster processing delay is denoted by $P_i(x)$, where $i = 1, 2, \cdots, N$, and x represents the amount of data bytes allocated to the data route. We define $T_i(x)$ as total delay on the i-th data route, which betweens the beginning of the data transmission to the ending of data processing by JStorm. $T_i(x)$ can be calculated by

$$T_i(x) = C_i(x) + P_i(x) \tag{1}$$

where $C_i(x)$ and $P_i(x)$ are mutually independent. A K-byte large data block needs to be split into N blocks, and x_i bytes data is allocated to the i-th data route:

$$\begin{cases} \sum_{i=1}^{N} x_i = K, x_i \geq 0, \\ i = 1, 2, \cdots, N \end{cases} \tag{2}$$

According to (1) and (2), we can conclude that the system delay is determined by a route with the longest latency and then compute the delay of the whole system as

$$max_i\{T_i(x_i)\} = max_i\{C_i(x_i) + P_i(x_i)\} \tag{3}$$

However, we need to find an optimal data distribution method that minimizes the delay of the system. The corresponding model can be calculated by

$$min_{\{x_i\}_{i=1}^N} \, max_i\{C_i(x_i) + P_i(x_i)\}, \tag{4}$$

which subjects to (2). By solving the optimization problem (4), we can obtain a data set $\vec{x} = \{x_1, x_2, \cdots, x_N\}$, where $\vec{x}$ is the optimum solution to minimize the system delay.

3.3 Optimal Data Scheduling Policy

To illustrate the functionality of this system, we simplify the mathematical model of $C_i(x)$ and $P_i(x)$. The function of the communication delay is defined as follows:

$$C_i(x) = x/v_i \tag{5}$$

where v_i is the network speed in the *i-th* communication channel. Since JStorm is based on stream data processing, we denote U_i as a data processing unit in the JStorm cluster on the *i-th* data route, which has the longest latency by processing one unit of data and decides the waiting time of the whole data stream. On this data route, we use t_{w_i} to denote the delay processing one unit of data, namely waiting time, by U_i, and t_{p_i} to denote the delay processing one unit of data completely by the JStorm cluster. The function of the processing delay of the JStorm cluster on the *i-th* data route is defined:

$$P_i(x) = x * t_{w_i} + t_{p_i} - t_{w_i} \tag{6}$$

According to (4), (5) and (6), mathematically, we can formulate the problem as

$$min_{\{x_i\}_{i=1}^N} \, max_i\{x_i/v_i + x_i * t_{w_i} + t_{p_i} - t_{w_i}\}, \tag{7}$$

which subjects to (2). To solve the problem (7), it is transformed into

$$min_{\{x_i\}_{i=1}^n} \, t$$
$$subject \ to \begin{cases} \sum_{i=1}^N x_i = K, \\ x_i/v_i + (x_i - 1)t_{w_i} + t_{p_i} \leq t, \\ x_i \geq 0, i = 1, 2, \cdots, N. \end{cases} \tag{8}$$

where t is the optimal value of (7). We define the corresponding Lagrangian function:

$$\mathcal{L}(t, \vec{x}, \lambda, \vec{\mu}) = t + \lambda \left(\sum_{i=1}^N x_i - K \right) + \sum_{i=1}^N \mu_i \left[\left(\frac{1}{v_i} + t_{w_i} \right) x_i - t_{w_i} + t_{p_i} - t \right], \tag{9}$$

Where $\vec{x} = \{x_1, x_2, \cdots, x_N\}$. And then we have Karush-Kuhn-Tucker Conditions:

$$
\begin{cases}
\nabla_{(t,\vec{x})}\mathcal{L} = \begin{pmatrix} \frac{\partial \mathcal{L}}{\partial t} \\ \frac{\partial \mathcal{L}}{\partial x_1} \\ \vdots \\ \frac{\partial \mathcal{L}}{\partial x_N} \end{pmatrix} = \begin{pmatrix} 1 - \sum_{i=1}^{N} \mu_i \\ \lambda + \mu_1 \left(\frac{1}{v_1} + t_{w_1} \right) \\ \vdots \\ \lambda + \mu_N \left(\frac{1}{v_N} + t_{w_N} \right) \end{pmatrix} = \begin{pmatrix} 0 \\ 0 \\ \vdots \\ 0 \end{pmatrix} \\
\mu_i \left[\left(\frac{1}{v_i} + t_{w_i} \right) x_i - t_{w_i} + t_{p_i} - t \right] = 0, i = 1, 2, \cdots, N \\
\lambda \geq 0, \\
\frac{x_i}{v_i} + (x_i - 1) t_{w_i} + t_{p_i} - t \leq 0, i = 1, 2, \cdots, N \\
\sum_{i=1}^{N} x_i - K = 0, i = 1, 2, \cdots, N \\
x_i \geq 0, i = 1, 2, \cdots, N
\end{cases}
\tag{10}
$$

By solving the equations above, we can obtain

$$
x_i = \frac{\frac{K + \sum_{i=1}^{N} \frac{t_{p_i} - t_{w_i}}{\frac{1}{v_i} + t_{w_i}}}{\sum_{i=1}^{N} \frac{1}{\frac{1}{v_i} + t_{w_i}}} - \left(t_{p_i} - t_{w_i} \right)}{\frac{1}{v_i} + t_{w_i}},
\tag{11}
$$

$$
t = \frac{K + \sum_{i=1}^{N} \frac{t_{p_i} - t_{w_i}}{\frac{1}{v_i} + t_{w_i}}}{\sum_{i=1}^{N} \frac{1}{\frac{1}{v_i} + t_{w_i}}}.
\tag{12}
$$

According to (11) and (12), once K, v_i, t_{w_i} and t_{p_i} are known, we can easily obtain the optimal data scheduling policy $\vec{x} = \{x_1, x_2, \cdots, x_N\}$ to make the system have the minimum delay t.

4   Simulation Results

In this section, we evaluate the performance of the proposed optimal data scheduling policy by simulations. we compare it with two baseline data scheduling policies based on typical policies frequently used in the industrial environment.

Single-Route Policy. Single-route policy only has one channel to transmit data and one JStorm cluster to process data, simulating a centralized system that only adopts cloud computing in the industrial environment.

Balanced Scheduling Policy. Balanced scheduling policy, where a large data block is split into N blocks with the same size and transmitted to multiple JStorm clusters, simulated a distributed system using fog computing in most IIoT scenarios such as [3] [6]. This policy has the same number data routes as the optimal scheduling policy.

By analyzing the delay of processing the same size data under three different policies, we evaluate the real-time computing power and stability of the system. We consider that network speed v obeys a normal distribution over time with a mathematical expectation of μ and a variance of σ^2, denoted as $N(\mu, \sigma^2)$. In simulations, we assume there are N data routes in the system, and v_i obeys normal distribution but μ_i, σ_i^2, t_{w_i} and t_{p_i} are constants but unequal in different routes. We assume that time is divided into equal-length time slots, and in every time slot the data can be completely processed with the average delay T. Then we randomly choose 100 consecutive time slots, and there is a K-byte data block needing to be processed in every time slot. The system adopting the single-route policy means that $N = 1$. Since the larger number N is, the more resources, such as bandwidth, the system occupies, we assume that N is not greater than 5.

The average delay of the systems that are executed by different scheduling policies are shown in Fig. 2. When the network is reliable, curves are relatively smooth and steady. And the curves changing drastically indicates that the network has a large delay suddenly. It can be observed intuitively from the figures that when network is stable, the average delay is reduced achieved by optimal data scheduling policy comparing with the other two. And with the increasing of N (In Single-route policy N is always equal to 1), the system can obtain a better behavior with lower latency. However, even when $N = 5$, it can be calculated that there are over 15% reduction of system delay relative to the behavior of the balanced scheduling policy.

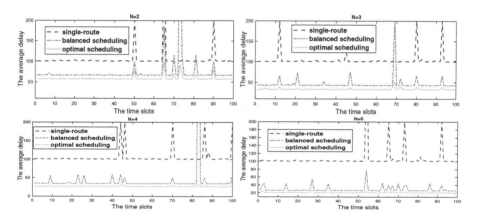

Fig. 2. The average delay

To illustrate the stability of the systems, we calculate the system delay standard deviation with the changing of the network, which is shown in Fig. 3. The result is same as we expect that the system adopting optimal scheduling policy has the lowest standard deviation, which represents that the system is most stable. Both balanced scheduling policy and the single-route policy are hardly to achieve stability requirements in IIoT if there is a problem such as the failure of cluster or the interruption of network.

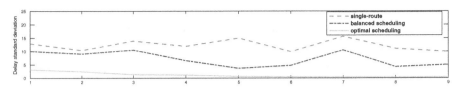

Fig. 3. Delay standard deviation

5   Conclusions

In this paper, we propose a four-layer scheme essentially based on fog computing in IIoT. In supposed scheme, we use JStorm to integrate geographically large-scale distributed fog nodes into multiple clusters so that system can process big data. And then we provide an optimal data scheduling policy based on multi-channel transmission to solve the problem of the non-negligible network latency and fluctuations in the industrial environment. Based on the analysis of average delay and stability of the systems under three policies, we find that our proposed optimal data scheduling policy achieves the minimum delay and better stability compared to two baseline policies. Simulation results show that over 15% performance gain, in the system adopted optimal data scheduling policy, can be achieved according to different working scenarios, in which network communication conditions and processing power make the decisive contributions.

Acknowledgements. This paper is supported in part by NSFC China (61771309, 61671301, 61420106008, 61521062), Shanghai Key Laboratory Funding (STCSM15DZ2270400), CETC Key Laboratory of Data Link Technology Foundation (CLDL-20162306), and Medical Engineering Cross Research Foundation of Shanghai Jiao Tong University (YG2017QN47).

References

1. O'Donovan, P., Gallagher, C., Bruton, K., et al.: A fog computing industrial cyber-physical system for embedded low-latency machine learning Industry 4.0 applications. Manuf. Lett. **15**, 139–142 (2018)
2. Gonçalves, P., Ferreira, J., Pedreiras, P., Corujo, D.: Adapting SDN datacenters to support Cloud IIoT applications. In: 2015 IEEE 20th Conference on Emerging Technologies and Factory Automation (ETFA), pp. 1–4. IEEE (2015)
3. Peralta, G., Iglesias-Urkia, M., Barcelo, M., Gomez, R., Moran, A., Bilbao, J.: Fog computing based efficient IoT scheme for the Industry 4.0. In: 2017 IEEE International Workshop of Electronics, Control, Measurement, Signals and their Application to Mechatronics (ECMSM), pp. 1–6 (2017)
4. Ghaderi, J., Shakkottai, S., Srikant, R.: Scheduling storms and streams in the cloud. In: ACM SIGMETRICS Performance Evaluation Review, vol. 43, no. 1, pp. 439–440 (2015)
5. da Silva Morais, T.: Survey on frameworks for distributed computing: Hadoop, Spark and storm. In: Proceedings of the 10th Doctoral Symposium in Informatics Engineering-DSIE, vol. 15 (2015)

6. Mukherjee, M., Shu, L., Wang, D., Li, K., Chen, Y.: A fog computing-based framework to reduce traffic overhead in large-scale industrial applications. In: 2017 IEEE Conference on Computer Communications Workshops (INFOCOM WKSHPS), pp. 1008–1009. IEEE (2017)
7. Bonomi, F., Milito, R., Zhu, J., Addepalli, S.: Fog computing and its role in the internet of things. In: Proceedings of the First Edition of the MCC Workshop on Mobile Cloud Computing, pp. 13–16 (2012)
8. Yan, J., Meng, Y., Lu, L., et al.: Industrial big data in an industry 4.0 environment: challenges, schemes and applications for predictive maintenance. IEEE Access **PP**(99), 1 (2017)
9. Wu, D., et al.: A fog computing-based framework for process monitoring and prognosis in cyber-manufacturing. J. Manuf. Syst. **43**, 25–34 (2017)
10. Su, K., Li, J., Fu, H.: Smart city and the applications. In: 2011 International Conference on Electronics, Communications and Control (ICECC), pp. 1028–1031. IEEE (2011)
11. Zhang, W., Zhang, Z., Chao, H.C.: Cooperative fog computing for dealing with big data in the internet of vehicles: architecture and hierarchical resource management. IEEE Commun. Mag. **55**(12), 60–67 (2017)
12. Lin, C.C., Yang, J.W.: Cost-efficient deployment of fog computing systems at logistics centers in industry 4.0. IEEE Trans. Ind. Inf. **PP**(99), 1 (2018)
13. Yen, C.T., Liu, Y.C., Lin, C.C., Kao, C.C., Wang, W.B., Hsu, Y.R.: Advanced manufacturing solution to industry 4.0 trend through sensing network and cloud computing technologies. In: 2014 IEEE International Conference on Automation Science and Engineering (CASE), pp. 1150–1152. IEEE (2014)

Research on CNN Parallel Computing and Learning Architecture Based on Real-Time Streaming Architecture

Yuting Zhu[1](✉), Liang Qian[1], Chuyan Wang[1], Lianghui Ding[1], Feng Yang[1], and Hao Wang[2]

[1] School of Electronic Information and Electrical Engineering,
Shanghai Jiao Tong University, Shanghai, China
{kris_ting,lqian,cywang_xxx,
lhding,yangfeng}@sjtu.edu.cn
[2] The Air Force of Military Representative Office in Shanghai-Nanjing,
Nanjing, China
worest@163.com

Abstract. Convolutional neural network (CNN) is a deep feed-forward artificial neural network, which is widely used in image recognition. However, this mode highlights the problems that the training time is too long and memory is insufficient. Traditional acceleration methods are mainly limited to optimizing for an algorithm. In this paper, we propose a method, namely CNN-S, to improve training efficiency and cost based on Storm and is suitable for every algorithm. This model divides data into several sub sets and processes data on several machine in parallel flexibly. The experimental results show that in the case of achieving a recognition accuracy rate of 95%, the training time of single serial model is around 913 s, and in CNN-S model only needs 248 s. The acceleration ratio can reach 3.681. This shows that the CNN-S parallel model has better performance than single serial mode on training efficiency and cost of system resource.

Keywords: CNN · Parallel computing · Apache storm · Real time

1 Introduction

Convolutional neural network is a deep neural network model with convolution structure [1]. It extracts image features by pooling, sharing weight and convolution, which makes it widely applied in picture recognition, face detection and target tracking. Nowadays CNN could achieve higher recognition accuracy, but serial mode constrains the improvement of efficiency. With the development of big data, needs of data analyzing sharply increase. The shortcomings of single-machine serial mode become more and more prominent [2]. In order to achieve a certain accuracy, we require a long training time and a large memory usage, which are difficult to solve. If we use multiple integrated CPUs, high equipment costs are also a big problem.

Storm is a free and open source distributed real-time computing system [3]. Storm can easily and reliably process unlimited data streams to process data in real time.

© Springer Nature Switzerland AG 2019
G. Fahrnberger et al. (Eds.): ICDCIT 2019, LNCS 11319, pp. 150–158, 2019.
https://doi.org/10.1007/978-3-030-05366-6_12

Storm uses parallel processing to process massive amounts of data. It makes multiple computers to process one task possible, which also solves the problem of equipment costs.

In this paper, we propose a new method based on Storm, namely CNN-S. Storm assign CNN tasks to work nodes to minimize the latency, CPU resource and cost of memory. We compare two methods in experiment of Lenet-5. In the experiment, CNN-S method uses high parallelism to reduce running time reaching some recognition accuracy, and use Storm to control the high costs of multiple integrated CPUs.

2   Related Work

2.1   Convolutional Neural Network

Convolutional neural network was proposed firstly by Yann Lecun and widely used in image recognition and speech recognition [4]. CNN is a multi-layered neural network. It faces more challenges, such as training speed and recognition accuracy. Many papers focus on how to change the algorithms of CNN to improve the performance of task. In [5], author proposed R-Storm to make overall throughput higher. In [6], a new adaptive topology decomposition algorithm is presented for Storm.

2.2   Distributed Computing System

Nowadays, Hadoop and Storm are two important and popular distributed computing systems. Considering latency, Storm's memory of read and write is n orders of magnitude faster than Hadoop's. In terms of throughput, Storm's streaming eliminates time to collect batch data. It needn't the time of scheduling. To some extend, Storm is faster than Hadoop. Moreover, it has a high degree of fault tolerance during task execution. By comparison, we find that Storm is more suitable for distributed optimization of convolutional neural networks.

2.3   Real-Time Distributed Computing System—Apache Storm

Storm is a free, open source, distributed, highly fault-tolerant real-time computing system. It is divided into two components, Nimbus and Supervisor.

Nimbus is responsible for sending code to the cluster, assigning work to the machine, and monitoring the status. Supervisor listens to the work assigned to it and starts/closes the worker process as needed. Zookeeper is an external resource that Storm focuses on. Nimbus and Supervisor even actually run the Worker to save the heartbeat information on Zookeeper [7]. Nimbus also performs scheduling and task assignment based on heartbeat and task health on the Zookeeper. The smallest message unit processed by Topology is a Tuple, which is an array of arbitrary objects. Topology consists of Spout and Bolt. Spout is the node that sends the Tuple [8] (see Fig. 1).

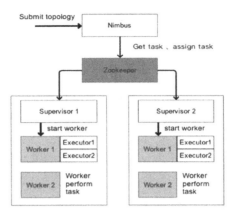

Fig. 1. Flow chat of storm

3 Parallel Algorithm for Convolutional Neural Network

3.1 Storm-Based CNN-S Parallel Model

Two parallel strategies are widely used. First one is model parallelism. It splits the model to different computing units. Different machines in a distributed system are responsible for different parts of the network model. The second method is data parallelism. Different machines have multiple copies of the same model, each machine is assigned different data, and then calculation results of all machines are combined. The CNN-S model combines the data parallel of CNN algorithm with the storm system. After submitting the topology to the nimbus, zookeeper starts the scheduling work. It splits the task and distributes it to the workers of each supervisor. After the task distribution process is completed, the CNN-S model starts training. Then, the network training of CNN is performed. And the weight of the network of each layer and the arithmetic mean of the parameters are calculated after each training. Finally, we get a batch weight update. Then, repeat the above cycle until all data training is completed.

Here we use three bolts to simplify the training process of CNN. Spout reads the input data, and the bolts are each executor body in order. We see that the red line below represents a data stream, Task1 completes the data input, and then transferred to task3 in Bolt A. After Task3 processes the input, it passes the output to the next executor Bolt B, and so on, and finally outputs the result. The process of blue line is the same as the red line. This means two different data streams can be performed simultaneously and are not affected by each other at the same time (see Figs. 2 and 3).

CNN-S model	CNN training model based on storm system

Task distribution process:

    1 Submit the topology to nimbus

    2 Zookeeper completes the scheduling work

    3 Zookeeper distributes the task to the supervisor.

The process of forward propagation of the model:

    Input: $< offset, data >$

    Setup: $CNN_{in} \leftarrow$ read CNN_{set};

    Storm: $dataSet_i \leftarrow < offset, data >$

    1 for each data in $dataSet_i$

    2    $CNN_{intermediate} \leftarrow train(CNN_{in})$;

    3   output $(<1, CNN_{intermediate}>)$;

    4 end for

    Output: $<1, CNN_{intermediate}>$

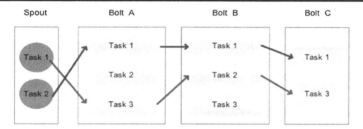

Fig. 2. Logical topology of CNN-S (Color figure online)

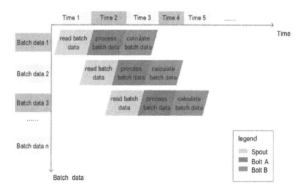

Fig. 3. Spout and bolts of CNN-S

4 Evaluation

4.1 Environment of Experiment

In this experiment, seven Mac Minis are used to build a Storm cluster with one master node and six slave nodes. The configuration of the cluster are as follows (Table 1):

Table 1. Cluster configuration

Node name	Configuration
Master & Supervisor 1, 2, 3, 4, 5, 6	2 core 2.6 GHz CPU 8 GB RAM
Storm	V 1.2.1
Zookeeper	V 3.4.10

4.2 Experimental Dataset

This experiment uses the MNIST (Mixed National Institute of Standards and Technology) data set, which is one of the benchmark data sets of commonly used in convolutional neural networks. The data set contains 70 000 scanned images of handwritten Arabic numerals from "0" to "9" and their correct classification labels. 60 000 images are training sets used to model the image recognition; other 10 000 images are test sets used to test the accuracy of the model.

4.3 Image Recognition Experiment

This experiment selects Lenet-5 as an example. Lenet-5 uses a 9-layer convolutional neural network model (see Fig. 4).

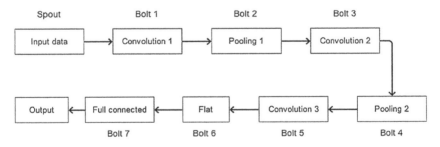

Fig. 4. Spout and bolts of CNN-S

The data input for each round of training is a grayscale image. The size of the image is 32 pixels * 32 pixels, and the image is converted into a matrix format for storage by preprocessing. The convolutional layer C1 has a convolution kernel size of 5 * 5 and 6 convolution kernel. By the convolution operation to the input data on the convolution kernel, six feature vectors with the size of 28 * 28 are generated. The pooling layer S2 down samples the output of the upper layer, and the size of the pooling window is 2 * 2. The output of pooled layer 1 is 6 * 14 * 14 neurons. The convolutional layer C3 use the output vector of the S2 layer to make convolution through the convolution kernel, and the convolution kernel size of C3 is 5 * 5. The output of C3 layer is 16 feature vectors of size 10 * 10. The pooling layer S4 includes 16 feature vectors having a size of 5 * 5, and 120 feature maps are obtained through a pooling window of 2 * 2 and a convolution layer C5 having a size of 5 * 5. Finally, through transition layer F6 and fully connected layer F7, 10 neurons are finally output, and a training process of data is completed.

The single-machine serial training experiment is performed from the input layer to the output layer in sequence according to the above process, and 60,000 rounds of training experiments are completed in order. After the current round of training is completed, the next round of data training can be started. The results of the previous training will update the parameters of the model. After receiving the uploaded task, the storm cluster automatically distributes the task according to the number of workers set in the task and the number of nodes in the cluster. The spout and bolt are assigned to each supervisor according to the default scheduling rule. convolutional layers are assigned as different task performers to different supervisors for parallel calculation and data processing, the weights and parameters in the training model are updated online.

4.4   Experiment Analysis

In this experiment, the accuracy results of Lenet-5 training in different cases are shown in the figure (see Fig. 5).

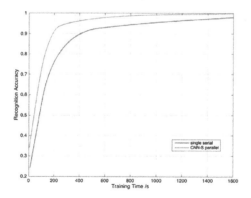

Fig. 5. Curve of training time and recognition accuracy

It can be seen from figure that both time curves showed a positive correlation growth trend. Under the same training time, the parallel training has higher accuracy than under a single machine. The training accuracy rate of the model will also fluctuate up and down within the normal range. In the serial mode from 0 to 200 s, the recognition accuracy is rapidly increasing from 14% to about 76%. During the period of 200 s to 900 s, the overall growth trend is flat, increasing from about 76% to 95%. In the latter part of the experiment, the accuracy tends to be stable and gradually approaches 100%. In the CNN-S parallel model, from 0 s to 180 s, and the recognition accuracy is rapidly increasing from 15% to 90%, ranging from 180 s to 400 s, but overall it has a gradual growth trend, increasing from an accuracy rate of about 80% to 95%. At the end of experiment, the accuracy rate tends to be stable and gradually approaches 100%.

In order to more objectively compare the parallel and serial training efficiency, we use the speedup ratio to indicate the parallel acceleration effect. We set the training accuracy rate to over 95%, indicating that the training model is basically qualified. According to the experimental data, we get that in the case of single-machine serialization, the running time required to achieve 95% accuracy is 913 s, and in the CNN-S is 248 s. The formula for the acceleration ratio is as follows:

$$speedup\ ratio = \frac{training\ time\ of\ serial}{training\ time\ of\ storm\ parallel} \qquad (1)$$

We can see that the training efficiency under CNN-S model has been improved. The speed is 3.681 times that of serial training under the same algorithm model.

In CNN-S, before entering the CNN model training, Storm will distribute the tasks. This time is called the distribution time. This part of the time is the extra time overhead introduced by CNN-S. For the same algorithm topology, we make experiments on different numbers of storm clusters and record time of sending task (see Fig. 6, left):

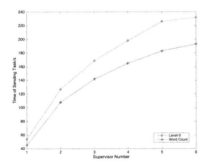 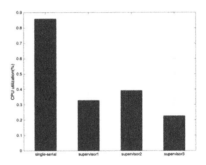

Fig. 6. Curve of sending task time with supervisor number (left) and CPU utilization of different models (right)

Combined with the distribution time of CNN-S and the training time of CNN, we set:

$$running\ Time = sending\ Time + training\ Time \qquad (2)$$

Then, when the number of clusters is 3, the running time of the CNN-S algorithm is 417 s, and the running time of the single-machine serial is 913 s. The acceleration ratio of the running time is significantly lower than that of the training time. To some extent, the extra distribution time brought by the Storm system has affected its overall acceleration effect to some extent. As can be seen from the figure, as the number of clusters grows, the distribution time grows more slowly. For a larger CNN training set, when the number of supervisors is increased, the training time acceleration ratio will be faster, and the effect of the distribution time on the training time will be lower. If the number of supervisors is increased, the acceleration effect is not necessarily better. Excessive supervisors will result in a significant increase in communication time overhead between nodes.

The single-machine serial training CNN algorithm often encounters the problem of insufficient memory, resulting in a decline in training speed. In a single serial experiment, the memory occupancy rate is high, which will affect the server performance and thus reduce the training efficiency of the algorithm. Under the CNN-S model, the memory usage of the three supervisors of the Storm cluster is less than 50%, and the program can run with good performance under each machine. At present, the problem of insufficient serial memory is solved by stacking CPU and GPU on a large number of machines which is expensive and inflexible. The CNN-S model combines multiple servers to solve not only the problem of insufficient memory, but also the hardware cost (see Fig. 6, right).

5 Conclusion

This paper proposes and implements a model CNN-S based on Storm distributed framework parallel adaptive training CNN. The experimental results show that the model has good parallelism and solves the problem of low efficiency and insufficient memory of the single-machine serial for training CNN algorithm. The CNN-S system has an acceleration ratio of 3.681. Factors affecting the acceleration of the system are those such as the number of clusters and the degree of parallelism of the algorithms. For any CNN algorithm, the CNN-S model can be adaptive, which does not require additional algorithm design, and is a highly flexible parallel optimization framework.

Acknowledgements. Yuting Zhu is also with Shanghai Microwave Research Institute and CETC Key Laboratory of Data Link Technology. This paper is supported in part by NSFC China (61771309, 61671301, 61420106008, 61521062), Shanghai Key Laboratory Funding (STCSM15DZ2270400), CETC Key Laboratory of Data Link Technology Foundation (CLDL-20162306), and Medical Engineering Cross Research Foundation of Shanghai Jiao Tong University (YG2017QN47).

References

1. Lecun, Y., Bottou, L., Bengio, Y., et al.: Gradient-based learning applied to document recognition. Proc. IEEE **86**(11), 2278–2324 (1998)
2. Venkatraman, S., Kulkarni, S.: Map Reduce neural network framework for efficient content based image retrieval from large datasets in the cloud. In: 12th International Conference on Hybrid Intelligent Systems, HIS (2012)

3. Yang, W., Liu, X., Zhang, L., et al.: Big data real-time processing based on storm. In: Proceedings of IEEE International Conference on Trust, Security and Privacy in Computing and Communications, pp. 1784–1787 (2013)
4. Hubel, D.H., Wiesel, T.N.: Binocular interaction and functional architecture in the cat's visual cortex. J. Physiol. **160**(1), 106–154 (1962)
5. Xiang, D., Wu, Y., Shang, P., Jiang, J., Wu, J., Yu, K.: RB-storm: resource balance scheduling in apache storm. In: 2017 6th IIAI International Congress on Advanced Applied Informatics, IIAI-AAI, Hamamatsu, pp. 419–423 (2017)
6. Xie, C., Qian, L., Ding, L., Yang, F.: Adaptive topology decomposition for storm. In: 2017 International Conference on Electrical Engineering and Informatics, ICELTICs, Banda Aceh, pp. 269–273 (2017)
7. Batyuk, A., Voityshyn, V.: Apache storm based on topology for real-time processing of streaming data from social networks. In: Proceedings of the 1st IEEE International Conference on Data Stream Mining & Processing. IEEE (2016)
8. Ranjan, R.: Streaming big data processing in datacenter clouds. IEEE Cloud Comput. **1**(1), 78–83 (2014)

Emerging Areas

Detection of Alcoholism: An EEG Hybrid Features and Ensemble Subspace K-NN Based Approach

Sandeep Bavkar, Brijesh Iyer$^{(\boxtimes)}$, and Shankar Deosarkar

Department of E & TC Engineering,
Dr. Babasaheb Ambedkar Technological University,
Lonere, District Raigad, Maharashtra, India
bavkar_ss@rediffmail.com, brijeshiyer@dbatu.ac.in,
sbdeosarkar@yahoo.com

Abstract. The excessive consumption of alcohol affects the brain neuronal system. Electroencephalogram signals convey information regarding alcoholic or normal status of a subject. The paper reports a novel method of detection of alcoholism using EEG hybrid features. Narrow band pass Butterworth filters are designed to separate the EEG rhythms. Linear, nonlinear and statistical feature are extracted to measure the complexity and nonlinearity in EEG signal. Alpha and Gamma rhythm gives very low p-value, indicating that gamma and alpha rhythms are capable to differentiate alcoholic EEG signal from nonalcoholic EEG signal. These rhythm features were applied to ensemble subspace K NN classifier with 10-fold cross validation. The proposed method with ensemble subspace KNN classifier delivers best classification accuracy (98.25%) as compared with other existing techniques.

Keywords: Alcoholic · Nonlinear features · EEG rhythm

1 Introduction

Alcoholism is a condition developed into a subject due to the excessive consumption of alcohol. It results into different psychological and physical problems and may be fatal also. A person suffers from alcoholism not only losses his health but also the social status too. According to World health organization (WHO) report, the destructive use of alcohol results in almost 2.5 million deaths each year [1].

Alcohol slowly affects every organ in the body including the brain. Over last few decades, percentage of alcohol consumption in India increased every year. According to National Crime Records Bureau (NCRB) press release, after every 96 min, one casualty is reported in India on account of alcoholism [2]. The rural part of India is worst affected by the alcoholism due to lack of educational awareness. Slowly but surely alcoholism penetrated its arms in the society irrespective of the social strata.

After knowing the drawbacks of excessive alcohol consumption, it becomes necessary to find out the way to differentiate the alcoholic and non-alcoholic subjects. The early detection of symptoms of alcoholism will be helpful to create a warning bell for

© Springer Nature Switzerland AG 2019
G. Fahrnberger et al. (Eds.): ICDCIT 2019, LNCS 11319, pp. 161–168, 2019.
https://doi.org/10.1007/978-3-030-05366-6_13

the particular subject. This may be helpful to prevent the permanent damage of the human subject. The questionnaire-based manual tools, physiological tools like stress measurement and blood test based analysis are commonly used methodologies to measure the effect of alcohol consumption. However, questionnaire-based analysis and stress measurement techniques are challengeable in terms of their accuracy of outcomes due to the human intervention. Blood test method is invasive, painful and costly one. Further, all these methods require cooperation from the subject under test. Hence, an automatic, accurate, non-invasive and cost-effective technique is required for the clinical diagnosis of alcoholism for the subject under test.

Electroencephalogram (EEG) signals are signature of neuronal activity of a human being. EEG records electrical activity of human brain by placing multiple electrodes on scalp. In recent research, it is reported that excessive alcohol consumption affects the brain activity of a human being as it destroys the white matter (connecting fiber) and gray matter (cell membrane) of brain. Reduction in white matter results in loss of functional connectivity between neurons and loss of gray matter results in the reduction of neurons [3].

The brain activities can be recorded by various techniques such as PET (Positron Emission Tomography), MRI (Magnetic Resonance Imaging), fMRI (Functional Magnetic Resonance Imaging). However, EEG signals is best choice to record the neuronal changes due to its non-invasiveness, accuracy in real-time mode of operation and best suited for the complex dynamism of human brain activities. With EEG based analysis, the medical practitioners do not require human cooperation during the diagnostic activities.

Researchers and academicians had reported notable contributions in the area of EEG based analysis of alcoholism detection. A second order autoregressive modeling was used to discriminate alcoholic subject. MLP-BP, LD and SFA classifiers were applied, which gives average of classification errors of 2.8%, 2.6% and 11.9% respectively [5]. Horizontal visibility graph entropy feature proposed by *Zhu et al.* This approach reported an accuracy of 87.5% using three HVGE features and 10-fold cross validation [6]. Analysis of Variance (ANOVA) statistical method was reported to analyses the EEG signal with BPNN classifier. Investigational results confirmed that the BPNN classifier is better than SVM classifier [7]. Kumar et al. focused on motor cortex of human brain by using only channels in that region. This method suffers from inferior accuracy with SVM clustering [8]. Empirical mode decomposition was proposed for EEG band separation in [9] using only statistical features for identification of alcoholic EEG signals. However, these features do not extract nonlinearity in signal. Hence, there is a requirement to have a methodology to extract the non-linearity of the EEG signals.

To extract nonlinearity, complexity present in signal, the paper reports the use of EEG hybrid features. These are the combination of linear, nonlinear and statistical features of each EEG rhythm. Linear features give difference between alcoholics and normal EEG. Generally alcoholic signals are highly unpredicted and complex, non-linear features are used to represent it. The statistical features extract variability present in EEG signal. Combination of these three features gives hybrid set of features to discriminate alcoholic EEG. Table 1 provides a brief state of the art alcoholic EEG classification.

Table 1. State of the art of alcoholic EEG classification

Sr. no.	Contribution	Sample size	Feature extraction	Classifier	Maximum accuracy
1	Acharya et al. [4]	60 samples (30 alcoholic + 30 normal)	Approximate entropy, largest lyapunov exponent, sample entropy	SVM with RBF kernel	91.7%
2	Palaniappan [5]	40 samples (20 alcoholic + 20 normal)	Autoregressive modeling	Fuzzy ARTMAP NN, MLP-BP NN	–
3	Zhu et al. [6]	60 samples (30 alcoholic + 30 normal)	13-dimension horizontal visibility graph entropy	K-NN and SVM	87.5%
4	Shri et al. [7]	20 samples (10 alcoholic + 10 normal)	Approximate entropy and ANVO test	BPNN and SVM	90%
5	Kumar et al. [8]	40 samples (20 alcoholic + 20 normal)	EEG absolute band power	SVM and LDA	88%
6	Taran et al. [9]	60 samples (30 alcoholic + 30 normal)	Mean absolute difference, inter quartile range, covariance and entropy	Extreme learning machine, LS SVM	93.75%

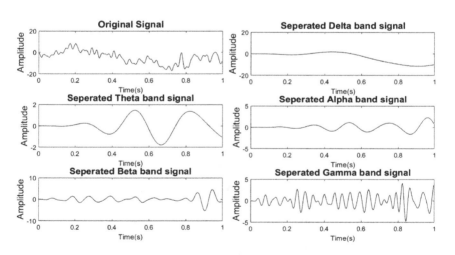

Fig. 1. EEG signal and its corresponding separated EEG band signal

In this paper, Butterworth narrow band pass filter is used for separation of non-stationary EEG signals into EEG rhythms. Figure 1 indicate original signal with it different EEG rhythm as per their frequency range.

The rest of the paper is organized as: Section 2 describes the EEG rhythms and impact of alcohol of each rhythm, details of database, feature extraction and classification. Section 3 present results and discussion of proposed method. Conclusion of paper is given in Sect. 4.

2   The Methodology

EEGs can be divided into different frequency bands. Each band shows their usefulness in EEG based analysis of brain physiological state. The bands that are normally distinguished delta 'δ' (0.5–4 Hz), theta 'θ' (4–8 Hz), alpha 'α' (8–13 Hz), beta 'β' (13–28 Hz), and gamma 'γ' (28–55 Hz).

The paper reports a new EEG rhythm-based methodology using hybrid features and ensemble subspace K-NN, for automatic discrimination of alcoholic and normal subjects. The block diagram of the proposed method is shown in Fig. 2.

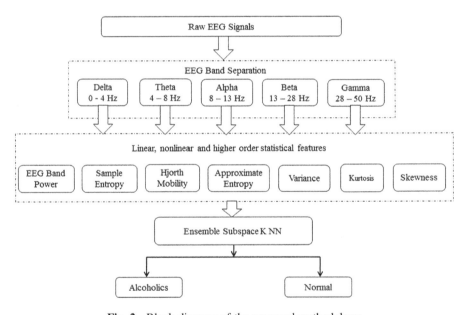

Fig. 2. Block diagram of the proposed methodology

2.1   The Database

The EEG database of the University of California, Irvine Knowledge Discovery in Database (UCI KDD) Archive is used for the present analysis [10]. This is a database of 64 electrodes placed on scalp of person with a visually evoked potential. Signals were sampled at 256 Hz (3.9 ms epoch) for one second. The stimuli contain pictures from the 1980 Snodgrass and Vander wart set. Database includes total 122 subjects. The control groups consists of 48 male subjects and mean age of control group is 25.81. Alcoholic group contains 77 male having mean age 35.83. While recording data all subjects are abstinent for at least 30 days.

2.2 Feature Extraction and Selection

The literature promotes the use of various types of features in individual manner. We propose the combination of those features to give best accuracy.

Linear Feature: For each rhythm absolute band power is calculated using power spectral density (PSD) of EEG signals. Figure 3 shows comparisons of absolute band power in alcoholics and normal person's EEG signal.

Nonlinear Feature: Approximate entropy (*ApEn*), Sample entropy (*SampEn*), Hjorth mobility, and Hjorth complexity are used as nonlinear feature for discrimination of alcoholic from normal EEG signal. *ApEn* signifies an index that represents the overall complexity and predictability of fluctuations in the signal. A time series with high regularity has lesser *ApEn* values, and vice versa.

$$ApEn(p,q,N) = \frac{1}{N-p+1} \sum\nolimits_{i=1}^{N-p+1} log C_i^p(q) - \frac{1}{N-p} \sum\nolimits_{i=1}^{N-p} log C_i^{p+1}(q) \quad (1)$$

Where

$$C_i^p(q) = \frac{1}{N-p+1} \sum\nolimits_{i=1}^{N-p+1} \varnothing (r - \|x_i - x_j\|) \quad (2)$$

is the correlation integral. N is the number of samples in signal, q is the radial distance around each reference point x_i and p is embedding dimension. In this experimentation embedding dimension p is chosen to be 2 and q radial distance is to be 0.2 times the standard deviation of data. $\varnothing$ is the Heaviside function and x_i, x_j are the sample value in signal.

SampEn is conceptually similar to *ApEn*, with additional features such as no self-matching count and independent of data size.

From given time series signal, data mobility and complexity were extracted using Hjorth mobility and complexity respectively.

Statistical Features. The statistical features like variance, skewness and kurtosis are used for investigation and classification of alcohol and nonalcoholic EEG signals.

2.3 Ensemble Subspace KNN

Merging several classifiers, known as ensemble techniques, will give considerable improvement in classification performance. Weak k nearest neighbor classifiers were used with random subspace to ensemble the result. Number of learning cycle value kept to 30. In our experimentation, ensemble subspace KNN is used with 10-fold cross validation approach [11]. *Statistics and Machine Learning Toolbox* present in MATLAB 2016 were used for classification.

3 Result and Discussion

This section elaborates the results of proposed method for classification of alcoholics and normal subjects. Absolute band power is used as a linear feature set, whereas four nonlinear features (*SampEn, ApEn*, Hjorth mobility and complexity) and three higher order statistical feature (variance, skewness and kurtosis) were extracted from each EEG rhythm. Extracted features were normalized using min-max normalization because they have large dynamic range of feature value. After normalization every feature value in the range of 0 to 1.

Figure 3 indicates that delta, theta and gamma power of EEG rhythm PSD is higher in alcoholic subject as compared to the signals of nonalcoholic subject. In alpha rhythm nonalcoholic person's signal has higher power. This indicates that these linear features can be used to differentiate alcoholic person's EEG signal.

Table 2 gives the quantitative analysis of different EEG rhythm based features. It indicates a lower Pearson Correlation Coefficient (p) value for alpha and gamma rhythm feature as compared to theta and beta rhythm. The p value analysis depicts close agreement with PSD, shown in Fig. 3. It shows large difference in alpha and gamma rhythm as compared to other rhythm. Thus alpha and gamma rhythms are dominant in the discrimination of alcoholic from a controlled subject.

Table 2. P-value of different rhythm-based feature.

Features	Delta	Theta	Alpha	Beta	Gamma
Rhythm power	5.31409×10^{-5}	0.2559	2.05261×10^{-17}	0.0363	9.75332×10^{-7}
Variance	1.32121×10^{-5}	0.2579	2.0099×10^{-17}	0.0363	9.75332×10^{-7}
Skewness	0.0068	3.16903×10^{-8}	2.46376×10^{-8}	0.0449	0.1987
Kurtosis	0.0003	0.0155	1.87069×10^{-7}	0.332	8.79632×10^{-7}
SampEn	1.94605×10^{-5}	0.4459	3.5998×10^{-5}	0.9318	7.70484×10^{-12}
ApEn	0.007	0.3647	3.33511×10^{-11}	0.0043	0.0003

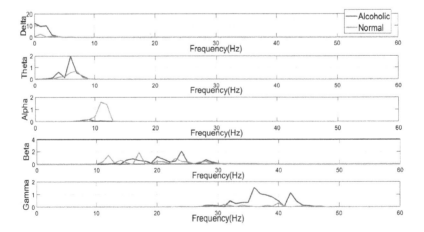

Fig. 3. Comparison of each EEG band power in alcoholic and nonalcoholic subject

Total 800 samples were used for training and testing with 10-fold cross validation. For analysis, original samples are randomly grouped into ten subgroups. Table 3 provides the qualitative comparative analysis of the proposed method with existing methodologies.

Recently, *Taran et al.* [9] proposed EEG rhythm-based method for classification of alcoholic subjects. The cost functions like mean absolute deviation (*MAD*), inter quartile range (*IQR*), coefficient of variation (*COV*), entropy (*En*), and negentropy features were used to extract statistical information from EEG signal with maximum accuracy of 97.92% using extreme learning machine (ELM). However complete signal information cannot be extracted using only those features as EEG signals are highly complex and nonstationary.

Ahmadi et al. proposed a method for alcoholism detection using nonlinear features with different classifier and achieved 99% detection accuracy [12]. However, the authors doesnot discussed the size of the database used for ROC plot. Hence, it is possible that the proposed result in [12] may vary with the database. Further, *Gopan et al.* [13] proposed hybrid feature (combination of raw EEG data and derived features) for alcoholic identification. However, the selected features did not provide the complete analysis of the complex EEG signals.

This drawback is overcome by the present work by using hybrid feature containing linear, nonlinear and statistical parameters of EEG signal. Further, *p* value hypothesis test is also applied to select robust EEG rhythm for identification of EEG signal and oval all accuracy was increased using ensemble subspace K NN classifier.

Table 3. Qualitative comparative analysis of the proposed method

Sr. no.	Contribution	Feature selection method	No. of features	Classifier	Accuracy %
1	Acharya et al. [4]	*APE, SPE, LLE, HOS* features	7	SVM with poly kernel	91.7
2	Zhu et al. [6]	Horizontal visibility graph entropy	13	SVM K NN	94.5
3	Kumar et al. [8]	Absolute power, relative power & peak power frequency	3	SVM FCM	88
4	Taran and Bajaj [9]	*MAD, IQR, COV*, negentropy and entropy	5	ELM LS-SVM	93.75
5	Gopika et al. [13]	Spectral entropy features with test ranking	–	KNN MLP classifier	93.08
6	**Proposed method**	**EEG rhythm hybrid features**	7	**Ensemble subspace K NN**	**98.25**

4 Conclusion

The paper reports a novel method for classification and identification of alcoholics and normal persons using EEG rhythm features. The EEG rhythms are used to compute linear feature (Absolute power), nonlinear features (SampEn, ApEn, Hjorth mobility) and statistical features (variance, skewness, and kurtosis). It is noticed that the skewness kurtosis has lesser variability in EEG of alcoholics and normal person. The absolute power, variance, sample entropy is strongest features that give more separability between alcoholic and normal. The p-value analysis of proposed features recommends that alpha and gamma rhythms are more statistically significant for classification. Alpha and gamma rhythm feature with ensemble subspace K-NN classifier provides highest classification accuracy 98.25%. In order to establish the usefulness of this method, we suggest to, evaluate using different database. Also accuracy can be improved using other robust features.

References

1. World Health Organization: Global Status Report on Alcohol and Health. World Health Organization, Geneva (2014)
2. NCRB report (2013). http://ncrb.gov.in/StatPublitions/ADSI/ADSI2013/ADSI-2013.pdf
3. Mukherjee, S.: Alcoholism and its effects on the central nervous system. Curr. Neurovascular Res. **10**(3), 256–262 (2013)
4. Acharya, U.R., Sree, S.V., Chattopadhyay, S., Suri, J.S.: Automated diagnosis of normal and alcoholic EEG signals. Int. J. Neural Syst. **22**(3) (2012). https://doi.org/10.1142/s0129065712500116
5. Palaniappan, R.: Discrimination of alcoholic subjects using second order autoregressive modelling of brain signals evoked during visual stimulus perception. World Acad. Sci. Eng. Technol. **12**, 640–645 (2005)
6. Zhu, G., Li, Y., Wen, P.P., Wang, S.: Analysis of alcoholic EEG signals based on horizontal visibility graph entropy. Brain Inform. **1**(1–4), 19–25 (2014)
7. Shri, T.K.P., et.al.: Characterization of EEG signals for identification of alcoholics using ANOVA ranked approximate entropy and classifiers. In: International Conference on Circuits, Communication, Control and Computing, Bangalore, pp. 109–112 (2014)
8. Kumar, A., Ghosh, S., Tetarway, S., Sinha, R.: Support vector machine and fuzzy C-mean clustering-based comparative evaluation of changes in motor cortex electroencephalogram under chronic alcoholism. Med. Biol. Eng. Comput. **53**(7), 609–622 (2015)
9. Taran, S., Bajaj, V.: Rhythm-based identification of alcohol EEG signals. IET Sci. Measur. Technol. **12**(3), 343–349 (2018)
10. UCI KDD Database. https://archive.ics.uci.edu/ml/datasets/eeg+database
11. Gul, A., Perperoglou, A., Khan, Z., et al.: Adv. Data Anal. Classif. **12**, 827 (2018). https://doi.org/10.1007/s11634-015-0227-5
12. Ahmadi, N., Pei, Y., Pechenizkiy, M.: Detection of alcoholism based on EEG signals and functional brain network features extraction. In: 2017 IEEE 30th International Symposium on Computer-Based Medical Systems (CBMS), Thessaloniki, pp. 179–184 (2017)
13. Gopan, G.K., Sinha, N., Babu, D.J.: Hybrid features based classification of alcoholic and non-alcoholic EEG. In: IEEE International Conference on Electronics, Computing and Communication Technologies, Bangalore, pp. 1–6 (2015)

On the Growth of the Prime Numbers
Based Encoded Vector Clock

Ajay D. Kshemkalyani$^{(\boxtimes)}$ and Bhargav Voleti

University of Illinois at Chicago, Chicago, IL 60607, USA
{ajay,bvolet2}@uic.edu

Abstract. The vector clock is a fundamental tool for tracking causality in parallel and distributed applications. Unfortunately, it does not scale well to large systems because each process needs to maintain a vector of size n, where n is the total number of processes in the system. To address this problem, the encoded vector clock (EVC) was recently proposed. The EVC is based on the encoding of the vector clock using prime numbers and uses a single number to represent vector time. The EVC has all the properties of the vector clock and yet uses a single number to represent global time. However, the single number EVC tends to grow fast and may soon exceed the size of the traditional vector clock. In this paper, we evaluate the growth rate of the size of the EVC using a simulation model. The simulations show that the EVC grows relatively fast, and the growth rate depends on the mix of internal events and communication events. To overcome this drawback, the EVC can be used in conjunction with several scalability techniques that can allow the use of the EVC in practical applications. We then present a case study of detecting memory consistency errors in MPI one-sided applications using EVC.

Keywords: Causality · Vector clock · Prime numbers · Encoding
Happened-before relation · Scalability · Performance

1 Introduction

The ordering of events and states is a basic operation in the analysis of parallel and distributed executions. It is used in parallel applications such as dynamic race detection in multithreaded programs. It is used in distributed applications such as checkpointing and rollback recovery, mutual exclusion, debugging, and replication-based data stores. For example, in replication-based data stores, the ordering of reads and updates to a shared object is required to determine the object's most recent value. Logical clocks have been proposed to order events without the need for tightly synchronized physical clocks. These logical clocks order events based on the *causality* relation on events, defined by Lamport [13]. The ordering of events based on the causality relation is also required for enforcing causal consistency in data stores. Thus, tracking causality and evaluating causality between different events and between different states of a distributed execution is an important problem.

© Springer Nature Switzerland AG 2019
G. Fahrnberger et al. (Eds.): ICDCIT 2019, LNCS 11319, pp. 169–184, 2019.
https://doi.org/10.1007/978-3-030-05366-6_14

The simplest form of logical clocks, proposed by Lamport [13], uses a scalar clock at each process in the system. If two events are related by causality, their scalar clock values are so ordered. However, the causality relation between events cannot be inferred from the values of the scalar clocks of events. To overcome this drawback, vector clocks have been proposed [5,14]. The vector clock is a fundamental tool for tracking causality in distributed applications. Unfortunately, vector clocks do not scale well to large systems because each process needs to maintain a vector of size n, where n is the total number of processes in the system. To address this problem, the encoding of the vector clock using prime numbers to use a single number to represent vector time was proposed [9]. This encoding preserves the properties of the vector clock by maintaining only a single number – a big integer – at each process. The tick, merge, and comparison operations on the encoded vector clock (EVC) were proposed in [9]. This result also showed how to timestamp global states and how to perform operations – namely, the union, intersection, common causal past computation, and comparison – on the global states using the EVC. All these operations on the EVCs of events and on the EVCs of global states have equal or lower time complexity than the corresponding operations on traditional vector clocks in the uniform cost model. As the EVC values are big integers, the time complexities of the operations on EVCs are also expressed in the logarithmic cost model. However, these complexities are incomparable with the complexities of operations on traditional vector clocks in the uniform cost model.

Contributions: Although the EVC is a single big integer rather than a vector of integers, the drawback of the EVC is that it appears to grow fast. In this paper, using a simulation model, we evaluate the growth rate of the size of the EVC. Assuming that the integer data type used by programming languages is represented in 32 bits, we compute the number of events in the execution until the EVC size reaches $32n$, as a function of n. We also study via simulations, how many system events it takes until the size of the single big integer number EVC at some process becomes $32n$. We do this by computing the size of the EVC as a function of the number of events in the execution, for a fixed n. We also show that the growth rate of the EVC depends on the ratio of internal events to communication events, and analyze this dependency. Our simulation results confirm the intuition that the single number EVC grows fast.

To overcome the drawback that the EVC grows quite fast, we can use four techniques. These are: ticking the clock only at application-relevant events, the use of detection regions within which the EVC is tracked, resetting the EVC in the system when the size of the EVC at some process reaches a threshold such as $32n$ or when a global synchronization is performed, and using logarithms of the EVC rather than the EVC itself. A judicious use of these scalability techniques can control the size of the EVC, and can be used to guarantee that the size of the EVC never exceeds the size of the traditional vector clock.

Outline: In Sect. 2, we give the system model and present preliminaries. In Sect. 3, we give the simulation results on the growth of the EVC. Section 4 gives scalability techniques for the EVC. In Sect. 5, we discuss the application of the scalability techniques in a case study of detecting memory consistency errors in MPI one-sided applications using EVC. We give concluding remarks in Sect. 6.

2   System Model and Preliminaries

2.1   System Model

A distributed system is modeled as an undirected graph (P, L), where P is the set of processes and L is the set of communication links connecting them. Let $n = |P|$. Between any two processes, there may be at most one logical channel over which the two processes communicate asynchronously. A logical channel from P_i to P_j is formed by paths over links in L. We do not assume FIFO logical channels; thus the messages may be delivered out of order.

The execution of process P_i produces a sequence of events $E_i = \langle e_i^0, e_i^1, e_i^2, \cdots \rangle$, where e_i^k is the kth event at process P_i. An event at a process can be an *internal* event, a *message send* event, or a *message receive* event. Let $E = \bigcup_{i \in P} \{e \mid e \in E_i\}$ denote the set of events in a distributed execution. The causal precedence relation between events induces an irreflexive partial order on E. This relation is defined as Lamport's "happened before" relation [13], and denoted as $\rightarrow$. An execution of a distributed system is thus denoted by the tuple $(E, \rightarrow)$. Lamport designed the scalar clock, which is a function C that assigns integer timestamps to events such that if $e \rightarrow f$, then $C(e) < C(f)$. However, the drawback of scalar clocks is that $C(e) < C(f)$ does not imply that $e \rightarrow f$.

2.2   Vector Clocks

Mattern [14] and Fidge [5] designed the vector clock which assigns a vector V to each event such that: $e \rightarrow f \iff V(e) < V(f)$. This is called the *strong clock consistency condition*. Thus, the vector clock overcomes the drawback of the scalar clock. Each process P_i maintains a vector clock V. Events are timestamped by the current clock value. The vector clocks, initialized to the 0-vector, are updated by the following rules.

1. Before an internal event happens at process P_i, $V[i] = V[i] + 1$ (local tick).
2. Before process P_i sends a message, it first executes $V[i] = V[i]+1$ (local tick), then it sends the message piggybacked with V.
3. When process P_i receives a message piggybacked with timestamp U, it executes
   $\forall k \in [1 \ldots n], V[k] = \max(V[k], U[k])$ (merge);
   $V[i] = V[i] + 1$ (local tick)
   before delivering the message.

The vector clock is a fundamental tool to characterize causality in distributed executions [10,17]. Charron-Bost has shown that to capture the partial order $(E, \rightarrow)$, the size of the vector clock is the dimension of the partial order [2], which is bounded by the size of the system, n. Thus, each process needs to maintain a vector of size n to represent the local vector clock. Unfortunately, this does not scale well to large systems. Several works in the literature attempted to reduce the size of vector clocks [11,12,15,19–21], they had to make some compromises in accuracy or alter the system model, and in the worst-case, were as lengthy as vector clocks. To address this problem, the encoding of the vector clock using prime numbers to use a single number to represent vector time was proposed [9].

---

1. Initialize $t_i = 1$.
2. Before an internal event happens at process P_i,
   $t_i = t_i * p_i$ (local tick).
3. Before process P_i sends a message, it first executes $t_i = t_i * p_i$ (local tick),
   then it sends the message piggybacked with t_i.
4. When process P_i receives a message piggybacked with timestamp s, it executes
   $t_i = LCM(s, t_i)$ (merge);
   $t_i = t_i * p_i$ (local tick)
   before delivering the message.

Fig. 1. Operation of EVC t_i at process P_i [9].

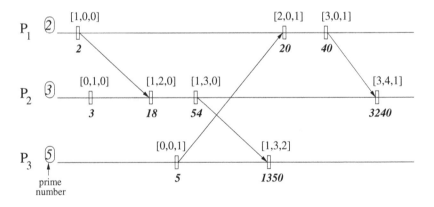

Fig. 2. Illustration of using EVC. The vector timestamps and EVC timestamps are shown above and below each timeline, respectively. In real scenarios, only the EVC is stored and transmitted.

2.3   Encoded Vector Clock

Instead of using a vector of size n, [9] proposed that the vector can be encoded into a single number using n distinct prime numbers. The encoding of vector clocks using primes was used for detecting locality-aware conjunctive predicates in large-scale systems [18]. Each process P_i is associated with a unique prime number p_i. A vector clock containing n elements, $V = [v_1, v_2, \cdots, v_n]$, can be encoded by n distinct prime numbers $p_1, p_2, \cdots, p_n$ as:

$$Enc(V) = p_1^{v_1} * p_2^{v_2} * \cdots * p_n^{v_n}.$$

However, only being able to encode a vector clock into a single number is insufficient to track causal relations. The EVC technique was developed [9] to show how to implement the basic operations of a vector clock, namely, local tick, merge, and compare. The encoded vector clock t_i (initialized to 1) is operated at process P_i as shown in Fig. 1. To manipulate the EVC, each process needs to know only its own prime and not the primes of other processes.

- For a local tick, t_i is multiplied by p_i.
- For a merge of timestamps t_i and s, the $LCM(t_i, s) = \frac{t_i * s}{GCD(t_i, s)}$ is computed. Merging two EVCs requires computing the LCM, which does not require factorization.

The operations using EVC are illustrated in Fig. 2 using an example execution over three processes.

3   Simulations

For n processes in the system and f_i events at each process P_i, the maximum EVC timestamp across all processes is at least as large as $O(\prod_{i=1}^{n} p_i^{f_i})$. This is because at each event (send, receive, or internal) at P_i, the EVC gets multiplied by p_i, and in addition, at receive events, an LCM computation over two EVCs may significantly increase the EVC. From this observation, we can see that EVC timestamps grow fast. We ran simulations to test the growth rate of EVCs. The simulations were done in Rust and used the GMP library. We simulated distributed executions with a random communication pattern. As parameters, we used the number of processes, n, and the probability of a send (versus internal) event, denoted pr_s. The destination of a message from a send event was chosen at random. We timestamped events using EVCs, and measured the size of the EVC in bits. We used the first n prime numbers for the n processes.

We define the *overflow process* to be that process which is earliest to have its EVC size exceed $32n$ bits. The size $32n$ was chosen for comparison because this is the constant size used by traditional vector clocks, assuming each integer in the vector clock is represented by 4 bytes.

3.1   Simulation Results

Number of Events Until EVC Size Becomes $32n$ as a Function of n:
Figure 3 shows the number of events executed in the system until the EVC size reaches $32n$ bits at the overflow process, as a function of n. We varied n from 10

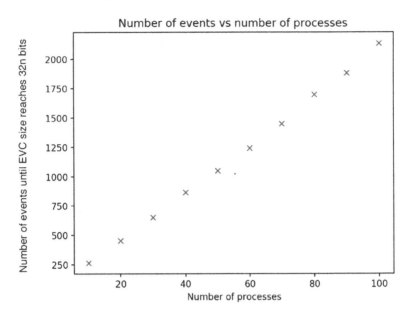

Fig. 3. Number of events needed for EVC to reach a size of $32n$ as a function of the number of processes n in the system.

to 100, and plotted the average of 10 runs for each setting, assuming that pr_s, the probability of send events (versus internal events), was 0.6. The plot turns out to be almost a straight line.

For the range of n tested (10–100), typically 21 to 25 events were executed at some process before the EVC size exceeded $32n$ at the overflow process. As this number in the interval $[21, 25]$ appears small, we conduct a worst-case strawman analysis to show that this number is reasonable. As $pr_s = 0.6$, $probability(send\ event) = probability(receive\ event) = 0.6/1.6$. We can approximate this as assuming that every third event is a receive event. Now consider, for example, $n = 60$. The simulation uses the 60 lowest prime numbers, and a significant number of them need 8 bits for representation. At each event, we multiply t_i by p_i, so the size of the EVC increases by 8 bits. In addition, at every third event (a receive event), the size of the EVC can double in the worst case due to the LCM operation. (Doubling of the size of the EVC due to LCM computation is more likely in the initial part of the execution because the LCM is likely to be computed over relative prime numbers.) So the worst-case progression of the size of the EVC in bits at a process P_i can be approximated as:

$$8, 16, 32 \text{ and } 40 \text{ (event } e_i^3), 48, 56, 112 \text{ and } 120 \text{ (event } e_i^6),$$
$$128, 136, 272 \text{ and } 280 \text{ (event } e_i^9), 288, 296, 592 \text{ and } 600 \text{ (event } e_i^{12}),$$
$$608, 616, 1232 \text{ and } 1240 \text{ (event } e_i^{15}), 1248, 1256, 2512 \text{ and } 2520 \text{ (event } e_i^{18}).$$

At the 18th event at P_i, the EVC size exceeds $60 \times 32 = 1920$ bits. As per the simulation, the overflow happens at the 1250/60th event, which is the 21st event, at the overflow process, so this worst-case analysis is reasonably accurate.

This analysis indicates that receive events cause the EVC to grow very fast due to the LCM computation.

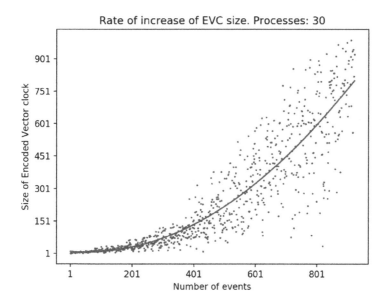

Fig. 4. Scatter-plot of the size of EVC in bits as a function of the number of events in the system. $n = 30$.

Size of EVC as a Function of Number of Events: In our next experiment, we measured the size of the EVC in bits as a function of the number of events executed in the system. Figures 4, 5, and 6, show the scatter-plots for a system with $n = 30, 60, 100$ processes, respectively. For these executions, pr_s, the probability of send event (versus internal event) was chosen as 0.5. In these plots, the number of events on the X-axis is such that the size of the EVC in bits is always less than that of the traditional vector clocks. The Y-axis shows the size of the EVC in bits until the size equals $32n$. The maximum size $32n$ was chosen because this is the constant size used by traditional vector clocks, assuming each integer in the vector clock is represented by 4 bytes.

Consider for example, Fig. 5, which uses parameters $n = 60$ and $pr_s = 0.5$. There were about 1800 events in the systemwide execution (or an average of $1800/60 = 30$ events at a process) until the EVC size reached $1920 (= 60 \times 32)$ bits at the overflow process.

Number of Events Until EVC Size Becomes $32n$ as a Function of Ratio of Event Types: We also varied the percentage of internal events (where the

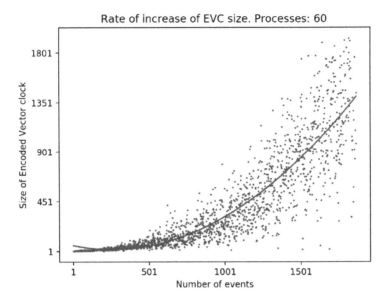

Fig. 5. Scatter-plot of the size of EVC in bits as a function of the number of events in the system. $n = 60$.

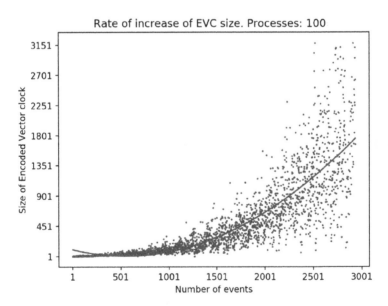

Fig. 6. Scatter-plot of the size of EVC in bits as a function of the number of events in the system. $n = 100$.

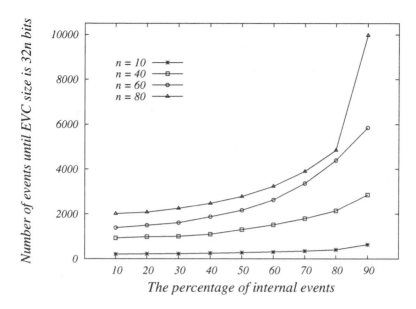

Fig. 7. Total number of events until EVC size reaches $32n$ bits, for different n and different percentages of internal events.

total number of events included send, receive, and internal events), and varied n, and observed the total number of events in the system until the EVC size reaches $32n$ bits at the overflow process. The observations are plotted in Fig. 7. For a given n, as the percentage of internal events increased, symbolizing an increasingly smaller proportion of receive events (and hence fewer LCM computations), the rate of increase of the total number of events until the EVC size reached $32n$ bits kept increasing. In particular, when $probability(internal\ event) > 0.8$, there was a more noticeable rate of increase of the total number of events (until the EVC size reached $32n$ bits at the overflow process). This shows that as the proportion of send events and corresponding receive events decreases progressively, particularly below 10%, due to the fewer resulting LCM computations at receive events, the EVC grows much less rapidly, thereby resulting in a much larger number of system events until the EVC size reaches $32n$ bits. This corroborates the earlier observation that receive events cause the EVC to grow very fast due to the LCM computation.

Consider, for example, the value for $n = 60$, $probability(internal\ event) = 0.9$ which implies that $probability(receive\ event) = 0.05$. We again conduct a strawman analysis. We assume the prime numbers take up to 8 bits representation. As before, let us assume each LCM computation causes the EVC size (in bits) to double because the execution has just begun and the LCM is likely to be computed over relative prime numbers. Then, the receive event occurs every 20 events, at which time the EVC size increases by a factor of 2. So the worst-case progression of the size of the EVC in bits at a process P_i can be approximated as:

$$8, \cdots 152, 304 \text{ and } 312 \text{ (event } e_i^{20}),$$
$$320, \cdots 464, 928 \text{ and } 936 \text{ (event } e_i^{40}),$$
$$944, \cdots 1088, 2176 \text{ and } 2184 \text{ (event } e_i^{60}).$$

At the 60th event at P_i, or equivalently at around the $60 \times 60 = 3600$th event in the execution, the EVC size exceeds $60 \times 32 = 1920$ bits. As per the simulation graph (Fig. 7), the overflow happens at around the 6000th event in the execution, and this can be justified by applying a correction to the worst-case strawman analysis. Note that in the simulation, there is a delay for the message transmission. Hence, in the small initial window (before steady state) that the results in Fig. 7 depict, actually $probability(receive\,event) < 0.05$ and hence there are more than 20 non-receive events per receive event. Hence, there are more than 60 events at the overflow process P_i and hence more than 3600 events in the system until overflow occurs. This supports the simulation result of 6000 events.

4   Scalability

As seen in Sect. 3, the EVC timestamps grow fast and eventually they will exceed the size of vector clocks. However, we can use several strategies to alleviate this problem and control the maximum size of the EVC. In particular, these strategies can be used to guarantee that the EVC size is always less than the vector clock size.

4.1   Relevant Events

It suffices if the local clock does not tick at every event but only at events that are relevant to the application. Thus, the EVC does not grow so fast. This strategy is used in the context of predicate detection [18]. The local clock ticks only when the variables in the predicate alter the truth value of the predicate. As another example, the local clock ticks only at synchronization events in MPI application programs [4]; see the case study in Sect. 5.

4.2   Detection Regions

In large-scale systems, the application requiring a vector clock may be confined to only a subset of m processes, where $m < n$. An example of this is locality-aware predicate detection [18]. The subset of m processes forms a detection region. Processes within the detection region maintain a single number for the EVC. Additionally, for processes outside the detection region, we can cut down the storage cost and make the solution more practical for large-scale systems. When a process P_j outside the region first receives a message piggybacked with an EVC timestamp, it simply stores this single number. Although P_j will not tick the EVC locally since there is no corresponding component in the vector clock for P_j, it may still receive multiple messages. Each time this happens, P_j simply executes the merge operation by calculating the LCM of two numbers. (P_j needs to store the EVC and to do the merge because it may later send messages back into the detection region, directly or transitively.)

4.3   Resetting EVC

We can adapt the clock resetting technique [22] to solve the problem when the clock overflows. This technique divides the execution of a distributed system into multiple phases. Each time the clock overflows at any process, the resetting algorithm terminates the current phase by sending control messages while ensuring there is no computation message sending from the current phase to the next phase, nor from the next phase to the current phase. The reset protocol involves a period of send inhibition of messages, and the local clock gets reset in a strongly consistent (i.e., transitless) global state [1,8]. The use of clock resetting also may require that the phase number be maintained along with the EVC, to enable (if required) the timestamp comparison of events in different phases.

It is up to the application to determine when the EVC overflows. If we say that the clock overflows when the size of the EVC equals $32n$ bits at some process, then we can guarantee that the size of EVC is always less than that of traditional vector clocks.

We can also reset the EVCs globally when there is a naturally occuring global system state in which all previous events are ordered (as per the "happened before" relation $\longrightarrow$) before all subsequent events. For example, such global synchronization occurs at a global barrier or fence instruction in MPI programs [7]; see the case study in Sect. 5. The system state immediately after a global synchronization is a transitless global state.

4.4   Using Logarithms of EVC

As the EVC technique uses exponentiation, logarithms can be used to store and transmit the EVCs. This can result in a significant reduction in the size of EVCs. We note that since logarithms involve finite-precision arithmetic, their use is subject to the introduction of errors due to the limited precision. This may potentially affect the outcome of the test of comparison of a pair of EVC timestamps in determining causality between the corresponding events.

5   Case Study

We review a case study of detecting memory consistency errors in MPI one-sided applications using EVC [4]. MPI one-sided communication, also known as MPI remote memory access, does not require sends to be matched with corresponding receive instructions [7]. Only one process takes part in the data movement (using unilateral instructions such as MPI_Put and MPI_Get rather than matching pairs of MPI_Send and MPI_Receive). It decouples data transfer between processes from synchronization between the processes. This eliminates overhead from unneeded synchronization and allows for greater concurrency. This also eliminates message matching and buffering overheads that are incurred in traditional two-sided communication, leading to significant reduction in communication costs. These advantages of one-sided communication come at a cost – the programs are more prone to synchronization bugs, such as memory consistency errors.

In simple terms, a memory consistency error is a write to a location (through a local store instruction or through a remotely issued MPI_Put) that is concurrent with another write or a read (through a local load instruction or a locally or remotely issued MPI_Get) to the same memory location at the same process [3]. We elaborate on "is concurrent with" semi-formally. The $\xrightarrow{hb}$ "happened before" relation between events a and b is the transitive closure of the union of the program order and synchronization order. The program order at a process specifies that a previous instruction is executed before a later instruction. The synchronization order across processes orders events by the order in which synchronization instructions are executed (e.g., MPI_Send at a source process completes before MPI_Receive at the destination process). The consistency order $\xrightarrow{co}$ on events a and b guarantees that the memory effects of a are visible before b [7]. This order is necessary because synchronization instructions such as MPI_Win_lock/unlock order memory accesses but do not synchronize processes. For example, if a is nonblocking, and a and b both access overlapping buffers, there is no consistency order because of a potential race condition due to a being nonblocking. Now, the $\xrightarrow{cohb}$ relation on events is the transitive closure of the intersection of the $\xrightarrow{co}$ and $\xrightarrow{hb}$ relations [7]. If the $\xrightarrow{cohb}$ does not hold between a pair of events, that pair of events is concurrent under $\xrightarrow{cohb}$. Thus, two memory operations are concurrent if there are no $\xrightarrow{co}$ and $\xrightarrow{hb}$ between them. If there are two concurrent events accessing the same memory location and at least one of them is an update operation (whether local or remote), then there is a memory consistency error in an MPI one-sided program execution. Note that a memory consistency error may be two types: either within an epoch at the same process, or across processes.

Although MPI one-sided communication calls may cause memory consistency errors with other such calls or load/store operations, not every pair of operations will cause such errors. This is because MPI applications use synchronization calls (such as MPI_Barrier and MPI_Win_fence) to enforce $\xrightarrow{co}$ and/or $\xrightarrow{hb}$ between two operations. Only when two operations fall within a concurrent program region may memory consistency errors arise. A *concurrent program region* is defined as a group of program regions across multiple (all) processes, that can be executed concurrently without $\xrightarrow{co}$ and $\xrightarrow{hb}$ ordering relations, i.e., program regions that are not ordered by $\xrightarrow{cohb}$ [3]. Each *program region* is formed of one or multiple epochs, where an *epoch* is formed by a pair of one-sided synchronization calls.

MC-Checker [3] is a tool for identifying memory consistency errors. Using trace files, it generates a dynamic data access DAG whose nodes are the events and edges represent the "happened before" relation. The DAG represents a set of concurrent regions. A concurrent region begins and ends with a global synchronization operation (such as MPI_Barrier and MPI_Win_fence). In the general case, the set of concurrent regions forms a partial order. However, the set of concurrent regions is totally ordered, assuming a single MPI communicator. Each concurrent region is modeled as a graph: the set of nodes are the events in MPI one-sided programs and the edges are the $\xrightarrow{cohb}$ relation. Each concurrent region is (independently) analyzed to detect memory consistency errors – such an error exists between each pair of conflicting operations that are not ordered by $\xrightarrow{cohb}$. MC-Checker detects conflicting operations within each epoch of a program region, and across processes within the concurrent region.

Typically, two-sided communication is used along with one-sided communication in high-performance computing applications. In order to detect memory consistency errors, transitive dependencies between processes, such as those induced by send and receive operations by several different processes, need to be captured. MC-Checker [3] suffers the drawback that it does not take into account such transitive dependencies, because capturing such dependencies would require building a complete DAG of dependencies between events for analysis, which would require maintaining vector clocks. However, vector clocks do not scale and they impose high overheads; as a result MC-Checker did not use vector clocks and this led to the introduction of false positives in reporting memory consistency errors.

The MC-CChecker tool [4] overcame this drawback by using the EVC, thereby eliminating the false positives reported by MC-Checker while still maintaining low overheads. As the $\xrightarrow{cohb}$ relation is specified only on synchronization events within and across processes (these are the relevant events), the EVC scheme also needs to timestamp only such events. MC-CChecker adapted the EVC rules of Fig. 1 [9] to MPI one-sided communication system as follows [4].

R1. For two consecutive synchronization events, if $e_i^x \xrightarrow{cohb} e_i^{x+1}$, then $t_i^{x+1} = t_i^x * p_i$.

R2. If e_i^x is fence (or barrier) and e_j^y is the corresponding fence (or barrier), then a message m from e_i^x to e_j^y is timestamped $tm = t_i^x$. On receipt at P_j, $t_j^y = LCM(tm, t_j^y)$.

R3/R4/R5. If e_i^x is post/complete/send and e_j^y is the corresponding start/wait/receive, then a message m from e_i^x to e_j^y is timestamped $tm = t_i^x$; and then a local tick is executed at P_i. On receipt at P_j, $t_j^y = LCM(tm, t_j^y)$.

For simplicity, it is assumed that post $\xrightarrow{cohb}$ start and complete $\xrightarrow{cohb}$ wait. Only synchronization operations are timestamped as the goal is to represent an area (termed as a *separate region*) formed between two consecutive synchronization operations, including the former but excluding the latter; the timestamps of all events within the separate region equal the timestamp of the representing (former) synchronization event's timestamp.

Along the lines of the test in [9], $e_i^x \xrightarrow{cohb} e_j^y$ if and only if t_i^x divides t_j^y. The two events are concurrent under $\xrightarrow{cohb}$ if and only if the EVC timestamp of neither event divides that of the other. MC-CChecker considers concurrent regions like MC-Checker, but using EVC timestamped information built after analyzing the trace files. MC-CChecker loads concurrent regions one by one from trace files. Once MC-CChecker loads one concurrent region, it detects memory consistency errors within each epoch similar to MC-Checker. However, for errors across processes, it examines the concurrency of each pair of separate regions for each concurrent region. If two separate regions are executed concurrently, MC-CChecker checks the accessed memory of each pair of operations belonging to the two separate regions to flag memory consistency errors (if the two operations are concurrent under $\xrightarrow{cohb}$, conflict, and access the same location).

Experiments run on HPC platforms using three different MPI applications showed that MC-CChecker used low processing time and memory usage, when checked for up to 128 processes. The scalability study compared MC-CChecker using EVC and using traditional vector clocks, for systems ranging from 512 up to 8192 processes. The study showed that with EVC, execution time and memory usage are linear (with respect to n), whereas with traditional vector clocks, both execution time and memory usage were significantly higher and increased in much larger proportion.

In this case study, the relevant events were the synchronization events; only these were timestamped by MC-CChecker using EVCs. Further, each concurrent region contained a program region from a different process. All the concurrent regions were totally ordered, assuming a single MPI communicator. (Without this assumption, the concurrent regions form a partial order.) The boundary between two adjacent concurrent regions was implemented by global synchronization calls such as `MPI_Barrier` and `MPI_Win_fence`. The start of each concurrent region corresponded to a global synchronization where there was no concurrency between events in the previous concurrent region and in the following one. Each concurrent region was a unit of computation [1,8], and the boundary between two adjacent/consecutive concurrent regions corresponded to a global transitless state. MC-CChecker safely reset the EVC of each process to 1 at the start of each concurrent region. Using the combination of these two techniques, viz., tick at relevant event, and reset at the start of each concurrent region, the size of the EVCs at the processes remained small and grew linearly (with n), as the MC-CChecker scalability study showed.

6   Conclusions

Vector clocks are important in distributed and parallel systems, but are not very scalable because they have a space complexity of $O(n)$. The encoding of the vector clock using prime numbers, to use a single number to represent vector time, has the potential to save on the space overheads of vector clocks. A drawback of EVCs is that they grow fast and soon overflow, i.e., exceeding the space used by traditional vector clocks soon occurs. To understand this growth phenomenon, we showed the results of simulations to examine how fast the EVC grows. The simulations confirm that the EVC grows relatively fast, and the growth rate also depends on the ratio of internal events to communication events. In particular, receive events which use an LCM computation cause the size of the EVC to grow more significantly.

Scalability approaches for the EVC to deal with the overflow problem can be used. These include ticking the clock only at application-relevant events and only at processes where such events occur, and resetting the EVC throughout the system at a transitless global state when it overflows at some process or at a global synchronization. A judicious use of these scalability approaches can control the size of the EVC and can be used to guarantee that the size of the EVC never exceeds the size of the traditional vector clock. We considered a case study of using EVC for detecting memory consistency errors in MPI applications that use one-sided communication. Using the combination of two scalability approaches, viz., ticking at relevant event, and resetting at the start of each concurrent region, the size of the EVCs at the processes remained small, grew linearly, and was significantly much less than that using traditional vector clocks.

The EVC timestamps in the case study were assigned after analyzing the program traces. It would be interesting to determine whether they can be assigned in an on-line manner efficiently. Another future direction is to examine whether the EVCs can be used instead of traditional vector clocks in tools for dynamic race detection in multithreaded programs, such as DJIT+ [16] and FastTrack [6].

Acknowledgements. We thank Rahul Sathe for his help with the simulations.

References

1. Ahuja, M., Kshemkalyani, A.D., Carlson, T.: A basic unit of computation in distributed systems. In: 10th International Conference on Distributed Computing Systems (ICDCS 1990), 28 May–1 June 1990, Paris, France, pp. 12–19 (1990)
2. Charron-Bost, B.: Concerning the size of logical clocks in distributed systems. Inf. Process. Lett. **39**(1), 11–16 (1991)
3. Chen, Z., Dinan, J., Tang, Z., Balaji, P., Zhong, H., Wei, J., Huang, T., Qin, F.: MC-Checker: detecting memory consistency errors in MPI one-sided applications. In: International Conference for High Performance Computing, Networking, Storage and Analysis, SC 2014, New Orleans, LA, USA, 16–21 November 2014, pp. 499–510 (2014)
4. Diep, T.D., Fürlinger, K., Thoai, N.: MC-CChecker: a clock-based approach to detect memory consistency errors in MPI one-sided applications. In: Proceedings of the 25th European MPI Users' Group Meeting, EuroMPI 2018, pp. 9:1–9:11 (2018)
5. Fidge, C.J.: Logical time in distributed computing systems. IEEE Comput. **24**(8), 28–33 (1991)
6. Flanagan, C., Freund, S.N.: FastTrack: efficient and precise dynamic race detection. In: Proceedings of the 2009 ACM SIGPLAN Conference on Programming Language Design and Implementation, PLDI 2009, Dublin, Ireland, 15–21 June 2009, pp. 121–133 (2009)

7. Hoefler, T., Dinan, J., Thakur, R., Barrett, B., Balaji, P., Gropp, W., Underwood, K.D.: Remote memory access programming in MPI-3. TOPC **2**(2), 9:1–9:26 (2015)
8. Kshemkalyani, A.D.: A framework for viewing atomic events in distributed computations. Theor. Comput. Sci. **196**(1–2), 45–70 (1998)
9. Kshemkalyani, A.D., Khokhar, A.A., Shen, M.: Encoded vector clock: using primes to characterize causality in distributed systems. In: Proceedings of the 19th International Conference on Distributed Computing and Networking, ICDCN 2018, Varanasi, India, 4–7 January 2018, pp. 12:1–12:8 (2018)
10. Kshemkalyani, A.D., Singhal, M.: Distributed Computing: Principles, Algorithms, and Systems. Cambridge University Press, Cambridge (2011)
11. Kulkarni, S.S., Demirbas, M., Madappa, D., Avva, B., Leone, M.: Logical physical clocks. In: Aguilera, M.K., Querzoni, L., Shapiro, M. (eds.) OPODIS 2014. LNCS, vol. 8878, pp. 17–32. Springer, Cham (2014). https://doi.org/10.1007/978-3-319-14472-6_2
12. Kulkarni, S.S., Vaidya, N.H.: Effectiveness of delaying timestamp computation. In: Proceedings of the ACM Symposium on Principles of Distributed Computing, PODC 2017, Washington, DC, USA, 25–27 July 2017, pp. 263–272 (2017)
13. Lamport, L.: Time, clocks, and the ordering of events in a distributed system. Commun. ACM **21**(7), 558–565 (1978)
14. Mattern, F.: Virtual time and global states of distributed systems. In: Proceedings of the Parallel and Distributed Algorithms Conference, pp. 215–226 (1988)
15. Meldal, S., Sankar, S., Vera, J.: Exploiting locality in maintaining potential causality. In: Proceedings of the Tenth Annual ACM Symposium on Principles of Distributed Computing, PODC 1991, pp. 231–239 (1991)
16. Pozniansky, E., Schuster, A.: MultiRace: efficient on-the-fly data race detection in multithreaded C++ programs. Concurr. Comput. Pract. Exp. **19**(3), 327–340 (2007)
17. Schwarz, R., Mattern, F.: Detecting causal relationships in distributed computations: in search of the holy grail. Distrib. Comput. **7**(3), 149–174 (1994)
18. Shen, M., Kshemkalyani, A.D., Khokhar, A.A.: Detecting unstable conjunctive locality-aware predicates in large-scale systems. In: IEEE 12th International Symposium on Parallel and Distributed Computing, ISPDC 2013, Bucharest, Romania, 27–30 June 2013, pp. 127–134 (2013)
19. Singhal, M., Kshemkalyani, A.D.: An efficient implementation of vector clocks. Inf. Process. Lett. **43**(1), 47–52 (1992)
20. Torres-Rojas, F.J., Ahamad, M.: Plausible clocks: constant size logical clocks for distributed systems. Distrib. Comput. **12**(4), 179–195 (1999)
21. Ward, P.A.S., Taylor, D.J.: A hierarchical cluster algorithm for dynamic, centralized timestamps. In: Proceedings of the 21st International Conference on Distributed Computing Systems (ICDCS 2001), Phoenix, Arizona, USA, 16–19 April 2001, pp. 585–593 (2001)
22. Yen, L., Huang, T.: Resetting vector clocks in distributed systems. J. Parallel Distrib. Comput. **43**(1), 15–20 (1997)

A Sensitivity Analysis on Weight Sum Method MCDM Approach for Product Recommendation

Gaurav Kumar and N. Parimala[✉]

School of Computer and Systems Sciences, JNU, New Delhi, India
gaurav37_scs@jnu.ac.in, dr.parimala.n@gmail.com

Abstract. The weights assigned to features, in an MCDM approach, play a crucial role in the computation of the ranking of alternatives. These weights can be varied which can result in a varied ranking of alternatives. In this paper, we present a method for conducting a sensitivity analysis of the weight assigned to decision criteria. In our earlier work, we have applied the Weighted Sum Method (WSM) multi criteria decision making approach to rank cameras. Using the results, a sensitivity analysis is performed in this paper. The weights are varied across thirty-four experiments. The result says that the minimum percentage of change required in the weight is 8.52% to alter the final ranking of alternatives.

Keywords: MCDM · Weighted Sum Method · Sensitivity analysis

1 Introduction

MCDM is a well-known strategic decision model that evaluates the ranking of alternatives in the presence of multiple, usually conflicting, decision criteria [1]. MCDM techniques structure the problems clearly and systematically. These characteristics enable decision makers to easily analyze the problem and scale it according to their requirements. In MCDM problems, assessment of data such as weight and type of decision attributes, and decision matrix play a crucial role in the evaluation of the ranking of alternatives. The results obtained by MCDM methods strongly depends on the actual value assigned to these data. Often input data in MCDM problems is imprecise and changeable. Due to uncertainty in the input data, the result obtained using MCDM methods are not stable. Therefore, it is an important step to conduct a sensitivity analysis on the input data in the applications of MCDM. The objective of sensitivity analysis is to determine the sensitivity of ranking of alternatives while varying the input data.

Dantzig [2] defines the sensitivity analysis as "a fundamental concept in the effective use and implementation of quantitative decision models, whose purpose is to assess the stability of an optimal solution under changes in the parameters." Insua [3] demonstrated that some reasonable variation in the input parameter might change the results of decision making problems. His conclusion justifies the necessity of sensitivity analysis in MCDM problems.

G. Fahrnberger et al. (Eds.): ICDCIT 2019, LNCS 11319, pp. 185–193, 2019.
https://doi.org/10.1007/978-3-030-05366-6_15

Numbers of methods have been proposed on sensitivity analysis in deterministic MCDM models. Barron and Schmidt [4] proposed two approaches which were, respectively, entropy-based and least-squares procedure based to accomplish sensitivity analysis. These procedures determine the closest set of weights for a given pair of alternatives that equates the ranking. One important finding of these approaches is that the weight of decision criteria do matter in the ranking of the alternatives.

Samson [5] defined a new approach that states "sensitivity analysis should be part of the decision analysis process, thinking in real time," i.e., the approach must be incorporated in every step of decision analysis. The weight assigned to the decision criteria in decision making modeling represents the genuine importance of the criteria.

Winston [6] stated that the criterion with the highest weight was the critical decision criteria. However, authors [7] argued that the highest weight criterion as the critical decision criteria may not always be true, and in some cases, the lowest weight criterion may represent the most critical decision criterion. If a decision maker can predetermine the criticality of each criterion, then decision maker can make a better decision about alternatives. Zavadskas et al. [8] proposed a multi-attribute utility analysis on SAW methods and concluded that only significant attributes relative to other attributes created an impact on the ranking of alternatives.

The main disadvantage of existing sensitivity analysis approach is that (i) it generally doesn't consider the combined effect of changes in the criteria weight, (ii) methods developed for specific MCDM algorithm can't be utilized in a broad range of MCDM applications, and (iii) the most critical criterion responsible for changing the ranking of alternatives is not defined.

Therefore, sensitivity analysis methods were incomplete and unsatisfactory. However, Hyde et al. [9] overcame some of the limitations of existing sensitivity analysis methods. But, these method requires the assignment of probability distribution to the criteria weights which might be difficult in some situations due to the paucity of data. Therefore, in this paper, we have formulated 34 different cases of changes in weight value to understand its effect on the ranking of alternatives. Thereafter, we determine what minimum percentage changes in the existing weight of the decision criterion affect the ranking of the alternatives. In this way, key weight and critical decision criteria are determined. We have conducted a sensitivity analysis of the results obtained in our previous experiments [10].

2   Sensitivity Analysis Methods

In our earlier work, we considered a product recommendation framework that consisted of M (=5) alternatives and N (=5) decision criteria. The objective of the product recommendation framework was to rank the alternatives based on their performance values obtained from the customers' reviews and to recommend the best product to the user. The proposed system used Weighted Sum Method (WSM) approach to compute the preference score of alternatives. The decision matrix for WSM consists of scores and an associated weight for the features. The reviews of customers were used as scores. The weights were the average number of customers who provided an opinion.

In this paper, we have performed the sensitivity analysis on the weights of decision criteria to analyze the ranking of alternatives. We have varied the weight as shown in Table 1, to determine its effect on the final ranking of alternatives. There are a total of thirty-four variations. The weights are varied by adding a value δ which varies between -0.45 and $+0.45$. We re-calculate the WSM score for each case to examine the ranking of alternatives.

Table 1. Thirty-four cases of variation in the weight

δ ($\pm0.01, \pm0.05, \pm0.1, \pm0.125, \pm0.15, \pm0.175, \pm0.2, \pm0.225, \pm0.25, \pm0.275, \pm0.3, \pm0.325,$
$\pm0.35, \pm0.375, \pm0.4, \pm0.425, \pm0.45$)

Then, the new weight of criterion (W_i^*) is computed as defined below. Here, W_i refers to the weight used in WSM and δ is as defined above.

$$W_i^* = |W_i \pm \delta|, \, for \, 1 \leq i \leq n \tag{1}$$

The weight is normalized using Eq. (2) so that the sum of the new weights is equal to 1.

$$W_i' = \frac{W_i^*}{\sum W_i^*} \, for \, 1 \leq i \leq n \tag{2}$$

2.1   Implementation of Sensitivity Analysis

We have re-produced the decision matrix and the ranking of alternatives as given [10] in Tables 2 and 3 respectively. Table 2 represents the decision matrix of five alternatives (digital camera) and five criteria where each cell contains the computed aggregate sentiment score of customers' opinion. Weights assigned to the decision criteria is also shown in Table 2.

The ranking of alternatives is shown in Table 3 after applying WSM approach. The current ranking of alternatives is **A2 > A3 > A4 > A1 > A5,** i.e., the most preferred digital camera is Camera (A2). Notice that in Table 2, C1 criterion (Picture) is considered to be the most important one according to its weight.

Now, we have performed a total of thirty-four experiments to compute the ranking of alternatives using the different weights as shown in Table 1. For each δ, new normalized weight (W_i') of each criterion C_i, is calculated using Eq. (2) and alternatives are ranked using WSM. The result is shown in Table 4.

Table 2. Decision matrix of digital camera

	Criterion				
	Picture (C1)	Cost (C2)	Zoom (C3)	Battery (C4)	Memory (C5)
Weight alternative	**0.5178**	**0.2566**	**0.1097**	**0.0792**	**0.0368**
Camera (A1)	0.5690	0.6002	0.6188	0.5000	0.4167
Camera (A2)	0.6781	0.6345	0.6440	0.5600	0.3251
Camera (A3)	0.6228	0.5801	0.6441	0.6394	0.4772
Camera (A4)	0.6124	0.6125	0.5495	0.5333	0.2992
Camera (A5)	0.5760	0.5662	0.3636	0.4972	0.2969

Table 3. Preference score of WSM approach

Alternative	Camera (A1)	Camera (A2)	Camera (A3)	Camera (A4)	Camera (A5)
Preference score	0.5714	0.6409	0.6103	0.5889	0.5338
Ranking	4	1	2	3	5

The criterion which requires the smallest change in the weight for changing the ranking of alternatives is said to be the most critical decision criterion. Now, to analyze the effect of weight on the ranking of alternatives, we adopted the approach of [7]. Here, the authors measure the change in weights in *absolute term* and *relative term*. These terms are explained below.

For example, let us consider the weight of two criteria C_1 and C_2 are defined as $W_1 = 0.20$ and $W_2 = 0.40$, respectively. Moreover, let's assume that when the new value of first weight becomes $W_1' = 0.24$, then the current ranking of alternatives changes. Similarly, when the new value of second weight becomes $W_2' = 0.48$, then the current ranking of alternatives changes. Minimum changes required in the weight for $C_1 = |W_1 - W_1'| = 0.04$, and for $C_2 = |W_2 - W_2'| = 0.08$ for changing the ranking of alternatives. The change for the first criterion C_1 is smaller than the second criterion C_2. Hence, C_1 criterion is the most critical decision criterion in terms of absolute measurement. When the relative term is considered for the measurement for the previous example, the relative change of weight for $C_1 = |W_1 - W_1'|$ *100/W_1 = 20.00, and for $C_2 = |W_2 - W_2'|*100/W_2 = 16.67$. Here, the result shows that relative change for the second criterion is smaller than the first criterion. Therefore, criterion C_2 is the most critical decision criteria in terms of relative measurement. The absolute change and relative change are defined in Eqs. (3) and (4) respectively below.

$$\delta_i' = |W_i' - W_i| \tag{3}$$

where δ_i' represents changes in absolute term, and n denotes the number of criteria.

$$\delta_i'' = (W_i' - W_i) \times \frac{100}{W_i}, \ for \ 1 \leq i \leq n. \tag{4}$$

where δ_i'' represents changes in relative term, and n denotes the number of criteria.

Table 4. Sensitivity analysis of the variation of weight change

Weight Change (δ)	New Normalized Weights of Criteria (W_i') (Existing Normalized Weight $W_1, W_2, \ldots W_5$) 0.5178 (W_1) 0.2566(W_2)0.1097 (W_3)0.0792(W_4) 0.0368 (W_5)					New Ranking of Alternatives (WSM Approach)
	C1(w_1')	C2(w_1')	C3(w_1')	C4(w_1')	C5(w_5')	
+0.01	0.5026	0.2539	0.1139	0.0849	0.0447	A2>A3>A4>A1>A5
-0.01	0.5344	0.2595	0.1049	0.0728	0.0282	A2>A3>A4>A1>A5
0.05	0.4542	0.2452	0.1277	0.1033	0.0694	A2>A3>A4>A1>A5
-0.05	0.6024	0.2660	0.0768	0.0376	0.0169	A2>A3>A4>A1>A5
0.1	0.411839	0.237717	0.139791	0.119459	0.091194	A2>A3>A4>A1>A5
-0.1	0.625355	0.234396	0.014519	0.031133	0.094597	A2>A3>A4>A1>A5
0.125	0.395545	0.234816	0.144422	0.125654	0.099563	A2>A3>A4>A1>A5
-0.125	0.583049	0.195339	0.02271	0.067983	0.130919	A2>A3>A4>A1>A5
0.15	**0.381578**	**0.23233**	**0.148392**	**0.130964**	**0.106737**	**A2>A3>A1>A4>A5**
-0.15	0.526406	0.152569	0.057679	0.101331	0.162015	A2>A3>A4>A1>A5
0.175	0.369474	0.230174	0.151832	0.135566	0.112954	A2>A3>A1>A4>A5
-0.175	**0.473677**	**0.112754**	**0.090231**	**0.132375**	**0.190963**	**A3>A2>A1>A4>A5**
0.2	0.358882	0.228289	0.154842	0.139593	0.118394	A2>A3>A1>A4>A5
-0.2	0.424469	0.075598	0.120609	0.161346	0.217978	A3>A2>A1>A4>A5
0.225	0.349536	0.226625	0.157498	0.143146	0.123194	A2>A3>A1>A4>A5
-0.225	0.378441	0.040843	0.149024	0.188445	0.243247	A3>A2>A1>A4>A5
0.25	0.341229	0.225146	0.15986	0.146305	0.127461	A2>A3>A1>A4>A5
-0.25	0.335295	0.008263	0.17566	0.213848	0.266934	A3>A2>A1>A4>A5
0.275	0.333796	0.223822	0.161972	0.149131	0.131279	A3>A2>A1>A4>A5
-0.275	0.282162	0.021383	0.192098	0.227542	0.276816	A3>A2>A1>A4>A5
0.3	0.327107	0.222631	0.163873	0.151674	0.134715	A3>A2>A1>A4>A5
-0.3	0.232817	0.046392	0.203421	0.236024	0.281347	A3>A2>A1>A4>A5
0.325	0.321054	0.221553	0.165594	0.153975	0.137823	A3>A2>A1>A4>A5
-0.325	0.190797	0.067689	0.213063	0.243246	0.285205	A3>A2>A1>A4>A5

0.35	0.315552	0.220574	0.167158	0.156067	0.140649	A3>A2>A1>A4>A5
-0.35	0.154583	0.086043	0.221373	0.24947	0.288531	A3>A2>A1>A4>A5
0.375	0.310528	0.219679	0.168585	0.157977	0.14323	A3>A2>A1>A4>A5
-0.375	0.12305	0.102025	0.228608	0.25489	0.291426	A3>A2>A1>A4>A5
0.4	0.305923	0.218859	0.169894	0.159728	0.145595	A3>A2>A1>A4>A5
-0.4	0.095346	0.116066	0.234966	0.259652	0.29397	A3>A2>A1>A4>A5
0.425	0.301686	0.218105	0.171099	0.161339	0.147771	A3>A2>A1>A4>A5
-0.425	0.070813	0.128501	0.240595	0.263869	0.296223	A3>A2>A1>A4>A5
0.45	0.297775	0.217409	0.17221	0.162826	0.14978	A3>A2>A1>A4>A5
-0.45	0.048935	0.139589	0.245615	0.267629	0.298232	A3>A2>A1>A4>A5

Having defined the minimum change, the next aspect to be considered is the manner in which analysis can be performed. The authors argue that the analysis can be performed in two ways-

(a) One may think of what minimum change in the weight of a criterion can change the rank of the best alternative.
(b) In the second case, one might think of the minimum changes that is required in the weight of a criterion that can lead to changes in the ranking of products which are below the product which is on top of the list.

Thus, a total of four possible terminologies can be defined to measure and analyze the ranking- (i) The minimum weight in terms of Absolute Top (AT) corresponds to minimum weight change (δ'), (ii) the minimum weight in terms of Absolute Any (AA) corresponds to minimum weight change $\left(\delta''\right)$, (iii) the minimum weight in terms of Relative Top (RT) corresponds to minimum weight change (δ'), (iv) the minimum weight in terms of Relative Any (RA) corresponds to minimum weight change $\left(\delta''\right)$.

The approach of computing absolute change might be ambiguous. For example, a small change 0.05 doesn't indicate any meaning until and unless one also specifies the original value. A change of 0.05 would represent very different meaning if the original value were 0.7 or 0.07. Therefore, it is more meaningful to use the relative change measurement in the decision making problem for criticality analysis. In this paper, we have emphasized relative measurement in the sensitivity analysis. The above-defined terminology of RA and RT is used to evaluate the most critical criterion. The positive sign represents the increase in the weight, and the negative sign represents the decrease in the weight before normalization.

2.2 Analysis of Ranking Using *Any* (RA)Alternative

According to the result obtained in Table 5, the minimum positive and negative change, δ, that is required for the weight W_i is 0.15 and -0.175, for i = 1, 2, 3, 4, and 5 to alter the ranks of A1 and A4. Positive sign represents the increase in the weight and Negative sign represents the decrease in the weight before normalization. Now, using Eq. (3), we have determined the most critical decision criterion.

Table 5. Most critical criterion evaluation for any two alternatives

		C1	C2	C3	C4	C5
Original Weight (W)		0.5178	0.2566	0.1097	0.0792	0.0368
Minimum Weight Change After Normal-ization	$\delta = 0.15$	0.381578	0.23233	0.148392	0.130964	0.106737
	$\delta = -0.175$	0.473677	0.112754	0.090231	0.132375	0.190963
		26.30	9.45	35.27	65.35	189.94
Relative Change (%)		8.52	56.05	17.74	67.14	418.92

If we increase the weight of the criteria by $\delta = 0.15$, then the ranking order of intermediate alternatives (A1 and A4) is changed. As a result, the smallest weight change in relative term is 9.45%, which corresponds to criterion C2 shown in Table 5. Therefore, the most critical criterion responsible for changing the ranking of any alternative (RA) is **C2,** when the current weight increases.

On the other hand, if we decrease the current weight of criteria by $\delta = -0.175$, then the ranking of intermediate alternatives (A1 and A4) is reversed as well as the ranking of the top alternative changes. As a result, the smallest weight change in relative term is 8.52%, which corresponds to Criterion C1. Therefore, the most critical criterion responsible for changing the ranking of any alternative (RA) is **C1,** when the current weight decreases.

2.3 Analysis of Ranking Using *Top* (RT)Alternative

According to the result obtained in Table 6, the minimum positive and negative change, δ, that is required for the weight W_i is 0.275 and -0.175, for i = 1, 2, 3, 4, and 5 to change the rank of top alternative A2. Now, using Eq. (2), we have determined the most critical criterion.

If we increase the weight of the criteria by $\delta = 0.275$, then the then the rank of top alternative (A2) is changed. As a result, the smallest weight change in relative term is 12.77%, which corresponds to criterion C2 shown in Table 6. Therefore, the most critical decision criterion responsible for changing the ranking of the top alternative (RT) is **C2**, when current weight increases.

On the other hand, if we decrease the current weight of criteria by $\delta = -0.175$, then the ranking of the top alternative (A2) is changed. As a result, the smallest weight change in relative term is 8.52%, which corresponds to criterion C1. Therefore, the most critical decision criterion responsible for changing the ranking of the top alternative (RT) is **C1**, when the current weight decreases.

Table 6. Most critical criterion evaluation for top alternative

		C1	C2	C3	C4	C5
Original Weight (W)		0.5178	0.2566	0.1097	0.0792	0.0368
Minimum Weight Change After Normalization	$\delta = 0.275$	0.333796	0.22382 2	0.16197 2	0.14913 1	0.13127 9
	$\delta = -0.175$	0.473677	0.11275 4	0.09023 1	0.13237 5	0.19096 3
Relative Change (%)		35.53	12.77	47.65	88.25	256.73
		8.52	56.05	17.74	67.14	418.92

3 Conclusion

In this paper, we have presented a sensitivity analysis method to understand the sensitivity of the weight of decision criteria on the ranking of alternatives. We have investigated the sensitivity of ranking of alternatives with varying weights of decision criteria. The experiment was performed using the result of the recommendation framework given in [10]. The results say that the minimum percentage of change in the weight required to change the final ranking of alternatives is 8.52%. The C_1 criterion is found to be the most critical decision criterion responsible for the changes in the ranking of alternatives.

Acknowledgment. One of the authors G. Kumar would like to thank Human Resource Development Group, Council of Scientific & Industrial Research (CSIR), Ministry of Science and Technology, Govt. of India for funding the fellowship (09/263(1001)/2013-EMR-1) throughout his research.

References

1. Pomerol, J.-C., Romero, S., Barba, R.: Multi-criterion Decision in Management: Principles and Practice, 1st edn. Kluwer Academic, Boston (2000)
2. Dantzig, G.B.: Linear Programming and Extensions. Princeton University Press, NJ (1963)
3. Rios Insua, D.: Sensitivity Analysis in Multi-objective Decision Making. Lecture Notes in Economics and Mathematical Systems. Springer, Germany (1990). https://doi.org/10.1007/978-3-642-51656-6
4. Barron, H., Schmidt, C.P.: Sensitivity analysis of additive multi-attribute value models. Oper. Res. **36**(1), 122–127 (1988)
5. Samson, D.: Managerial Decision Analysis. Irwin, Illinois (1988)
6. Winston, L.W.: Operations Research, 2nd edn. PWS-KentPublishing Co., Boston (1991)
7. Triantaphyllou, E., Sánchez, A.: A sensitivity analysis approach for some deterministic multi-criteria decision-making methods. Decis. Sci. **28**(1), 151–194 (1997)
8. Zavadskas, E.K., Turskis, Z., Dejus, T., Viteikiene, M.: Sensitivity analysis of a simple additive weight method. Int. J. Manag. Decis. Mak. **8**(5–6), 555–574 (2007)
9. Hyde, K.M., Maier, H.R., Colby, C.B.: Reliability-based approach to multi-criteria decision analysis for water resources. J. Water Resour. Plan. Manag. **130**(6), 429–438 (2004)
10. Gaurav, K., Parimala, N.: A weighted sum method MCDM approach for recommending product using sentiment analysis. Int. J. Bus. Inf. Syst. (2018, accepted)

Event Detection and Aspects in Twitter: A BoW Approach

Abhaya Kumar Pradhan$^{(\boxtimes)}$, Hrushikesha Mohanty$^{(\boxtimes)}$, and Rajendra Prasad Lal$^{(\boxtimes)}$

School of Computer and Information Sciences,
University of Hyderabad, Hyderabad, India
abhaya08csc007@gmail.com, h.mohanty@kiit.ac.in, rplcs@uohyd.ernet.in

Abstract. Tweets carry much information on the context people are tweeting. Finding the context of tweets or finding the event the tweets talk of is a hot research problem. Among several techniques like statistical, graph-based, machine learning, NLP based and many such techniques, bag-of-words technique is simple and elegant. This paper reports an event detection technique using clustering of bag-of-words of a given set of tweets. The method proposed follows three phase incremental clustering applying Jaccard similarity and Simpson similarity coefficients at different phases. Further, our method is capable of detecting different aspects of an event using a heuristic called EAAS (Event And Aspects Selection) based on tweeter participation, cluster quality and word commonality with the detected event. As a case study, we have used publicly available tweets, collected from Twitter streaming API with a keyword-based strategy. The obtained event detection result is presented and aspects of an event are evaluated in terms of precision and recall against human annotators. With concluding remark the paper presents its findings the possibility of enhancement in event detection as well as aspect finding capability.

Keywords: Event detection · Aspect detection
Social network mining · Microblog mining · Tweet processing

1 Introduction

Nowadays, Social Networking Services (SNS) like Twitter, Facebook, Google+, LinkedIn, and etc. have got increasing popularity and are able to attract a huge number of users form different parts of the globe. All these SNS provide a platform for users to report or opine on happenings around them, this enabling real-time dissemination of information to a large number of users across globe. Twitter launched in 15th July, 2006, has seen a tremendous growth in popularity, reaching approximately 313 million monthly active users[1] who make more than

---

[1] https://about.twitter.com/company.

G. Fahrnberger et al. (Eds.): ICDCIT 2019, LNCS 11319, pp. 194–211, 2019.
https://doi.org/10.1007/978-3-030-05366-6_16

500 million[2] tweets every day. Tweeters (i.e. Twitter users) post short messages with limited number of characters called tweets on starting from their daily life updates to interesting news and events happening around world. In order to take effective decisions on many domains, particularly affecting social interests, it is wishful to make use of information available from tweeters. For the purpose identifying events on processing tweets is a computational problem. There would be two different scenarios i.e. 1. finding events from repository of tweets, 2. identifying events in real-time from emerging tweets. Here we have taken up the problem of the first category.

Events are the things with contexts, space, time and people. Tweeters convey their observations on events; so it should be possible to identify events from tweets. Here we have assumed all the tweets are of single event but the event particulars are not known. Identifying events from tweets has problem that is typical to tweet processing [6]. The problem is due to i. short and at times cryptic, ii. advertisements, iii. meaningless communications etc. This makes detecting events from tweets challenging and inviting researchers attentions in exploring different techniques based on context similarity, syntactic analysis, geographical and temporal coherence.

In this work we have followed context similarity, to be specific word similarity and come up with an efficient bag-of-words based event detection model (BOWED) which detects events from accumulated tweets. Our approach is different than other bag-of-words based approaches is in the following ways.

1. Guided multi-phase clustering
2. Identifying aspects of an event

This paper introduces a new concept called 'aspect', that is a particular observation of an event. A direct relation between quality of cluster and precise event detection is a supportive observation found here through the experiments. Our proposed BOWED model pre-process tweets, cluster them incrementally and find probable event clusters. As we know tweets are noisy in nature and all of them are not informative. So all the output clusters are not event clusters. So we have proposed a heuristics called EAAS (Event And Aspects Selection) for choosing informative and meaningful clusters, out of them one will become an event others will be aspects of the detected event based on word commonality with the event. Efficiency of BOWED model is represented in terms of EDE (Event Detection Error) and F1 score for detected aspects.

The rest of this paper is organized as follows. Section 2 provides a brief review of literature. Section 3 introduces the architecture of the proposed BOWED model and various modules are explained subsequently. Section 4 presents experimental set-up, obtained results of our experiment and evaluation of BOWED model using our generated corpus. Finally Sect. 5 concludes with summary and further work.

---

[2] http://www.internetlivestats.com/twitter-statistics/.

2   Related Work

Event detection has gained focus of researchers long back. In early 2000, Topic Detection and Tracking (TDT) project [4], which intend to detect and track events from news streams. Two main approaches are found from literature, one is document-pivot approach and other one is feature-pivot approach [2]. The former aims to cluster documents related to the same events and then extract event based features from the document clusters [7,8,16–18]. The latter aims to first identify the representative features of the hidden event from the stream, which shows heavy bursty frequency patterns. Then events are detected by clustering these representative features [5,9,10,12,22,26]. our proposed BOWED model falls under the document-pivot method and specifically uses bag-of-words based technique, so in this section we are going to provide a brief literature survey for document-pivot techniques which are close our work.

Recently, event detection on twitter stream becomes a hot research topic. Unankard et al. [25] proposed a method for the early detection of emerging hotspot events in social network with location sensitivity. They have considered the message-mentioned locations for identifying the locations of the events. in this paper, they identified strong correlation between user locations and event locations in detecting the emerging events. In their approach tweets are represented as a term weight vector where each term weight will be calculate as the augmented normalized term frequency in the tweet and the cosine similarity used for calculating similarity between vectors while clustering the tweets. During the clustering for merging duplicate clusters they tried to find conceptual similarity between the clusters by utilizing the semantic information available from lexical resources such as WordNet [15]. In another work, Kumar et al. [13] investigated event detection in the context of real-time Twitter streams as observed in real-world crises. By looking at the challenging features of the Twitter stream such that the informal nature of text, high-volume and high-velocity, they proposed single-pass clustering and the compression distance to efficiently detect events in Twitter streams. They have modified entropy formula to compute User Diversity for each cluster and the clusters having the User Diversity score above a threshold become events. The intuition here is that a diverse user population lends credibility to the event and helps to filter out noise. In the above works researchers focused on only event detection but we are looking for events as well as aspects of events.

Rudra et al. proposed an approach to identify sub-events using a dependency parser to identify noun-verb pairs and generate summaries of big volume of messages around those events using an Integer Linear Programming (ILP) technique [20]. Srijith et al. proposed a probabilistic topic model based on hierarchical Dirichlet processes (HDP) for automatic sub-story detection. They showed, HDP performs hierarchical modelling of topics and is effective in modelling sub-stories by learning sub-topics associated with the common topic of the shared real-world [23]. In another work [21], a classification based framework is proposed for detection of traffic events in real-time. Geo-located tweets are classified into positive, negative, or neutral class using sentiment analysis and stress and relaxation strength detection is performed. Researchers have introduced a temporal approach to detect structural change of the social network that reflects an occurrence of an event using machine learning techniques [3].

3   Event Detection Model

3.1   Architecture of the BOWED Model

In this section we describe the complete architecture of our proposed BOWED model. The Model comprises of 3 key modules, as shown in Fig. 1. The modules are 1. Pre-processing module, 2. Clustering module and 3. Event and Aspect Identification module. Accumulated tweets from Twitter Streaming API are passed through each module one after another and get processed to extract event and aspects of event at the end. First, the Pre-processing module takes all the tweets and apply basic and standard pre-processing techniques for data curation and convert each tweet to it's bag-of-words form. Next, the Clustering module takes these bag-of-words and cluster them based on their content similarity in three different phases. Finally, in the Event and Aspect Identification module, our proposed EAAS heuristics is applied on the output clusters and event and it's associated aspects are identified.

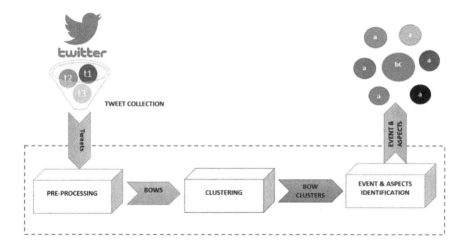

Fig. 1. Components of BOWED model

3.2   Pre-processing and Data Representation

As we have discussed earlier, tweets are short and often noisy. In order to improve the quality of input to our proposed model and the performance of the subsequent steps, the pre-processing module is designed to ignore common words that does not provide much information about events. The Twitter streaming API is used to download tweets and stored them in a JSON (JavaScript Object Notation) file. All the collected tweets are passed to this module. For each tweet Pre-Processing module removes irrelevant data e.g. removes the keyword RT (ReTweet) and the message-mentioned username such as @Abhaya, web address and non ASCII characters. Then "#" symbol is removed from hashtags and all the punctuations and stop words are removed. Then the tweets are converted into lower case and all the words are converted into their root form by applying NLTK WordNetLemmatizer[3]. At the end of pre-processing, all the input tweets are dismantled to sets of words, each called a bag-of-words for a given tweet. So a bag-of-words contain a set of root words of the words of a tweet undergone pre-processing. And these bag-of-words are given as input to the next module called Clustering module.

`Data Representation in the algorithm:`

Let's say a tweet is represented as "t" and each word in the tweet called "w"

$\langle t \rangle ::= \langle t_{id} \rangle \langle t_{bow} \rangle \langle t_{tr\_id} \rangle$

$\langle t_{bow} \rangle ::= \langle \{w\} \rangle$

$\langle c \rangle ::= \langle \langle c_{id} \rangle \langle \{t_{id}\} \rangle \rangle$

$\langle D \rangle ::= \langle \{t\} \rangle$

Where: "t_{id}" is the unique identifier of the tweet, "t_{tr_id}" is the unique identifier of the tweeter who has tweeted it and "t_{bow}" is the bag-of-word representation of the tweet. Similarly "c_{id}" is the unique identifier for the cluster.

3.3   Three Phase Based Clustering

Clustering module takes bag-of-words (i.e. the output of the Pre-processing module) as input and cluster them based on their content similarity. We have proposed a three phase based incremental clustering algorithm for clustering of tweet bag-of-words, extracted from tweets. As we are dealing with the retrospective event detection and not having any information or the zero knowledge about the events, clustering of tweets is the probable solution for detecting events. Among all clustering algorithms, incremental clustering algorithm based on the assumption that, it is possible to consider instances one at a time and assign them to the existing clusters, without significantly affecting the existing clusters. Only the cluster representations are stored in the main memory to alleviate the space limitations. The major advantage of using incremental clustering is, it is not necessary to store the entire dataset in the memory. Therefore the space and time requirements of incremental clustering algorithm is very small.

In the first phase of clustering, we form clusters of tweets (i.e. bag-of-words of each tweet), which are 100% matched with each other. Algorithm 1 is an incremental clustering, where each tweet bag-of-words is compared with all other tweet bag-of-words for exact match and all the 100% matched tweet bag-of-words are grouped into the same cluster called Seed Clusters (SC). It uses Jaccard

---

[3] http://www.nltk.org/_modules/nltk/stem/wordnet.html.

Similarity measure (see Eq. 1) for computing content similarity between tweet bag-of-words. All other tweets that are not matched with any other are grouped into a set called remaining tweets(*RBOW*). Both the SC and *RBOW* are passed for the second phase clustering.

Algorithm 1. Phase1_Clustering(D)

Input: D : All tweets
Output: SC : List of Seed Clusters, RBOW : List of Remaining Tweets
1 **begin**
2 $\quad$ $SC \longleftarrow NULL$;
3 $\quad$ $RBOW \longleftarrow D$;
4 $\quad$ **forall** $t \in RBOW$ **do**
5 $\quad\quad$ $c \longleftarrow Seed\_Cluster(t, RBOW)$; // Clustered using Jaccard
$\quad\quad\quad$ Similarity = 1.0, i.e. finding 100% matched clusters
6 $\quad\quad$ $ROBW \longleftarrow RBOW \ⓇR\ c$; // Remove cluster c from RBOW
7 $\quad\quad$ $SC \longleftarrow SC \ⓐ\ c$; // Append cluster c to SC
8 $\quad\quad$ $c \longleftarrow \phi$;
9 $\quad$ **end forall**
10 $\quad$ **return** $SC,\ RBOW$
11 **end**
12 Seed_Cluster(RBOW);
13 {
14 $c \longleftarrow \phi$;
15 $c \longleftarrow Create\_Cluster(t)$;
16 **forall** $t' \in RBOW$ **do**
17 $\quad$ $SIM \longleftarrow Jaccrad\_Sim(t \cdot t_{bow}, t' \cdot t_{bow})$;
18 $\quad$ **if** $SIM == 1.0$ **then**
19 $\quad\quad$ $c \longleftarrow c \ⓐ\ t'$;
20 $\quad$ **else**
21 $\quad\quad$ exit;
22 $\quad$ **end if**
23 $\quad$ **return** c
24 **end forall**
25 }

Now in the second phase of clustering, we are trying to add remaining tweets (RBOW) to the output Seed Clusters (SC) of Phase1_Clustering by reducing the similarity threshold. This provision is made considering different partial observations of different tweeters to the same event. So, similarity between two tweets could be partial. In order to take this reality into consideration, a further attempt on clustering is carried out to find out an association between a tweet to a cluster of tweets. Algorithm 2 also uses Jaccard Similarity measure to calculate similarity between tweet and cluster of tweets. Each cluster also has a centroid representation which is the set of most frequent terms in the cluster.

Algorithm 2. Phase2_Clustering(SC, RBOW)

Input: SC : List of Seed Clusters, RBOW : Remaining Tweets
Output: SP: List of Spread Clusters

1 **begin**
2     $SP \longleftarrow SC$;
3   **forall** $t \in RBOW$ **do**
4        $C_{bm} \longleftarrow \phi, SIM_{min} \longleftarrow 0.5$;
5        $C_{bm} \longleftarrow Best\_Matched\_Cluster(t, SP, SIM_{min})$;
6   **if** $C_{bm} == \phi$ **then**
7           $c \longleftarrow Create\_Cluster(t)$;
8           $SP \longleftarrow SP \text{Ⓐ} c$; // Append cluster c to SP
9   **else**
10          $SP \longleftarrow SP \text{Ⓡ} C_{bm}$; // Remove cluster C_{bm} from SP
11          $C_{bm} \longleftarrow C_{bm} \cup t$;
12          $SP \longleftarrow SP \text{Ⓐ} C_{bm}$; // Append cluster C_{bm} to SP
13   **end if**
14   **end forall**
15   **return** SP
16 **end**
17 $Best\_Matched\_Cluster(t, SP, SIM_{min})$;
18 {
19 **forall** $c \in SP$ **do**
20    $C_{bm} \longleftarrow \phi$;
21    $mft_c \longleftarrow Most\_Frequent\_Terms(c)$; // Finding most frequent terms set from cluster c
22    $c_{bow} \longleftarrow \cup_{\forall t \in c} t_{id} \cdot t_{bow}$; // Finding complete set of bag of words for each tweet in cluster c
23    $SIM \longleftarrow$
      $\frac{1}{2} * (Jaccard\_Sim(t \cdot t_{bow}, c_{bow}) + Jaccard\_Sim(t \cdot t_{bow}, mft_c))$;
24   **if** $SIM \geq SIM_{min}$ **then**
25       $SIM_{min} \longleftarrow SIM$;
26       $C_{bm} \longleftarrow c$; // Selected as Best Matched Cluster
27   **else**
28   Continue;
29   **end if**
30 **end forall**
31 **return** C_{bm};
32 }

A method called `Most_Frequent_Terms( )` find the set of most frequent terms in a cluster. It ranks all the terms present in a cluster based on their frequency and select top x terms, represent the set as centroid of the cluster. In experiment, x is the average tweet length of the dataset. The same procedure also followed in Algirthm 3.

Algorithm 3. Phase3_Clustering(SP)

Input: SP: List of Spread Clusters
Output: SP': List of Final Clusters
1 **begin**
2   **repeat**
3      $SP' \longleftarrow SP$;
4      $C_{bm} \longleftarrow \emptyset, SIM_{min} \longleftarrow 0.5$;
5   **forall** $c \in SP$ **do**
6        $C_{bm} \longleftarrow \phi, SIM_{min} \longleftarrow 0.5$;
7        $C_{bm} \longleftarrow Best\_Matched\_Cluster(c, SP, SIM_{min})$;
8   **if** $C_{bm}! = \phi$ **then**
9          $C_{bm} \longleftarrow C_{bm} \cup c$;
10          $SP \longleftarrow SP \, \textcircled{R} \, c$; // Remove cluster c from SP
11          $SP \longleftarrow SP \, \textcircled{A} \, C_{bm}$; // Append cluster C_{bm} to SP
12   **else**
13   Continue;
14   **end if**
15   **end forall**
16   **until** $SP \, \textcircled{E} \, SP'$;; // Until the clusters do not change
17
18   **return** SP'
19 **end**
20 $Best\_Matched\_Cluster(c, SP, SIM_{min})$;
21 {
22 $mft_c \longleftarrow Most\_Frequent\_Terms(c)$; // Finding most frequent terms set from cluster c
23 $c_{bow} \longleftarrow \cup_{\forall t \in c} t_{id} \cdot t_{bow}$; // Finding complete set of bag of words for each tweet in cluster c
24 **forall** $c' \in SP$ **do**
25    $C_{bm} \longleftarrow \phi$;
26    $mft_{c'} \longleftarrow Most\_Frequent\_Terms(c')$;
27    $c'_{bow} \longleftarrow \cup_{\forall t \in c'} t_{id} \cdot t_{bow}$;
28    $SIM \longleftarrow$ $\frac{1}{2} * (Simpson\_Sim(c_{bow}, c'_{bow}) + Jaccard\_Sim(mft_c, mft_{c'}))$;
29   **if** $SIM \geq SIM_{min}$ **then**
30      $SIM_{min} \longleftarrow SIM$;
31      $C_{bm} \longleftarrow c'$; // Selected as Best Matched Cluster
32   **else**
33   Continue;
34   **end if**
35 **end forall**
36 **return** C_{bm};
37 }

Now the content similarity between a tweet and a cluster computed as the normalized score of the Jaccard Similarity between the tweet bag-of-words and the cluster bag-of-words and Jaccard Similarity between the tweet bag-of-words and the cluster centroid. Here the intuition is to merge the tweet to the most appropriate Seed Cluster and improve the cluster quality. Phase2_Clustering starts with the minimum similarity threshold as 0.5, best matched clusters found based on the normalized similarity score and tweets are merged with it's best matched cluster. If the tweet doesn't match with any of the cluster, it creates a new cluster and become the first element of the newly created cluster. The output clusters of the Pahse2_Clustering called Spread Clusters (SP), will be the input for the next phase of clustering to find Final Clusters (SP').

$$Jaccard\ Similarity\ Coefficient = \frac{|\ t \cdot t_{bow} \cap t' \cdot t_{bow}\ |}{|\ t \cdot t_{bow} \cup t' \cdot t_{bow}\ |} \tag{1}$$

$$Simpson\ Similarity\ Coefficient = \frac{|\ t \cdot t_{bow} \cap t' \cdot t_{bow}\ |}{min(|\ t \cdot t_{bow}\ |, |\ t' \cdot t_{bow}\ |)} \tag{2}$$

On performing the second phase clustering each cluster contents may go in content changes. At a stage if a large number tweets get associated to some clusters then the resultant clusters may not remain absolutely different. This inclusion in second phase may give rise to some similarity among clusters. So, the need arises to test inter cluster similarity. For the purpose Simpson Similarity metric is used in Algorithm 3. Considering liberal austerity in reporting an event we have considered 0.5 as the minimum similarity between two clusters to consider those reporting the same event. In case of one cluster having the same equality with more than one clusters, we plan to consider other heuristics like cluster size, number of unique tweeters etc. into consideration to break the ties. Also a reasoning in choosing a threshold value can be worked out considering application domain into consideration, like tweeters of a particular location having good access to observe an event do have strong similarity among their tweets and so of respective clusters.

Finally, in the third phase of clustering, we are trying find out inter cluster similarity and the clusters having similarity score above the threshold are merged together. In this phase we are using Simpson Similarity metric (see Eq. 2) with minimum similarity score 0.5. Phase3_Clustering will provide Final Clusters (SP') as output. Like Phase2_Clustering, the content similarity between two clusters computed as the normalized score of the Simpson Similarity between the two clusters bag-of-words and Jaccard Similarity between the cluster centroids.

We have done an extensive experiment on different datasets with four different binary similarity measures (i.e. Jaccard similarity, Dice similarity, Simpson similarity, Braun & Banquet similarity) and combinations of them in different phase of the clustering algorithm. We found combination of Jaccard similarity and Simpson similarity yields good quality and meaningful clusters. The well known internal measure Silhouette Coefficient (see Sect. 3.4) is used to evaluate cluster quality. We consider estimation of best similarity measure and similarity threshold in an another study.

Now the outputs of Clustering module (SP') passed to the Event and Aspect Identification module for further processing.

3.4   Event and Aspect Identification

After Clustering of the tweet bag-of-words, we have to choose which cluster represents real-world and meaningful event. So we thought of two main characteristics for a cluster to be selected as an event. One is the quality of the cluster and other one is the number of users contributed tweets to the cluster.

Event And Aspects Selection (EAAS) is proposed to select event cluster and aspect clusters. We have used Silhouette Coefficient as a measure to check cluster quality. EASS is looking for the cluster which having highest Silhouette Coefficient and highest witness ratio and select that cluster as event. The intuition is, there are some tweeters who totally report on the event and some retweet the same confirming the event. Now a quality cluster with highest Silhouette Coefficient (SLC) and having largest number of tweeters participation makes a base description of the event. Such a cluster called a base cluster (bc) and detected as an event. In other words, the quality cluster which gained the focus of a large number of tweeters, become the core discussion or the base discussion for the event. And we call this as the base cluster. Algorithm 4 trying to find the such base cluster among the output clusters of Clustering module. It computes SLC and witness Ratio (WR) for each cluster and find the aggregate score for each cluster and choose the cluster having highest score as the base cluster. The set of unique words of the cluster will be displayed as event representation.

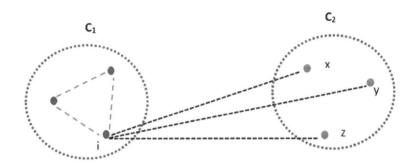

Fig. 2. Silhouette coefficient calculation for object "i"

Silhouette Coefficient: After clustering of tweet bag-of-words, we need to check the quality of clusters, in other words how well the clusters are formed. So we have used the well known internal measure Silhouette Coefficient [19, 24] to compute cluster quality. Internal measures are used to measure the goodness of a clustering structure without respect to external information. Silhouette Coefficient combine ideas of both cohesion and separation, for individual points, as well as clusters (see Fig. 2). Cluster cohesion says, how closely related objects are in a cluster and cluster separation deals, how distinct or well separated a cluster is from other clusters. For a object i in a cluster the Silhouette Coefficient can be calculated as follows:

1. For the ith object, calculate its average distance to all other objects in its cluster. Call the value a_i
2. For the ith object and any cluster not containing the object, calculate the object's average distance to all other objects in the given cluster. Find the minimum of such value with respect to all clusters. Call this value b_i
3. For the ith object, the Silhouette Coefficient is $s_i = \frac{b_i - a_i}{max(a_i, b_i)}$

Average Silhouette Coefficient Score for a cluster "C" $= \frac{1}{n} \sum_{i=1}^{n} s_i$, where: $|C| = n$. Typically, s_i vary between -1 and 1. The coefficient value closer to 1 is better cluster.

Algorithm 4. Selection_of_BC(SP', D)

Input: SP' : List of Final Clusters, D : Dataset of tweet bag_of_words
Output: bc: Base Cluster

1 **begin**
2 | $SLC \longleftarrow Calulate\_Silhouette\_Coeff(SP')$;
3 | $N \longleftarrow Unique\_Tweeters(D)$;
4 | Take **Any** $c \in SP'$;
5 | $WR_c \longleftarrow \frac{Unique\_Tweeters(c)}{N}$; // WR_c : Witness Ratio of cluster "c"
6 | $AW_c \longleftarrow w_1 \times SLC_c + w_2 \times WR_c$; // AW_c : Aggregate Weight of cluster "c"
7 | **foreach** $c' \in SP'$ **do**
8 | | $AW_{c'} \longleftarrow w_1 \times SLC_{c'} + w_2 \times WR_{c'}$;
9 | | **if** $CW_{c'} \geq CW_c$ **then**
10 | | | $bc \longleftarrow c'$; // Selecting the cluster having high SLC and high WR as Base Cluster (EAAS is applied for event selection)
11 | | **else**
12 | | | Continue;
13 | | **end if**
14 | **end foreach**
15 | **return** bc
16 **end**

Aspects of Event: After selecting base cluster (bc), **EAAS** finds the aspect clusters which are having strong association with the base cluster. Now among the output clusters the cluster, which having highest SLC and highest WR become the base cluster. Other clusters with good ($\alpha \geq 0.5$) Silhouette Coefficient and appreciable number of tweeter participation in each of the cluster are the Candidate Clusters (QC) to be considered for association with the base cluster (bc). The percentage of tweeters of base cluster with respect to total number of tweeters in the dataset and the same percentage of tweeters of the base cluster, is a criterion for selecting Candidate Clusters. Then these selected candidate clusters are checked for word commonality with the base cluster. The intuition here is, some tweeters tend to see other aspects of an event that a base cluster represents and the aspects are the particular observations made by tweeters other than the central observation i.e. the event. The relation with the base cluster is determined by word commonality i.e. reference of a word or some words of a base cluster in these candidate clusters.

Algorithm 5. Selection_of_QC(SP', bc)

Input: SP' : List of Final Clusters, bc : Base Cluster
Output: QC : Candidate Clusters considered for the association with bc
1 **begin**
2     $QC \longleftarrow NULL$;
3     $N \longleftarrow Unique\_Tweeters(D)$;
4     $p \longleftarrow \frac{n}{N} \times 100$;
5     $q \longleftarrow n \times p$;
6   **foreach** $c \in \{SP' - bc\}$ **do**
7        $TP_c \longleftarrow Unique\_Tweeters(c)$; // TP_c : Tweeter Participation in cluster "c"
8   **if** $TP_c \geq q$ **and** $SLC_c \geq \alpha$ **then** ; // $\alpha = 0.5$ (EAAS is applied for aspects selection)
9
10           $QC \longleftarrow Add(QC, c)$
11   **else**
12   Continue;
13   **end if**
14   **end foreach**
15   **return** QC
16 **end**

Word-ClusterIDs Inverted Index: Algorithm 5 find the set of Candidate Clusters(QC), which will be checked for the word commonality with the base cluster (bc). To find word commonality Algorithm 6 utilizes a Word-ClusterIDs inverted index(T) to provide a low computational cost solution for finding clusters having word commonality with the base cluster. Each entry in the Word-ClusterIDs inverted index (see Fig. 3) contains a word from the bag-of-words of the bc and a set of Candidate Cluster IDs, in which the word appeared. First Phase of Apriori algorithm [1] can be applied on the Word-ClusterIDs inverted index to find the set of clusters which are having word commonality with the base cluster, called Aspect Clusters (QC'). Algorithm 6 presents the detailed procedure for finding QC'.

Now the set difference between the bag-of-words of the base cluster and the clusters belongs to QC', become aspects of the event and displayed as aspects (see Algorithm 7).

Algorithm 6. Selection_of_QC'(QC, bc)

Input: QC : Candidate Clusters, bc : Base Cluster
Output: QC' : Aspect Clusters

1 **begin**
2    $T \longleftarrow$ **empty;** // Initialize Word-ClusterIDs Inverted Index T
3   **foreach** $w \in bc$ **do ;** // For each word in Base Cluster
4
5   **find all** $q_c \in QC$ **s.t.** $|w \cap q_c| = 1$; // Finding all such clusters from QC, which are having word "w" of bc
6      $T \longleftarrow \langle w, \{ClusterIDs\} \rangle$; // Add an entry to T for word "w"
7   **end foreach**
8    $F \longleftarrow Frequency\_of\_CIDs(T)$; // First step of Apriori Algorithm for Frequent itemset generation
9   **foreach** $q_c \in F$ **do**
10   **if** $Frequency(q_c) > 1$ **then**
11        $QC' \longleftarrow Add(QC', q_c)$
12   **else**
13   **Continue;**
14   **end if**
15   **end foreach**
16   **return** QC'
17 **end**

Algorithm 7. Aspect_Detection(QC', bc)

Input: QC' : Aspect Clusters, bc : Base Cluster
Output: A : List of Aspects

1 **begin**
2    $A \longleftarrow NULL$;
3   **foreach** $q'_c \in QC'$ **do**
4      $a_c \longleftarrow Set\_Diff(q'_c, bc)$; // Set difference of the BoWs of bc and q'_c
5      $A \longleftarrow Add(A, a_c)$
6   **end foreach**
7   **return** A
8 **end**

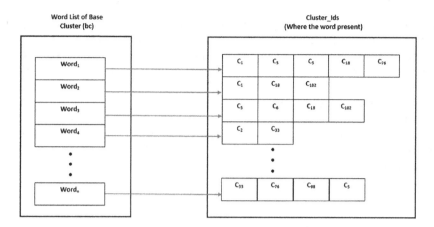

Fig. 3. Word-ClusterIDs inverted index

4   Experiment Results and Evaluation

Dataset

The efficacy of the proposed event detection algorithm has been studied by carrying out experiment on three sets of data collected from Twitter using Twitter streaming API. In absence of standard dataset, we have chosen to collect data (tweets written in English) from Twitter itself with keyword-based strategy on specific events. Table 1 provides the event names, the number of tweets appeared during occurrence of those events, in a time window, and the number of unique tweeters contributed for that event. As we have told earlier, the proposed algorithm is to find an event from a tweet repository. It is further assumed that a repository is of single event but the event descriptions are not known. The proposed technique aims to provide event description.

Table 1. Dataset description

Event name	No of tweets	No of unique tweeters
GST	5898	3949
Kulbhushan Jadav	24667	13718
NARI	1653	1019

Evaluation Metrics

In order to verify correctness of the proposed technique, we have resorted to a standard technique as followed by other researchers [11]. We have used three human annotators (Ph.D. students of Mass Communication, Sociology and Computer Science) to judge whether the detected events and aspects of the events are meaningful and valid. They have asked to read the keywords describing the event and aspects detected by our BOWED model and assign a rate to each description independently. If the annotators are agreed that the description is meaningful and related to the real world event(in the case of events) or an aspect of the detected event (in case of aspects), they rate it 1 or 0 in any other cases. The inter-annotator agreement measured with Cohen's kappa [14], is $\kappa \simeq 0.56$, showing a moderate agreement among annotators. As this proposed approach is to detect single event and associated aspects of it, we have calculated Event Detection Error(EDE) for each event in the dataset. EDE value is 0, if BOWED able to detect event successfully, otherwise is 1.

We have calculated precision, recall and F1 score for the evaluation of detected aspects of each event. Precision is the ratio of the number of detected aspects that two or more annotators have rated 1 called k', to the total number of detected aspects, k. Recall is defined as the fraction of k' to the number of Candidate Clusters (QC) selected by Algorithm 5 for which two or more annotator rated 1 called k" (i.e. these are the actual aspects should have been detected by the model but missed in the process of word commonality with the base cluster). The F1 score formula is given in Eq. 5. Table 2 shows the EDE, P, R and F1 score for each event. For illustration purpose, we present example of detected event and aspects of Kulbhushan Jadav dataset in Table 3.

$$Precision = \frac{k'}{k} \tag{3}$$

$$Recall = \frac{k'}{k''} \tag{4}$$

$$F1score = \frac{2 * Precision * Recall}{Precision + Recall} \tag{5}$$

Table 2. Results of BOWED model

Event name	EDE	Precision %	Recall %	F1 score %
GST	0	47.368	90	62.068
Kulbhushan Jadav	0	76.923	71.429	74.074
NARI	0	71.428	45.454	55.555

Observations

Our proposed BOWED model is experimented with three different datasets of different sizes and the experimental results are presented in Table 2. As our proposed model is to detect single events, experimental results shows, it detects events successfully for all the three datasets with 100% accuracy. The F1 score shows, BOWED is capable enough to detect aspects for each of the event. If we closely observe that more discussed event "Kulbhushan Jadav" has high F1 score (74.07%), whereas less discussed event "NARI" has low F1 score (55.55%)

Table 3. Detected event and aspects by BOWED for Kulbhushan Jadav dataset

ID	Detected event	Description
bc	'fabricate', 'story', 'kulbhushanjhadav', 'retract', 'do', 'damage', 'toast', 'pakista','pak'	Pakistan might be fabricating the entire story of alleged Indian spy Kulbhushan Jadhav's trial

ID	Detected aspects	Description
a_1	'treacherous', 'journalism', 'true', 'could', 'cost', 'kulbhushanjadhav', 'life', 'least', 'freedom'	Treacherous journalism could cost Kulbhushan Jadhav's life and his freedom
a_2	'basically', 'quint', 'want', 'kulbhushanjadhav', 'kill', 'modi', 'govt', 'look', 'bad', 'language', 'use', 'make', 'one', 'thing', 'clear', 'pakistan', 'nda", 'ppl', 'put', 'book'	The Quint wants Kulbhushan Jadhav killed so that Modi Govt. looks bad
a_3	'another', 'fake', 'video', 'pakistan', 'kulbhushan', 'jadhav', 'jail', '2', 'years', 'amponly', 'proof', 'theyve', 'con', 'confession', 'v', 'put', 'video', 'claim', 'hes'	Kulbhushan Jadav's confession Fake video released by Pakistan
a_4	'1st', 'abduction', 'bindi', 'shoesmangalsutra', 'doctor', 'video', 'cdr', 'kulbhushanjadhav', 'prove', 'pak', 'rogueinh','ro'	Jadhav's wife was asked to remove her 'bindi', 'mangal sutra' and shoes
a_5	'urge', 'fellows', 'indians', 'world', 'believe', 'do', 'great', 'disservice', 'nation'	I urge my fellows Indians all over the world who believe that @TheQuint has done a great disservice to the Nation
a_6	'media', 'thugs', 'publish', 'cookedup', 'stories', 'evidence', 'kulbhushanjadhav', 'pakistan', 'execut'	Media thugs are publishing cooked-up stories with cooked-up evidences against Kulbhushan Jadhav
a_7	'better', 'thousands', 'enemies', 'outside', 'country', 'one', 'single', 'enemy', 'inside', 'within', 'bt', 'hv', 'many', 'mor', 'kulbhushanjadhav', 'pain', 'liberals', 'get'	Better to Have Thousands Of Enemies Outside The Country Than To Have One Single Enemy Inside it
a_8	'statement', 'kulbhushanjadhav', 'meet', 'wife', 'mother', 'give', 'shut', 'call', 'indian', 'propaganda', 'rj', 'ameerabbas84', 'pr', 'propag'	Statement of Kulbhushan Jadhav after meeting with his wife and mother. He gives shut up call to Indian propaganda
a_9	'much', 'efforts', 'support', 'kulbhushanjadhav', 'morons', 'quint', 'run', 'fake', 'news', 'regrading', 'hence', 'block', 'h',	'The Quint' named Kulbhushan Jadhav an Indian spy and made a fake story
a_{10}	'outrage', 'quint', 'direct', 'people', 'directly', 'responsible', 'kulbhushanjadhav', 'article', 'must', 'al',	All Outrage against The Quint was directed at people directly responsible for Kulbhushan Jadhav article

which indicates that events which are having high popularity among tweeters, has discussed thoroughly and all the particular observations made by tweeters are detected successfully.

5 Conclusion

In this paper, we proposed BOWED, a bag-of-words based approach for event detection and finding aspects of an event in Twitter. For retrospective event detection a three phase based incremental clustering algorithm proposed for grouping similar tweets efficiently and explained each phase in detail. We also proposed a heuristics EAAS (Event And Aspects Selection) based on cluster quality, tweeter participation and word commonality for detecting event cluster and aspect clusters. Empirical analysis shows the efficiency of BOWED in detecting single event and it's aspects. As part of our future work, we intend to extend this technique for detecting multi events and their aspects. We are planning to incorporate spatio-temporal information for detecting more specific events in more precised location and time. Further, the proposed model can be converted to online version for precessing streaming tweets.

References

1. Agrawal, R., Srikant, R.: Fast algorithms for mining association rules. In: Proceedings of 20th International Conference on VLDB, pp. 487–499 (1994)
2. Aiello, L.M., et al.: Sensing trending topics in Twitter. IEEE Trans. Multimedia **15**(6), 1268–1282 (2013). https://doi.org/10.1109/TMM.2013.2265080
3. Aldhaheri, A., Lee, J.: Event detection on large social media using temporal analysis. In: 2017 IEEE 7th Annual Computing and Communication Workshop and Conference (CCWC), pp. 1–6, January 2017. https://doi.org/10.1109/CCWC.2017.7868467
4. Allan, J., Lavrenko, V., Jin, H.: First story detection in TDT is hard. In: Proceedings of the Ninth International Conference on Information and Knowledge Management, CIKM 2000, pp. 374–381. ACM, New York (2000). https://doi.org/10.1145/354756.354843
5. Alsaedi, N., Burnap, P., Rana, O.: Can we predict a riot? Disruptive event detection using Twitter. ACM Trans. Internet Technol. **17**(2), 18:1–18:26 (2017). https://doi.org/10.1145/2996183
6. Atefeh, F., Khreich, W.: A survey of techniques for event detection in twitter. Comput. Intell. **31**(1), 132–164 (2015). https://doi.org/10.1111/coin.12017
7. Becker, H., Naaman, M., Gravano, L.: Beyond trending topics: Real-world event identification on Twitter (2011). https://www.aaai.org/ocs/index.php/ICWSM/ICWSM11/paper/view/2745
8. Brants, T., Chen, F., Farahat, A.: A system for new event detection. In: Proceedings of the 26th Annual International ACM SIGIR Conference on Research and Development in Information Retrieval, SIGIR 2003, pp. 330–337. ACM, New York (2003). https://doi.org/10.1145/860435.860495
9. Cataldi, M., Di Caro, L., Schifanella, C.: Emerging topic detection on Twitter based on temporal and social terms evaluation. In: Proceedings of the Tenth International Workshop on Multimedia Data Mining, MDMKDD 2010, pp. 4:1–4:10. ACM, New York (2010). https://doi.org/10.1145/1814245.1814249
10. Fung, G.P.C., Yu, J.X., Yu, P.S., Lu, H.: Parameter free bursty events detection in text streams. In: Proceedings of the 31st International Conference on Very Large Data Bases, VLDB 2005, pp. 181–192. VLDB Endowment (2005). http://dl.acm.org/citation.cfm?id=1083592.1083616
11. Guille, A., Favre, C.: Event detection, tracking, and visualization in twitter: a mention-anomaly-based approach. Soc. Netw. Anal. Mining **5**(1), 18 (2015). https://doi.org/10.1007/s13278-015-0258-0
12. Kleinberg, J.: Bursty and hierarchical structure in streams. In: Proceedings of the Eighth ACM SIGKDD International Conference on Knowledge Discovery and Data Mining, KDD 2002, pp. 91–101. ACM, New York (2002). https://doi.org/10.1145/775047.775061
13. Kumar, S., Liu, H., Mehta, S., Subramaniam, L.V.: Exploring a scalable solution to identifying events in noisy twitter streams. In: Proceedings of the 2015 IEEE/ACM International Conference on Advances in Social Networks Analysis and Mining 2015, ASONAM 2015, pp. 496–499. ACM, New York (2015). https://doi.org/10.1145/2808797.2809389

14. Landis, J., Koch, G.: The measurement of observer agreement for categorical data. Biometrics **33**(1), 159–174 (1977). https://doi.org/10.2307/2529310

15. Miller, G.A.: Wordnet: a lexical database for English. Commun. ACM **38**(11), 39–41 (1995). https://doi.org/10.1145/219717.219748

16. O'Connor, B.T., Krieger, M., Ahn, D.: TweetMotif: exploratory search and topic summarization for Twitter. In: ICWSM (2010)

17. Petrović, S., Osborne, M., Lavrenko, V.: Streaming first story detection with application to Twitter. In: Human Language Technologies: The 2010 Annual Conference of the North American Chapter of the Association for Computational Linguistics, HLT 2010, pp. 181–189. Association for Computational Linguistics, Stroudsburg (2010). http://dl.acm.org/citation.cfm?id=1857999.1858020

18. Phuvipadawat, S., Murata, T.: Breaking news detection and tracking in Twitter. In: 2010 IEEE/WIC/ACM International Conference on Web Intelligence and Intelligent Agent Technology, vol. 3, pp. 120–123, August 2010. https://doi.org/10.1109/WI-IAT.2010.205

19. Rousseeuw, P.J.: Silhouettes: a graphical aid to the interpretation and validation of cluster analysis. J. Comput. Appl. Math. **20**, 53–65 (1987). https://doi.org/10.1016/0377-0427(87)90125-7, http://www.sciencedirect.com/science/article/pii/0377042787901257

20. Rudra, K., Goyal, P., Ganguly, N., Mitra, P., Imran, M.: Identifying sub-events and summarizing disaster-related information from microblogs. In: The 41st International ACM SIGIR Conference on Research & #38; Development in Information Retrieval, SIGIR 2018, pp. 265–274. ACM, New York (2018). https://doi.org/10.1145/3209978.3210030

21. Salas, A., Georgakis, P., Nwagboso, C., Ammari, A., Petalas, I.: Traffic event detection framework using social media. In: 2017 IEEE International Conference on Smart Grid and Smart Cities (ICSGSC), pp. 303–307, July 2017. https://doi.org/10.1109/ICSGSC.2017.8038595

22. Sayyadi, H., Hurst, M., Maykov, A.: Event detection and tracking in social streams (2009). https://www.aaai.org/ocs/index.php/ICWSM/09/paper/view/170

23. Srijith, P., Hepple, M., Bontcheva, K., Preotiuc-Pietro, D.: Sub-story detection in Twitter with hierarchical dirichlet processes. Inf. Process. Manag. **53**(4), 989–1003 (2017). https://doi.org/10.1016/j.ipm.2016.10.004

24. Tan, P.N., Steinbach, M., Kumar, V.: Introduction to Data Mining, 1st edn. Addison-Wesley Longman Publishing Co. Inc., Boston (2005)

25. Unankard, S., Li, X., Sharaf, M.A.: Emerging event detection in social networks with location sensitivity. World Wide Web **18**(5), 1393–1417 (2015). https://doi.org/10.1007/s11280-014-0291-3

26. Xie, W., Zhu, F., Jiang, J., Lim, E.P., Wang, K.: TopicSketch: real-time bursty topic detection from Twitter. IEEE Trans. Knowl. Data Eng. **28**(8), 2216–2229 (2016). https://doi.org/10.1109/TKDE.2016.2556661

A New Automatic Multi-document Text Summarization using Topic Modeling

Rajendra Kumar Roul[1(✉)], Samarth Mehrotra[2], Yash Pungaliya[2],
and Jajati Keshari Sahoo[3]

[1] Department of Computer Science, Thapar Institute of Engineering and Technology,
Patiala 147004, Punjab, India
`raj.roul@thapar.edu`
[2] Department of Computer Science, BITS-Pilani, K. K. Birla Goa Campus,
Zuarinagar, Pilani 403726, Goa, India
`samarth.1397@gmail.com, yashpungaliya@gmail.com`
[3] Department of Mathematics, BITS-Pilani, K. K. Birla Goa Campus, Zuarinagar,
Pilani 403726, Goa, India
`jksahoo@goa.bits-pilani.ac.in`

Abstract. This paper proposes a novel methodology to generate an
extractive text summary from a corpus of documents. Unlike most existing methods, our approach is designed in such a way that the final generated summary covers all the important topics from a corpus of documents. We propose a heuristic method which uses the Latent Dirichlet
Allocation technique to identify the optimum number of independent
topics present in the corpus. Some of the sentences are identified as the
important sentences from each independent topic using a set of word
and sentence level features. In order to ensure that the final summary is
coherent, we suggest a novel technique to reorder the sentences based on
sentence similarity. The use of topic modeling ensures that all the important content from the corpus of documents is captured in the extracted
summary which in turn strengthen the summary. Experimental results
show that the proposed approach is promising.

Keywords: Extractive · Multi-document · ROUGE · Summarization
Topic modeling

1 Introduction

Generating a brief summary from a large amount of textual data is an important research area in the field of computer science. A summary can be defined
as 'some brief statements that present the main aspects of a subject (i.e., a corpus of documents) in a concise manner' [1]. The tools and techniques used for
text summarization help to convert the raw textual information into a summary
without any human intervention. Based on the nature of the summary generated from text documents, summarization can be of two types: *abstractive* and

© Springer Nature Switzerland AG 2019
G. Fahrnberger et al. (Eds.): ICDCIT 2019, LNCS 11319, pp. 212–221, 2019.
https://doi.org/10.1007/978-3-030-05366-6_17

extractive [2]. Abstractive summaries are generated by interpreting the raw text and generating the same information in a different and concise form. Modern day abstractive summarization systems uses complex neural network based architectures such as RNNs and LSTMs. On the other hand, extractive summarization is implemented by identifying the important sections of the text, processing and combining them to form a meaningful summary [3]. Text summarization can be further divided into two categories: *single* and *multi-text* summarization. In single text summarization, text is summarized from one document where as Multi-document text summarization systems are able to generate reports that are rich in important information, and concisely present varying views that span multiple documents. Many researchers have worked in the field of text summarization [4–7], however research work in the domain of multi-document text summarization using topic modeling is limited.

Aiming in this direction, the paper proposes a four-step procedure to generate a concise and useful summary from a given corpus. In the first step, Latent Dirichlet Allocation (LDA) is used to select only a subset of sentences per topic. The second step identifies fifteen important features and accordingly compute the score for each sentence. In the third step, an aggregate score for each sentence is calculated using those fifteen features. This aggregate score is used to select the important sentences which are to be the part of the summary. In the fourth and final step, the important sentences are ordered to form a coherent summary. Empirical results on different DUC datasets justify the suitability and importance of the proposed approach for multi-document text summarization.

Rest of the paper is organized as follows: Sect. 2 describes the detailed methodology to summarize the corpus of documents. Results and analysis of the experimentation have been carried out in Sect. 3, which is followed by the conclusion of the work in Sect. 4.

2   Proposed Approach

Consider a corpus C of documents $d = \{d_1, d_2, \cdots, d_i\}$. Initially, all these documents are merged into a large document called D_{large}. Then D_{large} is split into n sentences, i.e., $\{s_1, s_2, \cdots, s_n\}$. The proposed approach reduces these n sentences to n/X (i.e., length of the final summary), where X is a user defined value and greater than 2^1. The experiments are carried out by using $X = 13^2$, as n is a reasonably large value in most collection of documents in the DUC dataset. Final summary is generated using the following steps.

1. *LDA is used to reduce number of sentences from n to 2n/X:*
   Assume that the set of sentences $\{s_1, s_2, \cdots, s_n\}$ consists of k independent topics. Although the problem of identification of the exact number of topics in a corpus is an unsolved problem, we propose a heuristic method which help us to decide the value of k. This heuristic method is discussed later in this

---

[1] Since reduction is being performed, $2/X < 1$.
[2] Experimental results generate a good summary for $X = 13$.

Table 1. Sentence-topic matrix.

	$Topic_1$	$Topic_2$	$Topic_3$	...	$Topic_k$
s_1	w_{11}	w_{12}	w_{13}	...	w_{1k}
s_2	w_{21}	w_{22}	w_{23}	...	w_{2k}
s_3	w_{31}	w_{32}	w_{33}	...	w_{3k}
$\vdots$	$\vdots$	$\vdots$	$\vdots$	$\ddots$	$\vdots$
s_n	w_{n1}	w_{n2}	w_{n3}	...	w_{nk}

Algorithm 1: Selection of $2n/Xk$ sentences from each topic

```
 1: Input: n × k sentence-topic matrix
 2: Output: 2n/Xk sentences
 3: reduced_matrix[iterations][k] ← φ
 4: for all t ∈ (0, k − 1)  do
 5:    for all i ∈ (0, iterations − 1)  do
 6:       max_elem ← max(sentence_topic_matrix[][t])
 7:       max_index ← index of max_elem in matrix
 8:       reduced_matrix[i][t] ← max_index
 9:       sentence_topic_matrix[max_index][t] ← 0
10:    end for
11: end for
12: return reduced_matrix
```

---

step. After identifying a reasonably good k, we perform topic modeling on the set of n-sentences (each sentence is consider as an individual document) using LDA [8]. Gensim[3], a python library is used for this purpose. Based on these k-topics that are generated from the n-sentences, a sentence-topic matrix is created as shown in Table 1 where, each entry w_{ij} denotes the weight of jth topic in i^{th} sentence. To ensure that the final summary covers all the topics, we select a total of $2n/(Xk)$ sentences from each topic (i.e., from each column of the Table 1) having maximum weight. Since this procedure is carried for k topics, we will get a total of $2n/X$ sentences. However, some sentences might be chosen from multiple columns, therefore, we will always have less than or equal to $2n/X$ sentences. Algorithm 1 illustrates the implementation.

Heuristic method to decide the number of independent topics (k):

To decide an appropriate number of independent topics[4] (k), the following steps are used and is illustrated in Algorithm 2.

i. Initially the number of topics i.e., $k_{initial}$ is set to a large value, say M (M is set to $2i$ where i is the number of documents of the corpus C).

ii. Topic modeling is performed on n sentences as discussed in Step 1 assuming that the number of topics as $k_{initial}$ and then the similarities between topics are calculated.

---

[3] https://radimrehurek.com/gensim/.

[4] By independent means low similarity between topics.

iii. Since each topic is a probability distribution over the vocabularies of C, the topic similarity is computed using KL-Divergence [9], Hellinger's Distance[5], and Jensen Shannon Divergence [10].

iv. A topic-topic similarity matrix is generated as shown in Table 2, where $Topic_{ij}$ denotes the aggregate similarity between $Topic_i$ and $Topic_j$, and $Topic_{ii} = 1$.

v. In the entire topic-topic similarity matrix, apart from the diagonal elements (as diagonal elements are 1), if any pair of topics which have a similarity greater than 0.40 (user defined threshold) is found out then that is an indication that the initial estimate of the number of topics $k_{initial}$ is higher than the appropriate number of independent topics (k). So, we reduce $k_{initial}$ by 1, i.e., $k_{initial} = k_{initial}$-1 and repeat the Steps (ii–v) again.

vi. Eventually a stage will come where we would have a number of topics k i.e., in the topic-topic similarity matrix between any pair of topics, the similarity score is less than 0.4. This will ensure that we will reach a suitable number of independent topics which serves the purpose of summarization as it covers the breadth of topics of the original corpus.

Table 2. Topic-topic matrix.

	$Topic_1$	$Topic_2$	$Topic_3$	...	$Topic_k$
$Topic_1$	$Topic_{11}$	$Topic_{12}$	$Topic_{13}$	...	$Topic_{1k}$
$Topic_2$	$Topic_{21}$	$Topic_{22}$	$Topic_{23}$	...	$Topic_{2k}$
$Topic_3$	$Topic_{31}$	$Topic_{32}$	$Topic_{33}$	...	$Topic_{3k}$
$\vdots$	$\vdots$	$\vdots$	$\vdots$	$\ddots$	$\vdots$
$Topic_k$	$Topic_{k1}$	$Topic_{k2}$	$Topic_{k3}$	...	$Topic_{kk}$

Algorithm 2: Selection of appropriate number of independent topics

---

```
1: Input: the set of sentences {s₁, s₂,..., sₙ}
2: Output:num_topics //number of topics
3: num_topics ← 2 * num_docs// number of documents
4: while num_topics >0 do
5:     ldamodel ← generate an LDA model using num_topics
6:     similairity_matrix[num_topics][num_topics] ← φ
7:     similarity_matrix ← generated topic-topic similarity matrix
8:     if (element ∈ similarity_matrix) >0.4 and element is not a diagonal element then
9:         num_topics ← num_topics − 1
10:    else
11:        exit
12:    end if
13: end while
14: return num_topics
```

---

[5] www.encyclopediaofmath.org/index.php?title=Hellinger_distance&oldid=16453.

2. *Identifying important word and sentence level features*:
   Fifteen important features are identified to generate an aggregate score for each sentence s of a document d. Those features are 'length', 'weight', 'density', 'title words', 'upper-case words', 'quoted text', 'numerical words', 'alphanumeric words', 'cue-phrase', 'similarity among sentences', 'similarity among paragraphs', 'LSI-based score', 'concept-based score', 'Doc2Vec score', and 'Word2Vec score' of each sentence s.
3. *Reducing $2n/X$ sentences to n/X sentences*:
   After performing the topic modeling with the appropriate number of topics k, and selecting $\frac{2n}{Xk}$ sentences from each topic, we are left with a total of $2n/X$ sentences. For each topic, the following steps are used:
   i. All fifteen word and sentence level features for each sentence s (as discussed in Step 2) are computed in the set of $2n/Xk$ sentences.
   ii. An aggregate score for each sentence is calculated using Eq. 1.

   $$\frac{\text{sum of all normalized feature scores}}{\text{total number of features}} \tag{1}$$

   iii. All the sentences are ranked based on their aggregate scores and the top n/Xk sentences are selected among them.
   iv. Steps (i–iii) are carried out for all k topics, hence we now have a total of n/X sentences. However, since some of the sentences might be chosen for more than one time as discussed in Step 1, therefore we will always have less than or equal to n/X sentences.
4. *Ordering of the sentences*:
   Now we have a list of n/X sentences, but these sentences have not yet been ordered. To ensure that the generated summaries are coherent, the following steps are followed:
   i. Since the corpus C contains a total of i documents, hence we have a total of i opening lines (opening line indicates the first sentence of a document), i.e., one line for each document.
   ii. After traversing through the list of n/X sentences, if we encounter an opening line OL during this traversal, then OL will be chosen as the summary's first sentence. Unlikely, when none of the n/X sentences contain any opening line then a sentence is selected randomly from this list of n/X sentences as the opening line.
   iii. A sentence-sentence similarity matrix is generated using WordNet-based similarity [1]. The order of the sentences is stored in a list. The first entry in this list is the starting sentence. We then go to the rth row of the sentence-sentence similarity matrix where r is the starting index. We traverse this row and find the maximum element in the row apart from the diagonal elements. Consider that this element is found in the jth column. We now add j to our list of ordered sentences and then jump to the jth row of the matrix. Then the element having the maximum score from the jth row excluding the previous selected sentence and the jth column is selected. This process is repeated till all the sentences are added to the list. This ensures that consecutive sentences are similar and so the summary will be coherent.

2.1 Generating Extractive Gold Summaries from Human Written Summaries

Python Natural Language Toolkit[6] has been used to tokenize the documents into sentences. The way extractive gold summaries are created from the human written gold summaries (available in DUC datasets) are explained below.

(i) Each document d of C is parsed sentence by sentence. For each sentence $s \in d$, calculate the number of keywords it has in common with each of the four human written gold summaries of the corpus C. The number of common words between each s and four human written gold summaries gives the score for the sentence s. This way the scores for all the sentences of a document are calculated.

(ii) Now rank all the sentences of a document d based on their scores computed in Step (i). Top-m important sentences are selected from the ranked sentences in order to form the extractive gold summary of d. For experimental purpose, we have taken $m = 5$, i.e., each document has an extractive gold summary of five sentences. Repeat Steps (i) and (ii) for all documents of the corpus C.

3 Experimental Analysis

For experimental purpose, Document Understanding Conference (DUC)[7] datasets are used, where each dataset having four human written summaries. DUC-2005 has 50 and DUC-2007 has 45 document sets. *ROUGE* or Recall-Oriented Understudy for Gisting Evaluation score [11] is used by the approach to measure the performance of text summarization. ROUGE-N measures the unigram, bigram, trigram, and higher order n-gram overlap between the summaries generated by the system (i.e., by the proposed approach) and the gold summary (either human written or extractive). ROUGE-1 and ROUGE-2 are used to compute the F-measure value for unigram and bigram matching respectively.

3.1 Discussion

For experimental purpose, the stop-words are removed from all DUC-datasets while computing the ROUGE score. Tables 3, 4, 5 and 6 show the performance of ROUGE-1 score of extractive and human written gold summary on different DUC datasets. Similarly, Tables 7, 8, 9 and 10 show the performance of ROUGE-2 score of extractive and human written gold summary on different DUC datasets. From the results of these tables, the following points can be observed:

---

[6] http://www.nltk.org/.
[7] http://www.duc.nist.gov.

Table 3. ROUGE-1 extractive (DUC-2005).

Doc-Id	Recall	Precision	F-Score
D301	0.43273	0.74537	0.54757
D307	0.44990	0.77817	0.57016
D311	0.37160	0.86547	0.51995
D313	0.47493	0.79914	0.59578
D321	0.55001	0.75214	0.63538
D324	0.20625	0.89593	0.33531
D331	0.71323	0.72054	0.71687
D332	0.74888	0.68653	0.71635
D343	0.40890	0.85114	0.55242
D345	0.33215	0.86331	0.47973
D346	0.47539	0.74505	0.58043
D347	0.78038	0.71554	0.74656
D350	0.45230	0.75985	0.56706
D354	0.47950	0.78655	0.59579
D391	0.68774	0.68914	0.68844
Average	0.50425	0.77692	0.58985

Table 4. ROUGE-1 human written (DUC-2005).

Doc-Id	Recall	Precision	F-Score
D301	0.46291	0.22785	0.30538
D307	0.51105	0.26882	0.35232
D311	0.47226	0.60594	0.53081
D313	0.68563	0.32934	0.44495
D321	0.59350	0.22408	0.32533
D324	0.19080	0.64404	0.29438
D331	0.76016	0.17862	0.28927
D332	0.58571	0.13851	0.22404
D343	0.54839	0.33601	0.41670
D345	0.35294	0.57365	0.43701
D346	0.51151	0.27370	0.35659
D347	0.61161	0.13117	0.21602
D350	0.54472	0.28926	0.37786
D354	0.52239	0.22173	0.31132
D391	0.57046	0.32261	0.41214
Average	0.52826	0.31768	0.35294

Table 5. ROUGE-1 extractive (DUC-2007).

Doc-Id	Recall	Precision	F-Score
D0701A	0.54533	0.11414	0.18877
D0702A	0.58369	0.20606	0.30459
D0703A	0.51667	0.23308	0.32124
D0705A	0.55703	0.21627	0.31157
D0706B	0.49161	0.17402	0.25705
D0707B	0.30196	0.24290	0.26923
D0708B	0.51429	0.25862	0.34417
D0709B	0.79960	0.15011	0.25277
D0710C	0.38978	0.29897	0.33839
D0711C	0.67520	0.29781	0.41332
D0712C	0.46970	0.26007	0.33477
D0713C	0.47486	0.20706	0.28838
D0714D	0.44698	0.24968	0.32039
D0715D	0.59544	0.27756	0.37862
D0716D	0.54277	0.22412	0.31724
Average	0.52699	0.22736	0.30936

Table 6. ROUGE-1 human written (DUC-2007)

Doc-Id	Recall	Precision	F-Score
D0701A	0.73705	0.05485	0.10210
D0702A	0.67704	0.08788	0.15557
D0703A	0.44531	0.28571	0.34809
D0705A	0.71311	0.17920	0.28642
D0706B	0.61508	0.13158	0.21678
D0707B	0.48606	0.38486	0.42958
D0708B	0.49407	0.35920	0.41597
D0709B	0.76384	0.07788	0.14135
D0710C	0.60079	0.31340	0.41192
D0711C	0.76378	0.13691	0.23221
D0712C	0.63878	0.28188	0.39115
D0713C	0.62451	0.19245	0.29423
D0714D	0.67969	0.11083	0.19058
D0715D	0.58120	0.18061	0.27558
D0716D	0.61089	0.19123	0.29128
Average	0.62874	0.19789	0.27885

Table 7. ROUGE-2 extractive (DUC-2005).

Doc-Id	Recall	Precision	F-Score
D301	0.26548	0.45738	0.33596
D307	0.30684	0.53084	0.38889
D311	0.26914	0.62703	0.37662
D313	0.34112	0.57410	0.42796
D321	0.37891	0.51822	0.43775
D324	0.17576	0.76435	0.28579
D331	0.46161	0.46634	0.46396
D332	0.50026	0.45860	0.47853
D343	0.31701	0.66007	0.42831
D345	0.26956	0.70092	0.38937
D346	0.29128	0.45659	0.35567
D347	0.57447	0.52673	0.54957
D350	0.29049	0.48812	0.36422
D354	0.32333	0.53047	0.40177
D391	0.41050	0.41134	0.41092
Average	0.34505	0.54474	0.40635

Table 8. ROUGE-2 human written (DUC-2005).

Doc-Id	Recall	Precision	F-Score
D301	0.11554	0.05650	0.07589
D307	0.12379	0.06471	0.08499
D311	0.13556	0.17274	0.15191
D313	0.22111	0.10552	0.14286
D321	0.17939	0.06729	0.09786
D324	0.07609	0.25529	0.11724
D331	0.30040	0.07011	0.11369
D332	0.16444	0.03862	0.06255
D343	0.15736	0.09580	0.11909
D345	0.07858	0.12686	0.09705
D346	0.09778	0.05198	0.06788
D347	0.13407	0.02856	0.04709
D350	0.11668	0.06156	0.08059
D354	0.07639	0.03218	0.04528
D391	0.12335	0.06924	0.08869
Average	0.14003	0.08646	0.09284

Table 9. ROUGE-2 extractive (DUC-2007).

oc-Id	Recall	Precision	F-Score
D0701A	0.15177	0.03173	0.05249
D0702A	0.17049	0.06013	0.08891
D0703A	0.18436	0.08291	0.11438
D0705A	0.18883	0.07321	0.10550
D0706B	0.20433	0.07222	0.10672
D0707B	0.07480	0.06013	0.06667
D0708B	0.18966	0.09510	0.12668
D0709B	0.36747	0.06887	0.11601
D0710C	0.13208	0.10124	0.11462
D0711C	0.25001	0.11017	0.15294
D0712C	0.18845	0.10420	0.13420
D0713C	0.12605	0.05488	0.07647
D0714D	0.13470	0.07521	0.09652
D0715D	0.23429	0.10904	0.14882
D0716D	0.18343	0.07561	0.10708
Average	0.18538	0.07831	0.10720

Table 10. ROUGE-2 human written (DUC-2007).

Doc-Id	Recall	Precision	F-Score
D0701A	0.28151	0.01987	0.03712
D0702A	0.16667	0.02072	0.03685
D0703A	0.17501	0.10553	0.13166
D0705A	0.22944	0.05464	0.08826
D0706B	0.16309	0.03229	0.05390
D0707B	0.12971	0.09810	0.11171
D0708B	0.14815	0.10375	0.12203
D0709B	0.22780	0.02221	0.04047
D0710C	0.18930	0.09504	0.12655
D0711C	0.24473	0.04096	0.07018
D0712C	0.22984	0.09580	0.13523
D0713C	0.21992	0.06463	0.09991
D0714D	0.22449	0.03505	0.06064
D0715D	0.21364	0.06250	0.09671
D0716D	0.23770	0.07073	0.10902
Average	0.20539	0.06145	0.08801

i. The ROUGE-N scores of human written summaries are less than the extractive summaries and this is because as in the original documents (i.e., the documents of the DUC dataset), people try to use different words and paraphrase the documents in their own way, hence most of the words of the human written summaries do not match with the original documents. However, the extractive gold summaries takes care of the words common between the sentence of the original documents and the four human gold summaries as discussed in Sect. 2.1.

ii. If the stop-words are removed from the corpus, then for every concise summary, ROUGE-1 score alone may suffice [11] which are reflected when we compared the obtained ROUGE-1 with the ROUGE-2 scores.

4 Conclusion

The paper developed an approach that generates a concise summary using multi-document text summarization. Initially, topic modeling using LDA is run on each single sentence of a corpus and a subset of sentences are selected per topic. Next, fifteen important word and sentence level features are identified and using these features, the aggregate score of each sentence is calculated. Important sentences are selected based on the aggregate scores and finally sentences are ordered to form a coherent summary. Unlike most of the other techniques, the generated summaries will not only contain sentences that have the best structural features, but also cover all the key topics of the corpus. Future work includes further improvement of the two heuristic methods i.e., identifying a suitable number of topics and reordering of the sentences. This work can also be extended by using abstractive text summarization technique in place of extractive one.

References

1. Miller, G.A.: Wordnet: a lexical database for English. Commun. ACM **38**(11), 39–41 (1995)
2. Ganesan, K., Zhai, C., Han, J.: Opinosis: a graph-based approach to abstractive summarization of highly redundant opinions. In: Proceedings of the 23rd International Conference on Computational Linguistics, pp. 340–348. Association for Computational Linguistics (2010)
3. Moratanch, N., Chitrakala, S.: A survey on extractive text summarization. In: 2017 International Conference on Computer, Communication and Signal Processing (ICCCSP), pp. 1–6. IEEE (2017)
4. Fang, C., Mu, D., Deng, Z., Wu, Z.: Word-sentence co-ranking for automatic extractive text summarization. Expert Syst. Appl. **72**, 189–195 (2017)
5. Nallapati, R., Zhai, F., Zhou, B.: SummaRuNNer: a recurrent neural network based sequence model for extractive summarization of documents. In: AAAI, pp. 3075–3081 (2017)
6. Roul, R.K., Sahoo, J.K., Goel, R.: Deep learning in the domain of multi-document text summarization. In: Shankar, B.U., Ghosh, K., Mandal, D.P., Ray, S.S., Zhang, D., Pal, S.K. (eds.) PReMI 2017. LNCS, vol. 10597, pp. 575–581. Springer, Cham (2017). https://doi.org/10.1007/978-3-319-69900-4_73

7. Narayan, S., Cohen, S.B., Lapata, M.: Ranking sentences for extractive summarization with reinforcement learning. In: 16th Annual Conference of the North American Chapter of the Association for Computational Linguistics: Human Language Technologies. US. ACL anthology, New Orleans (2018)

8. Blei, D.M., Ng, A.Y., Jordan, M.I.: Latent dirichlet allocation. J. Mach. Learn. Res. **3**(Jan), 993–1022 (2003)

9. Kullback, S., Leibler, R.A.: On information and sufficiency. Ann. Math. Stat. **22**(1), 79–86 (1951)

10. Fuglede, B., Topsoe, F.: Jensen-Shannon divergence and Hilbert space embedding. In: Proceedings, International Symposium on Information Theory. ISIT 2004, p. 31. IEEE (2004)

11. Lin, C.-Y.: Rouge: a package for automatic evaluation of summaries. In: Text Summarization Branches Out: Proceedings of the ACL-04 Workshop, vol. 8, pp. 74–81 (2004)

Improved Visible Light Communication Using Code Shift Keying Modulation

Ishrath Unissa[1]([✉]), Syed Jalal Ahmad[2], and P. Radha Krishna[3]

[1] Department of Electronics and Communication Engineering,
Mahatma Gandhi Institute of Technology, Hyderabad, India
ishrathunnisa94@gmail.com
[2] Department of Electronics and Communication Engineering,
Model Institute of Engineering and Technology, Jammu, India
jalal.ece@mietjammu.in
[3] Department of Computer Science and Engineering,
National Institute of Technology, Warangal, India
prkrishna@nitw.ac.in

Abstract. Visible light communication can provide higher bandwidth and bit rates without causing any interference to the Radio Frequency signals. Red-Green-Blue Light-Emitting Diodes are more suitable than other light sources as they have a smaller switching time, greater lifespan and cost-effective. Designing a communication scheme that avoids dimming and flickering, and that maximize the throughput and coverage area is challenging. Modulation schemes such as Amplitude Shift Keying, Frequency Shift Keying, and Phase Shift Keying exist in the literature for communication with controlled dimming and flickering effect. However, these schemes may not be efficient as they bound the bit rates with more Bit Error Rate. In this paper, a spread spectrum technique, Code Shift Keying along with Manchester (CSK-M) coding, is used to improve bit rates, a reduction in Bit Error Rate with an efficient control of fluctuations and dimming effect. The simulation results show that the presented approach outperforms the existing modulation schemes.

Keywords: Visible light communication · CSK-M · Dimming
BER · Bit rate

1 Introduction

Visible light communication (VLC) is used to transfer the data from the source to the destination by intensity modulation of light emitting sources such as fluorescent lights and light emitting diodes (LEDs). Predominantly LEDs are used as their switching time is minimum, more lifespan and cost effective when compared to fluorescent lights. Red-Green-Blue (RGB) LEDs are preferred over phosphorous LEDs as they provide higher data rates. The intensity of the LED is varied in accordance with the digital message signal. The photodetector is used at the receiver end to capture these intensity variations and convert them back to digital signals. The main advantage of VLC is that it provides higher data rates and bandwidth up-to terra hertz unlike the bandwidth provided by the use of radio frequency (RF) signal which is in the range of gigahertz.

© Springer Nature Switzerland AG 2019
G. Fahrnberger et al. (Eds.): ICDCIT 2019, LNCS 11319, pp. 222–232, 2019.
https://doi.org/10.1007/978-3-030-05366-6_18

The communication through visible light is bounded by several issues and challenges. In VLC, the input data is intensity modulated where the high-intensity value is represented as digital 1 and the low intensity is considered to be digital 0. When intensity modulation is performed, there are chances of dimming of the light intensity (that is, presence of continuous 0's in the input data) which effects the primary characteristic of the LED namely illumination. The flickering effect is due to the continuous variation of light intensity that a human eye can detect. If the intensity of light is varied with high frequencies (beyond human eye recognition) then this effect can be mitigated. These two parameters are very important in designing the transmitter and receiver for VLC.

The communication process using VLC is also interrupted by opaque objects present between transmitter and receiver as light cannot pass through it and Line of Sight is necessary for VLC. The coverage distance of VLC is restricted to a few meters (3 to 4 m), and also less bandwidth is available for modulation of data. In the literature, there are different modulation techniques for VLC such as On-Off Keying, Pulse Width Modulation (PWM), Pulse Position Modulation, Amplitude Shift Keying (ASK), Phase Shift Keying (PSK) and Frequency Shift Keying (FSK) to increase the data rate, control dimming and flickering of LED and to minimize the bit error rate (BER). But these techniques may fail to reduce the BER as the available modulation bandwidth is limited.

In this paper, Code-Shift keying (CSK) with fixed Manchester equal weighted binary hex code and chip size 4 is used for the intensity modulation of the digital message signal as well as to increase the bandwidth for modulation. As the input bits are spread over a large spectrum by CSK-M modulation, the scope of interference is reduced which lowers the BER. On the other hand, in the narrow spectrum, the probability of interference is more. In CSK-M coding, each symbol (of chip size 4) represents two input bits which double the bit rates when compared to conventional modulation techniques. Each of the data bits is spread by using the Manchester code to control dimming and minimizing the flickering of LED (as the input bits are modulated at high frequency.

The rest of the paper is organized as follows. In Sect. 2, we present the related work. The proposed approach is discussed in Sect. 3. In Sect. 4, we present simulation results, and we conclude the paper in Sect. 5.

2 Related Work

Komine and Nakagawa [1] discussed the importance of LEDs in VLC, analyzed the effect of radiation and interference by using multiple LEDs and concluded that VLC can be used for room communication purpose. Grobe et al. [2] presented a real-time bidirectional communication using LEDs with high data rates. The authors also discussed issues and challenges of VLC and its future perspective. Elgala et al. [3] designed orthogonal frequency division multiplexing (OFDM) with Quadrature phase shift keying (QPSK) transmitter and receiver to reduce the BER and increase the data rates. However, this method may be complex due to synchronization problem and less efficiency caused by guard bits interval.

The authors in [4–7] carried out a survey on VLC and discussed its issues and challenges. Rajagopal et al. [8] presented different modulation techniques and coding schemes for VLC. They discussed the importance of flickering and dimming effects in communication using visible light as a medium. In [9], an on-off keying demodulator is developed which is resistant to the interference from other light sources. Pradana et al. [10] designed Pulse width modulation (PWM) and demodulation technique to increase the data rates and reduce the BER. However, the coverage distance is very less as the design gives accurate results in less than a meter range. The authors also discussed pulse position modulation technique to control dimming and mitigate flickering effect [11].

Din and Kim [12] implemented Sub-carrier pulse positions modulation (SC-Pulse Position Modulation) technique to control the dimming and reduce the BER in VLC. Their approach increases complexity as the number of subcarriers increases. Jang et al. [13] proposed an approach that employs PWM along with Pulse Position Modulation to manage the dimming of the LEDs. The multiple-input-multiple-output orthogonal frequency division multiplexing (MIMO-OFDM) technique is proposed by Wang et al. [14] to analyze its performance for VLC. However, it may increase the complexity as multiple signals are used and the frequency synchronization problem persists in this method. Yao et al. [15] compared different shift keying techniques and analyzed their performance in communication using visible light. MIMO technique is employed to reduce the dimming and flickering effect in various modulation techniques used in VLC [16]. Costanzo et al. [17] presented a VLC system which employs decision making using fuzzy logic dynamically. They used white and red at front ends for better communication. However, the system performance is degraded when significant noise is present in the channel.

Chi et al. [18] discussed the visible light communication using different modulation techniques without a carrier, and distortion is reduced by employing Manchester coding and machine learning techniques to increase the data rates. Ahmad et al. [19] presented a modulation scheme using optical OFDM in the presence and absence of a direct current component to minimize BER. In this paper, CSK-M coding technique is proposed to provide higher bit rates, controlling the dimming effect, and minimizing the BER.

3 Proposed Approach

Code shift keying modulation is a spread spectrum modulation technique which increases the modulation frequency by reducing the time period of the input signal and increases the bit rate [20]. In the proposed technique, Manchester coding is used to reduce the direct current (DC) component (continuous 0's or continuous 1's) in the modulated signal. Dimming is controlled by Manchester symbol code sequence (MSCS) which is multiplied by the digital input signal. MSCS is developed from Fundamental Manchester symbol code (FMSC). In conventional CSK modulation, the input bits are multiplied by Pseudo-random codes (PRC) at the transmitter end and PRC synchronizer is used at the receiver end to obtain original data. However, it is difficult and complex to generate the accurate PRC at the receiver end. Hence in CSK-M, we fix the random codes by using Manchester coding of equal weighted binary hex code to reduce the synchronization complexity. Since the CSK modulation provides high bandwidth up-to

7 m of communication distance, the reduction of transmission speed by factor of 2 using Manchester code will not be significant in optical communication.

3.1   Generation of FMSC and MSCS

Design of FMSC is based on the chip size C_S and chip interval T_{CI}. The number of bits represented by each FMSC is given as [20]:

$$N = \log_2 P$$

$$\Rightarrow P = 2^N \tag{1}$$

where P represents the number of possible shifts of FMSC.

The equal-weighted binary hex code is used to generate FMSC by considering chip size as 4 (user defined). As the chip size is 4, equal weighted binary hex code ranging from 0 to15 decimal values (that is, 3, 5, 6, 9, 10 and 12) represented in binary number system as 0011, 0101, 0110, 1001, 1010, 1100 respectively in concatenation can be employed. These codes can be generated using Eqs. 2, 3 and 4 [21].

$$C_i = \prod_{z=1}^{s} b.Z \tag{2}$$

where $b = 3$ and $s = 4$.

Equation 2 generates only 3, 6, 9 and 12, the missing terms, $M_{T1} = 5$ and $M_{T2} = 10$ can be generated as

$$M_{T1} = \frac{C_f + C_l}{C_f} \tag{3}$$

$$M_{T2} = 2(M_{T1}) \tag{4}$$

where C_f is the first term of C_i, and C_l is the last term of C_i. One of these codes is selected to generate FMSC. For simplicity and ease of understanding, we consider the code 0 0 1 1. The Manchester coding of the bits 0 0 1 1 can be done by taking the transition from higher to lower level as 0 and transition from lower to higher level as 1. The FMSC symbol obtained from this code is represented as

$$M_1(t) = -\text{square}\left(2\pi t, \frac{r}{2}\right)$$
$$M_0(t) = \text{square}\left(2\pi t, \frac{r}{2}\right) \tag{5}$$

where $M_1(t)$ Manchester equation is for input bit 1 and $M_0(t)$ Manchester equation is for input bit 0. Here, 'r' is the total width of a single bit.

$$\text{FMSC}(t) = \sum_{v=1}^{C_s} M_{iv}(t) \tag{6}$$

where $i = 0$ or 1.

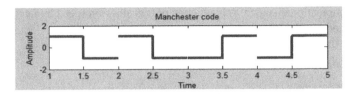

Fig. 1. FMSC (t)

Figure 1 represents FMSC (t) = 0 0 1 1 in Manchester form. The MSCS is developed by concatenation of the circularly shifted FMSC up to the length equal to that of input bits. For the chip size 4, the number of possible circular shifts of 0 0 1 1 is $P = 4$, that is, S_0 (t) to S_{p-1} (t) and N = 2 (from Eq. 1). The MSCS of 0 0 1 1 can be given as,

$$MSCS_j(t) = \sum_{q=0}^{S-1} S_j[q].rect\left(\frac{t - qT_{CI}}{T_{CI}}\right)$$ (7)

where q is an integer representing the shift number.
  $S_j[q]$ = FMSC (mod $[q-q_j, C_S]$)
  $j = 0, 1, ...,P-1, (P = 4)$

$$0011 \text{ can produce} \atop \text{on circular shift} \left\{ \begin{matrix} 0 & 0 & 1 & 1 \\ 1 & 0 & 0 & 1 \\ 1 & 1 & 0 & 0 \\ 0 & 1 & 1 & 0 \end{matrix} \right.$$

The concatenation of circularly shifted FMSC (t) is shown in Fig. 2. Suppose K is a number of times FMSC should be repeated (user defined) to represent the digital input bits so as to cover the maximum number of bits in the optimal time interval. In general, the CSK coding can be represented as (N, K). Then,

$$d_j(t) = \sum_{a=0}^{K-1} MSCS_j(t - aT_{MAN})$$ (8)

where T_{MAN} is the period length of the chip.

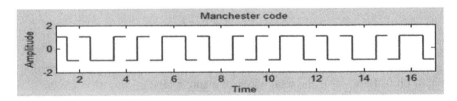

Fig. 2. Concatenation of circularly shifted FMSC (t)

We repeat the FMSC only once, that is, K = 1 which means each symbol of FMSC covers two digital input bits. Therefore, the CSK coding of the proposed approach is CSK-M (2, 1).

3.2   Design of CSK-M Transmitter and Receiver

Figure 3 shows the block diagram of the proposed technique with channel capacity 'CC'. The channel used in our approach is Additive white Gaussian noise (AWGN) channel with constant power spectral density. The capacity of the channel is directly proportional to the bandwidth and logarithmic value of the signal to noise ratio. CSK modulation is a spread spectrum modulation technique which increases the modulation frequency by reducing the time period of the input signal and increasing the bit rate. This type of modulation uses more spectrum than that of the data signal with the same signal power and hence interference is reduced when compared to narrow band signals, which increases the channel capacity. However, it is difficult for an unauthorized user to distinguish between noise and the original signal, and authorized users can use the symbol synchronization to recover the original data signal.

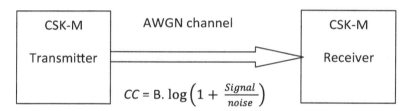

Fig. 3. Block diagram of proposed modulation method

Transmitter

Figure 4 represents the CSK-M modulator. The serial stream of input bits is converted into parallel bits by using serial to parallel (S/P) converter. These parallel bits are multiplied with the circular phase shifted fixed Manchester equal weighted code signals which are interleaved at a certain instant of time to spread the signal and assign a

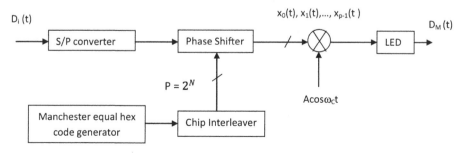

Fig. 4. CSK-M modulator

unique symbol to each input bit. Thus the resultant symbols are then mixed with the carrier signal and transmitted using an RGB LED. The transmitter and receiver block of CSKM is similar to that of conventional CSK except the fact that the PRC block is replaced by Manchester equal weighted hex code block at the transmitter end.

The modulated signal D_M (t) is represented as,

$$D_M(t) = \sqrt{2E_p} \sum_{h=-\infty}^{\infty} d_{j[h]}(t - hT_F) \tag{9}$$

where j[h] belongs to the set (0, P−1), E_p is transmitted power and $T_F = \alpha \, T_{MAN}$.

Receiver
The receiver consists of a photodetector which can capture the variations of the light intensity and convert it into electrical signals. The received signal $Y(t)$ is a combination of the transmitted signal and the noise incorporated while propagating through the channel. Synchronization block is used to get back the original signal. The demodulator (see Fig. 5) uses the synchronization of the carrier, chip inter-leaver, and Manchester bits. The synchronized signal is multiplied with the unique symbols (same as produced at transmitter end for each respective bit). The symbols obtained as the output of chip inter-leaver are given to the integrator as input. The output of the integrator at time interval t = T is given to the matched filters. The matched filters are used to obtain the maximum output function of each symbol received to recover the appropriate input bits. These filters select the phase shift which is most likely for that particular symbol and decodes it. The decoded output is converted into a serial stream of bits by using parallel to serial (P/S) converter and demodulated signal D_o (t) is obtained.

$$Y(t) = D_M(t) + N_C \tag{10}$$

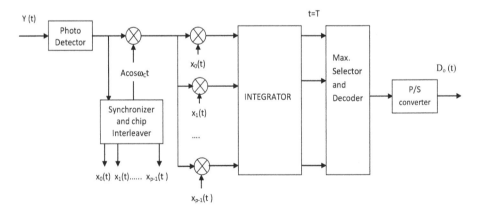

Fig. 5. CSK-M demodulator

Here, $D_i(t)$ is the digital input signal, $D_o(t)$ is the demodulated signal, and N_c is the noise or interference caused due to the channel. The output is less affected by channel noise as the transmitted signal is compressed. The bit rate is increased by a factor of 2 when compared to the traditional methods as each symbol is of chip size 4. In CSK-M modulation, a fixed equal weighted binary hex Manchester code is used to produce codes (symbols) instead of random codes to remove continuous 0's and 1's series and reduce the complexity at the receiver end (synchronization complexity). Thus by removing continuous 0's, dimming of LED is controlled. Flickering can be observed using *maximum flickering time period* which is the maximum period over which the intensity of the light is changed (from 0 to 1 or 1 to 0) without being noticed by the human eye. In the proposed approach, compression of each data bit into 4 bits reduces the time period by 4 times (than that of the original data time period), when compared to conventional techniques which in-turn reduces flickering and increases the bit rate. The interference in the transmitted signal is reduced as each input bit is multiplied with a unique Manchester symbol which can be accessed only by the authorized user. Hence, the interference is minimized with the reduction in bit error rate.

4 Simulation Results

In this section, we present the comparison of the proposed modulation method with the existing modulation techniques namely ASK, PSK and FSK. These modulation techniques are used for narrow bandwidth whereas the proposed technique is a similar type but used for wide bands. The parameters used are RGB Led with transmitting power of 20 W, photodetector with a physical area of 1 (cm^2), half power semi-angle 70° and variable distance of 5–6 m. The AWGN channel is introduced using Simulink. The input signal, the Manchester sequence, and the modulated signal are shown in Fig. 6 (a), (b) and (c) respectively.

Figure 7 shows signal to noise ratio (SNR) versus BER of CSK-M with chip size 4. Note that there is a decrease in the BER when compared to ASK, FSK and PSK techniques. As spread spectrum modulation technique is employed, the bit rate is doubled with unique patterns generated for the input data, and therefore, the bit errors are minimized. In the conventional shift keying modulation, no such patterns are developed and also it is more susceptible to interference (errors). Figure 8 represents the Data rate versus BER. CSK-M can transfer double the number of bits in the same bandwidth used to transfer single bit in ASK, FSK, and DPSK. Here, an increase in the data rate leads to an increase in the bit error rate. This is because the proposed method minimizes the interference and reduces the bit error rate at higher data rates when compared to existing methods.

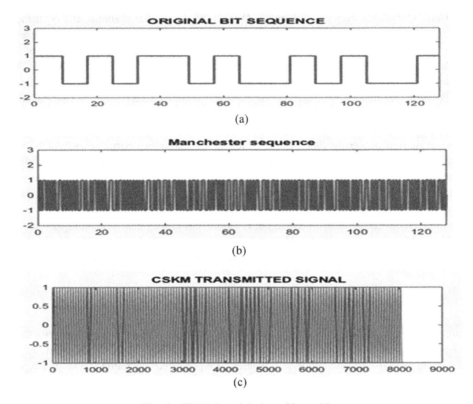

Fig. 6. CSK-M modulation of input bits

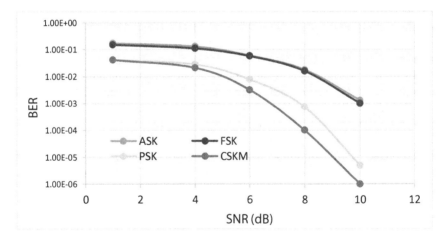

Fig. 7. SNR versus BER

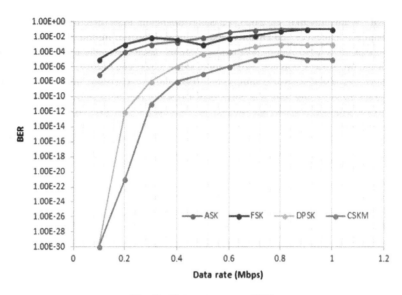

Fig. 8. Data rate versus BER

5   Conclusion

In this paper, CSK-M modulation is used to improve the performance of visible light communication with chip size 4 and the distance of communication is up-to 6 m without increasing the BER. The bit rate is doubled than that of original as each symbol represents two input bits. The Manchester code is used to control the dimming effect. As the proposed modulation technique uses high frequency, the flickering effect is decreased. The complexity of symbol synchronization is reduced due to application of fixed Manchester equal weighted hex code instead of random codes which increase the synchronization complexity. The simulation result shows that our technique reduces the BER and improves the bandwidth of modulation with higher data rates.

References

1. Komine, T., Nakagawa, M.: Fundamental analysis for visible-light communication system using LED lights. IEEE Trans. Consum. Electron. **50**(1), 100–107 (2004)
2. Grobe, L., et al.: High-speed visible light communication systems. IEEE Commun. Mag. **51** (12), 60–66 (2013)
3. Elgala, H., Mesleh, R., Haas, H., Pricope, B.: OFDM visible light wireless communication based on white LEDs. In: Vehicular Technology Conference, pp. 2185–2189 (2007)
4. Pathak, P.H., Feng, X., Hu, P., Mohapatra, P.: Visible light communication, networking, and sensing: a survey, potential and challenges. IEEE Commun. Surv. Tutor. **17**(4), 2047–2077 (2015)
5. Do, T.H., Yoo, M.: An in-depth survey of visible light communication-based positioning systems. Sensors **16**(5), 678 (2016)

6. Saadi, M., Wattisuttikulkij, L., Zhao, Y., Sangwongngam, P.: Visible light communication: opportunities, challenges and channel models. Int. J. Electron. Inform. **2**, 1–11 (2013)
7. Luo, J., Fan, L., Li, H.: Indoor positioning systems based on visible light communication: state of the art. IEEE Commun. Surv. Tutor. **19**(4), 2871–2893 (2017)
8. Rajagopal, S., Roberts, R.D., Lim, S.K.: IEEE 802.15.7 visible light communication: modulation schemes and dimming support. IEEE Commun. Mag. **50**(3) (2012)
9. Zhao, Y., Vongkulbhisal, J.: Design of visible light communication receiver for on-off keying modulation by adaptive minimum-voltage cancelation. Eng. J. **17**(4), 125–130 (2013)
10. Pradana, A., Ahmadi, N., Adiono, T.: Design and implementation of visible light communication system using pulse width modulation. In: International Conference on Electrical Engineering and Informatics (2015)
11. Pradana, A., Ahmadi, N., Adiono, T., Cahyadi, W.A., Chung, Y.H.: VLC physical layer design based on pulse position modulation (PPM) for stable illumination. In: Intelligent Signal Processing and Communication Systems (ISPACS) (2015)
12. Din, I., Kim, H.: Performance analysis of SC-L-PPM for energy-efficient visible light communication. In: The 18th IEEE International Symposium on Consumer Electronics (ISCE 2014) (2014)
13. Jang, H.J., Choi, J.H., Ghassemlooy, Z., Lee, C.G.: PWM-based PPM format for dimming control in a visible light communication system. In: International Symposium on Communication Systems, Networks & Digital Signal Processing (CSNDSP) (2012)
14. Wang, Q., Wang, Z., Dai, L.: Multiuser MIMO-OFDM for visible light communications. IEEE Photonics J. **7**(6), 1–11 (2015)
15. Yao, C., Guo, Z., Long, G., Zhang, H.: Performance comparison among ASK, FSK, and DPSK in visible light communication. Opt. Photonics J. **6**, 150–154 (2016)
16. Suban, A., Prabu, P., Manikandan, R., Pradeep, M.: Mitigating effect of flickering & dimming in visible light communication using MIMO. Int. J. Electr. Comput. Eng. **1**(1), 8–12 (2014)
17. Costanzo, A., Loscri', V., Costanzo, S.: Adaptive dual color visible light communication (VLC) system. In: Rocha, Á., Adeli, H., Reis, L.P., Costanzo, S. (eds.) WorldCIST'18 2018. AISC, vol. 746, pp. 1478–1487. Springer, Cham (2018). https://doi.org/10.1007/978-3-319-77712-2_143
18. Chi, N., et al.: LED-based high-speed visible light communications. In: Proceedings of SPIE 10559, Broadband Access Communication Technologies XII, p. 105590I, 29 January 2018
19. Ahmad, R., Srivastava, A., Selmy H.A.I.: Novel modulation scheme for VLC. In: Proceedings of SPIE 10559, Broadband Access Communication Technologies XII, p. 105590K, 29 January 2018
20. Garcia-Pena, A., Aubault-Roudier, M., Ries, L., Boucheret, M.L., Poulliat, C., Julien, O.: Code shift keying prospects for improving GNSS signal design. Inside GNSS **10**, 52–62 (2015)
21. Ahmad, S.J., Krishna, P.R.: BHQRSM: binary hex quadratic residue security model to enhance the trust in MANETs. Wireless Pers. Commun. **101**, 661–676 (2018)

Networks

Optimization of Transmission Range for a Fault Tolerant Wireless Sensor Network

Aditi, Rasita Pai, and S. Mini[✉]

Department of Computer Science and Engineering,
National Institute of Technology Goa, Farmagudi, Goa, India
aditinitgoa@gmail.com, rasitapai@gmail.com, mini2min2002@yahoo.co.in

Abstract. Applications of wireless sensor network face many censorious issues, fault tolerance being a prominent one. The problem of missing communication link(s), sensor node(s) and data is unavoidable in such networks. Fault tolerance is important for reliable delivery of data in WSN applications. This ensures the system's availability for use in case of any interruption or occurrence of fault, thus enhancing the availability and reliability. Current work introduces the fault-tolerance behavior of a dynamically generated system of wireless sensor network that comprises of super-nodes and sensor nodes having k - vertex disjoint paths. As the parameters involved in the process of determination of fault-tolerance of a network change, the capacity of the network to tolerate the fault changes accordingly. This paper proposes an algorithm that evaluates the fault tolerance of randomly generated networks based on k - vertex disjoint path connectivity and also evaluates the results.

Keywords: Wireless sensor network · Fault tolerance · Sensor node
Topology control · k - vertex-disjoint paths

1 Introduction

Wireless Sensor Network (WSN) can be visualized as a collection of numerous tiny sensors having the capability to sense, process as well as transmit data through wireless links. Sensor nodes generally co-operate traitorously in an autonomous and distributed manner in order to carry out a specific function, generally in a setup that has inadequate or no proper framework (or infrastructure) [1,2]. Fault tolerance and power efficiency are desired features in WSNs with the aim of achieving network functionality efficiently in case of alterations in energy levels, failures in hardware, errors in communication links, malicious attacks, detrimental environmental conditions, or events having a very high probability of occurrence in WSNs [3,4].

Adjusting the communication range of the nodes and/or choosing only specific nodes of the network to control the neighbor set of nodes that would be involved in transmitting the messages is known as topology control [5]. Approaches for topology control can be broadly grouped into two main categories, namely, heterogeneous and homogeneous [6]. When all the sensor nodes

© Springer Nature Switzerland AG 2019
G. Fahrnberger et al. (Eds.): ICDCIT 2019, LNCS 11319, pp. 235–242, 2019.
https://doi.org/10.1007/978-3-030-05366-6_19

used have equivalent transmission ranges, it is referred to as a homogeneous approach while in heterogeneous approach, all the sensor nodes used can have different transmission ranges [1].

In this paper, we have considered an algorithm to achieve fault resilient topology control for heterogeneous WSNs, consisting of super-nodes and sensor nodes. The super-nodes have more power reserves and better capabilities in terms of processing and storage capacities. The super-nodes may process the data from the sensor nodes before forwarding it [7,8,12–14]. Links between the super-nodes are considered to possess longer scope and greater data rates; however, due to their high cost, super-nodes are lesser in number. Super-nodes could also possess certain distinctive capabilities such as acting counter to an event or a specific condition.

A WSN is considered to be k-vertex super-node connected if by removing any $k - 1$ sensor nodes, the network is not being partitioned [7]. With the aim of minimizing the allocated transmission range and power of each sensor node and also maintaining k - vertex disjoint paths from each sensor node to the set of super-nodes, topology control can be modeled as a communication range allotment task for all the sensor nodes in the network such that there are a minimum of k - vertex disjoint paths from each sensor node to the set of super-nodes in the network.

The rest of this paper is organized as follows: In Sect. 2, the related work is detailed. Section 3 describes the proposed algorithm. Section 4 discusses the results of simulations and Sect. 5 concludes the paper.

2   Related Work

A noteworthy work about fault tolerance and topology control in heterogeneous wireless sensor networks for a two-layered architecture of the network under consideration has been put forth by Cardei et al. [7], taking both into consideration, the k - connectivity as well as the energy efficiency of the network. The focus is on k - degree Anycast Topology Control (k - ATC) problem, that intents to conform the communication scope of the sensor nodes in order to accomplish k - vertex super-node connectivity while curtailing the maximum communication capacity of the nodes. An acquisitive centralized algorithm known as Global Anycast Topology Control (GATC), in addition to a distributed algorithm termed as Distributed Anycast Topology Control (DATC), that yields k - vertex super-node connectivity through incremental regulation of the communication scope of the sensor nodes in the network has been proposed.

In [1], to attain fault-tolerant topologies, the aim is to ensure the existence of at least k - pairwise vertex disjoint paths from any of the sensor nodes to the super-node. A scale-free topology is useful for a WSN's performance, from the facets of both network strength as well as energy efficiency [9]. The Barabasi-Albert (BA) model depicts that in larger WSNs, a significantly small quantity of sensor nodes possess a high degree while a large quantity of nodes possesses a low degree [10]. In [11], the Adaptive Disjoint Path Vector (ADPV) algorithm is performed in two stages: the beginning one being a single initialization phase followed by the restoration phases. It is of great importance to have fault tolerance in the routing paths that originate from the sensor nodes to go up till the super-nodes and gateway nodes, which are considered to be additionally equipped in terms of power than the sensor nodes [4].

We aim at minimizing the transmission range and the cumulative transmission power of the sensor nodes which are used in the network for a heterogeneous topology whereas these papers consider flat homogeneous topographies. Also, we aim at providing a path between every sensor node to the super-node while they focus on the existence of path in between any pair of sensor nodes. The methodologies used in papers [12] and [13] do not consider k - connectivity between the sensor nodes and super-node and hence do not provide fault tolerance when k - 1 node failures may occur. The methods in [14] do consider the issue of k - connectivity but they do not contemplate the energy efficiency in the resultant topographies.

3   Proposed Algorithm

We initially assume that all the inter-node links are present. Algorithm 1 shows the proposed algorithm. The distance between a pair of nodes is taken as the weight of the edge between them. The initial phase is of edge weight updations in the matrix D wherein those edges whose weights are not within the threshold values' range are eliminated and those edges which satisfy this condition are retained. The next stage is the formation of k vertex disjoint paths on the new formed graph after elimination of edges having weights greater than the threshold value. We start by updating the distance matrix D to form minimum weighted paths between any given pair of nodes. This is done so that the obtained vertex disjoint paths will be formed on minimum inter-node distances.

Next, for all the sensor nodes, with the sensor node under consideration as the source s and the super-node as the destination t, we aim to form at least k vertex disjoint paths. Using Dijkstra's algorithm, we look for a path such that the length of the path is minimized by choosing the minimum weighted edges of the nodes in the path. From the obtained set of vertices, which denotes the shortest path from node s to t, note the maximum and the minimum inter-node distances in the path and delete the super-node. This forms the first path for that particular node. If the shortest path obtained was a direct edge between the node and the super-node, the compressed set of vertices in the path will be empty. Else these nodes are to be deleted from the original graph and we proceed by incrementing the k value. This is repeated until the incremented k value matches the k value provided. Among the k paths discovered for a particular sensor node, the paths are not assigned in the same sequence as they are formed. We arrange all the formed paths in the ascending order of the maximum range of the paths. Among these, the path with the least maximum range is assigned as the path for $k = 1$. Amongst the remaining unassigned paths, the next one with the lowest maximum transmission range is allocated as the path for $k = 2$ and the same pattern is followed for the rest of the k values. This process is then repeated for all sensor nodes to obtain k vertex disjoint paths from each sensor node to the super-node.

Algorithm 1

Input: G, N, k, t
Output: path from node to supernode
Algorithm:
    for $i = 1$ to N **do**
        for $j = 1$ to N **do**
            if $D_{i,j} \le t$ and $D_{i,j} \ne 0$ **then**
                retain edge between i and j
            else
                delete edge between i and j
            end if
        end for
    end for
    for $S_i = 1$ to $N - 1$ **do**
        $G_{new} = G$
        $x = 1$
        while $x \le k$ **do**
            find path from S_i to supernode (algorithm 2)
            form the set $S_i\_path_x$ by deleting supernode from the set denoting path from node S_i to supernode
            if $S_i\_path_x ==$ NULL **then**
                delete edge between S_i and supernode
            else
                delete nodes that occur in $S_i\_path_x$ from G_{new}
            end if
            $x = x + 1$
        end while
        form a set by sorting the paths as per their maximum range in ascending order
        for $K = 1$ to k **do**
            assign the path having least maximum range as path for K and eliminate it from the set
            return $S_i\_path_K$
        end for
    end for
end

Theorem 1. *For any vertex $v \in G$, we can compute the shortest distance $D_{v,u} \forall u \in V$ by successively considering the shortest distance in between each pair of intermediate vertices.*

Proof. We prove the above theorem by induction on l where l is the length of the path i.e. the number of edges from v to u.

Basis step: $l = 0$. This implies that the set S consisting of the vertices in the path contains only the start vertex v and $D_{v,v} = 0$ is minimum, is true.

Hypothesis: Assume the shortest distance between v and u to be $D_{v,u}$ for a path of length l.

Induction step: We assume that for some k, $l = k - 1$ such that there are k vertices in set S and let w be some vertex such that $w \notin S$ and $D_{v,w}$ is the smallest. One can update $S = S \cup \{w\}$. Using the induction hypothesis, one can claim that for any path to w emerging from S will have minimum distance as $D_{v,w}$. One can say that a path through any vertex $\notin S$ that later reaches w has length at the very least $D_{v,w}$ which is the minimum distance to reach to w from v. Now we know that by adding w to S, path to w from v has shortest length, we can similarly obtain a shortest path from w to u. Thus we can extend this induction hypothesis for $l + 1$ and so on.

4   Results and Discussion

We consider a $100\,\mathrm{m} \times 100\,\mathrm{m}$ region and vary the number of nodes from 10 to 50 for different values of k. The results are reported as an average of 100 instances. Instead of assuring the connectivity between any pair of nodes amongst the sensor nodes, we aim at providing the communication path from each sensor node to the super-node in the network. A threshold is set as the maximum transmission range possible for the nodes.

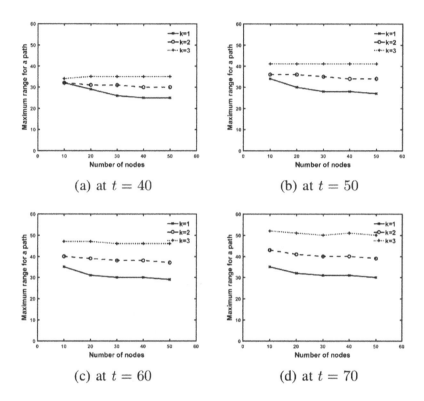

(a) at $t = 40$ (b) at $t = 50$

(c) at $t = 60$ (d) at $t = 70$

Fig. 1. Number of nodes vs maximum range in a path

Checking k - connectivity for each node in the graph formed ensures that any case of failure of any $k-1$ sensor nodes in WSN does not partition the network thus providing a fault-tolerant topology. Figure 1 shows the number of nodes against the maximum range in a path, which is the maximum distance between any pair of nodes in the path, for the k values $1, 2, 3$ and threshold values $40, 50, 60$ and 70 respectively. As we can see from the figure, for a fixed value of k, as the number of nodes increases, the maximum inter-node distance decreases for the given value of threshold. Also, when the number of nodes and the k value are kept constant and the threshold value is varied, the maximum range in a path increases with increase in threshold value. When the number of nodes is kept constant and k is varied, the maximum distance between any pair of nodes is found to be increasing for the given threshold value with increasing k. From these results, we could conclude that as the network grows more denser, the maximum distance between any pair of nodes in the paths, obtained to form a k vertex disjoint graph, decreases and increases with increasing k values.

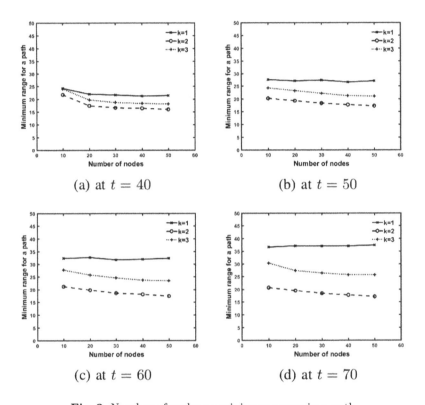

(a) at $t = 40$ (b) at $t = 50$

(c) at $t = 60$ (d) at $t = 70$

Fig. 2. Number of nodes vs minimum range in a path

Figure 2 shows the number of nodes against the minimum range in a path which is the smallest distance between any pair of nodes in the path obtained. From these figures, we can claim that the minimum distance between any pair of nodes in the resulting path decreases as the number of sensor nodes increases for a given value of k and for given number of nodes, with increasing value of k the minimum distance in the path decreases.

Figure 3 shows the number of nodes against the maximum transmission range of the network. This is based on the assumption that the number of nodes in the network vary from 30 to 70. The results obtained by using the proposed algorithm are compared to the results obtained with the GATC algorithm and the DPV algorithm. As we can see from the plots, the DPV algorithm provides a reduced maximum transmission range as compared to the GATC approach and we are able to provide better results than the DPV approach by being able to further reduce the maximum transmission ranges for the topologies obtained. Thus, our approach provides a better topology in terms of average path length as well as the reduced maximum transmission range and also reduces the average power consumed by the network for the randomly generated topologies.

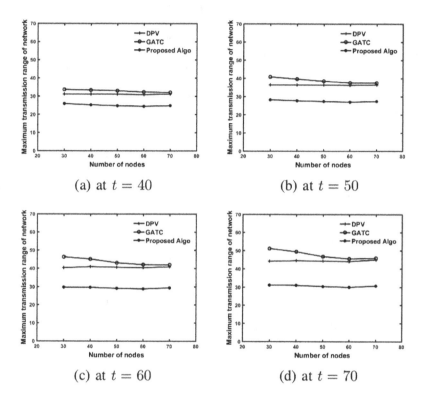

Fig. 3. Number of nodes vs maximum transmission range of the network

5 Conclusion and Future Work

In this paper, a fault tolerant topology was formed by minimizing the transmission range with the threshold values under consideration using the k - connectivity property of graphs. The obtained topology could be used to increase connectivity, reduce average path length and also to increase the network lifetime. The approach, being localized and distributed, can be used for large networks for real time applications. A comparison with the existing methods was carried out and the results obtained showed that the proposed approach yielded better results than the existing ones while maintaining the property of k - connectivity as well as providing a fault tolerant topology for the network. This model can be extended to form energy efficient weighted fault tolerant network topologies.

References

1. Bagci, H., Korpeoglu, I., Yazici, A.: A distributed fault-tolerant topology control algorithm for heterogeneous wireless sensor networks. IEEE Trans. Parallel Distrib. Syst. **26**(4), 914–923 (2015)
2. Yick, J., Mukherjee, B., Ghosal, D.: Wireless sensor network survey. Comput. Netw. **52**(12), 2292–2330 (2008)
3. Anastasi, G., Conti, M., Francesco, M., Passarella, A.: Energy conservation in wireless sensor networks: a survey. Ad Hoc Netw. **7**(3), 537–568 (2009)
4. Liu, H., Nayak, A., Stojmenovic, I.: Fault-tolerant algorithms/protocols in wireless sensor networks. In: Woungang, I., Misra, S., Misra, S. (eds.) Guide to Wireless Sensor Networks. CCN, pp. 261–291. Springer, London (2009). https://doi.org/10.1007/978-1-84882-218-4_10
5. Wang, Y.: Topology control for wireless sensor networks. In: Li, Y., Thai, M.T., Wu, W. (eds.) Wireless Sensor Networks and Applications. SCT, pp. 113–147. Springer, Boston (2008). https://doi.org/10.1007/978-0-387-49592-7_5
6. Rodolfo, C., Azzedine, B., Luiz, V., Antonio, L.: Underwater wireless sensor networks: a new challenge for topology control based systems. ACM Comput. Surv. (CSUR) **51**(1), 1–36 (2018)
7. Cardei, M., Yang, S., Wu, J.: Algorithms for fault-tolerant topology in heterogeneous wireless sensor networks. IEEE Trans. Parallel Distrib. Syst. **19**(4), 545–558 (2008)
8. Yarvis, M., Kushalnagar, N., Singh, H., Rangarajan, A., Liu, Y., Singh, S.: Exploiting heterogeneity in sensor networks. In: Proceedings of IEEE International Conference on Computer and Communications, vol. 2, pp. 878–890 (2005)
9. Wang, D., et al.: A flow-weighted scale-free topology for wireless sensor networks. IEEE Commun. Lett. **19**(2), 235–238 (2015)
10. Barabasi, A.L., Albert, R.: Emergence of scaling in random networks. Science **286**(5439), 509–512 (1999)
11. Deniz, F., Bagci, H., Korpeoglu, I., Yazici, A.: An adaptive, energy-aware and distributed fault-tolerant topology-control algorithm for heterogeneous wireless sensor networks. Ad Hoc Netw. **44**, 104–117 (2016)
12. Ozaki, K., Watanabe, K., Itaya, S., Hayashibara, N., Enokido, T., Takizawa, M.: A fault-tolerant model for wireless sensor-actor system. In: Proceedings of the 20th International Conference on Advanced Information Networking and Applications, vol. 2, April 2006
13. Dima, S.M., Christos, A., Stavros, K.: Resource aware sensor-to-actor allocation framework for WSANs based on Voronoi cells theory. J. Sens. **2017** (2017)
14. Wu, J., Yang, S., Cardei, M.: On maintaining sensor-actor connectivity in wireless sensor and actor networks. In: Proceedings of IEEE International Conference on Computer and Communications, pp. 888–896 (2008)

Community Detection Using an Enhanced Louvain Method in Complex Networks

Laxmi Chaudhary$^{(\boxtimes)}$ and Buddha Singh

Jawaharlal Nehru University, New Delhi 110067, India
laxmichaudari.iet@gmail.com, b.singh.jnu@gmail.com

Abstract. Recent developments and extensive usage of social networking applications have facilitated enormous amounts of essential data. It can be examined for numerous reasons by companies, governments, nonprofit organizations. The problem in social networks analysis mainly emerged of its vast scale and complicated relations in the networks. These networks can be analyzed and visualized using community structure properties. This paper introduces an agglomerative hierarchical community detection approach, Enhanced Louvain method (ELM), to identify communities in complex networks. We proposed a modularity and similarity measure-based approach that does not need the information of the communities as input and can find community structure in a rapid way. Experimental results on real world network datasets demonstrate the performance of the proposed ELM method over its counterparts to show that good results can be generated. The performance of methods evaluated in terms of communities, modularity value and quality of community obtained in the network.

Keywords: Community detection · Community structure · Modularity
Social network

1 Introduction

Community detection is a significant research issue with respect to complex networks and the objective of community detection is to discover the communities (community structure) in networks [1]. A community structure is a group of closely knit nodes having tight connections within the group and sparse connections with other groups in a network. Mostly, the nodes which are in same community have the similar features due to their closeness. Hence, detection of community plays a very predominant role in analyzing the structure of complex networks. For instance, it helps in identifying and visualizing the internal structure of the network, detecting potentially useful information, and mine the relationships between individuals. With the advancement of information technology, the scale of complex networks is expanding larger all the time. Social networks are a typical example. The number of active Facebook users exceeded 1.3 billion, and the active daily users of Twitter exceeded 66.6 million [2]. Thus, in a large-scale network environment, a high-speed and high-quality community detection algorithm is crucial. In the past decade, different community detection methods have been discovered and these methods can be categorized into three categories: graph partition methods, hierarchical clustering methods and, modularity optimization methods [2].

© Springer Nature Switzerland AG 2019
G. Fahrnberger et al. (Eds.): ICDCIT 2019, LNCS 11319, pp. 243–250, 2019.
https://doi.org/10.1007/978-3-030-05366-6_20

In this paper, we have introduced a new approach, Enhanced Louvain method (ELM), based on Jaccard and cosine similarity measure, and modularity metric is used to assess the quality of community. ELM is a greedy agglomerative hierarchical approach. This method is an extended version of Louvain method [3] and PyLouvain method [4]. It is a very efficient method and it can be used to analyze real world networks. The rest of the paper is organized as follows. Related works are discussed in Sect. 2. Section 3 introduces our proposed Enhanced Louvain method (ELM). The experiments and results description our proposed algorithm is given in Sect. 4. Section 5 concludes the paper.

2 Related Work

In recent years, a plethora of methods to unveil community structure have been introduced. Girvan et al. [5] method is a hierarchical based divisive technique. This method uses edge betweenness centrality to uncover the communities present in the network. The limitation of this approach is not to provide any information regarding the number of communities in which the network will spilt. Radicchi et al. [6] method is another hierarchical divisive method. It uses edge clustering coefficient instead of edge betweenness centrality measure. Its computation time is high. Newman developed [7], leading eigenvector method to detect communities in the network. This method uses the most positive eigenvector value of the modularity matrix and neglect all the other eigenvector, hence, losing the essential information present in these eigenvectors. Newman [8] developed an algorithm which is based on modularity. Here, to optimize the modularity value is very costly. Clauset et al. [9] suggested a method which is a hierarchical based agglomerative technique to unveil network communities using modularity function. But the computational time for this method is very high. Louvain [3] introduced a greedy modularity optimization method which works in an agglomerative hierarchical manner. The problem in this approach is the network size limits due to limited storage capacity. Odent et al. [4] developed a PyLouvain method based on Louvain method [3] to explore communities in networks.

3 Proposed Enhanced Louvain Method (ELM)

We have introduced a new approach, Enhanced Louvain method (ELM), to identify communities in complex network. ELM algorithm proceeds in an agglomerative greedy way, which is a bottom up approach. It detects the communities in large network using Jaccard and cosine similarity measure. Modularity [10] metric is a qualitative objective function to find the goodness of the community structure. This method is divided into three steps which is repeated iteratively.

- Similarity Measure
- Optimization of Modularity
- Aggregation of community.

1-Similarity Measure
In this step of proposed ELM method, we consider that every node of a given network act as an individual cluster. Therefore, the network has the communities same as the nodes present in the network. Additionally, consider each node of the network is depicted with p and the number of neighboring nodes i.e. adjacent nodes are represented with q. In this step of ELM method, the node p can form community with q adjacent nodes, it means node p have q communities for its movement on the other hand, node p must select the best adjacent node or community for its movement. To identify the best adjacent node or community, the node p is joining with all the adjacent nodes, for each movement of node p, we are calculating the new similarity measure Jaccard Cosine Shared measure (JCSM) which is a combination of Jaccard similarity measure [11], Cosine similarity measure [12], and shared link score. Consequently, we get q number of JCSM values with respect to all the neighbors of node p in a given network. The node p joins to its adjacent community based on maximum value of Jaccard cosine shared measure value. This step is applied reiteratively for every node until there is no change in the communities obtained.

Jaccard Cosine Shared Measure (JCSM). Cosine Similarity [12] is a similarity measure to find the resemblance between the nodes. It is the normalized dot product of the two attributes. It can measure the similarity between the nodes more efficiently. The cosine similarity [12], Sim_{pq} of moving node p to community q is calculated by

$$Sim_{pq} = \left(\frac{p.q}{||p|.|q||} \right) \qquad (1)$$

Jaccard Similarity [11] is a measure to get the similarity between the nodes. It is the ratio of the intersection of the neighborhoods to the union of neighborhoods. We define a new JCSM which will give more accurate similarity value between the nodes. The JCSM, J_{pq} of moving node p to community q is computed by

$$J_{pq} = \left(\frac{|\Gamma(p) \cap \Gamma(q)|}{|\Gamma(p) \cup \Gamma(q)|} \right) + Sim_{pq} + r \qquad (2)$$

where $\Gamma(p)$ and $\Gamma(q)$ are the neighborhoods of nodes p and q. Here, r represents the average shared edges and it value can be computed using

$$r = \left(2 * s - \frac{d_p * d_q}{l} \right) \qquad (3)$$

where s represents the shared links between the nodes p and q. d_p and d_q gives the degree of nodes p and q. l represents the number of connections between the nodes in the graph.

2- Optimization of Modularity
After exerting similarity measure step, we will attain communities depending on the JCSM, that tells how much a node is like other nodes. In this step of proposed ELM method, we will find the modularity metric [10] value of the communities. Modularity

metric is an objective function to quantify the community quality obtained in a given network. The communities for which the modularity metric value is more is considered as best communities among the other communities in the network. The modularity metric value, Q is computed by

$$Q = \frac{W}{2l} - \left(\frac{d_p d_q}{(2l)^2}\right) \tag{4}$$

where W is the weight of linking node p and node q.

3- Aggregation of Community

After optimization of modularity step of ELM method, we obtain community structure which is based on the modularity score and Jaccard cosine shared measure (JCSM). Moreover, we are applying the aggregation of community step of ELM method. In this step, we are aggregating the communities achieved during the optimization of modularity step. A new network community structure has been obtained in such a way that the nodes obtained during the similarity measure step becomes the communities. To obtain this community network, the link weights among the nodes is calculated as the total weights of the links within the nodes in the respective groups and the connections obtained among the same group lead to self-loops.

After this step, we are again employing all the steps of the ELM method to the resulted community network graph and repeat the steps until the communities with maximum modularity value is not attained.

4 Experiments and Results

The Enhanced Louvain method (ELM), proposed in this paper is explored on four diverse real-world networks. The ELM algorithm is tested through the comparison with algorithm of PyLouvain method [4] and Louvain method [3].

4.1 Analysis of Real World Networks

The analysis of the proposed ELM method and other existing methods on four real world networks are presented. The performance evaluation criteria adopted in the ELM methods is modularity [10], number of communities obtained in a given network.

Polbooks Network. The network used is Books about US politics network [13], The Polbooks network consists 105 nodes and 441 edges. We have tested the network using the ELM method in Polbooks network, we will get 4 communities and modularity score 0.526. The modularity score computed by proposed ELM method more than the existing methods. Hence, the community structure achieved by the proposed ELM method is better compared to other existing methods.

Facebook Network. The network used is Facebook network [14], The Facebook network consists 4,039 nodes and 88,234 edges. We have applied the ELM method in Facebook network, we will get 16 communities and modularity score 0.837. By applying the existing methods, we will get the same number of communities and less modularity value. Consequently, the community structure obtained by proposed ELM is better compared to other methods.

Soc-epinions. The network used is Soc-epinions which is an Epinions social networks [15], The Soc-epinions network consists 75,879 nodes and 5,08,837 edges. We have tested the network using ELM method, we will get 776 communities and modularity score 0.469. The modularity value of proposed ELM is greater than the existing methods. Therefore, the community structure achieved by ELM method is better than other methods.

Brightkite Network. The network used is Brightkite Location based online social networks [16], It consists 58,228 nodes and 2,14,078 edges. We have tested the network 1using ELM method, we will get 714 communities and modularity score 0.682. The modularity value of ELM method is more than the existing methods. Hence, the communities achieved by ELM method is better than other methods.

4.2 Simulation Results

The simulation results obtained by proposed ELM method, is demonstrated in Table 1. It shows that maximum modularity achieved by the ELM method as compared to other methods, PyLouvain method and, Louvain method. Hence, ELM performs well. The high modularity value helps in finding the best community structure of the real-world datasets. Therefore, the ELM method unveils the best community structure of the networks.

Table 1. Summarized results of the communities and modularity score of datasets

Network	ELM algorithm		PyLouvain method		Louvain method	
	Q	C	Q	C	Q	C
Polbooks network	0.526	4	0.521	4	0.521	4
Facebook network	0.837	16	0.835	16	0.835	16
Soc-epinions network	0.469	776	0.467	767	0.467	767
Brightkite network	0.682	714	0.679	724	0.675	853

Figure 1 shows the analogy of the modularity metric value obtained by proposed ELM method, and the existing approaches, PyLouvain and Louvain method, with respect to the different real-world networks. The modularity value obtained by ELM is greater than the other methods. It means the community detected by ELM is better than the PyLouvain method, and Louvain method. Figure 2 represents the comparison of the modularity value computed by the ELM, PyLouvain method and Louvain method relating to the number of nodes present in the network. Figure 3 represents the comparison of the modularity value computed by the ELM, PyLouvain method and Louvain method relating to the number of edges present in the network.

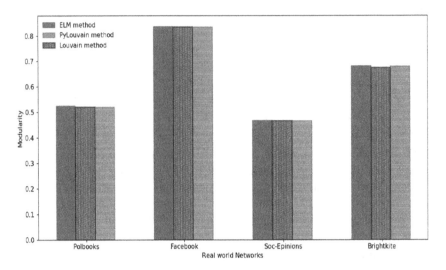

Fig. 1. Modularity vs real world networks

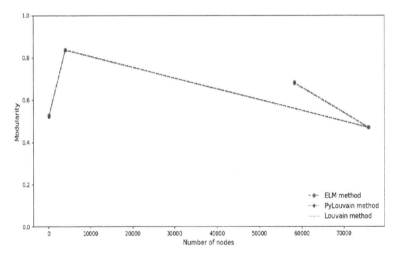

Fig. 2. Modularity versus number of nodes

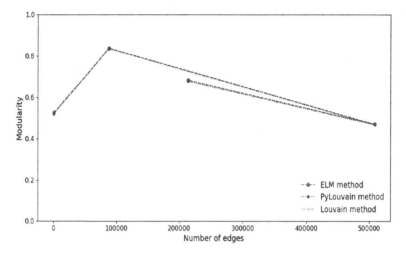

Fig. 3. Modularity versus number of edges

5   Conclusion and Future Scope

The community structure detection issue in large networks has been widely investigated during past years. A plethora of methods have been discussed in past years for detecting communities in complex networks. This paper proposed an agglomerative hierarchical approach, Enhanced Louvain method (ELM), to uncover communities in social networks. We have used modularity metric which assess the quality of the community structure in the network. We have used a new similarity measure, i.e. JCSM for finding community structure in networks. JCSM is a combination of Jaccard measure, cosine similarity, and shared link. The JCSM finds the similarity between two nodes. Then, the nodes with high JCSM are chosen and joined with the most similar node. Further, the result obtained by ELM are tested in real world networks. The result obtained by the ELM outperforms than the existing community detection approaches.

The proposed ELM method performance is evaluated and compared to existing methods and the output shows good results. The modularity value achieved using ELM is greater than the existing methods. It means the quality of community structure obtained by ELM is better than the other existing techniques. The performance of methods evaluated in terms of communities, modularity value and quality of community obtained in the network.

References

1. Fortunato, S.: Community detection in graphs. Phys. Rep. **486**(3), 75–174 (2010)
2. Chen, L., et al.: Fast community detection based on distance dynamics. Tsinghua Sci. Technol. **22**(6), 564–585 (2017)
3. Blondel, V.D., et al.: Fast unfolding of communities in large networks. J. Stat. Mech: Theory Exp. **2008**(10), 10008 (2008)

4. Odent, J., Saint-Guillain, M.: Automatic detection of community structure in networks (2012)
5. Girvan, M., Newman, M.E.J.: Community structure in social and biological networks. Proc. Natl. Acad. Sci. **99**(12), 7821–7826 (2002)
6. Radicchi, F., et al.: Defining and identifying communities in networks. Proc. Natl. Acad. Sci. U.S.A. **101**(9), 2658–2663 (2004)
7. Newman, M.E.J.: Finding community structure in networks using the eigenvectors of matrices. Phys. Rev. E **74**(3), 036104 (2006)
8. Newman, M.E.J.: Modularity and community structure in networks. Proc. Natl. Acad. Sci. **103**(23), 8577–8582 (2006)
9. Clauset, A., Newman, M.E.J., Moore, C.: Finding community structure in very large networks. Phys. Rev. E **70**(6), 066111 (2004)
10. Newman, M.E.J., Girvan, M.: Finding and evaluating community structure in networks. Phys. Rev. E **69**(2), 026113 (2004)
11. Jaccard, P.: Distribution de la flore alpine dans le bassin des Dranses et dans quelques régions voisines. Bulletin de la Société Vaudoise des Sciences Naturelles **37**, 241–272 (1901)
12. Singhal, A.: Modern information retrieval: a brief overview. Bull. IEEE Comput. Soc. Tech. Comm. Data Eng. **24**(4), 35–43 (2001)
13. Krebs, V.: A network of books about US politics (2004)
14. Leskovec, J., Mcauley, J.J.: Learning to discover social circles in ego networks. In: Advances in Neural Information Processing Systems (2012)
15. Richardson, M., Agrawal, R., Domingos, P.: Trust management for the semantic web. In: Fensel, D., Sycara, K., Mylopoulos, J. (eds.) ISWC 2003. LNCS, vol. 2870, pp. 351–368. Springer, Heidelberg (2003). https://doi.org/10.1007/978-3-540-39718-2_23
16. Cho, E., Myers, S.A., Leskovec, J.: Friendship and mobility: friendship and mobility: user movement in location-based social networks. In: ACM SIGKDD International Conference on Knowledge Discovery and Data Mining (KDD) (2011)

A Fast Handoff Technique for Wireless Mobile Networks

Debasis Das[(✉)]

Department of CS and IS, BITS Pilani, K.K. Birla Goa Campus, Zuarinagar 403726,
Goa, India
debasisd@goa.bits-pilani.ac.in

Abstract. To maintain user quality in IEEE 802.11 networks could
also be a troublesome issue, and conjointly the necessity for Multimedia Applications. To take care of the quality of the connections, these
Multimedia applications want fast handoffs between Base Stations (BS).
Previous work is based on maintaining a neighbor table by presently
associated Access Point (AP) and scan delay. In this paper, we have
made an attempt to propose a Neighboring approach where scan delay
has been reduced to some zero by exploiting the MH neighbor table. It
contains detailed knowledge of all the applications that unit at intervals. The MH neighbor table has been maintained by MH itself and its
updated once each 0.5 s interval therefore it ensures the MH neighbor
table contains details of exclusions that APs unit extremely neighbor
of MH nonetheless as MH context knowledge has been transferred by
presently associated AP to exclude that APs that's at intervals, or we'll
recommend that APs that details have been sent by MH to presently
associated AP. The result shows that this approach is better than all
existing approaches as a result of it reduces scan delay to some zero and
to boot reduces re-association delay, that the general handoff delay is
unbelievably low for Multimedia Applications.

Keywords: IEEE 802.11 · Fast handoff · Handoff delay
Re-association delay

1 Introduction

The IEEE 802 [1,2] customary contains a family of networking standards that
covers the physical layer specifications of technologies from LAN to wireless
medium [3,4]. The wireless network [5,6] protocol, IEEE 802.11 [6], permit high
speed secure dynamic wireless network access to a network infrastructure [5,6].
The most important characteristic of cellular systems [7] and the handoff is that
the tactic of adjusting the channel (i.e., bandwidth, frequency, slotted time, code,
or a combination of them) concerning this association whereas a choice is current.
The real time voice and multimedia based applications are the usual application
in continuous mobility as seen in the cellular networks, and we require real time
voice and multimedia applications will play as the compound for continuous

© Springer Nature Switzerland AG 2019
G. Fahrnberger et al. (Eds.): ICDCIT 2019, LNCS 11319, pp. 251–259, 2019.
https://doi.org/10.1007/978-3-030-05366-6_21

mobility in Wi-Fi networks much as they did for the cellular networks once multi-style handsets and end-user applications become more widely usable.

In this work, we tend to propose an advanced technique which nearly reduces scanning delay by zero in the neighbor table at MH. MH keeps records of each neighbor APs that are within the circle of radius 400 m. MH sends details of those designated neighbor AP, that are within the circle to current associated AP. Current associated AP sends context caching data of this MH to all or any neighbor AP whose details are sent by MH. Though MH can move in any direction, thus our planned approach repeat these works on each 0.5 s interval. If after 0.5 s, current associated AP is same because the previous one, then MH won't send details of the neighbor AP to the current associated AP, otherwise, MH can send details of neighbor AP, that is within the circle, to current associated AP.

2 Related Work of Fast Handoff in Wireless Networks

For fast and scalable handoffs for wireless internetworks [8,9], Caceres and Padmanabhan [7] proposed a scalable quality management scheme. Diverse proposals [6,8] for efficient and effective handoff techniques could also be found in the existing works. Chen et al. [6] propose a fast and economical handoff scheme [9,10] that supports handoff of mobile devices crossing wireless cell boundaries typically throughout interactive language sessions. They adopt an internet site spy to hide the quality of mobile nodes within the foreign domain from the factor. The DeuceScan [6] scheme could also be a pre-scan scheme that minimizes the layer-two handoff delays. Two factors of signal strength and variation of signal strength square measure used in the Deuce Scan scheme [8]. The measurements of the handoff latency of the APs and mobile nodes (MNs) from entirely completely different vendors have discovered that the probe delay occupies the foremost necessary a neighborhood of the handoff latency, accounting for over ninetieth of the latency [9,10]. The QoS [10] of the MNs is also degraded and thus the transmission is also complete as a result of too high handoff latency [11,12]. As pointed in [10], once every MN selects the AP to connect to severally, few APs is also connected by many MNs but others APs keep idle. Projected in [11], the QoS-based integrated load balancing (ILB) scheme leverage's on QoS-based fast relinquishing to produce seamless relinquishing and soft admission management to defend QoS of existing connections once resources unit low. It selects the AP of the lower packet delay and offers a definition of a handoff threshold [7,8] in step with the packet loss rate.

3 Preliminaries

There are 3 types of delays for handoff [1,2] within the IEEE 802.11 customary handoff method, which are

- Scanning latency.
- Re-authentication latency.
- Re-association latency.

3.1   Scanning Latency

The scanning part latency defines the time taken by the MH to scan all the WiFi channels so as to search out the most effective AP in the handoff method. In our proposed approach, MH creates one circle with the radius of 400 m. MH hear the beacon messages (i.e., BSSID, beacon interval, support rate, etc.) broadcasted sporadically by the APs, that are during a circle.

If the first Access Point doesn't answer the authentication request from the MH that means it is not accessible. Therefore, the MH tries to manifest with the second AP at intervals the neighbor's table. However, if the MH was not able to manifest with any of the AP at intervals the table, then the MH will perform a full scanning (i.e., IEEE 802.11 standard) completely different previous work additionally uses context transfer for fast handoff have targeted on PNC and Selective Neighbor Caching (SNC) schemes.

BSSID	Beacon Interval	Supported Rates
00-15-E9-2B-99-3C	100 Kilomicroseconds	Auto
00-16-41-34-2C-A6	200 Kilomicroseconds	Auto
00:1C:B3:09:85:15	90 Kilomicroseconds	Auto
00:10:18:90:1A:97	600 Kilomicroseconds	Auto
00:3C:B9:10:76:41	80 Kilomicroseconds	Auto

Fig. 1. Mobile Host (MH) neighbor table

Here MH creates the neighbor table supported the circle with the radius of 400 m. So all AP that is found in 400 m close of MH, MH has details data about them. Once the MH moves from the presently associated AP and a hand-off are required, the MH uses the MH neighbors table to manifest directly with the primary AP accessible within the table while not scanning. If the primary AP doesn't answer the authentication request from the MH meaning it is not accessible. Therefore, the MH tries to manifest with the second AP inside the neighbor's table then on. As a result of all APs that within the radius of MH, data about them are within the neighbor table of MH, MH will send the direct authentication request to all or any of them. Therefore know would like of scanning by MH. The time delay is simply to see the provision of AP within the table that is incredibly marginal.

3.2   Re-authentication Latency

The re-authentication latency is that the time taken to manifest the MH with the new AP. It depends on the authentication methodology used.

3.3   Re-association Latency

The re-association section latency is that the time taken to re-association the MH with the new Access Point. The MH sends a re-association request to the new AP and waits for a re-association response. Throughout this method, the new AP requests the MH context data from the recent AP mistreatment IAPP before causing the re-association response. In our planned approach, the candidate set of APs is known by the MH neighbor table. So as to enhance the re-association latency, the context transfer method (using IAPP), is completed by presently associated AP to all or any the APs that details has been held on in the MH neighbor table. It should be separated from the re-association method. Once MH requests Re-association to new AP, the new AP does not get to send a security block to a recent AP at the time of Hand-off, as a result of the new-AP gets the client-context before the handoff, or pro-actively. At the time of handoff, new AP has needed causing solely re-association response to MH. Therefore, we are able to say that, in our planned approach, total handoff latency is incredibly less compare to existing approach.

4   Improvised Fast Handoff

In our proposed approach, first work is to reduce scanning delay and second work is prepositioning the station's context.

4.1   Data Structure

$Propagate_{context}(AP, MH, AP_i)$, currently associated Access Point (AP) propagate context information of Mobile Host (MH) to neighbor Access Point (AP_i) of Mobile Host i.

Algorithm 1. Distance Calculation Algorithm

Algorithm execute on MH
Step 1: AP broadcast beacon message.
Step 2: Receive beacon message.
Step 3: MH calculate distance from received beacon AP to itself.
Step 4: Put MH current location in points (x_{cmh}, y_{cmh}).
Step 5: Put AP current location in points (x_{cap}, y_{cap}).
Step 6: Calculate distance between these two points by using the distance formula
$\sqrt{(x_{cap} - x_{cmh})^2 + (y_{cap} - y_{cmh})^2}$
Put this value into x
if Val(x) less than equals 4000 **then**
    AP is selected
    if AP information is already in MH neighbor table **then**
        Discard the information.
    else
        Put the AP details in MH neighbor table and update neighbor table.
    else
        Reject AP details.
        Step 10: Step 3 will be repeated on every 0.5s interval.
    end if
end if

MH_{Info}, It describes that AP_i (i = 1 to the total neighbor) contains the context caching information of MH or not. If AP_i contains information of MH then re-association occur.

First, MH creates one circle with a radius of four hundred meters (because of the minimum vary of base station within the urban area). The MH creates one neighbor's table (as shown in Fig. 1) that contains info concerning all AP during this circle. Table columns square measure BSSID, beacon interval, support rate, etc. i.e., all relevant info concerning AP. These all info generated by MH by taking note of the beacon messages broadcasted sporadically by the APs. The MH copy the contents of its neighbor's table, place the probe request (BSSID, Beacon Interval, Support Rate) and send it to the associated AP. Associated AP can send context info concerning MH to any or all these hand-picked AP. Whenever MH receives the beacon message from neighbor AP it checks whether or not the AP info already exists within its neighbor's table or not. If the AP info isn't in its table the MH stores the received AP info into its neighbor's table. Otherwise, if the AP already exists within the neighbor's table, then nothing is modified within the table. These all method are going to be recurrent by MH at each 0.5 s. In formula one, once the MH moves [7–9] far away from the presently associated AP and a handoff square measure required, the MH uses the neighbor's table to demonstrate directly with the primary AP out there within the table while not scanning. If the primary AP does not reply to the authentication request from the MH meaning it is not out there. Therefore, the MH tries to demonstrate with the second AP within the neighbor table then on. As a result, if we've got captured all neighbor AP of MH within the explicit circle, therefore, there is no likelihood for MH for unable to demonstrate with any of the APs within the table (as shown in Fig. 1). As an associate degree application, we tend to gift a proactive context caching algorithm (shown in Algorithm 2) supported a neighbor table that contains neighbor AP data of MH to boost the re-association latency.

The neighbor table of MH provides the idea for distinctive this candidate set.

Algorithm 2. Proactive Caching Algorithm

Algorithm executes on currently associated AP.
Step 1: MH send details of neighbor AP as a Probe request to currently associated AP.
Step 2:
for all APi belongs to probe-packet (MH) **do**
    $propagate_{context}(AP, MH, AP_i)$
end for
Step 3: MH reassociates with APi.
Step 4:
if MH_{Info}==true **then**
    Re-association
end if

---

5   Simulations and Results

If MH is furnished with a table of accessible APs, then NS 2.34 [7] simulation results show an enormous improvement at intervals the handoff technique [8]. Once a handoff is needed, then MH starts pattern the neighbor table and tries to connect with the first Access Point at intervals the table directly whereas not active or passive scanning. If the first Access Points are not responding then the MH tries to connect to the second AP at intervals the neighbour table thus on until associate in neighbouring access point respond. Providing accessible APs to the MH brings the football play delay right all the way down to 0.762229 ms (as shown in Fig. 2).

In our simulation, we have created neighbouring MH's table for 10 APs and if first AP is free at the time of handoff it has been shown that the handoff delay [6,7] reduces to 0.762229. Once the first AP at intervals the neighbor's table is obtainable, it is our greatest case and so the worst case was offered once the AP is that the last AP at intervals the neighbor's table. We've placed the simulation result in Table 1. Here one represents, at the time of handoff, MH check the neighbor table and first AP is free then handoff delay is barely 0.762229. In Table 1, a combine of represents, at the time of handoff first AP in the neighbor table is not free then MH checks second AP and if it's free then handoff delay is 0.762232 and 10 represents, at the time of handoff from one to 9 AP aren't free therefore it'll use tenth AP and if it's free then handoff delay is 0.762341 and simulation setting shown in Table 2.

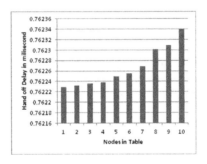

Fig. 2. Handoff delay calculation based on number of nodes

6   Distribution of Clients Across APs

We have presented a uniform distribution of clients across APs at the start of the simulation for both cases (i.e., neighbor graph-based approach and proposed scheme) for Multimedia Applications. Figure 3 shows the distribution of the Max. # of users linked with each AP during a simulation with five AP, and ten clients. Figure 3 shows that the proposed scheme performs the best among the existing scheme (i.e., Neighbor Graph-based approach [1,7]).

Table 1. Table for handoff delay calculation

Nodes in table	Total hand off delay (ms)
1	0.762229
2	0.762232
3	0.762236
4	0.762238
5	0.762250
6	0.762255
7	0.762269
8	0.762301
9	0.762309
10	0.762341

Table 2. Simulation parameters

Simulation parameters	Data values
# of Nodes	10, 20, 30, 40, 50
Total time in simulation	120 s
Simulation area	1000×1000
Speed	2, 5, 8, 10, 12 m/s
Time	0, 50, 100, 150, 200
Message size	512 bytes
Routing protocols	AODV, DSR
Traffic type	Constraint bit rate
Network simulator type	Network simulator 2.34
Mobility model	Random way point mobility model

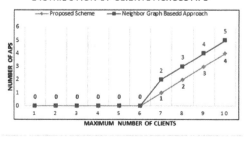

Fig. 3. Distribution of max. nos. of clients associated to an AP during a simulation with 5 APs and 10 users.

7   Conclusion

The scanning delay takes 90% times of total handoff delay. In this work, we propose a method which provides the fast handoff solution for Multimedia Applications. MH and AP both contains the neighbor table. MH contains information of neighbor APs by using beacon message. When the handoff occurs, MH first checks its neighbor table. If first AP in the table is freer than MH, it connects to that AP otherwise it checks second, third and so on. Due to this approach, sometimes scanning delay is equal to zero (if first AP in MH neighbor table is free). So we can see the handoff time decrease dramatically if last AP in the table is accessed by MH as well. Since all neighbors, APs details of MH are stored in the neighbor table so any AP is free for connection. AP uses the neighbor table for reducing re-association delay. MH sends the neighbor information to associated AP by using probe message. So that associated AP sends the context information to all neighbor AP of MH a priori. Elimination of scanning delay and re-association delay drops the total handoff delay time is 0.7 ms.

Acknowledgement. This work is partially supported by ECRA from SERB, DST, GoI, India (Project Number: ECR/2015/000256/ES).

References

1. Mishra, A., Shin, M., Arbaush, W.A.: Context caching using neighbor graphs for fast handoffs in a wireless network. In: Twenty-third Annual Joint Conference of the IEEE Computer and Communications Societies, pp. 351–361 (2004)
2. Nakhjiri, M., Perkins, C., Koodli, R.: Context transfer protocol. IETF Internet Draft (2003)
3. WG 802.11 - Wireless LAN Working Group: IEEE Recommended Practice for Multi-Vendor Access Point Interoperability via an Inter-Access Point Protocol Across Distribution Systems Supporting IEEE 802.11 Operation, IEEE Draft 802.1f/Final Version (2003)
4. Balachandran, A., Voelker, G.M., Jolla, L., Bahl. P., Rangan, P.V.: Characterizing user behaviour and network performance in a public wireless LAN. In: Proceedings of the 2002 ACM SIGMETRICS International Conference on Measurement and Modeling of Computer Systems, pp. 195–205 (2002)
5. Schwab, D., Bunt, R.: Characterising the use of a campus wireless network. In: Proceeding IEEE INFOCOM, pp. 862–870 (2004)
6. Chen, Y., Chuang, M., Chen, C.: DeuceScan: Deuce-based fast handoff scheme in IEEE 802.11 wireless networks. IEEE Trans. Veh. Technol. **57**(2), 1126–1141 (2008)
7. Mishra, A., Shin, M., Arbaugh, W.: An empirical analysis of the IEEE802.11 MAC layer handoff process. ACM SIGCOMM Comput. Commun. Rev. **33**, 93–102 (2004)
8. Das, D., Misra, R., Raj, A.: Approximating geographic routing using coverage tree heuristics for wireless network. Wirel. Netw. **21**(4), 1180–1188 (2015)
9. Lee, J., Ernst, T., Chilamkurti, N.: Performance analysis of PM IPv6 based network mobility for intelligent transportation systems. IEEE Trans. Veh. Technol. **61**(1), 74–85 (2012)

10. Wang, Y., Zhang, P., Zhou, Y., Yuan, J., Liu, F., Li, G.: Handover management in enhanced MIH framework for heterogeneous wireless networks environment. Wireless Pers. Commun. **52**(3), 615–636 (2010)
11. Abdullah, R.M., Zukarnain, Z.A., Iqbal, R.: Improved fast handover method for multiple node by using mobile nodes guide. Telecommun. Syst. (2016). https://doi.org/10.1007/s11235-016-0183-1.
12. Vallati1, C., Mingozzi, E., Benedetto, C.: Efficient handoff based on link quality prediction for video streaming in urban transport systems. Wirel. Commun. Mob. Com. (2016). https://doi.org/10.1002/wcm.2684

Adaptive Partitioning Using Partial Replication for Sensor Data

Bhumika Kalavadia[1], Tarushi Bhatia[1], Trupti Padiya[2],
Ami Pandat[1(✉)], and Minal Bhise[1(✉)]

[1] Distributed Database Group, DA-IICT, Gandhinagar, India
{201301167, 201311006, 201711032,
minal_bhise}@daiict.ac.in
[2] Friedrich Schiller Universität Jena, Jena, Germany
trupti.padiya@uni-jena.de

Abstract. There is a huge increase in IoT network size and applications. It has increased the amount of the IoT data that needs to be handled by the applications. State-of-the art workload based static partitioning methods scale poorly and often result in poor execution times as not all the queries are favoured by initial partition created. This work proposes an adaptive partitioning method that adapts the system to workload changes by reproducing the most frequent pattern among nodes. The scheme also adapts when new triples or properties are added into a system by ensuring proper placement of new triples in an appropriate partition by leveraging subject-object joins. The performance of this adaptive partitioning method is evaluated against the existing static partitioning scheme. The performance of the system for different query types such as linear, star, administrative and snowflakes are analysed. The experimental results verify that the adaptive partitioning method is scalable, adjusts to categories of dynamism and results in faster query execution by minimizing inter-node communication. Although Algorithm Execution Time (AET) for adaptive partitioning is greater than static partitioning, Query Execution Time (QET) increases at much faster rate for static partitioning for scaled data. Adaptive partitioning accelerates queries by 60% compared to static partitioning when averaged over types of queries.

Keywords: Adaptive partitioning · AET · Heat map · QET · RDF
Replication · Static partitioning

1 Introduction

The Semantic Web [1] is an effort by the W3C to enable integration and sharing of data across different applications and organizations. Due to its widespread use in real-world applications, an enormous growth is seen in semantic web data. Hence in order to exploit the full potential of semantic web vision, a shift from traditional centralized data storage systems to distributed storage systems was observed. Further, vital management of this semantic web data is desired so that it results in efficient data storage, low Query Execution Times (QET) and also minimal communication overheads between nodes while fetching data.

© Springer Nature Switzerland AG 2019
G. Fahrnberger et al. (Eds.): ICDCIT 2019, LNCS 11319, pp. 260–269, 2019.
https://doi.org/10.1007/978-3-030-05366-6_22

The data model that lies at the heart of the semantic web is the Resource Description Framework (RDF). In this framework, data is represented as a series of triples of the form <subject, property, object> wherein the property represents the relationship between the subject and object. Most prominent method for partitioning the data among different nodes is static partitioning method which uses a priori information of the query workload to place RDF triples into partitions. These static partitioning methods fail to accommodate when query load changes when the addition of new RDF triples or properties is carried out into the system. As a result, these schemes require inter-node communications for evaluating queries that are not supported by underlying initial partitioning.

Adaptive partitioning method can adjust to change in workload by screening the query patterns and then by reproducing and replicating the most frequent patterns among data nodes. This method adjusts, to addition of new RDF triples or properties by leveraging subject-object joins and then by placing the triples in an appropriate partition. As a result, this adaptive partitioning has the capacity to assess queries on massive RDF dataset in sub-seconds and helps in building faster applications for systems which exhibit dynamism.

If the data is initially partitioned among worker nodes as given in Figs. 1 and 2. Now if a query given in Fig. 3 is to be evaluated then in static partitioning method will result in inter node communication. This is because query pertains with fetching sampling times for systems. Here time for System_DEF and time for System_XYZ is in node 2 and node 1 respectively. So the nodes do not have entire data to evaluate query and will make use of join to compute the result. Since joins are expensive so proposed adaptive partitioning scheme will replicate the tuple <DEF_Rain, Sampling time, 13-01-2015> to node 1 and correspondingly <XYZ_humidity, Sampling time, 11-08-2016> to node 2 if they are frequent query patterns. This will ensure that each node has almost all the data needed to answer the query. This results in mini-missing inter-node communication and hence enhancing query performance.

Subject	Property	Object
System_ABC	GeneratedObservation	ABC_AirTemp
ABC_AirTemp	Type	TempObserv
ABC_AirTemp	Sampling time	20-04-2017
System_DEF	GeneratedObservation	DEF_Rain
XYZ_Humidity	Sampling time	11-08-2016

Fig. 1. Node 1 triples

Subject	Property	Object
System_XYZ	GeneratedObservation	XYZ_Humidity
XYZ_Humidity	Type	Humidity
XYZ_Humidity	Result	Measure_humidity
System_EFG	Type	WindObs
DEF_Rain	Sampling time	13-01-2015

Fig. 2. Node 2 triples

The contents of this paper are organised as follows. In next Section we discuss the literature reviewed for gaining a fundamental understanding of storage schemes in this area. Then our research methodology is described. Following section describes the experimental setup that was used to carry out the experiment. And last sections are highlighting the results and conclusion.

2 Related Work

In the most simplistic representation, RDF triples are stored in a three column format called triple store [2]. As it involves storing the entire information in a single table, most queries require several self-joins over the table and bring about poor QET. To overcome the limitations associated with the triple store approach, data partitioning schemes have been in use. The significant static data partitioning schemes that are widely used are the property table, vertical partitioning, column partitioning, and data-centric scheme.

In property table [2] approach subjects having similar properties are stored in denormalized flat structured tables. As the subjects having similar properties are likely to be queried together, it eliminates the need for subject-subject self-joins of the triple store scheme but may involve joins among several property tables. If the subjects do not contain certain properties applicable to them, then the number of NULL values in the table increases and thereby wastes storage space.

Find all systems that have snow depth defined on Instant_2004_8_9_7_00_00.

Fig. 3. SQL query

?s, generated Observation, ?o
?o, observedProperty, ?op
?o, sampling Time,? l

Fig. 4. Decomposed query pattern

Vertical Partitioning scheme [2] deals with the shortcoming of the property table approach by representing all the unique properties present in the RDF dataset as two column table. The first column in the table contains the subject that characterizes that property and second column contains the corresponding object data for those properties. However, if the query that is fired to the vertically partitioned scheme assesses several properties then merge joins are required over the two-column tables. In column orientated store approach, triples are stored as columns instead of the traditional row-based approach. It offers an advantage that only the column that is relevant for the query is fetched as opposed to row-based store in which entire rows needs to be read.

Further data-centric [3] storage scheme aims to strike a balance between property tables and binary tables. A two-phase algorithm consisting of clustering phase and partitioning phase helps in achieving that objective. It results in efficient query execution by maximizing the likelihood that queries will access properties in the same table without the need for a join and also by reducing the overhead associated with storing the nulls in the table.

In context of Static partitioning, to store RDF data three approaches were discussed by researchers: Property table, Vertical Partitioned Storage and Data Aware Hybrid Storage [4]. Data Aware Hybrid Storage approach combines both vertical partitioned and property table approach to resolve their respective performance issues. These approaches are not supported for distributed environment and also not able to manage data in adaptive manner.

DWAHP is dynamic workload aware hybrid partitioning. This technique is efficient for faster query joins and inter-node communication in distribution of RDF data [5]. This static workload based approach is not efficient for adaptive partitioning.

It can be seen that all the above static schemes suffer from inter-node communication and does not adapt when querying load changes or when new properties are added to a system. This adaptive partitioning scheme overcomes these limitations by controlled data replication of frequently accessed query patterns [6] among data nodes by leveraging subject-object bindings [7] for suitable placement of triples.

3   Research Methodology

The queries that are to be fired on the system are first decomposed into atomic query pattern forms. Since similar query patterns can occur in future, hence constants in the query must be replaced with generalized expressions. For example, Fig. 4 gives decomposed query pattern along with generalized query pattern for SQL query given in Fig. 3. We can see that in decomposed query pattern that constants such as snow depth is replaced with generalized expression?op. This will result in fetching all the properties that are there in the database and not just a particular property.

To record the frequency of the query patterns a heat map table is created which comprises four columns i.e. subject, property, object, and frequency count. If a new query pattern is encountered then it is inserted into the heat map table with a frequency count set to one and if an existing pattern is encountered then frequency count corresponding to that pattern is increased by one.

Different threshold values were set to control the amount of data replication in the system. When the frequency count of a particular pattern crosses the set threshold, the data corresponding to that query pattern is fetched into a table called the triple store and is termed as a frequent pattern. The triple store table contains the identified frequent patterns are to be replicated among data nodes so that it results in minimum inter-node communication for future queries. Algorithm 1 is used for the creation of heat map and triple store table.

As and when new subject parameters are encountered in the triple store table, a dictionary is created for that subject. The dictionary specifies to which data node among the three replica nodes, the frequent subject parameter is to be replicated. This it does by mapping the different subject categories to replica nodes. The core vertex amongst the subject parameters is assigned to replica data nodes using length (dictionary) mod N + 1 where N stands for the number of data nodes which in this case is 3. The remaining subject parameters are then assigned to replica data nodes using the subject-object bindings. Algorithm 2 describes the mechanism used behind the creation of dictionaries. The dictionaries were dumped in a pickle file so as to avoid creating them again.

Once the dictionary creation is completed, Incremental Redistribution (IR) is triggered for the data residing in the triple store table. In the incremental redistribution phase, the data in triple store table is replicated among the data nodes in the replica tables using the lookup dictionary that was created previously as it specified the data node to which a particular frequently occurring triple is to be replicated. Incremental Redistribution is described in Algorithm 3.

Algorithm 1

Input: query pattern <variable, property, variable>
Output: frequent subject category (one that crosses the threshold set)
Variables: Heatmap table as H, Triple Store table as T, Subject Category as S, query pattern as Q

If(S exist in H)
       Update the frequency count of corresponding Q by 1;
       If (S crosses the threshold):
            Insert the triples corresponding to this pattern Q into T;
            Return S;
Else:
       Insert the Q into H and set frequency count=1;

Once replication is successful, testing queries are fired. If the query pattern of this newly arrived query already exists in the heatmap then it is fired on replica table directly without accessing the main table for faster query evaluation, else new pattern is recorded in the heatmap and query is directed to the main table for evaluation. In this manner, the adaptive algorithm adapts to the newly arriving queries.

Two important challenges that static partitioning system faced were how to adapt to changing workload and how to cater to database updates. We already saw how heatmap concepts help to cater the former challenge easily with the considerable performance gain. On other hand, database updates can be in form of deletion or insertion. The delete operation can be carried out in parallel on each data node.

The triples to be deleted are removed from the main table as well as replica table parallel from each data node.In case of insertion, there are two possibilities:

1. Triples with similar properties, similar subject but different values are added. For example, system_ABC records air temperature values for some new instant.
2. Triples with similar properties but different subject and object values are added.
3. Triples with different new properties are added. Note that in this case subject category may change or remain the same as previous ones.

In case 1, the system checks whether the property of new triples is frequent or not. If not, triples are directly added to the main table otherwise newly inserted triples should also be replicated. Since these triples same similar subjects, it gets replicated to corresponding data nodes just by dictionary lookup.

Algorithm 2

Input: frequent subject category and access to main hash partitioned table
Output: lookup table which indicates replica node assigned to each triple of Triple Store table
Variables: Heatmap table as H, Triple Store table as T, Subject Category as S, query pattern as Q,
Main Table as L

If(S=core vertex)
        Rows = fetch all the triples from L corresponding to "system" category
        ($\forall$ Row $\in$ Rows)
                Create the dictionary using sub as key and len (dictionary) %N+1 as value
Else:
        Fetch the dictionary of the predecessor subject category S1
        Rows = fetch all the triples from main table corresponding to S
        For each row in rows:
                Create the dictionary using sub as key and key lookup in dictionary of S1;

In case 3, since triples with new properties are inserted it is not yet the frequently accessed triples. So these triples are inserted into the main table directly without any modification in replica tables or dictionaries. If the query patterns pertaining to these triples becomes frequent then it gets reflected in heatmap and algorithm to generate dictionaries gets triggered. Now if the subject category is the same as previous ones, these triples get replicated on corresponding data nodes identified by the dictionary. But if it is a new subject category then the system asks user its parent subject category for generating the new dictionary. Once the dictionary is created, triples are replicated to direct data node.

Algorithm 3

Input: pickle file containing dictionaries and access to triple store and replica tables
Output: all the frequent triples replicated to corresponding data nodes
Variables: Heatmap table as H, Triple Store table as T, Subject Category as S, query pattern as Q,
Main Table as L, Replica Table R

For each property that crosses threshold in H:
        Dict= load the dictionary of S corresponding to that property
        Rows=fetch all triples with this property from T
                ($\forall$ Row $\in$ Rows)
                    node_index= key corresponding to subject of row from dict
                    Insert this triple into R of datanode_ (%node_index)

4   Experimental Setup

For the purpose of carrying out the experiment, three data nodes on a single machine using POSTGRES-XL 9.5 R1.4, an open source scalable SQL database cluster. POSTGRES-XL has built-in MPP (Massively Parallel Processing) with apt query planning capability. Each data node had its own copy of the RDF data and handled SQL statements locally. The coordinator node was created for handling SQL statements and determining which data node to execute the query on. Unless explicitly mentioned coordinator fires the query on all the three data nodes. For the algorithmic implementation, we used Python and PL/PQSQL procedural language. The machine possessing three data nodes has an Intel 4th GenCore i7-4500U processor with 8 GB RAM and 1 TB HDD.

4.1   Dataset

LOD [8] (Linked Observation Data) was used as the benchmark for the experiment. The dataset comprised 10 unique properties and 5 subject categories. The number of triples was varied from 1lakh to 20 lakhs during the experiment. The dataset is available in standard RDF format comprising of triples <subject, predicate, object> in URI format. The dataset was parsed to retrieve only filenames associated with the URIs.

4.2   QuerySet

In order to evaluate the performance of the system we used 15 benchmark queries and categorized them into the following times: linear, star, snowflakes and administrative queries. Linear Queries retrieves a predetermined set of properties from the RDF dataset. These queries are atomic in nature and do not require any joins. Star Queries involve the selection of property values for a particular subject. Snowflakes Queries retrieves predetermined properties or subjects or both. Administrative Queries are range queries comprising of aggregate functions. Two static partitioning schemes i.e. distribute by round robin and distribute by hash based on the subject were also created in order to compare the performance with our adaptive partitioning scheme. Adaptive Partitioning Scheme follows two-tier partitioning approach wherein dataset is initially partitioned using hashing on the subject and later most frequent triples are again partitioned into replica nodes using locality-aware hashing.

5   Results and Analysis

The performance of adaptive partitioning algorithm proposed in this paper is evaluated against static partitioning scheme using the following parameters: QET, Scalability, Replication, Internode Communication and Algorithmic Time and Space Complexity.

5.1 QET

The query processing time for different types of QuerySet like linear, star, snowflakes and administrative queries on static as well as adaptive partitioned data. Figures 5 and 6 shows the results of QET. Adaptive partitioning scheme is almost 10 times faster in case of star, snowflakes and administrative queries and shows considerable performance gain in the case of linear queries. As the star queries fetch the properties associated with a particular subject only it gives exceptional performance due to subject based hashing. While snowflake and administrative queries require subject-object joins and aggregation over and above star access pattern, it takes more execution time compared to star queries. The optimum query performance is in view with the fact that each data node has most of the information it needs to answer the query in parallel fashion and requirement for internode communication is minimum.

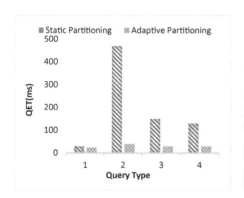
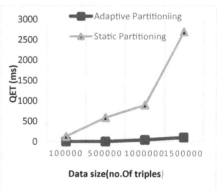

Fig. 5. QET for each type of query   **Fig. 6.** Average QET for all queries

5.2 Scalability

We carried out this experiment on different workloads. We used a LOD dataset of different sizes like 1 lakh, 5 lakhs, 10 lakhs, and 15 lakhs to verify the scalability of the proposed algorithm. The results verify that as the data size increases, query performance also increases compared to static partitioning schemes. By observation, it can be seen that snowflakes query shows better performance than star queries because a less frequent query is present in star QuerySet which requires communication as results are not cached in the replica tables. So even the small amount of internode communication results in a significant difference in QET.

5.3 Replication Cost

In order to control replication and at the same time get optimum QET with minimum inter-node communication, we varied the frequency threshold (upper limit beyond which query pattern in heatmap gets replicated) and recorded the QET, replication ratio and communication costs. From the graphical results, it can be verified that threshold 2 is the appropriate limit for categorizing the query pattern as the hot pattern because it records minimum execution time, minimum internode communication and considerable replication. Further, it was seen that as threshold increases execution time and communication cost both increases while replication drastically reduces. In this trade-off between efficient processing times versus minimizing memory usage, we gave more importance to the former parameter as processing time is more expensive whereas memory of system can be easily extended.

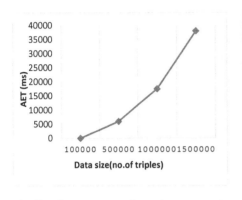

Fig. 7. Time complexity in generating dictionaries

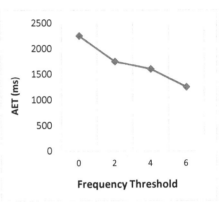

Fig. 8. Time complexity IR algorithm

5.4 Algorithmic Complexity Analysis

As discussed in the research methodology section of this paper, three main steps required in adaptive partitioning algorithm involves time and space complexities. The time taken to generate heatmap is constant and does not vary with data sizes and frequency threshold. The heat map table occupies nearly 8 KB of storage space. Time taken to run the Algorithm 2 and 3 on various data sizes and frequency threshold is shown in Figs. 7, 8, 9 and 10 respectively.

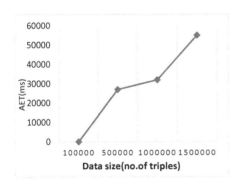

Fig. 9. Time complexity for IR algorithm of different data sizes.

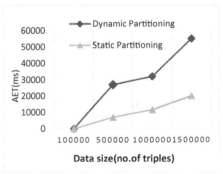

Fig. 10. Time complexity comparison

6 Conclusion

The proposed adaptive partitioning algorithm tries to ensure proper data placement using core vertex and their subject-object binding so that most of the queries can be evaluated in a parallel fashion. Apart from caching the frequently accessed triples, we replicated the triples in cache among three data nodes considering data locality using semantic hashing. Thus algorithm enabled each node to execute most of the queries in parallel, without internode communication. The experimental results successfully verify the query performance gain as well as the scalability of the system. Adaptive partitioning results presented in this work indicate a much better performance of the presented method for scaled data. Adaptive partitioning technique accelerates queries on an average by 60% compared to static partitioning technique. This will help in building faster applications for adaptive situations.

References

1. Lee, T.B., Hendler, J., Lassila, O.: The semantic web. In: Scientific American, pp. 1–4 (2001)
2. Abadi, D.J., Marcus, A., Madden, S.R., Hollenbach, K.: Scalable semantic web data management using vertical partitioning. In: Proceedings of the 33rd International Conference on Very Large Data Bases, pp. 411–422 (2007)
3. Levandoski, J.J., Mokbel, M.F.: RDF data-centric storage. In: IEEE International Conference on Web Services, ICWS 2009, Los Angeles, CA, USA, pp. 911–918 (2009)
4. Padiya, T., Bhise, M., Rajkotiya, P.: Data management for Internet of Things. In: IEEE Region 10 Symposium, pp. 62–65 (2015)
5. Padiya, T., Bhise, M.: DWAHP: workload aware hybrid partitioning and distribution of RDF data. In: IDEAS, pp. 235–241 (2017)
6. Al-Harbi, R.: Adaptive partitioning for very large RDF data. arxiv: 1505.02728 [cs.DB] (2015)
7. Lee, K., Liu, L.: Scaling queries over big RDF graphs with semantic hash partitioning. Proc. VLDB Endow. **6**, 1894–1905 (2013)
8. LinkedSensorData. http://wiki.knoesis.org/index.php/LinkedSensorData

Design and Implementation of Cognitive Radio Sensor Network for Emergency Communication Using Discrete Wavelet Packet Transform Technique

Mariappan Ramasamy[1]([✉]) and Rama Subramanian M.[2]

[1] Electronics and Communication Engineering,
Sri Venkateswara College of Engineering, Tirupati, India
prof.mariappan.r@gmail.com
[2] Madras Institute of Technology, Chennai 600 045, India
rama.mit2016@gmail.com

Abstract. The Cognitive Radio network is one of the challenging field, where researchers are working to utilize the underutilized spectrum bands for the needful and emergency purposes. This paper proposes one such possible solution to design Cognitive Radio network with Universal Software Radio Peripheral (USRP) based Software Defined Radio (SDR). It explores the efficient implementation of Software Defined Radio (SDR) to sense and detect white spaces in the spectrum for the use of emergency communication during disaster using Discrete Wavelet Packet Transform (DWPT). The SDR testbed setup was simulated using MATLAB and observed its performance parameters and it performs better in terms of detected Power level, SNR and detection accuracy. The simulation results prove that this new devised approach has zero interference to the primary user frequency bands and hence not affecting the existing users. Hence, this paper concludes the Proof- of-Concept proposed with improved Quality of Service (QoS).

Keywords: Cognitive radio · Emergency communications
Software defined radio (SDR)

1 Introduction

During natural disasters including heave floods, cyclones, etc., communication among the affected people plays a vital role. However, the existing communication technologies including, landline, wireless, mobile, Radio, TV communication, etc. fail during such scenarios of disasters. Moreover, everyone makes use of the communication channel for messaging, traffic support, recovery, etc., thereby the entire communication channel is overloaded and difficult to communicate easily one another. Hence, there is a need for an emergency communication technology to communicate among the people for a short duration. Cognitive Radio is one such challenging technology, which can be used for emergency communication without any assigned communication channel but sharing the unused frequency bands of other

© Springer Nature Switzerland AG 2019
G. Fahrnberger et al. (Eds.): ICDCIT 2019, LNCS 11319, pp. 270–278, 2019.
https://doi.org/10.1007/978-3-030-05366-6_23

communication channels like Radio, TV, etc. Thus, Cognitive Radio network can make use of the unused communication channels and hence increases the spectrum utilization and spectrum efficiency to the maximum. Therefore, this research paper addresses the issue of utilizing the unused frequency bands of other communication channels, by dynamic sensing of spectrum and assigning for emergency communication. The outline of this research paper is as follows. Section 2 reviews the current literature available in the field of Cognitive radio as well as emergency communication. Section 3 outlines the proposed work for the emergency communication using cognitive radio. Section 4 describes the design details of Cognitive radio network, followed by Sect. 5, showing the simulation results with MATLAB-SIMULINK. Finally, Sect. 6 concludes the paper with valuable remarks on cognitive radio networks.

2 Related Work

The Cognitive radio communication [1] is an emerging field of research and now-a-days it finds application in various sectors which include Defence, secure communication industry, etc. and it will occupy other sectors in near future. This new technology is no longer merely a concept of white space utilization in the allotted spectrum space but it is finding application in several areas such as grid communication, machine to machine communication, device to device communication, in cloud computing, military applications, medical science, etc. This section reviews most of the literature proposing sophisticated changes in such systems with the use of cognitive radio technology. Cognitive Radio technology [2] finds use in cognitive radio networks, applied in emergency communication, short messaging services, short term radio communication, defence communication, secure communication network, etc. In Worldwide, mobile communication frequency bands such as 2G, 3G, 4G, etc. almost fully loaded and seldom over-loaded. But, on the other side, military communication, amateur radio, etc. are less occupying h frequency bands and underutilized most of the times. Hence, the concept of cognitive radio was introduced by Royal Institute of technology to make use of the frequency bands of underutilized communication channels. It can be used in several ways like emergency communication, etc., even without having license to use the white spaces of primary user bands. The basic building blocks of a Cognitive radio are shown in Fig. 1.

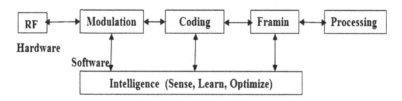

Fig. 1. Cognitive radio network

Haykin [3, 4] in 2005 defined cognitive radio as brain-Empowered Wireless Communications system. Cognitive radio basically works by making use of the regulated frequency spectrum into un-regulated frequency users. In general, the current researchers are focusing on horizontal and vertical spectrum sharing [5] of licensed frequency bands by the un-licensed users. The sharing of frequency resource is based on the regulatory status of radios working within the same spectrum. There are different types of spectrum sensing methods [6] found in literature.

3 Proposed System

In this paper, a number of spectrum sensors are placed in the disaster area. Sensors will start scanning the spectrum sequentially and forward the information towards the head node. A wifi based Mobile Ad Hoc Network (MANET) [7] will be used to share data among the sensor nodes. An enhanced version of IEEE 802.11 will be used for advanced mesh network. An emitter can be detected by multiple sensors. Channel model [8] for emergency environment will be employed on the sensors to predict the possible channel characteristics. Each sensor will extract the PHY parameters from the received signal and forward to the head node through the wifi link. The head node is responsible to develop and maintain the central database. Database will contain the following information: Emitter ID, Geo-location, Center Frequency, Modulation, Bandwidth, Association info and other PHY/MAC parameters. A cooperative algorithm [9] will be used to update database accordingly. A suitable Geo-location algorithm will be used to estimate the location of the emitters.

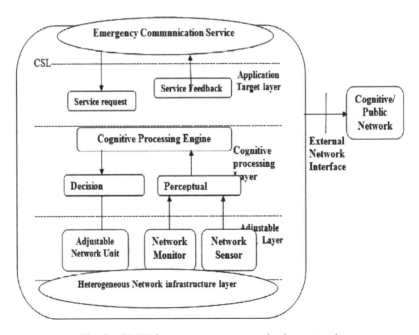

Fig. 2. CRSN for emergency communication network

In this research, it is proposed to use Cognitive Radio Sensor Network (CRSN) is shown in Fig. 2. It senses the real world parameters and to communicate through emergency setup established during disaster, using opportunistic spectrum access from the primary user licensed band 1 or 2. The CRSN uses the adhoc network or Coordinated Heterogeneous network topology [10]. The CRSN based emergency network considered in this project is having four layers as shown in Fig. 2. The layered design of Cognitive radio network for the emergency communication is shown in Table 1.

Table 1. Cognitive radio functionality

CR layer	Functionality
Application layer	Channel bandwidth, delay, reliability
Transport layer	Reliability, congestion control, flow control
	QoS requirement: packet loss &delay
Network layer	Routing and spectrum decision
Link layer control (LLC)	Link layer information, data & control channels
	Error control link layer reconfiguration
MAC layer	User channel control
Physical	Spectrum sensing, frequency, modulation,
	Topology reconfiguration

4 System Design

4.1 Physical Layer Design

The CRSN nodes will be different from WSN nodes in terms of energy efficiency, communication capability, processing power, memory, etc. The physical node structure of CRSN consists of sensor, central processor, CR unit.

4.2 Cognitive Radio Spectrum Sensing

This research work uses Discrete wavelet packet transform (DWPT) method to detect spectrum hole in wideband signals for dynamic spectrum access. The wavelet detection method is simple and flexible and it treats the entire spectrum as the combination of sub band frequencies and each band with smooth power characteristics with in the sub band and changes on the next sub band. This dynamic spectrum sensing can be used with enhanced Discrete Wavelet based Power Spectral Density (PSD) detection method as shown in Fig. 3. The CR spectrum sensing is a **Multi-Objective Problem,** which maximizes the spectral utilization using he multi-objective optimization algorithm as follows.

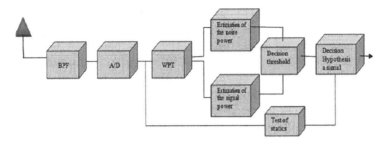

Fig. 3. Spectrum hole detection using discrete wavelet packet transform (DWPT)

Algorithm 1 Multi-Objective optimization

1: **begin**
2:   *minimise BER*: $F_{min-ber} = log\ 10\ (0.5)/\ log\ 10\ (P_{ber})$;
3:   *minimise.Power Transmission*: $F\ min\text{-}Power = P/P\ max$
4:   *minimise F min–inter* $f = \{(P + B + TDD)\text{-} P\ min + B\ min +1\{(Pmax + Bmax + Smax)$
5:   *maximise* $F_{max-Spectraleff} = 1\text{-}\ (M*B_{min} * S)/\ (B*M\ max * Smax)$
6:   *maximise Throughput*: $F\ max\ \text{--}throughput = 1\text{-}log_2(M)\ /\ log\ 2\ (M_{max})$
7: **end**

where M-modulation index, B- BW; P-power transmitted; *Pmax*- max.avl.power, *TDD*- Time div Dup; *Smax* – Max symbol rate

Algorithm 2 Spectrum sensing using DWPT

1: **begin**
2:   **for** *available N users, compute N-point FFT*
3:   *divide each each sub-band using DWPT*
4:   *compute n-level DWPT*
5:   *compute Energy of sub-band and average threshold value*
6:   **if** *the Energy level > 2x Threshold value* **then** *allocate the channel*
7:   **else** *wait and repeat the channel allocation steps until free slot available.*
8: **end**

4.3 MAC Layer Design

The MAC layer of CRSN has the following frame format. The CRSN node can share the MAC data frame to the CR sink. The MAC layer of the CRSN based emergency communication network uses enhanced version of Mobile adhoc network MAC protocol i.e. IEEE 802.11. The data channel for CRSN will be using OFDM baseband transceiver which optimally segments the spectrum as shown in Fig. 4, while the control channel uses unlicensed Ultra Wide band (UWB) transceiver.

Spectrum sensing (Primary channel)	Beacon Packet (Control Channel)	Network Entry (Control Channel)	Contention resolution (Control Channel)	Data (free Primary)

Fig. 4. OFDM data processing for cognitive radio network

4.4 Network Layer Design

The interaction between different layers of CRSN for the Emergency communication is considering essentially application layer QoS, transport layer handoff delay, network layer routing information, data link layer delay and physical layer sensing data for sharing the spectrum hole. The CR network will be reconfigured on transport layer or network layer or data link layer based on the shared information as shown in Fig. 5, the physical layer is initiating the spectrum sensing for the CR and it passes the spectrum sensing information to the spectrum hopping function. Then, the scheduling information as well as reconfiguration information is shared between Data link layer and spectrum management function. The spectrum sharing and link layer delay information are shared with spectrum hopping function. The upper layers respectively, network layer, transport layer and application layer is responsible for routing, reconfiguration and QoS Parameters.

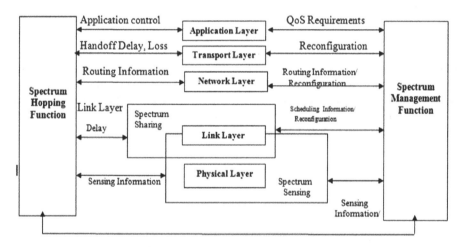

Fig. 5. Interaction between different layers of CRSN for emergency network

5   Simulation Results

In our simulation experiment, MATLAB version R2011 with standard MATLAB toolboxes and SIMULINK was used for the implementation of the algorithm and the wavelet coefficients. In this study, wideband spectra over the range 80Mz – 600 MHz, in the FM & TV frequency range are simulated. In 24 PSD models generated, we have assumed 50% spectrum occupancy rate and maintained the average PSD level in the

Table 2. Simulation parameters in MATLAB

Simulation parameters	Specifications
Frequency band	80 MHz–600 MHz
Sample size	1024
Number of wavelet scales	8
Number of PSD models per simulation	24
Spectral occupancy	50%
Ave PSD level in occupied channel	1 W/Hz
Number of channels	Max 20 (random generated)
Noise power	−20 to 40 dBW (AWGN)

occupied channels at 1 W/Hz. The rest of the parameters of each spectrum model are randomly selected such as the number of channels, the exact frequency location of each channel, etc. In each model, the spectrum is divided into a number of channels, which is unknown to the CR receiver. With the Monte-Carlo Simulation experiment in MATLAB R 2011, using the simulation parameters given in Table 2 was done for 1000 number of iterations.

The simulation experiment was carried out in MATLAB as follows. The CR was initialized with the carrier frequency fc = 85, 90, 95, 470, 475, 480 MHz and fs = 960 MHz. The Additive White Gaussian Noise (AWGN) was added to the modulating signal with a small attenuation. The user data was modulated by OFDM or Wavelet Packet division multiplexing. Then, all the modulated signals were added for transmission. If any new user enters, the available free slot will be given. If all the frequency bands are occupied, the user will be leaving the slot. The periodogram was used for the spectral estimation of the received signal. The Simulation setup in MATLAB and DWPT spectrum sensing is shown in Fig. 6. The PSD results and corresponding detection accuracy for different SNR is given in Table 3 for 5 channels.

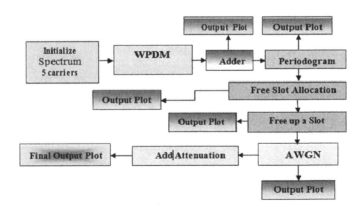

Fig. 6. Simulation setup in MATLAB and DWPT

The simulation results of PSD and the corresponding detection accuracy for different SNR is tabulated in Table 3 for 5 channels. From this table, it is observed that the DWPT dynamically senses the spectrum accurately even at low SNR and unoccupied hole will be assigned to CR and if the PU needs the band it will be vacated and given to the PU. This proves that Zero interference to the PU frequency bands.

Table 3. Simulation results of PSD & detection accuracy for different SNR

Channel	Freq range MHz	PSD level	P signal dBW	SNR at No = 15 dBW	SNR dB	Det. accuracy
1	85–90	5	23	10	−30	0.48
2	90–95	14	25	11	−25	0.52
3	95–100	0	–	–	−20	0.56
4	470–475	3	24	10	−10	0.62
5	475–480	3	24	10	0	0.76

6 Conclusion

In this paper, it is proposed that a new approach of using software defined radio based cognitive radio network for sensing the white spaces in the spectrum and to use for the emergency communication during disasters. The proposed spectrum sensing method using Discrete Wavelet Packet Transform (DWPT) applied on SDR setup was simulated using MATLAB and observed its performance parameters, which are better in terms of detected Power level, SNR and detection accuracy and QoS parameters. The MATLAB simulation proves that this new devised approach has zero interference to the primary user frequency bands and hence not affecting the existing users and hence it can be used for emergency communications during disasters.

References

1. IEEE Standard Definitions and Concepts for Dynamic Spectrum Access: Terminology Relating to Emerging Wireless Networks, System Functionality, and Spectrum Management, IEEE Std. 1900.1-2008, September 2008
2. Mitola III, J.: Cognitive radio: an integrated agent architecture for software defined radio. Ph. D. dissertation, Royal Institute of Technology, Stockholm, Sweden, May 2000
3. Haykin, S.: Cognitive radio: brain-empowered wireless communications. IEEE J. Sel. Areas Commun. **23**(2), 201–220 (2005)
4. Haykin, S.: Cognitive Radio. IEEE J. Sel. Areas Commn. **23**, 201–220 (2005)
5. Vo, Q.D., Choi, J.-P., Chang, H.M., Lee, W.C.: Green perspective cognitive radio-based M2 M communications for smart meters. In: Proceedings of International Conference on Information and Communication Technology Convergence (ICTC), pp. 382–383, November 2010

6. Ko, C.-H., Huang, D.H., Wu, S.-H.: Cooperative spectrum sensing in TV white spaces: when cognitive radio meets cloud. In: Proceedings of IEEE Conference on Computer Communications Workshops (INFOCOM WKSHPS), pp. 672–677, April 2011

7. Ge, F., et al.: Cognitive radio rides on the cloud. In: Proceedings of IEEE Military Communications Conference MILCOM, October– November 2010, pp. 1448–1453 (2010)

8. Abdulsattar, M.A., Hussein, Z.A.: Energy detection technique for spectrum sensing in cognitive radio: a survey. IJCNC **4**, 223 (2012)

9. Rawat, D.B., Yan, G.: Spectrum sensing methods and dynamic spectrum sharing in cognitive radio networks: a survey. IJRRWSN **1**(1), 1–3 (2011)

10. Jiang, Z.-L., Zhang, Q.-Y., Wang, Y., Shang, X.-Q.: Wavelet packet entropy based spectrum sensing in cognitive radio. In: IEEE 3rd ICCSN, Italy, pp. 121–125 (2011)

A Network Formation Model for Collaboration Networks

Ankur Sharma$^{(\boxtimes)}$ and S. Durga Bhavani$^{(\boxtimes)}$

School of Computer and Information Sciences, University of Hyderabad,
Hyderabad, India
ankurcusat123@gmail.com, sdbcs@uohyd.ernet.in

Abstract. In social networks, a network grows by following certain rules and patterns, e.g. a collaboration network in which authors come together and publish an article. These authors might have collaborated previously, or they may collaborate in the future with other authors. That is how a collaboration network grows. Collaboration networks are represented as graphs where nodes denote authors and edges between nodes indicate a collaboration between the corresponding authors. There are very few network formation models specific to collaboration networks in the literature. In this work, a novel network formation model that can imitate the growth of a collaboration network is proposed. The main idea is based on the arrival distribution of the numbers of authors collaborating for the papers. We find that Exponential distribution matches best for this process simulation. We have used DBLP dataset to analyze and find the patterns in the network. We show that the network generated by the proposed model is closer to the original network than that of Shi et al. The model has to be further refined in order to improve the results for average clustering coefficient and density of the network.

Keywords: Network formation model · Social networks
Collaboration network · DBLP

1 Introduction

Social networks such as friendship network, collaboration network etc. can be modelled as graphs. In a collaboration network, nodes denote authors and links represent collaborations. Whenever a network exists it has a past and a future. This present network will grow further or it has evolved from the past. The growth or the evolution of any social network is not random [6] and it is of research interest to predict the underlying growth model. Our objective in this work is to propose a network formation model for collaboration network such as DBLP. The network produced by the model should replicate the important characteristics [8] such as degree distribution, density, average clustering coefficient, assortativity of the original DBLP network. In a collaboration network G_t at time t, n number of papers get added to the network in Δt time. After Δt

© Springer Nature Switzerland AG 2019
G. Fahrnberger et al. (Eds.): ICDCIT 2019, LNCS 11319, pp. 279–294, 2019.
https://doi.org/10.1007/978-3-030-05366-6_24

time the network becomes $G_{t+\Delta t}$. Note that a paper coauthored by authors is a clique in the network formed by the authors. It is assumed that each paper that is being added to the network is authored by two or more authors.

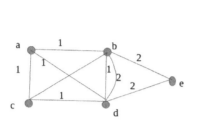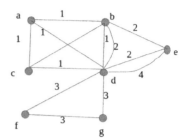

(a) A collaboration network G_t at time t

(b)   The   collaboration   network $G_{t+\Delta t}$ after time Δt

Fig. 1. Collaboration network growth

In Fig. 1(a) a collaboration network G_t is shown at time t. At time t there are 2 papers in the network labeled as 1 and 2. Paper 1 is coauthored by a, b, c and d and paper 2 is authored by b, e and d. As we can see there are two cliques present in the graph one having the vertices a, b, c, d and other is having the vertices b, d, e.

In Fig. 1(b) two papers 3 and 4 which arrived in time period of Δt get added to the network. Paper 3 is authored by d, f and g where as e and d collaborate for paper 4. Paper 3 is authored by a mix of old and new authors as there are two new authors f and g who joined the network, while paper 4 is authored by only old authors as the authors d and e have already been present in the network.

1.1   Problem Statement

To develop a model which can simulate the formation of a collaboration network so that it exhibits global characteristics and properties [8] such as degree distribution, density, average clustering, number of edges and assortativity as the original network.

1.2   Related Literature

A network formation model is a network generating method, which best represents the structure and properties of the real network. The main application of a network formation model is to evolve a network so that it can be analyzed and the local or global parameters of a real-world network be predicted [17]. One of the earliest network formation models is proposed by Barabasi and Albert called the Barabási-Albert model [6]. This is popularly known as the Preferential Attachment model. The model exhibits the scale-free property observed in many real-world networks such as the world wide web, the internet, and the citation network. Another model, the DMC (Duplication Mutation with complementarity) model mimics the Protein-Protein Interaction network [13]. The DMC model is based on two phenomena, the duplication in which a protein is duplicated from an existing protein and the mutation process in which a protein is mutated to obtain a new functionality. More recently, a network formation model given by Leskovec et al. called as Forest Fire model [11] shows that as the network evolves, its density increases and the diameter reduces as in many real-world networks. A closely related problem in which formation of a future link is predicted called the *Link Prediction* problem has been addressed extensively in the literature [10, 12].

A Collaboration Network is a co-authorship network in which an article is added to the network as a clique graph where nodes represent the authors collaborating for this article. Newman [15, 16] analyze the collaboration networks of Medline, complete, astro-ph, cond-mat, hep-th, SPIRES and NCSTRL. Newman computed the various parameters and statistical properties such as the clustering coefficient, mean papers per author, mean authors per paper and the giant component. Many of the social networks are scale-free networks in which the degree distribution $p(q)$, the frequency distribution of nodes of degree q, $p(q) \sim q^{-\gamma}, \gamma > 0$ following the power-law property [17]. Newman found that these co-authorship networks are scale-free networks and exhibit power law properties. Barabási et al. also studied the properties of co-authorship networks of mathematics and neuro-science [5]. They computed the degree distribution and also found that degree distribution follows power laws with exponent $\gamma_{math} = 2.4$ and $\gamma_{Neuro} = 2.1$.

Shi et al. [19] proposed a model to generate a collaboration network. Their model is based on motifs discovered in the network. Motifs can be patterns or subgraphs present in a complex network [14]. They divided the authors into two categories: old author, an author who has already published and new author, the author who has published in the given instant of time and has not published earlier. They compute the strength of each author and show that the more strength an author has the more collaborations are present with the other authors.

We have compared various global properties [8] of social network generated by our model such as density, clustering coefficient, assortativity and degree distribution with the original DBLP network as well as the model of Shi et al.

2 The DBLP Dataset and Analysis

DBLP is a computer science bibliography, an online database which contains the information of published papers in journals, conferences worldwide. DBLP is itself a very huge and complex network. Our objective is to design a network formation model which simulates and produces a DBLP-like network.

The dataset used in this work is DBLP dataset [4] in which the year-wise information of authors collaborating for articles published during the years 2001 to 2006 is available. The data from the years 2001 to 2004 is used for analyzing and computing the important parameters and values, and the data pertaining to the years 2005 and 2006 are used for testing and verifying the proposed model.

2.1 Data Preprocessing

Table 1 shows a small sample of the dataset in its raw form.

Table 1. A paper authored by four authors found in the dataset.

Author1_ID	Author2_ID	Conference_ID	Paper_Title
88141	42513	25	Modeling and Querying Moving Objects
88141	69948	25	Modeling and Querying Moving Objects
88141	69949	25	Modeling and Querying Moving Objects

As can be seen from the table, a paper which has the title "Modeling and Querying Moving Objects" having four authors "88141", "42513", "69948" and "69949" is present in the DBLP dataset. An article in the dataset corresponds to a complete subgraph in the network where vertices are the authors who are collaborating for the article. Conference_ID is not needed so it is removed from the dataset and a unique ID is set for each paper.

2.2 Network Analysis

DBLP is a collaboration network consisting of many authors and their articles so it can be a very complex network. To propose a model, some of the fundamental characteristics and properties of the network must be analyzed so that we can have an insight on how a collaboration network grows and what are the important parameters to be considered. Some of the basic statistics of the DBLP dataset is given in Table 2.

Table 2. Basic statistics of the dataset for 2001–2006

Years	2001	2002	2003	2004	2005	2006
Total papers	1861	1518	2112	2117	2921	2036
Total authors	4011	3384	4604	4891	6445	4723

The properties such as density, average clustering and assortativity change as the network grows, so it would be better to compute these properties cumulatively. These properties are computed using NetworkX software [1] and Table 3 gives the values of the mentioned characteristics from 2001 to 2004 cumulatively.

Table 3. Global properties of dataset from 2001 to 2004

Properties	01	01-02	01-03	01-04
Density	0.000738	0.000544	0.000416	0.000351
Avg. clustering	0.651067	0.663339	0.665605	0.668547
Assortativity	0.584894	0.585080	0.426343	0.329860
Total edges	6614	12966	21487	31112

From the Table 3 it can be noticed that the density is decreasing from 0.000738 to 0.000351 which is understandable because the number of authors increases in the cumulative network, making the network sparser resulting in a reduction in density and assortativity; on the other hand there is a slight increment in the value of average clustering coefficient.

Authors collaborate for an article, most of the time an article is written by two, three, or four authors but there are very few articles written by as many as ten to fifteen authors. It is one of the important parameters to consider while proposing a model. Fig. 2 gives an overview of the number of authors collaborating for the number of papers. In the plot, it can be seen that around 5000 papers are written by only two authors while there are around 20 papers written by ten authors.

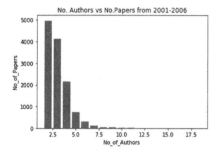

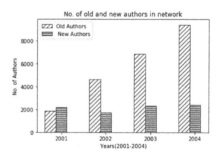

Fig. 2. Graph shows the number of authors co-authoring a paper

Fig. 3. Number of new and old authors

In the collaboration network of DBLP, along the lines of Shi et al., we divide the papers into three categories: old authors, new authors and old+new authors. New authors are those who are publishing the article for the first time and old authors are those who have already published. Whenever an article is published there are three possibilities. First one is that the article is written by only old authors, the second possibility is that authors who collaborated for the article are only new authors, and the third possibility is that the article is written by both new authors and the old authors. Figure 3 gives the details of the new authors who get added to the network while the Fig. 4 shows the percentage of papers written by authors among the three categories of *new*, *old* and *old+new*. In Fig. 4 we can see that the papers written by only new authors are gradually decreasing. In the year 2001 16% of papers are published by only new authors whereas in 2004 this number goes down to less than 12%. It is interesting to find that about one-third of the papers published every year are only by *Old Authors*, which means that collaborations increase among the authors who have published already.

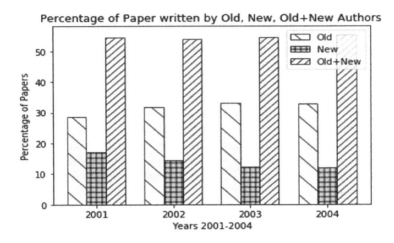

Fig. 4. Distribution of papers among the three categories

We also look at the mean papers per author and mean authors per paper. Mean papers per author give us the average number of papers an author has published while mean authors per paper extend the information we have obtained from analyzing the Fig. 2 i.e. mean authors per paper denotes the average number of authors collaborating for a paper. Figure 5 represents mean papers per author while Fig. 6 gives the plot of mean authors per paper.

As can be deduced from Fig. 5 that most of the authors have written, on an average, two papers in a period of six years from 2001 to 2006. Figure 6 shows that the average number of authors collaborating for a paper slightly increased from around 2.9 to 3.09.

Figure 7 is the degree distribution plot of the DBLP network and Fig. 8 is the log-log plot of the degree distribution. The heavy-tailed graph is an indication that the DBLP network is a scale-free network.

3   Parameter Estimation

In the previous section, it has been described that we have divided the papers into three categories either papers belong to the old category or the papers belong

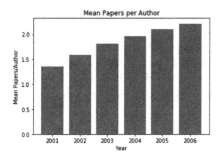

Fig. 5. Mean papers per author

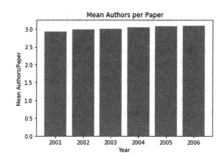

Fig. 6. Mean authors per paper

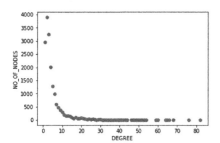

Fig. 7. Degree distribution

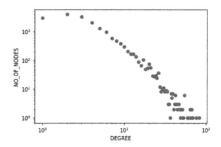

Fig. 8. Log-log plot of the degree distribution

to the new category or the papers belong to the new + old category. Figure 4 represents information of the percentage distribution of the authors among these three categories.

The data of each year is represented as a triple (*Old Authors*, *New Authors* and *Old* + *New Authors*) and the centroid of the points is calculated. The data from 2001 to 2004 is used to predict the composition for the 2005 network; and to predict the 2006 network, the data from 2001 to 2005 is used (Table 4).

Table 4. Percentage of papers belonging to either of the three categories

Categories	2001	2002	2003	2004	2005
Old authors	28.64	31.68	33.14	32.78	32.52
New authors	16.98	14.36	12.36	11.85	10.71
Old + new authors	54.38	53.95	54.49	55.36	56.76

The centroid value of *Old Authors* will be used as probability p and the value of *New Authors* + *Old Authors* will be used as the probability q in the proposed model.

4   Probability Distribution

To model the arrival of the number of authors of a paper, the underlying probability distribution needs to be studied. We modelled the number of authors per
paper using two probability distributions: Exponential distribution and Pareto
distribution. This choice is made based on the exponential-like behaviour seen
for the author-paper data shown in Fig. 2.

4.1   Exponential Vs Pareto Distribution

For each year, based on the number of papers published, random numbers
are generated using both Exponential distribution and Pareto distribution. For
example, in real dataset of 2001 a total of 1861 papers are published so a total
of 1861 random numbers have been generated using Exponential and Pareto distributions for the year 2001. A total of 10529 papers have been published during
2001–2004 so a total of 10529 random values have been generated using Exponential and Pareto distribution. Now t-Test is performed between the generated
and the actual distributions for the years 2001 to 2004. Table 5 shows the result
of t-Test.

Table 5. Results obtained by t-Test for the choice of Exponential and Pareto distributions

	Exponential			Pareto		
Year	T-stat	T-critical	P-val	T-stat	T-critical	P-val
2001	0.13437	2.10092	0.89460	0.55697	2.07961	0.58343
2002	0.11330	2.06865	0.91078	0.39249	2.04840	0.69766
2003	0.10092	2.06389	0.92045	0.22837	2.04523	0.82487
2004	0.10593	2.06389	0.91652	0.30204	2.04523	0.764706

It can be seen from the Table 5 that T-$stat$ value for both the distributions
(Exponential and Pareto) is less than the T-$critical$ value which means that the
hypothesis that the number of authors per paper of the DBLP network data is
similar to the numbers generated using Exponential and Pareto distribution is
true. We can notice from the table that p value of the Exponential distribution
is greater than the p value of Pareto distribution and the value of T-$stat$ of
Exponential distribution is lesser than the T-$stat$ value of the Pareto distribution. Hence it can be concluded that DBLP data is more similar to Exponential
distribution than the Pareto distribution [2].

4.2   QQ_plot

QQ plot [3] is another method to ascertain whether two samples arrive from
the same distribution. Figure 9(a) and (b) are the QQ plots for exponential and
Pareto distribution respectively.

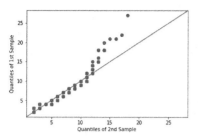
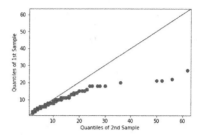

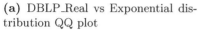

(a) DBLP_Real vs Exponential distribution QQ plot

(b) DBLP_Real vs Pareto Distribution QQ plot

Fig. 9. Quantile-Quantile plot

A total of 10529 papers have been published during 2001–2004 so a total of 10529 random values have been generated using Exponential and Pareto distribution. In both Fig. 9(a) and (b) quantiles of the 1st sample are DBLP real data and the quantiles of the 2nd sample are the data generated by Exponential or Pareto distribution respectively. As we can see in the figures, the scatter plot of Exponential data follows the line of 45 degree for larger length than the Pareto distribution hence this also goes in favor of Exponential distribution.

5 Proposed Model

The proposed model for DBLP collaboration network is given below (Fig. 10).

1. Generate $n_1, n_2, \ldots n_k$ randomly from the Exponential distribution, where $n_1, n_2, \ldots n_k$ are the number of authors collaborating for papers 1 to k respectively. k is the total number of papers published in a given time period.
2. Choose input value of p from the centroid value of *Old Authors* and input value of q as the sum of the centroid values of *New Authors* and *Old Authors* as explained in Sect. 3.
3. Choose integers x and y where $0 \leq x \leq n_i$ and $0 \leq y \leq n_i$ for $i = 1$ to k. The values x and y are the total number of old authors and new authors collaborating for paper i respectively. x and y will be determined in the following manner.
4. Generate a random value v in $(0, 1)$.
   (a) If v is less than the probability p then $x = n_i$ i.e. all the authors collaborating for paper i are only old authors. GOTO step 5.
   (b) If v is such that $p \leq v \leq q$ then $y = n_i$ i.e. all the authors collaborating for paper i will only be new authors. GOTO step 5.
   (c) If v is greater than q then generate a random value x such that $0 < x < n_i$ and $y = n_i - x$. This value of $(x + y)$ will be the total number of old and new authors collaborating for paper i.
5. Add $^{n_i}C_2$ edges to the network among all the authors new or old collaborating for the paper i.

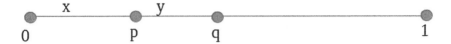

Fig. 10. A representation of the probability values of p and q. If the value of v is between 0 and p then the value x (old authors) is chosen, if v is between p and q then the value y (new authors) is chosen.

6   Experimentation and Result

We have used the data from 2001 to 2004 for estimating the parameters and obtained $p = 0.3$ and $q = 0.46$ and the real data of 2005 and 2006 is used to test the model. Results obtained using both Exponential and Pareto distributions are presented below.

6.1   Exponential Distribution

The algorithm given in Sect. 5 is implemented by simulating the number of authors per paper in a given year using Exponential distribution with rate parameter λ value varied between 1.44 to 1.56, this range has been decided using trial and error method.

Figures 11 and 12 are the degree distribution plots upto 2005 at different values of λ.

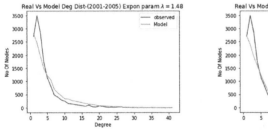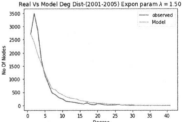

Fig. 11. Degree distribution comparison plot-2005

Table 6 gives the comparison of real and model generated network at different exponent values of Exponential distribution along with that obtained by the model of Shi et al.

Results are presented for cumulative DBLP network of years 2001–2005 as well as the network generated by the proposed model, i.e., a collaboration network is grown, estimating the parameters from the data of 2001–2004 and the network of 2005 has been generated. The same process is applied to generate the 2006 network.

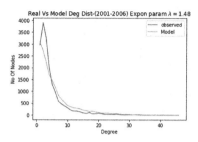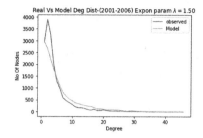

Fig. 12. Degree distribution comparison plot-2006

Table 6. Comparison of the degree distributions of DBLP-2006, proposed model at various exponent values and the network of Shi et al.

Degree D	No. of nodes of degree D at different exponent values								
	Real	1.44	1.46	1.48	1.50	1.52	1.54	1.56	Shi et al.
1	2965	3273	3133	3078	2957	2936	2871	2793	1533
2	3898	2743	2739	2738	2684	2566	2634	2545	1862
3	3256	2289	2258	2246	2225	2225	2182	2203	1593
4	2013	1802	1680	1701	1808	1724	1820	1843	343
5	1289	1394	1423	1451	1427	1390	1363	1389	318
6	976	1031	1145	1175	1100	1151	1134	1125	273
7	588	757	829	826	812	853	829	857	196
8	466	625	666	661	656	697	650	627	200
9	381	548	535	536	537	536	570	597	218
10	303	420	399	397	461	408	474	496	244
11	206	390	330	344	369	378	407	400	247
12	164	314	323	309	335	328	355	348	289
13	166	271	289	284	290	301	296	268	291
14	134	218	245	258	261	255	240	263	322
15	89	193	212	208	233	228	234	219	263
16	65	188	187	182	219	194	219	213	212
17	105	150	139	148	176	203	178	167	212
18	50	132	154	167	119	144	143	164	153
19	53	101	113	126	118	111	127	137	149
20	74	115	122	108	104	121	115	101	148

Apart from degree distribution, other properties such as density, average clustering, assortativity and the total number of edges have been computed. The resulting plots of these properties are shown in Figs. 13, 14, 15 and 16.

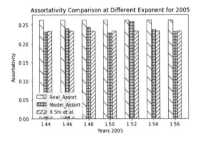
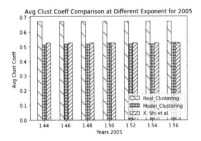

Fig. 13. Assortativity and average clustering-2005

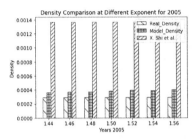
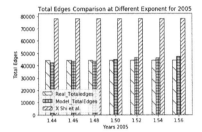

Fig. 14. Density and total edges-2005

From the Figs. 13, 14, 15 and 16 as it can be noticed that the value of assortativity and the total number of edges obtained from the model are similar to the real network. Assortativity is best obtained at $\lambda = 1.52$ and 1.50 for 2005 and 2006 respectively. The values obtained for density and average clustering coefficient are not matching very well to those of the real network. The density obtained for the model network is greater than the real network while the average clustering coefficient value is smaller. From the comparison of the proposed model and that of Shi et al. it can be concluded that the proposed model performs better than the existing model. The values of global properties obtained from the proposed model are closer than the values obtained from the model of Shi et al. In order to compare the degree distributions, two standard statistical measures, namely, Normalized root mean squared error (RMSE) and KL Divergence [7,9] are computed which is discussed below.

Normalized Root Mean Squared Error. Normalized root mean squared error (RMSE) is computed for the degree distributions of the predicted model networks from the original. The values obtained for various values of λ are given in Table 7 for the years 2005 and 2006 as well as the result of Shi et al. The value of RMSE has been normalized using the total number of nodes in the network.

From the Table 7 it can be seen that the root mean square value for the exponent 1.44 is lowest while the value obtained by the model of Shi et al. value is much higher.

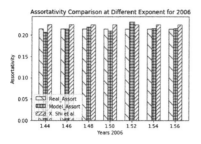
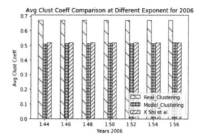

Fig. 15. Assortativity and average clustering-2006

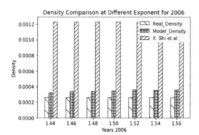
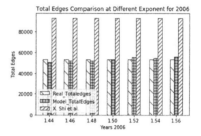

Fig. 16. Density and total edges-2006

Table 7. Normalized root mean squared error of degree distribution for year 2005 and 2006

	Exponent (λ) values							
Year	1.44	1.46	1.48	1.50	1.52	1.54	1.56	Shi et al.
2005	0.0149	0.0151	0.0152	0.0156	0.0163	0.0166	0.0164	0.0217
2006	0.0138	0.0140	0.0140	0.0143	0.0147	0.0145	0.0149	0.0206

KL Divergence. KL (Kullback-Leibler) Divergence is another measure to determine the loss of information when we are having two sets of data observed and original. The KL divergence is computed between the degree distributions of the actual and the proposed model and also with that of Shi et al. network. The results are shown in Table 8. Clearly, the value for KL divergence of the proposed model is less than that of Shi et al. model for both the years which means that the degree distribution of the proposed model is closer to that of the real network (Fig. 17).

Table 8. KL divergence of degree distribution for the networks of 2005 and 2006

Year	Model	Shi et al.
2005	0.0271	0.2263
2006	0.0262	0.2239

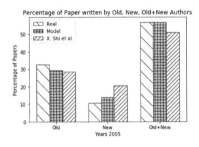 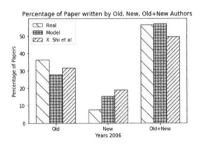

Fig. 17. Comparison of percentage of paper written by old, new, old + new authors in the year 2005 and 2006

6.2   Pareto Distribution

As it is previously described, we have chosen two probability distributions to simulate the event of papers being added to the model DBLP network, using Exponential distribution and Pareto distribution. It is shown that Exponential distribution performs better than Pareto using t-test and QQ plots. Following Figs. 18a and b present the degree distribution plots for 2005 and 2006 networks respectively.

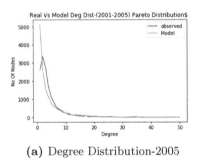 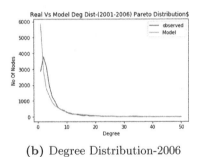

(a) Degree Distribution-2005   **(b)** Degree Distribution-2006

Fig. 18. Degree distribution comparison plot real Vs model generated using Pareto Distribution

Table 9 shows various network properties comparing the model generated using Pareto distribution and real networks of 2005 and 2006.

By looking at the Fig. 18 and Table 9 it can be seen that there is a difference between the result obtained using Pareto distribution and the real DBLP network. There is a bigger gap between the degree distributions with respect to degree 2 and 3 vertices and as far as the global properties are concerned, Pareto distribution performs worse than Exponential distribution. This is also confirmed by computing the normalized RMSE, which are 0.028282 and 0.027466 for the networks of 2005 and 2006 respectively, bigger than the values obtained for the Exponential distribution.

Table 9. Model vs real network properties

	2005		2006	
Properties	Model	Real	Model	Real
Density	0.000324	0.000289	0.000289	0.000262
Avg clust. coeff	0.402227	0673337	0.397183	0.673373
Assortativity	0.799772	0.263722	0.754504	0.215206
Total edges	35957	44310	42385	53232

7 Conclusion

We have proposed a network formation model that crucially depends on the arrival distribution of the number of authors per paper. When a new paper gets published, the algorithm helps in building a clique in the network by choosing nodes (i) from already existing nodes or (ii) the clique is formed by a combination of old and new nodes or (iii) only new nodes. We find that it is possible to simulate the process of papers getting added to the network using a probability distribution such as Exponential distribution. The proposed model is specific to collaboration networks and it may be interesting to work on similar models for other social networks. If worked backwards, a network formation model can be used for analyzing and predicting the past structures in the network. Network archeology [18] is an interesting area where the network evolution algorithms find applications.

References

1. https://networkx.github.io/
2. http://blog.minitab.com/blog/statistics-and-quality-data-analysis/what-are-t-values-and-p-values-in-statistics
3. https://data.library.virginia.edu/understanding-q-q-plots/
4. DBLP: Computer science bibliography. https://dblp.uni-trier.de
5. Barabasi, A.L., Jeong, H., Neda, Z., Ravasz, E., Schubert, A., Vicsek, T.: Evolution of the social network of scientific collaborations. Physica A: Statist. Mech. Appl. **311**, 590–614 (2002). https://doi.org/10.1016/S0378-4371(02)00736-7
6. Barabasi, A.L., Albert, R.: Emergence of scaling in random networks. Science **286**, 509–512 (1999)
7. Bishop, C.M.: Pattern Recognition and Machine Learning. Springer, Heidelberg (2006). https://doi.org/10.1007/978-1-4615-7566-5
8. Schreiber, F., Junker, B.H.: Analysis of Biological Networks. Wiley, Hoboken (2007)
9. Kullback, S., Leibler, R.: On information and sufficiency. Ann. Math. Statist. **22**(1), 79–86 (1951)
10. Lakshmi, T.J., Bhavani, S.D.: Temporal probabilistic measure for link prediction in collaborative networks. Appl. Intell. **47**(1), 83–95 (2017)

11. Leskovec, J., Kleinberg, J., Faloutsos, C.: Graphs over time: densification laws, shrinking diameters and possible explanations. In: 11th International Conference on Knowledge Discovery and Data mining, pp. 177–187 (2005)
12. Liben-Nowell, D., Kleinberg, J.: The link-prediction problem for social networks. J. Am. Soc. Inf. Sci. Technol. **58**(7), 1019–1031 (2007)
13. Middendorf, M., Ziv, E., Wiggins, C.H.: Inferring network mechanisms: the Drosophila melanogaster protein interaction network. Proc. Natl. Acad. Sci. **102**, 3192–3197 (2005)
14. Milo, R., Kashtan, N., Itzkovitz, S., Newman, M.E.J., Alon, U.: On the uniform generation of random graphs with prescribed degree sequences. arXiv e-prints (2003)
15. Newman, M.E.J.: Scientific collaboration networks. i. Network construction and fundamental results. Phys. Rev. E Stat. Nonlin. Soft Matter Phys. (2001). https://doi.org/10.1103/PhysRevE.64.016131
16. Newman, M.E.J.: The structure of scientific collaboration networks. Proc. Natl. Acad. Sci. **98**, 404–409 (2001)
17. Newman, M.E.J.: Networks: An Introduction. Oxford University Press, Oxford (2010)
18. Navlakha, S., Kingsford, C.: Network archaeology: uncovering ancient networks from present-day interactions. PLoS Comput. Biol. **7**(4), e1001119 (2011)
19. Shi, X., Wu, L., Yang, H.: Scientific collaboration network evolution model based on motif emerging. In: The 9th International Conference for Young Computer Scientists, pp. 2748–2752 (2008)

Bees Detection on Images: Study of Different Color Models for Neural Networks

Jerzy Dembski and Julian Szymański[✉]

Faculty of Electronic Telecommunications and Informatics,
Gdańsk University of Technology, Gdańsk, Poland
{jerzy.dembski,julian.szymanski}@eti.pg.gda.pl

Abstract. This paper presents an approach to bee detection in video streams using a neural network classifier. We describe the motivation for our research and the methodology of data acquisition. The main contribution to this work is a comparison of different color models used as an input format for a feedforward convolutional architecture applied to bee detection. The detection process has is based on a neural binary classifier that classifies ROI windows in frames taken from video streams to determine whether or not the window contains bees. Due to the type of application, we tested two methods of partitioning data into training and test subsets: video-based (some video for training, the rest for testing) and individual based (some bees for training, the rest for testing). The tournament-based algorithm was implemented to aggregate the results of classification. The manually tagged datasets we used for our experiments have been made publicly available. Based on our analysis of the results, we drew conclusions that the best color models are RGB and 3-channeled color models: RGB and HSV are significantly better than black & white or the H channel from HSV.

Keywords: Automatic bee's image classification
Deep neural networks · Bee farming

1 Introduction

One of the important factors in bee farming is an evaluation of the colonie's strength. Usually, it is performed by a beekeeper who, during hive inspection, estimates the number of bees that occupy each of the frames. This method requires opening the hive each time it is done, so it is invasive and of course it is not precise. The estimations may vary depending on the time of the day when the inspection is performed, as well as on the weather – e.g. during a sunny day there can be less bees in the hive as some of them would be out collecting pollen.

In our research we aim to provide more objective measures for evaluating the strength of a bee colony. Our method is based on the automatic counting of bees flying in or out of the hive, evaluated on videos recorded by a mobile camera. This

© Springer Nature Switzerland AG 2019
G. Fahrnberger et al. (Eds.): ICDCIT 2019, LNCS 11319, pp. 295–308, 2019.
https://doi.org/10.1007/978-3-030-05366-6_25

task requires a bee detection system that allows us to analyze a video stream. The detection process itself is based on a machine learning approach that scans an entire image using a scanning window from left to right, top to bottom, and for different window scales. In our approach, we use a binary classifier that distinguishes windows containing bees from windows without bees.

The bee-detection system allows us to measure correlations between bee activity and e.g. weather, as well as open new possibilities for the automatic analysis of bee behavior, e.g. tracing bees at a hive's entrance to detect movement patterns [1].

Our approach employs a mobile RGB camera that is placed at the hive's entrance. Then, a recorded video is analyzed using a dedicated algorithm that enables us to detect bees contained in frames of the video. The results presented in this paper show that the proposed neural network architecture is useful for the task of bee detection. We also publicly provide the dataset that we manually tagged to construct our model.

This paper is constructed as follows: in the next section we give a brief overview of the research and open source projects that use computers for analyzing bee activity. Section 3 describes our data acquisition process: the environment in which we recorded videos and the method for manually tagging the video-frames used as training data for the construction of our classifier. Section 4 describes the usage of different color models for classification algorithms. The classification results have been aggregated using the tournament method presented in Sect. 5. We performed a series of experiments presented in Sect. 6. The results of these experiments show that the proposed approach is useful and can be implemented in a real-world commercial application. We discuss possible extensions of our system and further work in the last section.

2   Automatic Analysis of Bee Activity

In this section we present current works in areas related to the subject of this paper. First, we present projects that aim to automate the process of analyzing bee behavior, with a focus on bee detection and the usage of neural networks with bee-related data.

Human interest in bee farming has a long history. The knowledge gathered during the ages allows us to better understand bee behavior, however a lot is still unknown. In recent years, technological progress has given us additional tools for more detailed environment monitoring [2] and gives us a closer look at the life of bees. The usage of smart sensing technologies and algorithms that analyze data from sensors allows us to draw new conclusions on bee behavior [3]. As the application of Information Technology for environment monitoring rapidly grows, we can find more and more research that employs computers for analyzing different aspects of a bee's life [4]. Below we present some of the research that focuses on bee detection.

Automatic image analysis has been employed for bee larvae detection. The authors of the research employ deep learning convolutional networks that, as is reported, is able to segment a frame containing a bee and differentiate empty cells and that with the laves to a high degree of accuracy. The project does not contain an in-depth description of the methods used in the form of publication, but it offers its code as open source[1].

The analysis of recorded bee sounds allows us to construct a classifier that indicates presence or absence of the bee queen in a hive. This is our initial project that employs IOT technology for bee farming. It shows that classifying bee sounds with an SVM [5] and using linear predictive coding [6] allows us to differentiate between the presence and absence of the queen bee in the hive. A detailed description of this method can be found in [7].

One of the first approaches for using cameras to detect and track bees at the entrance of a hive was proposed by Campbell et al. [8]. In this approach the camera was placed directly over the entrance to the hive. To detect bees on individual image frames, the authors first subtracted an empty background image from the current image frame and then found objects that matched with one of 16 fixed-size elliptic templates. The tracking method from frame-to-frame is based on bi-partite graph matching [9] on a graph composed of the current and previous frames' detections. The system works in a fixed environment and for every environmental change the algorithm requires additional templates.

The usage of 3D cameras to detect and track bees at the entrance of a hive has been also proposed by Chiron et al. [10]. Their method segments both the color and depth portions of images, and then finds bees by matching the segments with ellipses. In order to track bees across frames, the authors used a mixture of global nearest-neighbors and Kalman filtering [11]: individual bees were tracked across frames using the Kalman filter, and global nearest neighbors was used to track the paths of specific bees.

An approach for analyzing bees on video-data has been presented in "A Deep Learning Approach to Recognizing Bees in Video Analysis of Bee Traffic"[2]. The initial results reported [12] indicate that convolutional networks can be useful for the task. Unfortunately, the authors do not publicly provide the data used in their research, which in turn doesn't allow us to perform a comparison with our approach.

In another thesis "Fast detection of bees using deep learning and bayesian optimization"[3] an approach is presented for building a vision-based hive moni-toring system by training three deep learning-based object detection models that detect bees and predators using fast, region-based convolutional neural networks (Fast R-CNN). The results achieved on manually a created dataset report an F1 score below 0.5, which is insufficient for commercial applications.

Another project[4] aimed at counting bees using an artificial neural network has been made on Raspberry Pi. The authors use a standard convolutional net-work trained on half-resolution patches but run against full resolution images.

---

[1] https://github.com/metaflow-ai/hive.

[2] https://digitalcommons.usu.edu/cgi/viewcontent.cgi?article=8185&context=etd.

[3] https://mspace.lib.umanitoba.ca/handle/1993/32981.

[4] http://matpalm.com/blog/counting_bees/.

The approach has been published as open-source code and the authors claim it allows them to achieve good results that have been tested on a single hive. Unfortunately, the results have not been statistically analyzed and they have not been reported as scientific publication.

A system for the detection, localization, and tracking of honeybee body-parts from video at the entrance ramp of a hive has been reported in [13]. The approach employs a neural network composed of a first feature extraction part based on a pre trained VGG16 network [14] that serves as input for two convolutional network branches: the first branch predicts a confidence map with one channel per part of interest, and the second branch predicts affinity fields with one vectorial channel per connection. The proposed system shows very promising results with over 95entrance, without any prior tracking. It should be noted, however, that in order for the system to work correctly, it requires that the camera be placed exactly in the same position and orientation as it had while training data was acquired.

The problem of bee pose-estimation on single image has been analyzed in [15]. The authors used ConvNet [16] which had previously been employed for human pose-estimation using a fixed number of body joints. The proposed method applied to bee pose-estimation handles cases with a varying number of targets, which allows it to achieve very good results in terms of insect pose-estimation.

The aforementioned mentioned research relating to bee detection does not provide statistically reliable results nor present any publicly available data that would allow for the replication of said results. Some of the research only provides source code without any deeper analysis of the method used or a research paper. Thus, we propose our own approach that has been presented in detail in this paper and we have made the dataset we experiment on publicly available.

The continuous monitoring of bee hives requires the system to match two criteria: speed and accuracy of detection. In the beginning of the 21st century, the Adaboost algorithm [17] with Haar-like rectangular features [18] seems to be the best solution for these two criteria, especially in the face of detection tasks [19,20]. We investigated the usage of these techniques for bee detection and the results were not satisfactory, probably due to a significant difference between the domains of face and bee detection, such as a high percentage of blurry images and a smaller number of details.

In the recent decades, deep learned artificial neural networks with convolutional layers for image classification [21] have been used thanks to a greater generalization measured by the accuracy of test example classification, as well as better hardware allowing for faster calculation speed.

In recent years, newer ideas such as specialized network structures consisting of CNNs have been developed for object detection. One such idea is the region of interest (ROI) extraction from the whole image using very little calculation. Another method uses multitask learning connected with region-based CNN (R-CNN) [22] in which at the output of the CNN two kinds of information are presented: object probability and object position in the ROI area. Yet another idea uses pixel-wise segmentation [23] in which every pixel in an image is classified as belonging to an object or not.

3   Data Acquisition

For building our classifier we use 13 videos, each approximately 40 s long. Each video was shot during sunny weather using a mobile device camera without a tripod or any additional equipment. The videos capture a bee hive from different perspectives and different distance from the hive's entrance. In order to analyze the videos using machine learning classification, the data first needed to be tagged. This task can be completed using tools such as LabelImg[5] but we decided to develop our own software to have additional labeling possibilities such as marking the orientations of a bee's body, individual numbers, negative example areas, and areas excluded from detection during error evaluation, as was shown in Fig. 1. This extended information is not used in the experiments reported in this paper, but the dataset we acquired may be useful for future experiments. Thus, we made our dataset publicly available. The videos are accessible from the web url: https://goo.gl/KNV7sd. Each video has a corresponding metadata text file, wherein each line in the text file describes each video-frame. The text files are available under the url: http://julian.eti.pg.gda.pl/ramki.zip, and contain description of the frames stored in the following format:
<frame no> <x coordinate> <y coordinate> <radius> <1-bee, 0-background> <individual id> [6 fields not used now] <bee direction $(0,2\pi)$> <quality>

Our tagging tool allows us to tag video frames in such a way that a user can quickly mark all regions that contain an individual bee from frame-to-frame. Later, the user can append labels to the bee such as an ID number, information on a particular feature, e.g. whether or not the bee is arriving or returning to the hive, if the bee is bringing food to the hive, or if the bee is the queen bee.

Images with blurry objects such as the frame with individual number 3 in Fig. 1 lead to a marking dilemma. Fast moving bees recorded with ordinary cameras without shutter speed control can appear blurry and near transparent, which introduces difficulties in recognizing them, even for humans, who need to look at other neighboring frames for verification. This can also adversely influence classification, due to its proximity to background images. A similar problem is overlapping bee bodies. For these reasons we decided to only tag images containing recognizable bees, or fill in an image quality field as an additional attribute to preserve information of a bees position for tracking purposes.

Negative examples (background images) were prepared from the same videos as the positive samples were prepared from, keeping a similar proportion between the two. Such an approach guarantees proper data balance and provides images from the beekeeping environment, or the environment of particular beekeeper. In our acquisition system, a user should mark some ROI which do not contain bees (gray rectangle boxes in Fig. 1). These ROI are marked as negative examples

---

[5] https://github.com/qaprosoft/labelImg.

Fig. 1. Typical boxes of negative (gray) and positive (yellow) example images (Color figure online)

and are selected randomly. Additionally, for each negative ROI, a new image is generated from the ROI to enable the user to mark any artifacts that might be classified as false positives, such as bee shadows, wood grain, etc.

4   Training Bees Image Classifiers Using Deep Models

As input for the classifier, we test the usage of four different color models: RGB, HSV, black & white, and the Hue (H) component from the HSV model [24]. The black & white color model was obtained from an RGB model by calculating pixel intensity according to the formula: $J = 0.299R + 0.587G + 0.114B$ where R, G, B are red, green, and blue channel intensities for the same pixel.

Our approach for bee detection on a video frame consists two stages:

– binary classifiers trained to distinguish between images of bees and images of backgrounds,
– a detector algorithm that uses binary classifiers from the previous stage and that also can be trained.

To construct a model for processing the images we used deep convolutional neural networks that are composed of only a few convolutional layers and a few fully connected layers. This model has been used to construct a binary classifier that allows us to distinguish between frames containing bees and background images. The topology of the convolutional neural network was designed by trial and error testing during preliminary experiments, in such a way as to have enough capacity to enable the training error to decrease towards zero and not be too complex, mainly because of two reasons:

- overfitting avoidance in order to obtain a low test error,
- decreasing time complexity which is crucial for real-time detection applications.

Both of the aforementioned reasons were selected as our optimization criteria for creating a neural network topology. The neural network architectures used vary depending on the particular task, color model, and an input image resolution. The typical structure for a 48×48 3-channel RGB image has been shown in Fig. 2.

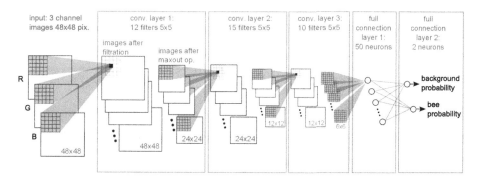

Fig. 2. Convolutional neural network structure used in color models comparison experiment

Each pixel intensity in a convolutional layer is calculated in the standard way as a ReLU activation function from a sum of weighted intensities of a 5×5 pixel area, in each input image from the previous layer. We use the padding option "same" to reduce the size of the input image. The resolution of each image after filtering is reduced two times by a maxout operation. In the last full connection layer we used a softmax activation function. About 27,000 positive examples (bee-boxes) were obtained for training and test purposes. We chose four types of partition into a training and test set, due to implementation purposes:

1. fully random division corresponding to the specific implementation for one beekeeper in a given season,
2. some bees for training and others for testing (bee based partition),
3. some videos for training and others for testing (video based partition),
4. some hives for training and other for test (hive based partition).

The difficulty grows from levels 1 to 4. Of course, the more representative set of examples is used for training, the small differences between the results are (test examples classification accuracy) because of these partitions.

5   Aggregation of Classification Results

The bee-detector described in the previous section can classify whether or not a window (that is a part of the frame) contains a bee.

In the task of counting the bees in a video frame, we need to scan the whole image assuming a minimal and a maximal size of the scanning window, the size change step, and the vertical and horizontal window shift steps. The typical result of such a scanning process is a huge amount of positive detection boxes around true bee occurrences, due to an inaccuracy of positive example acquisition as is shown in Fig. 3a. Such a cloud of boxes must be reduced to one detection box for each bee, which requires an algorithm for selecting boxes. The challenge becomes more sophisticated when bees are close to each other, which is manifested by the overlapping of positive detection clouds. In our research we use a fast greedy tournament algorithm [25].

a)   b)

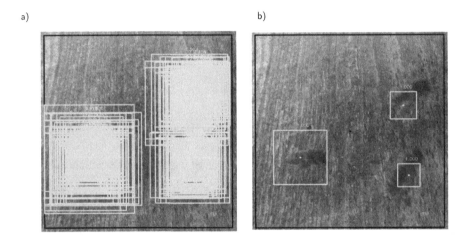

Fig. 3. Greedy tournament detection results: (a) set of frames after scanning the part of the image with a probability of bee appearance greater than 0.5, (b) frames selected based on the probability of a bees appearance. The probability is provided as a number over the box

The greedy tournament algorithm implemented by us is based on an iterative bee appearance probability comparison between overlapping random boxes after scanning a video frame. The overlapping threshold was chosen arbitrarily for 40

We think the aggregation stage can be improved using other approaches, such as:

- clique number minimization [26] from the graph theory domain,
- a weighted greedy C-means clustering algorithm [27].

It should be noted that the higher complexity of these algorithms can negatively influence detection-time.

6   Experiments and Results

In the first experiment we compared the four color models not only to find the best one, but also to compare them, taking into account their originality and time complexity.

The structure of our convolutional network was composed of a convolutional part with full-filter connections between neighboring layers and fully-connected layers at the end. During optimization we used the adaptive moment technique (ADAM) and a cross entropy loss function. The dropout technique was used in the fully-connected layers, excluding the last layer with a probability of 0.5. Training examples (input images + class numbers) were presented to the network in the form of packages – minibatches containing 100 randomly selected examples.

The results presented in Fig. 4 were obtained from the best-performing network architecture selected from several architectures tested on each color model, in order to maximize accuracy criterion. The Tensorflow library was used in the implementation of each CNN model.

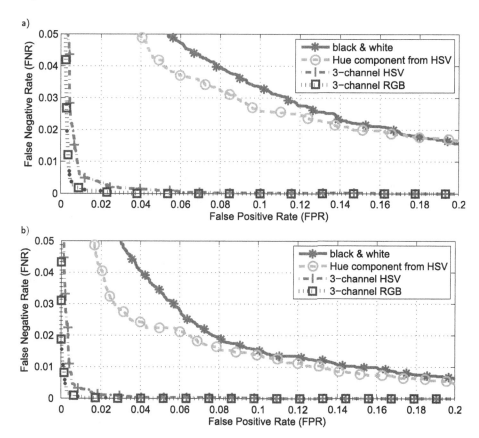

Fig. 4. ROC curves for 4 color models: (a) test example subset taken from videos not included in the training example subset, (b) test example subset with bees unseen in the training example subset. (Color figure online)

The ROC curves presented in Fig. 4 have been obtained by testing classifiers for different positive class probability thresholds. When the threshold is decreased, more images are classified as positive, which decreases the false negative rate (FNR) but increases the false positive rate (FPR). This causes the point in the ROC curve to shift to the right side of the chart.

The RGB color model, for the task of binary bee-detection in images (performed on our deep models), is the best color model by a significant margin, as is also shown in the 3-channel color models: HSV and RGB seem to be significantly better than one-channel models in general.

It should be noted that classifiers trained on one-channel models can be useful for two reasons: the classifier structures can be simpler and less computationally expensive, such a limitation of information can force a network to take into account other features than the ones given in any 3-channel color model, which may be useful in a classifiers ensemble. The black & white model, despite the worst, shows results that can be important in any extraordinary light conditions or artificial light, or in the case of atypical white balance setting in a digital camera. The Hue component from the HSV color model allows for better results than the black & white color model, which leads to another conclusion from this experiment, namely color information is very important in for bee detection, as opposed to other tasks such as face recognition.

The results presented in Fig. 4a were obtained for a video-based partition of training and test data. Each video was obtained from a different camera view and most often displays a unique beehive. We used 10 videos - 44970 examples for training and 3 videos for test - 10308 examples. Half of the examples are positive. The structure for the RGB color model is shown in Fig. 2. For the other models, the structures were slightly different.

Figure 4b displays the results for a bee-based partition into training and test data. It can be treated as the same camera view for the train and test subsets, but different individual bees were used for training and for testing. This is almost equivalent to training and testing on data from the same camera position and orientation but at different times in the video. We used images from 3/4 bees and 3/4 background images - 41913 examples for training and 13435 examples for testing. The network structure remains the same for all models.

The results for a bee-based partition are significantly better than for a video-based partition, which was expected due to a greater exposure to the environments than in the video-based partition, in which each video contains either a unique hive or a unique view. In Fig. 5 the best results for 3-channel color models are magnified.

Taking into account the results from the first experiment in the second experiment, we tested if the color information alone can be enough for a computationally cheap ROI indicator. The 24×24 RGB color images were transformed into HSV model and next were transformed into 9-point histograms of the hue (H) component. The results were unsatisfactory, so 9-component feature vectors were magnified by adding similar 9-point histograms of central 12×12 subimages and 9 values of difference between both histograms. The results are also poor,

a)

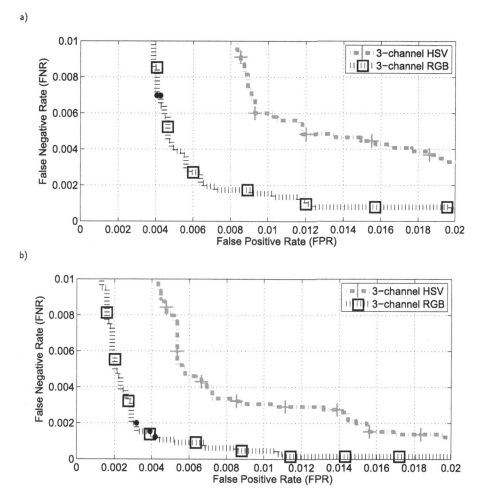

b)

Fig. 5. ROC curves in greater scale (a) test example subset taken from videos not contained in the training example subset, (b) test example subset with bee individuals not contained int the training example subset. (Color figure online)

which may indicate as to the importance of local dependencies between pixels, which are omitted in the color histograms.

7   Discussion and Future Works

In this paper we presented our system for the acquisition of data from images containing bees, based on a deep convolutional neural network classifier used to detect bees in 48×48 pixel images. We made a comparison of color models and proposed a tournament-based algorithm for the aggregation of classification results. We also provided publicly provided our data which allows for further research to extend on our results achieved in the domain of bee detection.

The results shown in Sect. 4 indicate the significant advantage 3-channel color models have over 1-channel models, as well as the small advantage that the RGB model has over the HSV model in the individual-bee data partition. In the future we plan to test how the influence of local or global color normalization affects the results.

We also have ideas to improve the results of the binary classifier accuracy. As for now, our model classifies single images. It is our contention that the usage of frame sequences could provide information that would yield better results. For instance, a previous and next frame can be added to the CNN's input images as additional channels or recurrent variants of the CNN can be used based on the whole sequence.

Manually creating the dataset is very laborious, but having a larger number of examples for the model should work better. We are planning on extending the dataset by building a semi-automatic data acquisition system which can find ROI areas based on existing classifiers.

We plan to automate the preparation of negative images from videos during parallel binary classifier training. The usage of this approach for detection tasks has been described in a cascade classifier training process in [20]. In such a setting, the negative images set will be periodically supplemented by images generated from false positive windows. Also usage SOM for visualizing ROI shell be considered [28].

The detector described in Sect. 5. can be additionally equipped with several binary classifiers to differentiate image areas. We are planning the following work in this field:

- as we mention at the end of the Sect. 5 aggregation algorithms other than tournament-based should be tested,
- a committee of binary classifiers trained on different color models and different resolutions,
- tracing algorithms and bee direction recognition to accelerate the detection process in video frames,
- a cascade of deep learned binary classifiers from simplest, fast, to complex, and more accurate,
- the pixel-wise detection approach verification [29],
- the genetic optimization of aggregation parameters with two criteria: speed and accuracy.

We plan to deploy our algorithms for bee detection on the Android mobile environment. This should allow us to collect more data as well as extend the research on bee image-processing. In the future we plan to conduct work on the identification of bees infected by Varroa mites[6]. The automatic detection of

---

[6] http://www.releasewire.com/press-releases/the-beescanning-app-is-saving-bees-worldwide-through-deep-learning-technology-808184.htm.

these parasites on bees should allow one to estimate the degree of an infection and suggest plan of treatment.

We also plan to perform an analysis on the videos with bees for the detection of abnormalities at a hive's entrance. This should allow us to detect a swarming moment [30] and immediately report it to a beekeeper.

Acknowledgements. This work was partially supported by funds from the Faculty of Electronics Telecommunications and Informatics, Gdansk University of Technology and Cost Action CA 15118 FoodMC "Mathematical and Computer Science Methods for Food Science and Industry".

References

1. Wario, F., Wild, B., Rojas, R., Landgraf, T.: Automatic detection and decoding of honey bee waggle dances. PloS one **12**, e0188626 (2017)
2. Othman, M.F., Shazali, K.: Wireless sensor network applications: a study in environment monitoring system. Proc. Eng. **41**, 1204–1210 (2012)
3. Tu, G.J., Hansen, M.K., Kryger, P., Ahrendt, P.: Automatic behaviour analysis system for honeybees using computer vision. Comput. Electron. Agric. **122**, 10–18 (2016)
4. Zacepins, A., Stalidzans, E., Meitalovs, J.: Application of information technologies in precision apiculture. In: Proceedings of the 13th International Conference on Precision Agriculture, ICPA 2012 (2012)
5. Scholkopf, B., Smola, A.J.: Learning with Kernels: Support Vector Machines, Regularization, Optimization, and Beyond. MIT Press, Cambridge (2001)
6. Bradbury, J.: Linear Predictive Coding. Mc G. Hill, New York (2000)
7. Cejrowski, T., Szymański, J., Mora, H., Gil, D.: Detection of the bee queen presence using sound analysis. In: Nguyen, N.T., Hoang, D.H., Hong, T.-P., Pham, H., Trawiński, B. (eds.) ACIIDS 2018. LNCS (LNAI), vol. 10752, pp. 297–306. Springer, Cham (2018). https://doi.org/10.1007/978-3-319-75420-8_28
8. Campbell, J., Mummert, L., Sukthankar, R.: Video monitoring of honey bee colonies at the hive entrance. Vis. Obs. Anal. Anim. Insect Behav. ICPR **8**, 1–4 (2008)
9. Riesen, K., Bunke, H.: Approximate graph edit distance computation by means of Bipartite graph matching. Image Vis. Comput. **27**, 950–959 (2009)
10. Chiron, G., Gomez-Krämer, P., Ménard, M.: Detecting and tracking honeybees in 3D at the beehive entrance using stereo vision. EURASIP J. Image Video Process. **2013**, 59 (2013)
11. Evensen, G.: Data Assimilation: The Ensemble Kalman Filter. Springer, Heidelberg (2009)
12. Tiwari, A.: A deep learning approach to recognizing bees in video analysis of bee traffic (2018)
13. Rodríguez, I., Branson, K., Acuña, E., Agosto-Rivera, J., Giray, T., Mégret, R.: Honeybee detection and pose estimation using convolutional neural networks. Technical report, RFIAP (2018)
14. Simonyan, K., Zisserman, A.: Very deep convolutional networks for large-scale image recognition. arXiv preprint arXiv:1409.1556 (2014)

15. Duan, L., Shen, M., Gao, W., Cui, S., Deussen, O.: Bee pose estimation from single images with convolutional neural network. In: 2017 IEEE International Conference on Image Processing (ICIP), pp. 2836–2840. IEEE (2017)
16. Krizhevsky, A., Sutskever, I., Hinton, G.E.: Imagenet classification with deep convolutional neural networks. In: Advances in Neural Information Processing Systems, pp. 1097–1105 (2012)
17. Freund, Y., Schapire, R.E.: A decision-theoretic generalization of on-line learning and an application to boosting. J. Comput. Syst. Sci. **55**, 119–139 (1997)
18. Porwik, P., Lisowska, A.: The Haar-wavelet transform in digital image processing: its status and achievements. Mach. Graph. Vis. **13**, 79–98 (2004)
19. Viola, P., Jones, M.J.: Robust real-time face detection. Int. J. Comput. Vis. **57**, 137–154 (2004)
20. Dembski, J., Smiatacz, M.: Modular machine learning system for training object detection algorithms on a supercomputer. In: Advances in System Science, pp. 353–361 (2010)
21. Hoo-Chang, S., et al.: Deep convolutional neural networks for computer-aided detection: CNN architectures, dataset characteristics and transfer learning. IEEE Trans. Med. Imaging **35**, 1285 (2016)
22. Girshick, R.B.: Fast R-CNN. In: 2015 IEEE International Conference on Computer Vision, ICCV 2015, 7–13 December 2015, Santiago, Chile, pp. 1440–1448 (2015)
23. Pinheiro, P.H.O., Collobert, R.: From image-level to pixel-level labeling with convolutional networks, pp. 1713–1721 (2015)
24. Zarit, B.D., Super, B.J., Quek, F.K.: Comparison of five color models in skin pixel classification. In: Proceedings of International Workshop on Recognition, Analysis, and Tracking of Faces and Gestures in Real-Time Systems, pp. 58–63. IEEE (1999)
25. Blickle, T., Thiele, L.: A mathematical analysis of tournament selection. In: ICGA, pp. 9–16. Citeseer (1995)
26. Erdos, P., Jacobson, M., Lehel, J.: Graphs realizing the same degree sequences and their respective clique numbers. Graph Theory Comb. Appl. **1**, 439–449 (1991)
27. Cannon, R.L., Dave, J.V., Bezdek, J.C.: Efficient implementation of the fuzzy c-means clustering algorithms. IEEE Trans. Pattern Anal. Mach. Intell. **2**, 248–255 (1986)
28. Szymański, J., Duch, W.: Self organizing maps for visualization of categories. In: Huang, T., Zeng, Z., Li, C., Leung, C.S. (eds.) ICONIP 2012. LNCS, vol. 7663, pp. 160–167. Springer, Heidelberg (2012). https://doi.org/10.1007/978-3-642-34475-6_20
29. Bach, S., Binder, A., Montavon, G., Klauschen, F., Müller, K.R., Samek, W.: On pixel-wise explanations for non-linear classifier decisions by layer-wise relevance propagation. PloS one **10**, e0130140 (2015)
30. Ferrari, S., Silva, M., Guarino, M., Berckmans, D.: Monitoring of swarming sounds in bee hives for early detection of the swarming period. Comput. Electron. Agric. **64**, 72–77 (2008)

Mobile Charging of Wireless Sensor Networks for Internet of Things: A Multi-Attribute Decision Making Approach

Abhinav Tomar$^{(\boxtimes)}$ and Prasanta Kumar Jana

Department of Computer Science and Engineering, Indian Institute of Technology
(Indian School of Mines) Dhanbad, Dhanbad, Jharkhand, India
profession.abhinav@gmail.com, prasantajana@iitism.ac.in

Abstract. The Internet of Things (IoT) has become an emerging and booming area of interest among the researchers and academia people. There is a rich set of IoT applications that include environment monitoring, e-healthcare, industry automation, and so on. Wireless sensor network (WSN) is a predominant alternative to make IoT more realistic as it connects physical devices to the Internet through a gateway. For real-time IoT applications, WSN with an ability to maintain energy efficient communication among sensor nodes for fast service delivery to the users is of utmost importance. However, the energy-limited battery remarkably limits the longer operability of nodes which hinders the continuous flow of sensory data to the Internet. In this regard, energy replenishment of energy-hungry nodes through wireless mobile chargers (MCs) is a promising alternative to alleviate the limited energy problem in the WSNs. To this end, we propose a multi-attribute decision making scheme that incorporates different network attributes (NAs), namely residual energy, distance to MC, neighborhood criticality, and charging significance. First, we determine the relative weights of different NAs by employing the entropy weight method (EWM). Next, the technique for order preference by similarity to ideal solution (TOPSIS) is applied for ranking the nodes in order to determine their charging schedule. Rigorous simulations are carried out to facilitate the quantitative evaluation of the proposed scheme. The comparison results reveal that our scheme outperforms the relevant state-of-the-art methods with respect to charging latency, number of dead nodes, and charging efficiency.

Keywords: Internet of Things · Wireless sensor networks
Mobile charging · Charging schedule

1 Introduction

The past few years have witnessed substantial interest in the Internet of Things (IoT). Wireless sensor network (WSN) plays a crucial role in IoT based applications such as healthcare, smart cities, and so on. The primary focus of IoT is to

© Springer Nature Switzerland AG 2019
G. Fahrnberger et al. (Eds.): ICDCIT 2019, LNCS 11319, pp. 309–324, 2019.
https://doi.org/10.1007/978-3-030-05366-6_26

provide any time connectivity to anywhere. WSN is a predominant alternative to provide such connectivity of virtual and real world. Moreover, the present day requirement of IoT is densely deployed sensor nodes. However, the nodes are operated with small batteries and thus their limited energy hinders the continuous working of WSNs. Recently, wireless energy transfer (WET) technology has been very promising to WSNs by powering energy-hungry nodes so as to realize the vision of IoT. Unlike charging the nodes through energy harvesting sources, that are temporally and spatially varying in nature [12], the deployment of mobile chargers (MCs) for empowering the nodes has come up as more emboldening technology. This guarantees that nodes can be charged in energy-balanced manner and thus they can work regularly [20].

In technical literature, the schemes based on mobile charging are either deterministic or real time in nature. The deterministic charging schemes are impractical for dynamic WSN since the MC should be known in advance about exact information, such as nodes' coordinate positions, energy consumption rates, etc. On the contrary, real time schemes conduct charging on demand basis only when nodes request for charging. We call such nodes the requesting nodes. Therefore, designing on-demand schemes is the recent trend among researchers as they meet dynamic requirements of the WSN and suitable for real-world IoT applications. However, in such schemes, determination of charging schedule of the requesting nodes becomes a leading issue. By charging schedule, we mean the sequence in which nodes are charged. To effectively deal with this issue, it is necessary that various attributes affecting network performance should be blended together for making a wise decision on nodes' charging preferences. In such situation, a multi-attribute decision making (MADM) approach can be quite effective.

In this paper, we propose a novel real time charging scheme that aims to determine efficient charging schedule of the requesting nodes by contemplating an integrated MADM approach. First, we apply Shannon's entropy weight method (EWM) [14] to assign weights to the multiple network attributes (NAs), such as residual energy, distance to MC, neighborhood criticality, and charging significance. The final charging schedule of the nodes is then obtained by the technique for order preference by similarity to ideal solution (TOPSIS) [6] that guides the movement of the MC. A numerical example is also presented for easy understanding of the proposed scheme. To signify the superiority of our scheme, we have conducted extensive simulations to compare it with state-of-the-art nearest-job-next with preemption (NJNP) [4] and first come first serve (FCFS) [5] charging schemes in diverse network scenarios. The rationale for adopting an EWM-TOPSIS based MADM approach is that it has a low time complexity and the decision making is very efficient [11]. To the best of our knowledge, any state-of-the-art charging scheme has neither incorporated multiple network attributes together nor used EWM and TOPSIS methods for the concerned problem.

The rest of this paper is organized as follows. Section 2 reviews the relevant literature. Section 3 introduces some important preliminaries. In Sect. 4, the proposed scheme is discussed in detail. In Sect. 5, simulations results are presented. Finally, Sect. 6 summarizes the paper.

2   Literature Review

With the advent of IoT as a new Internet paradigm, it is possible for machines/things to communicate autonomously without interacting with humans, thus rendering them the major source of generating Internet data. Recently, the usage of sensor nodes has made it possible to realize IoT as it connects Internet to the physical environment. However, ubiquitous service of sensor nodes is a key matter of concern since they have limited battery capacity. To ameliorate this problem, mobile charging of nodes has been very encouraging in the applications intended for long-term operation in IoT.

A considerable amount of researches have been done on mobile charging of nodes. Further, we present a comparative study of some existing notable literature that highlights the research gap which can not be overlooked. Most of the mobile charging schemes adopt periodical charging [16,19,21] that is deterministic in nature as the MC follows a preplanned path to charge the nodes. These schemes are either based on single-node charging or multi-node charging. The literature reveal that the schemes based on multi-node charging are more reliable compared to the other one since the charging latency is significantly reduced by simultaneously charging multiple nodes. It is noteworthy that the rate of energy consumption vary dynamically due to the uncertainty of environmental conditions, therefore, a periodical charging scheme is infeasible for complex and changeable networks.

On the contrary, an on-demand charging scheme supply energy to the nodes based on real time charging schedule, guiding the movement of the MC. In this context, the FCFS scheme [5] was presented in which the MC determines the charging schedule according to the temporal priorities of requesting nodes. However, due to random deployment of nodes in WSN, the MC travels a longer distance in FCFS, thereby significantly increasing the charging latency which is undesirable for real-time IoT applications. Furthermore, the preemption of the MC in any charging scheme negatively affects the charging performance. The NJNP scheme [4] allowed preemption of the MC, due to which the MC consumes a lot of energy in unnecessarily to and fro movement due to spatial constraints posed by the requesting nodes. As a result, energy of the nodes located farther from the MC gets exhausted inevitably. This is undesirable for IoT based applications since it affects perpetual flow of information from sensor nodes to the Internet. The TADP [8] charging scheme considered both temporal and spatial constraints imposed by nodes but it fails to cope with network dynamics. In [7,15], authors designed on-demand charging schemes aiming to determine charging schedule in real time. However, consideration of charging multiple nodes simultaneously and incorporation of multiple network attributes together was missing in these schemes.

Inspired by the above findings, we underpin the research of this paper. The objective of this research is to efficiently power the sensor nodes so that they

can be perpetually operated providing pervasive and ubiquitous service which is
the ultimate goal of IoT.

3 Preliminaries

3.1 Network Model

In the WSN, when the remaining energy of a node falls below a certain level,
it delivers the request for charging to MC. We assume that charging request
delivery time from a node to the MC is neglected as compared to the time
consumed by the MC for traveling or charging. This indicates that a charging
request can be delivered to the MC in real time [3]. However, finding the process
of routing the charging request is out of the scope of this paper. The charging
request message of node i can be denoted as $< ID, e_{res}(i), t_{request}, f = 1 >$,
where ID denotes node's ID, $e_{res}(i)$ represents node i's residual energy at the
time of charging request, $t_{request}$ is the time at which charging request is received.
Here, f is a flag set to be 1, indicating that it is a charging request message.
After collecting the charging requests, the MC determines the charging schedule
based on some predefined rules. A charging schedule $C_{schedule}$ is mathematically
expressed as follows.

$$C_{schedule} = \{MC \rightarrow i_1 \rightarrow i_2 \rightarrow \cdots \rightarrow i_r\} \tag{1}$$

where i_k represents the node that is charged by the MC at k^{th} position and r is
the total number of requesting nodes.

Note that location of any node can be identified using existing techniques
(e.g., [10]) or GPS and is reported to the MC via long-distance communications.
After completion of the charging task, the MC goes back to the service station
for maintenance and recharging purposes and waits for new charging requests.
The adopted WSN in our work consists of following components.

- A number of static nodes which are densely deployed in the WSN.
- An MC having sufficiently large battery capacity as compared to a node. We
  assume the energy of the MC is enough to fulfill charging demands of the
  nodes. The MC is capable to charge multiple nodes simultaneously falling
  under its charging range without significantly reducing the received power at
  each node [17].
- A service station.

Initially, all nodes have same amount of energy. The energy consumed by any
node at a specific time differs depending upon whether it is in transmitting,
receiving, listening or sleeping state [2].

We denote $t_{charge}(i)$ as the time taken by the MC to charge a node i that
can be calculated as:

$$t_{charge}(i) = \frac{e_{max} - [e_{res}(i) - (t_{wait}(i) \times e_{con}(i))]}{c_{rate}}, \forall i \in r \tag{2}$$

where e_{max} is the maximum energy of any node, $e_{con}(i)$ is the energy consumption rate of node i, c_{rate} is the charging rate of the MC, and $t_{wait}(i)$ is the waiting time of node i to be visited by the MC for charging (defined in Eq. 3). Here, $[e_{res}(i) - (t_{wait}(i) \times e_{con}(i))]$ represents remaining energy of node i at the time when the MC starts charging it. The waiting time of any node can be calculated by summing the charging time of previous node, the waiting time of previous node, and the time taken by the MC to travel from previous node to the current node i. We obtain $t_{wait}(i)$ by:

$$t_{wait}(i) = t_{charge}(i-1) + t_{wait}(i-1) + \frac{d(i, i-1)}{v_{MC}}, \ \forall i \in r \qquad (3)$$

where v_{MC} is moving speed of the MC and $d(i, i-1)$ is the distance between node i and its previous node. Next, Eq. 4 defines τ as the total time to charge multiple nodes by the MC which can be calculated as follows.

$$\tau = \max\{t_{charge}(1), t_{charge}(2)..., t_{charge}(k)\} \qquad (4)$$

where k is total number of nodes that are to be charged simultaneously and $t_{charge}(i)$ can be calculated from Eq. 2.

3.2   Network Attributes

The wise selection of network attributes (NAs) is of utmost importance as they play a critical role in decision making by MADM methods. In this paper, four NAs are considered those are: (1) residual energy, (2) distance to MC, (3) neighborhood criticality, and (4) charging significance. Next, we discuss the NAs in detail.

Residual energy(RE): Residual energy is an important NA as it directly reflects the criticality and thus charging necessity of a node. After network deployment, each node records its residual energy at regular time intervals. After receiving the charging request of a node, the MC records its residual energy based on its request message.

Distance to MC(D): It is the Euclidean distance between the locations of a node, e.g. i (x_i, y_i) and the MC (x_{MC}, y_{MC}) which can be defined as follows.

$$d(i, MC) = \sqrt{(x_i - x_{MC})^2 + (y_i - y_{MC})^2} \qquad (5)$$

Neighborhood criticality(NC): This paper leverages multi-node charging so that a number of nodes are charged simultaneously. It minimizes the MC's traveling time, thereby reducing the waiting time of other nodes. In this regard, we define a new metric, named as *Neighborhood criticality*. For a node i, it can be defined as total number of other requesting nodes that fall within the charging range of i. Let $n_{critical}(i)$ be the neighborhood criticality of a node i.

$$n_{critical}(i) = \sum_{y=1, \ y\neq i}^{r} x_{iy}, \qquad (6)$$

where

$$x_{iy} = \begin{cases} 1, & \text{if node } y \text{ is in the charging radius of } i \\ 0, & \text{otherwise} \end{cases}$$

Charging significance(CS): This attribute shows the importance of a node for charging according to its past history statistics. It signifies that the particular node belongs to that network area where event frequency is high, thereby having high probability to have higher energy consumption in future. Let $\eta_{schedule}$ be the total number of charging schedules followed by the MC till current network time and $c_{sig}(i)$ be the charging significance of node i. Then, it can be defined as follows.

$$c_{sig}(i) = \frac{c_{fq}(i)}{\eta_{schedule}}, \tag{7}$$

where $c_{fq}(i)$ denotes the number of times a node has been charged until current charging schedule and denoted by:

$$c_{fq}(i) = \sum_{z=1}^{\eta_{schedule}} y_{iz}, \tag{8}$$

where

$$y_{iz} = \begin{cases} 1, & \text{if MC charges node } i \text{ in the } z^{th} \text{ schedule} \\ 0, & \text{otherwise} \end{cases}$$

4   Proposed Method

In the proposed scheme, we follow an integrated MADM approach. First, we derive the weight of each NA using EWM. Next, TOPSIS is applied to determine the charging schedule of the nodes.

4.1   Deriving Relative Weights of Network Attributes by EWM

We introduce EWM in this study in order to differentiate the importance degree of various NAs. The entropy was first introduced in information theory by Shannon [14]. It is a very simple and convenient method that quantifies the uncertainty in terms of probability theory. The EWM derives the objective weights of NAs using mathematical computation. It is based on inherent information of NAs (as defined in Sect. 3.2). It deals with the unbiased data and thus it overcomes the man-made disturbances to make results more accurate. The stepwise procedure of EWM is as follows.

Step 1: Construct a decision matrix. We first build decision matrix $X(= [x_{ij}])$ for n number of requesting nodes with m number of NAs. The structure of X is as follows.

$$X = \begin{array}{c} \\ CN_1 \\ CN_2 \\ \vdots \\ CN_n \end{array} \begin{array}{cccc} NA_1 & NA_2 & \cdots & NA_m \\ \left[\begin{matrix} x_{11} & x_{12} & \cdots & x_{1m} \\ x_{21} & x_{22} & \cdots & x_{2m} \\ \vdots & \vdots & \ddots & \vdots \\ x_{n1} & x_{n2} & \cdots & x_{nm} \end{matrix}\right] \end{array} \tag{9}$$

where CN_i denotes the requesting node i, $i = 1, ..., n$; NA_j represents the jth network attribute, $j = 1, ..., m$, and x_{ij} is the value of network attribute NA_j for requesting node CN_i.

Example: We consider an example scenario of WSN (see Table 1) to illustrate the proposed MADM approach. In this example, there are six requesting nodes, i.e., $\{CN1, CN2, ..., CN6\}$. Let's assume a random decision matrix shown as follows.

Table 1. Decision matrix X.

	RE(J)	D(m)	NC	CS
CN1	0.92	43.20	1	0.1
CN2	0.58	28.90	1	0.1
CN3	0.68	42.40	1	0.2
CN4	0.23	29.60	1	0.2
CN5	0.85	48.80	0	0.1
CN6	0.43	27.60	2	0.2

Step 2: Normalize the decision matrix. The units of NAs may be different from each other having different ranges, thereby causing inconsistent comparisons. Therefore, the decision matrix X needs to be normalized to standardize the data. According to existing studies [9], vector normalization is mostly preferred in MADM methods. Thus, we employ vector normalization method and calculate the normalized decision matrix $R(= [r_{ij}])$ in which normalized value r_{ij} is calculated as follows.

If the network attribute is positive, i.e, it should be maximum for better performance, then normalization is done following Eq. 10.

$$r_{ij} = \frac{x_{ij}}{\sqrt{\sum_{i=1}^{n} (x_{ij})^2}}, \text{ for } i = 1, 2, \ldots, n; j = 1, 2, \ldots, m \tag{10}$$

If the network attribute is negative, i.e. it should be minimum for better performance, then normalization is done following Eq. 11.

$$r_{ij} = \frac{\frac{1}{x_{ij}}}{\sqrt{\sum_{i=1}^{n} \frac{1}{(x_{ij})^2}}}, \text{ for } i = 1, 2, \ldots, n; j = 1, 2, \ldots, m \tag{11}$$

It is worth mentioning that in our study, RE and D are negative NAs whereas NC and CS are the positive NAs.

Step 3: Characteristic proportion calculation for requesting nodes. As the values of a NA vary unpredictably with respect to the requesting nodes, we use characteristic proportion that implies the probability of a NA value for a particular requesting node in all the candidate requesting nodes. We consider p_{ij} to be the characteristic proportion of NA_j for CN_i, then:

$$p_{ij} = \frac{r_{ij}}{\sum_{i=1}^{n} r_{ij}}, \text{ for } i = 1, 2, \ldots, n; j = 1, 2, \ldots, m \tag{12}$$

The value of p_{ij} lies in the range [0,1].

Step 4: Entropy value estimation for each NA. By using characteristic proportion values, we can estimate entropy value for each NA according to Eq. 13.

$$e_j = -\frac{1}{\ln(m)} \sum_{i=1}^{n} p_{ij} \cdot \ln(p_{ij}), \text{ for } j = 1, 2, \ldots m \tag{13}$$

where e_j denotes the entropy measure of NA_j for all requesting nodes having the range as [0, 1]. For a particular NA j, if the difference among its values p_{ij} is higher for different i, then its entropy value e_j is small.

Step 5: Calculating the degree of divergence for each NA. Let d_j indicate the degree of divergence for NA_j, then we define d_j using Eq. 14.

$$d_j = 1 - e_j, \text{ for } j = 1, 2, \ldots m; \tag{14}$$

It is noteworthy that a large value of d_j reflects more variation among values of the NA_j, i.e., NA_j offers a larger amount of information. In other words, NA_j is more important than others when comparing different requesting nodes.

Step 6: Calculating the entropy weight for each NA. The entropy weight determines the objective weight of each NA. Let $w_e(j)$ be the entropy weight of the NA_j, we calculate $w_e(j)$ according to Eq. 15.

$$w_e(j) = \frac{d_j}{\sum_{j=1}^{m}(d_j)}, \sum_{j=1}^{m} w_e(j) = 1 \tag{15}$$

The results obtained from EWM computations on decision matrix X (see Table 1) using Eqs. 13, 14, and 15 are presented in Table 2. Note that the weights may vary based on the data since the WSN remains dynamic due to which the values of NAs alter significantly.

Table 2. Result summary of EWM.

	RE	D	NC	CS
Entropy value(e_j)	0.9546	0.9857	0.8710	0.9684
Degree of divergence(d_j)	0.0454	0.0143	0.1290	0.0316
Entropy weight($w_e(j)$)	**0.2060**	**0.0648**	**0.5857**	**0.1436**

4.2 Ranking the Requesting Nodes and Determine the Charging Schedule Using TOPSIS

The TOPSIS method has recently gained substantial interest among researchers for solving complex multi-attribute decision making problems which was originally developed by Hwang and Yoon [6]. TOPSIS is relatively simple and fast having a systematic procedure [13]. In TOPSIS, the requesting nodes are ranked according to their relative closeness to the ideal solutions. The best chosen node should be at closest distance from the positive ideal solution and at the same time it should be farthest from the negative ideal solution [1]. Note that the positive ideal solution maximizes the positive attributes, whereas the negative ideal solution maximizes the negative attributes [18]. The stepwise procedure of TOPSIS is as follows.

Step 1: Compute the weighted normalized decision matrix. We compute the weighted normalized decision matrix $Z(= [z_{ij}])$ by multiplying the normalized matrix $R(= [r_{ij}])$ (Eqs. 10 and 11) with the entropy weights of NAs (shown in bold in Table 2). The weighted normalized value z_{ij} is calculated as:

$$z_{ij} = r_{ij} \times w_e(j), \text{ for } i = 1, 2, \ldots, n; j = 1, 2, \ldots, m \qquad (16)$$

Table 3 shows the calculated matrix Z for the example data taken in Table 1.

Table 3. Weighted normalized decision matrix Z.

Requesting nodes	RE	D	NC	CS
CN1	0.1174	0.0303	0.2071	0.0371
CN2	0.0740	0.0203	0.2071	0.0371
CN3	0.0868	0.0298	0.2071	0.0741
CN4	0.0294	0.0208	0.2071	0.0741
CN5	0.1085	0.0343	0	0.0371
CN6	0.0549	0.0194	0.4141	0.0741

Step 2: Obtain the positive and negative ideal solution. We define the positive ideal solution as I^+ indicating the most suitable node and the negative ideal solution as I^- indicating the least suitable node for charging.

$$I^+ = \max \{z_{1j}, \ldots z_{nj}\} \text{ and } I^- = \min \{z_{1j}, \ldots z_{nj}\}, \text{for positive NA}$$
$$I^+ = \min \{z_{1j}, \ldots z_{nj}\} \text{ and } I^- = \max \{z_{1j}, \ldots z_{nj}\}, \text{for negative NA}$$

For positive NA, the larger the NA value is, the better the charging suitability of the corresponding node is. For example, a requesting node having higher NC or CS should be charged first for better charging performance. On the contrary, negative NAs have opposite meaning. The final value of I^+ and I^- for each of the criterion is shown in Table 4.

Table 4. Positive/negative ideal solutions for NAs.

Ideal solutions	RE	D	NC	CS
(PIS, I^+)	0.0294	0.0194	0.4141	0.0741
(NIS, I^-)	0.1174	0.0343	0	0.0371

Step 3: Determine separation measures for each node. Separation measures are calculated using Euclidean distance. The separation of each node from positive ideal solution I^+ and negative ideal solution as I^- is calculated using Eq. 17 as follows.

$$S_i^+ = \sqrt{\sum_{i=1}^{n}(z_{ij} - I^+)^2} \text{ and } S_i^- = \sqrt{\sum_{i=1}^{n}(z_{ij} - I^-)^2} \text{ where } j \in \{1, ..., m\}$$
(17)

Step 4: Calculation of relative closeness of each node to the ideal solution. The closeness coefficient CC_i (between $0-1$) indicates the relative closeness of ith node which is determined as follows.

$$CC_i = \frac{S_i^-}{S_i^- + S_i^+}, \text{ where } i \in \{1, ..., n\}$$
(18)

Step 5: Ranking the requesting nodes for charging schedule determination. In this step, we rank the requesting nodes by comparing their CC values. The values of CC_i for all $i \in r$ are sorted in descending order.

Table 5 shows the final ranking of the requesting nodes based on the values of S_i^+, S_i^-, and CC_i. It can be observed from shaded row in Table 5 that $CN6$ with highest value of CC_i as 0.9428 is ranked first. It means that $CN6$ is the most suitable node that should be charged next. Therefore, the charging schedule

$C_{schedule}$ is computed as $\{MC \rightarrow CN6 \rightarrow CN4 \rightarrow CN3 \rightarrow CN2 \rightarrow CN1 \rightarrow CN5\}$. The pseudo code of the proposed scheme is given in Algorithm 1.

Table 5. TOPSIS results.

Requesting nodes	S_i^+	S_i^-	CC_i	Rankings
CN1	0.2283	0.2071	0.4757	5
CN2	0.2150	0.2120	0.4965	4
CN3	0.2151	0.2126	0.4971	3
CN4	0.2071	0.2284	0.5245	2
CN5	0.4235	0.0089	0.0207	6
CN6	0.0255	0.4207	0.9428	1

Algorithm 1. CHARGING SCHEDULE DETERMINATION

Input   : r: number of requesting nodes; Information about residual energy $(e_{res}(i))$ of each requesting node $i \in r$.
Output: Charging schedule: $C_{schedule} \leftarrow \{MC\}$

---

1 **for** $i \leftarrow 1$ **to** r **do**
2 $\quad$ Determine $d(i, MC)$, $n_{critical}(i)$ and $c_{sig}(i)$ for each $i \in r$ using Eqs. 5, 6 and 7, respectively
3 Build decision matrix X by inserting each attribute value as defined in Eq. 9
4 Normalize the decision matrix for positive and negative NAs using Eqs. 10 and 11
5 Evaluate entropy weights for the NAs using EWM computations
$\qquad\qquad\qquad\qquad\qquad\qquad\qquad\qquad\qquad$ ▷ refer Section 4.1
6 Calculate weighted normalized matrix using Eq. 16
7 Find (PIS, I^+) and (NIS, I^-) for each NA
8 **for** $i \leftarrow 1$ **to** r **do**
9 $\quad$ Calculate separation measure of each node i with PIS and NIS using Eq. 17
10 $\quad$ Calculate closeness coefficient for each node i using Eq. 18
11 sort_nodes $\leftarrow$ sort the nodes according to descending order of CC_i values
12 $C_{schedule} \leftarrow C_{schedule} \cup$ sort_nodes
13 **return** $C_{schedule}$

Theorem 1. *The time complexity of proposed scheme is $O(n^2 m)$.*

Proof. Let n be the number of requesting nodes and m be the number of network attributes. Note that in Algorithm 1, r is the number of requesting nodes that is same as n here. Then, Steps 1 and 2 of Algorithm 1 requires $O(n)$ time. Step 3 is for building decision matrix by inserting values which takes $O(nm)$ time.

Step 4 requires $O(n^2m)$ time for normalization. Next, EWM computations are done using Eqs. 12, 13, 14, and 15, where each step requires $O(m)$ time. After EWM, weighted normalized matrix in Step 6 is calculated within $O(nm)$ time. Then, Steps 7, 8, 9, and 10 jointly requires $O(nm)$ time. In Step 11, sorting takes $O(n \log n)$ time. Thereafter, final $C_{schedule}$ is formed in $O(n)$ time. Therefore, the proposed scheme requires $O(n^2m)$ time.   □

5   Simulation Analysis

5.1   Simulation Setup

The simulations were accomplished in MATLAB R2016a on a system enabled with 4 GB RAM, Intel Core i7 processor running a 64-bit Windows 8.1 OS. For simulation purpose, a number of static rechargeable nodes $(500 - 1000)$ are randomly deployed over a $100\,\text{m} \times 100\,\text{m}$ rectangular region. Due to the randomness in the deployment pattern of nodes, the simulation results are averaged over 20 random simulation instances to achieve fair comparisons. The parameter settings used in the simulations are listed in Table 6 unless specified otherwise.

Table 6. Simulation parameter settings.

Parameters	Values
WSN	$100 \times 100\,\text{m}^2$
Number of sensor nodes	500–1000
Communication range	30 m
Speed of MC	1 m/s
Maximum battery capacity of a node	5 J
Initial energy of an MC	500 J
MC moving consumption rate	0.05 J/m
Charging range of an MC	5 m
Charging rate of MC	0.05 J/s
Simulation time (in rounds)	5000–10000

5.2   Performance Comparisons

We mainly evaluate simulation results in three network metrics, namely average charging latency, number of dead nodes, and charging efficiency. Moreover, we have shown the impact of two factors, i.e., different number of nodes and different simulation time for all performance metrics. Note that, the comparison results are recorded with first factor by setting the simulation time as 5000 *rounds*, while analyzing the impact of other factor, total number of nodes are considered to be 500.

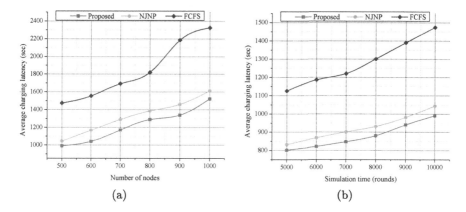

Fig. 1. Performance comparison of proposed scheme in terms of average charging latency against (a) number of nodes and (b) simulation time.

Average Charging Latency. The charging latency for a node is denoted as the time period between the time of its charging request and the time when it is completely charged by the MC. The mean of the charging latencies of all the requesting nodes is termed as the average charging latency. It can also be regarded as the average charging response time. This performance metric is important for any charging scheduling algorithm as it reflects the charging efficiency. The average charging latency is less, which means other requesting nodes have to wait for a shorter time period, thereby preventing them to die earlier due to energy exhaustion. It is clear to see in Figs. 1(a) and 1(b) that the average charging latency for the proposed scheme is less than that of NJNP and FCFS with respect to varying *number of nodes* and *simulation time*, respectively. It powerfully proves the efficacy of the proposed scheme. The reason is clear with the fact that the proposed scheme incorporates multiple attributes together, specially number of simultaneously charged requesting nodes (i.e., neighborhood criticality), resulting in efficient charging schedule. On the other hand, state-of-the-art schemes consider only temporal or spatial priority of nodes while scheduling their charging requests, thereby increasing the waiting times of other nodes.

Number of Dead Nodes. The comparison results in terms of the number of dead nodes are shown in Figs. 2(a) and 2(b). It is worth mentioning that a less number of dead nodes guarantees the longer connectivity and stability of WSN. It is possible only if more number of nodes get opportunity to be charged within their deadlines which is taken care of in our proposed scheme. It is clear in the referenced figures that the number of dead nodes using proposed scheme is always lower than that of NJNP and FCFS irrespective of both total number of nodes and simulation time. Furthermore, in Fig. 2(a), number of dead nodes increases with the increment in the total nodes as more number of charging requests are originated. On the other hand, with the simulation going on, number of dead

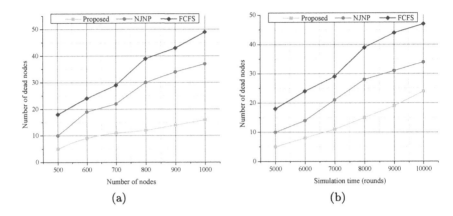

Fig. 2. Performance comparison of proposed scheme in terms of number of dead nodes against (a) number of nodes and (b) simulation time.

nodes get increased due to heavier burden on the MC for serving more requesting nodes. Contrarily to the proposed scheme, existing ones fail to attain the same due to inefficient scheduling of the MC in case of large number of charging requests.

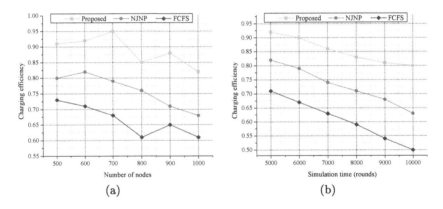

Fig. 3. Performance comparison of proposed scheme in terms of charging efficiency against (a) number of nodes and (b) simulation time.

Charging Efficiency. For an on-demand charging scheme, charging efficiency plays a vital role in achieving promising performance. It is the measure of energy transferred to the nodes per unit movement of the MC in the network. The higher charging efficiency reflects the betterment in the performance of a WSN. In Figs. 3(a) and 3(b), we observe that the charging efficiency of proposed scheme is comparatively high with that of other two schemes, regardless of the total number of nodes and simulation time, respectively. Moreover, charging efficiency of the proposed scheme is recorded highest to be 95% in case of 700 nodes. As discussed earlier, the average charging latency of our scheme is lowest. With this fact, MC makes more use of its energy to replenish the requesting nodes which makes proposed scheme more charging efficient as compared to existing ones. It can be also observed from Fig. 3(b) that charging efficiency of NJNP and FCFS decreases more abruptly with simulation time because nodes become dead more frequently due to unnecessary movement of the MC.

6   Concluding Remarks

In this study, we have presented an on-demand mobile charging scheme for powering the sensor nodes in order to ensure endless connectivity for real-world applications based on the Internet of Things. The proposed scheme utilizes a decision making approach by incorporating multiple network attributes related to nodes, such as residual energy, distance to mobile charger, neighborhood criticality, and charging significance. The prime objective of the scheme is to determine charging schedule of the nodes that guides the movement of mobile charger. Through rigorous simulations, we have shown the supremacy of proposed scheme over its contemporaries, i.e, NJNP and FCFS, revealing that proposed scheme boosts the charging performance with less number of dead nodes, low average charging latency, and high charging efficiency. In future, we will extend this work by considering the collaboration between multiple mobile chargers and the nodes.

References

1. Benitez, J.M., Martín, J.C., Román, C.: Using fuzzy number for measuring quality of service in the hotel industry. Tour. Manag. **28**(2), 544–555 (2007)
2. Feng, W., Alshaer, H., Elmirghani, J.M.: Optimization of energy consumption in rectangular ad-hoc wireless networks. In: Fourth International Conference on Communications and Networking in China, ChinaCOM 2009, pp. 1–5. IEEE (2009)
3. He, L., Gu, Y., Pan, J., Zhu, T.: On-demand charging in wireless sensor networks: theories and applications. In: 2013 IEEE 10th International Conference on Mobile Ad-Hoc and Sensor Systems, pp. 28–36. IEEE (2013)
4. He, L., Kong, L., Gu, Y., Pan, J., Zhu, T.: Evaluating the on-demand mobile charging in wireless sensor networks. IEEE Trans. Mob. Comput. **14**(9), 1861–1875 (2015)
5. He, L., Zhuang, Y., Pan, J., Xu, J.: Evaluating on-demand data collection with mobile elements in wireless sensor networks. In: 2010 IEEE 72nd Vehicular Technology Conference Fall, VTC 2010-Fall, pp. 1–5. IEEE (2010)
6. Hwang, C.L., Yoon, K.: Methods for multiple attribute decision making. Multiple Attribute Decision Making. Lecture Notes in Economics and Mathematical Systems, vol. 186, pp. 58–191. Springer, Heidelberg (1981). https://doi.org/10.1007/978-3-642-48318-9_3

7. Kaswan, A., Tomar, A., Jana, P.K.: An efficient scheduling scheme for mobile charger in on-demand wireless rechargeable sensor networks. J. Netw. Comput. Appl. **114**, 123–134 (2018)
8. Lin, C., Wang, Z., Han, D., Wu, Y., Yu, C.W., Wu, G.: TADP: enabling temporal and distantial priority scheduling for on-demand charging architecture in wireless rechargeable sensor networks. J. Syst. Archit. **70**, 26–38 (2016)
9. Lu, L., Yuan, Y.: A novel topsis evaluation scheme for cloud service trustworthiness combining objective and subjective aspects. J. Syst. Softw. **143**, 71–86 (2018)
10. Patwari, N., Hero, A.O., Perkins, M., Correal, N.S., O'dea, R.J.: Relative location estimation in wireless sensor networks. IEEE Trans. Sig. Process. **51**(8), 2137–2148 (2003)
11. Prakash, C., Barua, M.: Integration of AHP-TOPSIS method for prioritizing the solutions of reverse logistics adoption to overcome its barriers under fuzzy environment. J. Manuf. Syst. **37**, 599–615 (2015)
12. Ren, X., Liang, W., Xu, W.: Quality-aware target coverage in energy harvesting sensor networks. IEEE Trans. Emerg. Top. Comput. **3**(1), 8–21 (2015)
13. Shanian, A., Savadogo, O.: A methodological concept for material selection of highly sensitive components based on multiple criteria decision analysis. Expert. Syst. Appl. **36**(2), 1362–1370 (2009)
14. Shannon, C.E., Weaver, W., Burks, A.W.: The mathematical theory of communication (1951)
15. Tomar, A., Anwit, R., Jana, P.K.: An efficient scheme for on-demand energy replenishment in wireless rechargeable sensor networks. In: 2017 International Conference on Advances in Computing, Communications and Informatics (ICACCI), pp. 125–130. IEEE (2017)
16. Tomar, A., Nitesh, K., Jana, P.K.: An efficient scheme for trajectory design of mobile chargers in wireless sensor networks. Wirel. Netw. 1–16 (2018)
17. Tong, B., Li, Z., Wang, G., Zhang, W.: How wireless power charging technology affects sensor network deployment and routing. In: 2010 IEEE 30th International Conference on Distributed Computing Systems (ICDCS), pp. 438–447. IEEE (2010)
18. Wang, T.C., Chang, T.H.: Application of topsis in evaluating initial training aircraft under a fuzzy environment. Expert Syst. Appl. **33**(4), 870–880 (2007)
19. Xie, L., Shi, Y., Hou, Y.T., Lou, W., Sherali, H.D., Midkiff, S.F.: Bundling mobile base station and wireless energy transfer: modeling and optimization. In: 2013 Proceedings IEEE of INFOCOM, pp. 1636–1644. IEEE (2013)
20. Xie, L., Shi, Y., Hou, Y.T., Lou, W., Sherali, H.D., Midkiff, S.F.: Multi-node wireless energy charging in sensor networks. IEEE/ACM Trans. Netw. (ToN) **23**(2), 437–450 (2015)
21. Xie, L., Shi, Y., Hou, Y.T., Sherali, H.D.: Making sensor networks immortal: an energy-renewal approach with wireless power transfer. IEEE/ACM Trans. Netw. (TON) **20**(6), 1748–1761 (2012)

Security

Efficient Searching Over Encrypted Database: Methodology and Algorithms

Varad Deshpande and Debasis Das[(✉)]

Department of CS and IS, BITS Pilani-K.K. Birla Goa Campus, Zuarinagar 403726, Goa, India
debasisd@goa.bits-pilani.ac.in

Abstract. Database encryption is a process in which the data stored in the database are converted from plaintext (PT) to ciphertext (CT). The original data can be retrieved from the ciphertext with the help of a predefined key and a decryption scheme. This way, only the appropriate authority that has the key can access the data. Thus, encrypted databases help ensure data confidentiality and avoid data leaks. In this paper, we will describe a modification to the Secure K-Nearest Neighbours (SkNN) [3] technique to construct an encrypted database system. We briefly discuss some of the existing encryption models and the principles involved in their construction and look at some of the issues that plague these models. The motivation behind this paper is to devise a method that allows for strong database encryption, while at the same time facilitating efficient search over the encrypted data. In order to achieve this, we suggest an approach which combines RSA with the SkNN scheme.

Keywords: Database encryption
Secure K-nearest neighbours (SkNN) · RSA

1 Introduction

Database encryption [1] is a process in which the data stored in the database is converted from plaintext to ciphertext. The original data can be retrieved from the ciphertext with the help of a predefined key and a decryption scheme. This way, only the appropriate authority that has the key can access the data. Thus, encrypted databases help ensure data confidentiality [2] and avoid data leaks.

There are many techniques [1–3] available for database encryption [3–5]. Some of these include:

- Transparent Database Encryption
- Encryption of Database Columns
- Encryption of Database Fields
- Encrypting File System (EFS)
- Application-level Encryption.

G. Fahrnberger et al. (Eds.): ICDCIT 2019, LNCS 11319, pp. 327–338, 2019.
https://doi.org/10.1007/978-3-030-05366-6_27

1.1   External/Transparent Database Encryption

External Encryption refers to the encryption of the entire database [1–3]. It is said to be transparent because it is not visible to the applications and users that use the data, and does not require any changes in the logic of the application. The main use of this type of encryption is to prevent information leak due to the loss of physical media (disks, tapes etc.) containing the data.

1.2   Encryption of Database Columns

Column Level Encryption facilitates the encryption of specific columns of the tables that make up the database. The ability to encrypt only specific columns/fields allows this encryption scheme to be more adaptable when compared to external encryption. It is also possible to encrypt different columns with unique keys. This, however, leads to a loss of speed.

1.3   Encryption of Database Fields

Field Level Encryption allows us to operate on the encrypted fields of a database without having to decrypt them first. Since retrieval of data does not require the decryption of the ciphertext at any intermediate stage, this type of encryption prevents data leaks and is suitable for storing data on untrusted servers.

1.4   Encrypting File System (EFS)

A database system is taken care of by a Database Management System (DBMS) that executes on an existing operating system. This can lead to security risks as the database might be operating on a possibly weak operating system. EFS can encrypt data external to a database system, i.e. EFS widens the scope of database encryption. However, it also reduces the performance of the database and can lead to administrative issues.

1.5   Application Level Encryption

In this encryption scheme [4–6], it is the application layer that performs the data encryption. This enables the encryption process to be customized for every user depending upon the information that the application knows about its users. However, this encryption scheme has certain disadvantages. An important disadvantage is that the applications that are used by companies will need to be changed/modified so that they themselves can perform data encryption. This can require a lot of time and other resources [7]. Also, application level encryption can affect the performance of a database. Encrypting the data in the database using multiple applications can lead to difficulties in constructing the index and performing searches over the data.

In this paper, we will discuss some of the existing encrypted databases [3, 8–11]. We aim to provide a method to execute queries on encrypted data without decrypting them first. This allows us to not only save time but also avoid security leaks. Below, we give a general outline of our proposed model. Figure 1 describes the general structure of an encrypted database model.

- The user interacts with the database through the application.
- The proxy may or may not be included in the architecture and is largely determined by the design requirements. For instance, the Arx model consists of a client and a server proxy.
- The proxy is setup so that the application does not need to be modified.
- The proxy acts as a client to the database server. The database server stores the encrypted data.
- In practice, the process of encryption, decryption, key storing and data processing is done by the proxy.

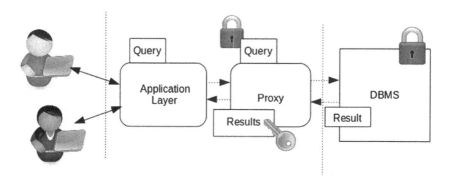

Fig. 1. Database model

In our approach, we make use of a type of field level encryption. Specifically, we make use of the RSA encryption scheme to encrypt the document index and queries and use garbled circuits to perform the computations necessary to return the required documents. We do not decrypt the entries of the index table or the query during any intermediate stage, thus providing more security and avoiding data leaks.

The rest of the paper is organised as follows. Section 2 discusses the connected work and Sect. 3 concisely discusses the Preliminaries. Section 4 grants our proposed scheme for Efficient Searching Over Encrypted Database. Section 5 discusses the Security Analysis of the proposed approach. Section 6 discusses the results of the proposed approach and finally, Sect. 7 concludes the work.

2 Existing Database Models

In this section, we list some of the previous work that has been carried out to construct secure databases.

2.1   Rank Based Keyword Search

In [3], Xia et al. proposed a secure K Nearest Neighbours scheme which supports multi keyword ranked search. In this paper, they present the Basic Dynamic Multi-Keyword Ranked Search (BDMRS) to allow for efficient search while at the same time maintaining index and query confidentiality as well as keyword privacy. However, this scheme is susceptible to the TF (Term Frequency) statistical attack. In order to remedy this, [3] also proposes an Enhanced Dynamic Multi-Keyword Ranked Search (EDMRS) which introduces some randomness in the calculation of the relevance score to obscure the TF distribution and thwart the TF statistical attack. We base our proposed scheme on the BDMRS model, making slight modification which can help reduce the computational cost.

2.2   Secure Database Using Homomorphic Encryption Schemes

Homomorphic encryption enables us to perform calculations on encrypted data. This produces a ciphertext which, after decryption, equals to the resulting computations performed on the original data. The encryption scheme mentioned in [2], makes use of a private key and a public key and defines certain security parameters. However, a model which is purely based on a homomorphic encryption [7,8] scheme requires a very high time to execute the queries [9] and hence, is not suitable for real time applications that involve a large database.

2.3   The Arx Model

Arx is a strongly encrypted database system [1]. Arx stores all the sensitive data on the database server. The Arx architecture has a client side, which consists of the application and a trusted client proxy, and a server-side consisting of a server proxy which acts like a regular client to the database server. The Arx model makes use of a modified AES encryption scheme. The encryption process takes place in the client proxy. The client proxy stores the master key. It processes queries, encrypts vital data, and sends this information to the server proxy. The client proxy also stores the metadata (schema information) and also processes the query results by decrypting them. The server does the majority of the work by filtering and aggregating the documents in a small result set. Arx provides IND-CPA, i.e., Indistinguishable under Chosen Plaintext Attack like security. Arx does not provide security underside channel attacks. Arx only supports a limited set of operations. Arx makes use of three encryption schemes. **BASE** is a standard encryption function, based on AES initialized with a random vector. **EQ** is a function that allows equality checks. EQ is capable of encrypting data and producing the necessary tokens. The token is used to check the value in the query against the values present in the database. The **AGG** function enables addition. Arx uses the Paillier cryptosystem. The Arx index is stored as a history independent treap. The drawback of Arx is that it can perform only a limited number of operations on the data.

3   Preliminaries

3.1   Searchable Encryption

Searchable Encryption (SE) [3,12] is an encryption scheme that allows searching of keywords over encrypted data. In order to understand how SE works, we need to be familiar with the concept of a trapdoor function. A trapdoor function $f(x)$ is a function which allows easy computation in one direction but finding the inverse of this function is hard without some special information. Keeping this definition in mind, we now state the two kinds of schemes based on searchable encryption.

Searchable Symmetric Encryption. In this type of SE scheme, the data owner generates a private key and only they can compute the ciphertext corresponding to the data as well as the trapdoor required for the query processing.

- $KeyGen(seed)$: This algorithm is used by the data owner who makes use of a random seed to generate a private key K_{pv}.
- $MakeIndex(K_{pv}, D)$: This function is used by the data owner to generate a keyword index I from the collection of documents D using the private key K_{pv}.
- $Trapdoor(K_{pv}, w)$: This is a keyword trapdoor generation algorithm run by an authorized user in order to generate the trapdoor T_w corresponding to the keyword w in the query Q.
- $Search(T_w, I)$ This function is executed by the cloud server in order to search for the keyword w using the trapdoor T_w provided by the user. This algorithm outputs the set of documents $D(w)$ which contain this keyword.

Public Key Encryption with Key Word Search. This scheme is similar to how SSE functions. However, in this scheme, the data owner generates a pair of keys: Public key(K_{pub}) and Private Key(K_{pv}). Any public key holder can produce the ciphertext for the data, but only the data owner having the private key can create the trapdoor function.

3.2   Secure Multi-Party Computation

Secure Multi-Party Computation (MPC) [5–7] is a field in cryptography for developing methods and protocols for parties to jointly compute a function over their inputs while keeping these inputs private. In our paper, we make use of Two Party Computation (Garbled Circuits). It is a cryptographic protocol that allows two parties to mutually compute a function over confidential inputs without relying on a trusted third party.

The MPC protocols ensure:

- Input Privacy: The messages exchanged during the execution of this proto-col do not reveal any information about the data belonging to the parties involved. The only information that can be gleaned is what is obtained by observing the function output.
- Correctness: An adversary cannot coerce honest parties to output incorrect results.

In this protocol, the operation to be performed is implemented as a boolean circuit. Both the parties are aware of this circuit. One party encrypts the circuit and along with the encrypted input, sends this circuit to the other party using oblivious transfer. The second party then evaluates the circuit to obtain the output.

The following are the two types of protocols that are used:

- Two Party Computation/Garbled Circuits: It is a cryptographic protocol that allows two parties to mutually compute a function over confidential inputs without relying on a trusted third party. In this protocol, the operation to be performed is implemented as a boolean circuit. Both the parties are aware of this circuit. One party encrypts the circuit and along with the encrypted input, sends this circuit to the other party using oblivious transfer. The second party then evaluates the circuit to obtain the output.
- Multiparty protocols: These protocols make use of secret sharing which involves dividing a secret into multiple shares which are then distributed among various parties. Thus, no party has the complete information.

4 Proposed Scheme: Algorithm for Efficient Searching over Encrypted Database

Our approach is similar to the Basic Dynamic Multi-Keyword Ranked Search (BDMRS) as suggested in [3,14]. However, the way in which we encrypt the data will differ. We will follow the following procedure:

- Generate the key pair (K_{pub}, K_{pv}) to be used in the RSA encryption scheme [13].
- Encrypt the keywords and the documents in the corpus using the private key K_{pv}.
- Build a secure keyword index I.
- Send the index I along with the encrypted document set D to the third party sever.
- In order the search for the keywords in the encrypted database, encrypt the query using the private key K_{pv} and send this encrypted query, along with the public key K_{pub} to the server.
- At each node, the garbled circuit having the encrypted query, encrypted term frequency vector and the public key as input, computes the score correspond-ing to that query.

– The $'k'$ documents closest to the query are returned as the result.

Here we assume that the users authorized to perform search over the encrypted database have access to the private key supplied by the data owner through a secure protocol such as Diffie-Hellman key exchange.

4.1 Key Generation

– Select to large random prime numbers p and q.
– Calculate $N = pq$. All operations are done modulo N.
– Calculate $\phi(N) = (p-1)(q-1)$.
– Select some e such that $1 < e < \phi(N)$, and e is co-prime to $\phi(N)$. The public key $K_{pub} = (e, N)$.
– Compute d such that $ed \equiv 1 mod(\phi(N))$. The private key $K_{pv} = (d, p, q)$.

4.2 Index Construction

The keyword index I we propose is similar to the one presented in [3]. Let $D = d_1, d_2, ..., d_n$ be a the documents present in the corpus. Let $W = w_1, w_2, ..., w_m$ be the set of all possible keywords. Let $T_i = t_1, t_2..., t_m$ represent the tuple which contains the normalized term frequency values of the words corresponding to the document d_i, i.e. $t_i = TF(w_i)$ in d_i. Henceforth, T and T_i will essentially mean the same thing. The size of the corpus is n and the number of unique keywords is m. The secure index is in the form of a keyword balanced binary tree. Construction of the tree is as follows:

– Corresponding to each document d_i, construct a leaf node.
– Obtain the tuple T_i consisting of the term frequencies of the keywords.
– Encrypt (RSA) every position in T_i using the private key K_{pv} to get the encrypted vector T_i'.

Let us denote each node in the index I by u. Thus, each node u consists of $< nodeID, T', c_l, c_r, DID >$, where $nodeID$ id the unique ID for the node, c_l and c_r are the left and right child of the node respectively and DID is the document ID. Along with this, each node also consists of a garbled circuit which takes as input $< T', Q', N, K_{pub} >$, calculates the $Score$ and outputs 1 if the score is greater than some minimum score x else it outputs 0. The score in the garbled circuit is computed as follows:

$$Score = \sum_{i=1}^{m}(t_i'q_i')^e modN = \sum_{i=1}^{m}(t_i^d q_i^d)^e modN = \sum_{i=1}^{m}(t_iq_i)^{ed} modN = \sum_{i=1}^{m}(t_iq_i)$$

Note that $t_i' = t_i^d modN$ and $q_i' = q_i^d modN$.

Before we describe the algorithm for index construction, we will like to establish the following notation:

– $Enc_{k_{pv}}$: The RSA encryption function.
– $TF_{d_{DID}}(w_i))$: The normalized term frequency of the keyword w_i in the document with document id DID.

- *CurrentSet*: The set of nodes currently being processed. They do not have a parent node yet.
- *TempSet*: The set of the newly generated nodes.

The algorithm for index construction is given below.

Algorithm 1. Index Construction

Input: The dataset D
Output: Index tree I
for *each entry d in the dataset* **do**
$\quad$ Construct a leaf node l for d where $l.ID = GenID()$,
$\quad l.left = l.right = null$ and $T'[i] = Enc_{k_{pv}}(TF_{d_{DID}}(w_i))$ for $i = 1, 2, .., n$;
$\quad$ Add the garbled circuit to l;
$\quad$ Add l to CurrentSet;
end
while $|CurrentSet| > 1$ **do**
$\quad$ **if** $|CurrentSet|$ *is even* **then**
$\quad\quad$ **for** *every node pair $\dot{l}$ and $\ddot{l}$ in CurrentSet* **do**
$\quad\quad\quad$ Initialize a parent node l for $\dot{l}$ and $\ddot{l}$, with $l.ID = 0$, $l.left = \dot{l}$,
$\quad\quad\quad l.right = \ddot{l}$ and $T'[i] = max\{\dot{l}.T'[i], \ddot{l}.T[i]\}$ for $i = 1, 2, .., n$;
$\quad\quad\quad$ Add l in TempSet;
$\quad\quad$ **end**
$\quad$ **end**
$\quad$ **else**
$\quad\quad$ **for** *every node pair $\dot{l}$ and $\ddot{l}$ of the $(2k - 2)$ nodes in CurrentSet* **do**
$\quad\quad\quad$ Initialize a parent node l for $\dot{l}$ and $\ddot{l}$;
$\quad\quad\quad$ Add l to TempSet;
$\quad\quad$ **end**
$\quad\quad$ Generate a parent node l_1 for the $(2k - 1)^{th}$ and $2k^{th}$ node, and a
$\quad\quad$ parent node l for l_1 and the $(2k + 1)^{th}$ node;
$\quad\quad$ Insert l in TempSet;
$\quad$ **end**
$\quad$ Replace CurrentSet with TempSet. Clear TempSet;
end
return Node in the CurrentSet, which is root of the index T;

In this algorithm, for each entry we construct a leaf node corresponding to that entry. Each node in the tree has a m-array which stores the encrypted TF values of the keywords. We iteratively construct each level of the tree by pairing the nodes at the lower nodes. CurrentSet is the set of nodes in current level while TempSet is the set of parent nodes for the nodes in the current level. When the algorithm terminates, CurrentSet only consists of the root of the index tree. We will now describe the algorithm used to search over the index. We will make use of a Greedy Depth First Search (GDFS). Again, this algorithm is similar to the one used in [3], with only a slight modification that garbled circuits at each node are used to perform the comparisons. In the algorithm given below, we use the symbol '$\leq$' operator to demonstrate how the algorithm works. The final result is stored in the *ResultSet*. Q' indicates the encrypted query string, K_{pub} is the public key. Each entry in the *ResultSet* is a tuple $< Score(T', Q'), l.ID >$ initialized to zero.

Algorithm 2. GDFS

Input: Index node u
Output: ResultSet
if *l is a non-leaf node* **then**
   | GDFS(l.left);
   | GDFS(l.right);
end
else
   if $k^{th} score < Score(T', Q')$ **then**
      | Remove entry having the least score from the ResultSet;
      | Insert $< Score(T', Q'), l.ID >$ in ResultSet;
   end
   return;
end

This algorithm returns the k documents closest to the query vector.

5   Security Analysis

Now, we present an analysis of our encryption model (shown in Table 1) based on the security goals.

– *Index and Query Confidentiality:* In the index stored at the third party server, the term frequency vector present at each node is in the encrypted format. As a result, it is not possible to obtain the original vector without the private key K_{pv}. Reconstructing the private key from the public key and the ciphertext requires factoring N into its constituent primes p and q. For large enough primes, any attempt at reconstructing the private key by the attacker is practically in-feasible. The same holds true for the query vector as well. Thus, no information regarding the documents and the query vector are revealed to the server.

– *Computational Privacy:* During any round of the search, the score is calculated between two encrypted vectors using garbled circuits and the output of the circuit determines whether a document is added to the result set. Since the actual keywords are not decrypted at any point during the computation,

Table 1. Table for security analysis and complexity analysis

Scheme	Confidentiality	Privacy	Time complexity	Space complexity
Proposed scheme	Yes	Yes	$O(mn)$	$O(mn)$
Xia et al. [3]	Yes	Yes	$O(nm^2)$	$O(mn)$

6   Results

Let n be the number of nodes in the index I. We visit each node exactly once. At each node we set the value of an m-tuple. Thus, the order of work done at any node is $O(m)$ and the total work done for index construction is $O(mn)$. We observe them by making use of the RSA encryption scheme and garbled circuits, we have reduced the time required to build the index as compared to the time required by the BDMRS scheme mentioned in [3] which happened to be $O(nm^2)$. The memory cost of the index tree is $O(nm)$, as each node consists of an m-tuple. The metric that we use to compare the performance of our model is the computational cost which is the amount of resources required, with our primary resource being time, to execute the algorithm. The graph in Fig. 2 shows the behaviour of the our proposed scheme in comparison to the BDRS model in terms of how the computational cost increases with the number of keywords. The *Blue* plot represents the BDMRS scheme while the *Red* plot represents our

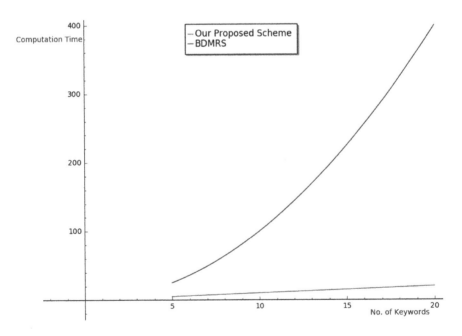

Fig. 2. Effect of number of keyword on index construction (Color figure online)

proposed scheme. We observe that in a corpus of fixed size, as the number of keywords increases, the computational cost associated with the BDMRS scheme increases much more rapidly in comparison to our proposed scheme.

Let x be the leaf nodes containing the keywords from the query. Since the index is a BBT, it's height is $log(n)$. Thus, the maximum number of nodes visited during $GDFS$ is $O(xlog(n))$. At each node we calculate the score which requires $O(m)$ time. Thus, the computational cost of retrieving data associated with our scheme is $O(xmlog(n))$. However, one drawback of our approach is that the garbled circuits have to be rebuilt every time the node is visited. This can add some overhead.

7   Conclusion

In this document, we proposed a scheme to obtain a secure database which supports efficient searching. We discussed two algorithms, one to obtain a secure index and another to enable searching over the constructed index. The security of the database is ensured by using the RSA encryption scheme while searching over this encrypted data without first needing to decrypt is facilitated by SkNN. While many other encryption schemes can be used to achieve data security, RSA allows us to reduce the computational cost associated with executing queries. Future work includes a detailed analysis of our suggested scheme against different threat models and performing comparisons with the existing models.

Acknowledgment. This work is partially supported by Early Career Research Award from Science and Engineering Research Board (SERB), Department of Science and Technology (DST), Govt. of India, New Delhi, India (Project Number: ECR/2015/000256).

References

1. Poddar, R., Popa, R., Boelter, T.: Arx: a strongly encrypted database system. IACR Cryptology ePrint Archive, p. 20 (2016)
2. Khatib, K., Guennoun, M., Gahi, Y.: A secure database system using homomorphic encryption schemes. In: The Third International Conference on Advances in Databases, Knowledge, and Data Applications, p. 5 (2011)
3. Wang, Q., Sun, X., Wang, X., Xia, Z.: A secure and dynamic multi-keyword ranked search scheme over encrypted cloud data. IEEE Trans. Parallel Distrib. Syst. **27**(2), 340–352 (2016)
4. Garay, J., Curtmola, R., Ostrovsky, R., Kamara, S.: Searchable symmetric encryption: improved definitions and efficient constructions. In: Proceedings of the 13th ACM Conference on Computer and Communications Security, pp. 79–88 (2006)
5. Cash, D., et al.: Dynamic searchable encryption in very-large databases: data structures and implementation. Cryptology ePrint Archive, p. 16 (2014)
6. Perrig, A., Song, D., Wagner, D.: Practical techniques for searches on encrypted data. In: Proceedings of the 2000 IEEE Symposium on Security and Privacy, SP 2000, p. 12 (2000)

7. Shmueli, E., Waisenberg, R., Elovici, Y., Gudes, E.: Designing secure indexes for encrypted databases. In: Jajodia, S., Wijesekera, D. (eds.) DBSec 2005. LNCS, vol. 3654, pp. 54–68. Springer, Heidelberg (2005). https://doi.org/10.1007/11535706_5

8. Athanasios, V., Mazhar, A., Samee, K.: Security in cloud computing: opportunities and challenges. Elsevier Inf. Sci. **305**, 357–383 (2015)

9. Daniel, M., Eduardo, F., Haralambos, M., Oscar, R.: Empirical evaluation of a cloud computing information security governance framework. Elsevier Inf. Softw. Technol. **58**, 44–57 (2015)

10. Kaiping, X., Jianan, H., Nenghai, Y., Peilin, H., Shaohua, L., Yingjie, X.: Two-cloud secure database for numeric-related SQL range queries with privacy preserving. IEEE Trans. Inf. Forensics Secur. **12**, 1596–1608 (2017)

11. Bony, C., Paul, C., Peter, C., Yu-Kwong, K.: CypherDB: a novel architecture for outsourcing secure database processing. IEEE Trans. Cloud Comput. 14 (2015)

12. Elmehdwi, Y., Samanthula, B.K., Jiang, W.: Secure k-nearest neighbor query over encrypted data in outsourced environments. In: 2014 IEEE 30th International Conference on Data Engineering (ICDE), pp. 664–675. IEEE (2014)

13. Rivest, R.L., Shamir, A., Adleman, L.: A method for obtaining digital signatures and public-key cryptosystems. Commun. ACM **21**(2), 120–126 (1978)

14. Popa, R.A., Redfield, C., Zeldovich, N., Balakrishnan, H.: CryptDB: protecting confidentiality with encrypted query processing. In: Proceedings of the Twenty-Third ACM Symposium on Operating Systems Principles, pp. 85–100. ACM (2011)

Tag-Reader Authentication System Guarded by Negative Identifier Filtering and Distance Bounding

Ruchi Kachhia, Prachi Agrawal$^{(\boxtimes)}$, and Manik Lal Das

DA-IICT, Gandhinagar, India
ruchi1496@gmail.com, prachiagrawal2396@gmail.com, maniklal@gmail.com

Abstract. In conventional authentication process, the legitimacy of communicating entity is directly checked with Authentication Server. This process is found efficient; however, it allows an illegitimate entity to get his/her attempts checked upon the authentication database (e.g. password table). In this paper, we present a two-layer entity authentication protocol in which the attempt by an illegitimate entity gets discarded at the first layer with the help of a negative filtering database. To filter illegitimate attempts 100% out the *negative database* is constructed such that no information about the *positive database that stores the credentials of legitimate users* can be obtained even if the negative database gets compromised. The proposed protocol is analytically simulated with a tag-reader authentication system, which provides mutual authentication and resists relay, impersonation and replay attacks.

Keywords: Authentication · Security · Privacy · Distance bounding

1 Introduction

Tag-Reader authentication (e.g. RFID system, Card-payment system) has found a wide range of applications such as consumer electronics, household appliances, and transmit system, where a chip-enabled tag can be attached to any objects pertaining to these applications [1–3]. Authentication of tag ensures its legitimacy to the authentication server based on application's requirements for one-way authentication or mutual authentication between communicating entities of the authentication system. Typically, a front-end interface scans the tag's data for checking its legitimacy with the help of the authentication server. The communication channel between tag and front-end interface is typically insecure wireless channel and between the front-end interface and the authentication server is a secure channel.

In recent times, many protocols [4–8] have been proposed in literature for tag-reader authentication using *tags database* stored in authentication server.

R. Kachhia and P. Agrawal—contributed equally to this work who worked for this project during their final year of undergrad study at DA-IICT, Gandhinagar.

© Springer Nature Switzerland AG 2019
G. Fahrnberger et al. (Eds.): ICDCIT 2019, LNCS 11319, pp. 339–348, 2019.
https://doi.org/10.1007/978-3-030-05366-6_28

We term *tags database*-based tag authentication as TPIN (Tags Positive Identification Information). The authentication system of these protocols works as follows: assume that P is the set of all valid tags credentials. The authentication system matches the request r against the set P. It checks whether the set P contains request r or not. If $r \in P$, then r is regarded as valid and the authentication is successful. One of the basic problems of this kind of authentication is the risk of malicious access to this stored user identity file. If the attacker gets hold of the file containing all the valid credentials, it can be misused by the attackers. Therefore, there is a potential threat to have unauthorized accessed to TPIN.

1.1   Our Contributions

To overcome the threat of the positive database being compromised or hacked as seen in positive credentials-based authentication model, we consider a negative database that is compliment of TPIN (i.e., the negative database contains identity information except the ones which stored in TPIN). We propose a protocol for authenticating RFID tags by *negative database filtering*. This additional layer of negative database filtering based authentication [10] works by the use of negative/false information rather than using positive/true information for checking the legitimacy of a valid tag. In other words, with the filtering of negative database, we focus more in checking if every request should go to the positive database for checking its legitimacy or illegitimate request should be stropped at the negative database. The most important part of our proposed protocol is that it is hard to discover the actual identity of a valid tag even if the negative counterpart is compromised. As an additional measure, the valid tags will get authenticated with the distance bounding phase, which can defend the proposed protocol against relay attack. The proposed protocol is shown secure against replay and impersonation attacks, and the computation cost for the reader to search for a particular tag is minimized with the help of linear probing structure.

1.2   Organization of the Paper

The paper is organized as follows. Section 2 discusses the related work. Section 3 presents the protocol and its analysis is provided in Sect. 4. The paper is concluded in Sect. 5.

2   Related Work

Tan et al. [4] proposed a protocol which provides mutual authentication between the tag and reader without the need for a persistent central database. In their protocol, every reader R has a unique identifier r and an access list L. The reader R gets access to this after authenticating itself to the certification authority (CA). Each tag T has a unique id and a secret t which is known by the tag itself and the CA. The list L_i is in form of $f_1(r_i, t_j)$, where $f_1(\cdot)$ is a cryptographic hash function. Unauthorized reader cannot obtain id_j since it does not know $f(r_i, t_j)$. The authorized reader checks its L_i for matching entries that have the same first m bits as $f_2(f_1(r_i, t_j))_m$, where $f_2(\cdot)$ is a cryptographic hash function. If there are no entries in L_i that match the first m bits, then either the tag is a fake or it is a tag that R_i is not authorized to access. Later the protocol [4] found vulnerable to the replay attack and relay attack. Jannati and Falahati proposed a server-less RFID search protocol [2], termed as SDB protocol. The SDB protocol uses distance bounding method to reduce the probability of the relay attack by $(1/2)^n$. In the SDB protocol, it is assumed that the secret key X_l and the identity ID_l are shared between the reader R and tag T_l before the protocol execution. Dasgupta and Saha presented a negative authentication filtering model [9], in which they constructed a set of anti-P (anti passwords). The user request was validated against the set of possible user credentials-valid credentials. If an attempt matches, then it is regarded as invalid and if not a match then valid. They used a V-Detector algorithm to generate anti-Ps from hashed passwords. Number of valid passwords, confusion parameter and Anti-P coverage were used to get a good detection rate. There are several other approaches [10–14] which generate the set of anti-Ps for negative filtering. We have addressed the problem by generating anti-Ps such that even if the database is compromised, there is no threat and invalid tags can be identified with 100% detection rate.

3   The Proposed Protocol

3.1   System Model

The tag T_i and the reader R establish a common secret k_i, which is unique for each tag. The server calculates the value of the function $f_1(k_1, tag_{id})$ and stores it in positive database and the reader calculates the value of function $f_2(f_1(k_1, tag_{id}, k_2)$ and stores it in negative database, where f_1 is a cryptographically secure hash function and f_2 is an expansion function. The system model is shown in Fig. 1.

The positive database in our model consists of the n_1 bit digest values corresponding to the valid tags, that is $f_1(k_1, tag_{id})$, where $f_1 : \{0, 1\}^* \rightarrow \{0, 1\}^{n_1}$ and tag_{id} is the unique identification number for a valid tag. Here, k_1 and k_2 are derived from master secret K, which is shared between the tag and the reader and is unique for each tag. The positive database is an important asset that allows the tags to access the system so it is stored in a secure region of central server. In the negative database we store information such that even if the adversary gets hold of the database, the adversary cannot retrieve any useful information from the database about the valid tags. To construct the negative database, we choose an expansion function $f_2 : \{0, 1\}^{n_1} \rightarrow \{0, 1\}^{n_2}$ such that $n_2 \geq n_1$. The positive database consists of $n1$ bit digests having the value $f_1(k_1, tag_{id})$. Suppose U be the set of all the possible n_1 bit numbers and P is the set of all the n_1 bit valid numbers stored in positive database. Let C be the set consisting of all the complements of P, i.e., $C = U - P$. We now compute the values $f_2(x, k_2)$,

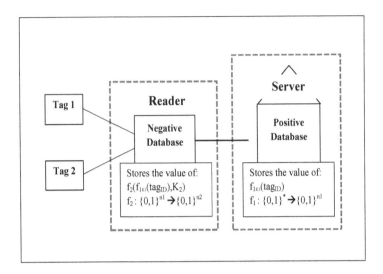

Fig. 1. System model

where $x \in C$ and k_2 is the key used for this expansion function. We compute this value for all $x \in C$ and construct n_2 bit digest values $(n_2 \geq n_1)$ which are stored in negative authentication table. All these n_2 bit digest values are stored in memory in the form of hash tables, to quickly locate an entry. We use linear probing hash function to efficiently locate all the entries present with constant search time. We assume that the clocks at both the ends (reader and tag) are synchronized and the master secret $K(k_1\|k_2)$ between the tag and the reader cannot be compromised.

3.2   Adversarial Model

A usual threat to negative databases is, if we store all the complements from the valid password space, the positive database is guessable from this negative database because all the entries not present in negative database will be valid passwords. Therefore, storing all the complements will be vulnerable. In order to avoid this threat, one can keep a subset of complements in the negative database, but will not be able to achieve a detection rate 100% for the false requests. To detect all the false requests, we need a detection rate of 100% which requires all (and even more) the complements stored in the database. The proposed system model achieves a detection rate of 100% without the positive database being guessable. The negative database consists of all the complements in positive database in expanded form, so it achieves 100% detection rate. The values stored in negative database are expanded to n_2 bit digest values. Not all the n_2 bit numbers are stored in the negative database, only the ones corresponding to complements of valid passwords are stored. Thus, some of the n_2 bit numbers missing from the negative database could be corresponding to the valid entries while some of them could be those of invalid entries. Therefore, the attacker cannot distinguish which of the missing are valid and which are invalid which leaves the attacker not being able to guess the entries of positive database. As a result, we can achieve a detection rate of 100% without the positive database being guessable. Even if the attacker gets hold of n_2 bit digest values, the attacker cannot obtain any useful information from it.

3.3   The Proposed Protocol

The protocol consists of two phases, the Setup phase to initiate the communication and the Authentication phase. The Authentication phase is further divided in two sub phases – the first phase is Negative filtering which is implemented to remove all the invalid tag requests and the second phase is distance bounding by which the possible valid tags after the first phase will have to authenticate themselves with the distance bounding approach to prevent the relay attack. The work-flow of the proposed authentication system is shown in Fig. 2.

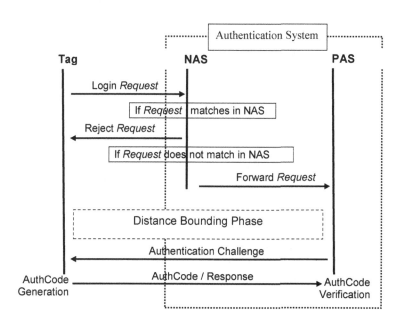

Fig. 2.   The   work-flow   of   the   proposed   authentication   system   [NAS: negative (database)authentication system; PAS: positive (database) authentication system]

Setup Phase. One common symmetric key K is established by the reader and is shared with the tag before deployment of the system. The symmetric key K made up of keys k_1 and k_2. Each tag has a unique tag-id and a unique secret key K shared between the tag and the reader. The reader R has the secret K for each tag and a negative database. The server contains the master key K and the positive database which consists of the values $f_1(k_1, tag_{id})$ (n_1 bit) for all the valid tags. The negative database consists of the values $f_2(x, k_2)$, where x is $f_1(k_1, tag_{id})$.

Authentication Phase 1: Negative Login Request Filtering
When the tag wants to initiate the communication, the tag chooses a random number N_c and computes the value of $A = f_1(k_1, tag_{id}, N_c)$. On receiving (N_c, A, tag_{id}), the reader computes the value of $f_1(k_1, tag_{id}, N_c)$ and checks whether it matches with the received value A from the tag. Both the values should be same which indicates the freshness of the session. Now, the reader computes the value of $x = f_1(k_1, tag_{id})$ and $f_2(x, k_2)$, where $f_2()$ is the expansion function. If this value is now present in negative database, then the reader discards the session, and if it is not present then the reader sends acknowledgement to the tag to continue the process. If a legitimate tag communicates, then the corresponding value will not be present in the negative database, which is identified in constant time by searching through the hash table.

Algorithm 1. Negative (Illegitimate) login request filtering

1: Tag computes $A = f_1(k_1 \| tag_{id} \| N_c)$ and send A to Reader.

2: Upon receiving A from the Tag the Reader validates it by computing the same at its end. If the received A is valid and fresh, then the Reader proceeds to Step 3; else, it discards the request.

3: Reader computes $x = f_1(k_1 \| tag_{id})$ and $B = f_2(x \| k_2)$.

4: If B exists in the negative database, then the request is illegitimate and the Reader discards the request. If B does not exist in the negative database, then the Reader send an acknowledgement to the Tag for further exchanges.

Authentication Phase 2: Distance Bounding
After the negative filtering phase, the distance bounding phase is invoked to prevent the possible relay attacks and also to authenticate the tag by the reader. There are three main stages of this phase:

1. *Initialization Stage*

    Reader $\rightarrow$ Tags: The reader R selects a random number N_r, loads t_c with current time. It computes $Q_r = f_3(k_2 \| tag_{id} \| t_c)$ and $W_r = f_4(N_r \| t_c)$, where f_3 and f_4 are pseudo-random function. Reader broadcasts Q_r, W_r and t_c.

    Tag $\rightarrow$ Reader: Each tag which is located in the vicinity of the reader R after receiving Q_r, W_r and t_c, checks the validity of t_c, that is, t_c must not be smaller than time stamp t. It checks the correctness of Q_r by using its secret key k_2, identity and the received t_c. If the computed Q_r does not match with the received Q_r, it aborts the session. Then, the tag selects a random number N_t and computes $W_t = f_4(N_t \| t_c)$, sends W_t and t_c to the reader.

Reader $\rightarrow$ Tag: The reader checks the validity of t_c. If it is smaller than the current time stamp t, the session is aborted; else, the next phase is executed.

2. *Rapid Bit Exchange Stage*

Reader $\rightarrow$ Tag: After the initialization, rapid bit exchange phase is started by reader through N rounds. Reader R selects a random bit c_i, sends it as a challenge bit c_i to the reader and starts the clock at the time t_s.

Tag $\rightarrow$ Reader: On the receipt of the challenge bit c_i, the tag generates a response bit r_i based on the value of the challenge bit. If the challenge bit is 0, the response bit should be N_{R_i}. If the challenge bit is 1, the response bit should be N_{T_i}. The sends the ith response bit to the reader. After receiving the response bit(r_i), the reader stops the clock and stores the delay time $\Delta t = (t_f - t_s)/2$.

3. *Verification Stage*

The reader R verifies the validity of the response bit r_i as well as the obtained distance Δt for all $i = 1$ to N. If the response bits are correct and the obtained distance values by R are shorter than the maximum distance t_{max}, reader R detects that the tag is located at a close proximity to R and so discover it, otherwise aborts the session.

4   Security Analysis

Low cost RFID tags are being used in various practical applications. Security features on these tags cover some or all of the aspects such as privacy, intractability and authentication. We analyze the security level of the proposed protocol with respect to achieve these features.

Database Hijacking Attacks: The threat of the database being hijacked from the reader's memory is addressed in our protocol. We claim that the adversary does not get any useful information from the attacked database. If the negative database is compromised that means the adversary can retrieve all the information from the database. The negative database consisted of n_2 bit numbers. These n_2 bit numbers correspond to the expanded form of complements of n_1 bit numbers from positive database. Since $n_2 \geq n_1$, when we take complement of these n_2 bit numbers, some complements correspond to actual n_1 bit numbers while some will be the extra numbers in n_2 bit space. Therefore, both the numbers can not be distinguished which makes it difficult for the attacker to figure out the contents of positive database from the negative database. Moreover, the expansion function f used to generate the n_2 bit values is not reversible. Therefore, the actual valid n_1 bit values corresponding to the positive database cannot be known from the negative database. Hence, the proposed protocol prevents the threat of database compromised in addition to achieving a detection rate of invalid users as 100%.

Denial of Service Attacks: The negative database consists of the expanded values corresponding to all complements of the valid secrets of the tags in the positive database. When a request arrives at the reader in the form of $f_1(k_1, tag_{id} \| N_c)$, the reader validates it and computes the value of $f_2(f_1(k_1, tag_{id}), k_2)$ and checks if this value exists in negative database. If it does, the reader aborts the session. The negative database actually consists of the complements of the valid values corresponding to $f_1(k_1, tag_{id})$. Now, suppose a request arrives at the reader which is corresponding to some invalid tag/attacker. The attacker takes tag-id of some valid tag and chooses some value of $k1$ and a random number N_c. This is not a valid value of k_1. Therefore, the value of $f_2(f_1(k_1, tag_{id}), k_2)$ will be present in negative database as we store all the complements. When the reader validates this request, this value will match with the ones present in negative database and the reader aborts the communication. Therefore, invalid requests can be recognized at the first step of the protocol without being processed further which minimizes the effect of denial of service attacks.

Replay Attacks: In the proposed protocol, suppose that one tag tries to use information of a previous session in the current session, that is, replaying the message to convince the Reader that the communication is valid. Suppose that the attacker tracks the value of A, tag_{ID}, and N_c in the previous session. Now it uses these values to initiate a new session. As the proposed protocol uses a random nonce N_c in the negative authentication phase which is stored by the reader, it rejects the request containing the replay messages as it will have the same N_c as in the previous session and the authentication fails. Therefore, the attacker will not be able to replay the previous message without being caught in the negative authentication phase. Suppose, the attacker tries to replay the messages Q_R and W_R from a previous session in the distance bounding phase. The tag checks the value of the time stamp t_C to prevent the replay attack and maintain the freshness property. If previous session's message is used, it will have an old timestamp and so the authentication fails.

Impersonation Attacks: For impersonation attack, suppose that the attacker tries to forge tag T_K, that is, it wants to convince the reader that it is a legitimate tag. To impersonate the tag, it will want to send the request to the reader with tag-id of T_K and it will have to pick his own random number N_c. However, to send a request to the reader the tag must know the shared secret k_1 between the tag and the reader which is unknown to others. As the attacker does not know the secret k_1 it cannot generate A. Furthermore, even if the tag is compromised, every tag has a unique secret. Attacker cannot use the secret of the compromised tag to impersonate another tag. Therefore, by the method of contradiction we can say that the reader can be sure that the message came from a legitimate tag. As a result, the protocol successfully resists impersonation attacks.

Relay Attacks: The relay attack is addressed by an attacker pretending as both tag (A_t) and the reader (A_r). The attacker convinces the reader that some other invalid/valid tag which is not in the proximity of the reader is actually in the proximity of the reader by making the other tag to communicate with the reader instead of valid tag and convincing that it's actually the valid tag with whom reader wants to communicate. A_r (is at the close proximity of the tag) communicates with the tag instead of actual reader and A_t(is at the close proximity of the reader) communicates with the reader instead of actual tag. In the rapid bit exchange, first the attacker A_r generates some challenge bits and sends them to the tag which then generates the response bits and sends them back to A_r. A_r forwards this to A_t. Now, the actual reader starts the rapid bit exchange phase. When the reader sends the challenge bits to the tag, the attacker A_t, instead of tag, responds to it with the response bits obtained from A_r. When the reader verifies the response bits in the verification phase, it will be correct only if the challenge bits selected initially by A_r matched exactly with the challenge bits generated by the reader because if the challenge bits are sent correctly, then the response bits are also correct which are in accordance to what the actual reader expects. So, the probability of this match taking place is $(1/2)^n$, where n is the number of challenge bits because A_r can guess each challenge bit correctly with the probability $(1/2)$. The attacker succeeds with the probability of $(1/2)^n$, which is negligible.

Known Key Attacks: We consider the case when the attacker compromises the tag T_K. Now, the attacker is able to make a fake tag T_j to fool the reader. As the tag T_K is compromised, the adversary can gather the information of T_K including the shared secret between T_K and the reader. To prevent the known key attack, we need to prevent the attacker from creating a fake tag T_j. To create a fake tag T_j, the attacker needs to generate A which uses the secret k_1. In the proposed protocol the secret k_1 is unique for each tag. Hence, the attacker cannot create fake T_j using the key of T_K to fool the reader.

5   Conclusion

Password based authentication is a classical approach in many real-world applications. In this paper, we discussed about the threats of maintaining only positive database of user's credential. As a countermeasure, we proposed a two-layer entity authentication protocol in which the attempt by an illegitimate entity gets discarded at the first layer with the help of a negative filtering database. The novelty of the proposed protocol lies in not having the threat of negative database being compromised by guaranteeing adversary gets no useful data from the compromised negative database. The digest values present in negative database are such that even if compromised, no useful information can be obtained. Even if the probability of detection of invalid tags is reduced due to the lack of storage, authentication of the possible valid tags after the first phase is done in the second phase. The proposed protocol can detect the invalid tags with 100% detection rate without the threat of the valid users database being compromised. The protocol provides mutual authentication and resists replay, relay, impersonation, known-key attacks and denial of service attacks.

References

1. Bertino, E., Choo, K.R., Georgakopolous, D., Nepal, S.: Internet of Things (IoT): smart and secure service delivery. ACM Trans. Internet Technol. **16**(4), 22 (2016)
2. Jannati, H., Falahati, A.: An RFID search protocol secured against relay attack based on distance bounding approach. Wireless Pers. Commun. **85**(3), 711–726 (2015)
3. Das, M.L.: Strong security and privacy of RFID system for *Internet of Things* infrastructure. In: Gierlichs, B., Guilley, S., Mukhopadhyay, D. (eds.) SPACE 2013. LNCS, vol. 8204, pp. 56–69. Springer, Heidelberg (2013). https://doi.org/10.1007/978-3-642-41224-0_5
4. Tan, C.C., Sheng, B., Li, Q.: Secure and serverless RFID authentication and search protocols. IEEE Trans. Wireless Commun. **7**(4), 1400–1407 (2008)
5. Hancke, G.P., Mayes, K.E., Markantonakis, K.: Confidence in smart token proximity: relay attacks revisited. Comput. Secur. **28**(7), 615–627 (2009)
6. Lee, Y.K., Batina, L., Verbauwhede, I.: Untraceable RFID authentication protocols: revision of EC-RAC. In: Proceedings of the IEEE International Conference on RFID, pp. 178-185 (2009)
7. Songhela, R., Das, M.L.: Yet another strong privacy-preserving RFID mutual authentication protocol. In: Chakraborty, R.S., Matyas, V., Schaumont, P. (eds.) SPACE 2014. LNCS, vol. 8804, pp. 171–182. Springer, Cham (2014). https://doi.org/10.1007/978-3-319-12060-7_12
8. Gope, P., Hwang, T.: A realistic lightweight authentication protocol preserving strong anonymity for securing RFID system. Comput. Secur. **55**(C), 271–280 (2015)
9. Dasgupta, D., Saha, S.: Password security through negative filtering. In: Proceedings of International Conference on Emerging Security Technologies, pp. 83–89 (2010)
10. Dasgupta, D., Azeem, R.: A negative authentication system. Technical report, The University of Memphis: CS-07-001 (2007)
11. Esponda, F.: Everything that is not important: negative databases. IEEE Comput. Intell. Mag. **3**(2), 60–63 (2008)
12. Esponda, F., Ackley, E.S., Helman, P., Jia, H., Forrest, S.: Protecting data privacy through hard-to-reverse negative databases. In: Katsikas, S.K., López, J., Backes, M., Gritzalis, S., Preneel, B. (eds.) ISC 2006. LNCS, vol. 4176, pp. 72–84. Springer, Heidelberg (2006). https://doi.org/10.1007/11836810_6
13. Esponda, F., Forrest, S., Helman, P.: Enhancing privacy through negative representations of data. Technical report, University of New, Mexico (2004)
14. González, F., Dasgupta, D., Niño, L.F.: A randomized real-valued negative selection algorithm. In: Timmis, J., Bentley, P.J., Hart, E. (eds.) ICARIS 2003. LNCS, vol. 2787, pp. 261–272. Springer, Heidelberg (2003). https://doi.org/10.1007/978-3-540-45192-1_25

RSA-Based Collusion Resistant Quorum Controlled Proxy Re-encryption Scheme for Distributed Secure Communication

Shravani Mahesh Patil[ID] and B. R. Purushothama[✉][ID]

Department of Computer Science and Engineering,
National Institute of Technology Goa, Farmagudi, Ponda 403401, Goa, India
patilmshravani@gmail.com, puru@nitgoa.ac.in

Abstract. In this paper, we analyze the quorum controlled proxy re-encryption scheme proposed by Jakobsson for the security. We show that the scheme is susceptible to collusion and cannot be used for secure communication. We design a new quorum controlled proxy re-encryption scheme based on RSA public key cryptosystem. We show that the proposed scheme is collusion resistant and non-transitive. Using the quorum/threshold controlled proxy re-encryption scheme, the trust on the proxy can be reduced and single point of failure problem can be solved. The proposed scheme can be used in any network application where distribution of trust and delegation of tasks are the requirements.

Keywords: Threshold proxy re-encryption · Distributed trust Collusion resistant

1 Introduction

Proxy re-encryption (PRE) is a cryptographic technique which allows the ciphertext encrypted for one party $\mathcal{X}$ to be transformed into ciphertext which can be decrypted by another party $\mathcal{Y}$ [1,3,11]. This transformation of ciphertext is performed by a third party which is referred to as the proxy and the transformation of the ciphertext is referred to as re-encryption. The re-encryption is performed in such a way that the message underlying the ciphertext is not revealed to the proxy. In this scenario of PRE, the party $\mathcal{X}$ for whom the ciphertext is originally intended is called as the delegator and the party $\mathcal{Y}$ for whom the ciphertext is transformed is called the delegatee. Transformation of the ciphertext by the proxy is enabled by a re-encryption key $rk_{\mathcal{X} \to \mathcal{Y}}$. The participation of the delegator in generating the re-encryption key is mandatory in order to ensure the authorization of $\mathcal{X}$ in transferring the ciphertext to the delegatee $\mathcal{Y}$. Ateneise et al. have enlisted the desirable properties for a PRE scheme [1]. The PRE schemes are in several applications such as email forwarding, access control delegation, group key management, etc. [1,4,10,12,15].

In securing the communication, there are highly likely scenarios where the nodes in the network want to delegate the responsibility to some of the other

© Springer Nature Switzerland AG 2019
G. Fahrnberger et al. (Eds.): ICDCIT 2019, LNCS 11319, pp. 349–363, 2019.
https://doi.org/10.1007/978-3-030-05366-6_29

nodes to carry out the task. The delegating node requires that the communications be learnt by only the authorized delegatee. In the traditional PRE scheme, there is only one proxy and that proxy needs to be trusted to carry out the re-encryption. If a network employs only one proxy for communication, it suffers from single point of failure apart from keeping trust on the proxy. To avoid both the problems, multiple proxies can be employed to carry out the task of delegation. By employing multiple proxies, trust as well as the re-encyrption task is distributed among the proxies. However, it is necessary to provide fault tolerance to the system employing multiple proxies and still be able to achieve delegation. Towards this, there is a need of quorum controlled PRE scheme that satisfies desirable properties of PRE scheme. Our focus is on analyzing the existing quorum controlled PRE scheme for its properties, identifying the weaknesses of the existing scheme and to propose a quorum controlled PRE scheme that satisfies some of the crucial properties of a PRE scheme such as collusion resistance and non-transitivity. In the next section, we highlight the properties that a PRE scheme should satisfy as listed by Ateniese et al. [1].

1.1 Properties of PRE Scheme

Ateniese et al. [1] enumerated some of the crucial properties of a PRE scheme, on the basis of which these schemes can be evaluated. These properties also allow the comparison of various PRE schemes. With the convention that a user $\mathcal{U}$ is identified by its public-private key pair $(pk_{\mathcal{U}}, sk_{\mathcal{U}})$, following are the desired properties of a PRE scheme:

1. Unidirectional
   Delegation of decryption rights from $\mathcal{Y}$ to $\mathcal{X}$ is not enabled by a delegation from $\mathcal{X}$ to $\mathcal{Y}$, i.e. given $rk_{\mathcal{X} \to \mathcal{Y}}$ it is impossible to compute $rk_{\mathcal{Y} \to \mathcal{X}}$.
2. Non Interactive
   The re-encryption key $rk_{\mathcal{X} \to \mathcal{Y}}$ computation can be done by $\mathcal{X}$ using the public key of $\mathcal{Y}$ and does not require any interaction with $\mathcal{Y}$, i.e. $sk_{\mathcal{Y}}$ is not required to compute $rk_{\mathcal{X} \to \mathcal{Y}}$.
3. Proxy Invisibility
   The existence of a proxy is concealed from the sender as well as the receiver, i.e. the distinction between a ciphertext produced by direct encryption under $pk_{\mathcal{Y}}$ and ciphertext produced by re-encryption using $rk_{\mathcal{X} \to \mathcal{Y}}$ for some entity $\mathcal{X}$ is not revealed to the entity $\mathcal{Y}$.
4. Key optimal
   The storage overhead at an entity accepting delegations remains constant and is not a function of the number of delegations it accepts.
5. Original access
   The ciphertexts which were originally encrypted for $\mathcal{X}$ can be decrypted by $\mathcal{X}$ after re-encryption to a delegatee $\mathcal{Y}$.
6. Collusion safe
   The secret key of the delegator is not exposed to a collusion of the proxy and the delegatee, i.e. knowledge of $rk_{\mathcal{X} \to \mathcal{Y}}$ and $sk_{\mathcal{Y}}$, does not facilitate the computation of $sk_{\mathcal{X}}$.

7. Non-transitive

The proxy cannot compute re-encryption keys to redelegate decryption rights, i.e. knowledge of $rk_{\chi \to y}$ and $rk_{y \to z}$, does not enable the computation of $rk_{\chi \to z}$.

8. Non-transferable

The decryption rights cannot be redelegated to a third party by a proxy colluding with a set of delegatees, i.e. knowledge of $rk_{\chi \to y}$, sk_y and pk_z, does not facilitate the computation of $rk_{\chi \to z}$.

9. Temporary

The authorization of re-encryption enabled by a re-encryption key, allows for re-encryption for only a specified time frame.

We focus on designing a PRE scheme based on threshold cryptosystem which satisfies the most crucial and desirable properties of a re-encryption scheme. To the best of our knowledge, the only threshold based PRE scheme was proposed by Jakobsson in [8]. Another PRE scheme in literature which claims to use threshold based re-encryption was proposed by Lin et al. [9]. Even though this scheme uses the concepts of threshold cryptography, it does not perform the re-encryption itself using the threshold based scheme. The threshold cryptography concepts are used in this scheme during the data retrieval phase which maps to the decryption phase of a PRE scheme. Whereas the scheme in [8] which we have targeted for analysis uses the threshold cryptosystem concepts for the re-encryption phase of the PRE scheme wherein the re-encryption key is itself distributed using the threshold cryptosystem concepts.

The existing PRE based schemes assume that the proxy is semi-trusted. Using the threshold based proxy cryptosystems, the trust can be distributed. Jakobsson [8] proposed a quorum based proxy re-encryption scheme. In a truly quorum based re-encryption scheme, the re-encryption key should be distributed to the collection of proxies and the proxies in collusion with the delegatee should not be able to obtain the secret key of the delegator. However, we show that in the scheme by Jakobsson, the secret key of the delegator is distributed to the proxies and any collusion among the proxies in the quorum can compromise the secret key of the delegator. This is a serious flaw in the existing scheme and cannot be used in practice. Also, we propose a scheme which is collusion resistant and non-transitive. These properties are necessary to use a PRE scheme in practice.

1.2 Our Contribution

In this section, we highlight the results of our analysis of the quorum controlled PRE scheme proposed by Jakobsson [8] and also emphasize on our contribution towards mitigating the limitations of this scheme.

– We analyze the scheme in [8] based on the desirable properties of a PRE scheme and identify the weaknesses of this scheme. We illustrate the collusion

susceptibility of this scheme which compromises the secret key of the delegator. We also identify that the scheme has the transitivity property which allows the proxies to redelegate the decryption rights to a third party.
- Further, we demonstrate how the scheme fails to satisfy the most basic requirement of a PRE scheme by allowing the proxies to have complete control over deciding the delegatee of the system.
- We also propose a new quorum based PRE scheme using the RSA algorithm as the base for encryption and decryption. The proposed scheme focuses on eliminating the major drawbacks of collusion susceptibility and transitivity of the scheme in [8].

Rest of the paper is organized as follows. In Sect. 2, we describe the existing quorum controlled scheme by Jakobsson [8], followed by the evaluation of it in Sect. 3 for its properties. Section 4 describes the drawbacks of Jakobsson's [8] scheme. In Sect. 5, we propose a new quorum controlled PRE scheme. The system model for the proposed scheme is elaborated in Sect. 5.2, followed by the construction of the scheme in the subsequent Sect. 5.3. Further, Sect. 6 evaluates the proposed scheme on the basis of the desired properties of a PRE scheme. Finally, the conclusion and future work is summarized in Sect. 7.

2   Quorum Controlled Proxy Re-encryption Scheme

Jakobsson [8] proposed a quorum controlled PRE scheme in which the concept of the proxy in a PRE scheme is extended to a set of proxies responsible for the re-encryption of the ciphertext. The scheme in [8] is such that the responsibility of ciphertext transformation using re-encryption is assigned to a group of proxies rather than a single proxy in such a way that any active quorum of proxies can perform the re-encryption of the ciphertext. This scheme is proposed under a model which consists of a delegator $\mathcal{X}$, delegatee $\mathcal{Y}$ and a set of proxies $P_1, P_2, \ldots P_n$. Elgamal based scheme is used for encryption with the primes being p and q such that $p = 2q + 1$ and g as the generator of the cyclic group Z_p^*.

1. Key Generation
   The public and private key pair $(pk_\mathcal{X}, sk_\mathcal{X})$ for a party $\mathcal{X}$ are generated such that

$$sk_\mathcal{X} = x \in Z_p^* \tag{1}$$

$$pk_\mathcal{X} = g^x \bmod p \tag{2}$$

2. Re-encryption Key Generation
   Shares of the private key of the delegator $\mathcal{X}$ are distributed using a (t, n) threshold scheme of secret sharing [14] to enable re-encryption.
   - A polynomial

$$\lambda(z) = \varphi_0 + \varphi_1 z + \varphi_2 z^2 + \ldots \varphi_{t-1} z^{t-1} \tag{3}$$

is chosen by $\mathcal{X}$ such that $\varphi_0 = sk_\mathcal{X} = x$ and $\varphi_1, \varphi_2, \ldots, \varphi_{t-1}$ are chosen uniformly at random from Z_p^*.

- A unique share of the polynomial $\lambda(z)$ is communicated securely by $\mathcal{X}$ to each proxy.
- The share $sk_{\mathcal{X}j}$ computed by evaluating the polynomial at a unique value z_j such that

$$sk_{\mathcal{X}j} = \lambda(z_j) , \quad \forall j \in \{1, 2, \ldots, n\} \tag{4}$$

is received by each proxy P_j.

3. Encryption
   A value $k \in Z_p^*$ is chosen uniformly at random and the encryption of message M is obtained by computing the ciphertext $C_\mathcal{X}$ such that

$$C_\mathcal{X} = Enc(M, pk_\mathcal{X}) = (u_\mathcal{X}, v_\mathcal{X}) = (M.pk_\mathcal{X}^k, g^k) \tag{5}$$

4. Decryption
   A ciphertext $C_\mathcal{X}$ encrypted under the public key $pk_\mathcal{X}$ of $\mathcal{X}$ can be decrypted by computing

$$M = \frac{u_\mathcal{X}}{v_\mathcal{X}^{sk_\mathcal{X}}} \tag{6}$$

5. Re-encryption
   An active quorum Q of the proxies perform the re-encryption of a ciphertext $C_\mathcal{X} = (u_\mathcal{X}, v_\mathcal{X})$ encrypted under $pk_\mathcal{X}$ to a ciphertext $C_\mathcal{Y} = (u_\mathcal{Y}, v_\mathcal{Y})$ which can be decrypted with $sk_\mathcal{Y}$. Each server $P_j \in Q$ enables this re-encryption by performing the following:
   - Computes its modified share as in [5,13] i.e.

$$sk'_{\mathcal{X}j} = sk_{\mathcal{X}j} * \prod_{\substack{P_s \in Q \\ j \neq s}} \frac{0 - z_s}{z_j - z_s} \tag{7}$$

   - Selects a random δ_j and computes

$$(c_j, d_j) = (v_\mathcal{X}^{-sk'_{\mathcal{X}j}} pk_\mathcal{Y}^{\delta_j}, g^{\delta_j}) \tag{8}$$

   and sends this pair (c_j, d_j) to all the other proxies in the active quorum. One of the servers or a third party can combine all the (c_j, d_j) pairs received from each $P_j \in Q$ and compute

$$C_\mathcal{Y} = (u_\mathcal{Y}, v_\mathcal{Y}) = (u_\mathcal{X} \prod_{P_j \in Q} c_j, \prod_{P_j \in Q} d_j) = (M.pk_\mathcal{Y}^\delta, g^\delta) \tag{9}$$

3   Evaluation of the Scheme

In this section, we evaluate the scheme by Jakobsson [8] with respect to the properties enumerated in Sect. 1.1. It can be observed that this scheme does not satisfy some of the crucial properties of a PRE scheme such as the collusion safe and non-transitive property.

1. Non-interactive
   The secret key of the delegatee $\mathcal{Y}$ is not required in the computation of the re-encryption key. The delegator can compute the re-encryption key without requiring any interaction with the delegatee.
2. Unidirectional
   The shares of the delegator's secret key $sk_{\mathcal{X}}$ are distributed to the proxies for a delegation from $\mathcal{X}$ to $\mathcal{Y}$. However, to allow for a re-encryption from $\mathcal{Y}$ to $\mathcal{X}$, shares of $sk_{\mathcal{Y}}$ are required to be available at the proxies. The shares of $sk_{\mathcal{X}}$ available due to $rk_{\mathcal{X} \to \mathcal{Y}}$ do not allow the proxies to construct $sk_{\mathcal{Y}}$ needed for $rk_{\mathcal{Y} \to \mathcal{X}}$.
3. Key optimal
   The delegatee is not required to store any additional keys to decrypt the re-encrypted ciphertext of a delegation. The decryption of the re-encrypted ciphertext is performed by using the delegatee's own secret key.
4. Proxy Invisible
   The decryption algorithm and key used to decrypt a ciphertext re-encrypted from $\mathcal{X}$ to $\mathcal{Y}$ using $rk_{\mathcal{X} \to \mathcal{Y}}$, is the same as that used for the decryption of a ciphertext directly encrypted under the public key $pk_{\mathcal{Y}}$ of a party $\mathcal{Y}$.
5. Not temporary
   The shares of the secret key $sk_{\mathcal{X}}$ of the delegator held by the proxies do not have any time interval specific information and thus enable the re-encryption permanently. This delegation of decryption rights can only be revoked by the delegator by updating its secret key $sk_{\mathcal{X}}$.
6. Not collusion safe
   The re-encryption key is itself the secret key $sk_{\mathcal{X}}$ of the delegator which is distributed using a (t, n) threshold secret sharing scheme. This allows a colluding quorum of at least t proxies to retrieve the secret key $sk_{\mathcal{X}}$.
7. Original access is not allowed
   The decryption of re-encrypted ciphertext $C_{\mathcal{Y}} = (M.pk_{\mathcal{Y}}^{\delta}, g^{\delta})$ is enabled only by $sk_{\mathcal{Y}}$ thus inhibiting the delegator $\mathcal{X}$ from decrypting $C_{\mathcal{Y}}$.
8. Transitive
   The shares of $sk_{\mathcal{X}}$ and $sk_{\mathcal{Y}}$ are available to the proxies possessing $rk_{\mathcal{X} \to \mathcal{Y}}$ and $rk_{\mathcal{Y} \to \mathcal{Z}}$. A new delegation from $\mathcal{X}$ to $\mathcal{Z}$ requires $rk_{\mathcal{X} \to \mathcal{Z}}$, which is created by distributing the shares of $sk_{\mathcal{X}}$ to the servers. The proxy servers already possess these shares due to $rk_{\mathcal{X} \to \mathcal{Y}}$ and thus can collude to delegate the decryption rights to $\mathcal{Z}$.
9. Transferable
   The shares of $sk_{\mathcal{X}}$ are held by the proxies which possess the re-encryption key $rk_{\mathcal{X} \to \mathcal{Y}}$. These shares are the only information required to create a delegation from $\mathcal{X}$ to $\mathcal{Z}$ without the authorization of $\mathcal{X}$. Here, not even the delegatee $\mathcal{Y}$ is required to collude with the proxies to transfer the decryption rights to a third party $\mathcal{Z}$.

4   Drawbacks of the Quorum Controlled Proxy Re-encryption Scheme

The quorum controlled PRE scheme described in Sect. 2 has significant drawbacks as indicated by evaluation of the scheme using the desirable properties enumerated in Sect. 1.1. In this section, we highlight the limitations of the scheme which compel the scheme to be used in a highly trusted environment of proxies.

- Re-encryption capability is provided to the proxies by distributing the shares of the secret key $sk_\mathcal{X}$ of the delegator across the set of n proxies in the system using a (t, n) threshold scheme [14]. This indicates that a quorum of t or more colluding proxies can employ Lagrange's interpolation [6] using their respective share to retrieve the secret key of the delegator. Consider a scenario wherein a quorum Q of t proxies is active. Each proxy $P_j \in Q$ has its share $sk_{\mathcal{X}j}$ of the secret key $sk_\mathcal{X}$ and can use it to compute its modified share $sk'_{\mathcal{X}j}$ such that

$$sk'_{\mathcal{X}j} = sk_{\mathcal{X}j} * \prod_{\substack{P_s \in Q \\ j \neq s}} \frac{0 - z_s}{z_j - z_s} \tag{10}$$

The modified share of each of the t proxies is further used to evaluate the Lagrange polynomial at 0 by means of Lagrange's interpolation, thus rendering the scheme susceptible to a collusion of proxies. The Lagrange's interpolation proceeds as follows:

$$\lambda(0) = \varphi_0 = sk_\mathcal{X} = \sum_{P_j \in Q} sk'_{\mathcal{X}j} \tag{11}$$

Thus it can be noted that this scheme is vulnerable to an active and colluding quorum of proxies and reveals the secret key $sk_\mathcal{X}$ of the delegator. The re-encryption in this scheme is enabled only by distributing the shares of the delegator's secret key and hence, a colluding quorum of proxies having access to this secret key can redelegate the decryption rights to a third party which is not authorized by the delegator.

- The re-encryption key for any delegation in this scheme does not have any delegatee specific information and is only dependent on the shares of the delegator's secret key. This implies that the entire trust is on the proxies in the system, to re-encrypt the ciphertext to the delegatee specified by the delegator and not to a third party. Consider the scenario wherein a delegation from $\mathcal{X}$ to $\mathcal{Y}$ has been authorized by $\mathcal{X}$ by constructing the re-encryption key $rk_{\mathcal{X} \to \mathcal{Y}}$ which refers to the distribution of shares of the secret key $sk_\mathcal{X}$ to the proxies. Even though, the delegator has authorized a delegation to $\mathcal{Y}$, the design of this scheme allows the proxies to decide the identity of the delegatee, without the need for authorization from the delegator. The proxies may deny to delegate the decryption capability to $\mathcal{Y}$ and instead choose any delegatee $\mathcal{Z}$ other than $\mathcal{Y}$ as the delegatee.

Each proxy $P_j \in Q$ can:

- Compute its modified share

$$sk'_{\chi j} = sk_{\chi j} * \prod_{\substack{P_s \in Q \\ j \neq s}} \frac{0 - z_s}{z_j - z_s} \tag{12}$$

- Select a random δ_j and compute

$$(c_j, d_j) = (v_\chi^{-sk'_{\chi j}} pk_{\mathcal{Z}}^{\delta_j}, g^{\delta_j}) \tag{13}$$

Each proxy P_j sends its partial ciphertext (c_j, d_j) to all other active proxies in the quorum. It should be noted that the public key of a third party $\mathcal{Z}$ is used during the re-encryption, thus generating a ciphertext which can be decrypted using the secret key $sk_{\mathcal{Z}}$ of the third party $\mathcal{Z}$. This allows the proxies to decide on the delegatee of a delegation without requiring authorization from the delegator.

Any one of the proxy servers or a trusted third party further can compute

$$C_{\mathcal{Z}} = (u_{\mathcal{Z}}, v_{\mathcal{Z}}) = (u_\chi \prod_{P_j \in Q} c_j, \prod_{P_j \in Q} d_j) = (M.pk_{\mathcal{Z}}^{\delta}, g^{\delta}) \tag{14}$$

The generated ciphertext $C_{\mathcal{Z}}$ which can be decrypted by $\mathcal{Z}$ provides an illustration of the fact that the delegator $\mathcal{X}$ does not hold any control over the re-encryption of a ciphertext once the shares of the secret key sk_χ are distributed over the proxy servers. Thus an active quorum of proxies can redelegate the decryption rights without even requiring to collude with a valid delegatee. This limitation of the scheme hampers the very basic property of any PRE scheme which is to establish a delegation which is specific to the delegator and the delegatee.

5   Proposed Quorum Controlled Proxy Re-encryption Scheme

In this section, we describe the motivation for the proposed scheme and detail the proposed quorum controlled proxy re-encryption scheme.

5.1   Motivation

The limitations of the quorum controlled scheme proposed by Jakobsson [8] are significant as the scheme fails at providing collusion resistance without the requirement of the delegatee as a party to the collusion. A colluding quorum of proxies can retrieve the secret key of the delegatee. This requires the PRE scheme to trust the proxies in order to ensure security of the private key of the delegator. Also, the scheme proposed by Jakobsson is such that a colluding quorum of proxies can transfer the decryption rights to a third party without the authorization of the delegator. More significantly, the scheme does not bind the delegator and the delegatee to a specific delegation, which is a primary requirement of a PRE scheme.

These limitations of the scheme proposed in [8] motivate us to propose a PRE scheme which primarily focuses on providing an alternative which achieves collusion resistance while retaining the quorum controlled nature of re-encryption. The proposed scheme is such that it ensures collusion resistance from a colluding set of proxies by preventing them from retrieving the delegator's secret key. The scheme proposed is also safe from a collusion of proxies and the delegatee. We also ensure that a specific delegation binds the delegator and the delegatee via a delegation key provided to the delegatee.

5.2   System Model for the Proposed Scheme

In this section, we present the proposed quorum controlled scheme based on the RSA encryption system which focuses on eliminating the limitations of the scheme proposed by Jakobsson [8]. The proposed scheme works under a system model which consists of a set of proxies $P_1, P_2, \ldots, P_n$ such that any proxy P_i where $i \in \{1, 2, \ldots n\}$ may or may not be active at any instance of time. The scheme proposed is based on the threshold secret sharing scheme in such a way that the re-encryption is enabled only when at least a desired number of proxies are active. Here, the desired number of proxies indicates the threshold in the scheme. Each user $\mathcal{U}$ in the proposed scheme is identified by a public-private key pair $(pk_\mathcal{U}, sk_\mathcal{U})$. We consider a scenario of the scheme where the user $\mathcal{X}$ identified by $(pk_\mathcal{X}, sk_\mathcal{X})$ is the delegator and the user $\mathcal{Y}$ identified by $(pk_\mathcal{Y}, sk_\mathcal{Y})$ is the delegatee. The system proceeds through five stages during its lifetime, namely key generation, re-encryption key generation, encryption, re-encryption and decryption.

The key generation phase of the scheme assigns to the delegator and the delegatee, their respective public-private key pairs. In the re-encryption key generation phase, the delegator computes the re-encryption key $rk_{\mathcal{X} \to \mathcal{Y}}$ to authorize the delegation of the decryption rights to the delegatee $\mathcal{Y}$. In this phase, the delegator also distributes the shares of this re-encryption key to the set of proxies such that each proxy receives one share of the re-encryption key which it can use to contribute to the re-encryption. In the encryption phase, the user encrypts the message M using the public key $pk_\mathcal{X}$ of the delegator. The transformation of the ciphertext takes place in the re-encryption phase wherein an active quorum of proxies transform the ciphertext encrypted under $pk_\mathcal{X}$ into a ciphertext which can be decrypted by the delegatee. The decryption phase follows this wherein the re-encrypted ciphertext is decrypted by the delegatee in order to retrieve the message M.

5.3   Construction of the Proposed Scheme

The quorum controlled PRE scheme is a tuple $(KGen, ReKGen, Enc_1, Dec_1, Enc_2, Dec_2, Re - Enc)$ of (probabilistic) polynomial time algorithms. We define each of the algorithms of this scheme in this Section.

1. Key Generation $(KGen)$
   This algorithm is run by each party $\mathcal{U}$ in order to generate its public-private key pair. Two large primes $p_\mathcal{U}$ and $q_\mathcal{U}$ are chosen. Further, the public-private key pair $(pk_\mathcal{U}, sk_\mathcal{U})$ is generated as follows:
   (a) Compute $N_\mathcal{U} = p_\mathcal{U} * q_\mathcal{U}$
   (b) Compute $\phi(N_\mathcal{U}) = (p_\mathcal{U} - 1) * (q_\mathcal{U} - 1)$
   (c) Choose a value $e_\mathcal{U}$ such that $1 < e_\mathcal{U} < \phi(N_\mathcal{U})$
   (d) Compute $d_\mathcal{U}$ such that $d_\mathcal{U} \equiv e_\mathcal{U}^{-1} \bmod \phi(N_\mathcal{U})$
   (e) The component $d_\mathcal{U}$ is split into $d_{1\mathcal{U}}$ and $d_{2\mathcal{U}}$ such that $d_\mathcal{U} \equiv (d_{1\mathcal{U}} * d_{2\mathcal{U}}) \bmod \phi(N_\mathcal{U})$. The computation proceeds as follows [2,7]:
      - Randomly select $d_{1\mathcal{U}} \in Z^*_{\phi(N_\mathcal{U})}$
      - Compute $d_{2\mathcal{U}} \equiv (d_\mathcal{U} * d_{1\mathcal{U}}^{-1}) \bmod \phi(N_\mathcal{U})$
      - Hence, $d_{1\mathcal{U}} * d_{2\mathcal{U}} \equiv d_{1\mathcal{U}} * (d_\mathcal{U} * d_{1\mathcal{U}}^{-1}) \bmod \phi(N_\mathcal{U}) \equiv d_\mathcal{U} \bmod \phi(N_\mathcal{U})$
      The public key of the entity $\mathcal{U}$ is $(N_\mathcal{U}, e_\mathcal{U}, e_\mathcal{U} d_{1\mathcal{U}})$ and the private key of the entity $\mathcal{U}$ is $d_\mathcal{U}$.

2. First Level Encryption (Enc_1)
   This algorithm is used to encrypt a message M for a party $\mathcal{X}$ such that it can only be decrypted by $\mathcal{X}$ and cannot be re-encrypted. The first level encryption takes place as follows:

$$C_{1\mathcal{X}} = Enc_1(M, e_\mathcal{X}) = M^{e_\mathcal{X}} \bmod N_\mathcal{X} \qquad (15)$$

3. First Level Decryption (Dec_1)
   To decrypt a first level encrypted ciphertext $C_{1\mathcal{X}}$, encrypted for $\mathcal{X}$, compute:

$$M = Dec_1(C_{1\mathcal{X}}, d_\mathcal{X}) = C_{1\mathcal{X}}^{d_\mathcal{X}} \bmod N_\mathcal{X} \qquad (16)$$

4. Second Level Encryption (Enc_2)
   To encrypt a message M for $\mathcal{X}$, which can be redelegated for decryption to other parties such as $\mathcal{Y}$, the following is computed:

$$C_{2\mathcal{X}} = Enc_2(M, e_\mathcal{X} d_{1\mathcal{X}}) = M^{e_\mathcal{X} d_{1\mathcal{X}}} \bmod N_\mathcal{X} \qquad (17)$$

5. Second Level Decryption (Dec_2)
   To decrypt a second level ciphertext $C_{2\mathcal{X}}$, compute:

$$M = Dec_2(C_{2\mathcal{X}}, d_{2\mathcal{X}}) = (C_{2\mathcal{X}})^{d_{2\mathcal{X}}} \bmod N_\mathcal{X} \qquad (18)$$

Since,

$$(C_{2\mathcal{X}})^{d_{2\mathcal{X}}} \bmod N_\mathcal{X} = (M^{e_\mathcal{X} d_{1\mathcal{X}}})^{d_{2\mathcal{X}}} \bmod N_\mathcal{X} = M^{e_\mathcal{X} d_\mathcal{X}} \bmod N_\mathcal{X} = M \bmod N_\mathcal{X}$$

6. Re-encryption Key Generation $(ReKGen)$
   For a delegation from $\mathcal{X}$ to $\mathcal{Y}$, a delegation key has to be provided to the delegatee $\mathcal{Y}$ for the decryption of the re-encrypted ciphertext. This delegation key is generated by the delegator using the same modulus $N_\mathcal{X}$ that it used to generate its own public-private key pairs. The delegator $\mathcal{X}$ computes

a new public private key pair $(e_{\mathcal{XY}}, d_{\mathcal{XY}})$ using $N_{\mathcal{X}}$ and the same key generation algorithm $(KGen)$. The $d_{\mathcal{XY}}$ component of this key is provided to the delegatee $\mathcal{Y}$ for decryption of the re-encrypted ciphertext whereas the $e_{\mathcal{XY}}$ component of this key is used for generating the re-encryption key $rk_{\mathcal{X} \to \mathcal{Y}}$ as follows:

$$rk_{\mathcal{X} \to \mathcal{Y}} = d_{2\mathcal{X}}e_{\mathcal{XY}} \bmod \phi(N_{\mathcal{X}}) \tag{19}$$

The re-encryption is performed by a quorum of proxies and to facilitate this, shares of the re-encryption key have to be distributed among the proxies. This sharing of the re-encryption key is done using a (t, n) threshold scheme for secret sharing [14].

- A polynomial

$$\lambda(z) = \varphi_0 + \varphi_1 z + \varphi_2 z^2 + \ldots \varphi_{t-1} z^{t-1} \tag{20}$$

  is chosen by $\mathcal{X}$ such that $\varphi_0 = rk_{\mathcal{X} \to \mathcal{Y}} = d_{2\mathcal{X}}e_{\mathcal{XY}}$ and $\varphi_1, \varphi_2, \ldots, \varphi_{t-1}$ are chosen uniformly at random from Z_p^*, where p is a prime.
- A unique share of the polynomial $\lambda(z)$ is securely communicated by $\mathcal{X}$ to each proxy.
- The share $s_{\mathcal{XY}j}$ such that

$$s_{\mathcal{XY}j} = \lambda(z_j), \quad \forall j \in \{1, 2, \ldots, n\} \tag{21}$$

  is received by each proxy P_j.

7. Re-encryption $(Re - Enc)$
   The re-encryption of the second level ciphertext $C_{2\mathcal{X}}$ for the delegation of the decryption rights to $\mathcal{Y}$ is performed by an active quorum Q of proxies. Each proxy $P_j \in Q$ performs the following:
   - Computes its modified share $s'_{\mathcal{XY}j}$ as,

$$s'_{\mathcal{XY}j} = s_{\mathcal{XY}j} * \prod_{\substack{P_k \in Q \\ j \neq k}} \frac{0 - z_k}{z_j - z_k} \tag{22}$$

   - Computes its share of the re-encrypted ciphertext as,

$$C_{\mathcal{Y}j} = (C_{2\mathcal{X}})^{s'_{\mathcal{XY}j}} \bmod N_{\mathcal{X}} \tag{23}$$

Any one of the proxies or a trusted third party can further compute

$$C_{1\mathcal{Y}} = \prod_{P_j \in Q} C_{\mathcal{Y}j} = M^{e_{\mathcal{XY}}} \bmod N_{\mathcal{X}} \tag{24}$$

Further, the decryption of the re-encrypted ciphertext, follows the algorithm Dec_1 for decryption of the first level ciphertext with the decryption key as $d_{\mathcal{XY}}$ provided for the specific delegation from $\mathcal{X}$ to $\mathcal{Y}$.

Proof of Correctness of the Proposed Scheme. The correctness of the proposed scheme relies on the secret reconstruction using the Lagrange's interpolation [6]. Lagrange's interpolation [6] allows for the reconstruction of a polynomial $\lambda(z)$ of degree $t-1$ by combining any t unique data pairs each having the form $(z_{value}, \lambda(z_{value}))$, where each z_{value} is a unique data point at which the interpolation polynomial $\lambda(z)$ is evaluated. In our proposed scheme, each of (z_j, s_{xy_j}) is the data pair used in Lagrange's interpolation since $s_{xy_j} = \lambda(z_j)$. For an active quorum Q of t proxies each holding its share, the polynomial $\lambda(z)$ can be reconstructed according to Lagrange's interpolation by computing:

$$\lambda(z) = \sum_{P_j \in Q} s_{xy_j} * \prod_{\substack{P_k \in Q \\ j \neq k}} \frac{z - z_k}{z_j - z_k} \tag{25}$$

Similarly, the evaluation of $\lambda(z)$ at $z = 0$, is thus obtained by computing:

$$\lambda(0) = \sum_{P_j \in Q} s_{xy_j} * \prod_{\substack{P_k \in Q \\ j \neq k}} \frac{0 - z_k}{z_j - z_k} = \sum_{P_j \in Q} s'_{xy_j} \tag{26}$$

where s'_{xy_j} is the modified share as described in Eq. 22.
We can observe that

$$\lambda(z) = \varphi_0 + \varphi_1 z + \varphi_2 z^2 + \dots \varphi_{t-1} z^{t-1} \tag{27}$$
$$= rk_{x \to y} + \varphi_1 z + \varphi_2 z^2 + \dots \varphi_{t-1} z^{t-1}$$
$$= d_{2x} e_{xy} + \varphi_1 z + \varphi_2 z^2 + \dots \varphi_{t-1} z^{t-1}$$

Hence, the evaluation of $\lambda(z)$ at $z = 0$, results in

$$\lambda(0) = \varphi_0 = rk_{x \to y} = d_{2x} e_{xy} \tag{28}$$

In our proposed scheme, each proxy $P_j \in Q$ computes C_{yj} using the modified share s'_{xy_j} of the re-encryption key provided to it and it can be observed that

$$C_{yj} = (C_{2x})^{s'_{xy_j}} \bmod N_x \tag{29}$$
$$= (M^{e_x d_{1x}})^{s'_{xy_j}} \bmod N_x$$

The C_{yj} values computed by a quorum of proxies are further used to compute the re-encrypted ciphertext by evaluating

$$C_{1y} = \prod_{P_j \in Q} C_{yj} \tag{30}$$
$$= \prod_{P_j \in Q} (C_{2x})^{s'_{xy_j}} \bmod N_x$$
$$= \prod_{P_j \in Q} (M^{e_x d_{1x}})^{s'_{xy_j}} \bmod N_x$$
$$= (M^{e_x d_{1x}})^{\sum_{P_j \in Q} s'_{xy_j}} \bmod N_x$$
$$= (M^{e_x d_{1x}})^{\lambda(0)} \bmod N_x$$

$$= (M^{e_X d_{1X}})^{rk_{X \to Y}} \bmod N_X$$
$$= (M^{e_X d_{1X}})^{d_{2X} e_{XY}} \bmod N_X$$
$$= M^{e_X (d_{1X} d_{2X}) e_{XY}} \bmod N_X$$
$$= M^{(e_X d_X) e_{XY}} \bmod N_X$$
$$= M^{e_{XY}} \bmod N_X$$

The decryption of the re-encrypted ciphertext follows the Dec_1 algorithm as follows:

$$Dec_1(C_{1Y}, d_{XY}) = C_{1Y}^{d_{XY}} \bmod N_X \qquad (31)$$
$$= (M^{e_{XY}})^{d_{XY}} \bmod N_X$$
$$= M^{e_{XY} d_{XY}} \bmod N_X$$
$$= M \bmod N_X$$

6   Evaluation of the Proposed Scheme

In this section, we evaluate the proposed quorum controlled PRE scheme, on the basis of the desired properties of a PRE scheme enumerated in Sect. 1.1.

1. Non-interactive
   Computation of the re-encryption key $rk_{X \to Y} = d_{2X} e_{XY} \bmod \phi(N_X)$ can be performed by the delegator alone and does not require any interaction with the delegatee. Even though the re-encryption key in itself does not require interaction with the delegatee, it should be noted that the delegation key d_{XY} is required to be delivered to the delegatee to ensure decryption capability at the delegatee.

2. Unidirectional
   Given $rk_{X \to Y} = d_{2X} e_{XY} \bmod \phi(N_X)$, the proxies cannot compute $rk_{Y \to X} = d_{2Y} e_{YX} \bmod \phi(N_Y)$. The re-encryption key $rk_{X \to Y}$ is such that it does not contain any information regarding d_{2Y} which is necessary to compute $rk_{Y \to X}$. Also, the e_{YX} component of $rk_{Y \to X}$ needs to be computed by Y using its secret parameter $\phi(N_Y)$, which is not available to the proxies.

3. Non-transitive
   Given $rk_{X \to Y} = d_{2X} e_{XY} \bmod \phi(N_X)$ and $rk_{Y \to Z} = d_{2Y} e_{YZ} \bmod \phi(N_Y)$, the proxies cannot compute $rk_{X \to Z} = d_{2X} e_{XZ} \bmod \phi(N_X)$, since the quorum of proxies cannot obtain d_{2X} from the re-encryption keys available to them and neither can they get an access to the public component e_{XZ} which is required for a delegation from X to Z.

4. Collusion safe
   A colluding set of proxies and the delegatee Y have an access to $rk_{X \to Y} = d_{2X} e_{XY} \bmod \phi(N_X)$ and d_{XY} and thus can at the most obtain $d_{2X} = rk_{X \to Y} * d_{XY}$ but cannot retrieve the secret key d_X of the delegator X.

5. Not key optimal

   The proposed scheme facilitates the delegation of decryption rights to a delegatee only with the help of a delegation key which is specific to the delegation. This requires a user to store one key per delegation that it accepts. The storage cost at a delegatee is not constant rather it is of the order of number of delegations accepted, thus rendering the scheme not key optimal.

6. Proxy visible

   The re-encrypted ciphertext for a party $\mathcal{Y}$ is decrypted using the delegation key specific to the delegation accepted by $\mathcal{Y}$ computed under the modulus of the delegator. Whereas, the ciphertext directly encrypted for $\mathcal{Y}$ is decrypted using the decryption key computed under its own modulus.

7. Original access is allowed

   The delegator computes the delegation key $(e_{\mathcal{X}\mathcal{Y}}, d_{\mathcal{X}\mathcal{Y}})$ specific to a delegation. The re-encrypted ciphertext has the form $C_{1\mathcal{Y}} = M^{e_{\mathcal{X}\mathcal{Y}}} \bmod N_{\mathcal{X}}$, which can be decrypted by $\mathcal{X}$ using the delegation key $d_{\mathcal{X}\mathcal{Y}}$ which it generated.

8. Not temporary

   A delegation from $\mathcal{X}$ to $\mathcal{Y}$ enabled by a re-encryption key $rk_{\mathcal{X} \to \mathcal{Y}}$ remains valid as long as the secret parameters of the delegator $\mathcal{X}$ do not change.

9. Transferable

   The decryption rights can be transferred by a delegatee $\mathcal{Y}$ directly to a third party $\mathcal{Z}$ by providing $\mathcal{Z}$ an access to the delegation key $d_{\mathcal{X}\mathcal{Y}}$ used to decrypt the re-encrypted ciphertexts.

7   Conclusion and Future Work

The proposed scheme for quorum controlled PRE is such that it avoids the collusion problem and thus satisfies this crucial desired property of a PRE scheme. The secret key of the delegator is not compromised by a colluding set of proxies and the delegatee. This is a significant improvement over the scheme proposed by Jakobsson which was susceptible to a collusion of proxies. The scheme also ensures that the delegation of decryption rights does not follow the transitivity property thus preventing the proxies from redelegating decryption rights to a third party without authorization of the delegator. The proposed scheme also binds the delegation key to a specific delegation thus indirectly binding the delegatee who owns the delegation key, to the delegation. The requirement of a delegation key for enabling re-encryption causes the scheme to not satisfy the key optimality property. Achieving key optimality in such a quorum controlled scheme which offers collusion resistance thus remains an open problem which we wish to explore.

Acknowledgements. This work is supported by Ministry of Human Resource Development (MHRD), Government of India.

References

1. Ateniese, G., Fu, K., Green, M., Hohenberger, S.: Improved proxy re-encryption schemes with applications to secure distributed storage. ACM Trans. Inf. Syst. Secur. (TISSEC 2006) **9**(1), 1–30 (2006). https://doi.org/10.1145/1127345.1127346
2. Bellare, M., Sandhu, R.S.: The security of practical two-party RSA signature schemes. IACR Cryptology ePrint Archive 2001, 60 (2001). https://eprint.iacr.org/2001/060.pdf
3. Blaze, M., Bleumer, G., Strauss, M.: Divertible protocols and atomic proxy cryptography. In: Nyberg, K. (ed.) EUROCRYPT 1998. LNCS, vol. 1403, pp. 127–144. Springer, Heidelberg (1998). https://doi.org/10.1007/BFb0054122
4. Chen, Y.R., Tygar, J.D., Tzeng, W.G.: Secure group key management using unidirectional proxy re-encryption schemes. In: Proceedings of the 2011 IEEE International Conference on Computer Communications INFOCOM 2011, pp. 1952–1960, April 2011. https://doi.org/10.1109/INFCOM.2011.5934999
5. Desmedt, Y., Frankel, Y.: Threshold cryptosystems. In: Brassard, G. (ed.) CRYPTO 1989. LNCS, vol. 435, pp. 307–315. Springer, New York (1990). https://doi.org/10.1007/0-387-34805-0_28
6. Horowitz, E., Sahni, S., Rajasekaran, S.: Fundamentals of Computer Algorithms, 2nd edn. Silicon Press, Summit (2007)
7. Ivan, A., Dodis, Y.: Proxy cryptography revisited. In: Proceedings of the Network and Distributed System Security Symposium (NDSS) (2003). https://www.ndss-symposium.org/ndss2003/proxy-cryptography-revisited/
8. Jakobsson, M.: On quorum controlled asymmetric proxy re-encryption. In: Imai, H., Zheng, Y. (eds.) PKC 1999. LNCS, vol. 1560, pp. 112–121. Springer, Heidelberg (1999). https://doi.org/10.1007/3-540-49162-7_9
9. Lin, H.Y., Tzeng, W.G.: A secure erasure code-based cloud storage system with secure data forwarding. IEEE Trans. Parallel Distrib. Syst. **23**(6), 995–1003 (2012). https://doi.org/10.1109/TPDS.2011.252
10. Liu, Q., Wang, G., Wu, J.: Time-based proxy re-encryption scheme for secure data sharing in a cloud environment. Inf. Sci. **258**, 355–370 (2014). https://doi.org/10.1016/j.ins.2012.09.034
11. Mambo, M., Okamoto, E.: Proxy cryptosystems: delegation of the power to decrypt ciphertexts. Inst. Electron. Inf. Commun. Eng. (IEICE) Trans. Fundam. Electron. Commun. Comput. Sci. **80**(1), 54–63 (1997)
12. Pareek, G., Purushothama, B.R.: On efficient access control mechanisms in hierarchy using unidirectional and transitive proxy re-encryption schemes. In: SECRYPT, pp. 519–524. SciTePress (2017). https://doi.org/10.5220/0006466405190524
13. Pedersen, T.P.: A Threshold cryptosystem without a trusted party. In: Davies, D.W. (ed.) EUROCRYPT 1991. LNCS, vol. 547, pp. 522–526. Springer, Heidelberg (1991). https://doi.org/10.1007/3-540-46416-6_47
14. Shamir, A.: How to share a secret. Commun. ACM **22**(11), 612–613 (1979). https://doi.org/10.1145/359168.359176
15. Tysowski, P.K., Hasan, M.A.: Hybrid attribute- and re-encryption-based key management for secure and scalable mobile applications in clouds. IEEE Trans. Cloud Comput. **1**(2), 172–186 (2013). https://doi.org/10.1109/TCC.2013.11

Extended Power Modulus Scrambling (PMS) Based Image Steganography with Bit Mapping Insertion

Srilekha Mukherjee$^{(\boxtimes)}$ and Goutam Sanyal

Department of Computer Science and Engineering,
National Institute of Technology, Durgapur, India
srilekha.mukherjee3@gmail.com, nitgsanyal@gmail.com

Abstract. With the technological advancement, security of information has become a sensitive and alarming issue since it is highly susceptible to many dangerous threats and attacks. In this context, we propose a steganographic methodology which endows a number of conditional evaluations in order to facilitate encryption and masking of the data. The Extended Power Modulus Scrambling (PMS) technique provides an encryption mask to the cover. It ensures the generation of randomized swapping sequence based on the estimated conditions, thus intensifying the security level. A new Bit Mapping Insertion strategy is implemented next. This method implants the data bits within the encrypted cover medium (in this case, image). Furthermore, the reverse scrambling technique zips and covers up the private data. This procedure accredits high payload in conjunction with retaining the quality of the image. The evaluation is done against various benchmarking parameters, which establishes the imperceptibility theory corresponding to the generated output images.

Keywords: Steganography · Extended Power Modulus Scrambling (PMS)
Peak Signal to Noise Ratio (PSNR) · Structural Similarity Measure (SSIM)

1 Introduction

Steganography [1] facilitates covert transmission of information over several communication channels, without any of the masked data being perceivable. It is often confused with cryptography, which protects information just by encryption. The major flaw of encrypted data [2] is that it attracts the attention of several hackers and crackers as all its encryptions are visible to any outsider. Steganography covers up this flaw with its unique feature of invisibility [3]. In this paper, we propose a methodology that serves as an add-on to the steganographic sphere. An extended form of the Power Modulus Scrambling (PMS) [4] technique is proffered. Here, a number of conditions model the trail of the chaotic progression mechanism. The carrier image is fed to the above procedure, which yields an encrypted form of the former. This stage endows a security [5] layer in the whole approach. The masking of the confidential data bits into the above generated form of the host takes place in the next stage. The concepts of upper and lower triangular matrix plays an important role in determining the fashion of

© Springer Nature Switzerland AG 2019
G. Fahrnberger et al. (Eds.): ICDCIT 2019, LNCS 11319, pp. 364–379, 2019.
https://doi.org/10.1007/978-3-030-05366-6_30

Bit Mapping Insertion and masking. Application of the inverse encryption step generates the final stego image [6]. In this approach, the non-linear embedding strategy enhances security of the methodology. The extended PMS technique actually improvises the base PMS strategy. We may also say that this new approach ameliorates its predecessor. Comparing the experimental results of both the approaches, we have better PSNR results of the new proposed approach (i.e. extended PMS strategy) than its respective base methodology (original PMS method). This serves to be an advantage for improvising the base method. Several other metrics are computed and plotted/tabulated to highlight the efficacy of the proposed approach.

This paper is subdivided into the following sections. Section 2 highlights some of the related works. The proposed approach is stated in Sect. 3. All the algorithms with their concerning methodologies is discussed in Sect. 4. Section 5 discloses the experimental results based on certain benchmarks. Section 6 draws the conclusion.

2 Related Work

All the assorted steganographic algorithms proposed in literature can broadly be classified into two categories, namely transform and spatial domain. The methods of the spatial domain are some of the simplest techniques with respect to the embedding and extraction complexity. The least significant bit (LSB) [7] method is one such technique that facilitates data hiding by direct substitution of the LSB's of cover with the secret bit. This method is quite liable to some of the changes made to the host image. To promote a difficile unmasking of the private data, LSB matching (LSBM) method was proposed by Luo, Huang and Huang. Both the techniques annotate the individual image pixels independently. LSB matching revisited (LSBMR) [8] is another efficient methodology proposed that speculates the existing relationship between the residing neighbors. Kumar and Sharma [9] proposed a Hash-LSB technique based on RSA algorithm, where a hash function is used to ascertain the embedding position. The RSA algorithm used facilitates the encryption of the secret information. One efficient methodology of hiding data is using the triple-A algorithm [10]. Every concept here is similar to the basic LSB approach. The main difference found here is that the selections of aggregate bits as well as the individual color channels are more randomized. This improves the overall capacity along with the complete system security, and thus more advantageous. The pixel value differencing (PVD) methodology [11] is another traditional technique which targets the existing disparity between the resident pixels neighbours. Mandal et al. [12] proposed a method based on the concept of PVD itself. Another distinguished method is the Gray level modification (GLM) [13], where the gray level values of elected pixels are emulated for the sake of mapping the confidential data bits. Combination of the PVD and GLM approaches, as proposed by Safarpour and Charmi [14], forms a hybrid methodology that serves an increase in the overall embedding capacity or payload. Ahmad et al. [15] proposed a technique of data hiding in the spatial domain, where dividing the host into uniform blocks forms the first stage. This is followed by hiding the secret bits in the selected edges according to the estimation of net number of 1's in the MSB's.

3 Proposed Approach

This specific section/unit, in particular embraces the detailed narration of the proposed methodology (sketched in Fig. 1). Here, the first step of the embedding phase is the encryption of the cover image so as to generate a chaotic form. This is done using the technique of Extended Power Modulus Scrambling (PMS). For all the resident pixels, certain intermediary evaluations are made so as to figure out their respective pairs for swapping. A randomized turbid anatomy of the cover or host image is the generated output. The extended frame of PMS takes into account several bit sequences of the resident pixels and their positions (as per Fig. 2). The computed values are used in the succeeding stages for the generation of final output. In the next step, the secret data bits are embedded in the above generated shuffled image. For Bit Mapping Insertion to take place, we first specify four conditions (illustrated in Table 3). Later, insertion strategies are prosecuted accordingly depending on whether the targeted pixel inherits the upper or lower triangular sector of the input image matrix. Application of the reverse Extended Power Modulus Scrambling (PMS) results in the final generation of the stego-image.

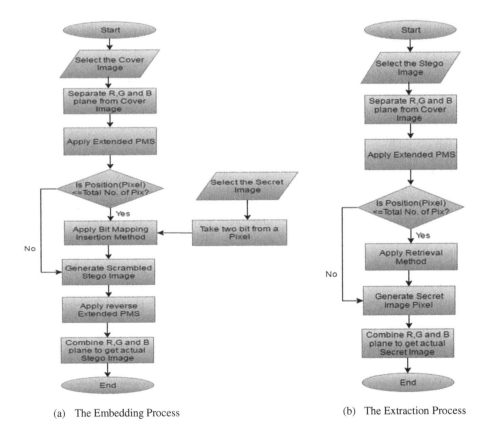

(a) The Embedding Process   (b) The Extraction Process

Fig. 1. Pictorial representation of: (a) The embedding process, (b) The extraction processes.

4 Algorithm

4.1 The Process of Embedding

In order to maintain the secrecy of the hidden data during communication, the embedding procedure embodies a number of stages that supports the stated. The steps are represented in Fig. 1(a).

   i. A host image is selected as input
   ii. Employ the Extended Power Modulus Scrambling (PMS) algorithm on it
  iii. Apply the Bit Mapping Insertion strategy
  iv. Reapply the reverse Extended PMS mechanism to get the stego

Extended Power Modulus Scrambling (PMS) Encryption. This is an extended form of the procedure of Power Modulus Scrambling (PMS). The step of determining the 1st variable 'a' in the basic method is modified in this approach and security is enhanced.

   i. Input the cover image matrix (say 'C_{img}' comprising of 'm * n' pixels, where, 'm' and 'n' signifies the total number of rows and columns resp.)
   ii. Trace out the position (say 'P(i, j)') of the pixels

$$P(i,j) = (i-1) * m + j \qquad (1)$$

  iii. Let's say 'Pix(i, j)' is the pixel residing at 'P(i, j)'
  iv. Take into consideration the four MSB's (say '4_MSB') of each 'Pix(i, j)' and compute the integer value (say 'V(i, j)') such that:

$$V(i,j) = decimal(b_1b_2b_3b_4)\forall Pix_{(i,j)} \qquad (2)$$

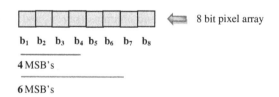

Fig. 2. 8 bit pixel array representation.

   v. Now, calculate the factorial of the integer formed in step iv and store it as an intermediary (say 'x')

$$x = fact(4\_MSB(Pix_{(i,j)})) \qquad (3)$$

$$\Rightarrow x = fact(V(i,j)) \qquad (4)$$

vi. Evaluate 'y' from Eq. 5

$$y = P(i,j)^x \% T + 1 \qquad (5)$$

Where 'T' is the total number of residing pixels

vii. Take into account the pixel residing at position 'y' (say 'pix_at_y') and consider its six MSB's as in step iv

viii. Trace out the values of 'a', 'b' and 'c' such that:

$$a = x * 6\_MSB(pix\_at\_y) \qquad (6)$$

$$b = (a\%((m/2) * n)) + 1 \qquad (7)$$

where, '(m/2) * n' is the last position of the '$(m/2)^{th}$' row

$$c = b + ((m/2) * n) \qquad (8)$$

'c' is the position of a pixel that is swapped with the pixel at position 'P(i, j)'

ix. If at any stage the pixel at 'c' is found to be swapped previously with some pixel, then the location is linearly probed. If not then swapping and insertion takes place as per previous logic

x. If 'c > P(m, n)', then the checking restarts from the position 'P((m/2), n)+1' and the process of linear probing continues.

Bit Mapping Insertion Strategy

A new strategy of Bit Mapping Insertion is described in this stage. We have matched the bits according to some condition (as given in Table 1). Also, the concept of triangular matrix is used to specify the individual locations, which directs the way of insertion.

i. Consider the total number of rows and columns (say 'r' and 'c' respectively) of the encrypted host.

ii. Trace out the total number of pixels, say 'n = r * c', for the same. Next, we estimate the total number of pixels (say 'T') such that 'T = m * n'.

iii. For each individual pixel (say 'pix(i, j)'), consider the 5th, 6th, 7th and 8th bits of a pixel.

iv. Match the 5th and 6th bits with that of the 7th and 8th according to the following specified conditions (illustrated in Table 1).

Table 1. Four conditional strategies of bit matching

Match	Conditions
Exact match	5th bit = 7th bit && 6th bit = 8th bit
Exact complement	5th bit = $(7^{th}$ bit$)'$ && 6th bit = $(8^{th}$ bit$)'$
Left complement	5th bit = $(7^{th}$ bit$)'$ && 6th bit = 8th bit
Right complement	5th bit = 7th bit && 6th bit = $(8^{th}$ bit$)'$

v. Next, for each 'pix(i, j)', check if it belongs to the upper triangular matrix i.e. if 'i ≤ j', insert secret data bits by following the direct insertion strategy according to the evaluated condition (mentioned in Table 2).

vi. Else, if pix(i, j) belongs to the lower triangular matrix i.e. if 'i > j', insert secret data bits by following the reverse insertion strategy according to the evaluated conditions (Table 2).

Table 2. Conditional table to delineate the matching conditions for insertion/extraction

Condition	Location of the pixel pix(i, j) in image matrix	Strategy
Exact match	Upper triangular matrix	Direct two bit direct insertion/extraction
	Lower triangular matrix	Reverse two bit direct insertion/extraction
Exact complement	Upper triangular matrix	Direct two bit complementary insertion/extraction
	Lower triangular matrix	Reverse two bit complementary insertion/extraction
Left complement	Upper triangular matrix	Two bit direct insertion/extraction with left bit complemented
	Lower triangular matrix	Two bit reverse insertion/extraction with left bit complemented
Right complement	Upper triangular matrix	Two bit direct insertion/extraction with right bit complemented
	Lower triangular matrix	Two bit reverse insertion/extraction with right bit complemented

4.2   The Process of Extraction

The confidential data bits are retrieved from the stego image in this phase. All the steps are executed in sequence so that no loss of data bits takes place.

i. The stego is the selected input
ii. Apply the Extended Power Modulus Scrambling (PMS) technique
iii. Implement the retrieval methodology to extract the secret bits
iv. All the extracted bits generate the masked image.

Pixel Retrieval Methodology

i. Consider the total number of rows, say 'r', and the total number of columns, say 'c', of the stego.
ii. Repeat steps ii to iv of the Bit Mapping Insertion strategy.
iii. For each 'pix(i, j)', check if it belongs to the upper triangular matrix, i.e. if 'i ≤ j', retrieve the secret data bits by following the direct extraction strategy according to the evaluated condition (mentioned in Table 2).

iv. Else, if 'pix(i, j)' belongs to the lower triangular matrix, i.e.
if 'i > j', retrieve the secret data bits by following the reverse extraction strategy according to the evaluated conditions given in Table 2.

5   Experimental Results

Several standard images like Lena, Pepper, Baboon, Airplane, Landscape, Goldhill, Sailboat, Barbara, etc are chosen for experimental purpose. The test images are evaluated with respect to certain quantitative and qualitative metrics, the results of which are represented in this section below. An example case corresponding to the experiment is shown next (Fig. 3).

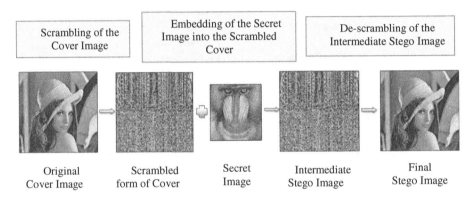

Fig. 3. Stages of execution of the proposed approach

The above figure (Fig. 3) shows the stepwise representation of the actual embedding process that is taking place. The original cover image is the chosen input. It is transformed into the scrambled form with the aid of the Extended Power Modulus Scrambling (PMS) procedure. Thereafter, the chosen secret file is inserted within the above scrambled form with the Bit Mapping Insertion strategy. Finally, on the application of reverse extended PMS, we get the stego-image.

Next, we present the results of the experimental analysis made. The tested benchmark parameters are highlighted as individual subsections.

5.1   Payload

Payload [16] is referred to as the peak amount of information that can be borne via any communicating medium. Here, in Fig. 4, we have plotted a comparative study of some of the existing methodologies on the basis of payload.

The plotted graph shown below (Fig. 4) depicts a comparison amongst several methodologies based on payload. According to the sculpted figure, the proposed approach achieves eminently high embedding capacity.

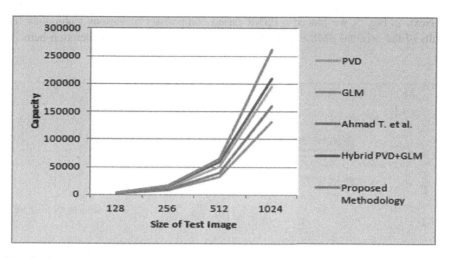

Fig. 4. A comparative study of the data load carrying capacity of different methodologies.

5.2 MSE, LMSE and PSNR

Peak signal to noise ratio (abbreviated as PSNR) [17] generally quantifies the quality of image reconstruction. This metric usually has a range of validation and can be estimated by computing MSE (Mean Squared Error) [18].

$$MSE = \frac{1}{(m*n)} \sum_{i=1}^{m} \sum_{j=1}^{n} [H(ij) - S(ij)]^2 \tag{9}$$

Where,

'H' is a host image (comprising m × n pixels) and 'S' is the stego-image.

Also, Laplacian Mean Squared Error can be evaluated from the following equation.

$$LMSE = \frac{\sum_{1}^{M} \sum_{1}^{N} [L(x(m,n)) - L(\hat{x}(m,n))]^2}{\sum_{1}^{M} \sum_{1}^{N} [L(x(m,n))]^2} \tag{10}$$

$L(m,n)$ is the Laplacian Operator, $x(m,n)$ signifies the cover pixels and $\hat{x}(m,n)$ represents the stego pixels

$$L(m,n) = x(m+1,n) + x(m-1,n) + x(m,n+1) + x(m,n-1) - 4x(m,n)$$

Finally, we acquire PSNR as follows:

$$PSNR = 10 \log_{10} 255^2 / MSE \quad db \tag{11}$$

Next, in Fig. 5, we placed a PSNR based comparison of various techniques. The results of the original PMS approach has also been taken into consideration here.

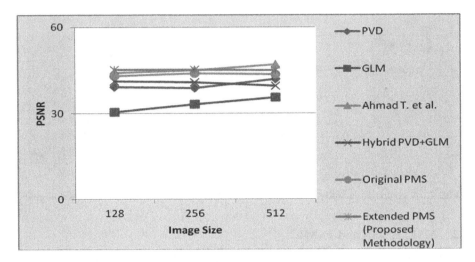

Fig. 5. A survey of PSNR for different methodologies

The above figure (Fig. 5) depicts the PSNR estimation for various methodologies. It is seen that the plotted values of PSNR for the proposed methodology is moderately good. Also, there is an improvement of the PSNR values for the Extended PMS methodology in comparison to the original PMS technique.

Table 3 displays an estimation of Mean Squared Error (MSE), Laplacian Mean Squared Error (LMSE) and Peak Signal to Noise Ratio (PSNR) for the proposed methodology. The low values of LMSE solace the affirmation of the generated good quality image. High LMSE values would have indicated poor image quality otherwise. It is noticed that the obtained values of PSNR lies within the valid range. This also proves that the quality of image is restored.

5.3   Cross Correlation Coefficient

The normalized cross correlation coefficient [19] can be estimated from the following Eq. (12):

$$r = \frac{\sum (H(i,j) - m_H)(S(i,j) - m_S)}{\sqrt{\sum (H(i,j) - m_H)^2}\sqrt{\sum (S(i,j) - m_S)^2}} \tag{12}$$

where,

'H' is the host/cover, 'S' is the obtained stego, 'm_H' is the mean value of the pixels of host/cover, 'm_S' is the mean value of the pixels of stego.

Table 3. Estimation of MSE, LMSE and PSNR

Image	Image size	Proposed methodology		
		MSE	LMSE	PSNR
Lena	128 × 128	16.90	0.003	45.08
	256 × 256	16.86	0.008	45.20
	512 × 512	16.86	0.030	44.87
Pepper	128 × 128	17.05	0.004	44.63
	256 × 256	16.98	0.011	44.50
	512 × 512	17.00	0.050	44.37
Baboon	128 × 128	16.95	0.005	43.80
	256 × 256	16.79	0.004	44.11
	512 × 512	16.85	0.003	44.52
Airplane	128 × 128	16.91	0.007	44.93
	256 × 256	16.90	0.010	44.75
	512 × 512	16.92	0.030	44.45

From the figure shown next (Fig. 6), we clearly see that the values of the cross correlation lies closer to 1. This signifies that the stego-image formed has high resemblance with that of the host image. Thus, the imperceptibility is well maintained.

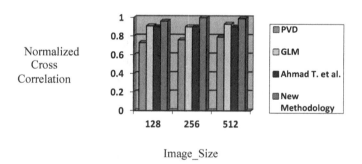

Fig. 6. Estimated similarity measure with reference to some of the methodologies

5.4 Skewness and Kurtosis

Skewness [20] and kurtosis are respectively the third and fourth order central moments of distribution. Considering a univariate set of data Y1, Y2, Y3…YN, skewness and kurtosis can be evaluated as per the following described Eqs. (13) and (14). Here, the mean is signified as 'μ' and the standard deviation is denoted as 'σ'. Also, 'N' is the number of pixel data.

$$\text{Skewness} = \frac{\sum_{i=1}^{N} (Y_i - \mu)^3 / N}{\sigma^3} \tag{13}$$

$$\text{Kurtosis} = \frac{\sum_{i=1}^{N} (Y_i - \mu)^4 / N}{\sigma^4} \tag{14}$$

The statistical estimation of the above stipulated moments (i.e. skewness and kurtosis), both for the cover and stego shows a negligible contrariety between each. This is exhibited in Table 4. Henceforth, we can infer that there is an occurrence of negligible distortion amidst the host and stego images.

Table 4. Estimation of skewness and kurtosis for different input test images used

Image	Image size	Components	Cover		Stego	
			Skewness	Kurtosis	Skewness	Kurtosis
Lena	512 × 512	R	−1.51	13.31	−1.52	13.38
		G	2.54	49.15	2.56	49.44
		B	1.38	18.78	1.38	18.76
	256 × 256	R	−1.47	13.38	−1.47	12.82
		G	2.63	53.71	2.65	52.06
		B	1.29	14.74	1.33	15.42
	128 × 128	R	−1.74	32.43	−1.75	31.83
		G	2.63	84.72	2.61	83.46
		B	1.14	18.92	1.11	17.89
Pepper	512 × 512	R	−1.05	9.02	−1.05	9.08
		G	−0.41	2.83	−0.41	2.84
		B	0.15	53.44	0.07	51.15
	256 × 256	R	−1.21	12.26	−1.21	12.35
		G	−0.42	2.81	−0.42	2.82
		B	−0.42	3.24	−0.42	3.22
	128 × 128	R	−1.12	11.42	−1.18	12.79
		G	−0.43	2.72	−0.43	2.71
		B	−0.38	3.93	−0.36	4.01

5.5   SSIM, KL Divergence and Entropy

The structural similarity index [21] also referred to as SSIM can be considered to be an improvement over various traditional methods that figure out the quality of similarity. It can be estimated from the following Eq. (15).

$$SSIM(c, s) = \frac{(2\mu_c\mu_s + v1)(2\sigma_{cs} + v2)}{(\mu_c^2 + \mu_s^2 + v1)(\sigma_c^2 + \sigma_s^2 + v2)} \tag{15}$$

Where,

μ_c is the average of cover pixels

μ_s is the average of stego pixels

σ_c^2 is the variance of cover pixels

σ_s^2 is the variance of stego pixels

σ_{cs} is the covariance of cover and stego

v1 and v2 are two variables having values (k1L)2 and (k2L)2, where L is $2^8 - 1$, k1 = 0.01 and k2 = 0.03.

KL Divergence (i.e. Kullback-Leibler Divergence) [22] is measured by Eq. (16):

$$D_{KL}(P_c||P_s) = \sum_i P_c(i) \log \frac{P_c(i)}{P_s(i)} \tag{16}$$

Where, Pc is the probability density function of the cover (say 'C'),

Ps is the probability density function of the stego (say 'S').

With respect to any data source, the entropy [23] rate can be signified as the mean or average quantity of bits per symbol assigned to encode it. It can be calculated from the following Eq. (17):

$$\text{Entropy} = -\sum_i P_i \log_2 P_i. \tag{17}$$

Where, 'P_i' is represented as the probability that the overall deviation between any two pixels (that are adjacent) is equivalent to 'i'.

Next, we have shown all the computations of SSIM, KL Divergence and Entropy with respect to the test images.

Figures 7 and 8 represent the plot for SSIM and KL divergence respectively, the values of which are obtained by varying the payload sizes for the test images [24]. All the SSIM values are very close to 1, and this establishes the condition of imperceptibility. The computed KL divergence values show that there is very less deviation of the stego from its respective cover.

Table 5 shows the tabulation of the computed values of the entropy parameter with respect to the cover and stego images. Very less difference is obtained between the two sets of values. This again supports the fact that the stego image is imperceptible and no perceived disturbance is measured in the final generated system output.

5.6   Results of RS Analysis

The RS analysis test has been performed so as to detect its resistance against certain attacks. Basically, this is a steganalysis detection algorithm. In the table shown below (Table 6), the difference between the R and S (i.e. regular and singular) components, each of the cover and stego is portrayed.

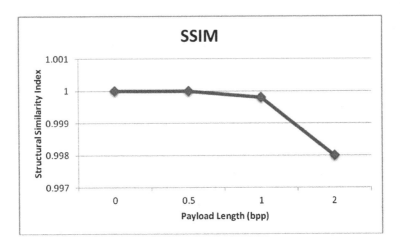

Fig. 7. Plotted values of structural similarity index by varying the payload sizes

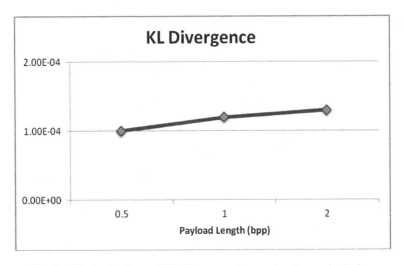

Fig. 8. Obtained values of KL divergence by varying the payload sizes

With the aid of R_S analysis, we obtain the tabulated values. It shows very negligible changes in the R_S values. Therefore, for the test images of various sizes with different hidden data, $R_C \approx R_S$ and $S_C \approx S_S$. Hence, this is quite resistant to such attacks.

Table 5. Measurement of entropy parameter

Entropy parameter				
Image	Component	Size	Entropy (Cover image)	Entropy (Stego-image)
Lena	R	512 × 512	7.25	7.25
	G		7.59	7.57
	B		6.96	6.91
	R	256 × 256	7.27	7.26
	G		7.63	7.62
	B		6.98	6.95
	R	128 × 128	7.32	7.32
	G		7.65	7.64
	B		7.03	6.97
Pepper	R	512 × 512	7.35	7.33
	G		7.59	7.61
	B		7.12	7.14
	R	256 × 256	7.37	7.34
	G		7.59	7.61
	B		7.14	7.15
	R	128 × 128	7.38	7.36
	G		7.58	7.61
	B		7.13	7.14
Baboon	R	512 × 512	7.75	7.72
	G		7.46	7.45
	B		7.77	7.75
	R	256 × 256	7.66	7.63
	G		7.37	7.36
	B		7.69	7.67
	R	128 × 128	7.56	7.53
	G		7.29	7.28
	B		7.61	7.59

Table 6. A comparative study on image parameters for original and stego-image

Image	Image size	Cover		Stego	
		R_C	S_C	R_S	S_S
Lena	512 × 512	32018	20765	32318	20415
	256 × 256	32020	20767	32321	20417
	128 × 128	32023	20769	32320	21419
Pepper	512 × 512	32013	20767	32329	20418
	256 × 256	32021	20766	32330	20418
	128 × 128	32025	20768	32331	20420

6 Conclusion

The proposed methodology is advantageous in a way that it serves several purposes critical to steganography. The prime of all is the security [25] lining that it adds to the data after actuating the Extended Power Modulus Scrambling (PMS) [26] algorithm on it. All the conditional assessment facilitates certain chaotic swapping series, which spawns the scrambled form. The Bit Mapping Insertion mechanism also implements several conditional comparisons that mask the bits accordingly, nailing two in one pixel. The evaluated experimental results show that there is no significant distortion [27] in the quality of the procured stego-image [28]. Also, the approximated statistical measures prove the above stated statement. Due to the perpetual 2-bit insertion procedure [29], high embedding capacity is another advantage of this methodology. Furthermore, this approach can be modified with the aim of intensifying the payload so that a higher volume of data can be communicated [30].

References

1. Mukherjee, S., Sanyal, G.: Enhanced position power first mapping (PPFM) based image steganography. Int. J. of Comput. Appl. **39**, 59–68 (2017)
2. Al-khasaaweneh, M.: Image encryption method based on using least square error techniques at the decryption stage. Int. J. Inf. Comput. Secur. **4**(4), 332–344 (2011)
3. Sahoo, A., Tiwari, R.: A novel approach for hiding secret data in program files. Int. J. Inf. Comput. Secur. **8**(1), 1–10 (2016)
4. Mukherjee, S., Ash, S., Sanyal, G.: A novel image steganographic methodology by power modulus scrambling with logistic mapping. In: IEEE Region 10th Conference on TENCON (2015)
5. Gayathri, J., Subashini, S.: A survey on security and efficiency issues in chaotic image encryption. Int. J. Inf. Comput. Secur. **8**(4), 347–381 (2016)
6. Singh, K.: A survey on image steganography techniques. Int. J. Comput. Appl. **97**, 10–20 (2014)
7. Gurav, J., et al.: High secured image by LSB steganography technique using matlab. Int. J. Recent Innov. Trends. Comput. Commun. **3**(4), 1836–1840 (2015)
8. Luo, W., Huang, F., Huang, J.: Edge adaptive image steganography based on LSB matching revisited. IEEE Trans. Inf. Forensics Secur. **5**, 201–214 (2010)
9. Kumar, A., Sharma, R.: A secure image steganography based on RSA algorithm and hash-LSB technique. Int. J. Adv. Res. Comput. Sci. Softw. Eng. **3**, 363–372 (2012)
10. Gutub, A., Al-Qahtani, A., Tabakh, A.: Triple-A: secure RGB image steganography based on randomization. In: IEEE/ACS International Conference on Computer Systems and Applications, Rabat, Morocco, pp. 400–403 (2009)
11. Sanchetti, A.: Pixel value differencing image steganography using secret key. Int. J. Innov. Technol. Exploring Eng. **2**, 2278–3075 (2012)
12. Mandal, J.K., et al.: Color image steganography based on pixel value differencing in spatial domain. Int. J. Inf. Sci. Tech. **2**(4) (2012)
13. Khan, M., et al.: A secure method for color image steganography using gray-level modification and multi-level encryption. KSII Trans. Internet. Inf. Syst. **9**(5), 1938–1962 (2015)

14. Safarpour, M., Charmi, M.: Capacity enlargement of the PVD steganography method using the GLM technique. CoRR abs/1601.00299 (2016)
15. Ahmad, T., et al.: A survey on digital image steganography. In: The 7th International Conference on Information Technology (2015)
16. Mukherjee, S., Sanyal, G.: A novel image steganographic technique using Position Power First Mapping. In: IEEE International Conference on Research in Computational Intelligence and Communication Networks, pp. 406–410 (2015)
17. Almohammad, A., Ghinea, G.: Stego-image quality and the reliability of PSNR. In: Image Processing Theory, Tools and Applications. IEEE (2010)
18. Subhedar, M., Mankar, V.: Current status and key issues in image steganography: a survey. J. Comput. Sci. Rev. **13**, 95–113 (2014)
19. Reddy, V., Subramanyam, A., Reddy, P.: A novel technique for JPEG image steganography and its performance evaluation. IJAMC **5**, 211–224 (2014)
20. Koo, H., Cho, N.: Skew estimation of natural images based on a salient line detector. J. Electr. Imaging **22**, 013020 (2013)
21. Moon, S., Raut, R.: Efficient performance analysis of data hiding technique for enhancement of information security, robustness and perceptibility. Int. J. Electr. Secur. Dig. Forensics **7** (4), 305–329 (2015)
22. Dukkipati, A.: On maximum entropy and minimum KL-divergence optimization by Gröbner basis methods. Appl. Math. Comput. **218**(23), 11674–11687 (2012)
23. Duncan, K., Sarkar, S.: Relational entropy-based saliency detection in images and videos. In: 19th IEEE International Conference on Image Processing, pp. 1093–1096 (2012)
24. Mohapatra, S., et al.: Adaptive threshold selection for impulsive noise detection in images using coefficient of variance. Neural Comput. Appl. **21**(2), 281–288 (2012)
25. Kasana, G., Singh, K., Bhatia, S.: Data hiding using lifting scheme and genetic algorithm. Int. J. Inf. Comput. Secur. **9**(4), 271–287 (2017)
26. Mukherjee, S., Sanyal, G.: A chaos based image steganographic system. Multimed. Tools Appl. **77**, 1–26 (2018)
27. Banerjee, I., et al.: Hiding and analysis data in image using extended PMM. In: International Conference on Computational Intelligence: Modeling Techniques and Applications, pp. 157–166 (2013)
28. Yang, C., et al.: Adaptive data hiding in edge areas of images with spatial LSB domain systems. IEEE Trans. Inf. Forensics Secur. **3**(3), 488–497 (2008)
29. Mahajan, M., Kaur, N.: Steganography in coloured images using wavelet domain-based saliency map. Int. J. Inf. Comput. Secur. **5**(3), 224–235 (2013)
30. Ash, S., Mukherjee, S., Sanyal, G.: A DWT based steganographic method using prime first mapping. In: Advances in Computing and Communicational Engineering, pp. 471–476 (2015)

Empirical Study on Malicious URL Detection Using Machine Learning

Ripon Patgiri$^{(\boxtimes)}$, Hemanth Katari$^{(\boxtimes)}$, Ronit Kumar$^{(\boxtimes)}$,
and Dheeraj Sharma$^{(\boxtimes)}$

National Institute of Technology Silchar, Silchar 788010, Assam, India
ripon@cse.nits.ac.in, hemanth.katari@gmail.com, ronit.kumar1194@gmail.com,
dheerajsharma.nits@gmail.com

Abstract. In this paper, the malicious URLs detection is treated as a binary classification problem and performance of several well-known classifiers are tested with test data. The algorithms Random Forests and support Vector Machine (SVM) are studied in particular which attain a high accuracy. These algorithms are used for training the dataset for classification of good and bad URLs. The dataset of URLs is divided into training and test data in 60:40, 70:30 and 80:20 ratios. Accuracy of Random Forests and SVMs is calculated for several iterations for each split ratio. According to the results, the split ratio 80:20 is observed as more accurate split and average accuracy of Random Forests is more than SVMs. SVM is observed to be more fluctuating than Random Forests in accuracy.

Keywords: Malicious URL detection · Network security
Machine Learning · Random Forest · Suport vector machine · SVM

1 Introduction

In today's world, there is a rapid advancement in technology. With the advancement of technology, there is a similar development in the Internet. Internet involvement in social and business fields is increasing in large scale. The increasing use of the internet for such purposes increases the scope for cyber criminal activities. As the connectivity and the number of users grow, there is a proportional increase in attackers. The Government, industry and individuals are the victims. It is a difficult task to predict the future threats and their nature, and practically unsolvable. Malware or malicious websites become one of the major threat for cyber security. Whereas malicious URLs, in particular, becomes a serious threat of cyber security. Malicious URL is a common and serious threat to cyber-security. Malicious URLs host content abnormalities, such as spamming, phishing attacks, exploiting users, etc. They allow unsuspected users as victims of attacks by drivers. They incur huge monetary loss of billions of dollars every year worldwide. It is very important to firstly detect and act on such attacks

© Springer Nature Switzerland AG 2019
G. Fahrnberger et al. (Eds.): ICDCIT 2019, LNCS 11319, pp. 380–388, 2019.
https://doi.org/10.1007/978-3-030-05366-6_31

frequently for security [5]. Generally, such detection's are done through the use of big blacklists [5]. In practice, it is not possible to have exhaustive blacklists [5]. Today's naive implementation of detection techniques is insufficient to address billions of URLs encountered in everyday life. Machine Learning techniques is used to address the problem as a binary classification problem in large scale [7]. There are various classifiers in Machine Learning which give high accuracy in classification of good and bad URLs [1,2,8]. Moreover, Huang et al. detects Malicious URL using a greedy selection algorithm [3]. Similarly, Liu et al. also provides experimental study on URL detection using Machine Learning algorithms [4]. Vu et al. performs cost-sensitive malicious URL detection using a Decision Tree algorithm [9]. In this empirical study, we perform- (a) collecting a dataset which consists of huge number of URL's which consists of both malicious and non malicious URLs, (b) divide the collected dataset into two subsets in the ratio of 80:20 for training purposes and testing purposes, (c) extract features from the training data categorized into lexical features, network based features and host based features, (d) training the system using the training data and Machine Learning algorithms like Random Forest algorithm and Support Vector Machines (SVM), and (e) testing the system by providing test data and calculating the accuracy using each of the algorithms. Our aim is to provide a comprehensive investigation on detection of Malicious URLs by using Machine Learning algorithms like SVM and Random Forest classification algorithm.

2   Proposed System

Our proposed system uses Machine Learning algorithms and analyzes using the various features obtained from the URL for classification purpose. Figure 1 represents the complete flow diagram of our proposed system which consists of the following phases- collection of data, features extraction, training model, testing the model, query phase and the final output phase. It also represents the source of data collection, extracted features and the models used for classification purposes and the output consisting of accuracy and classification result.

Data: Collection of reliable and informative dataset is a very important aspect in dealing with learning based problems for classification or regression. The data consisting of both malicious and non-malicious URLs with labels need to be collected for training and testing purpose from a reliable source in order to get better accuracy and classification result.

Feature Selection and Extraction: The selection of features is an important and difficult phase where the dataset in hand is very big. This makes detection of patterns and finding a correlation among features too heavy for computation. In Machine Learning, a feature is an individual measurable property or characteristic or an attribute of a phenomenon being observed. Choosing informative, differentiating and independent features is a vital step for efficient algorithms

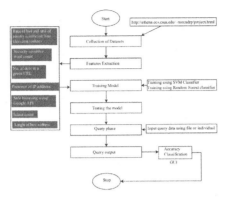

Fig. 1. Flow diagram representing the proposed solution

in pattern recognition, classification and regression purposes. Variable selection and attribute selection are referred for feature extraction. It includes the process of selecting selective features which are important for model training for classification. The problem requires to classify among the URLs as Benign or Malicious. So, in order to address the problem, we would require to design a model and train it using the features extracted from the training data. The next phase after the collection of data is extracting useful and informative features which are sufficient for the description of URLs and which can be mathematically interpreted for training using Machine Learning models. Simply, using an URL will not directly allow good classification method. So, it is important to select suitable features based on some rules or hypothesis to obtain a good feature from the set of URL. Thus, the quality of the extracted features from the URLs is prominent for the quality of the resulting malicious URL classification model. The features for classifying an URL can be of many types which can be classified into lexical features, host based features and web content features.

Lexical Features: lexical features are the features obtained based on the characteristics of the URL name or URL String. The most commonly used lexical features include statistical properties of the URL string, namely, (a) the length of the URL, (b) length of host name, (c) number of characters consisting of the host name, (d) length of path, (e) domain token count, (f) path token count, (g) average domain token length, (h) average path token length, (i) count of Security sensitive words, (j) number of dots, (k) presence of IP address, and (l) presence of .exe in URL.

Host Based Features: Host-based features are obtained from the host-name properties of the URL. The features include - safe browsing, rank of host and Country, and site popularity. Safe browsing is a Google service that lets client applications check URLs against Google's constantly updated lists of unsafe web resources. Rank of host and Country is a location based feature corresponding to an IP address corresponding to the URL. The Location information comprises the physical Geographic Location - e.g. country/city to which the IP address belongs. "Site popularity" is one of the prominent feature for URL classification. Site Popularity measured as the increase in traffic of web using competitive analytical methods. It is generally estimated by counting the number of incoming links from other web pages to these web pages. Link popularity refers to the number of backlinks (incoming links) that points to a given URL. It can be considered as a reputation measure of an URL. Malicious sites tend to have a lower value of link popularity, whereas many non-malicious URL, especially the popular ones, tends to have a higher value of link popularity. Both the link popularity of a URL and the link popularity of the URL's domain are used in our method. Link popularity (LPOP) can be easily obtained from a search engine. In our proposed solution, we have used traffic information obtained from Alexa.com. Alexa's traffic estimates and ranks are based on the browsing behavior of the people in our global data panel, which is a sample of all internet users.

Classification: Random Forest is a supervised classification algorithm. Random Forest can be used for regression and classification tasks. Random Forest classifier creates a set of decision trees from randomly selected features. Then, it calculates votes from different the decision tree for each predicted target and the highest voted class is considered the final prediction. The random-forest algorithm brings extra randomness into the model while growing the trees. Instead of searching best feature while splitting node, it searches for the best features among random subset of features. Similarly, Support Vector Machine (SVM) is a supervised classification algorithm. SVM is a discriminating classifier that separates defined by separating hyper-plane. More clearly, SVM takes training data and separates data into categories divided by a clear gap called the hyper-plane. SVM tries to find out the best or optimal hyper-plane, which has the largest distance from the nearest point, in high dimensions, which clearly separates training set into categories. Support vectors are the data points nearest to the hyper-plane. The goal is to choose a hyper-plane with the greatest possible margin between the hyper-plane and any point within the training set, giving a greater chance of new data being classified correctly.

Method Comparison: In order to evaluate the models, cross validation score is used to measure the accuracy. Accuracy is the overall success rate of the method in terms of predictions. The models Random Forest and SVM are compared using minimum, maximum and average accuracy's of test data.

3   Experimental Results and Discussions

The labeled data collected consists of malicious and benign URL undergoes the feature extraction process, and then, the data are divided into two, particularly, the training and the testing data [6]. The training data are passed through various methods for feature extraction and labelling the training data, and then, it is passed to various models such as Random Forest and SVM. And, the trained model is tested using the training dataset, i.e., one having features without labels and we calculate the accuracy of the model. The above process is repeated for 3 data splits, i.e., 80:20, 70:30, and 60:40, the antecedent being the training dataset and consequent being tested dataset. The Fig. 2 represents the experimental flow diagram. The dataset contain both Benign and Malicious URLs. A Uniform Resource Locator (URL) consists of protocol, domain name and path. From the URL, various lexical features, host-based features and site popularity features are extracted. A dataset containing Benign and Malicious URLs is collected from the following Source [6].

Fig. 2. Experimental flow diagram

3.1   Feature Selection and Extraction

Lexical Features: In order to extract these lexical features from URLs, the URL is first broken into a set of words or Tokens according to the delimiters ('.', '/', '?', '=', '-') in the URL. It is also very important to have the distinction between the tokens belonging to the host name, the path, the top-level domain and the primary domain name. **Tokenise(URL)** is the method used in implementation to generate tokens from an input URL string. This method takes the URL String as input and returns average token length, token count and largest token's length. Length of the URL is obtained by accessing the URL which is passed as an argument to **Feature_Extraction(URL)** method in the form of string and calculating the length of the string directly. After obtaining the tokens from the URL, we can similarly obtain other features by counting the number of tokens in the domain and path, and calculating the string length in other cases. The bag of words model is employed in order to count the number of security sensitive words. In this process, a security sensitive bag of words is created and stored in the form of an array and the collected tokens are checked if any of them matches with any of words present in the array, and if present, we can increase the counter for security sensitive words and have the final count. The security sensitive keywords consists of words, namely, 'confirm', 'account', 'banking', 'secure', 'ebayisapi', 'webscr', 'login', 'signin' and so on. This method takes in an array of words or tokens as input and returns an integer representing the count of security sensitive words. Number of dots is obtained by using a string matching algorithm. Ip Address presence can be determined by making use of regular expression. It is also checked if the URL has '.exe' extension using string matching algorithm.

Host Based Feature: Safe browsing information can be obtained by passing the URL as a request to safe browsing API of Google. The response is obtained in the form of a code which represent unique information about the URL passed as request. The response to the URL passed as a request to an online website Alexa.com is obtained which provides us with the rank of country which hosts the particular ip address. It is a fact that mostly malicious sites are registered in less reputable hosting centers or regions.

3.2 Training the Models for Classification

The data, which is in CSV format, are read using pandas package of python. The non-string columns from training data are extracted. The data are sent to Random Forests and SVM. Python consists a sklearn package which is used for Machine Learning applications. The Sklearn.ensemble package contains Random Forest Classifier module. Number of Trees is passed as an argument to Random

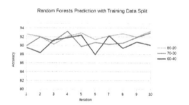

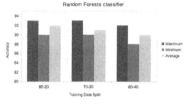

(a) Accuracy obtained in each iteration for different division ratio of data using Random Forest classifier

(b) Minimum,Maximum and Average accuracy obtained using Random Forest classifier at different split ratio of dataset

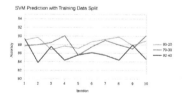

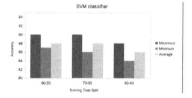

(c) Accuracy obtained in each iteration for different division ratio of data using SVM classifier

(d) Minimum, Maximum and Average accuracy obtained using SVM classifier at different split ratio of dataset

Fig. 3. Accuracy evaluation using difference Machine Learning algorithm.

Forests function. The model is trained using fit function which takes training data with output after feature extraction as arguments. The accuracy of trained model is tested using test data using **cross_val_score** function cross validation module. The test data and predicted values with accuracy is printed as output.

The accuracy of Random Forests is calculated for training data split ratios of 60:40, 70:30 and 80:20 for 10 iterations. For each iteration, the corresponding accuracy of each split ratio is depicted in Fig. 3a. It is clearly depicted that the Random Forests model varies from 88 to 92% in accuracy. The variance is smaller compared to SVMs. A histogram is also depicted in Fig. 3b for comparison of different ratios 60:40, 70:30 and 80:20 for minimum, maximum and average accuracy's. The average accuracy is calculated as the average of accuracy of 10 iterations. The minimum and maximum values are the smallest and biggest value in 10 iterations respectively.

3.3 Training with SVMs

The sklearn package contains SVM module. The function Support Vector Classification (SVC) is invoked for SVM object. The model is trained using fit function which takes training data, and outputs after feature extraction. The accuracy

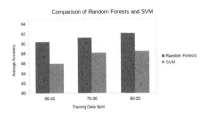

Iteration	Random Forest classifier	SVM classifier
1	0.89544	0.89415
2	0.88343	0.83842
3	0.91282	0.87556
4	0.91783	0.84368
5	0.92389	0.85610
6	0.92242	0.85542
7	0.89392	0.84423
8	0.92242	0.85542
9	0.90815	0.87933
10	0.90101	0.84610

(a) Comparison of Average accuracy obtained using both the models at different split ratio

(b) Accuracy for each iteration using both the classifiers at 60:40 split ratio

Iteration	Random Forest classifier	SVM classifier
1	0.92610	0.89080
2	0.91964	0.87967
3	0.91033	0.88464
4	0.93262	0.90067
5	0.89757	0.85514
6	0.90714	0.87504
7	0.90285	0.89010
8	0.90567	0.87949
9	0.91862	0.87051
10	0.92902	0.90148

Iteration	Random Forest classifier	SVM classifier
1	0.89985	0.87714
2	0.92048	0.89677
3	0.90291	0.86825
4	0.92086	0.87673
5	0.92885	0.87125
6	0.91379	0.88661
7	0.92188	0.89247
8	0.92714	0.89793
9	0.91953	0.87801
10	0.93302	0.88919

(c) Accuracy for each iteration using both the classifiers at 70:30 split ratio

(d) Accuracy for each iteration using both the classifiers at 80:20 split ratio

Fig. 4. Accuracy evaluation.

of trained model is tested using test data using **cross_val_score** function cross validation module. The test data and predicted values with accuracy is printed as output. The accuracy of SVM is calculated for training data split ratios of 60:40, 70:30 and 80:20 for 10 iterations. For each iteration the corresponding accuracy of each split ratio is depicted in Fig. 3c. It is clearly plotted that the Random Forests model varies from 82 to 90% in accuracy. The variance is more compared to SVM. The histogram is also plotted in Fig. 3d for comparison of different ratios 60:40, 70:30 and 80:20 for minimum, maximum and average accuracy.

3.4   Comparison of Models

The training models, Random Forests and SVM, are compared with their average accuracy of 10 iterations in plotted histogram in Fig. 4a. From the three split ratios 60:40, 70:30 and 80:20, the average accuracy of SVM is less compared to Random Forest Classifier. The accuracy of Random Forests and SVM are listed in the given in Figs. 4b, c, and d. The three figures consist of accuracy of models with training splits 80:20, 70:30 and 60:40 ratios for 10 iterations. The accuracy values are listed on a scale of 0 to 1. From the comparison, Random Forest gives more accuracy than SVM. SVM accuracy fluctuates more than Random Forests with iterations.

4   Conclusion

Malicious Web sites are the basis of most of the criminal activities over the internet. The dangers that arise due to the malicious sites are enormous and the end-users must be prohibited from visiting such sites. The users should prohibit themselves from clicking on such Uniform Resource Locator (URL). The detection of malicious URLs is a binary classification problem and several Machine Learning Algorithms, namely Random Forests, SVMs and Naive Bayes are implemented on training dataset. Also, it has been seen that the Random Forest classifier performs better for the particular problem than the SVM classifier.

References

1. Choi, H., Zhu, B.B., Lee, H.: Detecting malicious web links and identifying their attack types. WebApps **11**, 11 (2011)
2. Gabriel, A.D., Gavrilut, D.T., Alexandru, B.I., Stefan, P.A.: Detecting malicious URLs: a semi-supervised machine learning system approach. In: 2016 18th International Symposium on Symbolic and Numeric Algorithms for Scientific Computing (SYNASC), pp. 233–239. IEEE (2016)
3. Huang, D., Xu, K., Pei, J.: Malicious URL detection by dynamically mining patterns without pre-defined elements. World Wide Web **17**(6), 1375–1394 (2014)

4. Liu, C., Wang, L., Lang, B., Zhou, Y.: Finding effective classifier for malicious URL detection. In: Proceedings of the 2018 2nd International Conference on Management Engineering, Software Engineering and Service Sciences, ICMSS 2018, pp. 240–244. ACM, New York (2018)
5. Ma, J., Saul, L.K., Savage, S., Voelker, G.M.: Learning to detect malicious URLs. ACM Trans. Intell. Syst. Technol. (TIST) **2**(3), 30 (2011)
6. Narendra, P.: Malicious URL detection. http://athena.ecs.csus.edu/narendrp/project.html
7. Vanhoenshoven, F., Nápoles, G., Falcon, R., Vanhoof, K., Köppen, M.: Detecting malicious URLs using machine learning techniques. In: 2016 IEEE Symposium Series on Computational Intelligence (SSCI), pp. 1–8. IEEE (2016)
8. Verma, R., Das, A.: What's in a URL: fast feature extraction and malicious URL detection. In: Proceedings of the 3rd ACM on International Workshop on Security and Privacy Analytics, pp. 55–63. ACM (2017)
9. Vu, L., Nguyen, P., Turaga, D.: Firstfilter: a cost-sensitive approach to malicious URL detection in large-scale enterprise networks. IBM J. Res. Dev. **60**(4), 4:1–4:10 (2016)

Inter-family Communication in Hyperledger Sawtooth and Its Application to a Crypto-Asset Framework

Luke Owens, Benoit Razet$^{(\boxtimes)}$, W. Bryan Smith, and Theodore C. Tanner Jr.

PokitDok, Charleston, USA
{luke.owens,benoit.razet,bryan.smith,ted}@pokitdok.com

Abstract. Hyperledger Sawtooth is a general purpose blockchain project featuring pluggable consensus mechanisms and smart contracts that can be written in any general purpose programming language. We introduce a design pattern that enables communication between smart contracts for Hyperledger Sawtooth. The pattern is called Inter-Family Communication and we apply it to build a general crypto-asset framework where assets can be controlled by secondary smart contracts. The pattern is designed secure with formal models for Hyperledger Sawtooth and relevant concepts to the Inter-family Communication design pattern.

1 Introduction

Bitcoin [1] popularized the concepts of *cryptocurrency* and *blockchain* as a fundamental entity, planting the seed of *smart contracts* in the form of Bitcoin scripts [2]. There are a number of blockchain systems currently under development, in the vein of Ethereum [3], and most of them include both a cryptocurrency and smart contracts in different flavors.

The Hyperledger project [4] proposes a set of open-source Blockchain technologies for business applications, like Sawtooth [5], Fabric [6], and Iroha [7]. These platforms are designed to be general purpose to accommodate as many use cases as possible, putting forward and emphasizing different features[1]. None of them is built around a cryptocurrency. Nevertheless, many use cases of blockchain involve a form of asset/token transfer.

As a motivating example for this work, we are interested in developing a general crypto-asset framework. A crypto-asset framework allows a set of participants to manipulate an asset with transactions that are cryptographically secure. Examples of crypto-assets are certainly cryptocurrencies or cryptotokens, but could also be digital rights for music, reservations for restaurants, social governmental benefits, health benefits, *etc.* The simplest crypto-asset to consider is a cryptotoken, a system maintaining a set of accounts holding an amount of tokens, with the capability of transfering tokens from one account

---

[1] *e.g.* trusted executed environments, consensus mechanisms, public key infrastructure, certificate authorities, private channels, etc.

© Springer Nature Switzerland AG 2019
G. Fahrnberger et al. (Eds.): ICDCIT 2019, LNCS 11319, pp. 389–401, 2019.
https://doi.org/10.1007/978-3-030-05366-6_32

to another. It is possible to add a cryptotoken to a general purpose blockchain by developing the functionalities at the smart contract level. In contrast to Bitcoin and Ethereum, however, the immediate consequence with this design is that the cryptotoken smart contract is not granted any privileged role with respect to other smart contracts. This creates security and usability challenges. We address these challenges by introducing design patterns that provide (1) security to the cryptotoken within the ecosystem of other smart contracts deployed and (2) flexibility by enabling other smart contracts to control token transfers.

In this article we propose a solution to this problem for the permissioned blockchain Hyperledger Sawtooth [5]. Sawtooth is a general purpose blockchain with a global key-value store as the underlying ledger. The smart contracts are defined by rules performing get/set operations on the store, and they can be written in any programming language so long as it is able to interface with a Sawtooth validator to submit the get/set requests. There are currently SDKs available to program smart contracts in C++, Go, Java, Javascript, Python, and Rust. Both the global key-value store and language agnostic nature of Sawtooth are valuable features for smart contract developers. The security and correctness of smart contracts is challenging no matter which blockchain platform is used, but these Sawtooth features pose some additional challenges for developing smart contracts.

This article presents[2] a design pattern that enables smart contracts – operating in a global key-value store – to communicate with each other in a secure manner. We call this design pattern *Inter-Family Communication* and we show how to use it in a crypto-asset framework to implement a secure cryptotoken that is interoperable with other smart contracts. This is possible by leveraging several concepts inherent to Sawtooth that we will detail.

The remainder of this article is organized as follows. In Sect. 2 we provide a formal model describing a subset of Hyperledger Sawtooth. In Sect. 3 we develop the Inter-Family Communication design pattern. We illustrate the use of this design pattern in the crypto-asset framework with a general cryptotoken Sect. 4. Related works are presented in Sect. 5, and we conclude in Sect. 6.

2   A Model of Hyperledger Sawtooth

In this Section, we propose a formal model of a general purpose blockchain directly inspired by Hyperledger Sawtooth. The reader not familiar with Sawtooth may find the model interesting as it explains some of Sawtooth's core design. The reader more familiar with Sawtooth may find it relevant to conceptualize at a higher-level the capabilities of the system.

2.1   Formal Description of the Model

The formal description given below essentially describes a subset of the Hyperledger Sawtooth. It is the near minimal general purpose blockchain model required for the implementation of the design pattern presented in Sect. 4.

---

[2] Portions of this work is patent pending.

- The state of the blockchain is represented by a key-value store S, where a key is a sequence of 35 bytes (or 70 hexadecimal values), and a value is an arbitrarily long sequence of information. Let $\Sigma = \mathbb{B}^4$ be the set of 4 bit sequences (hexadecimal values), Σ^n be the set of n hexadecimal sequences, and Σ^* be the set of all finite sequences of hexadecimal values. Then,

$$S : K \rightarrow V, \quad \text{where} \quad K = \Sigma^{70} \text{ and } V = \Sigma^*.$$

We will refer to the keys of the key-value store as **addresses**; this will also avoid the confusion with public/private keys.
- To change the state of the blockchain, a user has to submit a **transaction**. A transaction is a function taking a state store and returning a new state store:

$$applyt : (T \times S) \rightarrow S, \quad \text{where } S = K \rightarrow V.$$

In practice, the transaction is defined as a pure function whose execution produces a sequence of gets and sets on S.
- The blockchain is **cryptographically secure** using public/private key pairs. In practice, a user owns a unique pair of public/private keys. He uses it to sign the transactions and includes the signature with its public key in the transaction:

$$T.pubkey, \quad T.signature.$$

The apply function is gated to verify the signature of the transaction with the pubkey and therefore certify that the owner of the public/private key pair is the originator of the transaction. This functionality can be coupled with an address design to map different addresses to different users and cryptographically secure the addresses. More specifically, when transactions only perform set/get operations on the store at addresses computed as

$$addr = hash(cst + T.pubkey)[0 : 70],$$

it is guaranteed that only the originator of transactions will be able to access and modify its corresponding address, hence the concept of **cryptographically secure address**. The $+$ operator is the string concatenation operation. The cst value in the equation is for a nonce or anything that is common and unique to a sequence of transactions.
- A **block** is a list of transactions, $B = T^*$. A block transforms a state into another state by applying successively the $applyt()$ function:

$$applyb : (B \times S) \rightarrow S$$
$$applyb([T_1, T_2, \ldots T_n], S) = applyt(T_n, \cdots applyt(T_2, applyt(T_1, S)) \cdots).$$

- Similarly, a list of blocks can be applied to a state to produce a new state. Such a list of blocks is called a blockchain, and we talk about **the** blockchain when a network of **validators** build and verify blocks, appending them in linear order in a chain. The uniqueness of the chain is guaranteed when validators follow a specific set of rules that enforce consensus over the blockchain.

– A **namespace** is a sequence of six hex that represents the prefix of every key address in the store. Precisely, for $k \in \Sigma^{70}$ a key in the store, we write $k = n+a$, where $n \in \Sigma^{6}$ is the namespace portion of the address and $a \in \Sigma^{64}$. Conceptually, the store S is partitioned into a set of namespaces. A key-value store S can be restricted to a set of keys in a namespace N with the following operation:

$$S|_N \; = \; \{(k, v) \in S \mid \exists a \in \Sigma^{64}, \; k = N + a\}.$$

This definition of restriction extends naturally to a set of namespaces.

– This namespace feature is an essential component of transaction families. A **transaction family** is simply a set of transactions, typically with related functionality. A transaction family can be viewed as a smart contract. Associated with each transaction family is a set of namespaces. For a given transaction family F, we let N_F denote the set of namespaces associated with F and N_T denote the set of namespaces associated with a transaction T. The set of namespaces associated with a transaction family are used to protect transactions from reading and writing outside the namespaces specified by their transaction family. Therefore, the $applyt()$ function above can be refined as $applyt'()$:

$$applyt'(T, S) = applyt(T, S|_{N_T}) \biguplus S|_{\overline{N_T}},$$

where $\overline{N_T}$ is the set of all other namespaces, and $\biguplus$ represents the disjoint union operator with the added side effect of throwing an exception if the sets are, in fact, not disjoint.[3] The function $applyb()$ is redefined accordingly.

The model presented above is an overview of Sawtooth and omits several design features[4]. Those features are not fundamental for the work presented in this article. We encourage the curious reader to look at the documentation of Sawtooth for further information.

2.2   Strict Isolation

In Sawtooth, smart contracts execute against a global state store. Without any restriction, any transaction family would be allowed to modify the content of the store used by another transaction family, which could create conflicts and raise security and correctness concerns. We introduce a first namespace restriction, called *strict isolation* that prevents such undesired behavior.

Definition 1 (Reserved Namespace, Strict Isolation)

– *A transaction family F has a **reserved** namespace N, if $N \in N_F$ and N is not a namespace for any other transaction family:*

$$N \in N_F \; \land \; \forall G \neq F, \; N \notin N_G.$$

---

[3] In Sawtooth 1.0, there is an onchain setting to list the namespaces for transaction families. The validator interprets these namespaces as write access control and does not limit the read access.

[4] Proof-of-Elapsed-Time, batch, input-output prefixes and nonce in transactions, state-delta events, dependencies, etc.

– F is **strictly isolated** if all its namespaces are reserved.

Throughout the rest of the paper, we mainly restrict our discussion to families with one reserved namespace, $|N_F| = 1.$[5] The main property we get by imposing strict isolation on a transaction family is that the behavior of the transaction family only depends on its own transactions.

Property 1. Let F be a transaction family that is strictly isolated and S a key-value store. Then, we have the following properties:

1. $\forall T \in F,\ applyt'(T,S)|_{\overline{N_F}} = S|_{\overline{N_F}}$
2. $\forall U \notin F,\ applyt'(U,S)|_{N_F} = S|_{N_F}$
3. $\forall T \in F,\ applyt'(T,S|_{N_F}) = applyt'(T,S)|_{N_F}$
4. For all $[T_1,\ldots,T_n]$ where $T_i \in F$ and $[U_1,\ldots,U_m]$ where $U_j \in \overline{F}$, and for all $[V_1,\cdots,V_{n+m}] \in ([T_1,\ldots,T_n] \odot [U_1,\ldots,U_m])$ where $\odot$ is the shuffle product[6] of two sequences, we have

$$applyb([T_1,\cdots,T_n],S)|_{N_F} = applyb([V_1,\cdots,V_{n+m}],S)|_{N_F} .$$

These properties can be proven directly using the definitions of $applyt'()$, $applytb()$, strict isolation, and by induction on the list of transactions.

2.3 Token Family Example

Assuming the model outlined in Sect. 2.1 with the separation of namespaces following Strict Isolation, we give an example of a Token Transaction Family that secures all token transactions on a blockchain network.

The Token Transaction Family is defined by a set of transactions for transferring tokens from one account to another. We implement these transactions in a Token Transaction Family, $\mathcal{T}$, with namespace $N_{\mathcal{T}} =$ hash(`token`)[0:6], referred to simply as the token namespace. Users on the blockchain will have an address in the token namespace where their token data is stored. Suppose that Alice has public key pubkeyA, then Alice's token data will be stored at a cryptograhically secure address of the form:

$$N_{\mathcal{T}} + \texttt{hash(`token-data' + pubkeyA)[0:64]},$$

with the token account data following the scheme:

```
TOKEN_ACCT = {
    'spendable_amount': 0,
    'approvals': {}, # Ex. {pubkey: {'amount': amt, 'release_time': rt}, ...}
}
```

---

[5] All results presented extend trivially to families with multiple reserved namespaces; however, focusing on a single namespace simplifies our presentation.

[6] For a definition of the Shuffle Product see any textbook on Automata Theory or Theory of Computation.

We implement handling basic token transfer functionalities motivated by the ERC-20 [8] standard. Namely, we implement

1. `transfer(to_pubkey, amount)`
2. `approve(to_pubkey, amount, release_time)`
3. `transfer_from(from_pubkey, to_pubkey, amount)`
4. `free_approvals()`

In summary, the transaction family designed as above with strict isolation and using cryptographically secure address design provides two levels of protection:

1. (*Namespace Protection*) The token transaction family is protected against an attack from any other transaction family.
2. (*User-address Protection*) The data associated with a user of the Token Transaction Family is protected against other users within the family.

In the remainder of this article, we propose to extend these ideas to provide more flexibility to cover more use cases, while maintaining the same type of protections.

3   Design Pattern for Inter-family Communication

First, we define the concept of *Relative Isolation*, a more flexible version of Strict Isolation. Second, we show how to secure individual addresses with the concept of a *Secure Communication Address*. Finally, we show how the two concepts together are used in a design pattern for *Inter-Family Communication*.

3.1   Relative Isolation

We use the namespace restriction feature of Sawtooth, in order to define the Relative Isolation principle.

Definition 2 (Refinement of Namespaces). *A family is defined with a set of read namespaces and write namespaces.[7] A namespace N is reserved for a transaction family F if (1) it belongs to its write namespaces and (2) no other family has N in its write namespaces.*

In the previous version of namespaces, it was impossible to give the transaction family G a read only access to the reserved namespace of F without giving also the write access. The refined namespace definition is essential to allow communication between two transaction families.

Definition 3 (Relative Isolation). *Let F and G be two families. We say that F **depends on** G when the following conditions are met:*

1. *F has a reserved namespace*
2. *F has read access on G's namespace*

It would be possible to define properties similar to Property 1 based on relative isolation, but we leave this as a future work. For the matter of this article the next coming patterns rely on relative isolation for security.

---

[7] The functions $applyt'()$ and $applyb()$ are straightforwardly updated according to different read and write namespaces.

3.2   Secure Communication Address

In this Section we work under the realistic assumption that the number of keys in the key-value store is much larger than the number of keys used in practice. Therefore we assume that the hash function used will not produce any collisions and that it is computationally hard to find collisions.

Let F and G be two transaction families that are in **co-relative isolation** (F depends on G and G depends on F). The transaction family F can communicate with G by identifying a specific address in F's reserved namespace that G has read access to. We call such an address a **communication address**. When the communication needs to be bidirectional, two communication addresses – one in each namespace – are required. It is important that F and G are co-relative to ensure that the addresses cannot be modified by other families.

Now let us leverage the cryptographic capabilities of the blockchain to multiple parties. If a communication address is computed from the pubkey keys of the parties involved, then the transaction families can guarantee that data written at this communication address is cryptographically secure. We extend the pattern of cryptographically secure address presented in Sect. 2.1 to multiparty.

Definition 4 (Multiparty Crypto Address). *Let F be a transaction family with a reserved namespace. An address is **cryptographically secure** for a set of public keys $\{pubkey_1, \cdots, pubkey_n\}$ if:*

- *The address is of the form:*
  $addr = N_F + hash(cst + pubkey_1 + \cdots + pubkey_n)[0 : 64]$
- *Any transaction T writing to addr is such that:*
  $T.pubkey \in \{pubkey_1, \cdots, pubkey_n\}$

Checking that a transaction family modifies only multiparty crypto addresses or global addresses for the family is tractable under the condition of (1) relative isolation of the transaction family, and (2) the addresses of key-value store that are accessed in the transaction are clearly identifiable.

Notice the *cst* part in the equation. This parameter can be a nonce to avoid replay attack during the execution of a smart contract. It is desirable that all the parties involved contribute to the creation of a nonce.

3.3   Inter-family Communication

In a smart contract environment, a desirable property is to have the capability for smart contracts to call other smart contracts. Ideally, this functionality should be as easy as having the ability to do a function call within another function in any programming language. Nevertheless, in a blockchain, the execution environment involves some form of cryptography, and it is challenging to pass along these cryptographic guarantees along smart contract calls without passing along more context. In Sawtooth, there is an additional challenge because the platform is language agnostic and transaction families can be written in different programming languages on the same blockchain deployment.

In the following example, we illustrate how the inter-family communication design pattern can be used to provide this general functionality while avoiding smart contract calls within other smart contracts. Assume that we have two smart contracts A and B, and the smart contract B calls the smart contract A within its execution body. Typically, the smart contract A is a payment transfer. This is shown in the left-hand side of the table below, where `contractB()` does some work before and after calling `contractA()` – this is indicated with `bodyA` and `bodyB` in the comments. We show on the right-hand side the pattern by splitting the smart contract B in two and using communication addresses.

```
def contractA(args):              def contractA(args):
    ... # bodyA                       addrB = make_addrB(T.pubkey)
                                      argsA = S.get(addrB)
                                      ... # bodyA
                                      addrA = make_addrA(T.pubkey)
                                      S.set(addrA, "Complete")


def contractB(args):              def contractB1(args):
    ... # bodyB1                       ... # bodyB1
    argsA = ...                       argsA = ...
    contractA(argsA)                  addrB = make_addrB(T.pubkey)
    ... # bodyB2                       S.set(addrB, argsA)


                                  def contractB2(args):
                                      addrA = make_addrA(T.pubkey)
                                      if S.get(addrA) == "Complete":
                                          ... # bodyB2
                                      else:
                                          raise InvalidTransaction
```

This example introduces two crypto addresses, namely `make_addrB(T.pubkey)` and `make_addrA(T.pubkey)`. Both addresses are secured by a single public key `T.pubkey`, the public key signing the transaction. These addresses are used for communicating information between smart contracts A and B. Notice that the addresses `addrA` and `addrB` are only used following the co-relative isolation principle where family A only performs `get` operations on B's namespace and conversely for family B. `addrA` is used to insure that `contractA()` executes before `contractB()`.

4   A Crypto-Asset Framework

We present an overview of a crypto-asset framework that relies on the inter-family communication design pattern presented above. A crypto-asset framework allows a set of participants to manipulate an asset with transactions that are cryptographically secure. Examples of crypto-assets are certainly cryptocurrencies or cryptotokens, but could also be digital rights for music, reservations for restaurants, social governmental benefits, health benefits, *etc.* In the rest of this Section we will use a token as an example of asset to illustrate the design of the crypto-asset framework.

4.1   Generic Token Transfer

We propose to extend the Token Transaction Family of Sect. 2.3 to allow secondary transactions to have an influence over a token transfer. We introduce a new type of token transfer called **generic token transfer**. Its design follows the inter-family design pattern where the Token Transaction Family and a secondary transaction family communicate through secure communication addresses.

A generic transfer is described as follows. Multiple users want to engage in monetary transfer where the distribution amounts are computed in some nontrivial manner by a secondary smart contract. The participants escrow a certain amount of tokens and delegate the final settlement to a well identified secondary smart contract. They do this by specifying a settlement address on the blockchain. This address can only be written to by the secondary smart contract that has both namespace and user-address protections (see Sect. 2.3). The workflow for performing a generic transfer uses the following transactions:

1. `init(nonce, amount, release_time, settle_addr, approved_joiners)`
   A user initiates a generic token transfer by escrowing a certain amount of tokens. The transfer is identified with a nonce parameter. The `settl_addr` argument is the address in the non-token namespace that will be used to settle the generic transfer. Other participants are allowed to join as indicated in the `approved_joiners` parameter, and `release_time` is the earliest time allowed to release a generic transfer.
2. `join(nonce, initer_pubkey, amount)`
   Allows another user to join a generic token transfer that was previously initialized. The nonce and `initer_pubkey` parameters are necessary to compute the address where the data for the generic transfer is stored.
3. `settle(nonce, initer_pubkey)`
   When the secondary transaction family has produced a settlement, anyone involved in the generic transfer is allowed to settle the total escrowed amount according to the data found in the `settle_addr`.
4. `add_release_sig(nonce, initer_pubkey, signature)`
   Any participant is allowed to add a signature of the nonce to eventually release the escrowed amount.
5. `release(nonce, initer_pubkey)`
   When all the participants involved have added their nonce signature, anyone is allowed to release the escrowed amount. Otherwise, if the blocktime is past the `release_time`, anyone is allowed to release the escrowed amount.

Notice that all the transactions have nonce[8] and `initer_pubkey` as first parameters – except for `init()` which uses the originator of the transaction as

---

[8] The nonce is used here to prevent replay attacks and is intended to be negotiated offchain among users, ideally by having all parties contribute to its elaboration.

`initer_pubkey`. These two fields determine the address where the data for a generic transfer is stored. The data onchain to safely track the progress of a generic transfer is the following json stored at a secure address made from the `nonce` and the `initer_pubkey`:

```
GENERIC_TRANSFER_DATA = {
    'nonce': None, 'amounts': {},   # {pubkey: amt, ...}
    'settle_addr': None, 'release_time': None,
    'approved_joiners': [],   # list of pubkeys
    'release_sigs': [],   # list of signatures
    'settle_amounts': {} } # {pubkey: amt, ...}
```

To keep track of the tokens engaged in generic transfer, we extend the `TOKEN_ACCT` with an additional field:

```
TOKEN_ACCT = {
    'spendable_amount': 0, 'approvals': {},
    'generic_transfers': {} } # Ex. {'nonce-initer_pubkey': amt, ...}
```

Figure 1 illustrates an example of generic transfer with a simple secondary smart contract. To specify thoroughly the valid sequences of transactions for generic transfers, we provide a state diagram in Fig. 2.

The generic transfer follows the design pattern because it is in relative isolation with secondary transaction families. It communicates through a secure address in its own namespace. The `settle_addr`, which is living in a secondary smart contract, is also intended to be secure.

4.2   Micropayment Channel and Other Applications

We have implemented a **micropayment channel** [9] functionality where two parties initiate a generic transfer with a settlement address controlled by a micropayment channel transaction family. The latter is able to receive bidirectional commit balances that are cryptographically signed. The channel is able to settle using timelocks guaranteeing fairness to parties involved, and the channel settlement is eventually `settled` in the `TOKEN_ACCT` data of the Token Transaction Family. As expected, our implementation provides transfer with low latency and high throughput by avoiding submitting the transactions on-chain.

Micropayment channel was our test case for the generic transfer, however, we envision many more applications of the generic token family and the inter-family communication pattern. Some of these include autoadjudication, crowdfunding, supply chain management, health care, identity, etc.

5   Related Works

This work is particularly relevant to the community of smart contracts developers on Hyperledger Sawtooth [5]. Sawtooth is general purpose, promulgates flexibility, and the set of good practices for its developers is still underway. This

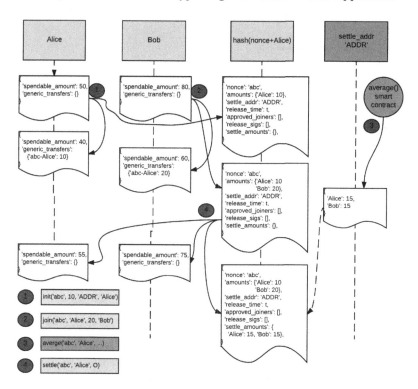

Fig. 1. Example of generic transfer. Each vertical line shows the content of the store, with yellow indicating the token namespace and blue the secondary namespace. The secondary smart contract computes the average of the amount escrowed and settled by splitting the funds in half. There are four transactions 1–4 indicated in the bottom left of the figure. The arrows demonstrate the flow of transactions. The dotted arrow represents read only access. In particular, the `settle()` transaction (4) of the token family reads the settlement at the `settle_addr`. (Color figure online)

work is a contribution to its community but may also provide insights to projects trying to solve the interoperability between different blockchains.

Our Inter-family Communication design pattern presented in Sect. 3 provides a way to call smart contracts within smart contracts. Ethereum also addresses this problem by providing a set of recommendations [10] (including the *Checks-Effects-Interactions* pattern) related to Solidity, to prevent unexpected funds retrievals by bypassing the cryptographically secure parameters.

We have presented this work with a formal development. There has been a lot of interest in formal verification with respect to blockchain technology [11,12] in particular since the DAO attack [13]. We envision developing further this aspect of the work and use formal verification tools [14–16] to verify the type of protection properties laid out in this article.

We have used our generic token transaction family and apply it to a micro-payment channel. We leave as future work the implementation of the off-chain

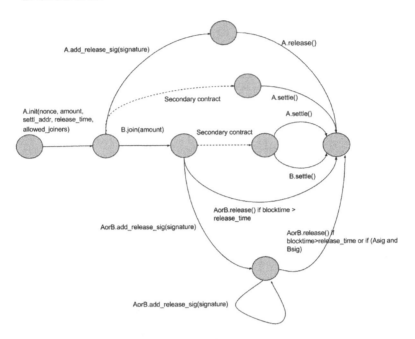

Fig. 2. Valid sequences of transactions for generic transfer. A complete path of generic transfer goes from the leftmost node (initiating a generic transfer) to the rightmost node (settling the transfer). From any state of this diagram, if a transaction is not indicated, it implies that it would raise an error during its execution. The transitions labelled "Secondary contract" in dashed line indicates it is an arbitrary sequence of transactions from the secondary smart contract.

part of the payment channel to use a trusted execution environment like SGX [17] and follow the approach developed in Teechan [18].

6   Conclusion

Sawtooth is a general purpose blockchain that can host smart contracts written in any general purpose programming language. Currently, there are SDK for developing smart contracts in C++, Go, Java, Javascript, Python, and Rust. This makes Sawtooth very flexible. Nevertheless Sawtooth does not come with a predefined mechanism allowing smart contracts to communicate with one another. In this article, we have introduced a design pattern – called Inter-Family Communication – that provides a design solution to enable smart contracts to communicate with one another, even in the case where the smart contracts are written in different programming languages. We have presented the desgin pattern with formal development that includes a model for Sawtooth with its address and namespace features. The protections operate both at the system level and at the user level.

We have demonstrated how to use the design pattern to define a general crypto-asset framework. The crypto-asset transactions are dependant upon secondary smart contracts, that can be arbitrary.

We believe this inter-family communication design pattern has many more applications and will be an essential building block to Sawtooth developers and more broadly to the Hyperledger community.

References

1. Nakamoto, S.: Bitcoin: a peer-to-peer electronic cash system (2008). http://bitcoin.org/bitcoin.pdf
2. Bitcoin Script. https://en.bitcoin.it/wiki/Script. Accessed Aug 2018
3. Wood, G.: Ethereum: A Secure Decentralized Generalised Transaction Ledger - EIP-150 Revision (2017). http://yellowpaper.io/
4. Hyperledger. Blockchain for Business. https://hyperledger.org/. Accessed Aug 2018
5. Hyperledger Sawtooth, v1.0 (2018). https://github.com/hyperledger/sawtooth-core. Accessed Aug 2018
6. Hyperledger Fabric, version 1.0. https://hyperledger.org/projects/fabric, https://github.com/hyperledger/fabric. Accessed Aug 2018
7. Hyperledger Iroha. http://iroha.tech/, https://github.com/hyperledger/iroha. Accessed Aug 2018
8. ERC20 Token Standard. https://theethereum.wiki/w/index.php/ERC20_Token_Standard. Accessed Nov 2017
9. Poon, J., Dryja, T.: The Bitcoin Lightning Network: Scalable Off-Chain Instant Payments, Version 0.5.9.2 (2016)
10. Ethereum. Security Considerations. https://solidity.readthedocs.io/en/develop/security-considerations.html. Accessed Aug 2018
11. Hildenbrandt, F.N., et al.: KEVM: A Complete Semantics of the Ethereum Virtual Machine (2017). http://hdl.handle.net/2142/97207
12. Hirai, Y.: Defining the Ethereum virtual machine for interactive theorem provers. In: 1st Workshop on Trusted Smart Contracts (2017)
13. Daian, P.: DAO attack (2016). http://hackingdistributed.com/2016/06/18/analysis-of-the-dao-exploit/. Accessed Aug 2018
14. The Coq Development Team: The Coq Reference Manual, version 8.6 (2017). https://coq.inria.fr/
15. Lamport, L.: Specifying Systems. Addison-Wesley (2002). http://www.lamport.org/. Accessed Nov 2017
16. Swamy, N., et al.: Dependent types and multi-monadic effects in F*. In: 43rd Annual ACM SIGPLAN-SIGACT Symposium on Principles of Programming Languages, POPL 2016, pp. 256–270. ACM (2016)
17. Intel: Intel Software Guard Extensions (Intel SGX) SDK (2018). https://software.intel.com/en-us/sgx-sdk
18. Lind, J., Eyal, I., Kelbert, F., Naor, O., Pietzuch, P.R., Sirer, E.G.: Teechain: scalable blockchain payments using trusted execution environments. In: The 4th Workshop on Bitcoin and Blockchain Research, BITCOIN 2017 (2017)

Attack Detection and Forensics Using Honeypot in IoT Environment

Rajesh Kumar Shrivastava$^{(\boxtimes)}$, Bazila Bashir, and Chittaranjan Hota

Birla Institute of Technology and Science-Pilani, Hyderabad Campus,
Hyderabad, India
{p20150005,2017h1030074,hota}@hyderabad.bits-pilani.ac.in

Abstract. The Internet of Things (IoT) is a collection of tiny devices deployed with sensors. IoT automates embedded devices and controls them over the Internet. Ubiquitous deployment of IoT introduces a vision for the next generation of the Internet where users, computing systems, and everyday objects possessing sensing and actuating capabilities cooperate with unprecedented convenience and economic benefits. Due to the increased usage of IoT devices, the IoT networks are vulnerable to various security attacks by remote login (like SSH and Telnet). This paper focuses on capturing the attacks on IoT devices using Cowrie honeypot. We employ various machine learning algorithms, namely, Naive Bayes, J48 decision tree, Random Forest and Support Vector Machine (SVM) to classify these attacks. This research classifies attacks into various categories such as malicious payload, SSH attack, XOR DDoS, Spying, Suspicious and clean. Feature selection is carried out using subset evaluation and best first search. Once features are selected, we use the proposed SVM model and evaluate its performance with baseline models like Random Forest, Naive Bayes, J48 decision tree. The trained model's fitness is evaluated on the basis of various metrics such as accuracy, sensitivity, precision, and F-score, where accuracy varies from 67.7% to 97.39%. This work exhibits the inclusion of machine learning module to classify attacks by analyzing the exhibit behavior. In the end, we discuss our observations of honeypot forensics over the commands executed by the attacker to execute malicious attack.

Keywords: Honeypot · Machine learning · Honeypot forensics
Behavior analysis

1 Introduction

The Internet of Things (IoT) is a collection of miniature devices which are equipped with various sensors to assist us in performing various day to day activities. IoT devices can be embedded devices attached to vehicles, home appliances etc. which enables these objects to connect and exchange data. Billions of IoT devices are already in use, and they are continuing to proliferate [11]. This may tempt an adversary mount a malicious attack by targeting IoT devices.

© Springer Nature Switzerland AG 2019
G. Fahrnberger et al. (Eds.): ICDCIT 2019, LNCS 11319, pp. 402–409, 2019.
https://doi.org/10.1007/978-3-030-05366-6_33

An adversary can change the default credentials of such devices and then using these devices can mount attacks on another system. Honeypot is a deception program, designed to identify an attacker's activity or behavior attempting to compromise the production systems [5]. A honeypot can serve as a surveillance tool and also capture an attack signature. The behavioral analysis of captured signatures provide useful insights into potential system loop-holes. Although honeypots can't secure IoT systems directly, they can be used to strengthen firewall and IDS (Intrusion Detection System) positioned at network periphery. A honeypot is able to capture new type of IP or attacks. There are various category of attacks using a remote server like Port scanning, DDoS attack, XOR-DDoS attack, brute-force attack, spying and mounting attack to different networks using a compromised server. However, an updated honeypot helps to capture these type of attack fingerprints. By analysing the system logs, analysts can categorise these attacks and strengthen or update the firewall rules [2]. In our deployment, we open two well-known remote login ports, SSH and Telnet. SSH protocol is mostly used for secure remote communications, but attackers can also use this protocol to mount an attack or upload malicious payload to victim machine. Cowrie honeypot stores all communicated sessions in log files. These log files provide fingerprint about the attackers and the commands used by them. The objective of this paper is to focus on capturing attacks and categorizing them into various types, which is also validated by the website www. virustotal.com. This research aims to strengthen firewall functionalities from the remote attack.

In this research, we apply various machine learning algorithms to classify attacks. Knowledge graph generated from Weka gives a comparison of all the approaches used in this research. We found that SVM (Support Vector Machine) and Random Forest give better accuracy and ROC curve. Honeypot forensics provide deep insights to understand, how an attack works? Analysis of the honeypot data is used to strengthen firewall rules.

The remainder of the paper is organized as follows. Related work on honeypot is presented in Sects. 2 and 3 lists the experimental results to support the solution and identify attacks. Section 4 gives post analysis i.e forensics report over captured data. Section 5 summarizes our result.

2   Related Work

Levine et al. [6] deployed Georgia Tech honeynet in Georgia Institute of Technology to identify rootkit attacks exploited by SSH. This honeypot was able to perform offline analysis and identified an attacker extracted the exploit code file within the r.tgz, a rootkit for SSH and then ran the exploit on the target system. Lin et al. [7] developed a honey-inspector to collect malware from malicious websites and perform behaviour analysis over collected data. Their research classify active and passive attacks. Gokul et al. [10] used Kippo honeypot to identify severe and not-so-severe attack. In his research they didn't clarify why attack in not-so-severe, and if attack is not-so-severe then what is the motive of attacker to break user id and password. Kippo is old generation honeypot which is easily identifiable by an attacker. If attacker sniffs and identifies the presence of honeypot then they immediately quit. Gokul et al. [10] identify this attack signature as not-so-severe. In our research we used Cowrie honeypot, which is a successor of Kippo and has additional features which look like a real system. Mushtakov et al. [8] implemented the Proxy server based honeypot which allows to log all activities on the proxy server. Main intention of their work is to analyze the log data and identification of patterns of attacks. Fraunholz et al. [4] deployed a honeypot to identify number of login attempts. They deployed a low interaction honeypot, which fails to collect attackers activities. But the author found a dependency between the number of login attempts and the protocol used. In the subsequent paper by Fraunholz et al. [3], authors investigated cyber crimes conducted by using weak passwords. In this work, we used honeypot data and try to identify successful attempts of login password with the help of machine learning algorithms. Paradise et al. [9] proposed a method to detect attacks on the social network user. The author created artificial profiles that were able to convince the attacker and appeared genuine for other users. Author claimed that more than 70% average acceptance rate when sending friend requests to members of the organization from the fake profiles. The fake profile received suspicious friend requests and emails. Brankovic et al. [1] proposed a feature selection and classification algorithm based on the randomized extraction of model populations. The author has evaluated and compared other well-known feature selection methods. An important feature of his method is the easy interoperability of the obtained models, which can be used to fine-tune the results and enhance the computational efficiency of the classification method.

3   Identification of Attacks

3.1   Pre-processing

A medium interaction honeypot Cowrie was installed in our Information security laboratory and we collected data for a period of 40 days, from 01/02/2018 to 12/03/2018. Cowrie captured all the interactions in the log files. In pre-processing phase, we classified attacks into six different categories, which helped us to prepare the database for supervised machine learning algorithms. To categorise attacks, message field is used, which contains commands executed by an attacker. The message field is analyzed by using virustotal.com and available literature, and resultant attacks were categorized into six different classes as follows:

1. Malicious: All the commands that tried to perform any malicious activity e.g., stealing server information, uploading payload etc. are kept in this class.
2. SSH attack: All the commands that tried to perform SSH-attacks were placed in this category.
3. XOR DDoS Attack: All the commands that tried to perform XOR DDoS attack were kept in this category.
4. Spying: All the commands that were checking if busy-box is there or not were placed in this category.

3.2 Feature Extraction

Feature extraction is an art to prune away dataset from irrelevant attribute or information and reduce the dimensionality of the dataset. The objective of feature extraction is to choose a subset of input variables by eliminating features, which are irrelevant or not helpful in producing useful information. Correctly chosen features effectively enhance learning efficiency, increasing predictive accuracy and reducing the complexity of learned results. The main goal of finding a feature subset from the dataset is to produce higher classification accuracy.

The attributes like geoip.ip and src_ip represent the same information. "message" and "input" provided the same information. Similarly, geoip.location contains both geoip.longitude and geoip.latitute. These kinds of attributes that are redundant were removed. Also, the attributes captured by Cowrie that were of our own machine like "host", "path", "sensor" were not considered for evaluation, because these attributes were same for all the instances. Feature selection is an important part of the analysis process. It reduces the dimensionality of the database and reduces search space. One of the most effective feature selection method "wrapper method" is used in pre-processing. Correct features create the correct predictive model. Wrapper method from Weka tool is a process that selects a minimal subset of features as a search problem. In wrapper method different combinations are prepared, evaluated and compared to other combinations.

3.3 Classification

10-fold cross-validation method was used for classification to improve the reliability of classifier evaluations. In this method, the database is randomly divided into 10 equal sized subsets. Here 90% of data are used as training set and the remaining 10% is used as testing set. The classifier is repeated for a total of 10 times to evaluate data. Each subset is used as a testing set once in each evaluation. The final evaluation is the averaging of the results of the 10 evaluations. Supervised machine learning algorithms are chosen to evaluate the performance of classification; the Table 1 contains results of machine learning algorithms. SVM is a binary linear classifier that outputs a hyperplane with a large margin between the positive and the negative samples. Multi-class SVM aims to assign labels to instances by using support vector machines, where the labels are drawn from a finite set of elements. The dominant approach for doing so is to reduce the single multi-class problem into multiple binary classification problems. Common methods for such reduction include building binary classifiers which distinguish (i) between one of the labels and the rest (one-versus-all) or (ii) between every pair of classes (one-versus-one). Classification of new instances for the one-versus-all case is done by a winner-takes-all strategy, in which the classifier with the highest output function assigns the class (it is important that the output functions be calibrated to produce comparable scores). For the one-versus-one approach, classification is done by a max-wins voting strategy, in which every classifier assigns the instance to one of the two classes, then the vote for the assigned class is

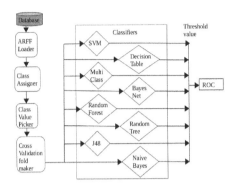

Fig. 1. Knowledge graph

Table 1. Result of classifier

Classifier	Accuracy	F1	ROC
SVM	97.39%	0.974	0.984
MultiClass	96.41%	0.964	0.978
Random Forest	94.29%	0.940	0.995
J48	92.33%	0.913	0.965
Decision Tree	87.92%	0.842	0.966
Bayes Net	86.62%	0.870	0.982
Naive Bayes	67.7%	0.686	0.868

increased by one vote, and finally, the class with the most votes determines the instance classification.

Sequential Minimal Optimization (SMO) computes the coefficients of the SVM algorithm. The Naive Bayesian classifier is based on Bayes theorem with the independence assumptions between features. Naive Bayes helps in predicting the probability of occurrence of all classes and chooses the one with the highest probability. J48 is a Java version of the popular decision tree algorithm C4.5. Random forests or random decision forests are an ensemble learning method for classification, regression and other tasks, that operate by constructing a multitude of decision trees at training time and outputting the class that is the mode of the class (classification) or mean prediction (regression) of the individual trees. Random decision forests correct decision trees habit of over-fitting to their training set. After performing supervised learning using SVM, Naive Bayes, Random Forest, Decision Tree, J48 etc., it was observed that maximum accuracy was obtained using Support Vector Machine with an accuracy of 97.39%. Thus, SVM is best suited for our problem.

3.4   Comparison Between Different Supervised Machine Learning Techniques

Sometimes percentage of accuracy is not a correct measure for classification because values of accuracy are highly dependent on the base rates of different classes. In that case, the Receiver Operating Characteristics (ROC) and F-Measure are used to evaluate the goodness of a classifier. Knowledge Flow tool in WEKA is used to compare different algorithms. The setup of the flow is shown in Fig. 1. "ARFF loader" is connected to "class assigner", which in turn is connected to class value picker using dataset. "CrossValidation" is connected to the supervised machine learning Algorithms using "training data" and "test data". It's result passes through Classifier Performance evaluator using batch classifier. The result is finally passed to "ModelPerformanceEvaluator" for visualization. Figure 2 shows, IP range of various category of attacks. Figure 3 shows the comparisons between different algorithms.

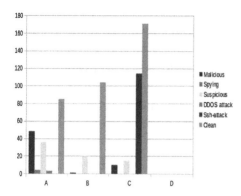

Fig. 2. IP class range wise attack

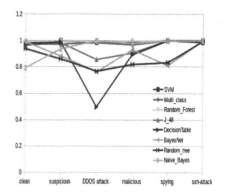

Fig. 3. Comparison between various ML methods

4   Honeypot Forensics

Forensics is one of the ways to confirm that the attackers tried to attack a system. There are two different ways to analyze attack commands, through offline and online means. Offline evaluation uses reverse engineering techniques, disassembly of binary etc. But obfuscations like cryptography, hashing, compression, randomization thwart forensics. Online forensics is done when binary is executed in the victim system. But in online forensics as infected binary contains malicious commands it can harm one's computer. The online evaluation must be done in controlled environment like docker, VM, jail-box etc. Forensics helps to identify following components when an attack takes place.

4.1   XOR DDoS Attack

```
$ wget http://xxxx.200.218.166/g33081
$ curl –O http://xxxx.200.218.166/g33081
$ chmod +x g33081
$ ./g33081
$ ls –la /var/run/gcc.pid
```

The attacker first selects the path where he/she wants to download the file. Using wget he or she downloads the file. The IP address in wget is the IP address of the source i.e., the attacker is downloading the XOR DDoS file from his or her own computer to the target computer. Once downloaded, he or she saves the XOR DDoS file with the same name as the one present in source. The attacker then changes the permissions of the file and executes it in the victim's machine.

4.2   Malicious Attack

```
$ scp −t /tmp/MvlFggnh
$ vcd /tmp && chmod +x MvlFggnh && bash −c ./MvlFggnh
$ ./MvlFggnh
```

The attacker copies the binary using secure copy and then he changes the permission of the file and executes it on the victim machine.

4.3   SSH Attack

```
$ sudo /bin/sh
$ mount ./gweerwe323f
$ echo −e '\x47\x72\x6f\x70/'⌴>⌴.nippon
$⌴cat⌴.nippon;⌴⌴⌴rm⌴−f⌴.nippon
$⌴echo⌴−e'\x47\x72\x6f\x70/proc'> /proc/.nippon
$ cat /proc/.nippon
$ rm −f /proc/.nippon
```

The attacker first mounts an attack and then checks whether a binary can be created and deleted in the victim's machine. If he or she succeeds then write malicious information in a binary file. After the successful execution he or she removes malicious file from the system.

4.4   Spying Attack

```
$ /bin/busybox echo −e \148\141\171\146\147\163
$ echo −e \148\141\171\146\147\163
$ /bin/busybox echii
```

These commands are used to check whether the device has a busybox or not. If busybox is not present, the attacker gets to know that he or she is not attacking an IoT device so he terminates the connection.

5   Conclusion and Future Work

Machine learning algorithm helps to classify remote attackers data. We also conclude that SVM is best classifier among all classifiers, it gives accuracy of 97.39%. By analyzing the commands it can be observed that the malicious commands are homogeneous as compared to clean commands which are heterogeneous. This is because clean commands include all the commands that can be executed on the Linux kernel, whereas a particular type of malicious command follows a particular pattern. Forensics study exactly identify how an attacker performs malicious activity on victim's system.

Acknowledgement. This work was supported by Department of Electronics and Information Technology (DeitY), Govt. of India and Netherlands Organization for Scientific research (NWO), Netherlands.

References

1. Brankovic, A., Falsone, A., Prandini, M., Piroddi, L.: A feature selection and classification algorithm based on randomized extraction of model populations. IEEE Trans. Cybern. **48**(4), 1151–1162 (2018)
2. Fan, W., Du, Z., Fernández, D., Villagrá, V.A.: Enabling an anatomic view to investigate honeypot systems: a survey. IEEE Syst. J. (2017)
3. Fraunholz, D., Krohmer, D., Anton, S.D., Schotten, H.D.: Investigation of cyber crime conducted by abusing weak or default passwords with a medium interaction honeypot. In: 2017 International Conference on Cyber Security And Protection Of Digital Services (Cyber Security), pp. 1–7. IEEE (2017)
4. Fraunholz, D., Zimmermann, M., Hafner, A., Schotten, H.D.: Data mining in long-term honeypot data. In: 2017 IEEE International Conference on Data Mining Workshops (ICDMW), pp. 649–656. IEEE (2017)
5. Kuman, S., Groš, S., Mikuc, M.: An experiment in using IMUNES and Conpot to emulate honeypot control networks. In: Information and Communication Technology, Electronics and Microelectronics (MIPRO), pp. 1262–1268. IEEE (2017)
6. Levine, J.G., Grizzard, J.B., Owen, H.L.: Using honeynets to protect large enterprise networks. IEEE Secur. Priv. **2**(6), 73–75 (2004)
7. Lin, Y.-D., Lee, C.-Y., Wu, Y.-S., Ho, P.-H., Wang, F.-Y., Tsai, Y.-L.: Active versus passive malware collection. Computer **47**(4), 59–65 (2014)
8. Mushtakov, R.E., Silnov, D.S., Tarakanov, O.V., Bukharov, V.A.: Investigation of modern attacks using proxy honeypot. In: 2018 IEEE Conference of Russian Young Researchers in Electrical and Electronic Engineering (EIConRus), pp. 86–89. IEEE (2018)
9. Paradise, A., et al.: Creation and management of social network honeypots for detecting targeted cyber attacks. IEEE Trans. Comput. Soc. Syst. **4**(3), 65–79 (2017)
10. Sadasivam, G.K., Hota, C., Anand, B.: Classification of SSH attacks using machine learning algorithms. In: 2016 6th International Conference on IT Convergence and Security (ICITCS), pp. 1–6. IEEE (2016)
11. Zanella, A., Bui, N., Castellani, A., Vangelista, L., Zorzi, M.: Internet of things for smart cities. IEEE Internet Things J. **1**(1), 22–32 (2014)

JSpongeGen: A Pseudo Random Generator for Low Resource Devices

Pranav Kumar Singh[✉], Anish V. Monsy, Rajan Garg, Sukanta Dey, and Sukumar Nandi

Department of Computer Science and Engineering, Indian Institute of Technology, Guwahati 781039, India
snghpranav@gmail.com, anishvmonsy2@gmail.com,
{rajan.garg,sukanta.dey,sukumar}@iitg.ac.in

Abstract. In this paper, we develop a new lightweight pseudorandom number generator (PRNG) scheme for low-cost Radio-frequency identification (RFID) tags named JSpongeGen. EPC Gen2 RFID tags are used worldwide and considered as international standards. However, these are the low resource devices and even unable to support symmetric key based cryptographic operation. Although various promising PRNG generation schemes for RFID tags have been proposed, developing a lightweight and secure scheme which also fulfills the randomness criteria is one of the open research problems. To this end, we propose JSpongeGen, a lightweight and secure mechanism that satisfies NIST randomness tests and also fulfills EPC Gen2 randomness criteria. Our proposed scheme is based on multiple polynomial dynamic feedback shift register in which we added a sponge function to update the contents of the shift register during the change of feedback polynomial. We show that our scheme outperforms one of the promising lightweight schemes in certain randomness metrics while remaining lightweight and secure solution.

1 Introduction

Random Number Generators are an integral part of most cryptographic systems. However, due to inherent periodic characteristics in the world, there are believed to only a few sources of true randomness in the universe. A usual method for generating random numbers in a computing system involves using deterministic algorithms with the resultant numbers satisfying the properties of a true random number generator (TRNG) to a reasonable extent based on certain metrics. These algorithms are referred to as pseudo-random number generators (PRNGs). PRNGs are mainly used to generate secret keys, nonces, and challenges in the cryptography to provide security.

The security of the Electronic Product Code (EPC) Gen2 low-cost RFID System [1] relies primarily on its 16-bit PRNG and password protected operations. The outgoing sequences can be predicted easily if weak PRNGs mechanism is used which may introduce security flaws in EPC Gen2 communications. Such

© Springer Nature Switzerland AG 2019
G. Fahrnberger et al. (Eds.): ICDCIT 2019, LNCS 11319, pp. 410–421, 2019.
https://doi.org/10.1007/978-3-030-05366-6_34

security flaw might allow the attacker to exploit the commands which are password protected in EPC Gen2 standard [2,3]. Since RFID tags are low resource devices, implementation of resource intensive and complex mechanisms are also not possible. Thus, the proposed PRNG schemes must be secure, lightweight and fulfill randomness criteria required for the security.

Although various PRNG designs have been proposed in the literature for EPC Gen2 tags, the details of a very few have been disclosed. The PRNG designs whose details are available in the literature are not that much secure and have been found vulnerable to attacks.

The main objective of our work is to develop a more secure 16-bit lightweight PRNG for low resource device, mainly for use in the RFID generated EPC Gen2 tags. Our work is inspired by [4,5] and we try to improve the security of their proposed model by adding more features. Also, to make the proposed PRNG scheme a lightweight, we try to lower the computation cost, which is measured in terms of gate equivalents (GE). Our model also uses a TRNG source like thermal noise to add true randomness.

The major contribution of our paper is two-fold:

- We propose a more secure PRNG for EPC Gen2 RFID tags using a lightweight sponge function, named JSponge that prevents the cryptanalysis.
- We implemented our proposal and the enhanced version of J3Gen proposed in [5]. We compared our scheme with the proposal one of [5] against NIST test suites and the EPC Gen2 randomness criteria to demonstrate the effectiveness of our proposed mechanism.

The rest of the paper is arranged as follows. Section 2 describes the related work. In Sect. 3, we discuss the PRNG designs of J3Gen and Proposal one. Section 4 presents our proposed PRNG design, JSpongeGen. In Sect. 5, we discuss the implementation of our design, and the comparative results obtained. We do the security analysis of our proposal in Sect. 6 and finally our work is concluded in Sect. 7.

2   Related Work

As it is shown in Fig. 1, there are two main approaches for random number generation. In the first approach, TRNGs are generated using the physical source such as the thermal noise of diodes. However, this method is not practical and bare a common drawback of the TRNGs. The other approaches are PRNGs, which uses some mathematical techniques such as Linear Feedback Shift Register (LFSR) and Congruential Generator (LCG) to generate the PRNGs inside the RFID tag artificially. However, we found very few good PRNG design proposals for low-resource RFID tags in the literature. In this section, we discuss those proposed PRNG mechanisms for low-cost RFID tags.

In 2007, Lee et al. [6] proposed the self-shrinking generator for RFID, which is an optimized version of the shrinking generator proposed in [7]. The proposed approach combines two clocked LFSRs in which an output sequence of the first

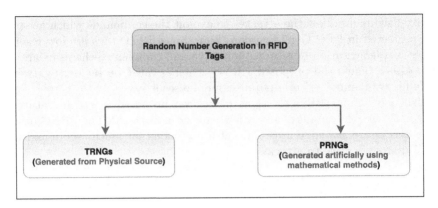

Fig. 1. Random number generation in RFID tags

LFSR discards some bits from the output sequence of the second LFSR. However, some of the techniques presented in [8] can be used to exploit the scheme.

In 2008, Che et al. [9] proposed another variant of the shrinking generator, which is based on TRNG (physical source: thermal noise) to handle the linearity of an underlying LFSR. However, in [10], the authors have shown that the scheme is vulnerable to attack and the PRNG configuration can be obtained with a confidence of 42 percent eavesdropping 128 bits of pseudorandom data only.

Some of the popular PRNG schemes proposed for low resource devices are Trivium (2005) [11], Grain (2007) [12], LAMED (2009) [13], and AKARI-X (2011) [14]. The manufacturers do not provide the design details of most of these schemes. There are very few PRNG designs whose details are present; however, various studies have raised concern related to their security claim.

J3Gen (2013) [2] and Warbler (2016) [15] are two other popular PRNGs for low resource devices. Although J3Gen fulfills the randomness criteria required by EPC Gen2 standard, the authors [16] questioned its security claims by performing two cryptanalytic attacks. These attacks are a probabilistic attack based on solving linear equation systems and a deterministic attack based on the decimation of the output sequence. In 2017, the authors of [17] claims that the Welch-Gong (WG) nonlinear feedback shift registers based schemes are vulnerable to linear attack, which is also a threat to the security of Warbler PRNGs that uses the same mechanism. In 2017, Nomaguchi et al. [18] proposed a new light-weight PRNG scheme which uses combination of NLFSR and DLFSR to achieve more efficiency and security than the existing approach. Authors have used larger key length and shown that their mechanism is resistant to existing attacks against Warbler and J3Gen.

In [5], an improvement was made on the approach of [4]. Two new proposals are made to solve the J3Gen security issues reported in [16]. One proposal involved replacing the final output logical AND gate with a logical XOR gate because the XOR operation provides less bias to the resultant bit value. The second proposal was inspired from a lightweight stream cipher called KATANTAN.

In this work, there are two LFSR units with their output bits being combined using an XOR gate. The output bit value of one LFSR is instead used for increasing internal randomness of the PRNG. For testing the pseudo-randomness, tests from the NIST testing suite and tests for checking EPC Gen2 criteria for randomness were used.

Our work is inspired from [5], and we have tried to further improve the security by introducing additional cryptographic complexity using lightweight Sponge function.

3 Background

In this section, we discuss the two PRNG schemes for EPC Gen2 RFID tags, J3Gen [2], and its improved version, proposal one of [5], which are closely related to our proposal.

3.1 J3Gen

Figure 2 shows the block diagram of the J3Gen. The J3Gen is inspired from a dynamic LFSR (DLFSR) based testing selection scheme of Hellebrand et al. [19]. It uses DLFSR of n cells. The four main components of the J3Gen are as follows:

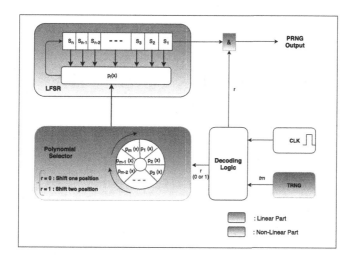

Fig. 2. Block diagram of J3Gen [2]

– **n-cell LFSR:** It produces good statistical values for pseudorandom sequences. Its hardware implementation is fast and efficient. Its computational requirements are also quite simple. Thus, it is well suited for the low resource or resource constrained environment (for both computational and energy constrained environments).

– **Thermal-Noise TRNG:** The J3Gen technique uses the oscillator-based high-frequency sampler proposed in [9]. The output generated by the TRNG is fed into the Decoding Logic, which in turn, helps in managing the Polynomial Selector.

– **Decoding Logic:** This module manages the internal PRNG clock of J3Gen. It activates and deactivates modules such as the LFSR or the TRNG for proper performance. For example, the sampling in the TRNG is activated only once for each PRNG output. It also manages the true random bit (trn) obtained from the TRNG and the corresponding output fed into Polynomial selector helps in rotating the polynomials.

– **Polynomial Selector:** This module of J3Gen helps in avoidance of the linearity. A set of m primitive feedback polynomials are used as a wheel, and each one of them is selected depending on the value of trn of TRNG.

3.2   Proposal One by Chen et al.

To develop a more secure 16-bit LFSR-based PRNG Chen et al. [5] proposed a modified version of J3Gen. The authors designed two proposals, proposal one and two. Since our work is an extension of proposal one, we provide the details of this proposal only. Figure 3 depicts the block diagram of the Proposal One. The modifications done in the J3Gen are as follows:

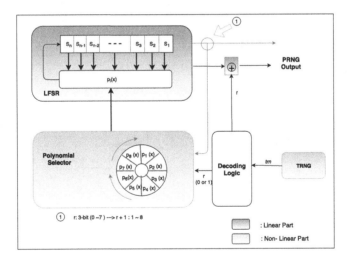

Fig. 3. Block diagram of proposal one by Chen et al. [5]

– **TRNG:** The authors used the same approach and used the oscillator-based high-frequency sampler by Che et al. [9]. However, the authors suggested that the system works even if TRNG has failed.

- **Feedback Polynomial:** In J3Gen, the feedback polynomials are implemented as wheels and rotates according to the r bits received from the decoder logic (shown in Fig. 2). However, in this mechanism, the selection of the multiple polynomials are more random. This approach makes it difficult for the adversary to predict the linear behavior of the random bit generation.
- **Output Computation:** The authors replaced the output AND computation of J3Gen with an XOR computation. Since XOR is perfectly balanced if $r = 1$, the output has less bias and it is independent of the seed bits value. Thus, enhances randomness property.

4 Proposed Method: JSpongeGen

In this section, we introduce our proposed mechanism JSpongeGen. The primary goal of our work is to propose a more secure PRNG than the J3Gen and the proposal of Chen et al. discussed in the previous section. To achieve that we increase cryptographic complexity by adding SPONGE function [20] in the model. Also, for a lightweight PRNG, we try to keep the computation resource cost (measured in terms of gate equivalents(GE)) as low as possible. Thus, the only additional component that we introduce is the SPONGE function. The TRNG in our proposed model is the same used in J3Gen, the oscillator-based high-frequency sampler proposed in [9] (Fig. 4).

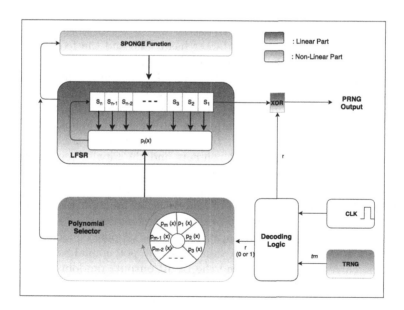

Fig. 4. Block diagram of our proposed method: JSpongeGen

The basic idea of the proposal is to make the key more strong and secure. In this model, the feedback polynomial used in the LFSR to generate the output is the key which is unknown to the attacker. The key strength should be at least 80 for low resource devices as found in previous works. In [2], the polynomial selector uses 16-degree polynomial functions which are primitive with a 16-bit LFSR and chooses eight random polynomial functions from the domain set. In [5], the domain set is increased for the 16-degree polynomial functions by including non-primitive polynomials, to increase the combinations. In our method, we propose to use polynomials of variable degree ranging from 12 to 16 and increase the domain set many folds. This increases the possible combination of 8 chosen polynomials exponentially making it more than 2^{80} which makes it difficult for an attacker to crack the polynomials.

As discussed in [2], an attacker requires $2n$ output bits to crack the polynomial and the LFSR state. So if one of the above is already known, then the attacker requires only n output bits to find the other by brute force. To avoid this, we use the polynomial function to generate only L bits at a time by running L iterations of LFSR using that polynomial. As given the n bits generated by the model, L bits of which are generated by one polynomial, there can be 2^{n-L+1} possible polynomials which can generate the remaining $n - L$ bits in the output. So the attacker can brute force to guess the polynomial function. So the computation of brute force is dependent on the value of L (as computation will be 2^{n-L+1}). We reduce the value of L to increase the uncertainty in cracking the feedback polynomial when the attacker has discovered n output bits. As the degree of the polynomial is variable which is n, thus, for a given n, we keep the value of L as $n/2$. We don't reduce the value of L further to prevent additional time complexity in changing polynomials.

As we discussed above, if the attacker has n bits and the feedback polynomial, then by brute force the state of the LFSR can be found. To prevent this, we change the contents of the LFSR after every L iterations of the model. While we change the polynomial function, we will also set a new value in the LFSR to include to prevent it from attacks. We use a sponge function, inspired from SPONGENT [21], every time we change the polynomial to reinitialize the contents in the shift register. As input to the sponge function, we use the 32-bit concatenation of the current LFSR contents and the bitwise representation of the coefficients of the previous polynomial.

In our sponge function, we use bitrate $r = 2$ and $c = 14$. We use a simple permutation function and simple 4-bit substitution function to transform the sponge state memory at each round of the sponge function.

Here, we present the working principle of the proposed model. The value in the LFSR is initialized to some value, and the polynomial selector chooses $p_1(x)$ as the current polynomial, and the LFSR outputs random bits using the bit output by LFSR XORed with the random bit coming from the true random source. After L iterations of the LFSR, the true random source generates another bit (0 or 1) based on which the polynomial wheel rotates by 1 or 2 respectively to choose the next polynomial and contents of LFSR are changed using the sponge function. Now the LFSR is set with the new value, and another L bits are generated using the LFSR output bit XORed with the true random bit.

5   Experiment and Results

In this section, we present implementation details, our experimental results, and a comparison of our schemes with the proposal one of [5]. Table 1 shows the details of our experiment. We used the Linear Feedback Shift Register implementation given in [22] as our reference.

Table 1. Implementation details

Parameter	Values
Operating system	Ubuntu 14.04 (64 Bit) Linux
Memory (RAM)	8 GB
CPU	Intel (R) Core (TM) i7-6700 CPU 3.40 GHz
Language	C
Compiler	gcc
Performance metrics	NIST randomness test (minimum set)
	EPC Gen2 randomness criteria
Schemes implemented	Our proposed scheme: JSpongeGen
	Proposal one of Che et al. [5]

We test the working of our proposed PRNG on a desktop personal computer to check if it satisfies the randomness requirements that are expected for a PRNG in an RFID application as per the following standards:

1. NIST Randomness Tests (Minimum Set)
2. EPC Gen2 Randomness criteria

5.1   NIST Randomness Test

For NIST randomness test, we use the Minimum Set of NIST SP800-22 [23] that consists of the following:

a. Frequency test
b. Block Frequency test
c. Linear Complexity Test
d. Rank Test
e. Cumulative Sums Test.

We took 20 million bits generated by the two generators, i.e., Proposal one and JSpongeGen and considered 100 binary streams of length 20000 each for input to the NIST test suite and compared the results. In the Table 2, the scores are given out of 100, which represents the correct proportion.

Table 2. NIST randomness tests score

Schemes/tests	Frequency	Block freq.	Linear compl.	Rank	Cumulative sums
Proposal one	99	99	99	100	98
JSpongeGen	100	100	96	100	100

5.2   EPC Gen2 Randomness Criteria

The EPC Gen2 randomness criteria [1] consists of the following.

a. **Criteria 1:** The probability that any single 16-bit number N drawn from the PRNG shall be bounded by the limits given below:
$1.22e - 5 < P(N) < 1.9e - 5$.
We generate 30 million random numbers using the PRNG to calculate Probability using the frequency definition of it. The results are shown in Table 3 and are for the numbers that appeared at least once.

b. **Criteria 2:** Probability of occurrence of same 16-bit sequence N in any two tags simultaneously shall be less than 0.1% for a population of up to ten thousand tags.
For testing this, 10000 instances of the PRNG are seeded randomly and then each of them generates 500 numbers. The probability is then calculated and listed in Table 4.

c. **Criteria 3:** The probability of finding next 16-bit random number generated by the tag shall be less than 0.025%, given all previous random numbers generated by PRNG are known to an adversary.
For satisfying this condition, we consider another metric distance correlation for comparing two PRNGs and present the results in Table 5 for the correlation scores of 10000 16-bit numbers generated by both the PRNGs.

Table 3. EPC Gen2 randomness criteria 1

Schemes/criteria	Min probability	Max probability
Proposal one	1.18 e-05	1.84 e-05
JSpongeGen	3.3 e-08	5.78 e-04

Table 4. EPC Gen2 randomness criteria 2

Schemes/criteria	Probability of simultaneous occurrence
Proposal one	7.62 e-06
JSpongeGen	1.85 e-01

Table 5. EPC Gen2 randomness criteria 3

Schemes/criteria	Correlation Score
Proposal one	3.99959
JSpongeGen	3.99953

6   Security Analysis

The security of a PRNG lies in the unpredictability of numbers generated in the future given numbers generated in the past. Given that the algorithm is known to the public, the hidden key in our algorithm is the exact combination of m feedback polynomials that are used in the polynomial selection phase.

For a simple PRNG which uses a single polynomial based LFSR of size n and period $2^n - 1$, Berlekamp-Massey algorithm [24] can be used to find out the polynomial with only $2n$ bits of output. This is based on the solution to the system of equations that can be formed due to the consistent use of one polynomial in the feedback phase of the LFSR.

However, for a dynamic feedback shift register based PRNG as in our case, the computational difficulty for an attacker in determining these polynomials depends on both the size of the set from which these polynomials are chosen as well as the polynomial update rate L.

In [5], they have considered taking polynomials other than primitive polynomials but of degree n = 16. We choose polynomials of degree 12 to 16 for increasing the size of the set of the polynomials that can be chosen and hence have a domain size of polynomials D given by:

$$D = (2^{15} - 1) + (2^{14} - 1) + (2^{13} - 1) + (2^{12} - 1) + (2^{11} - 1) = 63483$$

Choosing 8 polynomials from these can be done in $(63483C8)$ ways i.e. approximately $2^{120}/2^{16} = 2^{104}$, which is clearly greater than 2^{80}.

For RFID-based applications, a key strength of 80 has been found to be sufficient as mentioned in previous works [25] and [26]. Hence the key strength is adequate for the PRNG. We add more difficulties to the attacker's efforts by re-initializing the LFSR contents during every change in the feedback polynomial. Even if an attacker keeps track of output bits of the LFSR, it will be difficult to predict the new LFSR contents due to the use of a sponge function in the re-initialization stage.

7   Conclusion

We designed a new lightweight PRNG, named JSpongeGen, which is an extension of the existing design. We introduced additional cryptographic features called sponge function, and it is used to change the state of the LFSR. It is a lightweight solution to prevent the cryptanalysis in the case of the polynomial is known. We found through experiments that we do better than proposal one on specific randomness metrics of the NIST test suite, and also in some criteria of the EPC Gen2 standard. Our scheme gives comparable results. We hope that JSpongeGen PRNG may get adapted for low resource devices such as RFID tag-based applications.

Acknowledgments. The research work has been conducted in the Information Security Education and Awareness (ISEA) Lab of Indian Institute of Technology, Guwahati. The authors would like to acknowledge IIT Guwahati and ISEA MeitY, India for the support.

References

1. Global, E.: EPC radio-frequency identity protocols class-1 generation-2 UHF RFID protocol for communications at 860 MHz–960 MHz. Version **1**, 23 (2008)
2. Melià-Seguí, J., Garcia-Alfaro, J., Herrera-Joancomartí, J.: J3Gen: a PRNG for low-cost passive RFID. Sensors **13**(3), 3816–3830 (2013)
3. Garcia, F.D., et al.: Dismantling MIFARE classic. In: Jajodia, S., Lopez, J. (eds.) ESORICS 2008. LNCS, vol. 5283, pp. 97–114. Springer, Heidelberg (2008). https://doi.org/10.1007/978-3-540-88313-5_7
4. Melia-Segui, J., Garcia-Alfaro, J., Herrera-Joancomartí, J.: Multiple-polynomial LFSR based pseudorandom number generator for EPC Gen2 RFID tags. In: IECON 2011–37th Annual Conference on IEEE Industrial Electronics Society, pp. 3820–3825. IEEE (2011)
5. Chen, J., Miyaj, A., Sato, H., Su, C.: Improved lightweight pseudo-random number generators for the low-cost RFID tags. In: 2015 IEEE Trustcom/BigDataSE/ISPA, vol. 1, pp. 17–24. IEEE (2015)
6. Lee, H., Hong, D.: The tag authentication scheme using self-shrinking generator on RFID system. Trans. Eng. Comput. Technol. **18**, 52–57 (2006)
7. Coppersmith, D., Krawczyk, H., Mansour, Y.: The shrinking generator. In: Stinson, D.R. (ed.) CRYPTO 1993. LNCS, vol. 773, pp. 22–39. Springer, Heidelberg (1994). https://doi.org/10.1007/3-540-48329-2_3
8. Meier, W., Staffelbach, O.: The self-shrinking generator. In: Blahut, R.E., Costello, D.J., Maurer, U., Mittelholzer, T. (eds.) Communications and Cryptography, pp. 287–295. Springer, Heidelberg (1994). https://doi.org/10.1007/978-1-4615-2694-0_28
9. Che, W., Deng, H., Tan, W., Wang, J.: A random number generator for application in RFID tags. In: Cole, P., Ranasinghe, D. (eds.) Networked RFID Systems and Lightweight Cryptography, pp. 279–287. Springer, Heidelberg (2008). https://doi.org/10.1007/978-3-540-71641-9_16
10. Melià-Seguí, J., Garcia-Alfaro, J., Herrera-Joancomartí, J.: A practical implementation attack on weak pseudorandom number generator designs for EPC Gen2 tags. Wireless Pers. Commun. **59**(1), 27–42 (2011)
11. De Cannière, C.: TRIVIUM: a stream cipher construction inspired by block cipher design principles. In: Katsikas, S.K., López, J., Backes, M., Gritzalis, S., Preneel, B. (eds.) ISC 2006. LNCS, vol. 4176, pp. 171–186. Springer, Heidelberg (2006). https://doi.org/10.1007/11836810_13
12. Hell, M., Johansson, T., Meier, W.: Grain: a stream cipher for constrained environments. Int. J. Wireless Mobile Comput. **2**(1), 86–93 (2007)
13. Peris-Lopez, P., Hernandez-Castro, J.C., Estevez-Tapiador, J.M., Ribagorda, A.: LAMEDa PRNG for EPC class-1 generation-2 RFID specification. Comput. Stand. Interfaces **31**(1), 88–97 (2009)

14. Martin, H., San Millán, E., Entrena, L., Lopez, P.P., Castro, J.C.H.: Akari-X: a pseudorandom number generator for secure lightweight systems (2011)
15. Mandal, K., Fan, X., Gong, G.: Design and implementation of Warbler family of lightweight pseudorandom number generators for smart devices. ACM Trans. Embed. Comput. Syst. (TECS) **15**(1), 1 (2016)
16. Peinado, A., Munilla, J., Fúster-Sabater, A.: EPCGen2 pseudorandom number generators: analysis of J3Gen. Sensors **14**(4), 6500–6515 (2014)
17. Joseph, M., Sekar, G., Balasubramanian, R.: Distinguishing attacks on (ultra-)lightweight WG ciphers. In: Bogdanov, A. (ed.) LightSec 2016. LNCS, vol. 10098, pp. 45–59. Springer, Cham (2017). https://doi.org/10.1007/978-3-319-55714-4_4
18. Nomaguchi, H., Miyaji, A., Su, C.: Evaluation and improvement of pseudo-random number generator for EPC Gen2. In: Trustcom/BigDataSE/ICESS, pp. 721–728. IEEE (2017)
19. Hellebrand, S., Rajski, J., Tarnick, S., Venkataraman, S., Courtois, B.: Built-in test for circuits with scan based on reseeding of multiple-polynomial linear feedback shift registers. IEEE Trans. Comput. **44**(2), 223–233 (1995)
20. Bertoni, G., Daemen, J., Peeters, M., Van Assche, G.: Sponge functions. In: ECRYPT Hash Workshop, vol. 2007. Citeseer (2007)
21. Bogdanov, A., Knežević, M., Leander, G., Toz, D., Varıcı, K., Verbauwhede, I.: SPONGENT: a lightweight hash function. In: Preneel, B., Takagi, T. (eds.) CHES 2011. LNCS, vol. 6917, pp. 312–325. Springer, Heidelberg (2011). https://doi.org/10.1007/978-3-642-23951-9_21
22. Schneier, B.: Applied Cryptography: Protocols, Algorithms, and Source Code in C. Wiley, Hoboken (2007)
23. Bassham III, L.E., et al.: SP 800-22 rev. 1a. a statistical test suite for random and pseudorandom number generators for cryptographic applications (2010)
24. Massey, J.: Shift-register synthesis and BCH decoding. IEEE Trans. Inf. Theory **15**(1), 122–127 (1969)
25. Paar, C., Poschmann, A., Robshaw, M.: New designs in lightweight symmetric encryption. In: Kitsos, P., Zhang, Y. (eds.) RFID Security, pp. 349–371. Springer, Heidelberg (2008). https://doi.org/10.1007/978-0-387-76481-8_14
26. Bogdanov, A., et al.: PRESENT: an ultra-lightweight block cipher. In: Paillier, P., Verbauwhede, I. (eds.) CHES 2007. LNCS, vol. 4727, pp. 450–466. Springer, Heidelberg (2007). https://doi.org/10.1007/978-3-540-74735-2_31

Elliptic Curve Cryptography Based Mechanism for Secure Wi-Fi Connectivity

Pranav Kumar Singh$^{(\boxtimes)}$, Prateek Vij, Arpan Vyas, Sunit Kumar Nandi, and Sukumar Nandi

Department of Computer Science and Engineering, Indian Institute of Technology, Guwahati 781039, India
snghpranav@gmail.com, prateekvij55@gmail.com, {v.arpan,sukumar}@iitg.ac.in, sunitnandi834@gmail.com

Abstract. The connection establishment and client handover mechanism for Wi-Fi Protected Access (WPA/WPA2) Pre-Shared Key (PSK) networks described by the IEEE 802.11 standard are vulnerable to various attacks. The existing security protocols WPA/WPA2 use symmetric key cryptography to provide confidentiality and data authenticity. An attacker listening to the channel can eavesdrop on the four-way key handshaking and can also derive the encryption key. The well-known attacks are key recovery, man-in-middle, Hole 196, and de-authentication attack. Another key problem with the PSK mode is that all stations use the same key for authentication. In this paper, we propose an alternative to the existing mechanism for authentication and re-authentication during connection establishment and client handover, respectively that use Elliptic Curve Cryptography, a public key encryption technique. Our proposed mechanism uses a lesser number of frames during (re)-authentication and is immune to the existing vulnerabilities of WPA2 PSK.

1 Introduction

Wireless Local Area Networks (WLANs) have witnessed tremendous growth in the past two decades. With the recent growth in the number of mobile gadgets, more and more public places, homes and offices are now installed with WiFi networks to provide internet connectivity. Newer technologies, such as the Internet of Things (IoT) [1] and Intelligent Transport Service (ITS) [2] are also stressing the need for faster and secure wireless networks.

Despite the ever-growing demand, WLANs suffer from many challenges. The first significant issue is its coverage. Due to shorter coverage, it is not well suited for highly mobile users such as vehicles. The second issue is the transmission over the air is much more prone to errors and interferences, that in turn leads to retransmissions and further delays. These pose a problem, especially for real-time services such as Voice-over-IP. The excess time delay during Access Point (AP) switching or connection re-establishment can cause interruption for real-time services.

© Springer Nature Switzerland AG 2019
G. Fahrnberger et al. (Eds.): ICDCIT 2019, LNCS 11319, pp. 422–439, 2019.
https://doi.org/10.1007/978-3-030-05366-6_35

The third major issue is security. Since the communication medium is accessible to anyone, anyone can eavesdrop upon or modify the exchanged messages. WPA and WPA2 are the current security protocols for WLANs that provide confidentiality and data authenticity. Though being secure from any outside attacker, the protocols are vulnerable to malicious insiders that are authorized (MAC address is not blacklisted) to access the network. WPA/WPA2 Personal networks with shared PSK are vulnerable to Key recovery attack from anyone with authority to access the network. The existing vulnerabilities in WPA/WPA2 networks such as Hole 196 [3] can be exploited for attacking the network. Stealth Man-in-the-middle(SMitM) [4] attack and Advanced SMitM [5] attacks are examples of such attacks that exploit Hole 196 vulnerability.

Existing security protocols only use symmetric key encryption techniques for providing data confidentiality service. The alternate to symmetric key cryptography is Public Key Cryptography (PKC) or asymmetric key cryptography. These techniques are based on a pair of keys - a public key and a private key, and can also be used to provide this service. Since these techniques are computationally heavy, standalone usage of PKC for providing these services is infeasible. However, PKC can be used in combination with symmetric key encryption to improve both the security and speed of the communication protocol. Since many application of WLANs such as IoT involves resource constraint device, we need to consider the most computationally efficient approach.

The idea of using PKC for better security of WPA/WPA2 networks has already been proposed in many works. Lauter et al. [6] showed the advantage of using Elliptic Curve Cryptography (ECC) [7] over other PKC techniques such as RSA, especially for resource constraint devices. Namal et al. [8] proposed an approach, Host Identity Protocol (HIP)-WPA, for fast initial authentication (FIA) of hosts using ECC. This approach is a combination of HIP Diet EXchange (HIP-DEX) with some features of WPA technology. They tried to minimize the handover delay in intra basic service set (BSS) transition by reducing the number of frames in (re)authentication. However, Authors, also pointed out that some security considerations must be reviewed.

Noh et al. [9] proposed the use of a secondary key for Wi-Fi networks that use a pass-phrase for authentication. The secondary key was transmitted to the AP confidentially using PKC and was used for PMK generation. They [10] extended this idea to design a more secure 4-way handshake mechanism for establishing the Pairwise Transient Key (PTK) using ECC. The paper also showed how the approach is immune to some existing vulnerabilities in the WPA2 protocol.

In this paper, we propose an alternative to the traditional connection establishment and client handover mechanism in WPA/WPA2 networks based on PSK. Our approach is inspired by [10] and involve the use of ECC. In their mechanism, the PSK is generated only from the secondary key only. However, in our case, the PMK is made from both session key (SK) and pass-phrase which is different for each session to avoid some common attacks. Thus, SK acts kind of like salt added to the PSK (or passphrase) in our case rather than being just the Pairwise Master Key (PMK) generator. In their mechanism, they could not reduce the number of frames exchanged during the key handshake, which is four. Our proposed mechanism makes it three-way handshake during authentication as well re-authentication. This leads to minimizing the delay in initial connection establishment and during handover. Thus, our proposed approach is efficient in terms of the number of exchanged frames and also secure against attacks.

The paper is arranged as follows: Sect. 2 provides background information about WPA/WPA2, authentication, and the 4-way handshake. Section 3 provides details about the existing vulnerabilities in wireless security protocols. Section 4 introduces Public Key Cryptography, provides details about ECC and compares it with other techniques. In Sect. 5, we discuss our proposed approach for connection establishment and client handover. In Sect. 6, we present the performance comparison and finally conclude our paper in Sect. 7.

The description of various keys used in the paper are given in the Table 1 [11] for better readability.

2   Background

In this section, we discuss security frameworks, connection establishment procedure and handover mechanism in Wi-Fi.

2.1   WPA/WPA2

Introduced in IEEE 802.11i [12] draft, WPA, and WPA2 are security protocols for wireless communication. The draft was introduced to provide a solution to the security hole in the WEP protocol. These protocols provide confidentiality and authentication techniques for secure communication between a client station (STA) and Access Point (AP). For confidentiality and data authenticity, WPA uses Temporal Key Integrity Protocol (TKIP) based on per-packet RC4 keys, and WPA2 uses AES-CCMP (CTR mode with CBC-MAC Protocol), a more secure cipher suite. WPA or WPA2 protocol can be classified as WPA (or WPA2)-Personal and WPA (or WPA2)-Enterprise depending upon the mode of authentication. The former uses a Pre-shared Key (PSK) for authentication with the AP and doesn't require any authentication server. The latter needs an authenticator AP and a RADIUS authentication server [13], and use Extensible Authentication Protocol (802.1X/EAP) [14] based authentication mechanism.

2.2   Connection Establishment

The process of establishing a connection between AP and STA can be expressed in 3 steps:

1. Discovery
2. Authentication and Association
3. PMK generation
4. 4-way Handshake

Table 1. List of keys and their details

Abbr.	Full form	Description
PSK	Pre-Shared Key	PSK is the shared secret between the AP and the authorized STA. PSK is a 256-bit shared key, that can either be a 64 digit Hexadecimal string or can be generated from an ASCII passphrase (password) of length 8 to 63. In case of ASCII passphrase, PSK is derived by applying PBKDF2-SHA1 hash on the passphrase
PMK	Pairwise Master Key	PSK is used to generate another key referred to as PMK. In WPA(WPA2)-PSK network, the PSK is used as the PMK itself. In WPA2 Enterprise network, different authentication methods generate PMK differently
SK	Session Key	In our proposed approach, we generate an additional key called SK, which is used in combination with PSK for generating PMK
PTK	Pairwise Transient Key	The key used for encrypting (and decrypting) unicast traffic between STA and the AP. PTK is derived during the 4-way handshake. PTK, after generation, is split into 128-bit Key Confirmation Key (KCK), 128-bit Key Encryption Key and (KEK) and 256-bit Temporal Key (TK)
KCK	Key Confirmation Key	KCK is used for computing MIC of the exchanged EAPOL frames in the handshake
KEK	Key Encryption Key	KEK is used for encrypting (and decrypting) Key Data field of EAPOL frames (exchanged during 4-way handshake)
TK	Temporal Key	TK is used for encryption (and decryption) of Unicast data frames between AP and STA
GTK	Group Temporal Key	Used for encrypting (and decrypting) multicast and broadcast traffic from AP

The connection establishment process in WPA2/PSK mode is shown in Fig. 1 and are explained as follows.

Discovery

The STA first discover the AP for the initial association as well as association during handover. There are two ways in which the discovery of the target AP is performed: Passive Scanning and Active Scanning. In passive mode, the STA listens to the beacon frames periodically broadcasted by the AP. Beacon frame includes important information such as operating channel, data rate, Service Set Identifier (SSID), timestamp, etc. In Active scanning, the STA probes all the channels by sending a Probe request. The APs that receive the Probe request send Probe response frame to the STA. The Probe request is similar to beacons

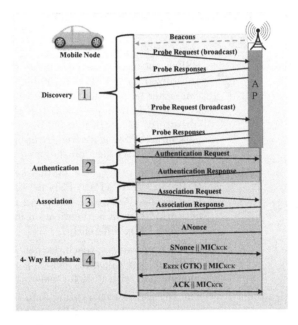

Fig. 1. Traditional way of connection establishment in WPA2/PSK [15]

and contains all the fundamental information about the network. Once beacons or Probe responses are received the STA selects the best suited AP for association based on some of the criteria such as RSSI.

Authentication and Association

After selecting the target AP, the next step is authentication. The initial authentication process is Open System Authentication, and any client can authenticate. This process involves an authentication request from STA to AP, followed by authentication response from AP to STA. Association then follows the authentication process. For association, the client sends an association request. The name of the desired cipher suite, which the STA would like to use for communication, is included in the request. The AP then respond with an association response if it was successful or not.

PMK Generation

After association, both STA and the AP generate the Pairwise Master Key (PMK). The PMK is generated using PSK (WPA/WAP2 Personal) or 802.1X EAP exchange (WPA/WPA2 Enterprise). PSK is itself used as PMK in the former case.

PSK is a 256-bit shared key, that can either be a 64 digit Hexadecimal string or can be generated from an ASCII passphrase (password) of length 8 to 63. In the case of ASCII passphrase, PSK is derived by applying PBKDF2-SHA1 hash on the passphrase.

In 802.1X EAP (WPA/WPA2 Enterprise) PMK is derived from the EAP parameters provided by the authentication server. The EAP framework, used in WPA2 Enterprise network, include many different authentication methods, such as PEAP, EAP-TLS, EAP-TTLS. This involves the use of a RADIUS server, and each method has its mechanism for generating the PMK. In PSK 802.1X/EAP authentication phase is not used.

4-Way Handshake

The final step is the 4-way handshake. The purpose of the 4-way handshake is to generate the Pairwise Transient Key (PTK) for Unicast communication between STA and AP, without any actual exchange of keys. The PTK is formed by concatenating PMK, Nonce from AP (ANonce), Nonce from STA (SNonce), AP MAC address and STA MAC address. The generated PTK is split into 128-bit Key Confirmation Key (KCK), 128-bit Key Encryption Key and 256-bit Temporal Key (TK). KCK is used for computing MIC of the exchanged EAPOL frames in the handshake, KEK is used for encrypting Key Data field of EAPOL frame, and TK is used for encryption of Unicast data frames between AP and STA.

The handshake happens in 4 steps as mentioned below. The handshake mechanism is shown in Fig. 1.

1. The AP sends ANonce to the STA. The STA can now construct the PTK, with its SNonce and the received ANonce.
2. The STA sends SNonce to the AP with a Message Integrity Code (MIC), computed via KCK. The AP can construct the PTK after receiving the frame and can authenticate the frame origin from the MIC.
3. The AP encrypts the GTK using KEK and sends it to AP along with computed frame MIC. The STA installs the PTK and GTK on receiving this message.
4. The STA sends the acknowledgment to the AP. AP installs PTK on receiving this frame.

2.3   Client Handover

If the client STA is mobile and switches from one AP to another, it needs to authenticate and associate with the new AP. The steps involved in this process are identical to the ones used for connection establishment: authentication, association or re-association, 802.1X authentication if required, and the 4-way handshake. IEEE 802.11r [16] introduced Fast BSS Transition (FT) Handshake to reduce the handover time between different APs of the same network. The FT handshake introduced two modifications in the traditional process. First, it uses the same PMK as established in the previous connection and thus, 802.1X authentication was not required every time a client switch AP. Second, rather than using 4-way handshake for establishing PTK after association, it piggybacks the Nonce values on the authentication and association messages itself. Thus, the PTK could be established just after association, taking away the need for the 4-way handshake. The FT handshake is shown in the Fig. 2.

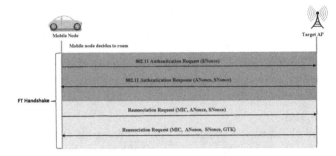

Fig. 2. IEEE 802.11r fast BSS transition (Over-the-Air) in WPA2/PSK [16]

The major challenge faced by 802.11r is backward compatibility. Many of the client devices do not have drivers that support IEEE 802.11r protocol [17]. The drivers fail to interpret the FT information element in the beacon frame and consider those frames as corrupted. Hence, 802.11r and the FT handshake is not yet popular, and most of the client handovers follow the traditional method.

3   Vulnerabilities of Existing WPA2/PSK

Though WPA/WPA2 is designed to ensure security from attackers outside the network, they are vulnerable to attacks from any malicious authorized user. These networks are susceptible to various attacks due to the openness of the medium [3,18]. Some of the existing popular attacks are as follows:

3.1   Key Recovery

In a WPA(WPA2)-PSK network, every authorized user share the same PSK, and hence PMK, which they use for authentication. Consider the case where one of the users is malicious and start eavesdropping on the network. When a new STA (victim, in this case) tries to connect to the AP, the attacker can recover the SNonce and Anonce by eavesdropping and generate PTK. The attacker can now decrypt and forge unicast packets between the victim and AP, without the knowledge of the victim or AP. Thus, it is important to ensure only trusted users possess the PSK. The attack is especially catastrophic for public Wi-Fi networks, where potentially any user can connect to the network and eavesdrop to attack other clients.

3.2   Hole 196

This vulnerability [19] allows malicious insiders to inject spoofed broadcast and multicast frames. These frames are encrypted with GTK in the WPA2/PSK enabled Wi-Fi networks. WPA/WPA2 use PTK for unicast and GTK for encrypting multicast and broadcast packets. The AP possess the GTK and is shared with every authorized user during 4-way handshake. As per 802.11 standards, only AP is authorized to send Multi/Broadcast packets encrypted with GTK. If the network has a malicious insider, it can spoof as AP and inject such packets after encrypting with GTK. The attacker needs to poison the ARP tables of the connected users to exploit this vulnerability.

3.3   Man-in-the-Middle

Advanced Stealth Man-in-The-Middle (ASMiTM) [5], Stealth Man-in-The-Middle (SMiTM) [20], and Wireless Denial of Service (WDoS) attacks occur due to the Hole 196 vulnerability. In these type of MiTM attack, an attacker usually performs Address Resolution Protocol (ARP) spoofing to intercept the client's traffic. An attacker tries to obtain PTK from the traffic by forcing target STA to perform 4-way handshake again. It analyzes the messages exchanged between STA and AP and obtains ANonce and SNonce. Using these parameters, an attacker can derive the PTK.

4   Public Key Crytography

Public Key Cryptography or Asymmetric Key Cryptography involves a pair of keys, one which is public to the network and other private with an entity. This provides two crucial security services, encryption, and authentication. Unlike the symmetric key cryptography, there is no need for a secure channel to transfer the keys. The figure of merit for this infrastructure is the work-factor, i.e., the computational work required to find the private key from the corresponding public key. The public key infrastructures are generally based upon problems having no efficient solutions like integer factorization, elliptic curve, and discrete logarithm.

Encryption
The public key of the recipient is used to encrypt the message to provide the secrecy. This means that anyone with the public key of the recipient can encrypt a message. Since only the recipient is in possession of the private key, this grants it the sole access to the plaintext message after decryption. Now the primary concern of the recipient is secrecy of their private key. Figure 3, shows the encryption process in PKC.

Authentication
Authentication or signing ensures that the message is sent by the entity claiming to send it. For this purpose, the sender signs the message by their private key, which serves as a digital signature. Since message was encrypted by the private key of sender, only sender could have created that message. This process ensures message is authenticated in terms of source and data integrity. Figure 4, shows the authentication process in PKC.

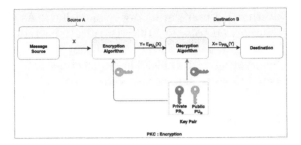

Fig. 3. Public key cryptography: encryption [21]

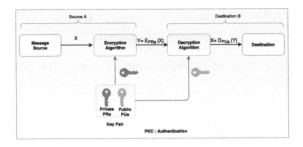

Fig. 4. Public key cryptography: authentication [21]

4.1 Types of Public Key Cryptography Techniques

RSA

The RSA technique, named after its founders, Rivest-Shamir-Adleman was first described in 1977. It is based on the mathematical difficulty of factorization of the product of two very large prime numbers.

ElGamal

Described by Taher ElGamal in 1985, it is a public key encryption and authentication technique. The former is widely used in many systems like PGP whereas the latter itself is seldom used but gave way to Digital Signature Algorithm. The encryption algorithm is based on the Diffie-Hellman Key Exchange and exploits the computational difficulty of determining discrete logarithms. ElGamal finds its best use in hybrid cryptography techniques where the asymmetric keys are used to encrypt the symmetric key which in turn encrypts the actual messages. This is due to the high computational complexity of applying asymmetric key encryption at every message transmission.

Elliptic Curve Cryptography

Elliptic Curve Cryptography or ECC said to be at the forefront of the second generation of modern cryptography techniques after the first generation of Diffie-Hellman and RSA. It is a complete mathematical framework based on an esoteric area of elliptic curves in a finite field. Built upon this ECC can provide a lot of functions not only limited to encryption but also digital signatures, key agreement and pseudo-random number generators. Its simple merit over RSA is that it requires much smaller keys to achieve the same level of security.

Elliptic Curve Equation. The elliptic curve over a prime finite field F_p is defined as

$$y^2 = x^3 + ax + b \quad mod \quad p$$

Here y, x, a and b are all over F_p. The parameters a and b are characteristic of the curve fulfilling $4a^3 + 27b^2 \neq 0$ to ensure that the curve does not contain any singularity. Any point P can be represented by its x and y coordinates satisfying the above curve as (p_x, p_y). It is to be noted that the point O at infinity is present on the curve.

Arithmetic Operations on Elliptic Curve. There are two basic operations addition and scalar multiplication on the elliptic curves.

Addition. The operation is not as simple as adding the x and y coordinates of the points. To add two points A and B we take the line joining them and get its third intersection on the curve C'. We then take the conjugate of C' to obtain $C = A + B$. In order to describe it mathematically we have to define a parameter called slope, s. The slope between the two points is $s = \frac{a_y - b_y}{a_x - b_x}$. The coordinates of the point C can be given as $c_x = s^2 - a_x - b_x$ and $c_y = s.(a_x - c_x) - a_y$. For point doubling i.e., $A = B$ and $C = 2A$, $s = \frac{3a_x^2 + a}{2a_y}$, $c_x = s^2 - 2a_x$ and $c_y = s.(a_x - c_x) - a_y$. It is to be noted that $A + O = A$.

Scalar Multiplication. This operation is derived from addition and doubling operation. This is written as $C = kA$. As an illustration, $C = 7A$ can be expressed as $C = A + 2A + 2(2A)$.

Cryptographic Operations. Along with the described p, a and b, there are two more parameters to be taken into consideration. G is the curve generator or base point and n the order of G which is the number of distinct points on the curve which can be obtained by its repeated scalar multiplication.

Key Pair Generation. We need to select a random number d in the range $\{1, 2, \ldots, n - 1\}$ which is the private key. Now $Q = d * G$ is the public key.

Encryption and Decryption. This works like any other public key technique where the sender encrypts the message using public key of the recipient.

- Considering m as the message we generate M which is corresponding point on the curve. There are a number of ways to generate M from m. Taking a random number k in the range $\{1, 2, \ldots, n - 1\}$ two cipher texts will now be generated $C_1 = k * G$ and $C_2 = M + k * Q$.
- On the receiver side, M can be obtained as $M = C_2 - d$. This works as $d * C_1$ can be expanded as $d * k * G$ which is equal to $k * Q$.

4.2   Comparison

The security of public key cryptographic technique lies in the computational effort or mathematical difficulty of breaking it. The cryptography algorithms are judged by the ratio of effort in the encryption-decryption with key versus the effort in decryption without the key. In the case of RSA, it is the difficulty in factoring a large into constituent primes. Thus if the public key is $\{d, N\}$ the problem essentially is to find the numbers p and q or the private key such that $N = p.q$. On the other hand in ECC it is a problem of computing discrete logarithm of a given number given the generator. This means that with $Q = d*G$ being the public key one needs to find d, the private given G.

Any function of the type where applying it is mathematically easier but finding its inverse is considerably harder is known as a trapdoor function. As it turns out, discrete factorization is not that of a strong trapdoor function. There have been specialized algorithms like Quadratic Sieve and the General Number Field Sieve which have made the problem a bit easier. To tackle these systems need to continually increase the key length which is infeasible for low-power embedded and mobile devices.

Discrete logarithm turns out to be a much better trapdoor function. A key size of 160 bits in ECC provides equivalent security with the key size of 1024 bits in RSA. This ratio of 1:7 key size translates to 1:3 computational effort required to apply the algorithm. Thus for such key size, equivalent security is provided at one-third of the computational cost. This difference widens with larger keys where 521 bit ECC keys equivalent to security with 15360 bit RSA key requires $\frac{1}{64}$ of the computational cost [22].

5   Proposed Mechanism

5.1   Connection Establishment

In this section, we provide the details about the proposed connection establishment mechanism. Authors in [10] recommended the use of a secondary key, exchanged using ECC, for better security. Our method extends this approach to make the handshake process more secure and efficient. The Fig. 5 describes the proposed mechanism. We explain the process in 4 steps below.

Discovery
The beacons and the probe request in the discovery phase are identical to the existing mechanism. The AP broadcast beacons at regular intervals. When an STA wants to connect to a specific AP, it sends a probe request to that AP along with the corresponding SSID (in our case STA knows about the available AP's SSIDs). When AP responds to the probe request, it also includes its Public Key KU_{AP} in the form of a certificate, signed by a certificate authority(CA), along with necessary domain parameters. Since we propose ECC over the prime field, these parameters include the (p, a, b, G, n, h). Where p is a k-bit prime number, a, b belongs to F_P that defines elliptic curve $E(F_P)$, G is the base point in $E_P(a, b)$, prime n in order of G, and integer h.

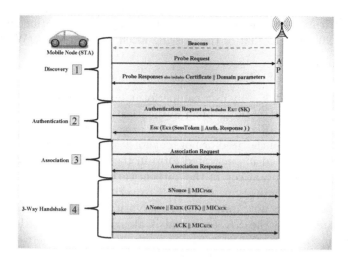

Fig. 5. Proposed ECC based mechanism for Wi-Fi connectivity

Security Analysis

In the discovery phase, if the public key KU_{AP} is sent as plaintext in probe response (as it is done in [10]) rather than as CA certificate, the network becomes vulnerable to MiTM Attack. The attacker can broadcast themselves as the AP and send their public-key $KU_{attacker}$ in probe response and sign with their private key $KR_{attacker}$ in the authentication response. Knowing the SK and the PSK, it is now possible for the attacker to generate PTK. The attacker can take Man-in-the-middle position, and both decrypt and forge frames. Thus, to guard the network against MiTM attack, we send public key as a certificate (signed by a certificate authority) that also contains the identity of the AP and digital signature. The domain parameters can be sent either in the certificate or as plaintext in the response.

Authentication and Association

Before sending the authentication request, the client generates a Session Key SK. The Session Key is generated at the STA end. The STA then encrypts the SK using the public key of AP KU_{AP} for secrecy. The STA include this encrypted message $E_{KU_{AP}}\{SK\}$ in its authentication request. The mechanism proposed by [9] sends the passphrase along with the SK, however, transmitting the passphrase, even in encrypted form, is a bad practice and hence not adopted.

On receiving the authentication request, the AP stores the SK and generate a session token $SessToken$ for the client. This token can be used during client handovers for faster authentication. The AP responds with the authentication response that includes the $SessToken$ digitally signed using KR_{AP}, followed by encryption using SK. The encryption ensures that the AP received the SK without any modification and the digital signature ensures the response is from AP. When using ECC, the ECDSA [23] algorithm is used for digital signature.

After authentication, the association is performed. The association request and response are identical to that of the existing mechanism in WPA/WPA2.

Security Analysis

We need to take note of a few important points here.

1. Similar to WPA2/PSK, any user can perform authentication and association. However, it does not perform open authentication but instead asks the AP to decrypt and use SK to prove it has the private key.
2. Any user, whether authorized or not, cannot learn the SK by eavesdropping since it is transmitted in encrypted form in the authentication request, and is used as an encryption key in the authentication response. The purpose of encryption in authentication response is to verify whether the SK has been received correctly or not. Rather than encryption, we can also compute MIC for the frame using the SK and send it along. In that case, however, the $SessToken$ could be read by anyone eavesdropping on the network.
3. The digital signing of authentication response using KR_{AP} ensures that the attacker if possessing the CA certificate of AP cannot forge its identity as AP to the STA. Hence, only the actual AP and the STA knows the SK.

PMK Generation

The problem of generating PMK from PSK has already been discussed in Sect. 3.1. Thus, rather than generating PMK from PSK as described in Sect. 2.2, we will use both PSK and SK. This will ensure that each STA has a fresh PMK each time it establishes a connection, different from other network users. The generated PMK is specific to a particular session and transmitted securely at the beginning of the connection establishment process. Hence, even if any malicious insider is eavesdropping, it cannot compute the PMK.

3-Way Handshake

The purpose of the proposed mechanism is to improve the process of connection establishment, which includes both efficiency and security. Since wireless communication is much slower and prone to noise, reducing the number of exchanged frames greatly improves the efficiency. Instead of using 4-way Handshake, a 3-way handshake is sufficient for both parties to authenticate themselves and establish PTK. The 3-way handshake is Phase 4 of the Fig. 5 and details are as follows:

1. The handshake starts with the STA sending $SNonce$ to the AP, after signing it with the PMK.
   On receiving the frame, the AP can verify the signature to ensure that STA is an authorized user. The AP, using the SNonce and ANonce it has, can now generate the PTK.
2. If the AP verifies the PMK by matching the MIC, it responds with ANonce and GTK. The GTK is encrypted using KEK (derived from PTK as in WPA/WPA2 4-way handshake). MIC for this frame computed using KCK is attached along with the message.
   STA uses the ANonce for computing the PTK. The STA then verifies the identity of AP by ascertaining the MIC. If verified, STA decrypts $E_{KEK}GTK$ and stores it. Both the parties are authenticated by each other at this point.

3. The STA now sends the acknowledgment to AP, along with the MIC. The MIC is used by AP to verify that the STA has derived the correct PTK.

Security Analysis

1. Conventionally, PMK is not used for encrypting or signing frames in WPA/WPA2 since it is derived directly from PSK and its compromise can lead to compromise of PSK itself. However, in our case, PMK is different for each session and hence, using it once for signature is not a security compromise.
2. The AP must install the PTK after receiving the second, and the STA must install after receiving the third frame of the handshake. To mitigate the vulnerability (KRACK) discovered by [24], ensure that the same PTK is never installed twice.
3. Eavesdropping on the handshake brings no benefit to the attacker since he is unaware of the PMK. Any attempt to modify or forge any frame won't go undetected due to MIC. Thus, the handshake is secure.
4. To protect the network from any attack based on Hole 96 vulnerability, the AP must digitally sign its broadcast messages after encrypting with GTK.

5.2 Alternative Approach for 3-Way Handshake During Client Handover

In this subsection, we discuss an alternative 3-way handshake mechanism using three frame exchange only, without the requirement of regenerating PMK or performing 802.1X authentication while handover.

During the handover, the first three phases remains same as it is shown in Fig. 5. However, the last phase, the 3-way handshake process is different during STA handover. It is also for connection re-establishment, the AP needs to maintain a list of active Session Tokens along with their corresponding PMK. For client handover, the same list can also be maintained by the authentication server (if present). The mechanism is of the 3-way handshake during handover is shown in Fig. 6, and details are as follows:

1. The STA sends *SNonce*, the previous session token *SessToken*, and the frame's MIC computed via the previously established PMK. The *SessToken* is used to identify the client, and the MIC is used to verify the client's identity. The AP looks up for the Session Token in the maintained list and verifies the client's identity from the MIC. If verified, the AP generates a new PTK' using the received *SNonce* and a fresh *ANonce*. The PTK' is used to derive the new KEK, KCK and TK.
2. The AP generates a fresh session token *SessToken'* and encrypt it using KEK. The AP responds to STA with *ANonce*, the new session token in the encrypted format $E_{KEK}(SessToken')$ and the MIC of the frame MIC_{KCK}. STA uses the *ANonce* for generating the new PTK'. The PTK' is then used to verify the frame integrity and message source using the attached MIC. If verified, the client updates the Session token from $E_{KEK}(SessToken')$.

3. The STA responds with an acknowledgment and the frame MIC computed via KCK. The AP verify the source and update the *SessToken*. The Unicast communication from now on is encrypted using TK.

Security Analysis

1. Any attacker eavesdropping on the network can read the first handshake message and store the *SessToken*. However, since no user possess the PMK, they can't use it to forge their identity as STA in future.
2. The attacker can store the first message of the handshake for replay attack, but since the last message requires the MIC, the attacker won't be able to forge its identity as STA.
3. The attacker cannot perform replay attack in future using the second message since the new connection request will have a different value of SNonce in the first message and hence, will have different PTK and MIC.
4. If the attacker drops the last message of the frame, the AP would be re-transmitting the second message after incrementing the replay counter. On receiving the second message from AP more than three times, the STA must revert to previous session key and restart the process. Similarly, the AP after sending the second message more than three times must be prepared to receive both, the message 3 for the new session token and the message 1 for new handshake request.
5. Since the PMK is different for every user, no user can modify any frame without being detected.

The current mechanism is secure from attacks from both inside or outside attackers and is performed using a simple 3-way handshake without the need for 802.1X authentication or new PMK generation.

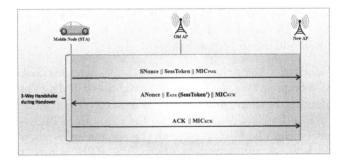

Fig. 6. Proposed 3-way handshake mechanism during handover

6   Performance Analysis

The computation time for encryption, decryption and key generation, as mentioned in [10] is given in Table 2. These values for ECC and AES-based operations they have obtained from the studies [25, 26], respectively. Based on these values, we compare the computation delay (CD) of our approach with WPA2-PSK and the work in [10], which is given in the Table 3. The computation delay has two parts: Delay in access authentication (CD_{AA}) and delay in key-handshake (CD_{KH}).

Since the number of frames exchanged during handshake in our approach are fewer in comparison, we save around 230 ms in the initial computation. This is a significant improvement, especially when using latency sensitive services such as VoIP. Although proposed ECC-based procedures have higher computational overheads at the initial stage of authentication (due to signification and verification) than WPA2-PSK, the delay in following encryption process for secure data transmission would be the same. Thus, the proposed scheme can enhance the security of the existing system at the cost of initial computation overheads.

Table 2. Computation time for various operations [10, 25, 26]

Operations	Algorithm	Time (ms)
Symmetric encryption (256 bits)	AES-CCMP	$T_{SE} = 100$
Symmetric decryption (256 bits)	AES-CCMP	$T_{SD} = 130$
Asymmetric encryption (384 bits)	ECC	$T_{AE} = 103$
Asymmetric decryption (384 bits)	ECC	$T_{AD} = 140$
Key generation (384 bits)		$T_{gen} = 31$

Table 3. Delay comparison

Steps	WPA2-PSK scheme	Work [10] with 384-bit keys	Proposed scheme with 384-bit keys
Authentication	$CD_{AA} = NoDelay$	$CD_{AA} = Tgen + 3(T_{AE} + T_{AD}) = 760ms$	$CD_{AA} = T_{gen} + 3(T_{AE} + T_{AD}) = 760ms$
Key-handshake	$CD_{KH} = 4(T_{SE} + T_{SD}) = 920ms$	$CD_{KH} = 4(T_{SE} + T_{SD}) = 920ms$	$CD_{KH} = 3(T_{SE} + T_{SD}) = 690ms$
Total	920 ms	1680 ms	1450 ms

7   Conclusion

In this paper, we propose a more secure connection establishment, re-establishment and session handover mechanism using Public Key Cryptography. We have discussed existing Wi-Fi vulnerabilities and also how ECC is a better option to help secure the WPA2/PSK based Wi-Fi. From the available PKC techniques, ECC seems to be the best alternative considering the resource-limitation in many wireless devices. For each proposed phase, we have done the critical security analysis which is given after each phase. The implementation of the mechanism can be much faster for devices having hardware support ECC encryption and decryption. Our work can also be extended in the context of IoT and ITS use cases. In our future work, we will try to demonstrate the robustness or security strength of the proposed protocol against the recent well-known attacks like KRACK and also evaluate its performance by using appropriate formal verification tools or via some implementation using the simulator.

Acknowledgments. The research work has been conducted in the Information Security Education and Awareness (ISEA) Lab of Indian Institute of Technology, Guwahati. The authors would like to acknowledge IIT, Guwahati and ISEA MeitY, India for the support.

References

1. Li, S., Da Xu, L., Zhao, S.: The internet of things: a survey. Inf. Syst. Front. **17**(2), 243–259 (2015)
2. Dimitrakopoulos, G., Demestichas, P.: Intelligent transportation systems. IEEE Veh. Technol. Mag. **5**(1), 77–84 (2010)
3. Sheldon, F.T., Weber, J.M., Yoo, S.M., Pan, W.D.: The insecurity of wireless networks. IEEE Secur. Priv. **10**(4), 54–61 (2012)
4. Kumar, V., Chakraborty, S., Barbhuiya, F.A., Nandi, S.: Detection of stealth man-in-the-middle attack in wireless Lan. In: 2012 2nd IEEE International Conference on Parallel Distributed and Grid Computing, PDGC, pp. 290–295. IEEE (2012)
5. Agarwal, M., Biswas, S., Nandi, S.: Advanced stealth man-in-the-middle attack in WPA2 encrypted wi-fi networks. IEEE Commun. Lett. **19**(4), 581–584 (2015)
6. Lauter, K.: The advantages of elliptic curve cryptography for wireless security. IEEE Wirel. Commun. **11**(1), 62–67 (2004)
7. Miller, V.S.: Use of elliptic curves in cryptography. In: Williams, H.C. (ed.) CRYPTO 1985. LNCS, vol. 218, pp. 417–426. Springer, Heidelberg (1986). https://doi.org/10.1007/3-540-39799-X_31
8. Namal, S., Georgantas, K., Gurtov, A.: Lightweight authentication and key management on 802.11 with elliptic curve cryptography. In: 2013 IEEE Wireless Communications and Networking Conference (WCNC), pp. 1830–1835. IEEE (2013)
9. Noh, J., Kim, J., Kwon, G., Cho, S.: Secure key exchange scheme for WPA/WPA2-PSK using public key cryptography. In: IEEE International Conference on Consumer Electronics-Asia (ICCE-Asia), pp. 1–4. IEEE (2016)
10. Noh, J., Kim, J., Cho, S.: Secure authentication and four-way handshake scheme for protected individual communication in public wi-fi networks. IEEE Access **PP**(99), 1 (2018)

11. Nakhila, O., Attiah, A., Jinz, Y., Zoux, C.: Parallel active dictionary attack on WPA2-PSK Wi-Fi networks. In: Military Communications Conference, MILCOM, pp. 665–670. IEEE (2015)
12. IEEE Std 802.11i, IEEE Standard for Wireless LAN Medium Access Control (MAC) and Physical Layer Specifications: Amendment 6: Medium Access Control Security Enhancements
13. RFC 2865: IETF Standard for Remote Authentication Dial in User Service (RADIUS)
14. IEEE Std 802.1X, I: IEEE Standard for Port-Based Network Access Control
15. Mishra, A., Shin, M., Arbaugh, W.: An empirical analysis of the IEEE 802.11 MAC layer handoff process. ACM SIGCOMM Comput. Commun. Rev. $33(2)$, 93–102 (2003)
16. IEEE Std 802.11r /D01.0, Draft Amendment to Standard for Information Technology - Telecommunications and Information Exchange Between Systems - LAN/MAN Specific Requirements Part 11: Wireless Medium Access Control (MAC) and Physical Layer Specifications: Amendment 8: Fast BSS Transition
17. Hintersteiner, J.: Wifi fast roaming. Accessed 03 Apr 2018
18. Sheldon, F.T., Weber, J.M., Yoo, S.M., Pan, W.D.: The insecurity of wireless networks. IEEE Secur. Priv. $10(4)$, 54–61 (2012)
19. Paladino, A., Phanse, K., Ahmad, S.: Hole 196 vulnerability in WPA2. Airtight Networks (2010)
20. Ahmad, M.S.: Wpa too! DEF CON 18 (2010)
21. Stallings, W.: Cryptography and Network Security: Principles and Practice. Pearson, Upper Saddle River (2017)
22. Bafandehkar, M., Yasin, S.M., Mahmod, R., Hanapi, Z.M.: Comparison of ECC and RSA algorithm in resource constrained devices. In: 2013 International Conference on IT Convergence and Security (ICITCS), pp. 1–3, December 2013
23. Johnson, D., Menezes, A., Vanstone, S.: The elliptic curve digital signature algorithm (ECDSA). Int. J. Inf. Secur. $1(1)$, 36–63 (2001)
24. Vanhoef, M., Piessens, F.: Key reinstallation attacks: Forcing nonce reuse in WPA2. In: Proceedings of the 2017 ACM SIGSAC Conference on Computer and Communications Security, pp. 1313–1328. ACM (2017)
25. Arif, M., Habib, A., Rufat, I., Azer, S.: Study and implementation of elliptic curve encryption algorithm for Azerbaijan E-ID card. Int. J. Innov. Res. Comput. Commun. Eng. $3(5)$, 3708–3713 (2015)
26. Sivakumar, C., Velmurugan, A.: High speed VLSI design CCMP AES cipher for WLAN (IEEE 802.11 i). In: International Conference on Signal Processing, Communications and Networking, ICSCN 2007, pp. 398–403. IEEE (2007)

Author Index

Printed in the United States
By Bookmasters